D1055425

TEN OF
THE BEST

The Reader's Digest Association, Inc.
Pleasantville, New York
Cape Town, Hong Kong, London, Montreal, Sydney

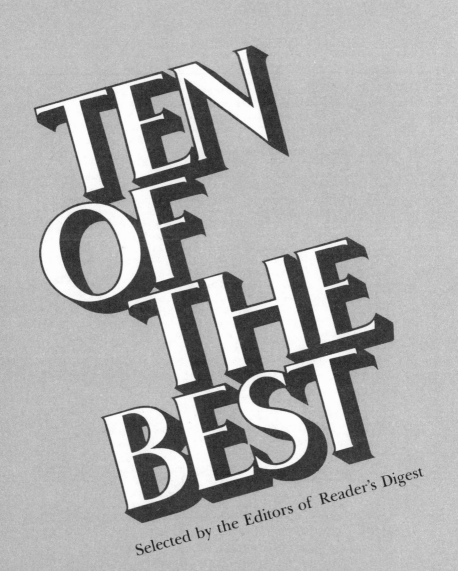

TEN OF THE BEST

Selected by the Editors of Reader's Digest

READER'S DIGEST CONDENSED BOOKS
Editor: John S. Zinsser, Jr.
Executive Editor: Barbara J. Morgan
Assistant Managing Editors: Anne H. Atwater, Ann Berryman,
Tanis H. Erdmann, Thomas Froncek, Marjorie Palmer
Senior Staff Editors: Jean E. Aptakin, Angela Weldon
Senior Editors: Olive Farmer, Angela C. Gibbs, Alice Murtha,
Virginia Rice (Rights), Margery D. Thorndike
Associate Editors: Linn Carl, Thomas S. Clemmons, Estelle T. Dashman,
Alice Jones-Miller, Mary Kirby, Joseph P. McGrath, Maureen A. Mackey, James J. Menick
Senior Copy Editors: Claire A. Bedolis, Jeane Garment
Associate Copy Editors: Rosalind H. Campbell, Jean S. Friedman, Jane F. Neighbors
Assistant Copy Editors: Maxine Bartow, Jean G. Cornell, Diana Marsh
Art Director: William Gregory
Executive Art Editors: Marion Davis, Soren Noring
Senior Art Editors: Angelo Perrone, Thomas Von Der Linn
Associate Art Editors, Research: George Calas, Jr., Katherine Kelleher

CB PROJECTS
Executive Editor: Herbert H. Lieberman
Senior Editors: Catherine T. Brown, John R. Roberson, Ray Sipherd
Associate Editor: Dana Adkins

CB INTERNATIONAL EDITIONS
Executive Editor: Francis Schell
Senior Staff Editor: Sigrid MacRae
Senior Editor: Istar H. Dole
Associate Editor: Gary Q. Arpin

The credits and acknowledgments that appear on page 608
are hereby made a part of this copyright page.

© 1985 by The Reader's Digest Association, Inc.
Copyright © 1985 by The Reader's Digest Association (Canada) Ltd.
© 1985 by Reader's Digest Services Pty. Ltd., Sydney, Australia
Copyright © 1985 by The Reader's Digest Association South Africa (Pty.) Limited
Copyright © 1985 by Reader's Digest Association Far East Limited
Philippines copyright 1985 by Reader's Digest Association Far East Limited

First Edition

All rights reserved. Reproduction in any manner, except as
authorized by the Copyright Act, is prohibited.

Library of Congress Cataloging in Publication Data
Main entry under title:
Ten of the best.
Contents: The Red Pony/by John Steinbeck—Good-bye, Mr. Chips/by
James Hilton—Night Flight/by Antoine de Saint–Exupéry—[etc.]
1. Fiction—20th century. I. Reader's Digest Association.
II. Reader's digest. III. Title: 10 of the best.
PN6120.2.T46 1985   808.83′04   84-27591
ISBN 0-89577-207-8

Printed in the United States of America

CONTENTS

THE
RED PONY

John Steinbeck

ILLUSTRATED BY BEN WOHLBERG

He was small in size, his mane was
tangled, and his coat was of rough red fur.
The boy's father had bought him for
little money at a local bankruptcy auction.
But to ten-year-old Jody, he was
the finest pony colt in the whole of
California's Salinas Valley—and perhaps in
the entire world.

From Nobel Prize–winning author John
Steinbeck comes this short novel that has been
honored as among the most beautiful,
sensitive and lyrical of all his stories.

CHAPTER 1
THE GIFT

AT DAYBREAK BILLY BUCK emerged from the bunkhouse and stood
for a moment on the porch looking up at the sky. He was a
broad, bandy-legged little man with a walrus mustache, with square
hands, puffed and muscled on the palms. His eyes were a contempla-
tive watery gray and the hair which protruded from under his
Stetson hat was spiky and weathered. Billy was still stuffing his shirt
into his blue jeans as he stood on the porch. He unbuckled his belt and
tightened it again. The belt showed, by the worn shiny places opposite
each hole, the gradual increase of Billy's middle over a period of years.

When he had seen to the weather, Billy cleared each nostril by
holding its mate closed with his forefinger and blowing fiercely.
Then he walked down to the barn, rubbing his hands together. He
curried and brushed two saddle horses in the stalls, talking quietly to
them all the time, and he had hardly finished when the iron triangle
started ringing at the ranch house. Billy stuck the brush and currycomb together and laid them on the rail and went up to breakfast.
His action had been so deliberate and yet so wasteless of time that he
came to the house while Mrs. Tiflin was still ringing the triangle. She
nodded her gray head to him and withdrew into the kitchen. Billy
Buck sat down on the steps because he was a cowhand and it wouldn't
be fitting that he should go first into the dining room. He heard Mr.
Tiflin in the house, stamping his feet into his boots.

The high jangling note of the triangle put the boy Jody in motion.

He was only a little boy, ten years old, with hair like dusty yellow grass and with shy, polite gray eyes, and with a mouth that worked when he thought. The triangle picked him up out of sleep. It didn't occur to him to disobey the harsh note. He never had; no one he knew ever had. He brushed the tangled hair out of his eyes and skinned his nightshirt off. In a moment he was dressed—blue chambray shirt and overalls. It was late in the summer, so of course there were no shoes to bother with. In the kitchen he waited until his mother got from in front of the sink and went back to the stove. Then he washed himself and brushed back his wet hair with his fingers. His mother turned sharply on him as he left the sink. Jody looked shyly away.

"I've got to cut your hair before long," his mother said. "Breakfast's on the table. Go on in, so Billy can come."

Jody sat at the long table, which was covered with white oilcloth washed through to the fabric in some places. The fried eggs lay in rows on their platter. Jody took three eggs on his plate and followed with three thick slices of crisp bacon. He carefully scraped a spot of blood from one of the egg yolks.

Billy Buck clumped in. "That won't hurt you," Billy explained. "That's only a sign the rooster leaves."

Jody's father came in then and Jody knew from the noise on the floor that he was wearing boots, but he looked under the table anyway to make sure. His father turned off the oil lamp over the table, for plenty of morning light now came through the windows.

Jody did not ask where his father and Billy Buck were riding that day, but he wished he might go along. His father was a disciplinarian. Jody obeyed him in everything without questions of any kind.

Carl Tiflin sat down and reached for the egg platter. "Got the cows ready to go, Billy?" he asked.

"In the lower corral," Billy said. "I could just as well take them in alone."

"Sure you could. But a man needs company. Besides your throat gets pretty dry." Carl Tiflin was jovial this morning.

Jody's mother put her head in the door. "What time do you think to be back, Carl?"

"I can't tell. I've got to see some men in Salinas. Might be gone till dark."

The eggs and coffee and big biscuits disappeared rapidly. Jody followed the two men out of the house. He watched them mount their horses and drive six old milk cows out of the corral and start over the hill toward Salinas. They were going to sell the old cows to the butcher.

When they had disappeared over the crown of the ridge, Jody walked up the hill in back of the house. The dogs trotted around the house corner hunching their shoulders and grinning with pleasure. Jody patted their heads—Doubletree Mutt, with the big thick tail and yellow eyes, and Smasher, who had killed a coyote and lost an ear in doing it. Smasher's one good ear stood up higher than a collie's ear should. Billy Buck said that always happened. After the frenzied greeting, the dogs lowered their noses to the ground in a businesslike way and went ahead, looking back now and then to make sure that the boy was coming. They walked up through the chicken yard and saw the quail eating with the chickens. Smasher chased the chickens a little to keep in practice in case there should ever be sheep to herd. Jody continued on through the large vegetable patch where the green corn was higher than his head. The cow-pumpkins were green and small yet. He went on to the sagebrush line where the cold spring ran out of its pipe and fell into a round wooden tub. He leaned over and drank close to the green mossy wood where the water tasted best. Then he turned and looked back on the ranch, on the low white-washed house girded with red geraniums, and on the long bunk-house by the cypress tree where Billy Buck lived alone.

Jody could see the great black kettle under the cypress tree. That was where the pigs were scalded. The sun was coming over the ridge now, glaring on the whitewash of the houses and barns, making the wet grass blaze softly. Behind him, in the tall sagebrush, the birds were scampering on the ground, making a great noise among the dry leaves; the squirrels piped shrilly on the side-hills. Jody looked along at the farm buildings. He felt an uncertainty in the air, a feeling of change and of loss and of the gain of new and unfamiliar things. Over the hillside two big black buzzards sailed low to the ground and their shadows slipped smoothly and quickly ahead of them. Some animal had died in the vicinity. Jody knew it. It might be a cow or it might be the remains of a rabbit. The buzzards overlooked nothing. Jody hated them as all decent things hate them, but they could not be hurt because they made away with carrion.

After a while the boy sauntered downhill again. The dogs had long ago given him up and gone into the brush to do things in their own way. Back through the vegetable garden he went, and he paused for a moment to smash a green muskmelon with his heel, but he was not happy about it. It was a bad thing to do, he knew perfectly well. He kicked dirt over the ruined melon to conceal it.

Back at the house his mother bent over his rough hands, inspecting his fingers and nails. It did little good to start him clean to school because too many things could happen on the way. She sighed over the black cracks on his fingers and then gave him his books and his lunch and started him on the mile walk to school. She noticed that his mouth was working a good deal this morning.

Jody started his journey. He filled his pockets with little pieces of white quartz that lay in the road, and every so often he took a shot at a bird or at some rabbit that had stayed sunning itself in the road too long. At the crossroads over the bridge he met two friends and the three of them walked to school together, making ridiculous strides and being rather silly. School had just opened two weeks before. There was still a spirit of revolt among the pupils.

It was four o'clock in the afternoon when Jody topped the hill and looked down on the ranch again. He looked for the saddle horses, but the corral was empty. His father was not back yet. He went slowly then, toward the afternoon chores. At the ranch house, he found his mother sitting on the porch, mending socks.

"There's two doughnuts in the kitchen for you," she said.

Jody slid to the kitchen, and returned with half of one of the doughnuts already eaten and his mouth full.

His mother asked him what he had learned in school that day, but she didn't listen to his doughnut-muffled answer. She interrupted, "Jody, tonight see you fill the woodbox clear full. Last night you crossed the sticks and it was only about half full. Lay the sticks flat tonight. And Jody, some of the hens are hiding eggs, or else the dogs are eating them. Look about in the grass and see if you can find any nests."

Jody, still eating, went out and did his chores. He saw the quail come down to eat with the chickens when he threw out the grain. For some reason his father was proud to have them come. He never allowed any shooting near the house for fear the quail might go away.

When the woodbox was full, Jody took his twenty-two rifle up to the cold spring at the brush line. He drank again and then aimed the gun at all manner of things—at rocks, at birds on the wing, at the big black pig kettle under the cypress tree—but he didn't shoot because he had no cartridges and wouldn't have until he was twelve. If his father had seen him aim the rifle in the direction of the house, he would have put the cartridges off another year. Jody remembered this and did not point the rifle down the hill again. Two years was enough to wait for cartridges. Nearly all of his father's presents were given with reservations, which hampered their value somewhat. It was good discipline.

The supper waited until dark for his father to return. When at last he came in with Billy Buck, Jody could smell the delicious brandy on their breath. Inwardly he rejoiced, for his father sometimes talked to him when he smelled of brandy, sometimes even told him about the things he had done in the wild days when he was a boy.

After supper Jody sat by the fireplace and his eyes sought the room corners, and he waited for his father to tell what it was he contained, for Jody knew he had news of some sort. But he was disappointed. His father pointed a stern finger at him.

"You'd better go to bed, Jody. I'm going to need you in the morning."

That wasn't so bad. Jody liked to do the things he had to do as long as they weren't routine things.

He looked at the floor and his mouth worked out a question before he spoke it. "What are we going to do in the morning—kill a pig?" he asked softly.

"Never you mind. You better get to bed."

When the door was closed behind him, Jody heard his father and Billy Buck chuckling and he knew it was a joke of some kind. And later, when he lay in bed trying to make words out of the murmurs in the other room, he heard his father protest, "But, Ruth, I didn't give much for him."

Jody heard the hoot-owls hunting mice down by the barn, and he heard a fruit tree limb tap-tapping against the house. A cow was lowing when he went to sleep.

WHEN THE TRIANGLE sounded in the morning, Jody dressed more quickly even than usual. In the kitchen, while he washed his face and combed back his hair, his mother addressed him irritably. "Don't you go out until you get a good breakfast in you."

He went into the dining room and sat at the long white table. He took a steaming hotcake from the platter, arranged two fried eggs on it, covered them with another hotcake and squashed the whole thing with his fork.

His father and Billy Buck came in. Jody knew from the sound on the floor that both of them were wearing flat-heeled shoes, but he peered under the table to make sure. His father turned off the oil lamp, for the day had arrived, and he looked stern and disciplinary, but Billy Buck didn't look at Jody at all. He avoided the shy, questioning eyes of the boy while he soaked a whole piece of toast in his coffee.

Carl Tiflin said crossly, "You come with us after breakfast!"

Jody had trouble with his food then, for he felt a kind of doom in the air. After Billy had tilted his saucer and drained the coffee which had slopped into it and had wiped his hands on his jeans, the two men stood up from the table and went out into the morning light together, and Jody respectfully followed a little behind them. He tried to keep his mind from running ahead, tried to keep it absolutely motionless.

His mother called, "Carl! Don't you let it keep him from school."

They marched past the cypress, where a singletree hung from a limb to butcher the pigs on, and past the black iron kettle, so it was not a pig killing. The sun shone over the hill and threw long, dark shadows of the trees and buildings. They crossed a stubble field to shortcut to the barn. Jody's father unhooked the door and they went in. They had been walking toward the sun on the way down. The barn was black as night in contrast and warm from the hay and from the beasts. Jody's father moved over toward the one box stall. "Come here!" he ordered. Jody could begin to see things now. He looked into the box stall and then stepped back quickly.

A red pony colt was looking at him out of the stall. Its tense ears were forward and a light of disobedience was in its eyes. Its coat was rough and thick as an Airedale's fur and its mane was long and tangled. Jody's throat collapsed in on itself and cut his breath short.

"He needs a good currying," his father said, "and if I ever hear of you not feeding him or leaving his stall dirty, I'll sell him off in a minute."

Jody couldn't bear to look at the pony's eyes anymore. He gazed down at his hands for a moment, and then he asked very shyly, "Mine?"

No one answered him. He put his hand out toward the pony. Its gray nose came close, sniffing loudly, and then the lips drew back and the strong teeth closed on Jody's fingers. The pony shook its head and seemed to laugh with amusement. Jody regarded his bruised fingers. "Well—" he said with pride. "Well, I guess he can bite all right."

The two men laughed, somewhat in relief. Carl Tiflin went out of the barn and walked up a sidehill to be by himself, because he was embarrassed, but Billy Buck stayed. It was easier to talk to Billy Buck. Jody asked again, "Mine?"

Billy became professional in tone. "Sure! That is, if you look out for him and break him right. I'll show you how. He's just a colt. You can't ride him for some time."

Jody put out his bruised hand again, and this time the red pony let his nose be rubbed. "I ought to have a carrot," Jody said. "Where'd we get him, Billy?"

"Bought him at a sheriff's auction," Billy explained. "A show went broke in Salinas and had debts. The sheriff was selling off their stuff."

The pony stretched out his nose and Jody stroked it a little. He said softly, "There isn't a—saddle?"

Billy Buck laughed. "I'd forgot. Come along."

In the harness room he lifted down a little saddle of red morocco leather. "It's just a show saddle," Billy Buck said disparagingly. "It isn't practical for the brush, but it was cheap at the sale."

Jody couldn't trust himself to look at the saddle either, and he couldn't speak at all. He brushed the shining red leather with his fingertips, and after a long time he said, "It'll look pretty on him though." He thought of the grandest and prettiest things he knew. "If he hasn't a name already, I think I'll call him Gabilan Mountains."

Billy Buck knew how he felt. "It's a pretty long name. Why don't you just call him Gabilan? That means hawk. That would be a fine name for him." Billy felt glad. "If you will collect tail hair, I might be able to make a hair rope for you sometime. You could use it for a hackamore."

Jody wanted to go back to the box stall. "Could I lead him to school, do you think—to show the kids?"

Billy shook his head. "He's not even halterbroke yet. We had a time getting him here. Had to almost drag him. You better be starting for school though."

"I'll bring the kids to see him here this afternoon," Jody said.

Six boys came over the hill half an hour early that afternoon, running hard, their heads down, their forearms working, their breath whistling. They swept by the house and cut across the stubble field to the barn. And then they stood self-consciously before the pony, and they looked at Jody with eyes in which there was a new admiration and a new respect. Before today Jody had been a boy, dressed in overalls and a blue shirt—quieter than most, even suspected of being a little cowardly. And now he was different. Out of a thousand centuries they drew the ancient admiration of the footman for the horseman. They knew instinctively that a man on a horse is spiritually as well as physically bigger than a man on foot. They knew that Jody now had been miraculously lifted out of equality with them and had been placed over them. Gabilan put his head out of the stall and sniffed them.

"Why'n't you ride him?" the boys cried. "Why'n't you braid his tail with ribbons like in the fair?" "When you going to ride him?"

Jody's courage was up. He too felt the superiority of the horseman. "He's not old enough. Nobody can ride him for a long time. I'm going to train him on the long halter. Billy Buck is going to show me how."

"Well, can't we even lead him around a little?"

"He isn't even halterbroke," Jody said. He wanted to be completely alone when he took the pony out the first time. "Come and see the saddle."

They were speechless at the red morocco saddle, completely shocked out of comment. "It isn't much use in the brush," Jody explained. "It'll look pretty on him though. Maybe I'll ride bareback when I go into the brush."

"How you going to rope a cow without a saddle horn?"

"Maybe I'll get another saddle for every day. My father might want me to help him with the stock." He let them feel the red saddle, and showed them the brass chain throatlatch on the bridle and the big brass buttons at each temple where the headstall and browband crossed. The whole thing was too wonderful. They had to go away after a little while, and each boy, in his mind, searched among his possessions for a bribe worthy of offering in return for a ride on the red pony when the time should come.

Jody was glad when they had gone. He took brush and currycomb from the wall, took down the barrier of the box stall and stepped cautiously in. The pony's eyes glittered, and he edged around into kicking position. But Jody touched him on the shoulder and rubbed his high arched neck as he had always seen Billy Buck do, and he crooned, "So-o-o, boy," in a deep voice. The pony gradually relaxed his tenseness. Jody curried and brushed until a pile of dead hair lay in the stall and until the pony's coat had taken on a deep red shine. Each time he finished, he thought it might have been done better. He braided the mane into a dozen little pigtails and he braided the forelock, and then he undid them and brushed the hair out straight again.

Jody did not hear his mother enter the barn. She was angry when she came, but when she looked in at the pony and at Jody working over him, she felt a curious pride rise up in her. "Have you forgot the woodbox?" she asked gently. "It's not far from dark and there's not a stick of wood in the house and the chickens aren't fed."

Jody quickly put up his tools. "I forgot, ma'am."

"Well, after this do your chores first. Then you won't forget. I expect you'll forget lots of things now if I don't keep an eye on you."

"Can I have carrots from the garden for him, ma'am?"

She had to think about that. "Oh—I guess so, if you only take the big tough ones."

"Carrots keep the coat good," he said, and again she felt the curious rush of pride.

JODY NEVER WAITED for the triangle to get him out of bed after the coming of the pony. It became his habit to creep out of bed even before his mother was awake, to slip into his clothes and to go quietly down to the barn to see Gabilan. In the quiet gray mornings when the land and the brush and the houses and the trees were silver-gray and black like a photograph negative, he stole toward the barn, past the sleeping stones and the sleeping cypress tree. The turkeys, roosting in the tree out of coyotes' reach, clucked drowsily. The fields glowed with a gray frostlike light and in the dew the tracks of rabbits and of field mice stood out sharply. The good dogs came stiffly out of their little houses, hackles up and deep growls in their throats. Then they caught Jody's scent, and their stiff tails rose up and waved a greeting—Doubletree Mutt, with the big thick tail, and Smasher, the would-be shepherd—then went lazily back to their warm beds.

It was a strange time and a mysterious journey, to Jody—an extension of a dream. When he first had the pony, he liked to torture himself during the trip by thinking Gabilan would not be in his stall, and, worse, had never been there. And he had other delicious little self-induced pains. He thought how the rats had gnawed ragged holes in the red saddle, and how the mice had nibbled Gabilan's tail until it was stringy and thin. He usually ran the last little way to the barn. He unlatched the rusty hasp of the barn door and stepped in, and no matter how quietly he opened the door, Gabilan was always looking at him over the barrier of the box stall, and Gabilan whinnied softly and stamped his front foot, and his eyes had big sparks of red fire in them like oakwood embers.

Sometimes, if the workhorses were to be used that day, Jody found Billy Buck in the barn harnessing and currying. Billy stood with him and looked long at Gabilan and he told Jody a great many things about horses. He explained that they were terribly afraid for their feet, so that one must make a practice of lifting the legs and patting the hooves and ankles to remove their terror. He told Jody how horses love conversation. He must talk to the pony all the time, and tell him the reasons for everything. Billy wasn't sure a horse could understand everything that was said to him, but it was impossible to say how much was understood. A horse never kicked up a fuss if someone he liked explained things to him. Billy could give examples, too. He had known, for instance, a horse nearly dead with fatigue to perk up when told it was only a little farther to his destination. And he had known a horse paralyzed with fright to come out of it when his rider told him what it was that was frightening him. While he talked in the mornings, Billy Buck cut twenty or thirty straws into neat three-inch lengths and stuck them into his hatband. Then during the whole day, if he wanted to pick his teeth or merely to chew on something, he had only to reach up for one of them.

Jody listened carefully, for he knew and the whole country knew that Billy Buck was a fine hand with horses. Billy's own horse was a stringy cayuse with a hammerhead, but he nearly always won the first prizes at the stock trials. Billy could rope a steer, make a double half hitch about the horn with his lariat and dismount, and his horse would play the steer as an angler plays a fish, keeping a tight rope until the steer was down or beaten.

Every morning after Jody had curried and brushed the pony, he let down the barrier of the stall, and Gabilan thrust past him and raced into the corral. Around and around he galloped, and sometimes he jumped forward and landed on stiff legs. He stood quivering, stiff ears forward, eyes rolling so that the whites showed, pretending to be frightened. At last he walked, snorting, to the water trough and buried his nose in the water up to the nostrils. Jody was proud then, for he knew that was the way to judge a horse. Poor horses only touched their lips to the water, but a fine-spirited beast put his whole nose and mouth under and only left room to breathe.

Then Jody stood and watched the pony, and he saw things he had never noticed about any other horse—the sleek, sliding flank muscles and the cords of the buttocks, which flexed like a closing fist, and the shine the sun put on the red coat. Having seen horses all his life, Jody had never looked at them very closely before. But now he noticed the moving ears, which gave expression and even inflection of expression to the face. The pony talked with his ears. You could tell exactly how he felt about everything by the way his ears pointed. Sometimes they were stiff and upright and sometimes lax and sagging. They went back when he was angry or fearful, and forward when he was anxious and curious and pleased; and their exact position indicated which emotion he had.

Billy Buck kept his word. In the early fall the training began. First there was the halterbreaking, and that was the hardest because it was the first thing. Jody held a carrot and coaxed and promised and pulled on the rope. The pony set his feet like a burro when he felt the strain. But before long he learned. Jody walked all over the ranch leading him. Gradually he took to dropping the rope until the pony followed him unled wherever he went.

And then came the training on the long halter. That was slower work. Jody stood in the middle of a circle, holding the long halter. He clucked with his tongue and the pony started to walk in a big circle, held in by the long rope. He clucked again to make the pony trot and again to make him gallop. Around and around Gabilan went thundering, enjoying it immensely. Then he called, "Whoa," and the pony stopped. It was not long until Gabilan was perfect at it. But in many ways he was a bad pony. He bit Jody in the pants and stomped on Jody's feet. Now and then his ears went back and he aimed a tremendous kick at the boy. Every time he did one of these bad things, Gabilan settled back and seemed to laugh to himself.

Billy Buck worked at the hair rope in the evenings before the fireplace. Jody collected tail hair in a bag, and he sat and watched Billy slowly constructing the rope, twisting a few hairs in order to make a string and rolling two strings together for a cord, and then braiding a number of cords to make the rope. Billy rolled the finished rope on the floor under his foot to make it round and hard.

The long-halter work rapidly approached perfection. Jody's father, watching the pony stop and start and trot and gallop, was a little bothered by it.

"He's getting to be almost a trick pony," he complained. "I don't like trick horses. It takes all the—dignity out of a horse to make him do tricks. Why, a trick horse is kind of like an actor—no dignity, no character of his own." And his father said, "I guess you better be getting him used to the saddle pretty soon."

Jody rushed for the harness room. For some time he had been riding the saddle on a sawhorse. He changed the stirrup length over and over, but he could never get it just right. Sometimes, mounted on the sawhorse in the harness room, with collars and hames and tugs hung all about him, Jody rode out beyond the room. He carried his rifle across the pommel. He saw the fields go flying by, and he heard the beat of the galloping hooves.

IT WAS A ticklish job, saddling the pony the first time. Gabilan reared and threw the saddle off before the cinch could be tightened. It had to be replaced again and again until the pony let it stay. And the cinching was difficult, too. Day by day Jody tightened the girth a little more until at last the pony didn't mind the saddle at all.

Then there was the bridle. Billy explained how to use a stick of licorice for a bit until Gabilan was used to having something in his mouth. Billy explained, "Of course we could force-break him to everything, but he wouldn't be as good a horse if we did. He'd always be a little bit afraid, and he wouldn't mind because he wanted to."

The first time the pony wore the bridle he whipped his head about and worked his tongue against the bit until the blood oozed from the corners of his mouth. He tried to rub the headstall off on the manger. His ears pivoted about and his eyes turned red with fear and with general rambunctiousness. Jody rejoiced, for he knew that only a mean-souled horse does not resent training.

And Jody trembled when he thought of the time when he would first sit in the saddle. The pony would probably throw him off. There was no disgrace in that. The disgrace would come if he did not get right up and mount again. Sometimes he dreamed that he lay in the dirt and cried and couldn't make himself mount again. The shame of the dream lasted until the middle of the day.

Gabilan was growing fast. Already he had lost the long-leggedness of the colt; his mane was getting longer and blacker. Under the constant currying and brushing his coat lay as smooth and gleaming as orange-red lacquer. Jody oiled the hoofs and kept them carefully trimmed so they would not crack.

The hair rope was nearly finished. Jody's father gave him an old pair of spurs and bent in the sidebars and cut down the straps and took up the chainlets until they fitted. And then one day Carl Tiflin said, "The pony's growing faster than I thought. I guess you can ride him by Thanksgiving. Think you can stick on?"

"I don't know," Jody said shyly. Thanksgiving was only three weeks off. He hoped it wouldn't rain, for rain would spot the red saddle.

Gabilan knew and liked Jody by now. He nickered when Jody came across the stubble field, and in the pasture he came running when his master whistled for him. There was a carrot for him every time.

Billy Buck gave him riding instructions over and over. "Now when you get up there, just grab tight with your knees and keep your hands away from the saddle, and if you get throwed, don't let that stop you. No matter how good a man is, there's always some horse can pitch him. You just climb up again before he gets to feeling smart about it. Pretty soon, he won't throw you no more, and pretty soon he *can't* throw you no more. That's the way to do it."

"I hope it don't rain before," Jody said.

"Why not? Don't want to get throwed in the mud?"

That was partly it, and also he was afraid that in the flurry of bucking Gabilan might slip and fall on him and break his leg or his hip. He had seen that happen to men before, and had seen how they writhed on the ground like squashed bugs, and he was afraid of it.

He practiced on the sawhorse how he would hold the reins in his left hand and a hat in his right hand. If he kept his hands thus busy, he couldn't grab the saddle if he felt himself going off. He didn't like to think of what would happen if he did grab the horn. Perhaps his father and Billy Buck would never speak to him again, they would be so ashamed. The news would get about and his mother would be ashamed too. And in the schoolyard—it was too awful to contemplate.

He began putting his weight on a stirrup when Gabilan was saddled, but he didn't throw his leg over the pony's back. That was forbidden until Thanksgiving.

Every afternoon he put the red saddle on the pony and cinched it tight. The pony was learning already to fill his stomach out unnaturally large while the cinching was going on, and then to let it down when the straps were fixed. Sometimes Jody led him up to the brush line and let him drink from the round green tub, and sometimes he led him up through the stubble field to the hilltop from which it was possible to see the white town of Salinas and the geometric fields of the great valley, and the oak trees clipped by the sheep. Now and then they broke through the brush and came to little cleared circles so hedged in that the world was gone and only the sky and the circle of brush were left from the old life. Gabilan liked these trips and showed it by keeping his head very high and by quivering his nostrils with interest. When the two came back from an expedition they smelled of the sweet sage they had forced through.

TIME DRAGGED ON toward Thanksgiving, but winter came fast. The clouds swept down and hung all day over the land and brushed the hilltops, and the winds blew shrilly at night. All day the dry oak leaves drifted down from the trees until they covered the ground, and yet the trees were unchanged.

Jody had wished it might not rain before Thanksgiving, but it did. The brown earth turned dark and the trees glistened. The cut ends of the stubble turned black with mildew; the haystacks grayed from exposure to the damp, and on the roofs the moss, which had been all summer as gray as lizards, turned a brilliant yellow-green. During the week of rain, Jody kept the pony in the box stall out of the dampness, except for a little time after school when he took him out for exercise and to drink at the water trough in the upper corral. Not once did Gabilan get wet.

The wet weather continued until little new grass appeared. Jody walked to school dressed in a slicker and short rubber boots. At length one morning the sun came out brightly. Jody, at his work in the box stall, said to Billy Buck, "Maybe I'll leave Gabilan in the corral when I go to school today."

"Be good for him to be out in the sun," Billy assured him. "No animal likes to be cooped up too long. Your father and me are going back on the hill to clean the leaves out of the spring." Billy nodded and picked his teeth with one of his little straws.

"If the rain comes, though—" Jody suggested.

"Not likely to rain today. She's rained herself out." Billy pulled up his sleeves and snapped his arm bands. "If it comes on to rain—why, a little rain don't hurt a horse."

"Well, if it does come to rain, you put him in, will you, Billy? I'm scared he might get a cold so I couldn't ride him when the time comes."

"Oh sure! I'll watch out for him if we get back in time. But it won't rain today."

And so Jody, when he went to school, left Gabilan standing out in the corral.

Billy Buck wasn't wrong about many things. He couldn't be. But he was wrong about the weather that day, for a little after noon the clouds pushed over the hills and the rain began to pour down. Jody heard it start on the schoolhouse roof. He considered holding up one finger for permission to go to the outhouse and, once outside, running for home to put the pony in. Punishment would be prompt both at school and at home. He gave it up and took ease from Billy's assurance that rain couldn't hurt a horse. When school was finally out, he hurried home through the dark rain. The banks at the sides of the road spouted little jets of muddy water. The rain slanted and swirled under a cold and gusty wind. Jody dogtrotted home, slopping through the gravelly mud of the road.

From the top of the ridge he could see Gabilan standing miserably in the corral. The red coat was almost black and streaked with water. He stood head down with his rump to the rain and wind. Jody arrived running and threw open the barn door and led the wet pony in by his forelock. Then he found a gunnysack and rubbed the soaked hair and rubbed the legs and ankles. Gabilan stood patiently, but he trembled in gusts like the wind.

When he had dried the pony as well as he could, Jody went up to the house and brought hot water down to the barn and soaked the grain in it. Gabilan was not very hungry. He nibbled at the hot mash, but he was not very much interested in it, and he still shivered now and then. A little steam rose from his damp back.

It was almost dark when Billy Buck and Carl Tiflin came home.

"When the rain started we put up at Ben Herche's place, and the rain never let up all afternoon," Carl Tiflin explained. Jody looked reproachfully at Billy Buck, and Billy felt guilty.

"You said it wouldn't rain," Jody accused him.

Billy looked away. "It's hard to tell, this time of year," he said, but his excuse was lame. He had no right to be fallible, and he knew it.

"The pony got wet, got soaked through."

"Did you dry him off?"

"I rubbed him with a sack and I gave him hot grain."

Billy nodded in agreement. "A little rain never hurt anything," Billy assured him.

Jody's father joined the conversation then and lectured the boy a little. "A horse," he said, "isn't any lapdog kind of thing." Carl Tiflin hated weakness and sickness, and he held a violent contempt for helplessness.

Jody's mother put a platter of steaks on the table and boiled potatoes and boiled squash, which clouded the room with steam. They sat down to eat. Carl Tiflin still grumbled about weakness put into animals and men by too much coddling.

Billy Buck felt bad about his mistake. "Did you blanket him?" he asked.

"No. I couldn't find a blanket. I laid some sacks over his back."

"We'll go down and cover him up after we eat, then." Billy felt better about it now. When Jody's father had gone in to the fire and his mother was washing dishes, Billy found and lighted a lantern. He and Jody walked through the mud to the barn. The barn was dark and warm and sweet. The horses still munched their evening hay. "You hold the lantern!" Billy ordered. And he felt the pony's legs and tested the heat of the flanks. He put his cheek against the pony's gray muzzle, and then he rolled up the eyelids to look at the eyeballs, and he lifted the lips to see the gums, and he put his fingers inside his ears. "He don't seem so chipper," Billy said. "I'll give him a rubdown."

Then Billy found a sack and rubbed the pony's legs violently and he rubbed the chest and the withers. Gabilan was strangely spiritless. He submitted patiently to the rubbing. At last Billy brought an old cotton comforter from the saddle room and threw it over the pony's back and tied it at the neck and chest with string. "Now he'll be all right in the morning," Billy said.

Jody's mother looked up when he got back to the house. "You're late up from bed," she said. She held his chin in her hard hand and brushed the tangled hair out of his eyes, and she said, "Don't worry about the pony. He'll be all right. Billy's as good as any horse doctor in the country."

Jody hadn't known she could see his worry. He pulled gently away from her and knelt down in front of the fireplace until it burned his stomach. He scorched himself through and then went in to bed, but it was a hard thing to go to sleep. He awakened after what seemed a long time. The room was dark, but there was a grayness in the window like that which precedes the dawn. He got up and found his overalls and searched for the legs, and then the clock in the other room struck two. He laid his clothes down and got back into bed. It was broad daylight when he awakened again. For the first time he had slept through the ringing of the triangle. He leaped up, flung on his clothes and went out of the door still buttoning his shirt. His mother looked after him for a moment and then went quietly back to her work. Her eyes were brooding and kind. Now and then her mouth smiled a little but without changing her eyes at all.

Jody ran on toward the barn. Halfway there he heard the sound he dreaded, the hollow rasping cough of a horse. He broke into a sprint then. In the barn he found Billy Buck with the pony. Billy was rubbing its legs with his strong thick hands. "He just took a little cold," Billy said. "We'll have him out of it in a couple of days."

Jody looked at the pony's face. The eyes were half closed and the lids thick and dry. In the eye corners a crust of hard mucus stuck. Gabilan's ears hung loosely sideways and his head was low. Jody put out his hand, but the pony did not move close to it. He coughed again and his whole body constricted with the effort. A little stream of thin fluid ran from his nostrils.

Jody looked back at Billy Buck. "He's awful sick, Billy."

"Just a little cold, like I said," Billy insisted. "You go get some breakfast and then go back to school. I'll take care of him."

"But you might have to do something else. You might leave him."

"No. I won't. I won't leave him at all. Tomorrow's Saturday. Then you can stay with him all day." Billy had failed again and he felt badly about it. He had to cure the pony now.

Jody walked up to the house and took his place listlessly at the table. The eggs and bacon were cold and greasy, but he didn't notice it. He ate his usual amount. He didn't even ask to stay home from school. His mother pushed his hair back when she took his plate. "Billy'll take care of the pony," she assured him.

He moped through the whole day at school. He couldn't answer any questions nor read any words. He couldn't even tell anyone the pony was sick, for that might make him sicker. And when school was finally out, he started home in dread. He walked slowly and let the other boys leave him. He wished he might continue walking and never arrive at the ranch.

Billy was in the barn, as he had promised, and the pony was worse. His eyes were almost closed now, and his breath whistled shrilly past an obstruction in his nose. A film covered the part of the eyes that was visible at all. It was doubtful whether the pony could see anymore. Now and then he snorted to clear his nose, and by that action seemed to plug it tighter. Jody looked dispiritedly at the pony's coat. The hair lay rough and unkempt and seemed to have lost all of its old luster. Bill stood quietly beside the stall. Jody hated to ask, but he had to know.

"Billy, is he—is he going to get well?"

Billy put his fingers between the bars under the pony's jaw and felt about. "Feel here," he said, and he guided Jody's fingers to a large lump under the jaw. "When that gets bigger, I'll open it up and then he'll get better."

Jody looked quickly away, for he had heard about lumps like that. "What is it the matter with him?"

Billy didn't want to answer, but he had to. He couldn't be wrong three times. "Strangles," he said shortly, "but don't you worry about that. I'll pull him out of it. I've seen them get well when they were worse than Gabilan is. I'm going to steam him now. You can help."

"Yes," Jody said miserably. He followed Billy into the grain room and watched him make the steaming bag ready. It was a long canvas nose bag with straps to go over a horse's ears. Billy filled it one-third full of bran, and then he added a couple of handfuls of dried hops. On top of the dry substance he poured a little carbolic acid and a little turpentine. "I'll be mixing it all up while you run to the house for a kettle of boiling water," Billy said.

When Jody came back with the steaming kettle, Billy buckled the straps over Gabilan's head and fitted the bag tightly around his nose. Then through a little hole in the side of the bag he poured the boiling water on the mixture. The pony started away as a cloud of strong steam rose up, but then the soothing fumes crept through his nose and into his lungs, and the sharp steam began to clear out the nasal passages. He breathed loudly. His legs trembled in an ague, and his eyes closed against the biting cloud. Billy poured in more water and kept the steam rising for fifteen minutes. At last he set down the kettle and took the bag from Gabilan's nose. The pony looked better. He breathed freely, and his eyes were open wider than they had been.

"See how good it makes him feel," Billy said. "Now we'll wrap him up in the blanket again. Maybe he'll be nearly well by morning."

"I'll stay with him tonight," Jody suggested.

"No. Don't do it. I'll bring my blankets down here and put them in the hay. You can stay tomorrow and steam him if he needs it."

The evening was falling when they went to the house for their supper. Jody didn't even realize that someone else had fed the chickens and filled the woodbox. He walked up past the house to the dark brush line and took a drink of water from the tub. The spring water was so cold that it stung his mouth and drove a shiver through him. The sky above the hills was still light. He saw a hawk flying so high that it caught the sun on its breast and shone like a spark. Two blackbirds were driving him down the sky, glittering as they attacked their enemy. In the west, the clouds were moving in to rain again.

Jody's father didn't speak at all while the family ate supper, but after Billy Buck had taken his blankets and gone to sleep in the barn, Carl Tiflin built a high fire in the fireplace and told stories. He told about the wild man who ran naked through the country and had a tail and ears like a horse, and he told about the rabbit-cats of Moro Cojo that hopped into the trees for birds. He revived the famous Maxwell brothers who found a vein of gold and hid the traces of it so carefully that they could never find it again.

Jody sat with his chin in his hands; his mouth worked nervously, and his father gradually became aware that he wasn't listening very carefully. "Isn't that funny?" he asked.

Jody laughed politely and said, "Yes, sir." His father was angry and hurt then. He didn't tell any more stories. After a while, Jody took a lantern and went down to the barn. Billy Buck was asleep in the hay, and, except that his breath rasped a little in his lungs, the pony seemed to be much better. Jody stayed a little while, running his fingers over the red rough coat, and then he took up the lantern and went back to the house.

When he was in bed, his mother came into the room. "Have you enough covers on? It's getting winter."

"Yes, ma'am."

"Well, get some rest tonight." She hesitated to go out, stood uncertainly. "The pony will be all right," she said.

JODY WAS TIRED. He went to sleep quickly and didn't awaken until dawn. The triangle sounded, and Billy Buck came up from the barn before Jody could get out of the house.

"How is he?" Jody demanded.

Billy always wolfed his breakfast. "Pretty good. I'm going to open that lump this morning. Then he'll be better maybe."

After breakfast, Billy got out his best knife, one with a needle point. He whetted the shining blade a long time on a little Carborundum stone. He tried the point and the blade again and again on his callused thumb-ball, and at last he tried it on his upper lip.

On the way to the barn, Jody noticed how the young grass was up

29

and how the stubble was melting day by day into the new green crop of volunteer. It was a cold sunny morning.

As soon as he saw the pony, Jody knew he was worse. His eyes were closed and sealed shut with dried mucus. His head hung so low that his nose almost touched the straw of his bed. There was a little groan in each breath, a deep-seated, patient groan.

Billy lifted the weak head and made a quick slash with the knife. Jody saw the yellow pus run out. He held up the head while Billy swabbed out the wound with weak carbolic acid salve.

"Now he'll feel better," Billy assured him. "That yellow poison is what makes him sick."

Jody looked unbelieving at Billy Buck. "He's awful sick."

Billy thought a long time what to say. He nearly tossed off a careless assurance, but he saved himself in time. "Yes, he's pretty sick," he said at last. "I've seen worse ones get well. If he doesn't get pneumonia, we'll pull him through. You stay with him. If he gets worse, you can come and get me."

For a long time after Billy went away, Jody stood beside the pony, stroking him behind the ears. The pony didn't flip his head the way he had done when he was well. The groaning in his breathing was becoming more hollow.

Doubletree Mutt looked into the barn, his big tail waving provocatively, and Jody was so incensed at his health that he found a hard black clod on the floor and deliberately threw it. Doubletree Mutt went yelping away to nurse a bruised paw.

In the middle of the morning, Billy Buck came back and made another steam bag. Jody watched to see whether the pony improved this time as he had before. His breathing eased a little, but he did not raise his head.

The Saturday dragged on. Late in the afternoon Jody went to the house and brought his bedding down and made up a place to sleep in the hay. He didn't ask permission. He knew from the way his mother looked at him that she would let him do almost anything. That night he left a lantern burning on a wire over the box stall. Billy had told him to rub the pony's legs every little while.

At nine o'clock the wind sprang up and howled around the barn. And in spite of his worry, Jody grew sleepy. He got into his blankets and went to sleep, but the breathy groans of the pony sounded in his dreams. And in his sleep he heard a crashing noise which went on and on until it awakened him. The wind was rushing through the barn. He sprang up and looked down the lane of stalls. The barn door had blown open, and the pony was gone.

He caught the lantern and ran outside into the gale, and he saw Gabilan weakly shambling away into the darkness, head down, legs working slowly and mechanically. When Jody ran up and caught him by the forelock, he allowed himself to be led back and put into his stall. His groans were louder, and a fierce whistling came from his nose. Jody didn't sleep anymore then. The hissing of the pony's breath grew louder and sharper.

He was glad when Billy Buck came in at dawn. Billy looked for a time at the pony as though he had never seen him before. He felt the ears and flanks. "Jody," he said, "I've got to do something you won't want to see. You run up to the house for a while."

Jody grabbed him fiercely by the forearm. "You're not going to shoot him?"

Billy patted his hand. "No. I'm going to open a little hole in his windpipe so he can breathe. His nose is filled up. When he gets well, we'll put a little brass button in the hole for him to breathe through."

Jody couldn't have gone away if he wanted to. It was awful to see the red hide cut, but infinitely more terrible to know it was being cut and not to see it. "I'll stay right here," he said bitterly. "You sure you got to?"

"Yes. I'm sure. If you stay, you can hold his head. If it doesn't make you sick, that is."

The fine knife came out again and was whetted again just as carefully as it had been the first time. Jody held the pony's head up and the throat taut, while Billy felt up and down for the right place. Jody sobbed once as the bright knife point disappeared into the throat. The pony plunged weakly away and then stood still, trembling violently. The blood ran thickly out and up the knife and across Billy's hand and onto his shirt-sleeve. The sure square hand sawed out a round hole in the flesh, and the breath came bursting out of the hole, throwing a fine spray of blood. With the rush of oxygen, the pony took a sudden strength. He lashed out with his hind feet and tried to rear, but Jody held his head down while Billy mopped the new wound with carbolic salve. It was a good job. The blood stopped flowing and the air puffed out the hole and sucked it in regularly with a little bubbling noise.

The rain brought in by the night wind began to fall on the barn roof. Then the triangle rang for breakfast. "You go up and eat while I wait," Billy said. "We've got to keep this hole from plugging up."

Jody walked slowly out of the barn. He was too dispirited to tell Billy how the barn door had blown open and let the pony out. He emerged into the wet gray morning and sloshed up to the house, taking a perverse pleasure in splashing through all the puddles. His mother fed him and made him put dry clothes on. She didn't question him. She seemed to know he couldn't answer questions. But when he was ready to go back to the barn she brought him a pan of steaming meal. "Give him this," she said.

But Jody did not take the pan. He said, "He won't eat anything," and ran out of the house. At the barn, Billy showed him how to fix a ball of cotton on a stick, with which to swab out the breathing hole when it became clogged with mucus.

Jody's father walked into the barn and stood with them in front of the stall. At length he turned to the boy. "Hadn't you better come with me? I'm going to drive over the hill."

Jody shook his head.

"You better come on, out of this," his father insisted.

Billy turned on him angrily. "Let him alone. It's his pony, isn't it?"

Carl Tiflin walked away without saying another word. His feelings were badly hurt.

All morning Jody kept the wound open and the air passing in and out freely. At noon the pony lay wearily down on his side and stretched his nose out.

Billy came back. "If you're going to stay with him tonight, you better take a little nap," he said. Jody went absently out of the barn. The sky had cleared to a hard thin blue. Everywhere the birds were busy with worms that had come to the damp surface of the ground.

Jody walked to the brush line and sat on the edge of the mossy tub. He looked down at the house and at the old bunkhouse and at the dark cypress tree. The place was familiar, but curiously changed. It wasn't itself anymore, but a frame for things that were happening. A cold wind blew out of the east now, signifying that the rain was over for a little while. At his feet Jody could see the little arms of new weeds spreading out over the ground. In the mud about the spring were thousands of quail tracks.

Doubletree Mutt came sideways and embarrassed up through the vegetable patch, and Jody, remembering how he had thrown the clod, put his arm about the dog's neck and kissed him on his wide black nose. Doubletree Mutt sat still, as though he knew some solemn thing was happening. His big tail slapped the ground gravely. Jody pulled a swollen tick out of Mutt's neck and popped it dead between his thumbnails. It was a nasty thing. He washed his hands in the cold spring water.

Except for the steady swish of the wind, the farm was very quiet. Jody knew his mother wouldn't mind if he didn't go in to eat his lunch. After a little while he went slowly back to the barn. Mutt crept into his own little house and whined softly to himself for a long time.

Billy Buck stood up from the box and surrendered the cotton swab. The pony still lay on his side and the wound in his throat bellowed in and out. When Jody saw how dry and dead the hair looked, he knew at last that there was no hope for the pony. He had seen the dead hair before on dogs and on cows, and it was a sure sign. He sat heavily on the box and let down the barrier of the box stall. For a long time he kept his eyes on the moving wound, and at last he dozed, and the afternoon passed quickly. Just before dark his mother brought a deep dish of stew and left it for him and went away. Jody ate a little of it and when it was dark, he set the lantern on the floor by the pony's head so he could watch the wound and keep it open. And he dozed again until the night chill awakened him. The wind was blowing fiercely, bringing the north cold with it. Jody brought a blanket from his bed in the hay and wrapped himself in it. Gabilan's breathing was quiet at last; the hole in his throat moved gently. The owls flew through the hayloft, shrieking and looking for mice. Jody put his head down on his hands and slept. In his sleep he was aware that the wind had increased. He heard it slamming about the barn.

It was daylight when he awakened. The barn door had swung open. The pony was gone. He sprang up and ran out into the morning light.

The pony's tracks were plain enough, dragging through the frost-like dew on the young grass, tired tracks with little lines between them where the hooves had dragged. They headed for the brush line halfway up the ridge. Jody broke into a run and followed them. The sun shone on the sharp white quartz that stuck through the ground here and there. As he followed the plain trail, a shadow cut across in front of him. He looked up and saw a high circle of black buzzards, and the slowly revolving circle dropped lower and lower. The solemn birds soon disappeared over the ridge. Jody ran faster then, forced on by panic and rage. The trail entered the brush at last and followed a winding route among the tall sagebrushes.

At the top of the ridge Jody was winded. He paused, puffing noisily. The blood pounded in his ears. Then he saw what he was looking for. Below, in one of the little clearings in the brush, lay the red pony. In the distance, Jody could see the legs moving slowly and convulsively. And in a circle around him stood the buzzards, waiting for the moment of death they knew so well.

Jody leaped forward and plunged down the hill. The wet ground muffled his steps and the brush hid him. When he arrived, it was all over. The first buzzard sat on the pony's head and its beak had just risen dripping with dark eye fluid. Jody plunged into the circle like a cat. The black brotherhood arose in a cloud, but the big one on the pony's head was too late. As it hopped along to take off, Jody caught its wing tip and pulled it down. It was nearly as big as he was. The free wing crashed into his face with the force of a club, but he hung on. The claws fastened on his leg and the wing elbows battered his head on either side. Jody groped blindly with his free hand. His fingers found the neck of the struggling bird. The red eyes looked into his face, calm and fearless and fierce; the naked head turned from side to side. Then the beak opened and vomited a stream of putrefied fluid. Jody brought up his knee and fell on the great bird. He held the neck to the ground with one hand while his other found a piece of sharp white quartz. The first blow broke the beak sideways and black blood spurted from the twisted, leathery mouth corners. He struck again and missed. The red fearless eyes still looked at him, impersonal and unafraid and detached. He struck again and again, until the buzzard lay dead, until its head was a red pulp. He was still beating the dead bird when Billy Buck pulled him off and held him tightly to calm his shaking.

Carl Tiflin wiped the blood from the boy's face with a red bandanna. Jody was limp and quiet now. His father moved the buzzard with his toe. "Jody," he explained, "the buzzard didn't kill the pony. Don't you know that?"

"I know it," Jody said wearily.

It was Billy Buck who was angry. He had lifted Jody in his arms and had turned to carry him home. But he turned back on Carl Tiflin.

"Course he knows it," Billy said furiously. "Jesus Christ, man, can't you see how he'd feel about it?"

CHAPTER 2
THE GREAT MOUNTAINS

IN THE HUMMING HEAT of a midsummer afternoon the little boy Jody listlessly looked about the ranch for something to do. He had been to the barn, had thrown rocks at the swallows' nests under the eaves until every one of the little mud houses broke open and dropped its lining of straw and dirty feathers. Then at the ranch house he baited a rattrap with stale cheese and set it where Doubletree Mutt, that good big dog, would get his nose snapped.

Jody was not moved by an impulse of cruelty; he was bored with the long hot afternoon. Doubletree Mutt put his stupid nose in the trap and got it smacked, and shrieked with agony and limped away with blood on his nostrils. No matter where he was hurt, Mutt limped. It was just a way he had. Once when he was young, Mutt got caught in a coyote trap, and always after that he limped, even when he was scolded.

When Mutt yelped, Jody's mother called from inside the house, "Jody! Stop torturing that dog and find something to do."

Jody felt mean then, so he threw a rock at Mutt. Then he took his slingshot from the porch and walked up toward the brush line to try to kill a bird. It was a good slingshot, with store-bought rubbers, but while Jody had often shot at birds, he had never hit one. He walked up through the vegetable patch, kicking his bare toes into the dust. And on the way he found the perfect slingshot stone, round and slightly flattened and heavy enough to carry through the air. He fitted it into the leather pouch of his weapon and proceeded to the brush line. His eyes narrowed, his mouth worked strenuously; for the first time that afternoon he was intent. In the shade of the sagebrush the little birds were working, scratching in the leaves, flying restlessly a few feet and scratching again. Jody pulled back the sling and advanced cautiously. One little thrush paused and looked at him and crouched, ready to fly. Jody sidled nearer, moving one foot slowly after the other. When he was twenty feet away, he carefully raised the sling and aimed. The stone whizzed; the thrush started up and flew right into it. And down the little bird went with a broken head. Jody ran to it and picked it up.

"Well, I got you," he said.

The bird looked much smaller dead than it had alive. Jody felt a little mean pain in his stomach, so he took out his pocketknife and cut off the bird's head. Then he disemboweled it and took off its wings, and finally he threw all the pieces into the brush. He didn't care about the bird, or its life, but he knew what older people would say if they had seen him kill it; he was ashamed because of their potential opinion. He decided to forget the whole thing as quickly as he could and never to mention it.

The hills were dry at this season and the wild grass was golden, but where the spring pipe filled the round tub and the tub spilled over, there lay a stretch of fine green grass, deep and sweet and moist. Jody drank from the mossy tub and washed the bird's blood from his hands in cold water. Then he lay on his back in the grass and looked up at the dumpling summer clouds. By closing one eye and destroying perspective he brought them down within reach so that he could put up his fingers and stroke them. He helped the gentle wind push them down the sky; it seemed to him that they went faster for his help. One fat white cloud he helped clear to the mountain rims and pressed it firmly over, out of sight. Jody wondered what it was seeing then. He sat up the better to look at the great mountains where they went piling back, growing darker and more savage until they finished with one jagged ridge, high up against the west. Curious secret mountains; he thought of the little he knew about them.

"What's on the other side?" he asked his father once.

"More mountains, I guess. Why?"

"And on the other side of them?"

"More mountains. Why?"

"More mountains on and on?"

"Well, no. At last you come to the ocean."

"But what's in the mountains?"

"Just cliffs and brush and rocks and dryness."

"Were you ever there?"

"No."

"Has anybody ever been there?"

"A few people, I guess. It's dangerous, with cliffs and things. Why, I've read there's more unexplored country in the mountains of Monterey County than anywhere in the United States." His father seemed proud that this should be so.

"And at last the ocean?"

"At last the ocean."

"But," the boy insisted, "but in between? No one knows?"

"Oh, a few people do, I guess. But there's nothing there to get. And not much water. Just rocks and cliffs and greasewood. Why?"

"It would be good to go."

"What for? There's nothing there."

Jody knew something was there, something very wonderful because it wasn't known, something secret and mysterious. He could feel within himself that this was so. He said to his mother, "Do you know what's in the big mountains?"

She looked at him and then back at the ferocious range, and she said, "Only the bear, I guess."

"What bear?"

"Why, the one that went over the mountain to see what he could see."

Jody questioned Billy Buck, the ranchhand, about the possibility of ancient cities lost in the mountains, but Billy agreed with Jody's father.

"It ain't likely," Billy said. "There'd be nothing to eat unless a kind of people that can eat rocks live there."

That was all the information Jody ever got, and it made the mountains dear to him, and terrible. He thought often of the miles of ridge after ridge until at last there was the sea. When the peaks were pink in the morning, they invited him among them. And when the sun had gone over the edge in the evening and the mountains were a purplelike despair, then Jody was afraid of them; then they were so impersonal and aloof that their very imperturbability was a threat.

Now he turned his head toward the mountains of the east, the Gabilans, and they were jolly mountains, with hill ranches in their creases, and with pine trees growing on their crests. People lived there, and battles had been fought against the Mexicans on the slopes. He looked back for an instant at the Great Ones and shivered a little at the contrast. The foothill cup of the home ranch below him was sunny and safe. The house gleamed with white light and the barn was brown and warm. The red cows on the farther hill ate their way slowly toward the north. Even the dark cypress tree by the bunkhouse was usual and safe. The chickens scratched about in the dust of the farmyard with quick waltzing steps.

Then a moving figure caught Jody's eye. A man walked slowly over the brow of the hill on the road from Salinas, and he was headed in the direction of the house. Jody stood up and moved down toward the house too, for if someone was coming, he wanted to be there to see. By the time the boy had got to the house the walking man was only halfway down the road, a lean man, very straight in the shoulders. Jody could tell he was old only because his heels struck the ground with hard jerks. As he approached, Jody saw that he was dressed in blue jeans and in a coat of the same material. He wore clodhopper shoes and an old flat-brimmed Stetson. Over his shoulder he carried a gunnysack, lumpy and full. In a few moments he had trudged close enough so that his face could be seen. And his face was as dark as dried beef. A mustache, blue-white against the dark skin, hovered over his mouth, and his hair was white too, where it showed at his neck. The skin of his face had shrunk back against the skull until it defined bone, not flesh, and made the nose and chin seem sharp and fragile. The eyes were large and deep and dark, with eyelids stretched tightly over them. Irises and pupils were one, and very black, but the eyeballs were brown. There were no wrinkles in the face at all. This old man wore a blue denim coat buttoned to the throat with brass buttons, as all men do who wear no shirts. Out of the sleeves came strong bony wrists and hands gnarled and knotted and hard as peach branches. The nails were flat and blunt and shiny.

The old man drew close to the gate and swung down his sack when he confronted Jody. His lips fluttered a little and a soft impersonal voice came from between them.

"Do you live here?"

Jody was embarrassed. He turned and looked at the house, and he turned back and looked toward the barn where his father and Billy Buck were. "Yes," he said, when no help came from either direction.

"I have come back," the old man said. "I am Gitano, and I have come back."

Jody could not take all this responsibility. He turned abruptly and ran into the house for help, and the screen door banged after him. His mother was in the kitchen poking out the clogged holes of a colander with a hairpin and biting her lower lip with concentration.

"It's an old man," Jody cried excitedly. "It's an old *paisano* man, and he says he's come back."

His mother put down the colander and stuck the hairpin behind the sink board. "What's the matter now?" she asked patiently.

"It's an old man outside. Come on out."

"Well, what does he want?" She untied the strings of her apron and smoothed her hair with her fingers.

"I don't know. He came walking."

His mother smoothed down her dress and went out, and Jody followed her. Gitano had not moved.

"Yes?" Mrs. Tiflin asked.

Gitano took off his old black hat and held it with both hands in front of him. He repeated, "I am Gitano, and I have come back."

"Come back? Back where?"

Gitano's whole straight body leaned forward a little. His right hand described the circle of the hills, the sloping fields and the mountains, and ended at his hat again. "Back to the *rancho*. I was born here, and my father, too."

"Here?" she demanded. "This isn't an old place."

"No, there," he said, pointing to the western ridge. "On the other side there, in a house that is gone."

At last she understood. "The old 'dobe that's washed almost away, you mean?"

"Yes, *señora*. When the *rancho* broke up, they put no more lime on the 'dobe, and the rains washed it down."

Jody's mother was silent for a little, and curious homesick thoughts ran through her mind, but quickly she cleared them out. "And what do you want here now, Gitano?"

"I will stay here," he said quietly, "until I die."

"But we don't need an extra man here."

"I cannot work hard anymore, señora. I can milk a cow, feed chickens, cut a little wood—no more. I will stay here." He indicated the sack on the ground beside him. "Here are my things."

She turned to Jody. "Run down to the barn and call your father."

Jody dashed away, and he returned with Carl Tiflin and Billy Buck behind him. The old man was standing as he had been, but he was resting now. His whole body had sagged into a timeless repose.

"What is it?" Carl Tiflin asked. "What's Jody so excited about?"

Mrs. Tiflin motioned to the old man. "He wants to stay here. He wants to do a little work and stay here."

"Well, we can't have him. We don't need any more men. He's too old. Billy does everything we need."

They had been talking over him as though he did not exist, and now, suddenly, they both hesitated and looked at Gitano and were embarrassed.

He cleared his throat. "I am too old to work. I come back where I was born."

"You weren't born here," Carl said sharply.

"No. In the 'dobe house over the hill. It was all one *rancho* before you came."

"In the mud house that's all melted down?"

"Yes. I and my father. I will stay here now on the *rancho*."

"I tell you you won't stay," Carl said angrily. "I don't need an old man. This isn't a big ranch. I can't afford food and doctor bills for an old man. You must have relatives and friends. Go to them. It is like begging to come to strangers."

"I was born here," Gitano said patiently and inflexibly.

Carl Tiflin didn't like to be cruel, but he felt he must. "You can eat here tonight," he said. "You can sleep in the little room of the old bunkhouse. We'll give you breakfast in the morning, and then you'll have to go. Go to your friends. Don't come to die with strangers."

Gitano put on his black hat and stooped for the sack. "Here are my things," he said.

Carl turned away. "Come on, Billy, we'll finish down at the barn. Jody, show him the little room in the bunkhouse."

He and Billy turned back toward the barn. Mrs. Tiflin went into the house, saying over her shoulder, "I'll send some blankets down."

Gitano looked questioningly at Jody. "I'll show you where it is," Jody said.

There was a cot with a shuck mattress, an apple box holding a tin lantern, and a backless rocking chair in the little room of the bunk-house. Gitano laid his sack carefully on the floor and sat down on the bed. Jody stood shyly in the room, hesitating to go. At last he said, "Did you come out of the big mountains?"

Gitano shook his head slowly. "No, I worked down the Salinas Valley."

The afternoon thought would not let Jody go. "Did you ever go into the big mountains back there?"

The old dark eyes grew fixed, and their light turned inward on the years that were living in Gitano's head. "Once—when I was a little boy. I went with my father."

"Way back, clear into the mountains?"

"Yes."

"What was there?" Jody cried. "Did you see any people or any houses?"

"No."

"Well, what was there?"

Gitano's eyes remained inward. A little wrinkled strain came between his brows.

"What did you see in there?" Jody repeated.

"I don't know," Gitano said. "I don't remember."

"Was it terrible and dry?"

"I don't remember."

In his excitement, Jody had lost his shyness. "Don't you remember anything about it?"

Gitano's mouth opened for a word and remained open while his brain sought the word. "I think it was quiet—I think it was nice."

Gitano's eyes seemed to have found something back in the years, for they grew soft and a little smile seemed to come and go in them.

"Didn't you ever go back in the mountains again?" Jody insisted.

"No."

"Didn't you ever want to?"

But now Gitano's face became impatient. "No," he said in a tone that told Jody he didn't want to talk about it anymore.

The boy was held by a curious fascination. He didn't want to go away from Gitano. His shyness returned. "Would you like to come down to the barn and see the stock?" he asked.

Gitano stood up and put on his hat and prepared to follow.

It was almost evening now. They stood near the watering trough while the horses sauntered in from the hillsides for an evening drink. Gitano rested his big twisted hands on the top rail of the fence. Five horses came down and drank, and then stood about, nibbling at the dirt or rubbing their sides against the polished wood of the fence. Long after they had finished drinking, an old horse appeared over the brow of the hill and came painfully down. It had long yellow teeth; its hooves were flat and sharp as spades, and its ribs and hip-bones jutted out under its skin. It hobbled up to the trough and drank water with a loud sucking noise.

"That's old Easter," Jody explained. "That's the first horse my father ever had. He's thirty years old." He looked up into Gitano's old eyes for some response.

"No good anymore," Gitano said.

Jody's father and Billy Buck came out of the barn and walked over.

"Too old to work," Gitano repeated. "Just eats and pretty soon dies."

Carl Tiflin caught the last words. He hated his earlier brutality toward old Gitano, and so he became brutal again. "It's a shame not to shoot Easter," he said. "It'd save him a lot of pains and rheumatism." He looked secretly at Gitano to see whether he noticed the parallel, but the big bony hands did not move, nor did the dark eyes turn from the horse. "Old things ought to be put out of their misery," Jody's father went on. "One shot, a big noise, one big pain in the head maybe, and that's all. That's better than stiffness and sore teeth."

Billy Buck broke in. "They got a right to rest after they worked all of their life. Maybe they like to just walk around."

Carl had been looking steadily at the skinny horse. "You can't imagine now what Easter used to look like," he said softly. "High neck, deep chest, fine barrel. He could jump a five-bar gate in stride. I won a flat race on him when I was fifteen years old. I could of got two hundred dollars for him anytime. You wouldn't think how pretty he was." He checked himself, for he hated softness. "But he ought to be shot now," he said.

"He's got a right to rest," Billy Buck insisted.

Jody's father had a humorous thought. He turned to Gitano. "If ham and eggs grew on a sidehill, I'd turn you out to pasture too," he said. "But I can't afford to pasture you in my kitchen."

He laughed to Billy Buck about it as they went on toward the house. "Be a good thing for all of us if ham and eggs did grow on the sidehills."

Jody knew how his father was probing for a place to hurt in Gitano. He had been probed often himself. His father knew every place in the boy where a word would fester.

"He's only talking," Jody said. "He didn't mean it about shooting Easter. He likes Easter. That was the first horse he ever owned."

The sun sank behind the mountains as they stood there. Gitano seemed to be more at home in the evening. He made a curious sharp sound with his lips and stretched one of his hands over the fence. Old Easter moved stiffly to him, and Gitano rubbed the lean neck.

"You like him?" Jody asked softly.

"Yes—but he's no damn good."

The triangle sounded at the ranch house. "That's supper," Jody cried. "Come on up to supper."

As they walked up toward the house Jody noticed again that Gitano's body was as straight as that of a young man. Only by a jerkiness in his movements and by the scuffling of his heels could it be seen that he was old.

The turkeys were flying heavily into the lower branches of the cypress tree by the bunkhouse. A flat sleek ranch cat walked across the road carrying a rat so large that its tail dragged on the ground. The quail on the sidehills were still sounding the clear water call.

Jody and Gitano came to the back steps and Mrs. Tiflin looked out through the screen door at them.

"Come running, Jody. Come in to supper, Gitano."

Carl and Billy Buck had started to eat at the long oilcloth-covered table. Jody slipped into his chair without moving it, but Gitano stood holding his hat until Carl looked up and said, "Sit down, sit down. You might as well get your belly full before you go on." Carl was afraid he might relent and let the old man stay, and so he continued to remind himself that this couldn't be.

Gitano laid his hat on the floor and diffidently sat down. He wouldn't reach for food. Carl had to pass it to him. "Here, fill yourself up." Gitano ate very slowly, cutting tiny pieces of meat and arranging little pats of mashed potato on his plate.

The situation would not stop worrying Carl Tiflin. "Haven't you got any relatives in this part of the country?" he asked.

Gitano answered with some pride, "My brother-in-law is in Monterey. I have cousins there, too."

"Well, you can go and live there, then."

"I was born here," Gitano said in gentle rebuke.

Jody's mother came in from the kitchen, carrying a large bowl of tapioca pudding.

Carl chuckled at her. "Did I tell you what I said to him? I said if ham and eggs grew on the sidehills, I'd put him out to pasture like old Easter."

Gitano stared, unmoved, at his plate.

"It's too bad he can't stay," said Mrs. Tiflin.

"Now don't you start anything," Carl said crossly.

When they had finished eating, Carl and Billy Buck and Jody went into the living room to sit for a while, but Gitano, without a word of farewell or thanks, walked through the kitchen and out the back door. Jody sat and secretly watched his father. He knew how mean his father felt.

"This country's full of these old *paisanos,*" Carl said to Billy Buck.

"They're damn good men," Billy defended them. "They can work older than white men. I saw one of them a hundred and five years, and he could still ride a horse. You don't see any white men as old as Gitano walking twenty or thirty miles."

"Oh, they're tough, all right," Carl agreed. "Say, are you standing up for him too? Listen, Billy," he explained, "I'm having a hard enough time keeping this ranch out of the Bank of Italy without taking on anybody else to feed. You know that, Billy."

"Sure, I know," said Billy. "If you was rich, it'd be different."

"That's right, and it isn't like he didn't have relatives to go to. A brother-in-law and cousins right in Monterey. Why should I worry about him?"

Jody sat quietly listening, and he seemed to hear Gitano's gentle voice and its unanswerable, "But I was born here." Gitano was mysterious, like the mountains. There were ranges back as far as you could see, but behind the last range piled up against the sky there was a great unknown country. And Gitano was an old man, until you got to the dull dark eyes. Behind them was some unknown thing. He didn't ever say enough to let you guess what was inside, under the eyes. Jody felt himself irresistibly drawn toward the bunkhouse. He slipped from his chair while his father was talking, and he went out the door without making a sound.

The night was very dark and far-off noises carried in clearly. The hame bells of a wood team sounded from way over the hill on the country road. Jody picked his way across the dark yard. He could see a light through the window of the little room of the bunkhouse. Because the night was secret he walked quietly up to the window and peered in. Gitano sat in the rocking chair and his back was toward the window. His right arm moved slowly back and forth in front of him. Jody pushed the door open and walked in. Gitano jerked upright, and, seizing a piece of deerskin, he tried to throw it over the thing in his lap, but the skin slipped away. Jody stood overwhelmed by the thing in Gitano's hand, a lean and lovely rapier with a golden basket hilt. The blade was like a thin ray of dark light. The hilt was pierced and intricately carved.

"What is it?" Jody demanded.

Gitano only looked at him with resentful eyes, and he picked up the fallen deerskin and firmly wrapped the beautiful blade in it.

Jody put out his hand. "Can't I see it?"

Gitano's eyes smoldered angrily and he shook his head.

"Where'd you get it? Where'd it come from?"

Gitano regarded him profoundly, as though he pondered. "I got it from my father."

"Well, where'd he get it?"

Gitano looked down at the long deerskin parcel in his hand. "I don't know."

"Didn't he ever tell you?"

"No."

"What do you do with it?"

Gitano looked slightly surprised. "Nothing. I just keep it."

"Can't I see it again?"

The old man slowly unwrapped the shining blade and let the lamplight slip along it for a moment. Then he wrapped it up again.

"You go now. I want to go to bed." He blew out the lamp almost before Jody had closed the door.

As he went back toward the house, Jody knew one thing more sharply than he had ever known anything. He must never tell anyone about the rapier. It would be a dreadful thing to tell anyone about it, for it would destroy some fragile structure of truth. It was a truth that might be shattered by division.

On the way across the dark yard Jody passed Billy Buck. "They're wondering where you are," Billy said.

Jody slipped into the living room, and his father turned to him. "Where have you been?"

"I just went out to see if I caught any rats in my new trap."

"It's time you went to bed," his father said.

JODY WAS FIRST at the breakfast table in the morning. Then his father came in, and last, Billy Buck. Mrs. Tiflin looked in from the kitchen.

"Where's the old man, Billy?" she asked.

"I guess he's out walking," Billy said. "I looked in his room and he wasn't there."

"Maybe he started early to Monterey," said Carl. "It's a long walk."

"No," Billy explained. "His sack is in the little room."

After breakfast Jody walked down to the bunkhouse. Flies were flashing about in the sunshine. The ranch seemed especially quiet this morning. When he was sure no one was watching him, Jody went into the little room and looked into Gitano's sack. An extra pair of long cotton underwear was there, an extra pair of jeans and three pairs of worn socks. Nothing else was in the sack. A sharp loneliness fell on Jody. He walked slowly back toward the house. His father stood on the porch talking to Mrs. Tiflin.

"I guess old Easter's dead at last," he said. "I didn't see him come down to water with the other horses."

In the middle of the morning Jess Taylor from the ridge ranch rode down.

"You didn't sell that old gray crow-bait of yours, did you, Carl?"

"No, of course not. Why?"

"Well," Jess said, "I was out this morning early, and I saw a funny thing. I saw an old man on an old horse, no saddle, only a piece of rope for a bridle. He wasn't on the road at all. He was cutting right up straight through the brush. I think he had a gun. At least I saw something shine in his hand."

"That's old Gitano," Carl Tiflin said. "I'll see if any of my guns are missing." He stepped into the house for a second. "Nope, all here. Which way was he heading, Jess?"

"Well, that's the funny thing. He was heading straight back into the mountains."

Carl laughed. "They never get too old to steal," he said. "I guess he just stole old Easter."

"Want to go after him, Carl?"

"Hell no, just save me burying that horse. I wonder where he got the gun. I wonder what he wants back there."

Jody walked up through the vegetable patch, toward the brush line. He looked searchingly at the towering mountains—ridge after ridge after ridge until at last there was the ocean. For a moment he thought he could see a black speck crawling up the farthest ridge. Jody thought of the rapier and of Gitano. And he thought of the great mountains. A longing caressed him, and it was so sharp that he wanted to cry to get it out of his breast. He lay down in the grass near the round tub at the brush line. He covered his eyes with his crossed arms and lay there a long time, full of a nameless sorrow.

CHAPTER 3
THE PROMISE

IN A MIDAFTERNOON of spring, the little boy Jody walked martially along the brush-lined road toward his home ranch. Banging his knee against the golden lard bucket he used for school lunch, he contrived a good bass drum, while his tongue fluttered sharply against his teeth to fill in snare drums and occasional trumpets.

Sometime back the other members of the squad that walked so smartly from the school had turned into the various little canyons and taken the wagon roads to their own home ranches. Now Jody marched seemingly alone, with high-lifted knees and pounding feet; but behind him there was a phantom army with great flags and swords, silent but deadly.

The afternoon was green and gold with spring. Underneath the spread branches of the oaks the plants grew pale and tall, and on the hills the feed was smooth and thick. The sagebrushes shone with new silver leaves and the oaks wore hoods of golden green. Over the hills there hung such a green odor that the horses on the flats galloped madly and then stopped, wondering; lambs, and even old sheep, jumped in the air unexpectedly and landed on stiff legs and went on eating; young clumsy calves butted their heads together and drew back and butted again.

As the gray and silent army marched past, led by Jody, the animals stopped their feeding and their play and watched it go by.

Suddenly Jody stopped. The gray army halted, bewildered and nervous. Jody went down on his knees. The army stood in long uneasy ranks for a moment, and then, with a soft sigh of sorrow, rose up in a faint gray mist and disappeared. Jody had seen the thorny crown of a horny-toad moving under the dust of the road. His grimy hand went out and grasped the spiked halo and held firmly while the little beast struggled. Then Jody turned the horny-toad over, exposing its pale gold stomach. With a gentle forefinger he stroked the throat and chest until the horny-toad relaxed, until its eyes closed and it lay languorous and asleep.

Jody opened his lunch pail and deposited the first game inside. He moved on now, his knees bent slightly, his shoulders crouched; his bare feet were wise and silent. In his right hand there was a long gray rifle. The brush along the road stirred restively under a new and unexpected population of gray tigers and gray bears. The hunting was very good, for by the time Jody reached the fork of the road where the mailbox stood on a post, he had captured two more horny-toads, four little lizards, a blue snake, sixteen yellow-winged grasshoppers and a damp newt from under a rock. This assortment scrabbled unhappily against the tin of the lunch bucket.

At the road fork the rifle evaporated and the tigers and bears melted from the hillsides. Even the moist and uncomfortable creatures in the lunch pail ceased to exist, for the little red metal flag was up on the mailbox, signifying that something was inside. Jody set his pail on the ground and opened the mailbox. There was a Montgomery Ward catalog and a copy of the *Salinas Weekly Journal*. He slammed the box, picked up his lunch pail and trotted over the ridge and down into the cup of the ranch. Past the barn he ran, and past the used-up haystack and the bunkhouse and the cypress tree. He banged through the front screen door of the ranch house calling, "Ma'am, ma'am, there's a catalog."

Mrs. Tiflin was in the kitchen spooning clabbered milk into a cotton bag. She put down her work and rinsed her hands under the tap. "Here in the kitchen, Jody. Here I am."

He ran in and clattered his lunch pail on the sink. "Here it is. Can I open the catalog, ma'am?"

Mrs. Tiflin took up the spoon again and went back to her cottage cheese. "Don't lose it, Jody. Your father will want to see it." She scraped the last of the milk into the bag. "Oh, Jody, your father wants to see you before you go to your chores." She waved a cruising fly from the cheese bag.

Jody closed the new catalog in alarm. "Ma'am?"

"Why don't you ever listen? I say your father wants to see you."

The boy laid the catalog gently on the sink board. "Do you—is it something I did?"

Mrs. Tiflin laughed. "Always a bad conscience. What did you do?"

"Nothing, ma'am," he said lamely. But he couldn't remember, and besides it was impossible to know what action might later be construed as a crime.

His mother hung the full bag on a nail where it could drip into the sink. "He just said he wanted to see you when you got home. He's somewhere down by the barn."

Jody turned and went out the back door. Hearing his mother open the lunch pail and then gasp with rage, a memory stabbed him and he trotted away toward the barn, conscientiously not hearing the angry voice that called him from the house.

Carl Tiflin and Billy Buck stood against the lower pasture fence. Each man rested one foot on the lowest bar and both elbows on the top bar. They were talking slowly and aimlessly. In the pasture half a dozen horses nibbled contentedly at the sweet grass. The mare, Nellie, stood backed up against the gate, rubbing her buttocks on the heavy post.

Jody sidled uneasily near. He dragged one foot to give an impression of great innocence and nonchalance. When he arrived beside the men he put one foot on the lowest fence rail, rested his elbows on the second bar and looked into the pasture too. The two men glanced sideways at him.

"I wanted to see you," Carl said in the stern tone he reserved for children and animals.

"Yes, sir," said Jody guiltily.

"Billy here says you took good care of the pony before it died."

No punishment was in the air. Jody grew bolder. "Yes, sir, I did." He felt a sudden warm friendliness for the ranchhand.

Billy put in, "He trained that pony as good as anybody I ever seen."

Then Carl Tiflin came gradually to the point. "If you could have another horse, would you work for it?"

Jody shivered. "Yes, sir."

"Well, look here, then. Billy says the best way for you to be a good hand with horses is to raise a colt."

"It's the *only* good way," Billy interrupted.

"Look here, Jody," continued Carl. "Jess Taylor, up to the ridge ranch, has a fair stallion, but it'll cost five dollars. I'll put up the money, but you'll have to work it out all summer. Will you do that?"

Jody felt that his insides were shriveling. "Yes, sir," he said softly.

"And no complaining? And no forgetting when you're told to do something?"

"Yes, sir."

"Well, all right, then. Tomorrow morning you take Nellie up to the ridge ranch and get her bred. You'll have to take care of her, too, till she throws the colt."

"Yes, sir."

"You better get to the chickens and the wood now."

Jody slid away. In passing behind Billy Buck he very nearly put out his hand to touch the blue-jeaned legs. His shoulders swayed a little with maturity and importance.

He went to his work with unprecedented seriousness. This night he did not dump the can of grain to the chickens so that they had to leap over each other and struggle to get it. No, he spread the wheat so far and so carefully that the hens couldn't find some of it at all. And in the house, after listening to his mother's despair over boys who filled their lunch pails with slimy, suffocated reptiles and bugs, he promised never to do it again. Indeed, Jody felt that all such foolishness was lost in the past. He was far too grown-up ever to put horny-toads in his lunch pail anymore. He carried in so much wood and built such a high structure with it that his mother walked in fear of an avalanche of oak. When he was done, when he had gathered eggs that had remained hidden for weeks, Jody walked down again past the cypress tree and past the bunkhouse toward the pasture. A fat warty toad that looked out at him from under the watering trough had no emotional effect on him at all.

Carl Tiflin and Billy Buck were not in sight, but from a metallic ringing on the other side of the barn Jody knew that Billy Buck was just starting to milk a cow.

The other horses were eating toward the upper end of the pasture, but Nellie continued to rub herself nervously against the post. Jody walked slowly near, saying, "So, girl, so-o, Nellie." The mare's ears went back naughtily and her lips drew away from her yellow teeth. She turned her head around; her eyes were glazed and mad. Jody climbed to the top of the fence and hung his feet over and looked paternally down on the mare.

The evening hovered while he sat there. Bats and nighthawks flicked about. Billy Buck, walking toward the house carrying a full milk bucket, saw Jody and stopped. "It's a long time to wait," he said gently. "You'll get awful tired waiting."

"No I won't, Billy. How long will it be?"

"Nearly a year."

"Well, I won't get tired."

The triangle at the house rang stridently. Jody climbed down from the fence and walked to supper beside Billy Buck. He even put out his hand and took hold of the milk bucket to help carry it.

The next morning Carl Tiflin folded a five-dollar bill in a piece of newspaper and pinned the package in the bib pocket of Jody's overalls. Billy Buck haltered Nellie and let her out of the pasture.

"Be careful now," he warned. "Hold her up short here so she can't bite you. She's crazy as a coot."

Jody took hold of the halter leather itself and started up the hill toward the ridge ranch with Nellie skittering and jerking behind him. In the pasturage along the road the wild oat heads were just clearing their scabbards. The warm morning sun shone on Jody's back so sweetly that he was forced to take a serious stiff-legged hop now and then in spite of his maturity. On the fences the shiny blackbirds with red epaulets clicked their dry call. The meadowlarks sang and the wild doves, concealed among the leaves of the oaks, made a sound of restrained grieving. In the fields the rabbits sat sunning themselves, with only their forked ears showing above the grass.

After an hour of steady uphill walking, Jody turned into a narrow road that led up a steeper hill to the ridge ranch. He could see the red roof of the barn sticking up above the oak trees, and he could hear a dog barking unemotionally near the house.

Suddenly Nellie jerked back and nearly freed herself. From the direction of the barn Jody heard a shrill whistling scream and a splintering of wood, and then a man's voice shouting. Nellie reared and whinnied. When Jody held to the halter rope she ran at him with bared teeth. He dropped his hold and scuttled out of the way, into the brush. The high scream came again, and Nellie answered it. With hooves battering the ground the stallion appeared and charged down the hill trailing a broken halter rope. His eyes glittered feverishly. His stiff, erect nostrils were as red as flame. His sleek black hide shone in the sunlight. The stallion came on so fast that he couldn't stop when he reached the mare. Nellie's ears went back; she whirled and kicked at him as he went by. The stallion spun around and reared. He struck the mare with his front hoof, and while she staggered under the blow, his teeth raked her neck and drew an ooze of blood.

Instantly Nellie's mood changed. She became coquettishly feminine. She nibbled his arched neck with her lips. She edged around and rubbed her shoulders against his shoulder. Jody stood half-hidden in the brush and watched. He heard the steps of a horse behind him, but before he could turn, a hand caught him by the overall straps and lifted him off the ground. Jess Tayor sat the boy behind him on the horse.

"You might have got killed," he said. "Sundog's a mean devil sometimes. He busted his rope and went right through a gate."

Jody sat quietly, but in a moment he cried, "He'll hurt her—he'll kill her. Get him away!"

Jess chuckled. "She'll be all right. Maybe you'd better climb off and go up to the house for a little. You might get a piece of pie up there."

But Jody shook his head. "She's mine, and the colt's going to be mine. I'm going to raise it up."

Jess nodded. "Yes, that's good. Carl has good sense sometimes."

In a little while the danger was over. Jess lifted Jody down and then caught the stallion by its broken halter rope. And he rode ahead, while Jody followed, leading Nellie.

It was only after he had unpinned and handed over the five dollars, and after he had eaten two pieces of pie, that Jody started for home again. And Nellie followed docilely after him. She was so quiet that Jody climbed on a stump and rode her most of the way home.

The five dollars his father had advanced reduced Jody to peonage for the whole late spring and summer. When the hay was cut, he drove a hay rake. He led the horse that pulled on the Jackson-fork tackle, and when the baler came, he drove the circling horse that put pressure on the bales. In addition, Carl Tiflin taught him to milk, and he put a cow under his care, so that a new chore was added night and morning.

The bay mare Nellie quickly grew complacent. As she walked about the yellowing hillsides or worked at easy tasks, her lips were curled in a perpetual fatuous smile. She moved slowly, with the calm importance of an empress. When she was put to a team, she pulled steadily and unemotionally. Jody went to see her every day. He studied her with critical eyes and saw no change whatever.

One afternoon Billy Buck leaned the many-tined manure fork against the barn wall. He loosened his belt and tucked in his shirttail and tightened the belt again. He picked one of the little straws from his hatband and put it in the corner of his mouth. Jody, who was helping Doubletree Mutt, the big serious dog, to dig out a gopher, straightened up as the ranchhand sauntered out of the barn.

"Let's go up and have a look at Nellie," Billy suggested.

Instantly Jody fell into step with him. Doubletree Mutt watched them over his shoulder; then he dug furiously, growled, sounded little sharp yelps to indicate that the gopher was practically caught. When he looked over his shoulder again and saw that neither Jody nor Billy was interested, he climbed reluctantly out of the hole and followed them up the hill.

The wild oats were ripening. Every head bent sharply under its load of grain, and the grass was dry enough so that it made a swishing sound as Jody and Billy stepped through it. Halfway up the hill they could see Nellie and the iron-gray gelding, Pete, nibbling at the heads from the wild oats. When they approached, Nellie looked at them and backed her ears and bobbed her head up and down rebelliously. Billy walked to her and put his hand under her mane and patted her neck, until her ears came forward again and she nibbled delicately at his shirt.

Jody asked, "Do you think she's really going to have a colt?"

Billy rolled the lids back from the mare's eyes with his thumb and forefinger. He felt the lower lip and fingered the black, leathery teats. "I wouldn't be surprised," he said.

"Well, she isn't changed at all. It's three months gone."

Billy rubbed the mare's flat forehead while she grunted with pleasure. "I told you you'd get tired waiting. It'll be five months more before you can even see a sign, and it'll be at least three months more before she throws the colt, about next January."

Jody sighed deeply. "It's a long time, isn't it?"

"And then it'll be about two years more before you can ride."

Jody cried out in despair, "I'll be grown up."

"Yep, you'll be an old man," said Billy.

"What color do you think the colt'll be?"

"Why, you can't ever tell. The stud is black and the dam is bay. Colt might be black or bay or gray or dappled. You can't tell. Sometimes a black dam might have a white colt."

"Well, I hope it's black, and a stallion."

"If it's a stallion, we'll have to geld it. Your father wouldn't let you have a stallion."

"Maybe he would," Jody said. "I could train him not to be mean."

Billy pursed his lips, and the little straw that had been in the corner of his mouth rolled down to the center. "You can't ever trust a stallion," he said critically. "They're mostly fighting and making trouble. Sometimes when they're feeling funny they won't work. They make the mares uneasy and kick hell out of the geldings. Your father wouldn't let you keep a stallion."

Nellie sauntered away, nibbling the drying grass. Jody skinned the grain from a grass stem and threw the handful into the air, so that each pointed, feathered seed sailed out like a dart. "Tell me how it'll be, Billy. Is it like when the cows have calves?"

"Just about. Mares are more sensitive. Sometimes you have to be there to help the mare. And if it's wrong, you have to—" He paused.

"Have to what, Billy?"

"Have to tear the colt to pieces to get it out, or the mare'll die."

"But it won't be that way this time, will it, Billy?"

"Oh, no. Nellie's thrown good colts."

"Can I be there, Billy? Will you be certain to call me? It's my colt."

"Sure, I'll call you. Of course I will."

"Tell me how it'll be."

"Why, you've seen the cows calving. It's almost the same. The mare starts groaning and stretching, and then, if it's a good right birth, the head and forefeet come out, and the front hooves kick a hole just the way the calves do. And the colt starts to breathe. It's good to be there, 'cause if its feet aren't right maybe he can't break the sack, and then he might smother."

Jody whipped his leg with a bunch of grass. "We'll have to be there, then, won't we?"

"Oh, we'll be there, all right."

They turned and walked slowly down the hill toward the barn. Jody was tortured with a thing he had to say, although he didn't want to. "Billy," he began miserably, "you won't let anything happen to the colt, will you?"

And Billy knew he was thinking of the red pony, Gabilan, and of how it died of strangles. Billy knew he had been infallible before that, and now he was capable of failure. This knowledge made Billy much less sure of himself than he had been. "I can't tell," he said roughly. "All sorts of things might happen, and they wouldn't be my fault. I can't do everything." He felt badly about his lost prestige, and so he said meanly, "I'll do everything I know, but I won't promise anything. Nellie's a good mare. She's thrown good colts before. She ought to this time." And he walked away from Jody and went into the saddle room beside the barn, for his feelings were hurt.

Jody TRAVELED OFTEN to the brush line behind the house. There, a rusty iron pipe ran a thin stream of spring water into an old green tub, and where the water spilled over and sank into the ground there was a patch of perpetually green grass. Even when the hills were brown and baked in the summer that little patch was green. The water whined softly into the trough all the year round. This place had grown to be a center point for Jody. When he had been punished, the cool green grass and the singing water soothed him. When he had been mean, the biting acid of meanness left him at the brush line. When he sat in the grass and listened to the purling stream, the barriers set up in his mind by the stern day went down to ruin.

On the other hand, the black cypress tree by the bunkhouse was as repulsive as the water tub was dear; for to this tree all the pigs came, sooner or later, to be slaughtered. Pig killing was fascinating, with the screaming and the blood, but it made Jody's heart beat so fast that it hurt him. After the pigs were scalded in the big iron tripod kettle and their skins were scraped and white, Jody had to go to the water tub to sit in the grass until his heart grew quiet. The water tub and the black cypress were opposites and enemies.

When Billy left him and walked angrily away, Jody turned up toward the house. He thought of Nellie as he walked, and of the little colt. Then suddenly he saw that he was under the very singletree where the pigs were hung. He brushed his hair off his forehead and hurried on. It seemed to him an unlucky thing to be thinking of his colt in the very slaughter place, especially after what Billy had said. To counteract any evil result of that bad conjunction he walked quickly past the ranch house, through the chicken yard, through the vegetable patch, until he came at last to the brush line.

He sat down in the grass. The trilling water sounded in his ears. He looked over the farm buildings and across at the hills, rich and yellow with rain. He could see Nellie on the slope. As usual, the water place eliminated time and distance. Jody saw a black long-legged colt butting against Nellie's flanks, demanding milk. And then he saw himself breaking a large colt to halter. All in a few moments the colt grew to be a magnificent animal, deep of chest, with a neck as high and arched as a sea horse's neck, with a tail that tongued and rippled like flame. This horse was terrible to everyone but Jody. In the schoolyard the boys begged rides, and Jody smilingly agreed. But no sooner were they mounted than the black demon pitched them off. Why, that was his name, Black Demon! For a moment the trilling water and the grass and the sunshine came back, and then . . .

Sometimes in the night the ranch people, safe in their beds, heard a roar of hooves go by. They said, "It's Jody, on Demon. He's helping out the sheriff again." And then . . .

The golden dust filled the air in the arena at the Salinas Rodeo. The announcer called the roping contests. When Jody rode the black horse to the starting chute, the other contestants shrugged and gave up first place, for it was well known that Jody and Demon could rope and throw and tie a steer a great deal quicker than any roping team of two men could. Jody was not a boy anymore, and Demon was not a horse. The two together were one glorious individual. And then . . .

The President wrote a letter and asked them to help catch a bandit in Washington. Jody settled himself comfortably in the grass. The little stream of water whined into the mossy tub.

THE YEAR PASSED slowly on. Time after time Jody gave up his colt for lost. No change had taken place in Nellie. Carl Tiflin still drove her to a light cart, and she pulled on a hay rake and worked the Jackson-fork tackle when the hay was being put into the barn.

The summer passed, and the warm bright autumn. And then the frantic morning winds began to twist along the ground, and a chill came into the air, and the poison oak turned red. One morning in September, when he had finished his breakfast, Jody's mother called him into the kitchen. She was pouring boiling water into a bucket full of dry middlings and stirring the materials to a steaming paste.

"Yes, ma'am?" Jody asked.

"Watch how I do it. You'll have to do it after this every other morning."

"Well, what is it?"

"Why, it's warm mash for Nellie. It'll keep her in good shape."

Jody rubbed his forehead with a knuckle. "Is she all right?" he asked timidly.

Mrs. Tiflin put down the kettle and stirred the mash with a wooden paddle. "Of course she's all right, only you've got to take better care of her from now on. Here, take this breakfast out to her!"

Jody seized the bucket and ran, down past the bunkhouse, past the barn, with the heavy bucket banging against his knees. He found Nellie playing with the water in the trough, pushing waves and tossing her head so that the water slopped out on the ground.

Jody climbed the fence and set the bucket of steaming mash beside her. Then he stepped back to look at her. And she was changed. Her stomach was swollen. When she moved, her feet touched the ground gently. She buried her nose in the bucket and gobbled the hot breakfast. And when she had finished and had pushed the bucket around the ground with her nose a little, she stepped quietly over to Jody and rubbed her cheek against him.

Billy Buck came out of the saddle room and walked over. "Starts fast when it starts, doesn't it?"

"Did it come all at once?"

"Oh, no, you just stopped looking for a while." He pulled her head around toward Jody. "She's goin' to be nice, too. See how nice her eyes are! Some mares get mean, but when they turn nice, they just love everything." Nellie slipped her head under Billy's arm and rubbed her neck up and down between his arm and his side. "You better treat her awful nice now," Billy said.

"How long will it be?" Jody demanded breathlessly.

The man counted in whispers on his fingers. "About three months," he said aloud. "You can't tell exactly. Sometimes it's eleven months to the day, but it might be two weeks early, or a month late, without hurting anything."

Jody looked hard at the ground. "Billy," he began nervously, "Billy, you'll call me when it's getting born, won't you? You'll let me be there, won't you?"

Billy bit the tip of Nellie's ear with his front teeth. "Carl says he wants you to start right at the start. That's the only way to learn. Nobody can tell you anything. Like my old man did with me about the saddle blanket. He was a government packer when I was your size, and I helped him some. One day I left a wrinkle in my saddle blanket and made a saddle sore. My old man didn't give me hell at all. But the next morning he saddled me up with a forty-pound stock saddle. I had to lead my horse and carry that saddle over a whole damn mountain in the sun. It darn near killed me, but I never left no wrinkles in a blanket again. I couldn't. I never in my life since then put on a blanket but I felt that saddle on my back."

Jody reached up a hand and took hold of Nellie's mane. "You'll tell me what to do about everything, won't you? I guess you know everything about horses, don't you?"

Billy laughed. "Why, I'm half horse myself, you see," he said. "My ma died when I was born, and being my old man was a government packer in the mountains, and no cows around most of the time, why, he just gave me mostly mare's milk." He continued seriously, "And horses know that. Don't you know it, Nellie?"

The mare turned her head and looked full into his eyes for a moment, and this is a thing horses practically never do. Billy was proud and sure of himself now. He boasted a little. "I'll see you get a good colt. I'll start you right. And if you do like I say, you'll have the best horse in the county."

That made Jody feel warm and proud, too; so proud that when he went back to the house he bowed his legs and swayed his shoulders as horsemen do. And he whispered, "Whoa, you Black Demon, you! Steady down there and keep your feet on the ground."

The winter fell sharply. A few preliminary gusty showers, and then a strong steady rain. The hills lost their straw color and blackened under the water, and the winter streams scrambled noisily down the canyons. The mushrooms and puffballs popped up and the new grass started before Christmas.

But this year Christmas was not the central day to Jody. Some undetermined time in January had become the axis day around which the months swung. When the rains fell, he put Nellie in a box stall and fed her warm food every morning and curried her and brushed her.

The mare was swelling so greatly that Jody became alarmed. "She'll pop wide open," he said to Billy.

Billy laid his strong square hand against Nellie's swollen abdomen. "Feel here," he said quietly. "You can feel it move. I guess it would surprise you if there were twin colts."

"You don't think so?" Jody cried. "You don't think it will be twins, do you, Billy?"

"No, I don't, but it does happen sometimes."

During the first two weeks of January it rained steadily. Jody spent most of his time, when he wasn't in school, in the box stall with Nellie. Twenty times a day he put his hand on her stomach to feel the colt move. Nellie became more and more gentle and friendly to him. She rubbed her nose on him. She whinnied softly when he walked into the barn.

Carl Tiflin came to the barn with Jody one day. He looked admiringly at the groomed bay coat, and he felt the firm flesh over ribs and shoulders. "You've done a good job," he said to Jody. And this was the greatest praise he knew how to give. Jody was tight with pride for hours afterward.

The fifteenth of January came and the colt was not born. And the twentieth came; a lump of fear began to form in Jody's stomach. "Is it all right?" he demanded of Billy.

"Oh, sure."

And again, "Are you sure it's going to be all right?"

Billy stroked the mare's neck. She swayed her head uneasily. "I told you it wasn't always the same time, Jody. You just have to wait."

When the end of the month arrived with no birth, Jody grew frantic. Nellie was so big that her breath came heavily, and her ears were close together and straight up, as though her head ached. Jody's sleep grew restless, and his dreams confused.

On the night of the second of February he awakened crying. His mother called to him, "Jody, you're dreaming. Wake up and start over again."

But Jody was filled with terror and desolation. He lay quietly a few moments, waiting for his mother to go back to sleep, and then he slipped his clothes on and crept out in his bare feet.

The night was black and thick. A little misting rain fell. The cypress tree and the bunkhouse loomed and then dropped back into the mist. The barn door screeched as he opened it, a thing it never did in the daytime. Jody went to the back and found a lantern and a tin box of matches. He lighted the wick and walked down the long straw-covered aisle to Nellie's stall. She was standing up. Her whole body weaved from side to side. Jody called to her, "So, Nellie, so-o, Nellie," but she did not stop her swaying nor look around. When he stepped into the stall and touched her on the shoulder, she shivered under his hand.

Then Billy Buck's voice came from the hayloft right above the stall. "Jody, what are you doing?"

Jody started back and turned miserable eyes up toward the nest where Billy was lying in the hay. "Is she all right, do you think?"

"Why sure, I think so."

"You won't let anything happen, Billy, you're sure you won't?"

Billy growled down at him, "I told you I'd call you, and I will. Now you get back to bed and stop worrying that mare. She's got enough to do without you worrying her."

Jody cringed, for he had never heard Billy speak in such a tone. "I only thought I'd come and see," he said. "I woke up."

Billy softened a little then. "Well, you get to bed. I don't want you bothering her. I told you I'd get a good colt. Get along now."

Jody walked slowly out of the barn. He blew out the lantern and set it in the rack. The blackness of the night struck him and enfolded him. He wished he believed everything Billy said as he had before the pony died. It was a moment before his eyes could make any form of the darkness. The damp ground chilled his bare feet. At the cypress tree the roosting turkeys chattered in alarm, and the two dogs responded to duty and came charging out, barking to frighten away the coyotes they thought were prowling under the tree.

As he crept through the kitchen, Jody stumbled over a chair. Carl called from his bedroom, "Who's there? What's the matter there?"

And Mrs. Tiflin said sleepily, "What's the matter, Carl?"

The next second Carl came out of the bedroom and found Jody before he could get into bed. "What are you doing out?"

Jody turned shyly away. "I was down to see the mare."

For a moment anger at being awakened fought with approval in Jody's father. "Listen," he said finally, "there's not a man in this country that knows more about colts than Billy. You leave it to him."

Words burst out of Jody's mouth. "But the pony died—"

"Don't you go blaming that on him," Carl said sternly. "If Billy can't save a horse, it can't be saved."

Mrs. Tiflin called, "Make him clean his feet and go to bed, Carl. He'll be sleepy all day tomorrow."

It seemed to Jody that he had just closed his eyes to try to go to sleep when he was shaken violently by the shoulder. Billy Buck stood beside him, holding a lantern in his hand. "Get up," he said. "Hurry up." He turned and walked quickly out of the room.

Mrs. Tiflin called, "What's the matter? Is Nellie ready?"

"Yes, ma'am."

"All right, I'll get up and heat some water in case you need it."

Jody jumped into his clothes so quickly that he was out the back door before Billy's swinging lantern was halfway to the barn. There was a rim of dawn on the mountaintops, but no light had penetrated into the cup of the ranch yet. Jody ran frantically after the lantern and caught up to Billy just as he reached the barn. Billy hung the lantern to a nail on the stall side and took off his blue denim coat.

Nellie was standing rigid and stiff. While they watched, she crouched. Her whole body was wrung with a spasm. The spasm passed. But in a few moments it started over again, and passed.

Billy muttered nervously, "There's something wrong." His bare hand disappeared. "Oh, Jesus," he said. "It's wrong."

The spasm came again, and this time Billy strained, and the muscles stood out on his arm. He heaved, his forehead beaded with perspiration. Nellie cried with pain. Billy was muttering, "It's wrong. I can't turn it. It's way wrong. It's turned all around wrong."

He glared wildly toward Jody. And then his fingers made a careful, careful diagnosis. His cheeks were growing tight and gray. He looked for a long questioning minute at Jody standing back of the stall. Then Billy stepped to the rack under the manure window and picked up a horseshoe hammer with his wet right hand.

"Go outside, Jody," he said.

The boy stood still and stared dully at him.

"Go outside, I tell you. It'll be too late."

Jody didn't move.

Then Billy walked quickly to Nellie's head. He cried, "Turn your face away, damn you, turn your face."

This time Jody obeyed. His head turned sideways. He heard Billy whispering hoarsely in the stall. And then he heard a hollow crunch of bone. Jody looked back in time to see the hammer rise and fall again on the flat forehead. Then Nellie fell heavily to her side and quivered for a moment.

Billy jumped to the swollen stomach; his big pocketknife was in his hand. He lifted the skin and drove the knife in. He sawed and ripped at the tough belly. The air filled with the sick odor of warm living entrails. The other horses reared back and squealed and kicked.

Billy dropped the knife. Both of his arms plunged into the terrible ragged hole and dragged out a big white dripping bundle. His teeth tore a hole in the covering. A little black head appeared through the tear, and little slick, wet ears. A gurgling breath was drawn, and then another. Billy shucked off the sac and found his knife and cut the string. For a moment he held the little black colt in his arms and looked at it. And then he walked slowly over and laid it in the straw at Jody's feet.

Billy's face and arms and chest were dripping red. His body shivered and his teeth chattered. His voice was gone; he spoke in a throaty whisper. "There's your colt. I promised. And there it is. I had to do it—had to." He stopped and looked over his shoulder into the box stall. "Go get hot water and a sponge," he whispered. "Wash him and dry him the way his mother would. You'll have to feed him by hand. But there's your colt, the way I promised."

Jody stared stupidly at the wet, panting foal. It stretched out its chin and tried to raise its head. Its blank eyes were navy blue.

"God damn you," Billy shouted, "will you go now for the water? *Will you go?*"

Then Jody turned and trotted out of the barn into the dawn. He ached from his throat to his stomach. His legs were stiff and heavy. He tried to be glad because of the colt, but the bloody face and the haunted, tired eyes of Billy Buck hung in the air ahead of him.

CHAPTER 4
THE LEADER OF THE PEOPLE

ON SATURDAY AFTERNOON Billy Buck raked together the last of the old year's haystack and pitched small forkfuls over the wire fence to a few mildly interested cattle. High in the air small clouds like puffs of cannon smoke were driven eastward by the March wind. The wind could be heard whishing in the brush on the ridge crests, but no breath of it penetrated down into the ranch cup.

The little boy, Jody, emerged from the house eating a thick piece of buttered bread. He saw Billy working on the last of the haystack. Jody tramped down, scuffing his shoes in a way he had been told was destructive to good shoe leather.

A flock of white pigeons flew out of the black cypress tree as Jody passed, and circled the tree and landed again. A half-grown tortoise-shell cat leaped from the bunkhouse porch, galloped on stiff legs across the road, whirled and galloped back again. Jody picked up a stone to help the game along, but he was too late, for the cat was under the porch before the stone could be discharged. He threw the stone into the cypress tree and started the white pigeons on another whirling flight.

Arriving at the used-up haystack, the boy leaned against the barbed wire fence. "Will that be all of it, do you think?" he asked.

The middle-aged ranchhand stopped his careful raking and stuck his fork into the ground. He took off his black hat and smoothed down his hair. "Nothing left of it that isn't soggy from ground moisture," he said. He replaced his hat and rubbed his dry leathery hands together.

"Ought to be plenty mice," Jody suggested.

"Lousy with them," said Billy. "Just crawling with mice."

"Well, maybe, when you get all through, I could call the dogs and hunt the mice."

"Sure, I guess you could," said Billy Buck. He lifted a forkful of the damp ground-hay and threw it into the air. Instantly three mice leapt out and burrowed frantically under the hay again.

Jody sighed with satisfaction. Those plump, sleek, arrogant mice were doomed. For eight months they had lived and multiplied in the haystack. In that time they had been immune from cats, from traps, from poison and from Jody. They had grown smug in their security, overbearing and fat. Now the time of disaster had come; they would not survive another day.

Billy looked up at the top of the hills that surrounded the ranch. "Maybe you better ask your father before you do it," he suggested.

"Well, where is he? I'll ask him now."

"He rode up to the ridge ranch after dinner. He'll be back pretty soon."

Jody slumped against the fence post. "I don't think he'd care."

As Billy went back to his work, he said ominously, "You'd better ask him anyway. You know how he is."

Jody did know. His father insisted upon giving permission for anything that was done on the ranch, whether it was important or not. Jody sagged farther against the post until he was sitting on the ground. He looked up at the little puffs of wind-driven cloud. "Is it like to rain, Billy?"

"It might. The wind's good for it, but not strong enough."

"Well, I hope it don't rain until after I kill those damn mice." He looked over his shoulder to see whether Billy had noticed the mature profanity. Billy worked on without comment.

Jody turned back and looked at the sidehill where the road from the outside world came down. The hill was washed with lean March sunshine. Silver thistles, blue lupines and a few poppies bloomed among the sagebrushes. Halfway up the hill Jody could see Doubletree Mutt, the black dog, digging in a squirrel hole. He paddled for a while and then paused to kick bursts of dirt out between his hind legs, and he dug with an earnestness which belied the knowledge he must have had that no dog had ever caught a squirrel by digging in a hole.

Suddenly, while Jody watched, the black dog stiffened, and backed out of the hole and looked up the hill toward the cleft in the ridge where the road came through. Jody looked up too. For a moment Carl Tiflin on horseback stood out against the pale sky, and then he moved down the road toward the house. He carried something white in his hand.

The boy started to his feet. "He's got a letter," Jody cried. He trotted toward the ranch house, for the letter would probably be read aloud and he wanted to be there. He reached the house before his father did, and ran in. He heard Carl dismount from his creaking saddle and slap the horse on the side to send it to the barn, where Billy would unsaddle it and turn it out.

Jody ran into the kitchen. "We got a letter!" he cried.

His mother looked up from a pan of beans. "Who has?"

"Father has. I saw it in his hand."

Carl strode into the kitchen then, and Jody's mother asked, "Who's the letter from, Carl?"

He frowned quickly. "How did you know there was a letter?"

She nodded her head in the boy's direction. "Big-Britches Jody told me."

Jody was embarrassed.

His father looked down at him contemptuously. "He *is* getting to be a Big-Britches," Carl said. "He's minding everybody's business but his own. Got his big nose into everything."

Mrs. Tiflin relented a little. "Well, he hasn't enough to keep him busy. Who's the letter from?"

Carl still frowned on Jody. "I'll keep him busy if he isn't careful." He held out a sealed letter. "I guess it's from your father."

Mrs. Tiflin took a hairpin from her head and slit open the flap. Her lips pursed judiciously. Jody saw her eyes snap back and forth over the lines. "He says," she translated, "he says he's going to drive out Saturday to stay with us for a little while. Why, this is Saturday. The letter must have been delayed." She looked at the postmark. "This was mailed day before yesterday. It should have been here yesterday." She looked up questioningly at her husband, and then her face darkened angrily. "Now what have you got that look on you for? He doesn't come often."

Carl turned his eyes away from her anger. He could be stern with her most of the time, but when occasionally her temper arose, he could not combat it.

"What's the matter with you?" she demanded again.

In his explanation there was a tone of apology Jody himself might have used. "It's just that he talks," Carl said lamely. "Just talks."

"Well, what of it? You talk yourself."

"Sure I do. But your father only talks about one thing."

"Indians!" Jody broke in excitedly. "Indians and crossing the plains!"

Carl turned fiercely on him. "You get out, Mr. Big-Britches! Go on, now! Get out!"

Jody went miserably out the back door and closed the screen with elaborate quietness. Under the kitchen window his shamed, downcast eyes fell upon a curiously shaped stone, a stone of such fascination that he squatted down and picked it up and turned it over in his hands.

The voices came clearly to him through the open kitchen window. "Jody's damn well right," he heard his father say. "Just Indians and crossing the plains. I've heard that story about how the horses got driven off about a thousand times. He just goes on and on, and he never changes a word in the things he tells."

When Mrs. Tiflin answered, her tone was so changed that Jody, outside the window, looked up from his study of the stone. Her voice had become soft and explanatory. Jody knew how her face would have changed to match the tone. She said quietly, "Look at it this way, Carl. That was the big thing in my father's life. He led a wagon train clear across the plains to the coast, and when it was finished, his life was done. It was a big thing to do, but it didn't last long enough. Look," she continued, "it's as though he was born to do that, and after he finished it, there wasn't anything more for him to do but think about it and talk about it. If there'd been any farther west to go, he'd have gone. He's told me so himself. But at last there was the ocean. He lives right by the ocean, where he had to stop."

She had caught Carl, caught him and entangled him in her soft tone.

"I've seen him," he agreed quietly. "He goes down and stares off west over the ocean." His voice sharpened a little. "And then he goes up to the Horseshoe Pub in Pacific Grove, and he tells people how the Indians drove off the horses."

She tried to catch him again. "Well, it's everything to him. You might be patient with him and pretend to listen."

Carl turned impatiently away. "Well, if it gets too bad, I can always go down to the bunkhouse and sit with Billy," he said irritably. He walked through the house and slammed the front door after him.

Jody ran to his chores. He dumped the grain to the chickens without chasing any of them. He gathered the eggs from the nests. He trotted into the house with the wood and interlaced it so carefully in the woodbox that two armloads seemed to fill it to overflowing.

His mother had finished the beans by now. She stirred up the fire and brushed off the stove top with a turkey wing. Jody peered cautiously at her to see whether any rancor toward him remained. "Is he coming today?" Jody asked.

"That's what his letter said."

"Maybe I better walk up the road to meet him."

Mrs. Tiflin clanged the stove lid shut. "That would be nice," she said. "He'd probably like to be met."

"I guess I'll just do it then."

Outside, Jody whistled shrilly to the dogs. "Come on up the hill," he commanded. The two dogs waved their tails and ran ahead. Along the roadside the sage had tender new tips. Jody tore off some pieces and rubbed them on his hands until the air was filled with the sharp wild smell. With a rush the dogs leaped from the road and yapped into the brush after a rabbit. That was the last Jody saw of them, for when they failed to catch the rabbit, they went back home.

Jody plodded on up the hill toward the ridge top. When he reached the little cleft where the road came through, the afternoon wind struck him and blew up his hair and ruffled his shirt. He looked down on the little hills and ridges below and then out at the huge green Salinas Valley. He could see the white town of Salinas far out in the flat and the flash of its windows under the waning sun. Directly below him, in an oak tree, a crow congress had convened. The tree was black with crows all cawing at once.

Then Jody's eyes followed the wagon road down from the ridge where he stood, and lost it behind a hill, and picked it up again on the other side. On that distant stretch he saw a cart slowly pulled by a bay horse. It disappeared behind the hill. Jody sat down on the ground and watched the place where the cart would appear again. The wind sang on the hilltops and the puffball clouds hurried eastward.

Then the cart came into sight and stopped. A man dressed in black dismounted from the seat and walked to the horse's head. Although it was so far away, Jody knew he had unhooked the checkrein, for the horse's head dropped forward. The horse moved on, and the man walked slowly up the hill beside it. Jody gave a glad cry and ran down the road toward them. The squirrels bumped along off the road, and a roadrunner flirted its tail and raced over the hill and sailed out like a glider.

Jody tried to leap into the middle of his shadow at every step. A stone rolled under his foot and he went down. Around a little bend he raced, and there, a short distance ahead, were his grandfather and the cart. The boy stopped his unseemly running and approached at a dignified walk.

The horse plodded stumble-footedly up the hill and the old man walked beside it. In the lowering sun their giant shadows flickered darkly behind them. The grandfather was dressed in a black broadcloth suit and he wore kid congress gaiters and a black tie on a short, hard collar. He carried his black slouch hat in his hand. His white beard was cropped close and his white eyebrows overhung his eyes like mustaches. The blue eyes were sternly merry. About the whole face and figure there was a granite dignity, so that every motion seemed an impossible thing. Once at rest, it seemed the old man would be stone, would never move again. His steps were slow and certain. Once made, no step could ever be retraced; once headed in a direction, the path would never bend nor the pace increase or slow.

When Jody appeared around the bend, Grandfather waved his hat slowly in welcome, and he called, "Why, Jody! Come down to meet me, have you?"

Jody sidled near and turned and matched his step to the old man's step and stiffened his body and dragged his heels a little. "Yes, sir," he said. "We got your letter only today."

"Should have been here yesterday," said Grandfather. "It certainly should. How are all the folks?"

"They're fine, sir." He hesitated and then suggested shyly, "Would you like to come on a mouse hunt tomorrow, sir?"

"Mouse hunt, Jody?" Grandfather chuckled. "Have the people of this generation come down to hunting mice? They aren't very strong, the new people, but I hardly thought mice would be game for them."

"No, sir. It's just play. The haystack's gone. I'm going to drive out the mice to the dogs. And you can watch, or even beat the hay a little."

The stern, merry eyes turned down on him. "I see. You don't eat them, then. You haven't come to that yet."

Jody explained, "The dogs eat them, sir. It wouldn't be much like hunting Indians, I guess."

"No, not much—but then later, when the troops were hunting Indians and shooting children and burning teepees, it wasn't much different from your mouse hunt."

They topped the rise and started down into the ranch cup, and they lost the sun from their shoulders. "You've grown," Grandfather said. "Nearly an inch, I should say."

"More," Jody boasted. "Where they mark me on the door, I'm up more than an inch since Thanksgiving even."

Grandfather's rich throaty voice said, "Maybe you're getting too much water and turning to pith and stalk. Wait until you head out, and then we'll see."

Jody looked quickly into the old man's face to see whether his feelings should be hurt, but there was no will to injure, no punishing nor putting-in-your-place light in the keen blue eyes. "We might kill a pig," Jody suggested.

"Oh, no! I couldn't let you do that. You're just humoring me. It isn't the time and you know it."

"You know Riley, the big boar, sir."

"Yes. I remember Riley well."

"Well, Riley ate a hole into that same haystack, and it fell down on him and smothered him."

"Pigs do that when they can," said Grandfather.

"Riley was a nice pig, for a boar, sir. I rode him sometimes, and he didn't mind."

A door slammed at the house below them, and they saw Jody's mother standing on the porch waving her apron in welcome. And then they saw Carl Tiflin walking up from the barn to be at the house for the arrival.

The sun had disappeared from the hills by now. The blue smoke from the house chimney hung in flat layers in the purpling ranch cup. The puffball clouds, dropped by the falling wind, hung listlessly in the sky.

Billy Buck came out of the bunkhouse and flung a washbasin of soapy water on the ground. He had been shaving in midweek, for Billy held Grandfather in reverence, and Grandfather said that Billy was one of the few men of the new generation who had not gone soft. Although Billy was in middle age, Grandfather considered him a boy. Now Billy was hurrying toward the house too.

When Jody and Grandfather arrived, the three were waiting for them in front of the yard gate.

Carl said, "Hello, sir. We've been looking for you."

Mrs. Tiflin kissed Grandfather on the side of his beard, and stood still while his big hand patted her shoulder. Billy shook hands solemnly, grinning under his straw mustache. "I'll put up your horse," said Billy, and he led the rig away.

Grandfather watched him go, and then, turning back to the group, he said as he had said a hundred times before, "There's a good boy. I knew his father, old Mule-tail Buck. I never knew why they called him Mule-tail except he packed mules."

Mrs. Tiflin turned and led the way into the house. "How long are you going to stay, Father? Your letter didn't say."

"Well, I don't know. I thought I'd stay about two weeks. But I never stay as long as I think I'm going to."

In a short while they were sitting at the white oilcloth table eating their supper. The lamp with the tin reflector hung over the table. Outside the dining-room windows the big moths battered softly against the glass.

Grandfather cut his steak into tiny pieces and chewed slowly. "I'm hungry," he said. "Driving out here got my appetite up. It's like when we were crossing. We all got so hungry every night we could hardly wait to let the meat get done. I could eat about five pounds of buffalo meat every night."

"It's moving around does it," said Billy. "My father was a government packer. I helped him when I was a kid. Just the two of us could about clean up a deer's ham."

"I knew your father, Billy," said Grandfather. "A fine man. They called him Mule-tail Buck. I don't know why except he packed mules."

"That was it," Billy agreed. "He packed mules."

Grandfather put down his knife and fork and looked around the table. "I remember one time we ran out of meat—" His voice dropped to a curious low singsong, dropped into a tonal groove the story had worn for itself. "There was no buffalo, no antelope, not even rabbits. The hunters couldn't even shoot a coyote. That was the time for the leader to be on the watch. I was the leader, and I kept my eyes open. Know why? Well, just the minute the people began to get hungry they'd start slaughtering the team oxen. Do you believe that? I've heard of parties that just ate up their draft cattle. Started from the middle and worked toward the ends. Finally they'd eat the lead pair, and then the wheelers. The leader of a party had to keep them from doing that."

In some manner a big moth got into the room and circled the hanging kerosene lamp. Billy got up and tried to clap it between his hands. Carl struck with a cupped palm and caught the moth and broke it. He walked to the window and dropped it out.

"As I was saying," Grandfather began again, but Carl interrupted him. "You'd better eat some more meat. All the rest of us are ready for our pudding."

Jody saw a flash of anger in his mother's eyes. Grandfather picked up his knife and fork. "I'm pretty hungry, all right," he said. "I'll tell you about that later."

When supper was over, when the family and Billy Buck sat in front of the fireplace in the other room, Jody anxiously watched Grandfather. He saw the signs he knew. The bearded head leaned forward; the eyes lost their sternness and looked wonderingly into the fire; the big lean fingers laced themselves on the black knees. "I wonder," he began, "I just wonder whether I ever told you how those thieving Piutes drove off thirty-five of our horses."

"I think you did," Carl interrupted. "Wasn't it just before you went up into the Tahoe country?"

Grandfather turned quickly toward his son-in-law. "That's right. I guess I must have told you that story."

"Lots of times," Carl said cruelly, and he avoided his wife's eyes. But he felt the angry eyes on him, and he said, "Course I'd like to hear it again."

Grandfather looked back at the fire. His fingers unlaced and laced again. Jody knew how he felt, how his insides were collapsed and empty. Hadn't Jody been called a Big-Britches that very afternoon? He rose to heroism and opened himself to the term Big-Britches again. "Tell about Indians," he said softly.

Grandfather's eyes grew stern again. "Boys always want to hear about Indians. It was a job for men, but boys want to hear about it. Well, let's see. Did I ever tell you how I wanted each wagon to carry a long iron plate?"

Everybody but Jody remained silent. Jody said, "No. You didn't."

"Well, when the Indians attacked, we put the wagons in a circle and fought from between the wheels. I thought that if every wagon carried a long plate with rifle holes, the men could stand the plates on the outside of the wheels when the wagons were in the circle and they would be protected. It would save lives. But of course the party wouldn't do it. No party had done it before and they couldn't see why they should go to the expense. They lived to regret it, too."

Jody looked at his mother and knew from her expression that she was not listening at all. Carl picked at a callus on his thumb and Billy Buck watched a spider crawling up the wall.

Grandfather's tone dropped into its narrative groove again. Jody knew in advance exactly what words would fall. The story droned on. Jody sat watching Grandfather. The stern blue eyes were detached. He looked as though he were not very interested in the story himself.

When it was finished, Billy Buck stood up and stretched. "I guess I'll turn in," he said. Then he faced Grandfather. "I've got an old powder horn and a cap-and-ball pistol. Did I ever show them to you?"

Grandfather nodded slowly. "Yes, I think you did, Billy. Reminds me of a pistol I had when I was leading the people across." Billy stood politely until the little story was done, and then he said, "Good night," and went out of the house.

Carl Tiflin tried to turn the conversation then. "How's the country between here and Monterey? I've heard it's pretty dry."

"It is dry," said Grandfather. "There's not a drop of water in the Laguna Seca. But it's a long pull from '87. The whole country was powder then. We had fifteen inches of rain this year."

"Yes, but it all came too early. We could do with some now." Carl's eye fell on Jody. "Hadn't you better be getting to bed?"

Jody stood up obediently. "Can I kill the mice in the old haystack, sir?"

"Mice? Oh! Sure, kill them all off. There isn't any good hay left."

Jody exchanged a secret and satisfying look with Grandfather. "I'll kill every one tomorrow," he promised.

Jody lay in his bed and thought of the impossible world of Indians and buffalo, a world that had ceased to be forever. He thought of the wide plains and of the wagons moving across like centipedes. He thought of Grandfather on a huge white horse, marshaling the people. Across his mind marched the great phantoms, and they marched off the earth and they were gone.

He came back to the ranch for a moment then. He heard the dull rushing sound that space and silence make. He heard one of the dogs, out in the doghouse, scratching a flea and bumping his elbow against the floor with every stroke. Then the wind arose again and the black cypress groaned and Jody went to sleep.

He was up half an hour before the triangle sounded for breakfast. His mother was rattling the stove to make the flames roar when Jody went through the kitchen. "You're up early," she said. "Where are you going?"

"Out to get a good stick. We're going to kill the mice today."

"Who is 'we'?"

"Why, Grandfather and I."

"So you've got him in it. You always like to have someone in with you in case there's blame to share."

"I'll be right back," said Jody. "I want to have a good stick ready."

He closed the screen door after him and went out into the cool blue morning. Doubletree Mutt and Smasher moved, sniffing along the edge of the brush, but when Jody whistled, their heads jerked up and their tails waved. They plunged down to him, wriggling their skins and yawning. Jody patted their heads seriously and moved on to the weathered scrap pile. He selected an old broom handle and a short piece of inch-square scrap wood. From his pocket he took a shoe-lace and tied the ends of the sticks loosely together to make a flail. He struck the ground experimentally, while the dogs leapt aside.

Jody turned and started down past the house toward the old haystack ground to look over the field of slaughter, but Billy Buck, sitting patiently on the back steps, called to him, "You better come back. It's only a couple of minutes till breakfast."

Jody changed his course and moved toward the house. He leaned his flail against the steps. "That's to drive the mice out," he said. "I'll bet they don't know what's going to happen to them today."

"No, nor you either," Billy remarked philosophically, "nor me, nor anyone."

Jody was staggered by this thought. He knew it was true. His imagination twitched away from the mouse hunt. Then his mother came out and struck the triangle, and all his thoughts fell in a heap.

Grandfather hadn't appeared at the table when they sat down. Billy nodded at his empty chair. "He's all right? He isn't sick?"

"He takes a long time to dress," said Mrs. Tiflin. "He combs his whiskers and rubs up his shoes and brushes his clothes."

Carl scattered sugar on his mush. "A man that's led a wagon train across the plains has got to be pretty careful how he dresses."

Mrs. Tiflin turned on him. "Don't do that, Carl! Please don't!"

"Well, how many times do I have to listen to the story of the iron plates and the thirty-five horses? That time's done. Why can't he forget it, now it's done?" His voice rose. "Why does he have to tell those stories over and over? He came across the plains. All right! Now it's finished. Nobody wants to hear about it over and over."

The door into the kitchen closed softly. The four at the table sat frozen. Carl laid his mush spoon on the table.

Then the kitchen door opened and Grandfather walked in. His mouth smiled tightly and his eyes were squinted. "Good morning," he said, and he sat down and looked at his mush dish.

Carl could not leave it there. "Did—did you hear what I said?"

Grandfather jerked a little nod.

"I don't know what got into me, sir. I didn't mean it."

Jody glanced in shame at his mother, and he saw that she was looking at Carl, and that she wasn't breathing. It was an awful thing that he was doing. He was tearing himself to pieces. It was a terrible thing to him to retract a word, but to retract it in shame was infinitely worse.

Grandfather looked sidewise. "I'm trying to get right side up," he said gently. "I'm not being mad. I don't mind what you said, but it might be true, and I would mind that."

"It isn't true," said Carl. "I'm not feeling well. I'm sorry."

"Don't be sorry, Carl. An old man doesn't see things sometimes. Maybe you're right. The crossing is finished. Maybe it should be forgotten, now it's done."

Carl got up from the table. "I've had enough to eat. I'm going to work. Take your time, Billy!" He walked quickly out of the dining room. Billy gulped the rest of his food and followed soon after. But Jody could not leave his chair.

"Won't you tell any more stories?" Jody asked.

"Why, sure, but only when—I'm sure people want to hear them."

"I like to hear them, sir."

"Oh! Of course you do, but you're a little boy. It was a job for men, but only little boys like to hear about it."

Jody got up from his place. "I'll wait outside for you, sir. I've got a good stick for those mice."

He waited by the gate until the old man came out on the porch. "Let's go down and kill the mice now," Jody called.

"I think I'll just sit in the sun, Jody. You go kill the mice."

"You can use my stick if you like."

"No, I'll just sit here awhile."

Jody turned disconsolately away and walked down toward the old haystack. He tried to whip up his enthusiasm with thoughts of the fat juicy mice. He beat the ground with his flail. The dogs coaxed and whined about him, but he could not go. Back at the house he could see Grandfather sitting on the porch, looking small and thin.

Jody gave up and went to sit on the steps at the old man's feet.

"Back already? Did you kill the mice?"

"No, sir. I'll kill them some other day."

The morning flies buzzed close to the ground and the ants dashed about in front of the steps. The smell of sage slipped down the hill.

Jody hardly knew when Grandfather started to talk. "I shouldn't stay here, feeling the way I do." He examined his strong old hands. "I feel as though the crossing wasn't worth doing. I tell those old stories, but they're not what I want to tell. I only know how I want people to feel when I tell them.

"It wasn't Indians that were important, nor adventures, nor even getting out here. It was a whole bunch of people made into one big crawling beast. And I was the head. I was westering and westering. Every man wanted something for himself, but the big beast that was all of them wanted only westering. I was the leader, but if I hadn't been there, someone else would have been the head. The thing had to have a head.

"When we saw the mountains at last, we cried—all of us. But it wasn't getting here that mattered, it was movement and westering.

"We carried life out here and set it down the way those ants carry eggs. And I was the leader. The westering was as big as God, and the slow steps that made the movement piled up and piled up until the continent was crossed.

"Then we came down to the sea, and it was done." He stopped and wiped his eyes. "That's what I should be telling instead of stories."

When Jody spoke, Grandfather started and looked down at him. "Maybe I could lead the people someday," Jody said.

The old man smiled. "There's no place to go. There's the ocean to stop you. There's a line of old men along the shore hating the ocean because it stopped them."

"In boats I might, sir."

"No place to go, Jody. Every place is taken. But that's not the worst—no, not the worst. Westering has died out of the people. Westering isn't a hunger anymore. It's all done. Your father is right. It is finished." He laced his fingers on his knee and looked at them.

Jody felt very sad. "If you'd like a glass of lemonade, I could make it for you."

Grandfather was about to refuse, and then he saw Jody's face. "That would be nice," he said. "Yes, it would be nice."

Jody ran into the kitchen where his mother was wiping the dishes. "Can I have a lemon to make a lemonade for Grandfather?"

His mother mimicked, "And another to make a lemonade for you."

"No, ma'am. I don't want one."

"Jody! You're sick!" Then she stopped suddenly. "Take a lemon out of the cooler," she said softly. "Here, I'll reach the squeezer down for you."

GOOD-BYE,
MR. CHIPS

GOOD-BYE, MR. CHIPS

JAMES HILTON

ILLUSTRATED BY GUY DEEL

To all those who had known him,
whether as a student in his classroom
or as a teaching colleague, he was
an institution at Brookfield School.
Indeed, Chips *was* Brookfield School—as
venerable a tradition of that English
boarding school as the buildings and the
courtyards through which he had
walked for more than half a century.

Out of loving memory of his
own schoolmaster father, novelist
James Hilton has created this
warm, endearing portrait of a modest
man whose name has become
famous worldwide.

CHAPTER 1

WHEN YOU ARE getting on in years (but not ill, of course), you get very sleepy at times, and the hours seem to pass like lazy cattle moving across a landscape. It was like that for Chips as the autumn term progressed and the days shortened till it was actually dark enough to light the gas before call-over. For Chips, like some old sea captain, still measured time by the signals of the past; and well he might, for he lived at Mrs. Wickett's, just across the road from the school. He had been there more than a decade, ever since he finally gave up his mastership; and it was Brookfield far more than Greenwich time that both he and his landlady kept. "Mrs. Wickett," Chips would sing out, in that jerky, high-pitched voice that had still a good deal of sprightliness in it, "you might bring me a cup of tea before prep, will you?"

When you are getting on in years it is nice to sit by the fire and drink a cup of tea and listen to the school bell sounding dinner, call-over, prep, and lights-out. Chips always wound up the clock after that last bell; then he put the wire guard in front of the fire, turned out the gas and carried a detective novel to bed. Rarely did he read more than a page of it before sleep came swiftly and peacefully, more like a mystic intensifying of perception than any changeful entrance into another world. For his days and nights were equally full of dreaming.

He was getting on in years (but not ill, of course); indeed, as Dr. Merivale said, there was really nothing the matter with him. "My dear fellow, you're fitter than I am," Merivale would say, sipping a glass of sherry when he called every fortnight or so. "You're past the age when people get these horrible diseases; you're one of the few lucky ones who're going to die a really natural death. That is, of course, if you die at all. You're such a remarkable old boy that one never knows." But when Chips had a cold or when east winds roared over the fenlands, Merivale would sometimes take Mrs. Wickett aside in the lobby and whisper, "Look after him, you know. His chest . . . it puts a strain on his heart. Nothing really wrong with him—only anno Domini, but that's the most fatal complaint of all, in the end."

Anno Domini . . . by Jove, yes. Born in 1848, and taken to the Great Exhibition as a toddling child—not many people still alive could boast a thing like that. Besides, Chips could even remember Brookfield in Wetherby's time. A phenomenon, that was. Wetherby had been an old man in those days—1870—easy to remember because of the Franco-Prussian War. Chips had put in for Brookfield after a year at Melbury, which he hadn't liked, because he had been ragged there a good deal. But Brookfield he *had* liked, almost from the beginning. He remembered the day of his preliminary interview—sunny June, with the air full of flower scents and the plick-plock of cricket balls on the pitch. Brookfield was playing Barnhurst, and one of the Barnhurst boys, a chubby little fellow, made a brilliant knock. Queer that a thing like that should stay in the memory so clearly. Wetherby himself was very fatherly and courteous; he must have been ill then, poor chap, for he died during the summer vacation, before Chips began his first term. But the two had seen and spoken to each other, anyway.

Chips often thought, as he sat by the fire at Mrs. Wickett's, I am probably the only man in the world who has a vivid recollection of old Wetherby. . . . Vivid, yes; it was a frequent picture in his mind, that summer day with the sunlight filtering through the dust in Wetherby's study. "You are a young man, Mr. Chipping, and Brookfield is an old foundation. Youth and age often combine well. Give your enthusiasm to Brookfield, and Brookfield will give you something in return. And don't let anyone play tricks with you. I—er—gather that discipline was not always your strong point at Melbury?"

"Well, no, perhaps not, sir."

"Never mind; you're young; it's largely a matter of experience.

You have another chance here. Take up a firm attitude from the beginning—that's the secret of it."

Perhaps it was. He remembered that first tremendous ordeal of taking prep; a September sunset more than half a century ago; Big Hall full of lusty barbarians ready to pounce on him as their legitimate prey. His youth, fresh-complexioned, high-collared and side-whiskered (odd fashions people followed in those days), at the mercy of five hundred unprincipled ruffians to whom the baiting of new masters was a fine art, an exciting sport, and something of a tradition. The sudden hush as he took his place at the desk on the dais; the scowl he assumed to cover his inward nervousness; the tall clock ticking behind him; the smells of ink and varnish; the last blood-red rays slanting in slabs through the stained-glass windows. Someone dropped a desk lid. Quickly, he must take everyone by surprise; he must show that there was no nonsense about him. "You there in the fifth row—you with the red hair—what's your name?" "Colley, sir." "Very well, Colley, you have a hundred lines." No trouble at all after that. He had won his first round.

And years later, when Colley was an alderman of the city of London and a baronet and various other things, he sent his son (also red-haired) to Brookfield, and Chips would say, "Colley, your father was the first boy I ever punished when I came here twenty-five years ago. He deserved it then, and you deserve it now." How they all laughed; and how Sir Richard laughed when his son wrote home the story in the next Sunday's letter!

A great joke, this growing old—but a sad joke, too, in a way. And as Chips sat by his fire with autumn gales rattling the windows, the waves of humor and sadness swept over him until tears fell, so that when Mrs. Wickett came in with his tea she did not know whether he had been laughing or crying. And neither did Chips himself.

CHAPTER 2

ACROSS THE ROAD behind a rampart of ancient elms lay Brookfield, russet under its autumn mantle of creeper. A group of eighteenth-century buildings centered upon a quadrangle, and there were acres of playing fields beyond; then came the small dependent village and the open fen country. Brookfield, as Wetherby had said, was an old foundation; established in the reign of Elizabeth, it might, with better luck, have become as famous as Harrow. Its luck, however, had been not so good; the school went up and down, dwindling almost to nonexistence at one time, becoming almost illustrious at another.

It was during one of these latter periods that the main structure had been rebuilt and large additions made. Later, after the Napoleonic Wars and until mid-Victorian days, the school declined again, both in numbers and in repute. Wetherby, who came in 1840, restored its fortunes somewhat; but its subsequent history never raised it to front-rank status. It was, nevertheless, a good school of the second rank. Several notable families supported it, it supplied fair samples of the history-making men of the age—judges, members of Parliament, colonial administrators, a few peers and bishops. Mostly, however, it turned out merchants, manufacturers and professional men, with a good sprinkling of country squires and parsons. It was the sort of school which, when mentioned, would sometimes make snobbish people confess that they rather thought they had heard of it.

But if it had not been this sort of school, it would probably not have taken Chips. For Chips, in any social or academic sense, was just as respectable as, but no more brilliant than Brookfield itself.

It had taken him some time to realize this, at the beginning. Not that he was boastful or conceited, but he had been, in his early twenties, as ambitious as most other young men at such an age. His dream had been to get a headship eventually, or at any rate a senior mastership in a really first-class school; it was only gradually, after repeated trials and failures, that he realized the inadequacy of his qualifications. His degree, for instance, was not particularly good, and his discipline, though good enough and improving, was not absolutely reliable under all conditions. He had no private means and no family connections of any importance. About 1880, after he had been at Brookfield a decade, he began to recognize that the odds were heavily against his being able to better himself by moving elsewhere; but about that time, also, the possibility of staying where he was began to fill a comfortable niche in his mind. At forty, he was rooted, settled and quite happy. At fifty, he was the doyen of the staff. At sixty, under a new and youthful Head, he *was* Brookfield—

the guest of honor at Old Brookfeldian dinners, the court of appeal in all matters affecting Brookfield history and traditions. And in 1913, when he turned sixty-five, he retired, was presented with a check and a writing desk and a clock, and went across the road to live at Mrs. Wickett's. A decent career, decently closed; three cheers for old Chips, they all shouted at that uproarious end-of-term dinner.

Three cheers, indeed; but there was more to come, an unguessed epilogue, an encore played to a tragic audience.

CHAPTER 3

IT WAS A SMALL but very comfortable and sunny room that Mrs. Wickett let to him. The house itself was ugly and pretentious, but that didn't matter. It was convenient—that was the main thing. For he liked, if the weather was mild enough, to stroll across to the playing fields in an afternoon and watch the games. He liked to smile and exchange a few words with the boys when they touched their caps to him. He made a special point of getting to know all the new boys and having them to tea with him during their first term. He always ordered a walnut cake with pink icing from Reddaway's in the village, and during the winter term there were crumpets, too—a little pile of them in front of the fire, soaked in butter so that the bottom one lay in a little shallow pool. His guests found it fun to watch him make tea—mixing careful spoonfuls from different caddies. And he would ask the new boys where they lived and if they had family connections at Brookfield. He kept watch to see that their plates were never empty, and punctually at five, after the session had lasted an hour, he would glance at the clock and say, "Well—umph—it's been very delightful—umph—meeting you like this—I'm sorry—umph—you can't stay. . . ." And he would smile and shake hands with them on the porch, leaving them to race across the road to the school with their comments. "Decent old boy, Chips. Gives you a jolly good tea, anyhow, and you *do* know when he wants you to push off. . . ."

And Chips also would be making his comments—to Mrs. Wickett when she entered his room to clear away the remains of the party. "A most—umph—interesting time, Mrs. Wickett. Young Branksome tells me—umph—that his uncle was Major Collingwood—the Collingwood we had here in—umph—nought-two, I think it was. Dear me, I remember Collingwood very well. I once thrashed him—umph—for climbing onto the gymnasium roof—to get a ball out of the gutter. Might have—umph—broken his neck, the young fool. Do you remember him, Mrs. Wickett? He must have been in your time."

Mrs. Wickett, before she saved money, had been in charge of the linen room at the school.

"Yes, I knew 'im, sir. Cheeky 'e was to me, gener'ly. But we never 'ad no bad words between us. Just cheeky-like. 'E never meant no harm. That kind never does, sir. Wasn't it 'im that got the medal, sir?"

"Yes, a Distinguished Service Order."

"Will you be wanting anything else, sir?"

"Nothing more now—umph—till chapel time. He was killed—in Egypt, I think. . . . Yes—umph—you can bring my supper about then."

"Very good, sir."

A pleasant, placid life at Mrs. Wickett's. He had no worries; his pension was adequate and there was a little money saved up besides. He could afford everything and anything he wanted. His room was furnished simply and with schoolmasterly taste: a few bookshelves and sporting trophies; a mantelpiece crowded with fixture cards and signed photographs of boys and men; a worn Turkish carpet; big easy chairs; pictures on the wall of the Acropolis and the Forum. Nearly everything had come out of his old housemaster's room in School House. The books were chiefly classical, the classics having been his subject there; there was, however, a seasoning of history and belles lettres. There was also a bottom shelf piled up with cheap editions of detective novels. Chips enjoyed these. Sometimes he took down Virgil or Xenophon and read for a few moments, but he was soon back again with Dr. Thorndyke or Inspector French. He was not, despite his long years of assiduous teaching, a very profound classical scholar; indeed, he thought of Latin and Greek far more as dead languages from which English gentlemen ought to know a few quotations than as living tongues that had ever been spoken by living people. He liked those short leading articles in the *Times* that introduced a few tags that he recognized. To be among the dwindling number of people who understood such things was to him a kind of secret and valued fellowship; it represented, he felt, one of the chief benefits to be derived from a classical education.

So there he lived, at Mrs. Wickett's, with his quiet enjoyments of reading and talking and remembering; an old man, white-haired and only a little bald, still fairly active for his years, drinking tea, receiving callers, busying himself with corrections for the next edition of the *Brookfeldian Directory*, writing his occasional letters in thin, spidery, but very legible script. He had the new masters to tea, as well as the new boys. There were two of them that autumn term, and as they were leaving after their visit one of them commented, "Quite a character, the old boy, isn't he? All that fuss about mixing the tea— a typical bachelor, if ever there was one."

Which was oddly incorrect; because Chips was not a bachelor at all. He had married; though it was so long ago that none of the staff at Brookfield could remember his wife.

CHAPTER 4

THERE CAME TO HIM, stirred by the warmth of the fire and the gentle aroma of tea, a thousand tangled recollections of old times. Spring— the spring of 1896. He was forty-eight—an age at which a permanence of habits begins to be predictable. He had just been appointed housemaster; with this and his classical forms, he had made for himself a warm and busy corner of life. During the summer vacation he went up to the Lake District with Rowden, a colleague; they walked and climbed for a week, until Rowden had to leave suddenly on some family business. Chips stayed on alone at Wasdale Head, where he boarded in a small farmhouse.

One day, climbing on Great Gable, he noticed a girl waving excitedly from a dangerous-looking ledge. Thinking she was in difficulty, he hastened toward her, but in doing so slipped himself and wrenched his ankle. As it turned out, she was not in difficulty at all, but was merely signaling to a friend farther down the mountain; she was an expert climber, better even than Chips, who was pretty good. Thus he found himself the rescued instead of the rescuer; and neither role was one for which he had much relish. For he did not, he would have said, care for women; he never felt at home or at ease with them; and that monstrous creature beginning to be talked about, the New Woman of the nineties, filled him with horror. He was a quiet, conventional person, and the world, viewed from the haven of Brookfield, seemed to him full of distasteful innovations; there was a fellow named George Bernard Shaw who had the most reprehensible opinions; there was Ibsen, too, with his disturbing plays; and there was this new craze for bicycling, which was being taken up by women equally with men. Chips did not hold with all this modern newness and freedom. He had a vague notion, if he ever formulated it, that nice women were weak, timid and delicate, and that nice men treated them with a polite but rather distant chivalry. He had not, therefore, expected to find a woman on Great Gable; but, having met one who seemed to need masculine help, it was even more terrifying that she should turn the tables by helping him. For she did. She and her friend had to. He could scarcely walk, and it was a hard job getting him down the steep track to Wasdale Head.

Her name was Katherine Bridges; she was twenty-five—young enough to be Chips's daughter. She had blue, flashing eyes and freckled cheeks and smooth straw-colored hair. She too was staying at a farm, on holiday with a girlfriend, and as she considered herself responsible for Chips's accident, she used to bicycle to the house in which the quiet, serious-looking man lay resting.

That was how she thought of him at first. And he, because she rode a bicycle and was unafraid to visit a man alone in a sitting room, wondered what the world was coming to. His sprain put him at her mercy, and it was soon revealed to him how much he might need that mercy. She was a governess out of a job, with a little money saved up; she read and admired Ibsen; she believed that women ought to be admitted to the universities; she even thought they ought to have the vote. In politics she was a radical, with leanings toward people like George Bernard Shaw and William Morris. All her ideas and opinions she poured out to Chips during those summer afternoons; and he did not at first think it worthwhile to contradict them. Her friend went away, but she stayed; what *could* you do with such a person, Chips thought. He used to hobble with sticks along a footpath leading to the tiny church; there was a stone slab on the wall, and it was comfortable to sit down, facing the sunlight and the green-brown majesty of the Great Gable and listening to the chatter of—well, yes, Chips had to admit it—a very beautiful girl.

He had never met anyone like her. He had always thought that the modern type, this New Woman business, would repel him; and here she was, making him positively look forward to the glimpse of her bicycle careering along the lakeside road. And she, too, had never met anyone like *him*. She had always thought that middle-aged men who read the *Times* and disapproved of modernity were terrible bores; yet here he was, claiming her interest and attention far more than youths of her own age. She liked him, initially, because he was so hard to get to know; because he had gentle and quiet manners; because his opinions dated from those utterly impossible seventies and eighties and even earlier—yet were, for all that, so thoroughly honest; and because—because his eyes were brown and he looked charming when he smiled. "Of course, *I* shall call you Chips, too," she said when she learned that was his nickname at school.

Within a week they were head over heels in love; before Chips could walk without a stick, they were engaged; and they were married in London a week before the beginning of the autumn term.

CHAPTER 5

WHEN CHIPS, DREAMING through the hours at Mrs. Wickett's, recollected those days, he used to look down at his feet and wonder which one it was that had performed so signal a service. That, the trivial cause of so many momentous happenings, was the one detail which evaded him. But he resaw the glorious hump of the Great Gable (he had never visited the Lake District since), and the mouse-gray depths of Wast Water under the Screes; he could resmell the washed air after heavy rain, and refollow the ribbon of the pass across to Sty Head. So clearly it lingered, that time of dizzy happiness, those evening strolls by the waterside, her cool voice and her gay laughter. She had been a very happy person, always.

They had both been so eager, planning a future together; but he had been rather serious about it, even a little awed. It would be all right, of course, her coming to Brookfield; other housemasters were married. And she liked boys, she told him, and would enjoy living among them. "Oh, Chips, I'm so glad you are what you are. I was afraid you were a solicitor or a stockbroker or a dentist or a man with a big cotton business. When I first met you, I mean. Schoolmastering's so different, so important, don't you think? To be influencing those who are going to grow up and matter to the world . . ."

Chips said he hadn't thought of it like that—or, at least, not often. He did his best; that was all anyone could do in any job.

"Yes, of course, Chips. I do love you for saying things like that."

And one morning—another memory gem-clear when he reflected on it—he had for some reason been afflicted with an acute desire to depreciate himself and all his attainments. He had told her of his only mediocre degree, of his occasional difficulties with discipline, of the certainty that he would never get a promotion, and of his complete ineligibility to marry a young and ambitious girl. And at the end of it all she had laughed in answer.

She had no parents and was married from the house of an aunt in London. On the night before the wedding, when Chips left the house to return to his hotel, she said, with mock gravity, "This is an occasion, you know—this last farewell of ours. I feel rather like a new boy beginning his first term with you. Not scared, mind you—but just, for once, in a thoroughly respectful mood. Shall I call you 'sir'—or would 'Mr. Chips' be the right thing? 'Mr. Chips,' I think. Good-bye, then—good-bye, Mr. Chips. . . ."

(A hansom clop-clopping in the roadway; green-pale gas lamps flickering on a wet pavement; newsboys shouting something about South Africa; Sherlock Holmes in Baker Street.)

"Good-bye, Mr. Chips. . . ."

CHAPTER 6

THERE HAD FOLLOWED then a time of such happiness that Chips, remembering it long afterward, hardly believed it could ever have happened before or since in the world. For his marriage was a triumphant success. Katherine conquered Brookfield as she had conquered Chips; she was immensely popular with boys and masters alike. Even the wives of the masters, tempted at first to be jealous of one so young and lovely, could not long resist her charms.

But most remarkable of all was the change she made in Chips. Till his marriage he had been a dry and rather neutral sort of person; liked and thought well of by Brookfield in general, but not of the stuff that makes for great popularity. He had been at Brookfield for over a quarter of a century, long enough to have established himself as a decent fellow and a hard worker; but just too long for anyone to believe him capable of ever being much more. He had, in fact, already begun to sink into that creeping dry rot of pedagogy that is the worst and ultimate pitfall of the profession: giving the same lessons year after year had formed a groove into which the other affairs of his life adjusted themselves with insidious ease. He worked well; he was conscientious; he was a fixture that gave service, satisfaction, confidence—everything except inspiration.

And then came this astonishing girl-wife whom nobody had expected—least of all Chips himself. She made him, to all appearances, a new man; though most of the newness was really a warming to life of things that were old, imprisoned and unguessed. His eyes gained sparkle; his mind, which was adequately if not brilliantly equipped, began to move more adventurously. The one thing he had always had, a sense of humor, blossomed into a sudden richness to which his years lent maturity. He began to feel a greater sureness; his discipline improved to the point where it became, in a sense, less rigid. When he had first come to Brookfield he had aimed to be loved, honored and obeyed—but obeyed, at any rate. Obedience he had secured, and honor had been granted him; but only now came love, the sudden love of boys for a man who was kind without being soft, who understood them well enough, but not too much, and whose private happiness linked them with their own. He began to make little jokes, the sort that schoolboys like—mnemonics and puns that raised laughs and at the same time imprinted something in the mind.

And Katherine broadened his views and opinions also, giving him an outlook far beyond the roofs and turrets of Brookfield, so that he saw his country as something deep and gracious to which Brookfield was but one of many feeding streams. She had a cleverer brain than his, and he could not refute her ideas even if and when he disagreed with them. He remained, for instance, a conservative in politics, in spite of all her radical-socialist talk. But even where he did not accept, he absorbed; her young idealism worked upon his maturity to produce an amalgam very gentle and wise.

Sometimes she persuaded him completely. For example, Brookfield ran a mission in East London, to which boys and parents contributed generously with money but rarely with personal contact. It was Katherine who suggested that a team from the mission should come up to Brookfield and play one of the school's elevens at soccer. The idea was so revolutionary that had it come from anyone but Katherine, it could not have survived its first frosty reception. To introduce a group of slum boys to the serene playing fields of better-class youngsters seemed at first a wanton stirring of all kinds of things that had better be left untouched. The whole staff was against it, and the Brookfield boys, if their opinion could have been taken, were probably against it too. Everyone was certain that the East End lads would be hooligans, or else that they would be made to feel uncomfortable; anyhow, there would be "incidents," and everyone would be confused and upset. Yet Katherine persisted.

"Chips," she said, "they're wrong, you know, and I'm right. I'm looking ahead to the future, they and you are looking back to the past. England isn't always going to be divided into officers and 'other ranks.' And those East End boys are just as important—to England—as Brookfield is. You've got to have them here, Chips. You can't satisfy your conscience by writing a check for a few guineas and keeping them at arm's length. Years hence, maybe, boys of that sort will be coming here—a few of them, at any rate. Why not? Why ever not? Chips, dear, remember this is eighteen ninety-seven—not sixty-seven, when you were up at Cambridge. You got your ideas well stuck in those days, and good ideas they were too, a lot of them. But a few—just a few, Chips—want unsticking. . . ."

Rather to her surprise, he gave way and suddenly became a keen advocate of the proposal, and the turnabout was so complete that the authorities found themselves consenting to the dangerous experiment. The boys from London arrived at Brookfield one Saturday afternoon, played soccer with the school's second team, were honorably defeated by seven goals to five, and later had high tea with the school team in the Dining Hall. They then met the Headmaster and were shown the school, and Chips saw them off at the railway station in the evening. Everything had passed without the slightest hitch of any kind, and it was clear that the visitors were taking away with them as fine an impression as they had left behind.

They took back with them also the memory of a charming woman who had met them and talked to them; for once, years later, during the war, a private stationed at a big military camp near Brookfield called on Chips and said he had been one of that first visiting team. Chips gave him tea and chatted with him, till at length, shaking hands, the man said, "And 'ow's the missus, sir? I remember her very well."

"Do you?" Chips answered eagerly. "Do you remember her?"

"Rather. I should think anyone would."

And Chips replied, "They don't, you know. At least, not here. Boys come and go; new faces all the time; memories don't last. Even masters don't stay forever. Since last year—when old Gribble retired—he's—um—the school butler—there hasn't been anyone here who ever saw my wife. She died, you know, less than a year after your visit. In ninety-eight."

"I'm real sorry to 'ear that, sir. There's two or three o' my pals, anyhow, who remember 'er clear as anything, though we did only see 'er that once. Yes, we remember 'er, all right."

"I'm very glad. . . . That was a grand day we all had—and a fine game, too."

"One o' the best days I ever 'ad in me life. Wish it was then and not now—straight, I do. I'm off to France tomorrow."

A month or so later Chips heard that he had been killed at Passchendaele.

CHAPTER 7

AND SO IT STOOD, a warm and vivid patch in his life, casting a radiance that glowed in a thousand recollections. Twilight at Mrs. Wickett's, when the school bell clanged for call-over, brought them back to him in a cloud—Katherine scampering along the stone corridors, laughing beside him at some "howler" in an essay he was marking, taking the cello part in a Mozart trio for the school concert, her creamy arm sweeping over the brown sheen of the instrument. She had been a good player and a fine musician. And Katherine furred and muffed for the December house matches, Katherine at the garden party that followed Speech Day prize giving, Katherine tendering her

advice in any little problem that arose. Good advice, too—which he did not always take, but which always influenced him.

"Chips, dear, I'd let them off if I were you. After all, it's nothing very serious."

"I know. I'd like to let them off, but if I do, I'm afraid they'll do it again."

"Try telling them that frankly, and give them the chance."

"I might."

And there were other things, occasionally, that *were* serious.

"You know, Chips, having all these hundreds of boys cooped up here is really an unnatural arrangement, when you come to think about it. So that when anything does occur that oughtn't to, don't you think it's a bit unfair to come down on them as if it were their own fault for being here?"

"Don't know about that, Kathie, but I do know that for everybody's sake we have to be pretty strict about this sort of thing. One black sheep can contaminate others."

"After he himself has been contaminated to begin with. After all, that's what probably *did* happen, isn't it?"

"Maybe. We can't help it. Anyhow, I believe Brookfield is better than a lot of other schools. All the more reason to keep it so."

"But this boy, Chips . . . you're going to sack him?"

"The Head probably will, when I tell him."

"And you're going to tell the Head?"

"It's a duty, I'm afraid."

"Couldn't you think about it a bit . . . talk to the boy again . . . find out how it began? . . . After all—apart from this business—isn't he rather a nice boy?"

"Oh, he's all right."

"Then, Chips dear, don't you think there *ought* to be some other way . . ."

And so on. About once in ten times he was adamant and wouldn't be persuaded. In about half of these exceptional cases he afterward rather wished he had taken her advice. And years later, whenever he had trouble with a boy, he was always at the mercy of a softening wave of reminiscence; the boy would stand there, waiting to be told his punishment, and would see, if he were observant, the brown eyes twinkle into a shine that told him all was well. But he did not guess that at such a moment Chips was remembering something that had happened long before he was born; that Chips was thinking, Young ruffian, I'm hanged if *I* can think of any reason to let him off, but I'll bet *she* would have done it!

But she had not always pleaded for leniency. On rather rare occasions she urged severity where Chips was inclined to be forgiving. "I don't like his type, Chips. He's too cocksure of himself. If he's looking for trouble, I should certainly let him have it."

What a host of little incidents, all deep-buried in the past—problems that had once been urgent, arguments that had once been keen, anecdotes that were funny only because one remembered the fun. Did any emotion really matter when the last trace of it had vanished from human memory; and if that was so, what a crowd of emotions clung to him as to their last home before annihilation! He must be kind to them, must treasure them in his mind before their long sleep. That affair of Archer's resignation, for instance—a queer business, that was. And that affair about the rat that Dunster put in the organ loft while old Ogilvie was taking choir practice. Ogilvie was dead and Dunster drowned at Jutland; of others who had witnessed or heard of the incident, probably most had forgotten. And it had been like that, with other incidents, for centuries. He had a sudden vision of thousands and thousands of boys, from the age of Elizabeth onward; dynasty upon dynasty of masters; long epochs of Brookfield history that had left not even a ghostly record. Who knew why the old fifth-form room was called "the Pit"? There was probably a reason, to begin with; but it had since been lost—lost like the lost books of Livy. And what happened at Brookfield when Cromwell fought at Naseby, nearby? Was there a whole holiday when news came of Waterloo? And so on, up to the earliest time that he himself could remember—1870, and Wetherby saying, by way of small talk after their first and only interview, "Looks as if we shall have to settle with the Prussians ourselves one of these fine days, eh?"

When Chips remembered things like this he often felt that he would write them down and make a book of them; and during his years at Mrs. Wickett's he sometimes went even so far as to make desultory notes in an exercise book. But he was soon brought up against difficulties—the chief one being that writing tired him, both mentally and physically.

Somehow, too, his recollections lost much of their flavor when they were written down; that story about Rushton and the sack of potatoes, for instance—it would seem quite tame in print, but Lord, how funny it had been at the time! It was funny, too, to remember it; though perhaps if you didn't remember Rushton . . . and who would, anyway, after all those years? It was such a long time ago . . . Mrs. Wickett, did you ever know a fellow named Rushton? Before your time, I daresay . . . went to Burma in some government job . . . or was it Borneo? . . . Very funny fellow, Rushton. . . .

And there he was, dreaming again before the fire, dreaming of times and incidents in which he alone could take secret interest. Funny and sad, comic and tragic, they all mixed up in his mind, and someday, however hard it proved, he *would* sort them out and make a book of them. . . .

CHAPTER 8

AND THERE WAS always in his mind that spring day in ninety-eight when he had paced through Brookfield village as in some horrifying nightmare, half struggling to escape into an outside world where the sun still shone and where everything had happened differently. Young Faulkner had met him there in the lane outside the school. "Please, sir, may I have the afternoon off? My people are coming up."

"Eh? What's that? Oh yes, yes. . . ."

"Can I miss chapel, too, sir?"

"Yes . . . yes . . ."

"And may I go to the station to meet them?"

He nearly answered, "You can go to blazes for all I care. My wife is dead and my child is dead, and I wish I were dead myself."

Actually he nodded and stumbled on. He did not want to talk to anybody or to receive condolences; he wanted to get used to things, if he could, before facing the kind words of others. He took his fourth form as usual after call-over, setting them grammar to learn by heart while he himself stayed at his desk in a cold, continuing trance. Suddenly someone said, "Please, sir, there are a lot of letters for you."

So there were; he had been leaning his elbows on them; they were all addressed to him by name. He tore them open one after the other, but each contained nothing but a blank sheet of paper. He thought in a distant way that it was rather peculiar, but he made no comment; the incident made hardly any impact upon his vastly greater preoccupations. Not till days afterward did he realize that it had been a piece of April foolery.

THEY HAD DIED on the same day, the mother and the child just born; on April 1, 1898.

CHAPTER 9

CHIPS CHANGED HIS more commodious apartments in School House for his old original bachelor quarters. He thought at first he would give up his housemastership, but the Head persuaded him otherwise, and later he was glad. The work gave him something to do, filled up an emptiness in his mind and heart. He was different; everyone noticed it. Just as marriage had added something, so did bereavement; after the first stupor of grief he became suddenly the kind of man whom boys, at any rate, unhesitatingly classed as "old." It was not that he was less active; he could still knock up a long hit on the cricket field. Nor was it that he had lost any interest or keenness in his work. Actually, too, his hair had been graying for years; yet now, for the first time, people seemed to notice it. He was fifty. Once, after some energetic game, during which he had played as well as many a fellow half his age, he overheard a boy saying, "Not half bad for an old chap like him."

Chips, when he was over eighty, used to recount that incident with many chuckles. "Old at fifty, eh? Umph—it was Naylor who said that, and Naylor can't be far short of fifty himself by now! I wonder if he still thinks that fifty's such an age? Last I heard of him, he was lawyering, and lawyers live long—look at Halsbury—umph—chancellor at eighty-two, and died at ninety-nine. There's an—umph—age for you! Too old at fifty—why, fellows like that are too *young* at fifty. . . . I was myself . . . a mere infant. . . ."

And there was a sense in which it was true. For with the new century there settled upon Chips a mellowness that gathered all his developing mannerisms and his oft-repeated jokes into a single harmony. No longer did he have those slight and occasional disciplinary troubles, or feel diffident about his own work and worth. He found that his pride in Brookfield reflected back, giving him cause for pride in himself and his position. It was a service that gave him freedom to be supremely and completely himself. He had won, by seniority and ripeness, an uncharted no-man's-land of privilege; he had acquired the right to those gentle eccentricities that so often attack schoolmasters and parsons. He wore his gown till it was almost too tattered to hold together; and when he stood on the wooden bench by Big Hall steps to take call-over, it was with an air of mystic abandonment to ritual. He held the School List, a long sheet curling over a board; and each boy, as he passed, spoke his own name for Chips to verify and then tick off on the list. That verifying glance was an easy and favorite subject of mimicry throughout the school—steel-rimmed spectacles slipping down the nose, eyebrows lifted, one a little higher than the other, a gaze half rapt, half quizzical. And on windy days, with gown and white hair and School List fluttering in uproarious confusion, the whole thing became a comic turn sandwiched between afternoon games and the return to classes.

Some of those names, in little snatches of a chorus, recurred to him ever afterward without any effort of memory . . . Ainsworth, Attwood, Avonmore, Babcock, Baggs, Barnard, Bassenthwaite, Battersby, Beccles, Bedford-Marshall, Bentley, Best . . .

Another one:

. . . Unsley, Vailes, Wadham, Wagstaff, Wallington, Waters Primus, Waters Secundus, Watling, Waveney, Webb . . .

And yet another that comprised, as he used to tell his fourth-form Latinists, an excellent example of a hexameter:

. . . Lancaster, Latton, Lemare, Lytton-Bosworth, MacGonigall, Mansfield . . .

Where had they all gone to, he often pondered; those threads he had once held together, how far had they scattered, some to break, others to weave into unknown patterns? The strange randomness of the world beguiled him, that randomness that never would, so long as the world lasted, give meaning to those choruses again.

And behind Brookfield, as one may glimpse a mountain behind

another mountain when the mist clears, he saw the world of change and conflict; and he saw it, more than he realized, with the remembered eyes of Katherine. She had not been able to bequeath him all her mind, still less the brilliance of it; but she had left him with a calmness and a poise that accorded well with his own inward emotions. It was typical of him that he did not share the general jingo bitterness against the Boers. Not that he was a pro-Boer—he was far too traditional for that and he disliked the kind of people who *were* pro-Boers; but still, it did cross his mind at times that the Boers were engaged in a struggle that had a curious similarity to those of certain English history-book heroes—Hereward the Wake, for instance, or Caractacus. He once tried to shock his fifth form by suggesting this, but they only thought it was one of his little jokes.

However heretical he might be about the Boers, he was orthodox about Mr. Lloyd George and the famous budget. He did not care for either of them. And when, years later, Lloyd George came as the guest of honor to a Brookfield Speech Day, Chips said, on being presented to him, "Mr. Lloyd George, I am nearly old enough—umph—to remember you as a young man, and—umph—I confess that you seem to me—umph—to have improved—umph—a great deal." The Head, standing with them, was rather aghast; but Lloyd George laughed heartily and talked to Chips more than to anyone else during the ceremonial that followed.

"Just like Chips," was the comment afterward. "He gets away with it. I suppose at that age anything you say to anybody is all right. . . ."

CHAPTER 10

IN 1900 OLD MELDRUM, who had succeeded Wetherby as Head and had held office for three decades, died suddenly from pneumonia; and in the interval before the appointment of a successor, Chips became Acting Head of Brookfield. There was just the faintest chance that the governors might make the appointment a permanent one; but Chips was not really disappointed when they brought in a youngster of thirty-seven, glittering with honors and with the kind of personality that could reduce Big Hall to silence by the mere lifting of an eyebrow. Chips was not in the running with that kind of person; he never had been and never would be, and he knew it. He was an altogether milder and less ferocious animal.

Those years before his retirement in 1913 were studded with sharply remembered pictures.

A May morning; the clang of the school bell at an unaccustomed time; everyone summoned to assemble in Big Hall. Ralston, the new Head, very pontifical and aware of himself, fixing the multitude with a cold, presaging severity. "You will all be deeply grieved to hear that His Majesty King Edward the Seventh died this morning. . . . There will be no school this afternoon, but a service will be held in the chapel at four thirty."

A summer morning on the railway line near Brookfield. The railway men were on strike; soldiers were driving the engines; stones had been thrown at trains. Brookfield boys were patrolling the line, thinking the whole business great fun. Chips, who was in charge, stood a little way off, talking to a man at the gate of a cottage. Young Cricklade approached. "Please, sir, what shall we do if we meet any strikers?"

"Would you like to meet one?"

"I—I don't know, sir."

God bless the boy—he talked of them as if they were queer animals out of a zoo! "Well, here you are, then—umph—you can meet Mr. Jones—he's a striker. When he's on duty he has charge of the signal box at the station. You've put your life in his hands many a time."

Afterward the story went around the school: There was Chips, talking to a striker. Talking to a striker. Might have been quite friendly, the way they were talking together.

Chips, thinking it over a good many times, always added to himself that Katherine would have approved and would have been amused.

Because always, whatever happened and however the avenues of politics twisted and curved, he had faith in England, in English flesh and blood, and in Brookfield as a place whose ultimate worth depended on whether she fitted herself into the English scene with dignity and without disproportion. He had a vision of an England for which the days of ease were nearly over, of a nation steering into channels where a hairbreadth of error might be catastrophic. He remembered the Diamond Jubilee; there had been a whole holiday at Brookfield, and he had taken Katherine to London to see the procession. Queen Victoria sitting in her carriage like some crumbling wooden doll, had symbolized so many things that, like herself, were nearing an end. Was it only the end of a century, or of an epoch?

And then that frenzied Edwardian decade, like an electric lamp that goes brighter and whiter just before it burns itself out.

Strikes and lockouts, champagne suppers and unemployed marchers, Chinese labor, tariff reform, H.M.S. *Dreadnought*, Marconi, Home Rule for Ireland, Dr. Crippen, suffragettes . . .

An April evening, windy and rainy; the fourth form construing Virgil, not very intelligently, for there was exciting news in the papers; young Grayson, in particular, was careless and preoccupied. A quiet, nervous boy.

"Grayson, stay behind—umph—after the rest."

Then: "Grayson, I don't want to be—umph—severe, because you are generally pretty good in your work, but today—you don't seem— umph—to have been trying at all. Is anything the matter?"

"N-no, sir."

"Well—umph—we'll say no more about it, but—umph—I shall expect better things next time."

Next morning it was noised around the school that Grayson's father had sailed on the *Titanic*, and that no news had yet come through as to his fate.

Grayson was excused from his lessons; for a whole day the school centered emotionally upon his anxieties. Then came news that his father had been among those rescued.

Chips shook hands with the boy. "Well—umph—I'm delighted, Grayson. A happy ending. You must be pleased."

"Y-yes, sir."

A quiet, nervous boy. And it was Grayson Senior, not Junior, with whom Chips was destined later to condole.

CHAPTER 11

AND THEN THE ROW with Ralston. Funny thing, Chips had never liked him. Efficient and ambitious, he had, admittedly, raised the status of Brookfield as a school, and for the first time in memory there was a longish waiting list. He was a live wire, but you had to beware of him.

Chips had never bothered to beware of him, though he served him willingly enough and quite loyally. Or, rather, he served Brookfield. He knew that Ralston did not like him, either; but that didn't seem to matter. He felt himself sufficiently protected by age and seniority from the fate of other masters whom Ralston had failed to like.

Then suddenly in 1908, when he had just turned sixty, came Ralston's urbane ultimatum. "Mr. Chipping, have you ever thought you would like to retire?"

Chips stared about him in that book-lined study, startled by the question, wondering why Ralston should have asked it. He said, at length, "No—umph—I can't say that—umph—I have thought much about it—umph—yet."

"Well, Mr. Chipping, the suggestion is there for you to consider."

Abruptly Chips flamed up. "But—umph—I don't want—to retire. I don't—umph—need to consider it."

"Nevertheless, I suggest that you do."

"But—umph—I don't see—why—I should!"

"In that case, things are going to be a little difficult."

"Difficult? Why—difficult?"

And then they set to, Ralston getting cooler and harder, Chips getting warmer and more passionate, till at last Ralston said icily, "Since you force me to use plain words, Mr. Chipping, you shall have them. For some time past, you haven't been pulling your weight here. Your methods of teaching are slack and old-fashioned; your personal habits are slovenly; and you ignore my instructions in a way which, in a younger man, I should regard as rank insubordination. It won't do, Mr. Chipping."

"But—" Chips began in sheer bewilderment; and then he took up isolated words out of that extraordinary indictment. "*Slovenly*—umph—you said—?"

"Yes, look at the gown you're wearing. I happen to know that that gown is a subject of continual amusement throughout the school."

Chips knew it, too, but it had never seemed to him a very regrettable matter. He went on: "And—you also said—umph—something about—*insubordination*—?"

"No, I didn't. I said that in a younger man I should have regarded it as that. In your case it's probably a mixture of slackness and obstinacy. This question of Latin pronunciation, for instance—I think I told you years ago that I wanted the new style used. But you prefer to stick to your old methods."

At last Chips had something tangible that he could tackle. "Oh, *that!*" he answered scornfully. "Well, I—umph—I admit that I don't agree with the new pronunciation. I never did. A lot of nonsense, in my opinion. Making boys say 'Kickero' at school when—umph—for the rest of their lives they'll say 'Cicero'—if they ever—umph—say it at all." He chuckled momentarily, forgetting that he was in Ralston's study and not in his own friendly form room.

"Well, there you are, Mr. Chipping—that's just an example of what I complain of. You hold one opinion and I hold another, and since you decline to give way, there can't very well be any alternative, can there? I aim to make Brookfield a thoroughly up-to-date school. I understand, Mr. Chipping, that your Latin and Greek lessons are exactly the same as they were when I began here ten years ago?"

Chips answered, slowly and with pride, "For that matter—umph—they are the same as when your predecessor—Mr. Meldrum—came here, and that—umph—was thirty-eight years ago. We began here, Mr. Meldrum and I—in—umph—eighteen seventy. And it was—um—Mr. Meldrum's predecessor, Mr. Wetherby—who first approved my syllabus. 'You'll take the Cicero for the fourth,' he said to me. Cicero, too—not Kickero!"

"Very interesting, Mr. Chipping, but once again it proves my point—you live too much in the past. Times are changing, whether you realize it or not. Modern parents are beginning to demand something more for their school fees than a few scraps of languages that nobody speaks. Besides, your boys don't learn even what they're supposed to learn. None of them last year got through the Lower Certificate."

And suddenly, in a torrent of thoughts too pressing to be put into words, Chips made answer to himself. All this efficiency and up-to-dateness—what did *that* matter, either? Ralston was trying to run Brookfield like a factory—a factory for turning out a snob culture based on money and machines. The old gentlemanly traditions of family and broad acres were changing, as doubtless they were bound to; but instead of widening them to form a genuine inclusive democracy of duke and dustman, Ralston was narrowing them upon the single issue of a fat bank account. There never had been so many rich men's sons at Brookfield. Ralston met these wealthy fellows in London clubs and persuaded them that Brookfield was *the* coming school, and since they couldn't buy their way into Eton or Harrow, they greedily swallowed the bait. Awful fellows, some of them—though others were decent enough. Financiers, company promoters, pill manufacturers. One of them gave his son five pounds a week pocket money. Vulgar . . . ostentatious . . . no sense of proportion. And it was a sense of proportion, above all things, that Brookfield ought to teach—not so much Latin or Greek or chemistry or mechanics. . . .

All this flashed through his mind in an instant of protest and indignation, but he did not say a word of it. He merely gathered his tattered gown together and with an "umph—umph" walked a few paces away. He had had enough of the argument. At the door he turned and said, "I don't—umph—intend to resign—and you can—umph—do what you like about it!"

Looking back upon that scene from the calm perspective of a quarter of a century, Chips could find it in his heart to feel a little sorry for Ralston. Particularly when, Ralston had been in such complete ignorance of the forces he was dealing with. So, for that matter, had Chips himself. Neither had correctly estimated the toughness of Brookfield tradition and its readiness to defend itself and its defenders. For it had so chanced that a small boy, waiting to see Ralston that morning, had been listening outside the door during the whole of the interview; he had been thrilled by it, naturally, and had told his friends. Some of these, in a surprisingly short time, had told their parents; so that very soon it was common knowledge that Ralston had insulted Chips and had demanded his resignation.

The amazing result was a spontaneous outburst of sympathy and partisanship such as Chips, in his wildest dreams, had never envisaged. He found, rather to his astonishment, that Ralston was thoroughly unpopular; he was feared and respected but not liked; and in this issue of Chips, the dislike rose to a point where it conquered fear and demolished even respect. There was talk of having a public riot if Ralston banished Chips. The masters, many of them young men who agreed that Chips was hopelessly old-fashioned, rallied round him nevertheless because they hated Ralston's slave driving and saw in the old veteran a likely champion. And one day the chairman of the governors, Sir John Rivers, visited Brookfield, ignored Ralston and went direct to Chips. "A fine fellow, Rivers," Chips would say, telling the story for the dozenth time. "Not—umph—a very brilliant boy in class. I remember he could never—umph—master his verbs. And now—umph—I see in the papers—they've made him—umph—a baronet. It just shows you—umph—it just shows you."

Sir John had said, on that morning in 1908, taking Chips by the arm as they walked around the deserted cricket fields, "Chips, old boy, sorry to hear about your row with Ralston—but the governors are with you to a man. We don't like the fellow a great deal. A bit too clever, if you ask me. He wants watching. So if he starts chucking his weight about with you, tell him very politely he can go to the devil. The governors all know that. Brookfield wouldn't be the same without you. You can stay here till you're a hundred if you feel like it— indeed, it's our hope that you will."

And at that—both then and often when he recounted it afterward—Chips broke down.

CHAPTER 12

SO HE STAYED ON at Brookfield, having as little to do with Ralston as possible. And in 1911 Ralston left "to better himself"; as head of one of the greater public schools. His successor was a man named Chatteris, whom Chips liked; he was even younger than Ralston had been—thirty-four. He was supposed to be very brilliant; at any rate, he was friendly and sympathetic. Recognizing in Chips a Brookfield institution, he wisely accepted the situation.

In 1913 Chips had had bronchitis and was off duty for nearly the whole of the winter term. That made him decide to resign that summer, when he was sixty-five; he felt that it would not be fair to hang on if he could not decently do his job. Besides, he would not sever himself completely. He would take rooms across the road, with the excellent Mrs. Wickett; he could visit the school whenever he wanted and could still, in a sense, remain a part of the school.

At that final end-of-term dinner in July 1913, Chips received his farewell presentations and made a speech. It was not a very long speech, but it had a good many jokes in it and was made twice as long, perhaps, by the laughter that impeded its progress. There were several Latin quotations in it, as well as a reference to the captain of the school, who, Chips said, had been guilty of exaggeration in speaking of his (Chips's) services to Brookfield. "But then—umph—he comes of an—umph—exaggerating family. I—um—remember—once—having to thrash his father—for it. [Laughter] I gave him one mark—umph—for a Latin translation, and he—umph—exaggerated the one into a seven! Umph—umph!" Roars of laughter and tumultuous cheers! A typical Chips remark, everyone thought.

And then he mentioned that he had been at Brookfield for forty-two years, and that he had been very happy there. "It has been my life," he said simply. *"O mihi praeteritos referat si Jupiter annos. . . .* Umph—I need not—of course—translate. . . ." Much laughter. "I remember lots of changes at Brookfield. I remember when there was no gas or electric light and we used to have a member of the domestic staff called a lampboy—he did nothing else but clean and trim and light lamps throughout the school. I remember when two thirds of the school went down with German measles and Big Hall was turned into a hospital ward. I remember the great bonfire we had on Mafeking night. I remember so much that I often think I ought to write a book. Well, well, perhaps I shall write it, someday. But I'd rather tell you about it, really. I remember . . . I remember . . . but chiefly I remember all your faces. I never forget them—the faces of boys. If you come and see me again in years to come—as I hope you all will—I shall try to remember those older faces of yours, but it's just possible I shan't be able to—and you'll say to yourself, 'The old boy doesn't remember me.' [Laughter] But I *do* remember you—as you are *now*.

"That's the point. In my mind you never grow up at all. Never. Sometimes, for instance, when people talk to me about our respected chairman of the governors, I think to myself, Ah yes, a jolly little chap with hair that sticks up on top. Well, well, I mustn't go on—umph—all night. Think of me sometimes as I shall certainly think of you. *Haec olim meminisse juvabit* . . . again, I need not translate." Much laughter and shouting and prolonged cheers.

August 1913. Chips went for a cure to Wiesbaden, where he lodged at the home of the young German master at Brookfield, Herr

Staefel, with whom he had got on excellently. In September, when term began, Chips returned and took up residence at Mrs. Wickett's. He felt a great deal fitter after his holiday, and almost wished he had not retired. Nevertheless, he found plenty to do. He had all the new boys to tea. He watched all the important matches on the Brookfield ground. Once a term he dined with the Head, and once also with the masters. He took on the preparation and editing of a new *Brookfeldian Directory*. He wrote occasional articles, full of jokes and Latin quotations, for the Brookfield magazine. He read his *Times* every morning—very thoroughly; and he also began to read detective stories—he had been keen on them ever since the first thrills of Sherlock Holmes. Yes, he was quite busy, and quite happy, too.

A year later, in 1914, he again attended the end-of-term dinner. There was a lot of war talk of trouble between Austria and Serbia. Herr Staefel, who was leaving for Germany the next day, told Chips he thought the Balkan business wouldn't come to anything.

CHAPTER 13

THE WAR YEARS.

The first shock, and then the first optimism. The Battle of the Marne, the Russian steamroller, Kitchener.

"Do you think it will last long, sir?"

Chips, questioned as he watched the first trial game of the season, gave quite a cheery answer. He was, like thousands of others, hopelessly wrong; but, unlike thousands of others, he did not afterward conceal the fact. "We ought to have—um—finished it—um—by Christmas. The Germans are already beaten. But why? Are you thinking of—um—joining up, Forrester?"

It was a joke because Forrester was the smallest new boy Brookfield had ever had—about four feet high above his muddy football boots. (But not much of a joke, when you came to think of it afterward; for he was killed in 1918—shot down in flames over Cambrai.) But one didn't guess what lay ahead. It seemed tragically sensational when the first Old Brookfeldian was killed in action—in September.

1915. Armies clenched in deadlock from the sea to Switzerland. The Dardanelles. Gallipoli. Military camps springing up quite near

Brookfield; soldiers using the playing fields for sports and training. Most of the younger masters gone or in uniform.

Every Sunday night, in the chapel after evening service, Chatteris read out the names of old boys killed, together with short biographies. Very moving; but Chips, in the back pew under the gallery, thought, They are only names to him; he doesn't see their faces as I do. . . .

1916. The Somme Battle. Twenty-three names read out one Sunday evening.

Toward the close of that catastrophic July, Chatteris talked to Chips one afternoon at Mrs. Wickett's. He was overworked and overworried and looked very ill. "To tell you the truth, Chipping, I'm not having too easy a time here. I'm thirty-nine, you know, and unmarried, and lots of people seem to think they know what I ought to do. I happen to be diabetic, but I don't see why I should pin a medical certificate on my front door."

Chips hadn't known anything about this; it was a shock to him, for he liked Chatteris.

The latter went on: "You see how it is. Ralston filled the place up with young men—all very good, of course—but now most of them have joined up and the substitutes are pretty dreadful, on the whole. The boys poured ink down a man's neck in prep one night last week—the silly fool got hysterical. I have to take classes myself, take prep for fools like that, work till midnight every night and get cold-shouldered as a slacker on top of everything. I can't stand it much longer. If things don't improve next term, I shall have a breakdown."

"I do sympathize with you," Chips said.

"I hoped you would. And that brings me to what I came here to ask you. If you felt equal to it and would care to—how about coming back here for a while? You needn't take anything strenuously—just a few odd jobs here and there, as you choose. What I'd like you for more than anything else is your help in other ways—in just *belonging* here. There's nobody ever been more popular than you were, and are still—you'd help to hold things together if there were any danger of them flying to bits. And perhaps there *is* that danger. . . ."

Chips answered, breathlessly and with a holy joy in his heart, "I'll come. . . ."

CHAPTER 14

HE STILL KEPT his rooms with Mrs. Wickett, but every morning, about half past ten, he put on his coat and muffler and crossed the road to the school. He felt very fit, and the actual work was not taxing. Just a few forms in Latin and Roman history—the old lessons, even the old pronunciation. He felt a little like a music-hall favorite returning to the boards after a positively last appearance.

They all said how marvelous it was that he knew every boy's name and face so quickly. They did not guess how closely he had kept in touch from across the road.

He was a grand success altogether. In some strange way he did—and they all knew and felt it—help things. For the first time in his life he felt *necessary*—and necessary to something that was nearest his heart. There is no sublimer feeling in the world, and it was his at last.

He made new jokes, too—about the food-rationing system and the air-raid blinds that had to be fitted on all the windows. There was a mysterious kind of rissole that began to appear on the school menu on Mondays, and Chips called it *abhorrendum*—"meat to be ab-horred." The story went around—heard Chips's latest?

Chatteris fell ill during the winter of 1917, and again, for the second time in his life, Chips became Acting Head of Brookfield. Then in April Chatteris died, and the governors asked Chips if he would carry on "for the duration." He said he would if they would refrain from appointing him officially. From that last honor, within his reach at last, he shrank instinctively, feeling himself in so many ways unequal to it. He said to Rivers, "You see, I'm not a young man and I don't want people to—um—expect a lot from me. I'm like all these new colonels and majors you see everywhere—just a wartime fluke. A ranker—that's all I am really."

1917. 1918. Chips lived through it all. He sat in the head-master's study every morning, handling problems, dealing with complaints and requests. Out of vast experience had emerged a kindly, gentle confidence in himself. To keep a sense of propor-tion—that was the main thing. So much of the world was losing it; as well keep it where it had, or ought to have, a congenial home.

On Sundays in chapel it was he who now read out the tragic list, and sometimes it was seen and heard that he was in tears over it. Well, why not, the school said; he was an old man. They might have despised anyone else for the weakness.

One day he got a letter from Switzerland, from friends there. On the following Sunday, after the names and biographies of old boys, he paused a moment and then added, "Those few of you who were here before the war will remember Max Staefel, the German master. He was in Germany visiting his home when war broke out. He was popular while he was here and made many friends. Those who knew him will be sorry to hear that he was killed last week—on the western front."

He was a little pale when he sat down afterward, aware that he had done something unusual. He had consulted nobody about it, anyhow; no one else could be blamed. Later, outside the chapel, he heard an argument.

"On the western front, Chips said. Does that mean he was fighting for the Germans?"

"I suppose it does."

"Seems funny, then, to read his name out with all the others. After all, he was an *enemy*."

"Oh, just one of Chips's ideas. The old boy still has 'em."

Chips was not displeased by the comment. Yes, he still had those ideas of dignity and generosity that were becoming increasingly rare in a frantic world. And he thought, Brookfield will take them, too, from me; but it wouldn't from anyone else.

Once, asked for his opinion of bayonet practice being carried on near the cricket pavilion, he answered, with that lazy, slightly asthmatic intonation that had been so often and so extravagantly imitated, "It seems—to me—umph—a very vulgar way of killing people."

The yarn was passed on and joyously appreciated—how Chips had told some big brass hat from the War Office that bayonet fighting was vulgar. Just like Chips. And they found an adjective for him—an adjective just beginning to be used: he was prewar.

CHAPTER 15

AND ONCE, ON A night full of moonlight, the air-raid warning was given while Chips was taking his lower fourth in Latin. The guns began almost instantly and, as there was plenty of shrapnel falling about outside, it seemed to Chips that they might just as well stay where they were, on the ground floor of School House. It was pretty solidly built and made as good a dugout as Brookfield could offer; and as for a direct hit, well, they could not expect to survive that, wherever they were.

So he went on with his Latin, speaking a little louder amid the reverberating crashes of the guns and the shrill whine of antiaircraft shells. Some of the boys were nervous; few were able to be attentive. He said gently, "It may possibly seem to you, Robertson—at this particular moment in the world's history—umph—that the affairs of Caesar in Gaul some two thousand years ago—are—umph—of somewhat secondary importance—and that—umph—the irregular conjugation of the verb *tollo* is—umph—even less important still. But believe me—umph—my dear Robertson—that is not really the case." Just then there came a particularly loud explosion—quite near. "You cannot—umph—judge the importance of things—umph—by the noise they make. Oh dear me, no." A little chuckle. "And these things—umph—that have mattered—for thousands of years—are not going to be—snuffed out. Another explosion—nearer still. "Let us—um—resume our work. If it is fate that we are soon to be—umph—interrupted, let us be found employing ourselves in something—umph—really appropriate. Is there anyone who will volunteer to construe?"

Maynard, chubby, clever and impudent, said, "I will, sir."

"Very good. Turn to page forty and begin at the bottom line."

The explosions still continued deafeningly; the whole building shook as if it were being lifted off its foundations. Maynard found the page, which was some way ahead, and began shrilly, *"Genus hoc erat pugnae—this was the kind of fight—quo se Germani exercuerant—in* which the Germans busied themselves. Oh, sir, that's good—that's really very funny indeed, sir—one of your very best—"

Laughing began, and Chips added, "Well—umph—you can see—now—that these dead languages—umph—can come to life again—sometimes—eh? Eh?"

Afterward they learned that five bombs had fallen in and around Brookfield, the nearest of them just outside the school grounds. Nine persons had been killed.

The story was told, retold, embellished. "The dear old boy never turned a hair. Even found something in Caesar about the way the Germans fought. You wouldn't think there were things like that in Caesar, would you? And the way Chips laughed . . . you know the way he *does* laugh . . . the tears all running down his face . . . never seen him laugh so much. . . ."

He was a legend.

With his old and tattered gown, his walk that was just beginning to break into a stumble, his mild eyes peering over the steel-rimmed spectacles, and his quaintly humorous sayings, Brookfield would not have had an atom of him different.

November 11, 1918. News came through in the morning; a whole holiday was decreed for the school. There was much cheering and singing, and a bread fight across the Dining Hall. When Chips entered in the midst of the uproar there was an instant hush, and then wave upon wave of cheering; everyone gazed on him with eager, shining eyes, as on a symbol of victory. He walked to the dais, seeming as if he wished to speak; but he shook his head after a moment, smiled and walked away again.

It had been a damp, foggy day, and the walk across the quadrangle to the Dining Hall had given him a chill. The next day he was in bed with bronchitis, and he stayed there till after Christmas. But already, on that night of November 11, after his visit to the Dining Hall, he had sent in his resignation to the board of governors.

At his own request there were no more farewells or presentations, nothing but a handshake with his successor and the word "Acting" crossed out on official stationery. The "duration" was over.

CHAPTER 16

AND NOW, FIFTEEN YEARS later, he could look back upon it all with a deep and sumptuous tranquillity. He was not ill, of course—only a little tired at times and bad with his breathing during the winter months. But there were warm fires and books, and you could look forward to the summer. It was the summer that he liked best, of course; apart from the weather, which suited him, there were the continual visits of old boys. Every weekend some of them motored up to Brookfield and called at his house. Sometimes they tired him, if too many came at once; but he did not really mind; he could always rest and sleep afterward. And he enjoyed their visits—more than anything else in the world that was still to be enjoyed. "Well, Gregson—umph—I remember you—umph—always late for everything—eh—eh? Perhaps you'll be late in growing old—umph—like me—umph—eh?"

And sometimes when the bell rang for call-over, he would go to the window and look across the road and over the school fence and see, in the distance, the thin line of boys filing past the bench. New times, new names . . . but the old ones still remained . . . Jefferson, Jennings, Jolyon, Jupp, Kingsley Primus, Kingsley Secundus, Kingsley Tertius, Kingston . . . Where are you all, where have you all gone to? . . . "Mrs. Wickett, bring me a cup of tea, will you, please?"

The postwar decade swept through with a clatter of change and maladjustments; Chips, as he lived through it, was profoundly disappointed when he looked abroad. The Ruhr, Corfu—there was enough to be uneasy about in the world. But near him at Brookfield and even, in a wider sense, in England, there was something that charmed his heart because it was old—and had survived. More and more he saw the rest of the world as a vast disarrangement for which England had sacrificed enough—and perhaps too much. But he was satisfied with Brookfield. It was rooted in things that had stood the test of time and change and war. Curious, in this deeper sense, how little it *had* changed. Boys were a politer race; bullying was nonexistent; there was more swearing and cheating. There was a more genuine friendliness between master and boy—less pomposity on the one side, less unctuousness on the other. One of the new masters, fresh from Oxford, even let the sixth-formers call him by his Christian name. Chips didn't hold with that; indeed, he was just a little bit shocked. "He might as well—umph—sign his terminal reports— umph—'yours affectionately'—eh—eh?" he told somebody.

Laughter . . . laughter . . . whatever he said, there was laughter. He had earned the reputation of being a great jester, and jests were expected of him. Whenever he rose to speak at a meeting, or even when he talked across a table, people prepared their minds and faces for the joke. It was easy to satisfy them. They laughed sometimes before he came to the point. "Old Chips was in fine form," they would say afterward. "Marvelous the way he can always see the funny side of things. . . ."

After 1929, Chips did not leave Brookfield—even for Old Boys' dinners in London. The late nights began to tire him too much. He came across to the school, however, on fine days, and he still kept up a wide and continual hospitality in his room. His small capital, invested in gilt-edged stocks, did not suffer when the slump set in, and he gave a lot of money away—to people who called on him with a hard-luck story, and to various school funds. In 1930 he made his will. Except for legacies to the mission and to Mrs. Wickett, he left all he had to found an open scholarship to the school.

1931 . . . 1932 . . .

Sometimes, when he was strolling about the school, boys of the cheekier kind would ask him questions, merely for the fun of getting Chips's "latest" to retell.

"Sir, do you think Germany wants to fight another war?"

"Have you been to the new cinema, sir? I went with my people the other day. Quite a grand affair for a small place like Brookfield. They've got a Wurlitzer."

"And what—umph—on earth—is a Wurlitzer?"

"It's an organ, sir—a cinema organ."

"Dear me. . . . I've seen the name on the billboards, but I always—umph—imagined—it must be some kind of—umph—sausage."

Laughter. . . . Oh, there's a new Chips joke, you fellows, a perfectly lovely one. I was gassing to the old boy about the new cinema, and . . .

CHAPTER 17

HE SAT IN HIS front parlor at Mrs. Wickett's on a November afternoon in 1933. It was cold and foggy, and he dared not go out. He had not felt too well since Armistice Day; he fancied he might have caught a slight chill during the chapel service. Doctor Merivale had been that morning for his usual fortnightly chat. "Everything all right? Feeling hearty? That's the style—keep indoors this weather—there's a lot of flu about. Wish I could have your life for a day or two."

His life . . . and what a life it had been! The whole pageant of it swung before him as he sat by the fire that afernoon. The things he had done and seen: Cambridge in the sixties; Brookfield throughout the years. And, for that matter, the things he had *not* done and would never do now that he had left them too late—he had never traveled by air, for instance, and he had never been to a talkie. So that he was both more and less experienced than the youngest new boy at the school might well be; and that, that paradox of age and youth, was what the world called progress.

Mrs. Wickett had gone out and had left the tea things ready on the table, with bread and butter and extra cups laid out in case anybody called. On such a day, however, with the fog thickening hourly outside, he would probably be alone.

But no. About a quarter to four a ring came, and Chips, answering the front door himself, encountered a rather small boy wearing a Brookfield cap and an expression of anxious timidity. "Please, sir," he began, "does Mr. Chips live here?"

"Umph—you'd better come inside," Chips answered. And in his room a moment later he added, "I am—umph—the person you want. Now what can I—umph—do for you?"

"I was told you wanted me, sir."

Chips smiled. It was an old joke—an old leg-pull. It amused him to cap it with one of his own. So he said, with eyes twinkling, "Quite right, my boy. I wanted you to take tea with me. Will you—umph—sit down by the fire? Umph—I don't think I have seen your face before. How is that?"

"I've only just come out of the sanatorium, sir—I've been there since the beginning of term with measles."

"Ah, that accounts for it."

Chips began his usual ritualistic blending of tea from the different caddies; luckily there was half a walnut cake with pink icing in the cupboard. He found out that the boy's name was Linford, that he lived in Shropshire, and that he was the first of his family at Brookfield.

"You know—umph—Linford—you'll like Brookfield—when you get used to it. It's not half such an awful place—as you imagine. You're a bit afraid of it—um, yes—eh? So was I, my dear boy—at first. But that was—um—sixty-three years ago. When I—um—first went into Big Hall and—I saw all those boys—I tell you—I was quite scared. Indeed—um—I don't think I've ever been so scared in my life. But—umph—it didn't last long—the scared feeling, I mean. I soon made myself—um—at home."

"Were there a lot of other new boys that term, sir?" asked Linford shyly.

"Eh? But—God bless my soul—I wasn't a boy at all—I was a man—a young man of twenty-two! And the next time you see a young man—a new master—taking his first prep in Big Hall—umph—just think—what it feels like!"

"But if you were twenty-two then, sir—"

"Yes? Eh?"

"You must be—very old—now, sir."

Chips laughed quietly and steadily to himself. It was a good joke. "Well—umph—I'm certainly—umph—no spring chicken."

He laughed quietly to himself for a long time.

Then he talked of other matters, of schools and school life in general, of the news in that day's papers.

At the front door he shook hands.

"Good-bye, my boy."

And the answer came in a shrill treble: "Good-bye, Mr. Chips. . . ."

Chips sat by the fire again, with those words echoing along the corridors of his mind. "Good-bye, Mr. Chips. . . ." An old leg-pull, to make new boys think that his name was really Chips; the joke was almost traditional. He did not mind. "Good-bye, Mr. Chips. . . ." He remembered that on the eve of his wedding day Katherine had used that same phrase, mocking him gently for the seriousness he had had in those days. He thought, Nobody would call me serious today, that's very certain. . . .

Suddenly the tears began to roll down his cheeks—an old man's failing; silly, perhaps, but he couldn't help it. He felt very tired; talking to Linford like that had quite exhausted him. But he was glad he had met Linford. Nice boy. Would do well.

Over the fog-laden air came the bell for call-over, tremulous and muffled. Chips looked at the window, graying into twilight; it was time to light up. But as soon as he began to move, he felt that he couldn't; he was too tired; and, anyhow, it didn't matter. He leaned back in his chair. No spring chicken—eh, well—that was true enough. And it had been amusing about Linford. A neat score off the jokers who had sent the boy over. Good-bye, Mr. Chips . . . odd, though, that he should have said it just like that. . . .

CHAPTER 18

WHEN HE AWOKE, for he seemed to have been asleep, he found himself in bed, and Merivale was there, stooping over him and smiling. "Well, you old ruffian––feeling all right? That was a fine shock you gave us!"

Chips murmured, after a pause, and in a voice that surprised him by its weakness, "Why—um—what—what has happened?"

"Merely that you threw a faint. Mrs. Wickett came in and found you. You're all right now. Sleep again if you feel inclined."

He was glad someone had suggested such a good idea. He felt so weak that he wasn't even puzzled by the details of the business—how they had got him upstairs, what Mrs. Wickett had said and so on. But then, suddenly, at the other side of the bed, he saw Mrs. Wickett. She was smiling. He thought, God bless my soul what's she doing up here? And then, in the shadows behind Merivale, he saw Cartwright, the new Head (he thought of him as "new," even though he had been at Brookfield since 1919), and old Buffles, commonly called "Roddy." Funny, the way they were all here. He felt, Anyhow, I can't be bothered to wonder why about anything. I'm going to go to sleep.

But it wasn't sleep and it wasn't quite wakefulness, either; it was a sort of in-between state, full of dreams and faces and voices. Old scenes and old scraps of tunes: a Mozart trio that Katherine once played in—cheers and laughter and the sound of guns—and, over it all, Brookfield bells, Brookfield bells. . . .

Once he heard them talking about him in the room.

Cartwright was whispering to Merivale, "Poor old chap—must have lived a lonely sort of life, all by himself."

Merivale answered, "Not always by himself. He married, you know."

"Oh, did he? I never knew about that."

"She died. It must have been—oh, quite thirty years ago. More, possibly."

"Pity. Pity he never had any children."

And at that, Chips opened his eyes as wide as he could and sought to attract their attention. It was hard for him to speak out loud, but he managed to murmur something, and they all looked around and came nearer to him.

He struggled, slowly, with his words. "What—was that—um—you were saying—about me—just now?"

Old Buffles smiled and said, "Nothing at all, old chap—nothing at all. We were just wondering when you were going to wake out of your beauty sleep."

"But—umph—I heard you—you *were* talking about me—"

"Absolutely nothing of any consequence, my dear fellow—really, I give you my word. . . ."

"I thought I heard you—one of you—saying it was a pity—umph— a pity I never had—any children . . . eh? . . . But I have, you know . . . I have . . ."

The others smiled without answering, and after a pause Chips began a faint and palpitating chuckle.

"Yes—umph—I have," he added, with quavering merriment. "Thousands of 'em . . . thousands of 'em . . . and all boys."

And then the chorus sang in final harmony, more grandly and sweetly than he had ever heard it before, and more comfortingly too. . . . Pettifer, Pollet, Porson, Potts, Pullman, Purvis, Pym-Wilson, Radlett, Rapson, Reade, Reaper, Reddy Primus . . . come around me now, all of you, for a last word and a joke. . . . Harper, Haslett, Hatfield, Hatherley . . . my last joke . . . did you hear it? . . . Did it make you laugh? . . . Bone, Boston, Bovey, Bradford, Bradley, Bramhall-Anderson . . . wherever you are, whatever has happened, give me this moment with you . . . this last moment . . . my boys . . .

And soon Chips was asleep.

He seemed so peaceful that they did not disturb him to say good night; but in the morning, as the school bell sounded for breakfast, Brookfield had the news. "Brookfield will never forget his lovableness," said Cartwright in a speech to the school. Which was absurd, because all things are forgotten in the end. But Linford, at any rate, will remember and tell the tale: "I said good-bye to Chips the night before he died. . . ."

NIGHT FLIGHT

NIGHT FLIGHT

Antoine de Saint-Exupéry

ILLUSTRATED BY CHUCK HAMRICK

Each in his or her own way was alone
and waiting for whatever fate would bring—the
youthful pilot who flew the treacherous
air route over the Andes Mountains to transport
the mail; his wife who waited at home,
worried and uncertain of his safe return;
his steely supervisor who believed in
commitment to one's duty above all.

   No other novel of its length captures the
perils and the poetry of the early days
of commercial aviation as does *Night Flight*.
Ironically and tragically, its author,
Antoine de Saint–Exupéry, was himself lost
on a solo flight between France and
North Africa in 1944.

CHAPTER 1

ALREADY, BENEATH HIM, through the golden evening, the shadowed hills had dug their furrows and the plains grew luminous with long-enduring light. For in these lands the ground gives
off this golden glow persistently, just as, even when winter goes, the
whiteness of the snow persists.

Fabien, the pilot bringing the Patagonia airmail from the far south
to Buenos Aires, could mark night coming on by certain signs that
called to mind the waters of a harbor—a calm expanse beneath,
faintly rippled by lazy clouds—and he seemed to be entering a vast
anchorage, an immensity of blessedness.

Or else he might have fancied he was taking a quiet walk in the
calm of evening, almost like a shepherd. The Patagonian shepherds
move, unhurried, from one flock to another; and he, too, moved
from one town to another, the shepherd of those little towns. Every
two hours he met another of them, drinking at its riverside or
browsing on its plain.

Sometimes, after a hundred miles of steppes as desolate as the
sea, he encountered a lonely farmhouse that seemed to be sailing
backward from him in a great prairie sea, with its freight of human
lives; and he saluted with his wings this passing ship.

"San Julián in sight. In ten minutes we shall land."

The radio operator gave their position to all the stations on the
line. From the Strait of Magellan to Buenos Aires the airports were

strung out across fifteen hundred miles and more, but this one led toward the frontiers of night, just as in Africa the last conquered hamlet opens onto the unknown.

The radio operator handed the pilot a slip of paper. "There are so many storms about that the static is fouling my earphones. Shall we stop for the night at San Julián?"

Fabien smiled; the sky was calm as an aquarium and all the stations ahead were signaling: *Clear sky: no wind.*

"No, we'll go on."

But the radio operator was thinking, These storms had lodged themselves somewhere or other, as worms do in a fruit; a fine night, but they would ruin it, and he loathed entering this shadow that was ripe to rottenness.

As he slowed down his engine for the San Julián landing, Fabien knew that he was tired. All that endeared life to man was looming up to meet him; men's houses, friendly little cafés, trees under which they walk. He was like some conqueror who, in the aftermath of victory, bends down upon his territories and now perceives the humble happiness of men. A need came over Fabien to lay his weapons down and feel the aching burden of his limbs—for even our misfortunes are a part of our belongings—and to stay, a simple dweller here, watching from his window a scene that would never change. This tiny village, he could gladly have made friends with it. Fabien would have wished to live a long while here—here to possess his morsel of eternity. These little towns where he lived an hour, their gardens girdled by old walls over which he passed, seemed something apart and everlasting. Now the village was rising to meet the plane, opening out toward him. And there, he mused, were friendliness and gentle girls, white napery spread in quiet homes; all that is slowly shaped toward eternity. The village streamed past beneath his wings, yielding the secrets of closed gardens that their walls no longer guarded. He landed; and now he knew that he had seen nothing at all, only a few men slowly moving among their stones. The village kept, by its mere immobility, the secret of its passions and withheld its kindly charm; for to master that he would have needed to give up an active life.

The ten-minute halt was ended and Fabien resumed his flight. He glanced back toward San Julián; all he now could see was a cluster of lights, then stars, then twinkling stardust that vanished, tempting him for the last time.

"I can't see the dials; I'll light up."

He touched the switches, but the red light falling from the cockpit lamps upon the dials was so diluted with the blue evening glow that they did not catch its color. When he passed his fingers before a bulb, they were hardly tinged at all.

"Too soon."

But night was rising like a tawny smoke and already the valleys were brimming over with it. No longer were they distinguishable from the plains. The villages were lighting up, constellations that greeted each other across the dusk. And, at a touch of his finger, his flying lights flashed back a greeting to them. The earth grew spangled with light signals as each house lit its star, searching the vastness of the night as a lighthouse sweeps the sea. Now every place that sheltered human life was sparkling. And it invited him to enter into this one night with a measured slowness, as into an anchorage.

He bent down into the cockpit; the luminous dials were beginning to show up. The pilot read their figures one by one; all was going well. He felt at ease up here, snugly ensconced. He passed his fingers along a steel rib of the plane and felt the life that flowed in it; the metal did not vibrate, yet it was alive. The engine's five-hundred horsepower bred in its texture a very gentle current. Once again the pilot in full flight experienced neither giddiness nor any thrill; only the mystery of metal turned to living flesh.

So he had found his world again. . . . A few digs of his elbow, and he was quite at home. He tapped the dashboard, touched the contacts one by one, shifting his limbs a little, and, settling himself more solidly, felt for the best position whence to gage the faintest lurch of his five tons of metal, now jostled by the heaving darkness. Groping with his fingers, he plugged in his emergency lamp, let go of it, felt for it again, made sure it held; then lightly touched each switch to be certain of finding it later, training his hands to function in a blind man's world. Now that his hands had learned their role by heart, he ventured to turn on a lamp, making the cockpit bright with polished fittings, and then, as on a submarine about to dive, watched his passage into night on the dials only. Nothing shook or rattled, neither gyroscope nor altimeter flickered in the least, the engine was running smoothly; so now he relaxed his limbs a little, let his neck sink back into the leather padding and fell into the deeply meditative mood of flight, mellow with inexplicable hopes.

Now, a watchman from the heart of night, he learned how night betrays man's presence, his voices, lights, and his unrest. That star down there in the shadows, alone; a lonely house. Yonder a fading star; that house is closing in upon its love. . . . Or on its lassitude. A house that has ceased to flash its signal to the world. Gathered around their lamplit table, those peasants do not know the measure of their hopes; they do not guess that their desire carries so far out into the vastness of the night that hems them in. But Fabien has met it on his path when, coming from a thousand miles away, he feels the heavy ground swell raise his panting plane and let it sink, when he has crossed a dozen storms like lands at war, between them neutral tracts of moonlight, to reach at last those lights, one following the other—and knows himself a conqueror. They think, these peasants, that their lamp shines only for that little table; but, from fifty miles away, someone has felt the summons of their light, as though it were a desperate signal from some lonely island, flashed by shipwrecked men toward the sea.

CHAPTER 2

THUS THE THREE planes of the airmail service, from Patagonia, Chile and Paraguay, would converge from south, west and north on Buenos Aires. Their arrival with the mail would give the signal for the departure, about midnight, of the Europe postal plane.

Three pilots, each behind a cowling as heavy as a river barge, intent upon his flight, were hastening through the distant darkness, soon to come slowly down, from a sky of storm or calm, like wild, outlandish peasants descending from their highlands.

Rivière, who was responsible for the entire service, was pacing to and fro on the Buenos Aires landing strip. He was in a silent mood, for until the three planes came in, he could not shake off the feeling of apprehension that had been haunting him all day. Minute by minute, as the telegrams were passed to him, Rivière felt that he had scored another point against fate, reduced the quantum of the unknown and was drawing his charges in out of the clutches of the night toward their haven.

One of his assistants came up to Rivière with a radio message.

"Chile mail reports: Buenos Aires in sight."

"Good."

Presently, then, Rivière would hear its drone; already the night was yielding up one of them. And soon the night would give him back the other two.

Then today's work would be over. Worn-out, the crews would go to sleep, fresh crews would replace them. Rivière alone would have no respite; then, in its turn, the Europe mail would weigh upon his mind. And so it would always be. Always. For the first time in his life this veteran fighter caught himself feeling tired. Never could an arrival of the planes mean for him the victory that ends a war and preludes a spell of smiling peace. For him it meant just one more step, with a thousand more to follow, along a straight, unending road. Rivière felt as though for an eternity he had been carrying a crushing load on his uplifted arms; an endless, hopeless effort.

I'm aging, he thought. If he no longer found a solace in work and work alone, surely he was growing old. He caught himself puzzling over problems that hitherto he had ignored. There surged within his mind murmuring regrets, all the gentler joys of life that he had thrust aside. Can it be coming on me—so soon? He realized that he had always been postponing for his declining years, "when I have time for it," everything that makes life kind to men. As if it were ever possible to "have time for it" one day and realize at life's end that dream of peace and happiness! No, peace there could be none; nor any victory, perhaps. Never could all the airmail land in one swoop once and for all.

Rivière paused before Leroux; the old foreman was hard at work. Leroux had forty years of work behind him. All his energies were for his work. When at ten o'clock or midnight Leroux went home, it certainly was not to find a change of scene or to escape into another world. When Rivière smiled toward him, he raised his heavy head and pointed at a burned-out axle. "Jammed it was, but I've fixed it up."

Rivière bent down to look; duty had regained its hold upon him. "You should tell the shop to set them a bit looser." He passed his finger over the trace of seizing, then glanced again at Leroux. As his eyes lingered on the stern old wrinkled face, an odd question hovered on his lips and made him smile.

"Ever had much to do with love, Leroux, in your time?"

"Love, sir? Well, you see—"

"Hadn't the time for it, I suppose—like me."

"Not a great deal, sir."

Rivière strained his ears to hear if there was any bitterness in the reply; no, not a trace of it. This man, looking back on life, felt the quiet satisfaction of a carpenter who has done a good job of planing down a board: There you are! *That's* done.

There you are, thought Rivière. My life's done.

Then, brushing aside the swarm of somber thoughts his weariness had brought, he walked toward the hangar—the Chile plane was droning down toward it.

CHAPTER 3

THE SOUND OF the distant engine swelled and thickened; a sound of ripening. Lights flashed out. The red lamps on the light tower silhouetted a hangar, radio standards, a square landing area. The setting of a gala night.

"There she comes!"

A sheaf of beams had caught the plane as it landed, making it shine as if brand-new. No sooner had it come to rest before the hangar than mechanics and airport hands hurried up to unload the mail. Only Pellerin, the pilot, did not move.

"Well, aren't you going to get down?"

The pilot, intent on some mysterious task, did not deign to reply. Listening, perhaps, to sounds that he alone could hear, long echoes of the flight. Nodding reflectively, he bent down and tinkered with some unseen instrument. At last he turned toward the officials and his comrades, gravely taking stock of them as though of his possessions. He seemed to pass them in review, to weigh them, take their measure, saying to himself that he had earned his right to them, as to this hangar with its gala lights and solid concrete and, in the offing, the city, full of movement, warmth and women. In the hollow of his large hands he seemed to hold these people; they were his subjects, to touch or hear or curse, as the fancy took him. His impulse now was to curse them for a lazy crowd, so sure of life they seemed, gaping at the moon, but he decided to be genial instead.

". . . Drinks are on you!"

Then he climbed down.

He wanted to tell them about the trip.

"If only you knew . . . !"

Evidently, to his thinking, that summed it up, for now he walked off to change out of his flying gear.

As the car was taking him to Buenos Aires in the company of a morose inspector and Rivière in a silent mood, Pellerin suddenly felt sad. Of course, he thought, it's a fine thing for a fellow to have gone through it and, when he's got his footing again, let off a healthy volley of curses. Nothing finer in the world! But afterward . . . when you look back on it all, you wonder; you aren't half so sure!

A struggle with a storm, that at least is a straight fight, it's *real*. But not that curious look things wear, the face they have when they think they are alone. His thoughts took form. Like a revolution it is; men's faces turning only the least shade paler, yet utterly unlike themselves.

He bent his mind toward the memory.

He had been crossing peacefully the cordillera of the Andes. A snowbound stillness brooded on the ranges; the winter snow had brought its peace to all this vastness, as in dead castles the passing centuries spread peace. Two hundred miles without a man, a breath of life, a movement; only sheer peaks that, flying at twenty thousand feet, you almost graze, straight-falling cloaks of stone, an ominous tranquillity.

It had happened somewhere near Tupungato Peak. . . .

He reflected. . . . Yes, it was there he saw a miracle take place.

For at first he had noticed nothing much, felt no more than a vague uneasiness—as when a man believes himself alone but is not; someone is watching him. Too late, and how he could not comprehend, he realized that he was hemmed in by anger. Where was it coming from, this anger? What told him it was oozing from the stones, sweating from the snow? For nothing seemed on its way to him, no storm was lowering. And still—another world, like it and yet unlike, was issuing from the world around him. Now all those quiet-looking peaks, snowcaps and ridges, growing faintly grayer, seemed to spring to life, a people of the snows. And an inexplicable anguish gripped his heart.

Instinctively he tightened his grasp on the controls. Something he did not understand was on its way and he tautened his muscles, like a beast about to spring. Yet, as far as eye could see, all was at peace. Peaceful, yes, but tense with some dark potency.

Suddenly all grew sharp; peaks and ridges seemed keen-edged prows cutting athwart a heavy headwind. Veering around him, they deployed like dreadnoughts taking their positions in a battle line. Dusk began to mingle with the air, rising and hovering, a veil above the snow. Looking back to see if retreat might still be feasible, he shuddered; the cordillera behind him was in seething ferment.

"I'm gone!"

On a peak ahead of him the snow swirled up into the air—a snow volcano. On his right flared up another peak and, one by one, all the summits grew lambent with gray fire, as if some unseen messenger had touched them into flame. Then the first squall broke and all the mountains around the pilot quivered.

Violent action leaves little trace behind it, and he had no recollection of the gusts that buffeted him from side to side. Only one clear memory remained; the battle in a welter of gray flames.

He pondered. A whirlwind, that's nothing. A man just saves his skin! It's what comes before it—the thing one meets upon the way!

But already even as he thought he had recalled it, that one face in a thousand, he had forgotten what it was like.

CHAPTER 4

RIVIÈRE GLANCED at the pilot. In twenty minutes Pellerin would step from the car, mingle with the crowd and know the burden of his lassitude. Perhaps he would murmur, "Tired out as usual. It's a dog's life!" To his wife he would, perhaps, let fall a word or two. "A fellow's better off here than flying above the Andes!" And yet that world to which men hold so strongly had almost slipped from him; he had come to know its wretchedness. He had returned from a few hours' life on the other side of the picture, not knowing if it would be possible for him ever to retrieve this city with its lights, ever to know again his little human frailties, irksome yet cherished childhood friends.

In every crowd, Rivière mused, are certain persons who seem just like the rest, yet they bear amazing messages. Unwittingly, no doubt, unless— Rivière was chary of a certain type of admirer, blind to the higher side of this adventure, whose vain applause perverted its meaning, debased its human dignity. But Pellerin's inalienable greatness lay in this—his simple yet sure awareness of what the world, seen from a special angle, signified, and his massive scorn of vulgar flattery. So Rivière congratulated him. "Well, how did you bring it off?" And loved him for his knack of only talking shop, referring to his flight as a blacksmith to his anvil.

Pellerin began by telling how his retreat had been cut off. It was almost as if he were apologizing about it. "There was nothing else for it!" Then he had lost sight of everything, blinded by the snow. He owed his escape to the violent air currents that had driven him up to twenty-five thousand feet. "I guess they held me all the way just above the level of the peaks." He mentioned trouble with the gyroscope and how he had had to shift the air inlet, as the snow was clogging it. After that another set of air currents had driven Pellerin down, and when he was only at ten thousand feet or so, he was puzzled as to why he had not run into anything. As a matter of fact, he was already above the plains. "I spotted it all of a sudden when I came out into a clear patch." And he explained how it had felt at that moment; just as if he had escaped from a cave.

"Storm at Mendoza, too?"

"No. The sky was clear when I made my landing, not a breath of wind. But the storm was at my heels all right!"

It was such a damned queer business, he said; that was why he mentioned it. The summits were lost in snow at a great height while the lower slopes seemed to be streaming out across the plain, like a flood of black lava that swallowed up the villages one by one. "Never saw anything like it before. . . ." Then he relapsed into silence, gripped by some secret memory.

Rivière turned to the inspector. "That's a Pacific storm; it's too late to take any action now. Anyhow they never cross the Andes."

No one could have foreseen that this particular storm would continue its advance toward the east.

The inspector, who had no ideas on the subject, agreed. Then he hesitated, turned toward Pellerin, and his Adam's apple stirred. But he held his peace and, after a moment's thought, resumed his air of melancholy dignity, looking straight before him.

That melancholy of his he carried about with him everywhere, like a briefcase. No sooner had he landed in Argentina than Rivière had appointed him to certain vague functions, and now his large hands and inspectorial dignity got always in his way. He had no right to admire imagination or ready wit; it was his business to commend punctuality and punctuality alone. He had no right to take a glass of wine in company, to call a comrade by his Christian name or risk a joke; unless, of course, by some rare chance, he came across another inspector on the same run.

It's hard luck, he thought, always having to be a judge.

As a matter of fact, he never judged; he merely wagged his head. To mask his utter ignorance he would slowly, thoughtfully, wag his head at everything that came his way, a movement that struck fear into uneasy consciences and ensured the proper upkeep of the plant.

He was not beloved—but then, inspectors are not made for love and such delights, only for drawing up reports. He had desisted from proposing changes of system or technical improvements since Rivière had written: *Inspector Robineau is requested to supply reports, not poems. He will be putting his talents to better use by speeding up the personnel.* From that day forth Inspector Robineau had battened on human frailties as on his daily bread; on the mechanic who had a glass too much, the airport overseer who stayed up of nights, the pilot who bumped a landing.

Rivière said of him, "He is far from intelligent, but very useful to us, such as he is." One of the rules that Rivière rigorously imposed— upon himself—was a knowledge of his men. For Robineau the only knowledge that counted was knowledge of the *orders*.

"Robineau," Rivière had said one day, "you must cut the punctuality bonus whenever a plane starts late."

"Even when it's nobody's fault? In case of fog, for instance?"

"Even in case of fog."

Robineau felt a thrill of pride in knowing that his chief was strong enough not to shrink from being unjust. Surely Robineau himself would win reflected majesty from such overweening power!

"You postponed the start till six fifteen," he would say to the airport superintendents. "We cannot allow your bonus."

"But, Monsieur Robineau, at five thirty, one couldn't see ten yards ahead!"

"Those are the *orders.*"

"But, Monsieur Robineau, we couldn't sweep the fog away with a broom!"

He alone among all these nonentities knew the secret: if you only punish men enough, the weather will improve!

"He never thinks at all," said Rivière of him, "and that prevents him from thinking wrong."

The pilot who damaged a plane lost his no-accident bonus.

"But supposing his engine gives out when he is over a woods?" Robineau inquired of his chief.

"Even when it occurs above a woods."

"I regret," Robineau would inform the pilots with cheerful zest, "I regret it very much indeed, but you should have had your breakdown somewhere else."

"But, Monsieur Robineau, one doesn't choose the place to have it."

"Those are the orders."

The orders, thought Rivière, are like the rites of a religion; they may look absurd, but they shape men in their mold. It was of no concern to Rivière whether he seemed just or unjust. Perhaps the words were meaningless to him. The little townsfolk of the little towns promenade each evening around a bandstand, Rivière thought. It's nonsense to talk of being just or unjust toward them; they don't exist.

For him, a man was a mere lump of wax to be kneaded into shape. It was his task to furnish this dead matter with a soul, to inject willpower into it. Not that he wished to make slaves of his men; his aim was to raise them above themselves. In punishing them for each delay he acted, no doubt, unjustly, but he bent the will of every crew to punctual departure; or, rather, he bred in them the will to keep to time. Denying his men the right to welcome foggy weather as the pretext for a leisure hour, he kept them so breathlessly eager for the fog to lift that even the humblest mechanic felt a twinge of shame for the delay. Thus they were quick to profit by the least rift in the armor of the skies.

"An opening on the north; let's be off!"

Thanks to Rivière, the service of the mails was paramount over twenty thousand miles of land and sea.

"The men are happy," he would say, "because they like their work, and they like it because I am hard."

And hard he may have been—still he gave his men keen pleasure for all that. They need, he would say to himself, to be urged on toward a hardy life, with its sufferings and its joys; only that matters.

As the car approached the city, Rivière instructed the driver to take him to the Head Office. Presently Robineau found himself alone with Pellerin and a question shaped itself upon his lips.

CHAPTER 5

ROBINEAU WAS FEELING tired tonight. Looking at Pellerin—Pellerin the Conqueror—he had just discovered that his own life was a gray one. Worst of all, he was coming to realize that, for all his rank of inspector and authority, he, Robineau, cut a poor figure beside this travel-stained and weary pilot crouching in a corner of the car, his eyes closed and his hands all grimed with oil. For the first time, Robineau was learning to admire. A need to speak of this came over him and, above all, a need to make a friend.

He was tired of his journey and the day's rebuffs and felt perhaps a little ridiculous. That very evening, when verifying the gasoline reserve, he had botched his figures, and the agent, whom he had wanted to catch out, had taken compassion and totted them up for him. What was worse, he had commented on the fitting of a Model B.6 oil pump, mistaking it for the B.4 type, and the mechanics with ironic smiles had let him maunder on for twenty minutes about this "inexcusable stupidity"—his own stupidity.

He dreaded his room at the hotel. From Toulouse to Buenos Aires, straight to his room he always went once the day's work was over. Safely ensconced and darkly conscious of the secret he carried in his breast, he would draw from his bag a sheet of paper and slowly inscribe the word Report on it, write a line or two at random, then tear it up. He would have liked to save the company from some tremendous peril, but it was not in any danger. All he had saved so far was a slightly rusted propeller hub. He had slowly passed his finger over the rust with a mournful air, eyed by an airport overseer, whose only comment was: "Better call up the last stop; this plane's only just in." Robineau was losing confidence in himself.

At a venture he essayed a friendly move. "Would you care to dine with me?" he asked Pellerin. "I'd enjoy a quiet chat; my job's pretty exhausting at times."

Then, reluctant to quit his pedestal too soon, he added, "The responsibility, you know."

His subordinates did not much relish the idea of intimacy with Robineau; it had its dangers.

But Robineau's mind this evening was full of his personal afflictions. He suffered from an annoying eczema, his only real secret; he would have liked to talk about his trouble, to be pitied and, now that pride had played him false, find solace in humility. Then again, there was his mistress over there in France, who had to hear the nightly tale of his inspections whenever he returned. He hoped to impress her thus and earn her love but—his usual luck!—he only seemed to aggravate her. He wanted to talk about her, too.

"You'll come to dinner?"

Good-naturedly Pellerin assented.

CHAPTER 6

THE CLERKS WERE drowsing in the Buenos Aires office when Rivière entered. He had kept his overcoat and hat on, like the incessant traveler he always seemed to be. His spare person took up so little room, his clothes and graying hair so aptly fitted into any scene, that when he went by hardly anyone noticed it. Yet, at his entry, a wave of energy traversed the office. The staff bustled, the head clerk hurriedly piled the papers remaining on his desk, typewriters began to click.

Noting the telegrams in a bulky register, Rivière sat down to read them.

All that he read, the Chile episode excepted, told of one of those favored days when things go right of themselves and each successive message from the airports is another bulletin of victory. The Patagonia mail, too, was making headway; all the planes were ahead of time, for fair winds were bearing them on a favoring tide.

"Give me the weather reports."

Each airport vaunted its fine weather, clear sky, and clement breeze. The mantle of a golden evening had fallen on South America. And Rivière welcomed this friendliness of things. True, one of the planes was battling with the perils of the night, but the odds were in its favor.

Rivière pushed the book aside.

"That will do."

Then, as a night warden whose charge was half the world, he went out to inspect the men on night duty, and came back.

Later, standing at an open window, he took the measure of the darkness. It contained Buenos Aires yonder, but also, like the hull of some huge ship, America. He did not wonder at this feeling of immensity; the sky of Santiago de Chile might be a foreign sky, but once the airmail was in flight toward Santiago you lived, from end to journey's end, under the same dark vault of heaven. Even now the Patagonian fishermen were gazing at the navigation lights of the plane whose messages were being awaited here. The vague unrest of an airplane in flight brooded not only on Rivière's heart but, with the droning of the engine, upon the capitals and little towns.

Glad of this night that promised so well, he recalled another night of chaos, when a plane had seemed hemmed in with dangers, its rescue a forlorn hope, and how its desperate calls came faltering through to the Buenos Aires radio post, fused with the atmospherics of the storm. Under the leaden weight of sky the golden music of the waves was tarnished. A lament in a minor key for the plane that sped arrowwise against the blinding barriers of darkness—no sadder sound than this!

Rivière remembered that when the staff is on night duty the place of an inspector is in the office.

"Send for Monsieur Robineau."

Robineau had all but made a friend of his guest, the pilot. Under his eyes he had unpacked his suitcase and revealed those trivial objects that link inspectors with the rest of men; some shirts in execrable taste, a dressing-set, a photograph of a lean woman, which the inspector pinned to the wall. Humbly thus he imparted to Pellerin his needs, affections and regrets. Laying before the pilot's eyes his sorry treasures, he laid bare all his wretchedness. A moral eczema. His prison.

But a speck of light remained for Robineau, as for every man, and it was in a mood of quiet ecstasy that he drew from the bottom of his valise a little bag carefully wrapped up in paper. He fumbled with it some moments without speaking. Then he unclasped his hands. "I brought this from the Sahara."

The inspector blushed to think that he had thus betrayed himself. For all his chagrins, domestic misadventures, for all the gray reality of life, he had a solace in these little blackish pebbles—talismans to open doors of mystery.

His blush grew a little deeper. "You find exactly the same kind in Brazil."

Then Pellerin had slapped the shoulder of an inspector poring over Atlantis and, as if duty bound, had asked a question. "Keen on geology, eh?"

"Keen? I'm mad about it!"

All his life long only the stones had not been hard on him.

Hearing that he was wanted at the Head Office, Robineau felt sad but forthwith resumed his air of dignity.

"I must leave you. Monsieur Rivière needs my assistance for certain important problems."

When Robineau entered the office, Rivière had forgotten all about him. He was musing before a wall map on which the company's routes were traced in red. The inspector awaited his chief's orders. Long minutes passed before Rivière addressed him, without turning his head.

"What is your idea of this map, Robineau?"

He had a way of springing conundrums of this sort when he came out of a brown study.

"The map, Monsieur Rivière? Well—"

As a matter of fact he had no ideas on the subject; nevertheless, frowning at the map, he roved over all Europe and America with an inspectorial eye. Meanwhile Rivière, in silence, pursued his train of thought. On the face of it, a pretty enough scheme—but it's ruthless.

When one thinks of all the lives, young fellows' lives, it has cost us! It's a fine, solid thing and we must bow to its authority, of course; but what a host of problems it presents! With Rivière, however, nothing mattered save the end in view.

Robineau, standing beside him with his eyes fixed on the map, was gradually pulling himself together. Pity from Rivière was not to be expected; that he knew. Once he had chanced it, explaining how that grotesque infirmity of his had spoiled his life. All he had got from Rivière was a jeer. "Stops you sleeping, eh? So much the better for your work!"

Rivière spoke only half in jest. One of his sayings was "If a composer suffers from loss of sleep and his sleeplessness induces him to turn out masterpieces, what a profitable loss it is!" One day, too, he had said of Leroux: "Just look at him! I call it a fine thing, ugliness like that—so perfect that it would warn off any sweetheart!" And perhaps, indeed, Leroux owed what was finest in him to his misfortune, which obliged him to live only for his work.

"Pellerin's a great friend of yours, isn't he, Robineau?"

"Well—"

"I'm not reproaching you."

Rivière made a half-turn and with bowed head, taking short steps, paced to and fro with Robineau. A bitter smile, incomprehensible to Robineau, came to his lips.

"Only . . . only you are his superior, you see."

"Yes," said Robineau.

Rivière was thinking how tonight, as every night, a battle was in progress in the southern sky. A moment's weakening of the will might spell defeat; there was, perhaps, much fighting to be done before the dawn. He weighed his words. "You may have to order this pilot tomorrow night to start on a dangerous flight. He will have to obey you."

"Yes."

"The lives of men worth more than you are in your hands." He seemed to hesitate. "It's a serious matter." For a while Rivière paced the room in silence, taking his little steps. "If they obey you because they like you, Robineau, you're fooling them. You have no right to ask any sacrifice of them."

"No, of course not."

"And if they think that your friendship will get them off disagreeable duties, you're fooling them again. They have to obey in any case. Sit down."

With a touch of his hand Rivière gently propelled Inspector Robineau toward the desk.

"I am going to teach you a lesson, Robineau. If you feel run down, it's not these men's business to give you energy. You are their chief. Your weakness is absurd. Now write!"

"I—"

"Write: Inspector Robineau imposes the penalty stated hereunder on Pellerin, pilot, on the following grounds. . . . You will discover something to fill in the blanks."

"Sir!"

"Act as though you understood, Robineau. Love the men under your orders—but do not let them know it."

So, once more, Robineau would supervise the cleaning of each propeller hub with zest.

AN EMERGENCY LANDING field sent in a radio message. *Plane in sight. Plane signals: Engine trouble; about to land.*

That meant half an hour lost. Rivière felt that mood of irritation the traveler knows when his express is held up by a signal and the minutes no longer yield their toll of passing hedgerows. The large hand of the clock was turning an empty semicircle, within whose compass so many things might have fitted in. To while away the interval Rivière went out, and now the night seemed hollow as a stage without an actor. Wasted—a night like this! He nursed a grudge against that cloudless sky with its wealth of stars, the moon's celestial beacon, the squandered gold of such a night. . . .

But once the plane had taken off, the night once more grew full of beauty and enthrallment; for now the womb of night was carrying life, and over it Rivière kept his watch.

"What weather have you?"

He had the query transmitted to the crew. Ten seconds later the reply came in: *Very fine.*

There followed a string of names, towns over which the plane had passed and, for Rivière's ears, these were so many names of cities falling one by one before a conqueror.

CHAPTER 7

AN HOUR LATER the radio operator on the Patagonia mail felt himself gently lifted as though someone were tugging at his shoulders. He looked around; heavy clouds were putting out the stars. He leaned toward the earth, trying to see the village lights shining like glowworms in the grass, but in those fields of darkness no light sparkled.

He felt depressed; a hard night lay before him, marches and countermarches, advances won and lost. He did not understand the pilot's tactics; a little further on and they would hit against that wall of blackness.

On the rim of the horizon in front he now could see a ghostly flicker, like the glow above a smithy. He tapped Fabien's shoulder, but the pilot did not stir.

Now the first eddies of the distant storm assailed them. The mass of metal heaved gently up, pressing itself against the operator's limbs; and then it seemed to melt away, leaving him for some seconds floating in the darkness, levitated. He clung to the steel bulwarks with both hands. The red lamp in the cockpit was all that remained to him of the world of men and he shuddered to know himself descending helpless into the dark heart of night, with only a little thing, a miner's safety lamp, to see him through. He dared not disturb the pilot to ask his plans; he tightened his grip on the steel ribs and, bending forward, fixed his eyes on the pilot's shadowed back.

In that obscurity the pilot's head and shoulders were all that showed themselves. His torso was a block of darkness, inclined a little to the left; his face was set toward the storm, bathed intermittently, no doubt, by flickering gleams. The radio operator could not see that face; all the feelings thronging there to meet the onset of the storm were hidden from his eyes; lips set with anger and resolve, a white face holding elemental colloquy with the leaping flashes ahead.

Yet he divined the concentrated force that brooded in that mass of shadow, and he loved it. True, it was carrying him toward the tempest, yet it shielded him. True, those hands gripping the controls pressed heavy on the storm, as on some huge beast's neck, but the strong shoulders never budged, attesting to vast reserves of force.

And after all, he said to himself, the pilot's responsible. So, carried like a pillion-rider on this breakneck gallop into the flames, he could relish to its full the solid permanence, the weight and substance implicit in that dark form before him.

On the left, faint as a far beacon, a new storm center kindled.

The radio operator made a gesture as if to touch Fabien's shoulder and warn him, but then he saw him slowly turn his head, fix his eyes awhile on this new enemy and then as slowly return to his previous position, his neck pressed back against the leather pad, his shoulders unmoving as before.

CHAPTER 8

RIVIÈRE WENT OUT for a short walk, hoping to shake off his malaise, which had returned. Toward eleven he was breathing more easily and turned back toward the Head Office, slowly shouldering his way through the stagnant crowds around the cinemas. He glanced up at the stars that glinted on the narrow street, well-nigh submerged by glaring signs, and said to himself, Tonight, with my two airmails on their way, I am responsible for all the sky. That star up there is a sign that is looking for me among this crowd—and finds me. That's why I'm feeling out of things, a man apart.

A phrase of music came back to him, some notes from a sonata that he had heard the day before in the company of friends. They had not understood. "That stuff bores us and bores you too, only you won't admit it!"

"Perhaps," he had replied.

Then, as tonight, he had felt lonely, but soon had learned the bounty of such loneliness. The music had breathed its message, to him alone among these ordinary folk, whispering its gentle secret. And now the star. Across the shoulders of these people a voice was speaking to him in a tongue that he alone could understand.

On the pavement they were hustling him about. No, he said to himself, I won't get annoyed. I am like the father of a sick child walking in the crowd, taking short steps, who carries in his breast the hushed silence of his house.

He looked upon the people, seeking to discover which of them, moving with little steps, bore in his heart discovery or love—and he remembered the isolation of the lighthouse keeper.

BACK IN THE OFFICE, the silence pleased him. As he slowly walked from one room to another, his footsteps echoed emptiness. The typewriters slept beneath their covers. The cupboard doors were closed upon the serried files. Ten years of work and effort. He felt as if he were visiting the cellars of a bank, where wealth lies heavy on the earth. But these registers contained a finer stuff than gold—a stock of living energy, living but, like the hoarded gold of banks, asleep.

Somewhere he would find the solitary clerk on night duty. Somewhere here a man was working in order that life and energy should persevere and thus the work go on from post to post so that, from Toulouse to Buenos Aires, the chain of flights should stay unbroken.

That fellow, thought Rivière, doesn't know his greatness.

Somewhere, too, the planes were fighting forward; the night flights went on and on like a persistent malady, and on them watch must be kept. Help must be given to these men who were wrestling with the darkness, who knew and only knew an unseen world of shifting things, whence they must struggle out, as from an ocean. And the things they said about it afterward were—terrible! "I turned the light onto my hands so as to see them." Velvet hands bathed in a dim red darkroom glow; last fragment that must be saved of a lost world.

Rivière opened the door of the Traffic Office. A solitary lamp shone in one corner, making a little pool of light. The clicking of a single typewriter gave meaning to the silence but did not fill it. Sometimes the telephone buzzed faintly and the clerk on duty rose obediently to its sad, reiterated call. As he took down the receiver that invisible distress was soothed and a gentle, very gentle murmur of voices filled the shadows.

Impassive, the man returned to his desk, for drowsiness and solitude had sealed his features on a secret unconfessed. And yet—what menace it may hold, a call from outer darkness when two postal planes are on their way! Rivière thought of telegrams that invaded the peace of families sitting around their lamp at night and that grief which, for seconds that seem unending, keeps its secret on the father's face. Waves, so weak at first, so distant from the call they carry, and so calm; and yet each quiet purring of the bell held, for Rivière, a faint echo of that cry. Each time the man came back from the shadow toward his lamp, like a diver returning to the surface, the solitude made his movements heavy with their secret, slow as a swimmer's in the undertow.

"Wait! I'll answer."

Rivière lifted the receiver and a world of murmurs hummed in his ears.

"Rivière speaking."

Confused sounds, then a voice: "I'll put you on the radio station."

Then another voice: "Radio station speaking. I'll pass you the messages."

Rivière noted them, nodding. "Good . . . Good . . ."

Nothing very important, the usual routine news. Rio de Janeiro asking for information, Montevideo reporting on the weather. Familiar sounds.

"And the planes?" he asked.

"The weather's stormy. We don't hear them tonight."

"Right!"

The night is fine here and starry, Rivière thought, yet those fellows can detect in it the breath of the distant storm.

"That's all for the present," he said.

As Rivière rose the clerk accosted him: "Papers to sign, sir."

Rivière discovered that he greatly liked this subordinate of his who was bearing, too, the brunt of night. A comrade in arms, he thought. But he will never guess, I fancy, how tonight's vigil brings us near each other.

CHAPTER 9

As HE WAS RETURNING to his private office, a sheaf of papers in his hand, Rivière felt the stab of pain in his right side that had been worrying him for some weeks past.

That's bad, he thought.

He leaned against the wall a moment.

It's absurd!

Then he made his way to his chair.

Once again he felt like some old lion fallen into a trap and a great sadness came upon him. To think I've come to this after all those years of work! I'm fifty; all that time I've filled my life with work, trained myself, fought my way, altered the course of events, and here's this damned thing getting ahold of me, obsessing me until it seems the only thing that matters in the world. It's absurd!

He wiped away a drop or two of sweat, waited till the pain had ebbed and settled down to work, examining the memoranda on his table.

In taking down Motor 301 at Buenos Aires we discovered that . . . The employee responsible will be severely punished.

He signed his name.

The Florianopolis staff, having failed to comply with orders . . .

He signed.

As a disciplinary measure, Airport Supervisor Richard is transferred on the following grounds . . .

He signed.

Then, as the pain in his side, slumbering but persistent, new as a new meaning in life, drove his thoughts inward, an almost bitter mood came over him.

Am I just or unjust? I've no idea. All I know is that when I hit hard, there are fewer accidents. It isn't the individual that's responsible but a sort of hidden force, and I can't get at it without—getting at everyone! If I were merely just, every night flight would mean a risk of death.

A sort of disgust came over him, that he had given himself so hard a road to follow. Pity is a fine thing, he thought. Lost in his musings, he turned the pages over.

Roblet, as from this day, is struck off the roster. . . .

He remembered the old fellow Roblet and their talk the evening before.

"There's no way out of it, an example must be made."

"But, sir. . . . It was the only time, just once in a way, sir . . . and I've been hard at it all my life!"

"An example must be made."

"But . . . but, sir. Please see here, sir."

A tattered pocket notebook, a newspaper picture showing young Roblet standing beside an airplane. Rivière saw how the old hands were trembling as they held this little scrap of fame.

"It was in nineteen ten, sir. That was the first plane in Argentina and I assembled it. I've been in aviation since nineteen ten, think of it, sir! Twenty years! So how can you say. . . ? And the young ones, sir, won't they just laugh about it in the shop! Won't they just chuckle!"

"I can't help that."

"And my kids, sir. I've a family."

"I told you you could have a job as a fitter."

"But there's my good name, sir, my name . . . after twenty years' experience. An old employee like me!"

"As a fitter."

"No, sir, I can't see my way to that. I somehow can't, sir!"

The old hands trembled and Rivière averted his eyes from their plump, creased flesh, which had a beauty of its own.

"No, sir, no. . . . And there's something more I'd like to say."

"That will do."

Not he, thought Rivière, it wasn't he whom I dismissed so brutally, but the mischief for which, perhaps, he was not responsible, though it came to pass through him. For, he mused, we can command events and they obey us; and thus we are creators. These humble men, too, are things and we create them. Or cast them aside when mischief comes about through them.

"There's something more I'd like to say." What did the poor old fellow want to say? That I was robbing him of all that made life dear? That he loved the clang of tools upon the steel of airplanes, that all the ardent poetry of life would now be lost to him . . . and then, a man must live?

"I am very tired," Rivière murmured and his fever rose, insidiously caressing him. "I liked that old chap's face." He tapped the sheet of paper with his finger. It came back to him, the look of the old man's hands, and he now seemed to see them shape a faltering gesture of thankfulness. "That's all right" was all he had to say. "That's right. Stay!" And then—he pictured the torrent of joy that would flow through those old hands. Nothing in all the world, it seemed to him, could be more beautiful than that joy revealed not on a face, but in those toilworn hands. Shall I tear up this paper? He imagined the old man's homecoming to his family, his modest pride.

"So they're keeping you on?"

"What do you think? I assembled the first plane in Argentina!"

The old fellow would get back his prestige, the youngsters would cease to laugh.

As he was asking himself if he would tear it up, the telephone rang. He picked it up.

There was a long pause, full of the resonance and depth that wind and distance give to voices.

"Airfield speaking. Who is there?"

"Rivière."

"No. 650 is on the tarmac, sir."

"Good."

"We've managed to fix it up, but the electric circuit needed overhauling at the last minute; the connections had been bungled."

"Yes. Who did the wiring?"

"We will inquire and, if you agree, we'll make an example. It's a serious matter when the lights give out on board."

"You're right."

If, Rivière was thinking, one doesn't uproot the mischief whenever and wherever it crops up, the lights may fail and it would be criminal to let it pass when, by some chance, it happens to unmask its instrument; Roblet shall go.

The clerk, who had noticed nothing, was busy with his typewriter.

"What's that?"

"The fortnightly accounts."

"Why not ready?"

"I . . . I . . ."

"We'll see about that."

Curious, mused Rivière, how things take the upper hand, how a vast dark force, the force that thrusts up virgin forests, shows itself whenever a great work is in the making! And he thought of temples dragged asunder by frail tendrils of liana.

A great work . . .

And, heartening himself, he let his thoughts flow on. These men of mine, I love them; it's not they whom I'm against but what comes about through them. . . . His heart was throbbing rapidly and it hurt him. . . . No, I cannot say if I am doing right or what precise value should be set on a human life, or suffering, or justice. How should I know the value of a man's joys? Or of a trembling hand? Of kindness, or pity?

disquieted her; did some danger threaten this young flesh of his?

"I know how strong you are, but—do take care!"

"Of course I'll take care."

Then he began dressing. For the occasion he chose the coarsest, roughest fabrics, the heaviest of leather—a peasant's kit. The heavier he grew, the more she admired him. She buckled his belt herself, helped to pull his boots on.

"These boots pinch me!"

"Here are the others."

She looked at him, set to rights the last flaw in his armor; all fell into place.

"You look splendid."

Then she noticed that he was carefully brushing his hair.

"For the benefit of the stars?" she questioned.

"I don't want to feel old."

"I'm jealous."

He laughed again and kissed her, pressing her to his heavy rough garments. Then he lifted her from the ground between his outstretched arms like a little girl and, laughing still, deposited her on the bed.

"Go to sleep!"

He shut the door behind him and, passing among the indistinguishable folk of night, took the first step toward his conquests.

She remained, sadly looking at the flowers and books, little friendly things that meant to him no more than the bottom of the sea.

CHAPTER 11

RIVIÈRE greeted him.

"That's a nice trick you played on me, your last trip! You turned back though the weather reports were good. You could have pushed through all right. Get the wind up?"

Surprised, the pilot found no answer. He slowly rubbed his hands together. Then, raising his head, he looked Rivière in the eyes.

"Yes," he answered.

Deep in himself Rivière felt sorry for this brave fellow who had been afraid. The pilot tried to explain.

"I couldn't see a thing. No doubt, further on . . . perhaps . . . the radio said . . . But my lamp was getting weak and I couldn't see my hands. I tried turning on my flying light so as to spot a wing anyhow, but I saw nothing. It was like being at the bottom of a huge pit, and no getting out of it. Then my engine started to rattle."

"No."

"No?"

"No, we had a look at it. It was in perfect order. But a man always thinks the engine's rattling when he gets the wind up."

"And who wouldn't? The mountains were above me. When I tried to climb I got caught in heavy squalls. Instead of climbing I lost three hundred feet or more. I couldn't even see the gyroscope or the manometers. It struck me that the engine was running badly and heating up, and the oil pressure was going down. And it was dark as a plague of Egypt. Damned glad I was to see the lights of a town again."

"You've too much imagination. That's what it is."

The pilot left him.

Rivière sank back into the armchair and ran his fingers through his grizzled hair.

The pluckiest of my men, he thought. It was a fine thing he did that night, but I've stopped him from being afraid.

He felt a mood of weakness coming over him again.

To make oneself beloved one need only show pity. I show little pity, or I hide it. Sure enough it would be fine to create friendships and human kindness around me. A doctor can enjoy that in the course of his profession. But I'm the servant of events and, to make others serve them too, I've got to temper my men like steel. That dark necessity is with me every night when I read over the flight reports. If I am slack and let events take charge, trusting to routine, always mysteriously something seems to happen. It is as if my will alone forbade the plane in flight from breaking or the storm delaying the mail. My power sometimes amazes me.

His thoughts flowed on.

Simple enough, perhaps. Like a gardener's endless labor on his lawn; the mere pressure of his hand drives back into the soil the virgin forest that the earth will engender time and time again.

His thoughts turned to the pilot.

I am saving him from fear. I was not attacking *him* but, across him, that stubborn inertia that paralyzes men who face the unknown. If I listen and sympathize, if I take his adventure seriously, he will fancy he is returning from a land of mystery, and mystery alone is at the root of fear. We must do away with mystery. Men who have gone down into the pit of darkness must come up and say—there's nothing in it! This man must enter the inmost heart of night, that clotted darkness, without even his little miner's light, which, falling only on a hand or wing, suffices to push the unknown a shoulder's breadth away.

Yet, a silent communion deep within them united Rivière and his pilots in the battle. All were like shipmates, sharing a common will to victory.

Rivière remembered other battles he had joined long ago to conquer night. In official circles darkness was dreaded as a desert unexplored. The idea of launching a craft at a hundred and fifty miles an hour against the storm and mists and all the solid obstacles night veils in darkness might suit the military arm; you leave on a fine night, drop bombs and return to your starting point. But regular night services were doomed to fail. "It's a matter of life and death," said Rivière, "for the lead we gain by day on ships and railways is lost each night."

Disgusted, he had heard them prate of balance sheets, insurance and, above all, public opinion. "Public opinion!" he exclaimed. "The public does as it's told!" But it was all a waste of time, he was saying to himself. There's something far above all that. A living thing forces its way through, makes its own laws to live by and nothing can resist it. Rivière had no notion when or how commercial aviation would tackle the problem of night flying, but its inevitable solution must be prepared for.

Those green tablecloths over which he had leaned, his chin propped on his arm, well he remembered them! And his feeling of power as he heard the others' quibbles! Futile these had seemed, doomed from the outset by the force of life. He felt the weight of energy that gathered in him. And I shall win, thought Rivière, for the weight of argument is on my side. That is the natural trend of things. They urged him to propose a utopian scheme, devoid of every risk. "Experience will guide us to the rules," he said. "You cannot make rules precede practical experience."

After a hard year's struggle, Rivière got his way. "His faith saw him through," said some, but others: "No, his tenacity. Why, the fellow's as obstinate as a bear!" But Rivière put his success down to the fact that he had lent his weight to the better cause.

Safety first was the obsession of those early days. Planes were to leave only an hour before dawn, to land only an hour after sunset. When Rivière felt surer of his ground, then and only then did he venture to send his planes into the depth of night. And now, with few to back him, disowned by nearly all, he plowed a lonely furrow.

Rivière rang up to learn the latest messages from the planes in flight.

CHAPTER 12

NOW THE PATAGONIA mail was entering the storm and Fabien abandoned all idea of circumventing it; it was too widespread for that, he reckoned, for the vista of lightning flashes led far inland, exposing battlement on battlement of clouds. He decided to try passing below it, ready to beat a retreat if things took a bad turn.

He read his altitude, five thousand five hundred feet, and pressed the controls with his palms to bring it down. The engine started thudding violently, setting all the plane aquiver. Fabien corrected the gliding angle approximately, verifying on the map the height of the hills below, some sixteen hundred feet. To keep a safety margin he determined to fly at a trifle above two thousand, staking his altitude as a gambler risks his fortune.

An eddy dragged him down, making the plane tremble still more harshly, and he felt the threat of unseen avalanches that toppled all about him. He dreamt an instant of retreat and its guerdon of a hundred thousand stars but did not shift his course by one degree.

Fabien weighed his chances; probably this was just a local storm, as Trelew, the next stop, was signaling a sky only three-quarters overcast. A bare twenty minutes more of solid murk and he would be through with it. Nevertheless the pilot felt uneasy. Leaning to his left, to windward, he sought to catch those vague gleams that, even in darkest night, flit here and there. But even those vagrant gleams were gone; at most there lingered patches in the mass of shadow where the night seemed less opaque, or was it only that his eyes were growing strained?

The radio operator handed him a slip of paper.

"Where are we?"

Fabien would have given much to know. "Can't say exactly," he answered. "We are flying by compass across a storm."

He leaned down again. The flame from the exhaust was getting on his nerves. There it was, clinging to the motor like a spray of fire-flowers, so pale it seemed that moonlight would have quelled it, but in this nothingness engulfing all the visible world. He watched it streaming stiffly out into the wind, like a torch flame.

Every thirty seconds Fabien bent down into the cockpit to check the gyroscope and compass. The luminous dials were ceaselessly emitting their pale and starry radiance. And in all those needles and printed figures the pilot found an illusive reassurance, as in the cabin of a ship swept by the waves. For, like a very sea of strange fatality, the night was rolling up against him with all its rocks and reefs and wreckage.

"Where are we?" the operator asked again.

Fabien drew himself up and, leaning to the left, resumed his tremendous vigil. He had no notion of how many hours more and what efforts would be needed to deliver him from fettering darkness. Would he ever come clear, he wondered, for he was staking his life on this little slip of dirty crumpled paper, which he unfolded and re-read a thousand times to nurse his hopes: *Trelew. Sky three-quarters overcast. Westerly breeze.* If there still remained a clear patch over Trelew, he would presently glimpse its lights across a rift in the clouds. Unless . . .

That promise of a faint gleam far ahead beckoned him on; but to make sure he scribbled a message to the radio operator. *Don't know if I can get through. Ask if the weather's holding out behind.*

The answer appalled him.

"Comodoro reports: Impossible return here. Storm."

He was beginning to measure this unforeseen offensive, launched from the cordillera toward the sea. Before he could make them, the storm would have burst upon the cities.

"Get the San Antonio weather report."

"San Antonio reports: West wind rising. Storm in the west. Sky three-quarters overcast. San Antonio picking up badly on account of interference. I'm having trouble too. I shall have to withdraw the aerial on account of the lightning. Will you turn back? What are your plans?"

"Stow your damned questions! Get Bahía Blanca!"

"Bahía Blanca reports: Violent westerly gale over Bahía Blanca expected in less than twenty minutes."

"Ask Trelew."

"Trelew reports: Westerly gale; rain squalls."

"Inform Buenos Aires: We are cut off on all sides; storm developing over a breadth of eight hundred miles; no visibility. What shall we do?"

A shoreless night, the pilot thought, leading to no anchorage (for every port was unattainable, it seemed), nor toward dawn. In an hour and twenty minutes the fuel would run out. Sooner or later he must blindly founder in the sea of darkness. Ah, if only he could have won through to daylight!

Fabien pictured the dawn as a beach of golden sand where a man might get a foothold after this hard night. Beneath him the plains, like friendly shores, would spread their safety. The quiet land would bear its sleeping farms and flocks and hills. And all the flotsam swirling in the shadows would lose its menace. If it were possible, how gladly he would swim toward the strand of daylight! But, well he knew, he was surrounded; for better or for worse, the end would come within this murk of darkness. . . . Sometimes, indeed, when daybreak came, it seemed like convalescence after illness.

What use to turn his eyes toward the east, home of the sun? Between them lay a gulf of night so deep that he could never clamber up again.

CHAPTER 13

"The Paraguay mail is making good headway from Asunción; it should be in at about two. The Patagonia mail, however, seems to be in difficulties and we expect it to be much overdue."

"Very good, sir."

"Quite possibly we won't make the Europe mail wait for it; as soon as the Asunción mail lands, come in for instructions, please. Hold yourself in readiness."

Rivière read again the weather reports from the northern sectors. *Clear sky; full moon; no wind.* The mountains of Brazil were standing stark and clear against the moonlit sky, the tangled tresses of their jet-black forests falling sheer into a silver tracery of sea. Upon those forests the moonbeams played and played in vain, tingeing their blackness with no light. Black, too, as drifting wreckage, the islands flecked the sea. But all the outward air route was flooded by that exhaustless fountain of moonlight.

If Rivière now gave orders for the start, the crew of the Europe mail would enter a stable world, softly illuminated all night long. A land that held no threat for the just balance of light and shade, unruffled by the least caress of those cool winds which, when they freshen, can ruin a whole sky in an hour or two.

Facing this wide radiance, like a prospector eyeing a forbidden goldfield, Rivière hesitated. What was happening in the south put Rivière, sole protagonist of night flights, in the wrong. His opponents would make such moral capital out of a disaster in Patagonia that all Rivière's faith would henceforth be unavailing. Not that his faith wavered; if, through a fissure in his work, a tragedy had entered in, well, the tragedy might prove the fissure—but it proved nothing else. Perhaps, he thought, it would be well to have lookout posts in the west. That must be seen to. After all, he said to himself, my previous arguments hold good as ever and the possibilities of accidents are reduced by one, the one tonight has illustrated. The strong are strengthened by reverses; the trouble is that the true meaning of events scores next to nothing in the match we play with men. Appearances decide our gains or losses and the points are trumpery. And a mere semblance of defeat may hopelessly checkmate us.

He summoned an employee. "Still no radio from Bahía Blanca?"

"No."

"Ring up the station on the phone."

Five minutes later he made further inquiries. "Why don't you pass on the messages?"

"We can't hear the mail."

"He's not sending anything?"

"Can't say. Too many storms. Even if he was sending, we couldn't pick it up."

"Can you get Trelew?"

"We can't hear Trelew."

"Telephone."

"We've tried. The line's broken."

"How's the weather your end?"

"Threatening. Very sultry. Lightning in the west and south."

"Wind?"

"Moderate so far. But in ten minutes the storm will break; the lightning's coming up fast."

Silence.

"Hullo, Bahía Blanca! You hear me? Good. Call me again in ten minutes."

Rivière looked through the telegrams from the southern stations. All reported alike: *No message from the plane.* Some had ceased by now to answer Buenos Aires and the patch of silent areas was spreading on the map as the storm swept upon the little towns and one by one, behind closed doors, each house along the lightless streets grew isolated from the outer world, lonely as a ship on a dark sea. And only dawn would rescue them.

Rivière, poring over the map, still hoped against hope to discover a haven of clear sky, for he had telegraphed to the police at more than thirty up-country police stations and their replies were coming in. And the radio posts over twelve hundred miles of country had orders to advise Buenos Aires within thirty seconds if any message from the plane was picked up, so that Fabien might learn at once whither to fly for refuge.

The employees had been warned to assemble at 1:00 a.m. and were now at their posts. Somehow, mysteriously, a rumor was gaining ground that perhaps the night flights would be suspended in the future and the Europe mail would leave by day. They spoke in whispers of Fabien, the storm and, above all, of Rivière, whom they pictured near at hand and capitulating point by point to this rebuff the elements had dealt.

Their chatter ceased abruptly; Rivière was standing at his door, his overcoat buttoned tightly across his chest, his hat well down upon his eyes, like the incessant traveler he always seemed. Calmly he approached the head clerk.

"It's one ten. Are the papers for the Europe mail in order?"

"I—I thought—"

"Your business is to carry out orders, not to think."

Slowly turning away, he moved toward an open window, his hands clasped behind his back. A clerk came up to him.

"We have very few replies, sir. We hear that a great many telegraph lines in the interior have been destroyed."

"Right!"

Unmoving, Rivière stared out into the night.

Thus each new message boded new peril for the Patagonia mail. Each town, when a reply could be sent through before the lines were broken, announced the storm on its way, like an invading horde. "It's coming up from the cordillera, sweeping everything before it toward the sea."

To Rivière the stars seemed overbright, the air too moist. Strange night indeed! The stars, in all their host, looked down on Buenos Aires—an oasis, and not to last. A haven out of Fabien's range, in any case. A night of menace, touched and tainted by an evil wind. A difficult night to conquer.

Somewhere in its depths an airplane was in peril; here, on the margin, they were fighting in vain to rescue it.

CHAPTER 14

Fabien's wife telephoned.

Each night she calculated the progress of the homing Patagonia mail. "He's leaving Trelew now," she murmured. Then she went to sleep again. Presently: "He's getting near San Antonio, he has its lights in view." Then she got out of bed, drew back the curtains and summed up the sky. "All those clouds will worry him." Sometimes the moon was wandering like a shepherd and the young wife was heartened by the faithful moon and stars, the thousand presences that watched her husband. Toward one o'clock she felt him near her. "Not far to go, Buenos Aires is in sight." Then she got up again, prepared a meal for him and a nice steaming cup of coffee. "It's so cold up there!" She always welcomed him as if he had just descended from a snow peak. "You *must* be cold!"

"Not a bit."

"Well, warm yourself anyhow!"

She had everything ready at a quarter past one. Then she telephoned. Tonight she asked the usual question.

"Has Fabien landed?"

The clerk at the other end grew flustered. "Who's speaking?"

"Simone Fabien."

"Ah! A moment, please . . ."

Afraid to answer, he passed the receiver to the head clerk.

"Who's that?"

"Simone Fabien."

"Yes. What can I do for you?"

"Has my husband arrived?"

After a silence, which must have baffled her, there came a monosyllable. "No."

"Is he delayed?"

"Yes."

Another silence. "Yes, he is delayed."

"Ah!"

The cry of a wounded creature. A little delay, that's nothing much, but when it lasts, when it lasts . . .

"Yes. And when—when is he expected in?"

"When is he expected? We . . . we don't know exactly . . ."

A solid wall in front of her, a wall of silence, which only gave her back the echo of her questions.

"Do please tell me, where is he now?"

"Where is he? Wait. . . ."

This suspense was like a torture. Something was happening there behind that wall.

At last, a voice! "He passed over Comodoro at seven thirty."

"Yes? And then?"

"Then—delayed, seriously delayed by stormy weather."

"Ah! A storm!"

The injustice of it, the sly cruelty of that moon up there, that lazing moon of Buenos Aires! Suddenly she remembered that it took barely two hours to fly from Comodoro to Trelew.

"He's been six hours on the way to Trelew! But surely you've had messages from him. What does he say?"

"What does he say? Well, you see, with weather like that . . . it's only natural . . . we can't hear him."

"Weather like—?"

"You may rest assured, madame, the moment we get news of him, we will ring you up."

"Ah! You've no news."

"Good night, madame."

"No! No! I want to talk to the director."

"I'm sorry, he's very busy just now; he has a meeting on—"

"I can't help that. That doesn't matter. I insist on speaking to him."

The head clerk mopped his forehead. "A moment, please."

He opened Rivière's door.

"Madame Fabien wants to speak to you, sir."

Here, thought Rivière, is what I was dreading. The emotional elements of the drama were coming into action. His first impulse was to thrust them aside; mothers and wives are not allowed into an operating theater. And all emotion is bidden to hold its peace on a ship in peril; it does not help to save the crew. Nevertheless he yielded.

"I will talk with her."

No sooner did he hear that far-off, quavering voice than he knew his inability to answer it. It would be futile for both alike, worse than futile, to meet each other.

"Do not be alarmed, madame, I beg you. In our calling it so often happens that a long while passes without news."

He had reached the point where it was not the problem of a small personal grief, but the very will to act that was at issue. Not so much Fabien's wife as another theory of life confronted Rivière now. Hearing that timid voice, he could but pity its infinite distress—and know it for an enemy! For action and individual happiness have no truck with each other; they are eternally at war. This woman, too, was championing a self-coherent world with its own rights and duties, that world where a lamp shines at nightfall on the table, flesh calls to mated flesh, a homely world of love and hopes and memories. She stood up for her happiness and she was right. And Rivière, too, was right, yet he found no words to set against this woman's truth. He was discovering the truth within him, his own inhuman and unutterable truth, by a humble light, the lamplight of a little home!

"Madame . . . !"

She did not hear him. Her hands were bruised with beating on the wall and she lay fallen, or so it seemed to him, almost at his feet.

ONE DAY AN engineer had remarked to Rivière, as they were bending above a wounded man beside a bridge that was being erected: "Is the bridge worth a man's crushed face?" Not one of the peasants using the road would ever have wished to mutilate this face so hideously just to save the extra walk to the next bridge. "The welfare of the community," the engineer had continued, "is just the sum of individual welfares and has no right to look beyond them." "And yet," Rivière had observed on a subsequent occasion, "even though human life may be the most precious thing on earth, we always behave as if there were something of higher value than human life. . . . But what thing?"

Thinking of the lost airmen, Rivière felt his heart sink. All man's activity, even the building of a bridge, involves a toll of suffering and he could no longer evade the issue.

These men, he mused, who perhaps are lost, might have led happy lives. He seemed to see as in a golden sanctuary the evening lamplight shine on faces bending side by side. Under what authority have I taken them from all this? he wondered. What was his right to rob them of their personal happiness? Did not the highest of all laws ordain that these human joys should be safeguarded? But he destroyed them. And yet one day, inevitably, those golden sanctuaries vanish like mirages. Old age and death, more pitiless than even he, destroy them. There is, perhaps, some other thing, something more lasting, to be saved; and, perhaps, it was to save this part of man that Rivière was working. Otherwise there could be no defense for action.

To love, only to love, leads nowhere. Rivière knew a dark sense of duty, greater than that of love. And deep within it there might lie another emotion and a tender one, but worlds away from ordinary feelings. He recalled a phrase that he once had read: "The one thing is to make them everlasting. . . . That which you seek within yourself will die." He remembered a temple of the sun-god, built by the ancient Incas of Peru. Tall monoliths on a mountain. But for these what would be left of all that mighty civilization that with its massive stones weighs heavy, like a dark regret, on modern man? Under the mandate of what strange love, what ruthlessness, did that primeval leader of men compel his hordes to drag this temple up the mountainside, bidding them raise up their eternity? And now another picture rose in Rivière's mind; the people of the little towns, strolling by nights around their bandstands. That form of happiness, those shackles . . . he thought. The leader of those ancient races may have had scant compassion for man's sufferings, but he had a boundless pity for his race, doomed to be blotted out beneath a sea of sand. And so he bade his folk set up these stones at least, something the desert could never engulf.

CHAPTER 15

THAT SCRAP OF folded paper might perhaps save him yet; gritting his teeth, Fabien unfolded it.

Impossible communicate Buenos Aires. Can't even touch the key, the shocks are numbing my hands.

In his vexation Fabien wanted to reply, but the moment his hands left the controls to write, a vast ground swell seemed to surge up across his body; the eddies lifted him in his five tons of metal and rocked him to and fro. He abandoned the attempt.

Again he clenched his hands upon the tempest and brought it down. Fabien was breathing heavily. If that fellow withdrew the aerial for fear of the storm, Fabien would smash his face in when they landed. At all costs they must get in touch with Buenos Aires—as though across the thousand miles and more a safety line might be flung to rescue them from this abyss! If he could not have one vagrant ray of light, not even the flicker of an inn lamp—of little help indeed, yet shining like a beacon, earnest of the earth—at least let him be given a voice, a single word from that lost world of his. The pilot raised his fist and shook it, hoping to make the man behind him understand the tragic truth, but the other was bending down to watch a world in ruins, with its buried cities and dead lights, and did not see him.

Let them shout any order whatever to him and Fabien would obey. If they tell me to go round and round, he thought, I'll turn in circles, and if they say I must head due south . . . For somewhere, even now, there still were lands of calm, at peace beneath the wide moon-shadows. His comrades down there, omniscient folk like clever scientists, knew all about them, poring over the maps beneath their hanging lamps, pretty as flower bells. But he, what could he know save squalls and night, this night that buffeted him with its swirling spate of darkness? Surely they could not leave two men to their fate in these whirlwinds and flaming clouds! No, that was unthinkable! They might order Fabien to set his course at two hundred and forty degrees, and he would do it. . . . But he was alone.

It was as if dead matter were infected by his exasperation; at every plunge the engine set up such furious vibrations that all the fuselage seemed convulsed with rage. Fabien strained all his efforts to control it; crouching in the cockpit, he kept his eyes fixed on the artificial horizon only, for the masses of sky and land outside were not to be distinguished, lost both alike in a welter as of worlds in the making. But the hands of the instruments oscillated more and more abruptly, grew almost impossible to follow. Already the pilot, misled by their vagaries, was losing altitude, fighting against odds, while deadly quicksands sucked him down into the darkness. He read his height, sixteen hundred feet—just the level of the hills. He guessed their towering billows hard upon him, for now it seemed that all these earthen monsters, the least of which could crush him into nothingness, were breaking loose from their foundations and careering about in a drunken frenzy. A dark earthly carnival was thronging close and closer around him.

He made up his mind. He would land no matter where, even if it meant cracking up! To avoid the hills anyhow, he launched his only landing flare. It sputtered and spun, illuminating a vast plain, then died away; beneath him lay the sea!

His thoughts came quickly. Lost—forty degrees' drift—yes, I've drifted, sure enough—where's land? He turned due west. Without another flare, he thought, I'm a goner. Well, it was bound to happen one day. And that fellow behind there! Sure thing he's pulled up the aerial. . . . But now the pilot's anger had ebbed away. He had only to unclasp his hands and their lives would slither through his fingers like a trivial mote of dust. He held the beating heart of each—his own, his comrade's—in his hands. And suddenly his hands appalled him.

In these squalls that battered the plane, to counteract the jerks of the wheel, which would have snapped the control cables otherwise, he clung to it with might and main, never relaxing his hold for an instant. But now he could no longer feel his hands, numbed by the strain. He tried to shift his fingers and get some signal they were there, but he could not tell if they obeyed his will. His arms seemed to end in two queer foreign bodies, insentient like flabby rubber pads. Better try hard to think I'm gripping, he said to himself. But whether his thought carried as far as his hands he could not guess. The tugs upon the wheel were only felt by him as sudden twinges in his shoulders. I'll let go for sure. My fingers will open. His rashness scared him—that he dared to even think such words!—for now he fancied that his hands, yielding to the dark suggestion of his thought, were opening slowly, slowly opening in the shadow, to betray him.

He might keep up the struggle, chance his luck; no destiny attacks us from outside. But, within him, man bears his fate and there comes a moment when he knows himself vulnerable; and then, as in a vertigo, blunder upon blunder lures him.

And, at this very moment, there gleamed above his head, across a rift in the storm, like a fatal lure within a deep abyss, a star or two.

Only too well he knew them for a trap. A man sees a few stars at the top of a pit and climbs toward them, and then—never can he get down again but stays up there eternally, chewing the stars. . . .

But such was his lust for light that he began to climb.

CHAPTER 16

HE CLIMBED AND it grew easier to correct the plunges, for the stars gave him his bearings. Their pale magnet drew him up; after that long and bitter quest for light, for nothing in the world would he forgo the frailest gleam. If the glimmer of a little inn were all his riches, he would turn around this token of his heart's desire until his death! So now he soared toward the fields of light.

Little by little he spiraled up out of the dark pit, which closed again beneath him. As he rose the clouds began to shed their slime of shadow, flowing past him in cleaner, whiter billows. Fabien rose clear.

And now a wonder seized him; dazzled by that brightness, he had to keep his eyes closed for some seconds. He had never dreamed the night clouds could dazzle thus. But the full moon and all the constellations were changing them to waves of light.

In a flash, the very instant he had risen clear, the pilot found a peace that passed his understanding. Not a ripple tilted the plane but, like a ship that has crossed the bar, it moved across a tranquil anchorage. In an unknown and secret corner of the sky it floated, as in a harbor of the Happy Isles. Below him still the storm was fashioning another world of squalls and cloudbursts and lightning, but turning to the stars a face of crystal snow.

Now all grew luminous—his hands, his clothes, the wings—and Fabien thought that he was in a limbo of strange magic; for the light did not come down from the stars but welled up from below, from all that snowy whiteness.

The clouds beneath threw up the flakes the moon was pouring on them; on every hand they loomed like towers of snow. A milky stream of light flowed everywhere, laving the plane and crew. When Fabien turned, he saw the radio operator smile.

"That's better!" he cried.

But his words were drowned out by the sound of the engine; they conversed in smiles. I'm daft, thought Fabien, to be smiling. We're lost.

And yet—at last a myriad dark arms had let him go; those bonds of his were loosed, as those of a prisoner whom they let walk awhile in liberty among the flowers.

Too beautiful, he thought. Amid the far-flung treasure of the stars he roved in a world where no life was, no faintest breath of life, save his and his companion's. Like plunderers of fabled cities they seemed, immured in treasure vaults from whence there is no escape. Among these frozen jewels they were wandering, rich beyond all dreams, but doomed.

ONE OF THE RADIO operators at the Comodoro station in Patagonia made a startled gesture and all the others keeping the helpless vigil there crowded around to read the message.

A harsh light fell upon the blank sheet of paper over which they bent. The operator's hand seemed loath to do its task and his pencil shook. The words to write were imprisoned in his hand, but already his fingers twitched.

"Storms?"

He nodded assent; he could hardly hear for the interference. Then he scrawled some illegible signs, then words; then, at last, the text came out.

Cut off at 12,000 feet, above the storm. Proceeding due west toward interior; found we had been carried above sea. No visibility below. Impossible know if still flying over sea. Report if storm extends interior.

By reason of the storms the telegram had to be relayed from post to post to Buenos Aires, bearing its message through the night like signal fires lit from tower to tower.

Buenos Aires transmitted a reply: *Storm covers all interior area. How much gasoline left?*

For thirty minutes. These words sped back from post to post to Buenos Aires.

In under half an hour the plane was doomed to plunge into a cyclone that would crash it to the earth.

CHAPTER 17

RIVIÈRE WAS MUSING, all hope lost; somewhere this plane would founder in the darkness. A picture rose in his mind of a scene that had impressed him in his boyhood; a pond being emptied to find a body. Thus, until this flood of darkness had been drained off the earth and daylight turned toward the plains and cornfields, nothing would be found. Then some humble peasants perhaps would come on two young bodies, like children asleep amid the grass and gold of some calm scene. Drowned by the night.

Rivière thought of all the treasure that was buried in the depth of night, as in deep, legendary seas. Night's apple trees that wait upon the dawn with all their flowers that serve as yet no purpose. Night, perfume-laden, that hides the lambs asleep and flowers that have no color yet.

Little by little the lush tilled fields, wet woods, and dew-cooled meadows would swing toward the light. But somewhere in the hills, no longer dark with menace, amid the fields and flocks, a world at peace again, two children would seem to sleep. And something would have flowed out of the seen world into that other.

Rivière knew all the tenderness of Fabien's wife, the fears that haunted her; this love seemed only lent to her for a while, like a toy to some poor child. He thought of Fabien's hand, which, firm on the controls, would hold the balance of his fate some minutes yet; that hand had given caresses and lingered on a breast, wakening a tumult there; a hand of godlike virtue, it had touched a face, transfiguring it. A hand that brought miracles to pass.

Fabien was drifting now in the vast splendor of a sea of clouds, but under him there lay eternity. Among the constellations still he had his being, their only denizen. For yet a while he held the universe in his hand, weighed it at his breast. That wheel he clutched upbore a load of human treasure and desperately, from one star to the other, he trafficked this useless wealth, soon to be his no more.

A single radio post still heard him. The only link between him and the world was a wave of music, a minor modulation. Not a lament, no cry, yet the purest of sounds that ever spoke despair.

CHAPTER 18

ROBINEAU BROKE IN upon his thoughts.

"I've been thinking, sir. . . . Perhaps we might try—"

He had nothing really to suggest but thus proclaimed his good intentions. A solution—how he would have rejoiced to find it! He went about it as if it was a puzzle to be solved. Solutions were his forte, but Rivière would not hear of them. "I tell you, Robineau, in life there are no solutions. There are only motive forces, and our task is to set them acting—then the solutions follow." The only force that Robineau had to activate was one that functioned in the mechanics' shop, a humble force that saved propeller hubs from rusting.

But this night's happenings found Robineau at fault. His inspectorial mandate could not control the elements, nor yet a phantom ship that, as things were, struggled no longer to win a punctuality bonus but only to evade a penalty that canceled all that Robineau imposed, the penalty of death. There was no use for Robineau now and he roamed the offices, forlorn.

Rivière was informed that Fabien's wife wished to see him. Tormented by anxiety, she was waiting in the clerk's office until Rivière could receive her. The employees were stealing glances at her face. She felt shy, almost shamefaced, and gazed nervously around her; she had no right to be here. They went about their tasks as usual, and to her it was as if they were trampling on a corpse. She looked for something that might speak to her of Fabien; at home all things confessed his absence—the sheets turned back upon the bed, the coffee on the table, a vase of flowers. Here there was nothing of him; all was at war with pity, friendship, memories. The only word she caught (for in her presence they instinctively lowered their voices) was the oath of an employee clamoring for an invoice. "The Dynamo account, God blast you! The one we send to Santos." Raising her eyes, she gazed toward this man with a look of infinite wonder, then toward the wall where a map hung. Her lips trembled a little, almost imperceptibly.

The realization irked her that in this room she was the envoy of a hostile creed and she almost regretted having come; she would have liked to hide somewhere and, fearful of being remarked, dared neither cough nor weep. She felt her presence here misplaced, indecent, as though she were standing naked before them. But so potent was *her* truth, the truth within her, that furtively their eyes strayed ever and again in her direction, trying to read it on her face. Beauty was hers and she stood for a holy thing, the world of human happiness. She vouched for the sanctity of that material something with which man tampers when he acts. She closed her eyes before their crowded scrutiny, revealing all the peace that in his blindness man is apt to shatter.

Rivière admitted her.

So now she was there to make a timid plea for her flowers, the coffee on the table, her own young body. Again, in this room, colder even than the others, her lips began to quiver. Thus, too, she bore witness to her truth, unutterable in this alien world. All the wild yearning of her love, her devotion, seemed here invested with a selfish, pestering aspect. And again she would have liked to leave this place.

"I am disturbing you—"

"No," said Rivière, "you are not disturbing me. But unfortunately neither you nor I can do anything except—wait."

There was a faint movement of her shoulders and Rivière guessed
its meaning. What is the use of that lamp, the dinner waiting, and the
flowers there when I return? Once a young mother confided in
Rivière, "I've hardly realized my baby's death as yet. It's the little
things that are so cruel—when I see the baby clothes I had ready, when
I wake up at night and there rises in my heart a tide of love, useless
now, like my milk . . . all useless!" And for this woman here, Fabien's
death would only just begin tomorrow—in every action, useless now in
trivial objects . . . useless. Little by little, Fabien would leave his home.
A deep, unuttered pity stirred in Rivière's heart.

"Madame—"

The young wife turned and left him with a weak smile, an almost
humble smile, ignoring her own power.

Rivière sat down again rather heavily. Still she is helping me to
discover the thing I'm looking for, he thought.

He fingered absentmindedly the messages from the northern airports. We do not pray for immortality, he thought, but only not to
see our acts and all things stripped suddenly of all their meaning; for
then it is that the utter emptiness of everything reveals itself.

His gaze fell on the telegrams.

These are the paths death takes to enter here—messages that have
lost their meaning, he thought.

He looked at Robineau. Meaningless, too, this fellow who served
no purpose now. Rivière addressed him almost gruffly.

"Have I got to tell you what your duties are?"

Then he pushed open the door that led into the Business Office
and saw how Fabien's disappearance was recorded there in signs his
wife could not have noticed. The slip marked *R.B. 9033*, Fabien's
machine, was already inserted in the wall index of unavailable air-
craft. The clerks preparing the papers for the Europe mail were
working slackly, knowing it would be delayed. The airport was ringing up for orders respecting the staff on night duty whose presence
was no longer necessary. The functions of life were slowing down.
That is death! thought Rivière. His work was like a sailing ship
becalmed upon the sea.

He heard Robineau speaking. "Sir, they had only been married six
weeks."

"Get on with your work!"

Rivière, watching the clerks, seemed to see beyond them the workmen, mechanics, pilots, all who had helped him in his task with the faith of men who build. He thought of those little cities of old time where men had murmured of the "Indies," built a ship and freighted it with hopes. That men might see their hope outspread its wings across the sea. All of them magnified, lifted above themselves and saved—by a ship! He thought, The goal, perhaps, means nothing, it is the thing done that delivers man from death. By their ship those men will live.

Rivière, too, would be fighting against death when he restored to those telegrams their full meaning, to these men on night duty their unrest and to his pilots their tragic purpose; when life itself would make his work alive again, as winds restore to life a sailing ship upon the sea.

CHAPTER 19

COMODORO COULD HEAR nothing now, but twenty seconds later, six hundred miles away, Bahía Blanca picked up a second message.

Coming down. Entering the clouds. . . .

Then two words of a blurred message were caught at Trelew.

. . . see nothing . . .

Shortwaves are like that; here they can be caught, elsewhere is silence. Then, for no reason, all is changed. This crew, whose position was unknown, had made itself heard by living ears, from somewhere out of space and out of time, and at the radio station phantom hands were tracing a word or two on white paper.

Had the fuel run out already or was the pilot, before catastrophe, playing his last card: to reach the earth again without a crash?

Buenos Aires transmitted an order to Trelew.

Ask him.

The radio station looked like a laboratory with its nickel and its copper, manometers and sheaves of wires. The operators on duty in their white overalls seemed to be bending silently above some simple experiment. Delicately they touched their instruments, exploring the magnetic sky, dowsers in quest of hidden gold.

No answer?

No answer.

Perhaps they yet might seize upon its way a sound that told of life. If the plane and its lights were soaring up to join the stars, it might be they would hear a sound—a singing star!

The seconds flowed away, like ebbing blood. Were they still in flight? Each second killed a hope. The stream of time was wearing life away. As for twenty centuries it beats against a temple, seeping through the granite, and spreads the fane in ruin, so centuries of wear and tear were thronging in each passing second, menacing the airmen.

Every second swept something away; Fabien's voice, his laugh, his smile. Silence was gaining ground. Heavy and heavier silence drowned their voices, like a heavy sea.

"One forty," someone murmured. "They're out of fuel. They can't be flying anymore."

Then silence.

A dry and bitter taste rose on their lips, like the dry savor of a journey's end. Something mysterious, a sickening thing, had come to pass. And all the shining nickel and trellised copper seemed tarnished with the gloom that broods on ruined factories. All this apparatus had grown clumsy, futile, out of use; a tangle of dead twigs.

One thing remained: to wait for daybreak. In a few hours all Argentina would swing toward the sun, and here these men were standing, as on a beach, facing the net that was being slowly, slowly drawn in toward them, no one knowing what its take would be.

To Rivière in his office came that quiet aftermath that follows only great disasters, when destiny has spent its force. He had set the police of the entire country on the alert. He could do no more; only wait.

But even in the house of death order must have its due. Rivière signaled to Robineau.

"Circulate a telegram to the northern airports: Considerable delay anticipated Patagonia mail. To avoid undue delay Europe mail, will ship Patagonia traffic on following Europe mail."

He stooped a little forward. Then, with an effort, he called something to mind, something important. Yes, that was it. Better make sure.

"Robineau!"

"Sir."

"Issue an order, please. Pilots forbidden to exceed nineteen hundred revs. They're ruining my engines."

"Very good, sir."

Rivière bowed his head a little more. To be alone—that was his supreme desire.

"That's all, Robineau. Good night."

And this, their strange equality before the shades, filled Robineau with awe.

CHAPTER 20

ROBINEAU WAS DRIFTING aimlessly about the office. He felt despondent. The company's life had come to a standstill, since the Europe mail, due to start at two, would be countermanded and only leave at daybreak. Morosely the employees kept their posts, but their presence now was purposeless. In steady rhythm the weather reports from the north poured in, but their "no wind," "clear sky," "full moon" evoked the vision of a barren kingdom. A wilderness of stones and moonlight. As Robineau, hardly aware what he was up to, was turning over the pages of a file on which the office superintendent was at work, he grew conscious that the official in question was at his side, waiting with an air of mocking deference to get his papers back. As if he were saying: "That's my show. Suppose you leave me to it, eh?"

Shocked though he was by his subordinate's demeanor, the inspector found himself tongue-tied and, with a movement of annoyance, handed back the documents. The superintendent resumed his seat. I should have told him to go to the devil, thought Robineau. Then, to save face, he moved away and his thoughts returned to the night's tragedy. For with this tragedy all his chief's campaign went under and Robineau lamented a twofold loss.

The picture of Rivière alone there in his private office rose in Robineau's mind. Never had there been a man so utterly unfriended as he, and Robineau felt an infinite compassion for him. He turned over in his mind vague sentences that hinted sympathy and consolation. He knocked gently at the door. There was no answer. Not daring in such a silence to knock louder, he turned the handle.

Rivière was there. For the first time Robineau entered Rivière's room
almost on an equal footing, almost as a friend; he likened himself to
the noncommissioned officer who joins his wounded general under
fire, follows him in defeat and, in exile, plays a brother's part.
"Whatever happens, I am with you—that was Robineau's unspoken
message.

Rivière said nothing; his head was bowed and he was staring at his
hands. Robineau's courage ebbed and he dared not speak; the old
lion daunted him, even in defeat. Phrases of loyalty, of ever-growing
fervor, rose to his lips; but every time he raised his eyes they encountered that bent head, gray hair and lips set tight upon their bitter
secret. At last he summoned up his courage.

"Sir."

Rivière raised his head and looked at him. So deep, so far away had
been his dream that till now he might well have been unconscious of
Robineau's presence there. And what he felt, what was the dream
and what his heart's bereavement, no one would ever know. . . . For a
long while Rivière looked at Robineau as at the living witness of some
dark event. Robineau felt ill at ease. An enigmatic irony seemed to
shape itself on his chief's lips as he watched Robineau. And the
longer his chief watched him, the more deeply Robineau blushed
and the more it grew on Rivière that this fellow had come, for all his
touching and unhappily sincere goodwill, to act as spokesman for the
folly of the herd.

Robineau by now had quite lost his bearings. The noncommissioned
officer, the general, the bullets—all faded into mist. Something inexplicable was in the air. Rivière's eyes were still intent on him. At last,
hardly knowing what he said, he stammered a few words.

"I've come for orders, sir."

Composedly Rivière pulled out his watch. "It is two. The Asunción
mail will land at two ten. See that the Europe mail takes off at two
fifteen."

Robineau bruited abroad the astounding news; the night flights
would continue. He accosted the office superintendent.

"Bring me that file of yours to check."

The superintendent brought the papers.

"Wait!"

And the superintendent waited.

CHAPTER 21

THE ASUNCIÓN MAIL signaled that it was about to land. Even at the darkest hour, Rivière had followed, telegram by telegram, its well-ordered progress. In the turmoil of this night he hailed it as the avenger of his faith, an all-conclusive witness. Each message telling of this auspicious flight augured a thousand more such flights to come. And, after all, thought Rivière, we don't get a storm every night! Once the trail is blazed, it must be followed up.

Coming down, flight by flight, from Paraguay, the pilot had just skirted the edge of a storm that never masked from him a single star. Nine passengers, huddled in their traveling rugs, had pressed their foreheads on the windows, as if they were shopfronts glittering with gems. For now the little towns of Argentina were stringing through the night their golden beads, beneath the paler gold of the star cities. And at his prow the pilot held within his hands his freight of lives, eyes wide open, full of moonlight, like a shepherd. The radio operator strummed with nimble fingers the final telegrams, last notes of a sonata he had played allegro in the sky—a melody familiar to Rivière's ears. Then he withdrew the aerial and stretched his limbs, yawning and smiling; another journey done.

The pilot who had just landed greeted the pilot of the Europe mail, who was lolling, his hands in his pockets, against the plane.

"Your turn to carry on?"

"Yes."

"Has the Patagonia come in?"

"We don't expect it; lost. How's the weather? Fine?"

"Very fine. Is Fabien lost then?"

They spoke few words of him, for that deep fraternity of theirs dispensed with unnecessary phrases.

The transit mailbags from Asunción were loaded into the Europe mail plane while the pilot stood motionless, watching the stars. He felt a vast power stirring in him and a potent joy.

"Loaded?" someone asked. "Then, contact!"

The pilot did not move. His engine was started. Now he would feel in his shoulders that pressed upon it the airplane come to life. At last, after all those false alarms—to start or not to start—his mind was easy. His lips were parted and in the moonlight his keen white teeth glittered like a jungle cub's.

"Watch out! The night, you know . . . !"

He did not hear his comrade's warning. His hands thrust in his pockets and head bent back, he stared toward the clouds, mountains and seas and rivers, and laughed silently. Soft laughter rustled through him like a breeze across a tree, and all his body thrilled with it. Soft laughter, yet stronger, stronger far, than all those clouds and mountains, seas and rivers.

"What's the joke?"

"It's that damned fool Rivière, who said . . . who thinks I've got the wind up!"

CHAPTER 22

IN A MINUTE he would be leaving Buenos Aires, and Rivière, on active service once again, wanted to hear him go. To hear his thunder rise and swell and die into the distance like the tramp of armies marching in the stars.

With folded arms Rivière passed among the clerks and halted at a window to muse and listen. If he had held up even one departure, that would be an end of night flights. But, by launching this other mail plane into the darkness, Rivière had forestalled the weaklings who tomorrow would disclaim him.

Victory, defeat—the words were meaningless. Life lies behind these symbols and life is ever bringing new symbols into being. One nation is weakened by victory, another finds new forces in defeat. Tonight's defeat conveyed perhaps a lesson that would speed the coming of final victory. The work in progress was all that mattered. Within five minutes the radio stations would broadcast the news along the line and across a thousand miles the vibrant force of life give pause to every problem.

Already a deep organ note was booming: the plane. Rivière went back to his work, and as he passed, the clerks quailed under his stern eyes: Rivière the Great, Rivière the Conqueror, bearing his heavy load of victory.

LOVE OF
SEVEN DOLLS

Love of Seven Dolls

Paul Gallico

ILLUSTRATED BY DON DAILY

Carrot Top, Mr. Reynardo, Madame Muscat,
Gigi, Dr. Duclos—they were about the only friends
and confidants the little orphan girl had.
That they were puppets fashioned out of wood
and cloth did not matter to her. She loved
them and they loved her, and because of the
bond that love created, she became the prize attraction
of the small traveling French puppet troupe of
"Capitaine Coq and His Family."

In this enchanting tale, Paul Gallico brings
to life a raffish and romantic world in which love
and hate, reality and unreality, are not always
what they seem. This story later became the basis
for the celebrated motion picture *Lili*.

PART ONE

IN PARIS, in the spring of our times, a young girl was about to throw herself into the Seine. In the drafty outdoor canvas-enclosed square that served as a dressing room for the shivering girls of a cheap grind-and-strip show called the *Moulin Bleu Revue*, Mouche, having surrendered the scanty bits of costume that had been lent her, donned her clothes and reflected for the last time upon the collapse of her hopes.

She was a thin, awkward creature with a wide mouth and short black hair. Her body was all bones and hollows where there should have been curves and flesh. Her face was appealing, but it was now gaunt with hunger and the misery of failure. Her eyes were haunting, large, liquid, dark and filled with despair.

Her name was Marelle Guizec, but her nickname was Mouche. She was an orphan, a Bretonnaise from the village of Plouha, near Saint-Brieuc. Wretched though she was, some of the mystery of this mysterious land still clung to her. It manifested itself in the grace with which she walked, as though still clad in swinging peasant skirts, the gravity of her glance, her innocence and primitive mind, in which for all her youth—she was only twenty-two—were dark corners of Celtic brooding. One of these was now leading her to her death.

She wished to die, for like many other girls from the provinces she had come to Paris to try to succeed in the theater. She had failed most miserably. There was truly no single soul in the world who cared what became of her now that she had been dismissed from the lowly *Moulin Bleu Revue* as incompetent and incapable of inspiring interest or desire among the patrons. There was no one who was her friend. The last paltry francs she would receive would feed and shelter her for only a few days. After that she must starve or sell herself.

Do you remember Paris that May when spring came early and the giant candelabra of the chestnut trees in bloom illuminated the beautiful city?

The sun-washed days were warm, but the nights still cold and often windy. By day Paris played at summer; the children appeared with their nurses by the Rond Point, the scent of perfumed women lingered on the boulevards, the gay shops glittered in the sunlight; the sky was a canopy of that particular blue that seems to exist only over France. But in the evening the chill drove people off the streets.

It was for this reason that the early-season street carnival beyond the Pont de Neuilly was preparing to pack up and depart in disappointment, for it had expected to do most of its business after dark.

Its chain of nakedly glaring electric light bulbs and smoking gasoline flares stretched along one side of the Avenue du Général de Gaulle from the Rond Point de la Défense all the way to the bridge across the Seine that gave entrance to Paris from the west.

The clangor of the street fair, the carousel music, the cries of the barkers and snapping of rifles in the shooting galleries, the ringing of bells and snorting of the engines that operated the rides had given way to the more prosaic sounds of dismantling, hammering and sawing, and the noise of boards and metal sheets being thrown to the ground and flats being loaded on trucks was drowning out the last of the mechanical music makers.

Only a few hardy stragglers defied the chill breeze and hung about as swings, whip rides, stages and tents began to come down. By morning, nothing but the litter in the street and the worn patches on the earth at the side of the broad avenue would indicate where the fair had been.

The *Moulin Bleu Revue* was packing to move on to Saint-Germain, but Mouche had not been good enough even to keep this job and go along. At the conclusion of the final performance that night, the manager had discharged her, saying, "Too thin, too thin, my child. Our girls run more to meat and juice. I heard someone in the audience say of you, 'Here comes that little plucked chicken again.' Sorry, but you won't do. If a girl cannot sing or dance, at least she must look like something."

It was true. Mouche excited pity rather than desire.

Her story was the usual one of the stagestruck girl encouraged by perhaps a local success at some amateur theatricals. Orphaned during the war, she had lived with a great-aunt, who had likewise died when she was but sixteen. She had then gone to Saint-Brieuc and secured a job cleaning the town hall, saving her money until she had sufficient funds to make the journey to Paris. And there she had come face to face with the fact that she had neither the talent nor the physical equipment to further her ambitions.

She had been pawed by dirty men and stripped by agents and managers who had examined the merchandise of her body and in the end had laughed and turned her out undamaged, for her innocence and chastity were an affront to their consciences and they wished to have her out of their sight.

Occasionally she had succeeded in securing a trial in the cabarets of Pigalle and Montmartre, and this had kept her from starvation. But she never was able to hold a job and, descending always lower, had ended with the strip revue in the street fair and now had been judged unfit for this most miserable of forms of entertainment. Not even to the tawdry audiences that filed through the tents for a few francs could her body deliver a single, solitary illusion.

It was this that determined her to do away with herself, for the dismissal pointed up the fact that even if she wished to sell herself to keep from starvation, she would find no buyers.

Mouche looked about her once more at the chattering girls who at least were useful in that they could walk across a plank stage and make men shout or laugh and whistle. Then she collected her few belongings and packed them into the small straw valise she had brought with her, as she had expected to be traveling with them in the bus to their next stop.

She would have no further need for these articles, but she could not bring herself to abandon them. The straw suitcase would be found standing on the parapet of the Pont de Neuilly in the morning when the police came with their long poles and fished her body out of the Seine.

She picked up the bag and without a backward glance went out of the enclosure. It seemed as if in anticipation of her rendezvous the light was already extinguished from her eyes. Her thin shoulders had the droop of the soon-to-be suicide. . . .

The manager emerged just then and, for a moment, was moved to pity and tempted to reverse his decision and call her back. But he hesitated. If one had pity on every little scarecrow from the provinces, where would one end?

And yet there was something appealing about the little one. He had felt it. Not what the customers wanted, but still—if one could catch what it was . . . By the time he had decided to yield to his better nature and called after her, "Allo! Mouche! Wait. Come back. Perhaps . . ." she was gone.

Mouche, marching unseeing, like one already dead, toward the Seine, thought of her childhood in Brittany and saw again the blue-green seas crashing in white foam onto the black rocks, the sunny fields cut by crooked stone walls, and the flames of the poppies from the midst of which rose the ancient stone crosses and still more ancient Druid monoliths.

The fishing boats beat their way home; children played in the sand; the postman on his bicycle rode by; women stopped to gossip outside the baker's cottage, and for a moment Mouche smelled the fresh bread and crisp rolls. She was in church again and heard the rustle of starched headdresses and the sigh of the organ. Snatches of melodies of old songs drifted through her mind and for an instant she saw her mother's work-worn hands arranging her First Communion dress. Recollections came to her of old friends, a gray rabbit she had once owned and a tortoise, a yellow cat and a duck that had only one leg. She remembered the eyes of wild things that sometimes peered from the depth of hedges in not unfriendly fashion.

Looking into this bright garden of life as through a door opened in a wall, she could not see how much there was to live for, that she was young and that one could build anew upon the ashes of failure. The black, smoky night, so noisy, cold and hostile, encouraged only the sunless corners of her mind. She hurried forward.

Something or someone cried out of the darkness, "Hello there, you with the suitcase! Where are you going and what's your hurry?"

Mouche paused, startled and bewildered, for the shrill little voice obviously was directed at her, but she could not make out whence it came. The impudence of the query angered her, for it had the effect of returning her to a world she had already departed in her mind.

The next words, reaching her out of the darkness, startled her even more.

"It's cold at the bottom of the river, little one, and the eels and the crayfish eat your flesh."

This was magic, and Mouche had all the superstition and belief in the supernatural of the Bretonnaise. Fearfully she gazed about her for the source of the voice that could guess her secret.

By the wavering light of a gasoline flare she saw only an empty puppet booth with an oilcloth sign across the top announcing: Capi-taine Coq and His Family. Nearby on one side a dirty-looking gypsy fortuneteller was quarreling with her husband over the small pickings while they occupied themselves with dismantling their tent. On the other, two men were engaged in loading a strength-testing machine onto a small truck. No one appeared to be aware of the presence of the girl.

The insistent piping voice attacked her again: "What's the big tragedy? Your boyfriend give you the air? There's plenty more fish in the sea."

Peering through the smoky haze, Mouche now saw that the puppet booth was not entirely deserted, as she had first thought. A doll was perched on the counter, or at any rate, half a doll, for no legs were visible. It was a boy with red hair, bulbous nose and pointed ears. He was regarding her with impertinent painted eyes and a curiously troubled expression on his countenance. In the shifting yellow flicker of the gasoline flare he seemed to be beckoning to her.

"Well?" he said. "Cat got your tongue? Speak up when you're spoken to."

In her first alarm Mouche had set down her valise. Now she picked it up and walked with it slowly to the booth to examine this astonishing little creature.

Still feeling strangely indignant at being thus unceremoniously accosted, she heard herself to her surprise reply, "Really, what makes you think it is any of your concern?"

The puppet looked her carefully up and down. "Oh," he said, "out of a job, down at the heels and huffy too. I was only trying to be polite and pass the time."

"By speaking to strangers to whom you have not been introduced?" Mouche chided. "And getting personal too. How would you like it if I . . . ?" She paused, realizing for the first time that she was addressing the little creature as though it were a human being. And yet it was not really strange that she should, for its attitudes and movements were so real and even the expression on the painted face seemed to change with the angle of the head.

"Oh, I wouldn't mind," he concluded for her. "Everyone likes to talk about themselves. Would you care to hear my life story? I was born in a tree on Christmas Eve . . ."

There was a swift movement, and a girl puppet appeared on the counter. She had golden ringlets, wide, staring eyes and a small, discontented mouth.

She turned this way and that, appearing to inspect Mouche from all angles. Then she said, "My goodness, Carrot Top, where do you find them?"

The other puppet took a bow and said, "Not bad, eh?"

The girl gave a little shriek. "My goodness, Carrots, you surely don't think she's pretty. . . . Why, she's nothing but skin and bones."

Carrot Top, with a twist of his head, managed to look reflective. "Well, I'll admit her legs aren't much to look at, Gigi, but she has nice eyes and there's something about her that . . ."

"Country trash, if you ask me, and probably no better than she should be," Gigi murmured, and, folding her hands piously, gazed skyward.

"Yes," Carrot Top agreed, "a country cousin all right. But still . . ."

Mouche felt that it was enough. She stamped her foot at the mocking little creatures and cried, "Really! How dare you two stand there and discuss me? Don't you know that is the worst manners?"

Carrot Top seemed taken aback and looked worried. He replied, "Dear me. Perhaps you are right. We've all been running somewhat wild of late. Maybe what we need is a little discipline. Why don't you try saying something rude to us?"

Gigi flounced petulantly. "Well, I for one don't intend to remain here to be abused by a scarecrow," she said and vanished beneath the counter.

Carrot Top looked after her and shook his head slowly. "She's not getting any better-tempered. Well, go ahead. I don't mind being insulted."

Mouche could not repress a smile. "I can't. I think I like you."

"Oh! Do you really?" Carrot Top contrived to look both pleased and startled. "That wants some thinking over. I'll see you later maybe."

He vanished likewise but was immediately replaced by the forepart of a red fox with a long, pointed nose and a sardonic grin. There was a leer in his avid eyes and a worse one in his voice. For a moment he watched the girl warily, then, appearing to smile a sly, oily smile, rasped at Mouche, "Hello, baby!"

Mouche gave him a severe look. "Don't you hello *me*," she admonished. "You're a wicked scoundrel if I ever saw one."

The fox turned his head on his neck so that he looked hurt. "I am not. I can't help my looks. Come on over here and see. Put your hand out."

Mouche moved closer to the booth and extended her hand gingerly. The expression on the pale brow beneath her cheap little hat was half worried, yet she felt herself being charmed. The fox gently snuggled his chin onto Mouche's palm and heaved a deep sigh. "There," he said, "you see how you've misjudged me?" He cocked an eye up at her.

Mouche was not to be deceived. She remarked, "I'm not sure I have at all."

"Heart like a kitten," the fox insisted, snuggling his chin deeper into the cup of Mouche's palm, and then added, "The trouble is, nobody trusts me. You would trust me, wouldn't you?"

She was about to reply that she wouldn't dream of doing so when he moved his head and looked up at her once more. His mouth opened and closed silently. Surely it was the smoky light and the dancing shadows, but Mouche thought she saw such an expression of yearning, such a desire for trust, on the sharp, clever face that she felt herself unaccountably touched and cried from her heart, "Oh yes, I would. . . ."

She had all but forgotten where she had been bound, or why.

Nor did it strike her as at all strange that she should be standing there by the counter of a puppet booth conversing with a scalawag of a fox. Where she came from, one talked not only with the little animals of the fields and the birds in the trees, but also with the trees themselves and the running brooks, and often one whispered one's innermost secrets or heart's desire to one of the gray dolmens that stood so mysteriously in a meadow.

The fox sighed again. "I knew I'd find someone innocent enough someday. What's your name, baby?"

"Marelle. But they call me Petite Mouche."

"Little fly, eh? My name is Mr. Reynardo. J. L. Reynardo—Rey to my friends. Where are you from?"

"Plouha, near Saint-Brieuc."

The fox suddenly raised his head so that he was looking at her sidelong out of one wicked eye. He quoted from an old proverb: "Beware a sleeping dog, a praying drunk or a Bretonnaise."

Mouche snatched her hand away and quoted back at him: "When the fox preaches, guard your geese. . . ."

Mr. Reynardo let out a yapping bark of laughter and retired to the side of the booth. "Kid, you've got some spunk in that skinny carcass of yours. Hasn't she, friends?"

This last was addressed to the two workmen, who had finished loading the truck and were now standing by, listening.

"She has your measure, old boy," one of them replied, grinning.

The fox yapped again and then called down below the counter, "Hey, Ali! Come up here a moment and see if you can scare this one."

The upper portion of a huge, tousle-headed, hideous, yet pathetic-looking giant rose slowly from beneath and stared fixedly at Mouche, who stared back. She could not help herself.

Mr. Reynardo performed the introductions: "This is our giant, Alifanfaron—Ali for short. Ali, this is Mouche. She's crazy about me."

Mouche started to reply indignantly, "I am not," but thought better of it and decided to let it go and see what would happen. The giant seemed to be trying desperately to recall something and finally said in a mild, friendly voice, "Fi-fo-fee . . . No, no—fo-fee-fi— Oh, dear, that isn't it either. I never seem to get it straight."

Mouche prompted him: "Fee-fi-fo . . ."

Ali nodded his head. "Of course. And then the last one is *fum*. But what's the use? I don't really frighten you, do I?"

On an odd impulse Mouche solemnly put her hand to her heart for a moment to test its beat and then replied, "Oh, I'm so sorry. I'm afraid you don't."

The giant said sadly, "Never mind. I'd really rather be friends. Then I can have my head scratched. Please scratch my head."

Obediently Mouche gently rubbed the wooden head while Ali sighed and pushed slightly against her fingers like a cat. Once more Mouche felt herself strangely moved, and even more so when the fox yipped, "Me too, me too," like a child that has been left out of something, and came whipping over and leaned his head against her shoulder.

A battered old Citroën with a luggage rack on the roof and a trunk fastened to the rear drove alongside the booth from out of the darkness, and a fearful and astonishing apparition climbed out.

He was a one-eyed black in the tattered remnants of the uniform of a Senegalese line regiment, a wrinkled old man with a large, rubbery face, naked, glistening skull, and a mouthful of gold teeth that testified he might once have known more opulent times.

He wore not a black but a soiled white patch over his blind left eye, which gave him a terrifying aspect, though this was belied by an innocent and childlike grin. There were sergeant's stripes on the uniform sleeve, and he had an old World War I kepi on the back of his head. Around his neck was slung a guitar.

He took in the group and shook his head in marvel, chuckling, "Whooeeeee! Who're you chasing up this time, Mr. Reynardo? Can't leave you alone two minutes before you go making eyes at something in skirts."

Mr. Reynardo leered at the Senegalese. "You, Golo! Cough up that ten-franc piece I saw you palm when you took up that last collection this evening."

The Senegalese grinned admiringly. "You saw that, Mr. Reynardo? By my life, you don't miss much, do you?" He fished the coin out of his pocket and laid it down on the counter, where the fox immediately pounced on it, saying to Mouche virtuously, "You see? It's good someone is honest around here. Golo, this is a friend of mine by the name of Mouche. We're thinking of getting married. Mouche, meet Golo. He's our orchestra."

Mouche found herself shaking hands solemnly with Golo,

who bowed courteously and carried her hand halfway to his lips as though she were a queen.

Mr. Reynardo rasped, "Break it up. You'll be giving her ideas." Then to Mouche: "By the way, kid, can you sing?"

Mouche replied, "A little. Can you?"

"Oh yes," Mr. Reynardo admitted. "Heroic tenor. And I've got a friend who is a pretty good basso. We could have a trio. Hey, Ali, send the Doc up. Golo, you play something for us."

The giant disappeared, to be replaced by a solemn-looking penguin who wore a pince-nez attached to a black ribbon and was introduced by the fox as Dr. Duclos, a member of the French Academy.

The penguin bowed and murmured, "Charmed, indeed. Forgive the formal clothes. I have just come from the annual dinner of the Anthropofumbling Society."

Golo leaned against the dented wing of the Citroën and fingered the advance ghost of a melody on his guitar, then struck a firm chord. Thereafter, without further introduction, Mouche found herself singing the Parisian song hit of the moment:

> *"Va t'en, va t'en, va t'en!*
> *Je ne suis plus ton amant . . ."*

She had not much voice, it was true, but there was a softness and an ingenuous earnestness in it, with a slight throaty quality that was young and pleasing and blended astonishingly well with the unctuous but not unmelodious tenor sung by Mr. Reynardo, supported and interlarded by deep basso "poom-pooms" contributed at the proper musical moments by Dr. Duclos.

> *"Be off, be off, be off!*
> *I am not your lover anymore . . .*
> *Another has taken your place . . ."*

The music completed the spell under which Mouche found herself and carried her further into this strangest of all strange lands of make-believe into which she had wandered out of the unhappy night.

The song was catching the ears of their neighbors too. The fortuneteller and her husband ceased quarreling and came nearer to listen, their gypsy eyes glistening in the torchlight. The workmen and the truckdriver were clapping their hands to punctuate the *"Va t'en."*

A passing cabdriver pulled up to the curb and got out. Late home-goers lingered. Other concessionaires came over from nearby tents that they had been engaged in dismantling. Soon a considerable crowd had formed a semicircle about the dingy little puppet booth.

These were hard, rough people mostly; the night was cold and the hour late, but they too succumbed to the spell of the odd little talking dolls, the music and the new ingredient that had been added—the waif.

Even this brief space of time had seen a transformation worked in Mouche. The listlessness and despair had been shed. If anything, her gauntness, the hunger-thin frame, and the large, tender, believing eyes shining from the pale countenance added to the attraction as in company with the sly-looking, amorous fox and the pompous, stuffy, overdignified penguin she acted out the verses of the song, playing first to one and then to the other, as though she had really changed lovers.

The song ended with a shout and a thump of Golo's guitar, and his hearty chuckle was heard above the applause and bravos of the audience. Mouche did not even notice Golo reaching behind the booth for a battered tin soldier's helmet, which he then passed swiftly through the crowd, nor the response to his collection in bills and coins, for she was too absorbed with Mr. Reynardo and Dr. Duclos, who were taking elaborate bows.

"You were in excellent voice tonight, my dear Reynardo."

"Permit me to compliment you likewise, friend Duclos."

To Mouche, Reynardo remarked, "You know, I could make something out of you, baby."

And Dr. Duclos added importantly, "Your *solfège* is not at all bad, my child. Of course, everything is diaphragm control. . . ."

From somewhere in the depths of the booth a bell rang. Mr. Reynardo let out a yelp. "Oops! Supper! Sorry. Nice to have met you, kid. Come on, Doc."

The fox and the penguin disappeared beneath the stage. Golo regarded Mouche for a moment with the sad creamy eyes of an old soldier who had seen much. He said, "Who are you, miss?"

Mouche replied, "Nobody."

"You brought us good luck."

"Did I? I'm glad."

"Where will you go now?"

"I don't know."

His question had restored the chill to the night and the feel of the hard earth beneath her feet. The fairy tale was over. Yet the echoes still lingered and her heart felt strangely light.

Golo nodded. To have no place to go was familiar to him. He said, "You excuse me, miss. I better get things ready to move."

He went to the car and unstrapped the big theatrical trunk from the rear. Someone at Mouche's elbow went "Pssst!" Another half-doll occupied the stage, an elderly woman with indignant eyebrows. She was wearing a coverall and mobcap and carried a dustcloth with which she took an occasional wipe at the counter. When Mouche turned to her she first peered furtively to both sides and then addressed her in a hoarse whisper. "Don't trust them."

Instantly Mouche was swept back to this other world. "Don't trust whom?" she asked.

"Don't trust *anyone*. I am a woman, and believe me, I know what I am talking about."

"But they were all so kind . . ." Mouche protested.

"Hah! That's just how they do it. I am Madame Muscat, the concierge here. I know everything that goes on. You look as though you might be a respectable girl. The things I could tell you . . . They're all a bad lot, and if you take my advice, you won't have anything to do with them."

Mouche was not one to listen to gossip, and Madame Muscat was exactly like all the concierges she had ever known. Nevertheless, she felt a pang at her heart, the kind one experiences when ill is spoken of dear friends. She cried, "Oh, surely that can't be so. . . ."

Golo went by carrying the trunk on his shoulders. He paused and said reprovingly, "You oughtn't say things like that, Madame Muscat. They ain't really so bad. They're just young and a little wild." To Mouche he said reassuringly, "Don't you pay her any attention, miss. Wait until I put her in this trunk again. That will keep her quiet."

Madame Muscat gave a little shriek at the threat and ducked quickly beneath the counter as Golo continued on behind the booth.

In her place there appeared finally one more puppet, an old gentleman who wore square steel-rimmed spectacles, a stocking cap and a leather apron. The expression painted on his face contrived sometimes to be quizzical and friendly; at others, when he moved his head, searching and benign. For a moment he appeared to look right through Mouche. Then in a gentle voice he spoke to her, saying, "Good evening to you. My name is Monsieur Nicholas. I am a maker and mender of toys. My child, I can see you are in trouble. Behind your eyes are many more tears than you have shed."

Mouche's hand flew to her throat because of the ache that had come to lodge there.

Monsieur Nicholas said, "Would you care to tell me about it?"

Golo appeared again. He said, "You tell *him*, miss. He is a good man. Everybody who has troubles tells them to Monsieur Nicholas."

Now the tears came swiftly to Mouche's eyes, and with their flow something loosened inside her, so that as she stood there in the garish light before the shabby puppet booth, with the single animated wooden doll listening so attentively to her, the story of her trials and failures poured from her in moving innocence, for she could not have confessed it thus to any human.

When she had reached the end of her unhappy tale, Monsieur Nicholas concluded for her, "And so you were going to throw your-self into the Seine tonight."

Mouche stared, marveling. "How did you know?"

"It was not hard to tell. But there is nothing to seek for one as young as you at the bottom of the river."

"But, Monsieur Nicholas—what shall I do? Where shall I go?"

The puppet bowed his head as he reflected gravely for a moment, a tiny hand held to his brow. Then he tilted his head to one side and asked, "Would you care to come with us?"

"Come with you? Oh, could I? Do you suppose I could?" It was as though suddenly a vista of heaven had opened for Mouche. For she loved them already, all of these queer, compelling little individuals who each, in a few brief moments, had captured her imagination or tugged at her heartstrings. To make believe forever—or as the day was long—to escape from reality into this unique world of fantasy . . . She held out her arms in supplication and cried, "Oh, Monsieur Nicholas! Would you really take me with you?"

The puppet contemplated the question silently for a moment and then said, "You must ask Carrot Top. Officially, he manages the show. Good-by."

The stage remained empty for an appreciable time. Then an insouciant whistling was heard and Carrot Top appeared, bouncing jauntily along the counter, looking nowhere in particular. As though surprised, he said, "Oh, hello, Mouche, you still here?"

The girl was uncertain how to approach him. He was mercurial. His mood now seemed to be quite different. She ventured, "Monsieur Nicholas said . . ."

Carrot Top nodded. "Oh yes. I heard about it."

"May I come, please, dear Carrot Top?"

The doll with the worried expression looked her over. "When you ask so prettily it is hard to refuse. . . . After all, it was I who discovered you, wasn't it? However, if you come with us, you wouldn't always be telling me what to do, would you? You know, I have a lot of responsibility with this show."

"Oh no . . ."

"But you'd look after us, wouldn't you?"

"If you'd let me . . ."

"Sew on buttons and things?"

"Darn socks . . ."

"We have no feet," Carrot Top said severely. "That's the first thing you'll have to learn."

"Then I'd knit you mittens."

Carrot Top nodded. "That would be nice. We've never had mittens. There'd be no money, you know."

"I wouldn't care . . ."

"Very well then . . . in that case you can come."

"Oh, Carrot Top!"

"Mouche!"

Mouche never knew exactly how it happened, but suddenly she was close to the booth, weeping with joy, and Carrot Top had his arms around her neck and was patting her cheek with one of his little wooden hands. He wailed, "Mouche, don't cry. I always meant you to come. I only had to pretend because I'm the manager. . . . Welcome from Carrot Top and the family of Capitaine Coq."

From below there sounded the sardonic yapping of the fox and the shrill voice of Gigi: "Why does she have to come with us? There isn't enough for everybody now." Madame Muscat whisked across the stage once, croaking, "Remember, I warned you." Ali arose and rumbled, "Gee, I'm glad. I need looking after because I'm so stupid. Scratch my head."

Carrot Top suddenly became efficient. "Not now, Ali. We've got to get cracking. Golo . . . Golo, where are you?"

"Right here, little boss." The Senegalese appeared from behind the booth.

"Mouche is coming with us. Find her a place in the car."

Golo shouted, "Bravo! That's mighty good luck for us. I'll find her a place in the car."

"Then come back and strike the set, Golo."

"Yes, sir, little boss. Strike the set. I'll do that. You come along with me, miss, and I'll fix you right up." He picked up Mouche's valise and went with her to the Citroën, where he stowed the valise in the luggage compartment. Then he looked into the backseat of the car, which was buried beneath pieces of old clothing, newspapers, maps, bits of costumes for the puppets, and props, packages, a bottle of beer, a half-eaten loaf of bread and some sausage, tools and a spare can of gasoline.

Golo began a futile rummaging. "Don't look like there's much room, but . . ."

Mouche took over. "Never mind, Golo. I promised Carrot Top I'd look after things. I'll have it tidied up in no time."

As she worked, Mouche hummed the melody of "Va t'en, va t'en, va t'en," but through her head were running new words to the old song: "Go away, Death! You are not my lover any longer. I have found a new one called Life. It is to him I shall always be faithful . . ."

She cleared a small space for herself on the seat, folded the clothing and the maps, stowed the costumes carefully where they would not get dirty, and while she was at it gave a good brushing and cleaning to the old car, which in a sense was to be her future home, one that she would share with Carrot Top, Reynardo, Ali, Madame Muscat, Dr. Duclos, Monsieur Nicholas, Gigi—and Golo.

So bemused and enchanted was she that not once did she give a thought to that other who would also be there, the unseen puppeteer who animated the seven dolls.

When she had finished, it was only the spare can of gasoline that had defeated her, and she emerged from the car searching for Golo to ask his advice.

Yet when Mouche discovered him nearby she found herself unable to call or even speak, so strange and ominous was the sight that met her eyes.

For the booth with all its endearing occupants had vanished from the spot it had occupied and now lay flat, a compact pile of boards, canvas, oilcloth and painted papier-mâché, tarpaulined and roped by Golo, who was finishing the job with the sure movements of long practice. None of the puppets was in sight; presumably they reposed in the trunk that stood nearby.

But the pole with the flaming gasoline torch was still there and against it leaned a man Mouche had not seen before. He was clad in corduroy trousers, rough shoes, and was wearing a turtleneck sweater under some kind of old army fatigue jacket. A stocking cap was pulled down on one side of his head and a cigarette hung from his lips.

In the wavering light it was not possible to judge his age, but his attitude and the expression on his face and mouth were cold, cynical and mocking. His eyes were fixed on Mouche and she could see their glitter reflecting the torchlight.

It was as if a chill hand had been laid upon her heart, for there was no warmth or kindliness in the figure lounging against the pole, his fists pressed deeply into the pockets of his jacket. The shine of his eyes was hostile and the droop of the cigarette from his lips contemptuous.

Mouche, in her marrow, knew that this was the puppet master, the man who had animated the little creatures that had laid such an enchantment upon her, yet she was filled with dread. For a moment, even, she hoped that somehow this was not he, the master of the dolls, but some other, a pitchman, a laborer or lounger from a neighboring concession.

Golo, straightening up from his task, looked from one to the other—the silent man, the frightened girl—and presented them to one another elaborately, as though they had never met before, as though the man had not been able to look through the one-way curtain behind which he sat as he gave life and voice to his puppets and study each curve and hollow of the girl's face and every line of her thin body.

"Miss Mouche, this is Capitaine Coq," Golo explained, and then turned to the man, who had not stirred. "Capitaine, this here is Miss Mouche. Carrot Top, he find her walking along in the dark by herself, crying, and he stop her and have a talk with her. Then Mr. Reynardo, he find out she a pretty damn good singer, and Monsieur Nicholas, he come up and ask maybe she like to come along with us, after that old gossip Madame Muscat, she try to make trouble. Then Carrot Top, he say okay she can come along with the show. I think that very good luck for everybody." He paused, satisfied. Golo was convinced that the little creatures thought and acted as individuals and that the puppeteer was not privy to what they said and did or what transpired among them.

Mouche, too, had been under the same spell, and the presence of the man confused and alarmed her and increased the turmoil of her emotions.

The man introduced as Capitaine Coq moved his eyes slightly so as to take in Golo and rasped, "Well, Golo, what do you expect me to do about it? What did Carrot Top tell you to do?"

"To get the gear on the car."

"Well, then, get on with it. And you drive. I want to get some sleep."

"Get the gear onto the car. Okay, sir." Golo picked up the heavy bundle but was slow in moving. Capitaine Coq barked *"Allez!"* at him and helped him with a kick.

Golo did not exclaim or protest. Mouche thought she would die of shame and sadness because of the manner in which Golo scuttled under the impetus of the blow, like one who has well learned the futility of protest against cruelty.

Reality as cold as the night engulfed Mouche. The man's personality and harshness were as acrid as the stench from the smoking flare above his head. Now he turned his calculating stare upon Mouche and for the first time spoke directly to her. He did not remove the cigarette from his lips, and it hung there, remaining horrifyingly motionless when he talked, for he had the professional ventriloquist's trick of speaking without moving his lips when he wished.

"You, Mouche! Come here."

She felt herself hypnotized. She was unable to resist moving slowly toward him. When she stood in front of him he looked her up and down.

"You needn't waste any sympathy on Golo," he said, having read her thoughts. "He has a better life than he would have elsewhere. Now you listen to me. . . ." He paused, and the cigarette end glowed momentarily. Mouche felt herself trembling. "You can stay with us as long as you behave yourself and help with the act. If you don't, I'll kick you out, no matter what Carrot Top says. Carrot Top likes you. Rey and Dr. Duclos seem to think you can sing. That baby bleat of yours makes me sick, but it pulled in the francs from that crowd tonight, and that's all I care about. Now get into the back of that car. You may have some bread and sausage if you're hungry. But not a sound out of you. March!"

Had she had her suitcase in her possession, Mouche would have turned and fled. But it was locked now in the luggage compartment and she had a woman's inability to part with her possessions, no matter how wretched they might be. And besides, where was she to go? Not the river anymore, at the bottom of which writhed eels and crayfish, as Carrot Top had warned her.

Half blinded with tears, Mouche got into the car.

She heard scraping and thudding as Golo fastened the dismantled puppet booth to the rack on the roof and then tied the trunk on behind.

Capitaine Coq got into the front seat, pulled his stocking cap over his eyes and went to sleep. The car, guided by Golo, moved off, crossing the bridge and turning north at the Porte de Neuilly. Soon they were on the highroad to Rheims.

Huddled in the backseat, Mouche dried her tears and nibbled on the bread and sausage. She managed to derive comfort from the fact that safe in the trunk tied behind her, tarpaulined against inclement weather, were all the little creatures who had seemed to like her. And she remembered that even Capitaine Coq had spoken of them in the third person, as though their lives were their own.

Just before she fell asleep she felt the trunk scrape against the rear of the car and she smiled, thinking of Carrot Top bowed beneath his managerial worries, the hypocritical but lovable fox, the unhappy giant, the sulky golden-haired girl, the pompous but friendly penguin, the gossipy concierge who at bottom was a woman who could be trusted, and the kind and touching mender of broken toys. Surely she would be meeting them all again. . . .

PART TWO

THE REAL NAME of the man who billed himself as Capitaine Coq was Michel Peyrot, and he was bred out of the gutters of Paris.

His had been a life without softness or pity. He had never known his father. When he was six his mother, who earned her living on the street, was murdered.

Michel was taken in by a carnival family. His foster mother, a worn-out singer, augmented their income by obliging clients behind the tent after the performance; his foster father was a fire-eater in the freak show and was rarely sober.

When Michel was twelve, the fire-eater engaged in a duel with a rival fire-eater from another fair but, being drunk, miscalculated the amount of gasoline he could store in his cheeks to blow out from his mouth in flames. So he swallowed some, it ignited simultaneously and he died horribly of internal combustion. His wife, already undermined by disease, did not survive him long, and at thirteen Michel was again alone in the world.

By the time he was fifteen he was a little savage practiced in all of the cruel arts and swindles of the street fairs and cheap carnivals. Now thirty-five, he was handsome in a rakish way, with wiry reddish hair, wide-spaced gray eyes in a pale face, and a virile crooked nose wrinkled still further by a blow that had flattened it during a brief experiment with pugilism and which, with his sensuous mouth, gave him something of the look of a satyr.

Throughout his life no one had ever been kind to him, or gentle, and he paid back the world in like. Wholly cynical, he had no regard or respect for man, woman, child or God. Not at any time he could remember in his thirty-five years of existence had he ever loved anything or anyone. He looked upon women as conveniences that his appetite demanded and, after he had used them, abandoned them or treated them badly. Why he had picked up the thin, wretched bit of flotsam known as Mouche he could not have told. Indeed, he would have insisted that it was not he at all who had added her to his queer family, but the members of that group themselves—Carrot Top, Mr. Reynardo, and Monsieur Nicholas—who had made the decision.

For in spite of the fact that it was he who sat behind the one-way curtain in the booth, animated them and supplied their seven voices, the puppets frequently acted strangely and determinedly as individuals over whom he had no control. Michel had never bothered to reflect greatly on this phenomenon but had simply accepted it as something that was so and which, far from interfering with the kind of life he was accustomed to living, brought him a curious kind of satisfaction.

Growing up with the people of the carnival acts, Michel had learned juggling, sword swallowing and leaping on the trampoline, but it was in ventriloquism that he had become most proficient.

The lives of the puppets had begun when Michel Peyrot was a prisoner of the Germans during the war and in their camps had received a kind of postgraduate course in all that was base in human nature.

In this evil period of an evil life he had first carved and clad the seven puppets, brought them to life for the entertainment of his fellow prisoners, and made the discovery that more and more they refused to speak the obscenities and vulgarities that make soldiers laugh, but instead were becoming individuals with lives of their own.

During those times that he sat hidden in the puppet booth, Michel Peyrot no longer existed, but the seven puppets did. Golo, the derelict Senegalese, understood this paradox perfectly. To him it was simply the primitive jungle magic by which a man's spirit was enabled to leave his body and enter into other objects, which then became imbued with his life. But there was yet another manifestation of which Michel Peyrot was unaware, and that was that under the scheme of creation it was not possible for a man to be wholly wicked and live a life entirely devoted to evil.

If Carrot Top, Gigi and Ali the giant were restoring to him the childhood of which he had been robbed, or Reynardo, Dr. Duclos, Madame Muscat and Monsieur Nicholas the means by which he could escape from himself, Michel was not consciously aware of it. Often he was cynically amused at the things done and the sentiments expressed by his creations, for they were completely foreign to him.

Yet the habit of the puppet booth grew, and when the war ended and he returned to France, Michel Peyrot became Capitaine Coq, and with Golo, whom he had found starving in the prison camp, as slave, orchestra and factotum, they took to the road.

The last night of the fair outside Paris it had been the experienced and cynical eye of Capitaine Coq that had instantly detected the despairing shoulder slope and the blind, suicide walk of the unhappy girl with the straw valise, but it had been Carrot Top, the puppet with the red hair and pointed ears, who had saved her, for Coq would not have given a fig for a whole troupe of despairing girls marching single file into the Seine. But it amused him to let Carrot Top and the others deal with the girl as they wished.

Nevertheless, once the strange little play had begun and the seven had proceeded independently with their work of capturing her, Coq's sharp showman's instincts had been quick to recognize the value of this trusting child speaking seriously and with complete belief across the booth to the inhabitants thereof. Whoever or whatever she was, she was possessed of that indefinable something that bridges the gap separating audience and performer and touches the heart of the beholder. He had noted her effect upon the hardened crowd of pitchmen, laborers and fellow rascals who had gathered about his booth. If the girl could be taught to work thus spontaneously with his family, standing out in front of the counter, she might become a definite business asset. If not, he could always kick her out.

But there was one more quality that had attracted him to her as he had peered through the scrim of the blind curtain and seen her pinched shoulders, hollow cheeks, dark unhappy eyes, and snow-white, blue-veined temples beneath the short-cut black hair. Or rather which had exasperated him and roused all of the bitterness and hatred of which he had so great a supply. This was her innocence and essential purity. Capitaine Coq was the mortal enemy of innocence. It was the one trait in human beings, man or woman, boy or girl, that he could not bear. He would, if he could, have corrupted the whole world.

In the back of the car Mouche had slept the sleep of mental and physical exhaustion. When she awoke, it was morning and she was alone. All of the panic of the night before returned and she sprang from the car, looking about her fearfully. But the bright sunlight and the surroundings helped to dissipate some of her fears. The dilapidated vehicle was parked in a tangled area behind booths and concessions of yet another fair. In the background she saw the twin towers of the war-damaged cathedral of Rheims.

There was a water pump nearby and she went to it and washed her face, the cold water helping to clear her head. When she ventured through the tangle of guy wires and stays supporting a nearby tent, she heard suddenly a voice with a familiar rasp call out "Hello, Mouche!"

She edged through the street on which the fair fronted. It was Mr. Reynardo. The booth that she had seen only by torch flare the night before was standing once more. It looked shabby in the morning light. But there was no disputing that Mr. Reynardo was a fine figure of an impudent red fox.

He whistled at her, opened his jaws and asked, "Wash your face, baby?"

"Of course," Mouche replied, and then asked pointedly, "Did you?"

"No, but don't tell anyone. I think I got away with it." He whipped below and was replaced by Carrot Top, who held a hundred-franc note in his two hands.

He said, "Oh, hello, Mouche. Sleep all right?"

"Oh yes, thank you. I think so." The most delicious relief pervaded her. Here they were again, her little friends of the night before. How natural it seemed to be standing there talking to them.

Carrot Top piped, "Go get yourself some bread and cheese for your breakfast," and handed her the note. "There's a shop just down the street. I've still got a lot to do to get the show ready. And bring back the change."

As she turned to go, somebody behind her went "Psssssst!"

She looked around and saw Mr. Reynardo in a corner of the booth, motioning to her with his head. She went to him and he stretched his snout up to her ear and whispered hoarsely, "There needn't *be* any change."

Mouche asked, "What do you mean, Mr. Reynardo?"

The fox contrived a wicked leer. "Call me Rey. Shhhh . . . Everybody knows prices are up. Say breakfast cost more and keep the difference. But remember, it was my idea. Fifty-fifty, kid . . ."

Mouche shook her head as earnestly as though she were reproving a child. "But, Rey . . . really! That isn't honest."

"Ha, ha!" yipped the fox. "Maybe not, but it's the only way you'll get any money out of this outfit. Don't say I didn't tip you off."

When Mouche returned from her breakfast with thirty francs left over, Carrot Top and Gigi, the ingenue, were holding the stage. Carrot Top was trying to comb Gigi's hair, the angle of his head giving a worried and concentrated expression to his face. A half dozen people were standing about, watching.

Carrot Top looked up. "Back again, Mouche? Had breakfast?"

Mouche replied politely, "Yes, thank you. And here's your change."

Carrot Top nodded absently, took the money, disappeared beneath the counter with it, and reappeared almost immediately, saying, "I'm trying to do Gigi's hair. It's full of mare's nests."

Gigi whined sulkily, "It is not. He's hurting me."

"Bird's nests, you mean," Mouche corrected. "Here, let me help. Girls know how to do that ever so much better."

Carrot Top looked severe. "Men make the best hairdressers," he announced but surrendered the comb to Mouche, who applied herself gently to reducing the snarls in Gigi's golden wig.

Gigi commanded, "I want braids. I'm tired of all that hair in my eyes. Braid my hair, Mouche."

"Certainly, Gigi," Mouche acquiesced. "And then we'll wind it about your ears in two buns, Breton fashion."

Unself-consciously, as though there were no one else watching, she set about combing and separating the hair into strands and then began to weave the braids, singing as she did so an ancient Breton hair-braiding song that for centuries mothers had sung to their little daughters to keep them quiet during the ceremony. It went:

> *"First,*
> *One and three*
> *then*
> *Three and two*
> *then*
> *Two and one,*
> *NOW—*
> *One and two*
> *and*
> *Three and one*
> *and*
> *Two and one . . ."*

It had a simple, repetitive, hypnotic melody and Golo, coming out from behind the booth with his guitar, fingered the strings softly for a moment and picked it up. Dr. Duclos appeared with some sheet music, which he read earnestly through the pince-nez affixed to his beak, and contributed basso "poom-pooms." Gigi beat time with her hands. In no time there was a fascinated and enchanted crowd, ten-deep, gathered about the booth.

When the hair was braided and bunned, Gigi and Dr. Duclos went away and Carrot Top took the empty stage to explain the plot of their play. He is in love with Gigi, but the girl is being compelled by her greedy mother, Madame Muscat, to marry wealthy, windy old Dr. Duclos. Carrot Top's friend, Reynardo, agrees to send the giant Alifanfaron to abduct Gigi, but since he is secretly in the employ of Dr. Duclos, the double-crossing fox arranges for the giant to steal Madame Muscat instead while he himself makes love to Gigi.

Without further preparation, Mouche was drawn into this plot by the puppets to stand outside the booth and explain, guide, mother and scold, keeping some secrets, sharing others with the audience, while playing a variety of roles—a maid, Mr. Reynardo's secretary, Dr. Duclos's sister, a friend of Madame Muscat . . .

She had a quick wit for situations, but above all she had the ability to forget herself and become wholly immersed in the goings-on. Because she believed so completely in the little creatures, she had the power of transferring this belief to the audience, and with a look, a laugh, or a single tender passage between herself and one of the puppets, she was able to transport the watchers away from the hard-packed earth on which they stood and into the world of make-believe, where the ordinary rules of life and living did not obtain.

Before the little play was over, all concerned had changed sides so often that Monsieur Nicholas had to appear to untangle the plot. And at the finish, to great applause, Carrot Top and Gigi, Dr. Duclos and Madame Muscat, and Ali and Mouche were paired off, for the poor giant made such a muddle of things that Mouche had to take him under her wing and he proceeded to fall desperately and moon-calf in love with her.

That day the collection made by Golo far surpassed anything Coq and his family had earned heretofore, and the puppeteer took a room in a cheap hotel for himself and a servant's room upstairs for

Mouche. Golo was relegated to sleeping in the car and watching over the puppets. He did not mind this, for he preferred to be with them.

And that night all three ate a good supper at the inn with red wine, of which Coq drank heavily. The drink did not make him mellower, but on the contrary still more scornful and contemptuous of Mouche.

He ate grossly, ignoring her presence, but once when he felt her large eyes upon him in the uneasy silence that lay over their table, he looked up from his eating and snarled at her, "What the devil got into you this afternoon when Carrot Top asked you what to do to win Gigi and get her to fly away with him in his helicopter? You stood there frozen and staring. Why didn't you tell him?"

It was not the reproof but the sudden shifting of the base of this new and marvelous world into which she had been ushered that disturbed Mouche. It was as though there had been an unwarranted intrusion by an outsider.

"Why," she explained carefully, "Carrot Top doesn't want to be told what to do. He made me promise before he let me come along that I would never tell him what to do. And besides," she concluded after a moment of reflection, "he doesn't really love Gigi at all, because—"

She broke off in alarm, for Capitaine Coq was staring at her, his face now flushed dark with rage.

"What makes you think you know who Carrot Top loves or doesn't love, you milk-faced little fool?"

For a moment Mouche thought the redheaded man was about to hurl his plate of food in her face.

She said, "I . . . I'm sorry. I really don't know . . . I suppose I just guessed. I won't do it again."

The fury did not abate from the countenance of Coq, but he did not speak to her again and instead took it out on Golo, shouting at him, "What are you lingering for? Haven't you stuffed yourself enough? Get back to the car before everything is pilfered. . . ."

Mouche and Coq continued to eat and drink in heavy silence until Mouche gathered the courage to speak to him again. In her simple, gentle way she asked, "Monsieur le Capitaine, why are you always so angry?"

He laid down his knife and fork and stared long at her out of his

cold hard eyes. "Because you are a fool," he replied finally, "and I have no time for fools, particularly women."

Mouche was not hurt, for she was used to outspoken men. And besides, she did not think she was clever or, since the disasters that had happened to her, even talented. Impulsively she reached over and placed her hand on his in a sweet conciliatory gesture, saying, "Dear Capitaine Coq, why cannot you be as kind and patient with me as Carrot Top, Dr. Duclos and Mr. Reynardo? I am sure they thought I was very stupid at times today, but they never showed it."

The touch of her gentle fingers seemed to sting Capitaine Coq, and he snatched his hand away. "Because your staring eyes and whining innocence make me sick."

The attack was so savage that tears came to Mouche's eyes and she nodded silently.

"As for them," Capitaine Coq continued, draining his glass, "it is no concern of mine what they do. Get along with them, if you know what is good for you, during working hours. And keep out of my way at other times. Understood?"

Mouche nodded again. "I'll try."

Yet in spite of the harshness of Capitaine Coq, which had the effect only of moving her to a kind of pity for him, for he seemed to be so wretched in his furies, the week of the street fair in Rheims was one of the happiest times Mouche had ever known.

The warmth of her relationship with the seven puppets seemed to grow by leaps and bounds, and soon she was familiar with their characteristics, their strengths and weaknesses: the striving and ambitious little Carrot Top with the soaring imagination that always wished to brush aside earthbound obstacles and yet was tied down by responsibility for running the show; the pompous, long-winded, fatuous Dr. Duclos, the prototype of every self-satisfied stuffed shirt, who still in his bumbling way was kind; and the vain, foolish, self-centered ingenue Gigi, who, of all the little dolls, was not.

Most dependent upon her was Alifanfaron, the giant, who frightened no one and was so kindhearted and slow-witted that everyone took advantage of him. He looked pathetically to Mouche for help and protection, and some of the most charming passages took place between the ugly, fearful-looking monster and the young girl who mothered him.

She got on best with Madame Muscat, for the madame was a woman who had seen life and buried husbands, understood men and felt that women should stick together for mutual protection. She was always Mouche's ally with advice or an aphorism, or a bit of useful gossip as to what was going on backstage or below the counter, that mysterious domain where the puppets dwelt.

But if Mouche had had to select a favorite of them all, it would have been Mr. Reynardo. He touched her most deeply because he was sly, wicked, not quite honest, knew it, and wished and tried, but not too fervently, to be better.

He amused her too. He baited and teased her and sometimes worked up little intrigues against her with the others, but when it came right down to it, he also seemed to love her the most and feel the deepest need for her affection. Much of his yapping was bravado, and the moments when Mouche felt almost unbearably touched and happy were when from time to time cracks appeared in his armor of cynicism and through them she caught glimpses of the small child within, wanting to be forgiven and loved.

Though he was her friend and counselor, Mouche remained a little in awe of Monsieur Nicholas, the mender of toys, for he was a dispenser of impartial justice as well as kindness. His glance through his square spectacles always seemed to penetrate her and reach to her innermost secret thoughts.

Childlike, too, but in the primitive fashion backed by the dark lore of his race, was Golo. He was indeed the slave who served the puppets and, now that Mouche had become as one of them, hers too. He was versed in the mechanics of the show, yet they meant nothing to him. One moment he could be behind the booth assisting Capitaine Coq in a costume change for one of the puppets, handing him props or hanging the dolls in proper order, head down, so that Coq could thrust his hands into them quickly for those lightning appearances and disappearances of the characters; and the next, he could be out front, looking on them as living, breathing creatures.

The belief in the separate existence of these little people was even more basic with Mouche, for it was a necessity to her and a refuge from the storms of life with which she had been unable to cope.

If fundamentally she must have been aware that it was Coq who animated them, she managed to obliterate the thought. For how could one reconcile the man and his creations? And further, she rarely saw Capitaine Coq enter or leave the booth, for he was moody and mysterious in his comings and goings. Sometimes he would sit inside for as long as an hour in the early morning or even late at night, without giving a sign of his presence there, until suddenly one or more of his puppets would appear onstage.

All orders were given, all business directed, through Carrot Top; all rehearsals were conducted, new songs learned, and plots and parts discussed with the puppets, until conversing with them became second nature to Mouche and it was almost impossible for her to associate this odd family of such diverse characters with the pale, bitter man who was their creator.

When the week of the fair in Rheims was at an end, they moved on to Sedan for three days and thence to Montmédy and Metz, for that year it was Capitaine Coq's intention to tour northeastern France and Alsace until the cold weather drove them south.

One night, without warning, Capitaine Coq emerged, half drunk and amorous, from the taproom of the sordid little inn on the outskirts of the city where they were quartered.

It was late. There were no women about, the regulars having long since paired off or disappeared. He bethought himself then of a piece of property he considered belonged to him—the thin girl asleep upstairs in the narrow bedroom under the eaves.

It was time, he thought as well, that the little ninny learned something and became a woman. And besides, since they were traveling together, it would be cheaper if henceforth they occupied one room—and perhaps, if she was not a stick, convenient too.

But there was yet another darker purpose that sent him prowling up the stairs that led to the attic chamber. It was the fact that her gentleness, innocence and purity of heart were a perpetual affront to him, the kind of man he was and the life that he led. It had been worming him ever since he had first laid eyes on her. Now he could no longer bear it unless he pulled her down to his level and made her as he was.

He tiptoed to her door, bent and listened for a moment, then, turning the handle swiftly, he whipped inside with the furtive speed of one of his own puppets and closed the door behind him.

When Mouche awoke the next morning, the sunshine was pouring in through the dormer window as if to deny the nightmare that had happened to her. She had thought she would not sleep that night, or ever sleep again. Yet, somehow, oblivion had come, and now the day.

She got out of bed and went to the window, which looked onto the rear courtyard of the inn, where a dog lolloped, a pig lay in the mud, chickens picked at the ground, and ducks and a goose waddled through puddles of dirty water.

They reminded her of her childhood and the farmyards of her village in Brittany, and she wondered how she could stand there so calmly contemplating them and the memories they aroused, she who would never be as a child again.

Mouche had neither protested nor resisted Capitaine Coq's act of darkness. Out of the darkness he had come, in darkness taken her, and to darkness returned, leaving her bruised, defiled and ashamed.

Startled out of her sleep by his presence, she had recognized him when a shaft of moonlight had fallen across his pale face with the crinkled nose, draining the red from his hair, turning it to purple.

For an instant her heart had leaped, for she thought that perhaps he loved her, and she would not have denied him.

But there was no love in his eyes or in his heart; no whisper came from his lips, and too late she knew what was afoot. It would have been no use to cry out. Besides, where could she have escaped to, naked, alone, friendless and penniless in a strange inn? He was there before she could make a move, intruding himself into her room, her consciousness, her bed, and then her person.

The brutality of his passion brought her close to a climax of her own, one of seemingly unbearable grief, anguish and pain, and once she had murmured his name, "Michel," piteously. She thought that surely she would die.

Then he was gone at last, leaving her shamed to death because he had abused her so callously without loving her, weeping miserably with humiliation and hurt because of his cynical contempt for her, the disgusting arrogance and carelessness of his possession of her person. He had not given her a single kindly glance or caress or kiss; no word, no gentleness. He had left not a solitary ray of hope to illuminate the despair that engulfed her, to show that within his strong, imprisoning, goatish body there beat a human heart.

And she was the more ashamed because of the instinct that told her that, despite the horror and brutality, she had yielded and the act and the moment might make her forever his.

These were the black memories, her thoughts and fears that morning as she washed and clad the body that was no longer a citadel, and prepared to face what the day would bring.

And yet the miracle occurred again, for that day was yet like any other, except, if anything, the troupe was still kinder and friendlier to her.

Carrot Top greeted her with a shrill cry of delight when she arrived at the booth. "Hey, Mouche! Where you been? Do you know what? There's sausage for breakfast. Golo! Give Mouche her sausage."

As the Senegalese appeared from behind the booth with garlic country sausage and fresh bread on a paper plate, Mr. Reynardo popped up from below with a large piece in his jaws and thrust it at her, saying, "Here. I saved a piece of mine for you. And you *know* how I love sausage. . . ."

Mouche said, "Oh, Rey. Did you really? That was sweet of you. . . ."

From below a protesting rumble was heard, and as Carrot Top vanished, Alifanfaron appeared. "Say, who stole that piece of sausage I was saving for Mouche?"

Shocked at such effrontery, Mouche cried, "Rey, you *didn't* . . ." But the fox's attitude of guilt condemned him. She said severely, memory of all her own troubles fading, "Rey, give it back to Ali at once. There. Now, Ali, you may give it to me."

The giant presented it. "It's only because I'm so stupid. Rey said he just wanted to borrow it to see if it was as big as his."

Mouche took it from him, leaned over and kissed the side of his cheek. "Poor, dear Ali," she said. "Never you mind. It's better to be trusting than to have no principles at all like some people around here. . . ."

Reynardo had the grace to look abashed and flattened himself like a dog at the end of the counter. He said, "I tried to save you a piece of mine, honestly I did, Mouche, but it got eaten."

The girl regarded him ruefully. 'Oh, Rey . . ." she cried, but there was tenderness in her voice as well as reproof. How had it happened so quickly that the iron bands that had clamped about her heart were easing, the sadness that had weighed her down was lifting? The play was on again.

Like a flash, at the first indication that she might be relenting, Reynardo whipped across the stage and with a hangdog look snuggled his head against her neck and shoulder. Madame Muscat made a brief appearance at the far side of the booth with a small feather duster and dusted the proscenium arch vigorously.

"I warned you, didn't I? You can't trust him for a minute." But she did not say who was not to be trusted. "When you've buried as many husbands as I have . . ." she began, and then vanished without concluding. Carrot Top reappeared, clutching a pale blue thousand-franc note.

"For you, Mouche," he said. "Salary for last week."

Mouche said, "Oh, Carrot Top, really? But ought you? I mean I never . . ."

"It's all right," the puppet replied. "We held a meeting this morning and voted you a share. Dr. Duclos presided. His speech from the chair lasted forty-seven minutes. . . ."

A crowd began to collect at the sight of a young girl in earnest conversation with a doll. The day's work began. . . .

All that summer and into the fall they trouped through eastern France and Alsace, slowly working southward, moving from town to town, sometimes part of a street fair or carnival, at other times setting up the booth in the marketplace or square of a small village in the country without so much as a by-your-leave from the police or local authorities.

When these officials came demanding permits, they found themselves disconcertingly having to deal with Carrot Top, Mr. Reynardo, Madame Muscat or Dr. Duclos, with Mouche endeavoring to help with the explanations. Usually their charm won the day and they were allowed to remain.

Since by virtue of Mouche's advent the lean days were over, there was always a bed in an inn, cheap hotel or farmhouse with a room to spare, and sometimes even the luxury of a bath at night after a day spent in the hot sun. Only now Capitaine Coq no longer bothered to engage two rooms but simply shared one and the bed in it with Mouche.

Thus Mouche, without realizing it, was possessed by him both by day and by night.

The days continued to be an enduring enchantment, the nights an everlasting torment, whether he used her for his pleasure or turned his back upon her without a word and fell into heavy sleep, leaving her lying there trembling. Sometimes he came to the room in a stupor, barely able to stand after hours of drinking in the taproom. When this happened, Mouche looked after him, undressed him, got him into bed, and when he cursed or moaned and tossed during the night, she got up to give him water to drink or to place a wet cloth upon his head.

Capitaine Coq was drinking to excess because he had impaled himself on the horns of a strange and insoluble dilemma and he did not know what to do, except consume wine until all sensation and memory were gone.

On the one hand, he was taking all that he wanted or needed from Mouche. She was a growing asset to the show and he was beginning to make money. Further, she was a captive bedmate for whom he need feel no responsibility. But on the other hand, he had made the discovery that while he had indeed been able to ravage her physically, he had never succeeded in destroying her innocence.

He hungered to annihilate it even though at the same time he knew that this was the very quality that drew the audiences and communicated itself to them. Wishing her as soiled and hardened as he was, he debauched her at night and then willy-nilly restored her in the daytime through the medium of the love of the seven dolls, so that phoenixlike she arose each day from the ashes of abuse of the night before, whether it was a tongue-lashing or a beating or being used like a woman of the streets. She was rendered each time as soft and dewy-eyed, as innocent and trusting, as she had been the night he had first encountered her on the outskirts of Paris.

The more cruelly he treated her, the kindlier and more friendly to her were the puppets the next morning. He seemed to have lost all control over them.

As for Mouche, she lived in a turmoil of alternating despair and entrancing joy.

One night in Besançon, in a horrible, culminating attempt to break her, Coq appeared in their room with a slut he had picked up in the tavern. They were both drunk.

He switched on the light and stood there looking down at her while she roused herself and sat up. "Get up and get out," he commanded.

She did not understand and sat there staring.

"Get out. I'm sick of you."

She still could not understand what he meant. "But, Michel . . . where am I to go?"

"To the devil, for all I care. Hurry up and get out. We want that bed. . . ."

That night Mouche reached a new depth of shame and humiliation as she dressed beneath the mocking eyes of the prostitute and went out of the room, leaving them there. She thought again of dying but was so confused she no longer knew how to die. For a time she wandered about in a daze through the streets, not knowing where she was going.

Then she came upon the Citroën. Golo was sitting at the wheel, smoking a cigarette, his white patch standing out in the light of the street lamp. He appeared to be waiting for her. He got out and took her by the arm.

"You come here and rest, Miss Mouche," he said. He had seen Capitaine Coq go in with the woman and Mouche emerge from the inn and had followed her. He opened the rear door and she climbed in, unseeing, and slumped onto the seat. Golo drove to the nearby fairgrounds and parked. The chimes of the musical clock of Besançon announced the hour of three. Mouche began to weep.

Golo reached back and took her small thin hand in his calloused mahogany paw whose fingers were hard and scaly from the steel strings of the guitar. But his grip was infinitely tender and his voice even more so as he said in his soft Senegal French, "Do not cry, my little one. It's bad for your pretty eyes."

Mouche continued to weep as though she would never be able to cease.

Golo got out of the car, was absent for a moment, and then returned. "Mouche," he called gently. "Miss Mouche. You look here. Please, Miss Mouche, you look. . . ."

The insistence of the soft pleading reached through to Mouche. She took her hands from her face and did as she was bidden. She stared, unbelieving, for a moment. Carrot Top and Mr. Reynardo were looking at her over the top of the front seat.

"Carrot Top! Rey! Oh, my darlings . . ." Mouche cried, her heart near to bursting.

The two stared at her woodenly. Between them shone the face of
Golo like the mask of an ancient African god carved out of ebony,
but an oddly compassionate god. He said sadly, "They not talk for
me, Miss Mouche. But they love you. That's why I brought them
here, so you remember that. They always love you."

Mouche reached over and took the two puppets from his hands
and cradled them. They brought her comfort until her sorely tried
spirit rebelled in an outcry that came from her depths: "But why
does he hate me so, Golo? Why is he so cruel, why is he so evil?"

The Senegalese reflected before he replied. "He bewitched. His
spirit go out from him. Another come in. I saw magic like this many
years ago in Touba in Senegal when I was a boy."

Mouche could understand this, for she herself came from a country where the supernatural was accepted.

She said, "Then you don't hate him, Golo?"

The Senegalese produced another Gaulois and lit it, and the match
illuminated the cream of his eyeballs. He replied, "Black man not
allowed to hate."

Mouche drew in her breath sharply. "Ah," she cried, "I hate him!
Dear God, how I hate him!"

Golo's cigarette glowed momentarily as he sighed. The noises of
the city and the fair were stilled except for the occasional shattering
protest of the mangy and hungry lion caged at the far end of the
fairgrounds. He said, "It good sometimes to hate. But I think it
better not to. Sometimes when you hate, you forget if you sing. . . ."

His guitar was by his side, and so softly that it was barely audible,
he plucked out the melody of a Breton lullaby and hummed it softly.
Goodness knows where he had picked it up during the long, rough
years of his perpetual exile from the land of his birth, in what camp,
prison or country he had heard it sung by another lonely expatriate
from the hard-rocked, sea-fringed shores of Brittany. He remembered the words after a moment or two:

> *"My young one, my sweeting . . .*
> *Rock in your cradle . . .*
> *The sea rocks your father,*
> *The sea rocks his cradle,*
> *God grant you sweet sleep . . .*
> *God grant him return . . ."*

When he played it again, Mouche began to sing it with him, rocking the two dolls in her arms, for that night she was more than half mad from what had been done to her.

Yet Golo had been right; the music worked its magic and the hatred seemed to fade. In its place there returned an echo of that odd compassion she had so often felt for this evil man and which she had never understood.

Golo's eyes were closed and he was singing, dreaming and swaying:

> *"The storm winds are blowing,*
> *God rules the storm winds,*
> *Love God, my sweeting,*
> *Safe rides your father,*
> *God rocks his cradle,*
> *God sends you sleep . . ."*

They sang it together in comfort and, not long after, in happiness. Golo left off playing. When the vibrations of the strings died away, Mouche went to sleep, the heads of Carrot Top and Mr. Reynardo still cradled to her breasts. Golo's cigarette glowed yet a while longer and then was extinguished. Darkness and quiet fell over the Citroën and its strangely assorted inhabitants.

Inextinguishable was the hatred that Capitaine Coq felt for the prostitute he had taken to his bed, and soon he pushed her from the room and lay there cursing helplessly, what or why he did not know, except it was the thought of Mouche, her simplicity, her gentleness, her inviolability, and the impossibility of reducing her to the state of the woman he had just flung from his bed.

Yet the next day life returned once more to Carrot Top and Mr. Reynardo and all the others. Mouche again appeared before the booth to look after, abet and interpret them to the children, large and small, infant and adult, who came to look and listen.

The tour was continued, but with a change. Thereafter Capitaine Coq took a second room for Mouche when they stayed overnight, and avoided contact with her as much as possible.

There was yet another difference, but this was more gradual in developing when they worked their way down through Annecy and Grenoble, heading for the South of France as the weather began to turn crisp and chill. The nature of the performance was changing.

More and more the stereotyped plot was abandoned, and the characters and the story wandered off into flights of imagination stemming from the schemes of Mr. Reynardo, the streak of poetry and imagination in Carrot Top, and Mouche's unique ability to enter into their make-believe instantly.

If they remained in a town for a week, a trip to the moon organized by Carrot Top with Dr. Duclos as scientific director might occupy them during the entire stay, with the result that people came back again and again to see how the affair was progressing, whether Gigi and Madame Muscat had succeeded in getting themselves taken along, and how Mouche was making out with Mr. Reynardo, who had a dishonest scheme for merchandising pieces of the moon as souvenirs.

The troupe appealed even more intimately to small communities where it played. Using local gossip, which seemed to collect astonishingly in the vicinity of the puppet booth, Carrot Top might call conspiratorially, "Psst—Mouche—Reynardo. Come here. I know a secret. . . ."

Mouche would move in closer, her plain face illuminated with excitement. "A secret. I love secrets. Oh, Carrots, tell me at once and I won't pass it on to a soul. . . ."

With his bogus smile Reynardo would insinuate, "Is there anything in it? Don't be a fool, Carrots. Tell me, maybe we can sell it—"

Carrots would protest, "Oh, Rey, it isn't *that* kind of a secret. It won't keep forever. In fact, it won't keep much longer. I understand that Renée Duval, the wife of Carpenter Duval back there in the audience, is expecting a little addition. . . ."

Reynardo would yap, "What? Why, they were only just married. Wait—let me count. . . ." And lifting one paw, he would pretend to tick off the months, "September, October, November . . ." until Mouche would go over and stop him with "Reynardo—you mustn't. That's none of your business."

Then for the next few minutes, while the audience roared, they would discuss the expected one: Dr. Duclos learnedly and stuffily would discourse on biology, Madame Muscat would give advice, Ali would offer himself as baby-sitter. Through the magic of Mouche's personality the villagers were swept into the middle of these odd doings and made a part of them.

Mouche was particularly adept at singling out wide-eyed children in the audience and summoning them over to meet the members of the cast—to shake hands with Ali to prove how harmless he was, to stroke Mr. Reynardo and to converse with Carrot Top.

Capitaine Coq and His Family were unique, and the parts of France through which they made their way were not long in discovering it. The reputation of the talking and singing puppets and the live girl who stood out front and conversed with them was beginning to precede them, and when they reached Nice on the Côte d'Azur, it had an effect that was to be far-reaching for all of them.

PART THREE

MOVING SOUTH, they remained for ten days in Lyons for the big October Fair, pressed on to Marseilles and Toulon, then ventured to rim the Côte d'Azur, the strip along the Mediterranean devoted to the wealthy. In Nice they joined up with a large circus playing in a vacant lot not far from the seashore. They set up on the midway as part of the sideshows. The rich came slumming from the big hotels, paused momentarily by the booth, and were unable to tear themselves away.

The morning of the final day of the circus, which was then going on to Monte Carlo, a fat, untidy-looking old gentleman with a veined nose, the calculating eyes of a pig, and wearing a bowler hat and carrying a gold-headed cane bustled up to Golo at the booth and demanded to see the proprietor.

The family was having its morning breakfast-get-together meeting before the day's performances began, which counted as a kind of warm-up during which plans for the day were discussed.

The old gentleman was immediately greeted by Carrot Top's shrill "Do you have an appointment?" and Reynardo's yapping laugh— "First he's got to have an appointment to make an appointment. That's my department. Who did you say you thought you were?"

Gigi bobbed up and sniggered unpleasantly, "Oh, I thought maybe it was somebody handsome."

Madame Muscat took her turn and reprimanded her. "Don't be a fool, Gigi. He's sure to be wealthy. Look at the fat on him. You don't get all that lard on your bones when there is a hole in your pocket."

It was obvious that the old fellow wasn't making a very good impression on the troupe, and Mouche apologized for them politely. "They're being very naughty today. You must forgive them. Perhaps I can help you."

It then turned out that he was an agent named Bosquet who booked acts for the Théâtre des Variétés in Nice and he wished to negotiate for the troupe to appear on the stage in the show.

The news threw the entire collection of puppets into a kind of frenzy of excitement, joy, worry, advice and counteradvice, plans and questions, with Mr. Reynardo yapping hysterically and thumping back and forth across the counter, shouting, "I'm going to be an actor. At last my true worth has been recognized. Ha, ha, it was me who gave you the idea, wasn't it, Bosquet, old boy? Mouche, did you hear? We're all going on the stage. I want to play Cyrano. I've got just the nose for it. . . ."

It was a somewhat harrowing experience for Monsieur Bosquet, who was made to show his credentials by Dr. Duclos and submit to an interview conducted by Madame Muscat on the state of the morals of the theater, and then deal with Monsieur Nicholas and Carrot Top, so that in the end he became confused into paying more for the act than he had intended.

He never did get to see Capitaine Coq, for when the contract was completed, Carrot Top took it below and returned with the document signed. Monsieur Bosquet then tried to make up for this by inviting Mouche to dine with him, for her thin, somewhat ungainly form, wide mouth and luscious eyes beneath the dark hair suddenly stirred him.

He was routed in confusion when Mr. Reynardo appeared, leaning on one elbow and regarding him sardonically as he grated, "Why, you dirty, dirty old man. At your age! Aren't you ashamed of yourself, going after a baby, you with all those hairs growing out of your ears? I know what *you're* after."

On the other side of the stage Madame Muscat, with her arms akimbo, snorted, "I suspected you from the first. I said so to Dr. Duclos. What are you prepared to give her if she goes with you— diamonds, furs, a car, perhaps? Not you, you old skinflint. . . . Don't listen to him, my dear. I know the kind. . . ."

Monsieur Bosquet fled while Reynardo roared with laughter.

The three weeks they took to prepare their act for the variety stage were not happy ones for Mouche, for while the rehearsals were as usual conducted by Carrot Top and Dr. Duclos, the sudden rise in the fortunes of the troupe seemed to have made Capitaine Coq even more bitter and violent. Aware that their engagement was due only to the catalytic presence of Mouche, he felt compelled to resent more than ever the fact that he owed to her an affluence and position he had never known before.

For some reason he had decided to abandon their successful formula and return to the puppet play they had given in the early days. But even the puppets appeared listless and seemed to respond mechanically to something in which they had long ago lost interest.

And so he was always at Mouche when they were together afterward—for her speech, her appearance, her country origins, endlessly reminding her, "I picked you up out of the gutter. When will you learn something better?" He criticized her walk, her clothes, her voice. It seemed as though he was almost determined to make their debut on the stage a failure.

But if so, he was doomed to disappointment and had forgotten the strange independent will of the seven dolls and the electric relationship that existed between them and the girl.

The first performance on any stage of Capitaine Coq and his family opened riotously on a Saturday evening to a packed house. With the first appearance of Mouche, the puppets individually and collectively threw away the script, so to speak, and for twenty minutes furnished the audience with entertainment that ranged from the hilarious, when Mr. Reynardo attempted to make himself up as Cyrano, to the touching, when Alifanfaron suffered an attack of stage fright.

They were presented against a set of a village square, with Golo strumming his guitar to attract a crowd. But with the first appearance of Carrot Top and his excitement and delight at discovering the audience and his shrill shouts for Mouche to come and see, all pretense of giving an orderly show was abandoned and they all, including Mouche, did exactly as they pleased.

Coq had originally provided a vulgar costume for Mouche. She came on instead in a simple skirt and peasant blouse as natural as she was, her short black hair and huge eyes shining in the spotlights that picked out the booth.

The puppets illuminated the theater with their excitement at being on a stage. They brought on embarrassed stagehands and electricians, whom Mouche at once put at ease; they attempted horribly garbled snatches from French classics; they made Mouche describe the members of the orchestra, whom they could not see; they demanded different-colored spotlights; they upset all tradition in a dozen different ways.

And as usual, Mouche forgot where she was and even who, and became the innocent and marveling playmate of the seven, and so carried them all straight to the hearts of the audience.

But while laughter ruled the evening, the highlight of the performance was reached perhaps when Alifanfaron, at the first sight of so large an audience, froze into such a ludicrous and stammering attack of stage fright that not even Mouche could coax him out of it!

Golo strolled on out of the wings, plucking at his guitar. He chuckled and said in his soft, rich, African French, "Sometimes when you're scared, it helps if you sing your scare away."

His fingers created the notes he had once played for Mouche on a certain night long ago in far-off Besançon. The girl picked up the thread at once. She went to the big, stupid giant, who was trembling and cowering in the booth, and put her arm about him and, rocking him gently, sang with Golo:

> *"My young one, my sweeting . . .*
> *Rock in your cradle . . .*
> *The sea rocks your father . . ."*

Carrot Top came up and joined in the chorus, and at the end the giant lifted his shaggy head, gazed out to all quarters of the audience and announced ineffably, "I'm not scared anymore." Carrot Top bounced over and patted Golo's cheek and kissed Mouche. The house was hushed as though it were a church. Many in the audience were crying.

The next moment Mouche and Reynardo were romping through their own version of *"Va t'en,"* with Gigi, the eternal coquette, and later Madame Muscat and Dr. Duclos.

In the wings, during the performance, there stood a young man in blue tights with gold spangles and an overcoat thrown over his shoulders. Never once did he take his large, moist, handsome brown eyes from the face and figure of the girl by the puppet booth.

His name was Balotte, and he was an acrobat, a member of a troupe waiting to go on the high trapeze in the act that followed the puppet number. Other artists were likewise gathered there to watch the new act and found themselves as captivated as the audience.

But Balotte, who was a good, simple boy of somewhat limited intelligence and overweening vanity, was for the first time in his life falling in love with someone other than himself.

Looking out onto the stage at this gentle, gay, sincere and motherly girl, he felt his heart touched as it had never been before. Yet at the same time he was filled with a professional's excitement at the show she was giving, for he appreciated what a girl who could make an audience sit up and take notice like that could do for him. He had long had it in his mind to go onstage as a single and had been looking for a girl partner to throw him the handkerchief and stand about while he performed his feats.

The act came to a close to ear-shattering applause. Wave after wave of it poured over Mouche. She brought on each of the puppets for a bow. When the curtain closed upon her for the last time, she was standing with her back to the booth. Carrot Top had his cheek pressed against hers, and Mr. Reynardo had an arm about her neck. Her eyes were shining. She had never been so happy.

When she came off, Balotte went to her and said, "Hello, little one. That was not bad, and I have seen many acts. Now stay here and watch me. Afterward I will have something to say to you."

And so, out of politeness, Mouche remained in the wings and looked upward at the handsome boy as he swung, leaped, whirled, and somersaulted with his partners and occasionally threw her a look as he sat resting on the trapeze high up in the flies or brushed his mustache self-consciously.

Capitaine Coq came by, clad in black corduroy trousers and a black turtleneck sweater, which emphasized his pallor, his fox-colored hair and the cold glitter of his eyes. It was a commentary on his art that, outside of the stage manager, hardly anyone knew who he was. He paused for a moment and followed Mouche's glance upward. "Kinkers," he sneered, using the showman's derogatory term for

acrobats, and spat. Then without another glance at Mouche he went on. He had made a date with a girl who played the flute in the orchestra. Now that he was becoming a success, it was time, he thought, to try it on with someone with a little class.

But Balotte, when he came sliding down the rope, was pleased, though not surprised, that Mouche had remained there watching him and said, "Well? All right, little one?"

Mouche replied sincerely, "Oh yes, indeed. I thought you were wonderful."

"Oh, that wasn't anything. Wait until you see the new routine I am working up. Something really sensational."

"But isn't it fearfully dangerous?" Mouche asked. "Without a net or anything?"

Balotte preened himself. "But of course. That is what the public likes. See here, what about coming out with me for something to eat and a glass of beer?"

He was amazed at the expression of panic that crossed Mouche's face. "I . . . I don't know whether I can. I've never been before . . ."

Balotte came quickly to the point. "Is he your husband, that one? The fellow who calls himself Capitaine Coq?" he asked.

Mouche shook her head quickly. "Oh no. He is not."

Balotte was intelligent enough not to inquire any further. "Well, then, put on your street clothes and I'll meet you inside the stage door as soon as I have changed."

It was several minutes before Mouche could bring herself to believe that she was free to accept such an invitation. The bondage in which Capitaine Coq held her had become almost a habit, but even more, she belonged to the seven dolls and felt as though she should have asked Carrot Top for permission.

She hurried then to keep the rendezvous but found herself wishing she might have discussed with Madame Muscat the propriety of going out with a young man who had just introduced himself to her.

Balotte arrived shortly, hair sleeked down, the inevitable acrobat's white silk scarf around his neck and inside his jacket, and smelling faintly of perspiration mingled with liniment.

He was delighted by his success and flashed magnificent white teeth at her. Also, he took her most solicitously by the arm to guide her, as though she were fragile. It had been so long since a man had been gentle with her that it quite warmed Mouche's heart. All of a sudden she remembered that she was a young girl and laughed happily and, leaning on the sturdy arm of the young man, asked, "Where shall we go?"

They went to a waterfront café at the far end of the Quai du Midi.

There, sitting out under the stars, they supped on highly seasoned bouillabaisse, which called for quantities of beer, which in turn made them lightheaded and merry.

They danced together. Contact with this strange girl made Balotte quite ardent and he held her close, but yet tenderly. The tenderness found an answering response in Mouche. Youth was wooing youth. For the first time in longer than she could remember, Mouche was enjoying herself in a normal manner. She felt as though she could never have enough of this magic night.

Everything was heightened: the sparkle of her eyes, the glitter of the stars, the swing of the music, the movement of her limbs and, of course, the good looks of Balotte and the impression he was making.

Indeed, she was almost insatiable for innocent pleasure and did not wish to go home. Balotte, certain that it was his person and enthralling tales about his triumphs in the circus and variety world and his plans for future successes that made her so happy and gay, humored her, for he was enjoying himself too. When at four in the morning the café finally closed, they were the last to leave.

Balotte, for all his vanity, came of a good circus family and therefore, in love as he felt himself to be with Mouche, was respectful of her and honorable in his attentions toward another in his own profession. He took her home on a tram and left her at the door of her hotel with no more than a warm pressure of the hand and a loving look from his dark, liquid eyes.

When Mouche went inside she found Capitaine Coq waiting for her. He was slumped in a chair in the dingy, ill-smelling lobby, a cigarette hanging from his lip, but he was sober. The flute player had proved flabby, damp, self-accusing, and had drenched him with tears. His temper was even more vile than usual and he took it out on Mouche.

He said, "Come over here. Where the devil have you been? You'll be getting a regular salary now. You don't have to go out whoring in the streets."

Mouche felt hatred of this man so intensely that she thought she would become ill or faint. Yet the small taste of freedom she had enjoyed, the echoes of the innocent evening, enabled her to face him. She replied, "I was out with Balotte. He asked me to have supper with him."

Coq laughed harshly. "Until four in the morning? That kind of dining we know. . . ."

"It is not true. We were dancing. Why shouldn't I dance with him? He is kind to me."

Capitaine Coq got up out of his chair, his hands and face working with rage. He ground his teeth and took her by the wrist so that she cried out with pain.

"That, and more of it," he shouted at her, applying more pressure. "If ever I catch you with that walking sweat gland again, I'll smash every bone in your body and in his too. Remember. Now get up to your room."

At the performance the next day Dr. Duclos, of all people, came up with a present for Mouche. It appeared he had been shopping and, passing a perfume counter, had so far abandoned caution as to invest in a small bottle. Oddly, it was the first perfume Mouche had ever had. They made her open it and try it on. Gigi jealously sampled some; Madame Muscat sniffed disdainfully; and Ali tried to drink it, because if it smelled so good, it must taste better. For twenty minutes they elaborated this slender theme to the enchantment of the audience and ended with Mr. Reynardo in Mouche's arms, quite overcome and swooning.

As Mouche came offstage, Balotte, waiting to go on, whispered, "Tonight again?"

Mouche looked about her in alarm. "I don't dare. He has threatened to do you an injury."

Balotte snorted, "Ho! I can take care of myself. I know of a place where the music is even better. Be at the stage door again the same time, little one, eh?"

Mouche replied, "I don't know."

But she went to the stage door, hoping that Coq would not be about. She longed so for the gaiety and the sweet ease of being with someone who was kind. She did not have to wait. Balotte was there. And Capitaine Coq stepped out of a shadowed corner.

Capitaine Coq said, "Well, I can see that you both are asking for it. Have it then!" He whipped the backs of five bony fingers across Mouche's face, knocking her up against the wall. "Gutter slut!" he bawled at her.

Balotte made a menacing movement. Coq turned on him. "As for you, you muscle-headed kinker, you can hang by your tail like a monkey, but you wouldn't lift a finger for her or anybody else. I'm going to teach you to keep away from her."

But Capitaine Coq was wrong. Balotte was no coward, and further-more, he had a body like iron, wrists of steel, and more than a little knowledge of the science of attack and defense.

The fight was short and savage, both men moiling, writhing and striking in silence with no sound but the whistling of their breathing, the thud of blows, and the grunts of pain. Then it was over, with Capitaine Coq lying in a battered, bloodied heap on the floor, stunned, whipped and unable to rise. He was bleeding from the nose and mouth and a gash in his cheek, and one eye was closing.

With his red hair, crinkled pale face and black outfit, he was the personification of the devil dethroned, evil conquered by good, as the young acrobat stood over him, panting but unmarked. Coq was the villain foiled, the wicked bully who at last receives his just deserts. He lay in an untidy heap like a horrid insect that has been squashed.

Mouche stood by the wall staring down at him. So had she prayed to see him, beaten, cowed, mastered. Yet she was conscious only of being filled with sadness and of an ache in her throat comparable to that she experienced sometimes in front of the puppet booth when one or another of its inhabitants was particularly moving. She had not known that a wish fulfilled could be so empty and that the physical destruction of the object of her hatred would yield no more than the desire to weep for the downfall of evil.

Balotte moved over to him, prepared to kick him unconscious if need be, and asked, "Want any more?"

The glassy eyes of Capitaine Coq filled with venom, but he shook his head, mumbling something unintelligible, and did not attempt to get up.

Balotte said, "Come along, then, Mouche. This fellow won't give you any more trouble."

They went out, arm in arm, and Mouche did not look back at the heap on the floor, for had she done so, she could not have gone. This time they did not dance, as if by mutual understanding they recognized it was not the time, but instead sat in a corner booth, eating and getting acquainted. And under the stimulus of the youth and wooing of Balotte, Mouche's mood of sorrow evaporated. They walked home and stood for a while by the promenade, looking out over the harbor with Nice's necklace of lights curving away from them and the stars cascading over the black, frowning wall of the mountains behind the city. Balotte kissed her, and gratefully Mouche returned his kisses.

At the next performance of Capitaine Coq and his family, Carrot Top appeared with a black eye and was raucously greeted by Mr. Reynardo and the rest of the cast demanding to know how it had happened. Carrot Top insisted that he had walked into a door in the dark. They devoted the act to discussing the truth of this plus the best remedies, Madame Muscat finally arriving with a small piece of steak, which Mouche solicitously bound to the eye. All through the show she felt herself unaccountably close to tears. Yet she was glad for the pressure of Balotte's hand as he passed her and whispered, "Petite Mouche, tonight we dance."

This was the night, too, that the manager of the theater stood at the door and counted more than two hundred patrons who had been there the week before and who had returned to see what mischief the family of Capitaine Coq was up to.

As the second month of the engagement drew to a close and it was obvious that the puppet show was as popular as ever and a decided drawing card, the management decided to retain them but change the rest of the bill. This meant that, among others, the company of aerialists of which Balotte was a member would be moving on.

One night, therefore, a little more than a week before this was to take place, as they sat on their favorite bench on the sea promenade and watched the moon set, Balotte asked Mouche to marry him and was accepted.

"You will see," he said. "As my assistant in my new act, you will make me famous, and yourself too. We will tour the world together."

But also he had told her that he loved her.

Mouche responded to his sincerity and his gentleness. She had been happy during those weeks that Balotte had been courting her.

Against the normality of their relationship and his simplicity, the walks they took together and the picnic lunches in the hills, she could recognize the nightmare of her relationship with Capitaine Coq and she knew that an end must be put to it. Mouche was sure that she loved Balotte, for he was handsome, kind and sympathetic to her, and there was no reason why she should not.

It had been a particularly trying week for Mouche, for although Coq had offered her no further violence or tried to interfere with her dates with Balotte since the beating, he was bitter and sneering and his tongue had never been nastier as he took her to task before stagehands and performers. His movements became more and more mysterious. Sometimes she would not see him for a whole day. Then the next he seemed always at her elbow, biting, mocking, sardonic or abusive.

It was said that he was spending long hours sitting in the puppet booth in silence, and once the night watchman, making his rounds in the theater between the hours of midnight and eight, when the scrubwomen came, swore that he heard the voices of the puppets coming from the booth in some kind of argument. But by the time he made his way from the balcony to the stage, there seemed to be no one there, and only the empty gloves of the Reynardo and Gigi puppets were found lying on the counter of the booth.

Capitaine Coq received the news of Mouche's forthcoming marriage and departure from the show with surprising calmness. Perhaps he had been expecting it. They went to him together, for Mouche had not the courage to face him alone. She declared her intention of remaining with the show until the end of the month, when the contract expired. Then she and Balotte would be married and she would leave.

He had listened to her with a curious expression on his cynical countenance and then had simply shrugged and turned away, vanishing in the direction of his dressing room, which was on the other side of the stage from that occupied by Mouche. And thereafter for the remainder of the engagement she never saw him again.

But if Coq appeared to accept with resignation Mouche's decision to marry Balotte and leave the act, the seven little creatures whom Mouche met twice daily in the pool of spotlights focused on the shabby little puppet booth onstage harped on the event endlessly.

Each reacted to Mouche's romance and engagement according to his or her nature. Madame Muscat's attempts to ascertain whether Mouche knew the facts of life and her advice to her for her wedding night made up one of the most hilarious evenings the old theater had ever known.

Day after day Mouche went through some kind of catechism with regard to her plans and her future. Where would she go? Where would she live? Where was she going to be married? Gigi wanted to know about her trousseau, and Dr. Duclos gave a pompous pseudo-scientific lecture on genetics and just why her children were likely to be acrobats. Mr. Reynardo tried to get the catering job for the wedding, and Alifanfaron applied for the job of nurse.

Yet to anyone witnessing one or more of these performances, it became evident that for all the childish interest and seemingly light-hearted banter, the fact of Mouche's approaching marriage and departure hung over them. They were filled with the tragic forebodings of children about to lose the security of the presence of one who has been both loved and loving.

Through every show there ran a vein of dread of the day, a forlornness, a helplessness, and a dumb pleading that wrung Mouche's heart, for with her departure becoming imminent, she herself did not know how she would be able to leave these little people who in the past year had become such a part of her and the only real friends, companions and playmates she had ever known.

Often, while Mouche would be in conversation with one character, another would appear from below, retire to the end of the booth, stare silently and longingly at her, then heave a large sigh and vanish again. The pressure upon Mouche was becoming intolerable and she did not know how she would be able to reach the final night without breaking, for Balotte could not help her. He was pleased with the publicity that had come his way and the applause that greeted his appearances now that he was the bridegroom-to-be in a romantic story that had been written up in the newspapers. He had no idea of what was happening to Mouche.

The final performance of Capitaine Coq and his family, which took place in the Théâtre des Variétés on the Saturday night of December 15, was one that Mouche would not forget as long as she lived.

The old theater with its red velvet drapes, gold-encrusted boxes and shimmering candelabra had been sold out for more than a week. Word had spread along the Côte d'Azur, and there were visitors from Cannes, Saint-Tropez, Antibes and Monaco. Half of the audience present were regulars who had fallen in love over the weeks with Mouche or the seven dolls and who had paid a premium for their tickets this evening. The front rows sparkled with jewels and décolletage and white shirtfronts. The playboys and playgirls of the gold coast had a wonderful nose for the unusual, the bittersweet in entertainment, the story behind the story, the broken heart palpitating onstage for all to see. The gossip had gone around the cocktail circuit: "My dear, it's frightfully amusing. She talks with all these little dolls, but there's supposed to be the most fantastic man behind them. No one has ever seen him. He's supposed to be madly in love with her. Philippe has four tickets. We're all driving over and dining at the Casino first."

It began as usual with the strains of *"Va t'en, va t'en"* dying away in the orchestra pit, followed by a curtain rise showing a corner of the village square with the puppet booth set up and Golo, the white patch gleaming over his vacant eye socket, strumming his guitar in front of it in a little song dedicated to calling the village folk together to see their show.

The spotlight on Golo would dim; the light pools by the booth would narrow. One of the puppets would appear with startling suddenness in the limelight and claim the attention of all. Mouche was never onstage as the curtain went up.

This night it began with Mr. Reynardo making a furtive appearance on the counter of the booth, looking carefully to the right and left and behind him as well. Then he called, "Pssssst! Golo!" And when Golo appeared from behind the booth: "Where's Mouche?"

"I don't know, Mr. Reynardo. You want me to call her?"

"In a minute. I've got something for her." He ducked down and appeared with a handsome red fox fur scarf tipped with a bushy tail at one end and a small fox mask at the other. He stretched it along the counter and for a moment snuffled up and down its length. "It's for her," he told Golo.

"Dieu!" remarked Golo. "But that's rich. I'll go fetch Mouche, Mr. Reynardo."

While Golo went off into the wings, Mr. Reynardo scrutinized the scarf closely. "Eeeeeh!" he said with some slight distaste. "Awfully familiar. Say, she was a nice-looking babe. . . . I seem to remember her from somewhere." He moved up to the head of the scarf and bestowed a surprisingly gentle kiss on the muzzle of the fox mask. *"Requiescat in pace,* kid," he said, "and keep Mouche warm."

Mouche walked onstage into a storm of applause that lasted for several minutes and brought the ache back to her throat. Whenever she was shown kindness or approval it brought her close to tears.

At last she was able to proceed. She began, "Golo said you were looking for me, Rey . . ."

"Uh-huh. Glad you got here before the others. Er . . . ah . . ." The fox was looking not entirely comfortable. He reached for the scarf and, taking it in his jaws, he held it out to the girl. "This is for you. It's a wed—" He seemed to gag over the words and switched: ". . . a going-away present for you."

Mouche's hand flew to her heart. "Oh, Rey! How beautiful. Oh, you shouldn't have . . . You know you shouldn't have spent so much . . ."

Her expression altered suddenly to the tender and slightly admonishing "Mother-knows-all-what-have-you-done-now" look that her audiences knew so well. "Rey! Come over here to me at once and tell me where you got that beautiful and expensive scarf."

The fox squirmed slightly. "Must I, Mouche?"

"Reynardo! You know what I have always told you about being honest. . . ."

By a twist of his neck Mr. Reynardo managed to achieve a look of injured innocence. "Well, if you must know, I bought it on the installment plan."

"Indeed. And what happens if you fail to keep up the payments? Oh, Rey! I suppose they'll come to my home and take it away from me."

The fox slowly shook his head. "Oh, now . . . You see, I made a kind of a deal."

Mouche was mock serious now and once more lost in their make-believe. She knew the kind of sharp practice to which he was prone. She asked, "And pray, what kind of a deal, Mr. Reynardo?"

"We-e-e-ll . . . If I fail to keep up the installments, the man gets something else in exchange. I signed a paper. It's all settled."

Mouche walked right into the trap. "Did you? And just what is he to have in exchange for this exquisite fur piece?"

The fox appeared to swallow once, then modestly turned his head aside before he replied meekly, "Me."

Struck to the heart, Mouche cried, "Oh, my dear— You mean you've pawned yourself— Oh, Rey . . . I don't know what to say. . . ."

For a moment Mouche glanced out across the footlights, and the balcony spot picked up two drops of light traversing her cheeks and splintered them so that they glowed like diamonds.

Like a flash the fox was across the stage of the booth and whipping his red, furry head with the black mask and long nose into the hollow of Mouche's shoulder. There he snuggled with a contented sigh in the manner of a naughty child that takes immediate advantage of any tenderness.

The contact came close to breaking Mouche's heart for love of this sly, wicked little creature whose mischief and amorality stemmed from his nature and the fact that he did not know any better. Yet he tried hard to please her and be honest for her sake.

Thereafter the other puppets appeared to delight and torture Mouche still further with their parting gifts and little made-up, awkwardly sincere speeches.

Dr. Duclos presented her with an encyclopedia. "Everything I know is inside this book," the formally dressed penguin pontificated. "Thought you might like to have it handy for information on all subjects when I am not around any longer."

Gigi gave her a trousseau negligee and nightgown set and a grudging kiss, while Madame Muscat handed her a rolling pin and an eggbeater, remarking significantly, "A marriage can be kept in order with these, my dear. And remember, all men are beasts, but necessary ones." From Alifanfaron she received a photograph of himself, and Monsieur Nicholas gave her an oddly turned piece of wood that was not one but many shapes.

"For your firstborn," he said. "It is a toy I have made for him that is not any, yet still is all toys, for in his imagination, when he plays with it, it will be whatever he sees in it or wishes it to be."

Golo came forward. He had a little African good-luck god he had carved for her out of a piece of ebon wood. Like the white-shafted spotlights beamed down from above, the emotions and tensions of everyone in the theater seemed to concentrate on this one spot—the shabby little booth, where Golo with the gleaming patch over one eye was crying unashamedly and the girl was trying desperately to hold herself together.

From where she was standing, Mouche could look into the wings and see the show girls, singers, dancers, acrobats and stagehands gathered there, watching and listening, as spellbound as the audience. She saw Balotte in his blue spangled tights, his beautiful body proud and erect, and he looked like a stranger to her.

Carrot Top appeared alone, contriving to look more worried and forlorn than usual. He was empty-handed. He tried to appear nonchalant by whistling, but it soon petered out when his lips seemed to have trouble pursing themselves for the whistle. Finally he gave it up, saying, "Oh, what's the use? I'm not fooling anybody. I came to say good-by, Mouche."

Mouche said, "Good-by, dear Carrot Top."

"Will you miss me?"

"Oh yes, Carrot Top. I shall miss you terribly."

"Shall you be having children of your own, Mouche?"

"Yes . . ."

"Will they be like us?"

"Oh, I hope so. . . . I do hope so. . . ."

Carrot Top was silent for a moment, and then he said to her, "I didn't get you anything. I couldn't. I'll give you my love to take with you, Mouche. . . ."

Now the ache was closing her throat again. "Carrot Top! Do you really love me?" In all the time they had been together, he had never once said it.

The puppet nodded. "Oh yes. I always have. Only you never noticed. Never mind. It's too late now. Mouche, will you give me a going-away present?"

"Oh yes, Carrots. Anything I have."

"Will you sing a song with me?"

"Of course, Carrots. What shall it be?"

The little doll said, "Golo knows."

The Senegalese appeared and picked out an introduction on his guitar. It was the Breton lullaby. Mouche had not expected this. She did not know whether she could get through it.

Carrot Top held out his hand to her and she took it in both of hers. They sang:

> *"My young one, my sweeting . . .*
> *Rock in your cradle . . .*
> *The storm winds are blowing,*
> *God rules the storm winds . . ."*

When they had finished, Golo wandered away quietly into the wings and Carrot Top reached up and kissed Mouche's cheek.

"Don't forget us when you have children of your own, Mouche." He vanished beneath the counter.

The others came whipping up by twos to cry, "Don't forget us, Mouche," and overwhelm her with pecks and kisses.

Mouche, her eyes now blinded by tears, opened her arms and cried to them as though there were no one else there but them and her, "Oh no, no! I can never forget you. My darlings, I will never forget you. You will always be like my own children and as dear to me—"

She hardly heard the band swing into its closing theme, or the heavy swish of the descending curtains, closing them off from the tempest of applause and cheers from the audience out front. The last thing that Mouche saw and heard was Alifanfaron with his head buried in the folds of the side curtains of the puppet booth and Mr. Reynardo, his muzzle turned skyward, howling like a coyote.

Then she fled to her dressing room, locked the door and, putting her head down on her arms, wept. Nor could she be persuaded by knocks or shouts from without to open the door and emerge to take her bows. She felt as though she would cry endlessly for the rest of her life.

She would not open even when Balotte came to fetch her. She begged him to go, promising to meet him at his hotel in the morning, and finally he too departed.

She remained sitting in the dark of her dressing room for a long while.

On every stage in the world at night after the performance is over, there stands a single naked electric light bulb. No spot seems as glaring as where the incandescent light sheds its halo, no shadows as long and deep and grotesque as those lurking at the bulb's extreme range, spilling over flats and props, pieces of sets and furniture.

Against the brick rear wall of the theater, almost at the farthest edge of the illumination, stood the deserted puppet booth, its white oilcloth sign, CAPITAINE COQ AND HIS FAMILY, barely legible.

Unseen in the shadows, squatting on his haunches, Golo sorrowed alone in the dark in the manner of his people. It was nearly four o'clock in the morning, and the theater was empty.

Mouche slipped from her dressing room for the last time. She carried a small valise in which she had packed her few personal belongings. Her wardrobe she was leaving behind her, just as she was leaving a part of herself behind, the Mouche that had been and would never be again.

To reach the stage door it was necessary for her to cross the dark, cavernous stage. From the passageway she stepped into the wings beyond the range of the single light that would have guided her across. And out of this darkness a hand reached and grasped her by the wrist and another was placed across her mouth before she could cry out with the fright that momentarily stopped her heart.

Had the distant light reflected upon the pale, hate-ravaged features and red hair of Capitaine Coq, Mouche's heart might never have started beating again.

But the hard calluses on the fingers covering her lips told their story, and a gleam of white eyeballs completed the identification.

Golo whispered into her ear, "For the love of the dear God, do not make a sound."

As quietly, Mouche asked against the pounding of her heart, "What is it, Golo?"

"I don't know. Something is happening. Stay here with me, Miss Mouche, but make no noise. I am very much afraid."

He pulled her gently down to her knees beside him, and she could feel that he was trembling.

"But, Golo . . ."

"Shhhhh, Miss Mouche. Don't speak. Listen . . ."

At first there was no sound but their own soft breathing. Then there came a faint rustling and scratching. It appeared to come from somewhere near the center of the stage. Sight came to the aid of straining ears, and Golo pressed Mouche's hand hard with his as the head of Carrot Top rose slowly above the counter of the puppet booth and reconnoitered carefully.

There was something horrible in the caution with which he looked to the right and to the left, and then, with that extraordinarily lifelike movement with which he was endowed, leaned out from the ends of the booth and gazed behind as well. Horrible, too, was the fact that no one was supposed to be there, that the performance was to an empty theater . . . or perhaps even more horrible still, that it was no performance at all. . . .

Golo whispered, "He gone away early, but *they* came back. I knew they were here. I felt it."

It was Mouche's turn to quiet him, and she pressed his arm gently and said, "Shhhhhhhh."

Having made certain there was no one about, Carrot Top retired to the far end of the counter and let his face sink into his hands and remained thus for a minute or two.

Then the quiet was disturbed by a rasping, gravelly whisper: "That you up there, Carrots?"

The redheaded puppet slowly lifted his head from his hands, looked down deliberately and replied, "Yes."

"Is the coast clear?"

"Yes. There's nobody here."

"Where's the watchman?"

"Asleep in the boiler room."

The head of the sharp-faced fox arose from below. He too reconnoitered for a moment, then, satisfied, leaned on the counter at the opposite end from Carrot Top. Finally the puppet said in a listless and woebegone voice, "Well, what do we do now?"

Reynardo sighed, then replied, "I don't know if you don't. You've been running the show, Carrot Top. Kind of messed it up, didn't you, old fellow?"

Carrot Top reflected. "Did I? I suppose I did. I never thought she'd leave us for that knucklehead. She'll never be happy with him."

"Why didn't you tip her off?"

"Madame Muscat tried, but it was no use. She's too young to see that monkey will never think of anyone but himself."

"Is she really going to marry him, Carrot Top?"

"Oh yes. It's all over."

The fox said, "Damn!"

Carrot Top reproved him. "Oh, cut it out, Rey. It won't help to use bad language. You know how *she* hated it. The thing is we've got to decide what to do. Is there any use in going on?"

Mr. Reynardo replied quickly, "Not as far as I'm concerned. She was the only thing I ever cared about. I'm ready to call it a day."

"Me too. I suppose we ought to put it to a vote."

"Uh-huh. Take the chair, Carrots. I'll call the roll. Ali?"

The voice of the giant came from below the counter. "I'm here, I think."

"Dr. Duclos?"

"Present."

"Gigi?"

"Yes."

"Madame Muscat?"

"Of course."

"Monsieur Nicholas?"

"Yes, yes."

Mr. Reynardo said, "All present and accounted for," and folded his arms.

Carrot Top then made a little speech in a not-too-firm voice. "Ladies and gentlemen of our company, inasmuch as our well-loved sister Mouche has left us to be married and will never return, I have called this meeting to decide what is to be done. The question before the committee of the whole is: Shall we try to continue without her?"

Dr. Duclos commented, "What's the use if nobody comes to see us, Mr. Chairman?"

Reynardo turned it around: "What's the use if we can't see her?"

Gigi's voice remarked, "We could get someone like her to take her place."

Alifanfaron was heard to rumble, "Gee, I'm stupid, but even I know there's no one like her. Nobody could take her place."

Madame Muscat contributed, "Well, we had a show we used to do before she came to us."

The deep voice of Monsieur Nicholas sounded from below. "Do you wish to return to that? And sleeping in haystacks again? One can never go back. . . ."

Gigi's girlish treble inquired anxiously, "But if there isn't anything forward?"

"Then," said Monsieur Nicholas, "perhaps it's best to go nowhere."

"Oh," exclaimed Carrot Top. "How?"

"Simply by ceasing to exist."

Carrot Top said "Oh" again and Reynardo rasped, "Ha-ha, suits me," while Dr. Duclos said pompously, "Logically sound, I must admit, however unpleasant the prospect." Ali complained, "I don't know what you're talking about. All I know is if I can't be with Mouche, I want to die."

Mr. Reynardo sniggered, "That's the general idea, Ali, old boy. You've hit it for once. Put it to a vote, Mr. Chairman."

There was a moment of silence. Then Carrot Top said firmly, "All in favor of ceasing to exist say 'Aye.'"

There was a scattered chorus of "Ayes" and one squeaky "No" from Gigi.

Reynardo graveled, "Motion carried. Proceed, Mr. Chairman."

"Now?" Carrot Top asked. There were no dissents.

He continued: "Next question—how?"

Dr. Duclos said, "I have always been fascinated by self-immolation—the Indian custom of suttee, where the widow casts herself upon the funeral pyre of her deceased spouse."

Reynardo said, "I don't see the connection, but the idea isn't bad. Fire is clean."

Carrot Top said, "There's a vacant lot back of the theater."

Gigi suddenly wailed, "But I don't want to die."

Reynardo ducked down beneath the counter swiftly and came up with the half-doll that was Gigi—empty, her eyes staring vacuously—clamped in his jaws. Then he carefully dropped her over the side of the booth onto the stage, where she fell with a small crash that echoed shockingly through the empty theater. "Then live, little golden-haired pig," he said.

Mouche drew in her breath and whispered, "Poor, poor little Gigi . . ."

Mr. Reynardo looked over the side of the booth at the little heap lying on the stage and then asked, "Anybody else want to back out?"

Madame Muscat pronounced Gigi's epitaph: "She was never much good anyway."

Alifanfaron said, "But she was so pretty."

Carrot Top sighed briefly. "One of the world's great illusions, the golden-haired fairy princess . . ."

"Who in the end turns out to be nothing more than a walking appetite," Reynardo concluded, for he had never liked Gigi much.

Monsieur Nicholas said from below, "It is not necessary to be unkind. God made her as she was, as He made us all."

Alifanfaron asked, "What will become of God when we are gone?"

The voice of Monsieur Nicholas replied after a moment of reflection, "I think perhaps God will destroy Himself too, if it is indeed true that He has created us all in His own image. . . ."

Carrot Top asked, "Why?"

"Because if He is God, He could not bear to contemplate such a miserable failure of His designs."

Mr. Reynardo stretched his neck and looked down below the counter. "Oh," he said. "That's clever of you. I hadn't thought about it in that way."

"Most profound," contributed Dr. Duclos, "not to mention praglatic—"

Carrot corrected him almost absentmindedly: "Pragmatic." He sighed then and added, "Well, then, it's good-by to Capitaine Coq and His Family."

Golo turned a stricken face toward Mouche. "They are going to die. Don't let them, Miss Mouche."

Mr. Reynardo went over to Carrot Top and stuck out his paw. "So long, kid. It wasn't a bad ride while it lasted."

Carrot Top took the paw and shook it solemnly. "Good-by, Rey. You've always been a friend. I'll go down and get things ready."

Mouche arose. Her knees were stiff from kneeling, her heart was pounding with excitement and her throat was dry. She picked up her small valise and marched across the stage, her heels clicking on the boards and the single standing light picking up her slender shadow, speeding it ahead of her and throwing it as a kind of prophecy of her coming toward the puppet booth and its single inhabitant.

It was astonishing, this repetition of the first time that Mouche had encountered the puppets of Capitaine Coq.

There was the same darkness with the single light to probe the shadows; there was the mysterious booth looming out of the shadows, the lone puppet perched on the counter, and the slender figure of a girl marching by, carrying a valise.

Except now the shoe was on the other foot, and it was Mouche who paused in the yellow light before the puppet booth and called to the small figure flattened on the counter there, "Hello, baby."

Mr. Reynardo, the composed, the cynical and the self-assured, was taken aback. His whole frame shuddered as he reared up and peered through the gloom, for he was handicapped by having to look directly into the light. His jaws moved silently several times and finally he managed to croak, "Mouche! Have you been around here long?"

Mouche paused before the booth and set her valise down. She contemplated the agitated and nonplussed fox jittering back and forth. Finally she said, "Never mind where I have been. I know where you are going. There is nothing to be found in the heart of flames but the ashes of regret. I'm ashamed of you all."

The fox stopped flapping and contemplated her long and hard. "We didn't know you were here." Then he added, "We voted . . ."

"Was it a fair vote?" Mouche asked.

The fox swallowed. "Well, maybe Monsieur Nicholas, Carrot Top and I rigged it a little. But it was only because of you—going away and leaving us, I mean."

"And Gigi here?" Mouche bent over and picked up the empty doll.

The fox looked uneasy. He flattened his head on the counter and thereby seemed to have moved his eyes guiltily. He said, "We pushed her out of the nest. We excommunicated her."

"We?"

"I did. She didn't love you. . . ."

"It was wrong, Rey."

He hung his head. "I know it. Don't leave us, Mouche."

"Rey, you're blackmailing me again, like always—with love. . . ."

There might have been the well-dressed, attentive, cultured audience of the night before out front instead of the blank staring, empty seats; there might have been the rabble from the slums, washed up from the edge of the street fair, gathered about the booth; there might have been the peasant children and the village people gathered about them on the village square—it made no difference. When the puppets were there and she talking with them, she lost herself, she lost reality, she lost the world. There remained only these, her friends and companions, and their need.

The hoarse voice of the fox dropped to a rattling whisper again. "This time it isn't blackmail, Mouche. If you must go, take me with you."

"And leave the others? Rey, you can't desert them now."

The wary figure of the fox stirred. He moved imperceptibly closer to where Mouche was standing. "Oh, yes, I can. I don't care about anything or anybody. Let me come, Mouche. I'm housebroken. And you know me—gentle with children."

The old habits were so hard to break. Momentarily Mouche forgot about herself and that she had parted from all this, that this was the beginning of the morning that was to see her wedded to Balotte and a new and normal life. She went to the booth and, bending over in her sweetly tender and concerned manner, admonished, "But don't you see, Rey, that's being disloyal."

Mr. Reynardo appeared to ponder this for a moment. Then he moved closer and barely nuzzled the tip of his snout into the back of Mouche's hand. He sighed deeply and said, "I know. But what's the dif? Everybody knows I'm a heel. They expect it of me. And to tell you the truth, it's a relief to be one again. I've tried to be a good fellow, but it doesn't work—not unless you're around to keep me from backsliding. . . ."

She could not help herself. She placed a caressing hand upon the bristly redhead. "My poor Rey . . ."

Instantly the fox whipped his head into the hollow between her neck and shoulder and whispered, "Mouche—take care of me. . . ."

The touch of him was, as always, an exquisitely tender agony. Her heart swelled with love for this unhappy creature. With startling suddenness Alifanfaron bobbed up.

"Oh gee, excuse me. Am I interrupting something? Goodness, it's Mouche. Are you back again, Mouche? If you're back again, I don't want to die anymore."

The fox grated, "Damn! Why did you have to come up just then? I nearly had her." He vanished.

Mouche said, "But, Ali dear, I cannot stay, I'm going to be married, and I don't want you to die. . . . What shall I do?" They had all the deadly logical illogicality of children.

"Take me along, Mouche. You don't know what it is to be a giant and stupid and lose a friend. . . ."

Mouche had heard herself say, "I'm going to be married," but it was like something someone else said about another person. Where was that real world now, the world of sanity and things as they ought to be, to which she had been fleeing to save herself from complete destruction? Now she could remember only how she had always felt about Alifanfaron's troubles.

"Oh, Ali," she cried, "you're not really stupid. It's just that you were born too big in a world filled with people who are too small."

"Ah hooom! Harrrumph! Exactly, my dear. A very trenchant remark. Most sage indeed." It was Dr. Duclos, the penguin, in formal attire as usual, his pince-nez attached to a black ribbon perched on the end of his beak. He peered at her for a moment and then said, "So glad to see you're back. We've all missed you frightfully." He went away.

Carrot Top appeared, whistling a snatch of *"Va t'en, va t'en,"* and then with simulated surprise discovered the girl standing at her accustomed place slightly to the right of the center of the booth. He said, "Oh, hello, Mouche. You still here?"

"I was just leaving. Carrot Top, come here . . ."

He edged tentatively a little closer, but was wary. Mouche said, "I overheard everything. I couldn't help it. Aren't you ashamed?"

Carrot Top said, "Oh," and was lost in thought for a moment. Then the small boy with the red hair, bulbous nose, pointed ears and wistful, longing face said reflectively, "It was going to be quite queer without you. Oh yes, quite queer. At first I thought I might be able to go places again. You were always holding me down, you know."

"Oh, Carrot Top—dear little Carrots," Mouche said. "I never wanted to."

Carrot Top mused, "I wonder. You were always pointing out my duty to Gigi, for instance. And there was never anything behind that pretty face. At first, after you left, I thought I might be able to—"

"Yes, yes, I know—fly," Mouche concluded for him as the sudden tears filled her eyes, and for a moment she was unable to see the booth or Carrot Top. "Fly then, Little Carrots. No one will keep you back now. Reach for the stars and they will tumble into your lap."

The puppet emitted a mortal wail. "But I don't want to fly, really. I don't want the stars. I only want to be with you forever, Mouche. Take me with you." He slithered across the counter and rested his head on Mouche's breast, and beneath the pressure of the little figure she could feel the wild beating of her heart.

"Carrots—dear Carrots . . . I have always loved you."

The doll turned his head and looked her full in the face. "Do you? But you don't really love us, Mouche, not really. Otherwise you couldn't go away."

A moan of pain almost animal in its intensity was torn from Mouche. She cried, "Oh, I do, I do. I love you all. I have loved you so much and with all my heart. It is only him I hate so terribly that there is room for nothing else, not even love anymore."

Standing there in the darkness, lost as it were in the center of the vast universe of the empty stage, she could bring herself to speak to a doll the truth that she had never spoken to a human.

"I loved him. I loved him from the first moment I saw him. I loved him and would have denied him nothing. He took me and gave me only bitterness and evil in return for all I had for him, all the tenderness and love, all the gifts I had saved for him. My love turned to hate. And the more I hated him, the more I loved you all. Carrots . . . how long can such deep love and fearful hatred live side by side in one human being before the host goes mad? Carrots, Carrots—let me go. . . ."

Yet she put up her hands and pressed the head of Carrot Top close to her neck, and suddenly Mr. Reynardo was there too, and the touch of the two little objects made her wish to weep endlessly and hopelessly. She closed her eyes, wondering if her mind would crack.

She was startled by the shrill voice of Carrot Top: "But who are *we*, Mouche?"

The remark was echoed by Mr. Reynardo, but when she opened her eyes the pair was gone and instead Monsieur Nicholas was regarding her from behind the panes of his square spectacles.

The little figure had the effect of calming her momentarily, for the old habits were still strong. Here was her reliable friend and philosopher and counselor who appeared inevitably in the booth when matters threatened to get out of hand. He was the mender of broken toys and broken hearts.

Yet he too asked the question that brought her again close to panic. "Who are we all, my dear—Carrot Top and Mr. Reynardo, Alifanfaron and Gigi, Dr. Duclos and Madame Muscat, and even myself?"

Mouche began to tremble and held to the side of the booth lest she faint. Worlds were beginning to fall; defenses behind which she had thought to live in safety and blindness were crumbling.

Who were they indeed? And what had been the magic that had kept them separate—the seven who were so different, yet united in love and kindness, and the one who was so monstrous?

Monsieur Nicholas spoke again. "Think, Mouche. Whose hand was it you just took to you so lovingly when it was Carrot Top or Mr. Reynardo or Alifanfaron, and held it close to your breast and bestowed the mercy of tears upon it?"

Mouche suppressed a cry of terror. "The hand that struck me across the mouth . . ." she gasped.

"Yet you loved it, Mouche. And those hands loved and caressed you—"

Mouche felt her senses beginning to swim, but now it was she who asked the question. "But who are you, then, Monsieur Nicholas? Who are you all?"

Monsieur Nicholas seemed to grow in stature, to fill the booth with his voice and presence as he replied, "A man is many things, Mouche. He may wish like Carrot Top to be a poet and soar to the stars, and yet be earthbound and overgrown, ugly and stupid like Alifanfaron. In him will be the seeds of jealousy, greed and the insatiable appetite for admiration and pleasure of chicken-brained, arrogant Gigi. Part of him will be a pompous bore like Dr. Duclos; and another the counterpart of Madame Muscat, gossip, busybody, tattletale and sage. And where there is a philosopher, there can also be a sly, double-dealing sanctimonious hypocrite, thief and self-forgiving scoundrel like Mr. Reynardo."

And Monsieur Nicholas continued, "The nature of man is a never-ending mystery, Mouche. There we are, Mouche, seven of us you have grown to love. And each of us has given you what there was of his or her heart. I think I even heard the wicked Reynardo offer to lay down his life for you—or his skin. He was trying to convey to you a message from Him who animates us all—"

"No, no—no more!" Mouche pleaded. "Stop. I cannot bear it."

"Evil cannot live without good," Monsieur Nicholas said in a voice that was suddenly unlike his own. "All of us would rather die than go on without you."

"Who is it? Who is speaking?" Mouche cried. And then on a powerful impulse, hardly knowing what she was doing, she reached across the booth to the curtain through which she could be seen but could not see, and with one motion stripped away the veil that for so long had separated her from the wretched, unhappy man hiding there.

He sat there immovable as a statue, gaunt, hollow-eyed, bitter, hard, uncompromising, yet dying of love for her.

The man in black with the red hair, in whose dead face only the eyes still lived, was revealed with his right hand held high, his fingers inside the glove that was Monsieur Nicholas. In his left was crumpled in a convulsive grip the limp puppet of Monsieur Reynardo. It was as though he were the balancing scale between good and evil, and evil and good. Hatred and love, despair and hope, played across his features, illuminating them at times like lightning playing behind storm clouds with an unearthly beauty—Satan before the fall.

And to Mouche, who passed in that moment over the last threshold from child to womanhood, there came as a vision of blinding clarity an understanding of a man who had tried to be and live a life of evil, who to mock God and man had perpetrated a monstrous joke by creating his puppets, like man, in His image, and filling them with love and kindness.

And in the awful struggle within him that confronted her she read his punishment. He who loved only wickedness and corruption had been corrupted by the good in his own creations. The seven dolls of his real nature had become his master and he their victim. He could live only through them and behind the curtain of his booth.

And in one last blinding flash Mouche knew the catalyst that could save him. It was herself. But he could not ask for her love. He would not and could not ask. In that flash she thought for an instant upon the story of Beauty and the Beast, which had always touched her oddly as a child, and knew that here was the living Beast who must die of the struggle if she did not take pity on him.

Yet it was not pity but love that made Mouche reach her arms toward him across the counter of the puppet booth where they had dueled daily for the past year and cry, "Michel—Michel! Come to me!"

No time seemed to have passed, yet he was out of the booth and they were clinging desperately to one another. Trembling, holding him, Mouche whispered, "Michel . . . Michel. I love you. I do love you, no matter who or what you are. I cannot help myself. It is you I love, you that I have always loved."

It was she who held him secure, his red head, as stiff and bristly as that of Mr. Reynardo, sheltered in the hollow of her neck and shoulder, where so often his hand, unrecognized, had leaned. And the desperation of his clinging was the greater as he murmured her name again and again, "Mouche . . . Mouche . . . Mouche . . ." and hid his face from hers.

"Michel . . . I love you. I will never leave you."

Then it was finally that Mouche felt the trickling of something warm over the hand that held the ugly, beautiful, evil, but now transfigured head to her and knew that they were the tears of a man who had never before in his life yielded to them and who, emerging from the long nightmare, would be made forever whole by love.

And thus they remained on that darkened empty stage for a long while as Michel Peyrot, alias Capitaine Coq, surrendered his person and his soul to what had been so fiercely hateful and unbearable to him, the cloister of an innocent and loving woman and the receiving and cherishing of love.

Nor did they stir even when an old black man with a white patch over one eye shuffled across the echoing stage and, looking down over the counter of the booth into the darkness of the mysterious quarters below, chuckled.

"Oh ho, little boss! You, Carrot Top! Mr. Reynardo! Dr. Duclos, Ali, Madame Muscat! Where are you all? You better come up here and learn the news. Miss Mouche is not going to leave us. She is going to stay with us forever."

MEETING WITH
A GREAT BEAST

Meeting
With
a
Great
Beast

Leonard Wibberly

ILLUSTRATED BY THOMAS BEECHAM

It would be an African safari unlike any
he had ever taken. It would also be his last. If he
had only a brief time to live, as his doctor had
informed him, why not spend part of that time at a
sport he enjoyed—big game hunting? And
now his quarry was to be an animal he had never
hunted before; an enormous aged elephant, which
had become legendary and which had
eluded the best hunters over scores of years.

Yet as he stalks his prey, the great beast
becomes something more than just the object of the
hunt. Rather, it is the instrument through
which the hunter comes to understand the world in
which he himself has lived and, far
too soon, must leave.

Writes the author, Leonard Wibberly, "I hope
this book will constitute a memorial to my
sister, Frances, who was generous and
lighthearted and brave, and who met the 'Great
Beast' in Pretoria, South Africa, May 1970."

CHAPTER 1

THE TEXT THAT comes most readily to mind is the one about living by the sword and dying by the sword, but I don't think that it really applies—not unless there is something far deeper in it than I can detect.

I understand, of course, that those who live by warfare are likely to die by warfare since their thinking turns them to war, and even in peace they are at war with their fellows. Beyond that I cannot go. I appear to have touched bottom and exhausted the text. In any case, I doubt that when Christ uttered these words He had in mind the as yet unwritten game laws of French Equatorial Africa, which, as Thompkins pointed out to me, were designed not to protect animals from man, but to protect man from man.

"The game laws say nothing whatever about the actions of animals," he said. "Animals are thoroughly reliable. They do exactly what is required of them and they never think of doing anything else. Their conduct does not have to be regulated. The lion will not kill unless he is hungry, and then he will most certainly kill. He does not kill to expand his personality. He kills because he personally needs to eat, and he will beat off his mate and his cubs until he has had enough. Only when he is full may they touch a morsel of his kill."

Thompkins took a sip of that sticky, sweet French coffee that I have never seen in France and never failed to find in Africa. It is sold all through the bush by little Hindu traders whom one comes upon

257

in all kinds of places—men about the size of English schoolboys and as cunning as a wreath of serpents. They have all the items that remind you of home—Ovaltine, Gold Flake cigarettes (Camels for Americans), Mazawatee tea and (again for Americans) Beech-Nut coffee. And for the French this horrible sticky liquid coffee in a bottle with a blue label that, as I say, you can find all over Africa and nowhere in France. I forget the name of it—Picar or maybe it is Pitot. Something like that.

When Thompkins had taken a suck of his coffee he bared his teeth, which were yellow and long like acorn shells, and the firelight flickered on the tuft of dirty gray hair that showed through the opening of his bush shirt.

"Man," he said, "does not behave as his creator intended him to. Therefore laws have to be laid down to govern his behavior. Laws that cover every aspect of his living, winding up with laws covering the killing of African game. As, for instance, no game is to be hunted with searchlights. And dogs are not to be employed in hunting the big cats or deer. And so on."

"To protect the animals," I said. "In fact, isn't that what the laws are called—Protection of Animals Act—or something of the sort? Nothing that I can see in them about protecting man."

Thompkins did not reply right away. That was one of the most irritating things I was finding out about him. He seemed to listen to me with only half an ear and a quarter of a mind, and then only when it amused him to do so. The rest of the time he appeared to be listening to Something else. I have used the capital on purpose—not for a cheap dramatic effect—but because it is the only way to raise a word to the dignity of whatever it was that Thompkins was listening to and conversing with. Was it night—the enormous and mysterious hemisphere of night that slides about the world with the rotation of the earth? No. That did not fit. Was it the mountains then—those great peaks over to the east in whose cool valleys ferns and strawberries flourished and bright waterfalls glittered under veils of mist? No. Not big enough. I am forced to return to Something. Thompkins listened to and lived with Something, and so did César, our African guide. What time Thompkins had left over, he listened to me.

This was annoying because I was paying Thompkins quite a sum of money for this safari. I had, in fact, arranged to have his services exclusively for six weeks. I had told Elliots in London that I wanted the best man available for elephants, that I wanted a big tusker (I think I even hinted that this was likely to be the last as well as the first time I would hunt elephant), and I had left the rest to them: the plane tickets, the gun licenses, the hunting licenses, the packing and transport of the guns—everything.

I am happy to report that in a world where service has all but disappeared, Elliots performed magnificently. Not a thing went wrong. I took the boat train to Paris for sentimental reasons and spent one night at the George V, again for sentimental reasons. There was pain rather than consolation, however, in these things and I was glad to get away from Paris; from a past that had, after all, gone and might be said to have died.

The following morning I took the plane to Fort Lamy—a monstrous switch from the carnival of Paris to the blinding African grasslands. At Fort Lamy I met Thompkins—tall, bony, red-faced and calm. He was there as I got off the plane, squinting in the sun, which in Africa, I think, is many times as bright as elsewhere on earth. He had already taken care of my guns. He had a jeep, fully equipped, gleaming in a shady corner of the parking lot.

We had one drink together while César got the luggage to the jeep. And then in an unfussed and unhurried manner I found myself in the jeep beside Thompkins, bowling down the macadam road toward a horizon that was, at that time, only a shapeless haze. I glanced at my watch as the jeep started and found that twenty-five minutes had sufficed for Thompkins to launch the safari.

A remarkable man then, but an annoying one, for in the jeep that afternoon I found him preoccupied with that Something of his to the extent that he rarely listened to me. It was disappointing and irritating because I came to realize that part of what I was paying Thompkins for was conversation. Conversation? Comfort, I think. Human communication. Consolation—a warming up of the cold empty spaces inside me. I wanted these things rather more than most men. Only I hadn't told Thompkins that was what I was hiring him for. I had told him I wanted to shoot an elephant.

"You mean kill an elephant," he said. He threw the dregs of his coffee into the fire and returned to the game laws. "Whatever their title," he said, "they are there to protect man from man. They are designed to improve man, to make him better than he would be without them, to raise him up and perhaps eventually to fit him for what may possibly be his proper station on earth."

"And what might that be—in your view?" I inquired.

"Ruler of all things," said Thompkins.

"Isn't that man's position right now?" I asked.

To my surprise César laughed. He looked me straight in the face and his laughter was so outright and genuine, without scorn or ridicule, that I could not get angry with him. He said something, smiling broadly in the friendliest way, and Thompkins said, "César thinks you have a great sense of humor."

"But man does rule all things," I said. "That's a statement of fact, not a joke. And it is so obvious. He is the master of every creature on earth and he is beginning to extend his control out into space."

César understood this, of course. He spoke French fluently, and this was the language in which we conversed. He looked at me puzzled, maybe a trifle dismayed, and then he decided that his doubts about me were absurd and he laughed again at the huge joke I had made, but which I did not understand myself.

Thompkins was a Canadian, coming from eastern Canada. I thought that it was in eastern Canada, in Montreal and Quebec City, that he had picked up his French, but this was not so. He had learned it all in Africa—not so strange a place, really, to learn a European tongue since Africa has been for so long divided among the countries of Europe. For instance, there are still places in Tanganyika, which was once German East Africa, where the Africans speak German.

Thompkins spoke French with the exaggeration of words that is typical of African French. So he was a Canadian who had been a hunter in his own country and then been drawn to Africa, which is the magnet of all big-game hunters. Now he was a professional hunter—a white hunter, as it is called—as opposed to César, who was a native hunter or, more properly speaking, a native guide.

The two types are essential on a safari and work excellently with each other. The white hunter not only knows the ways of the white men who have come to hunt, he also knows the ways of the government that permits them to hunt. He knows all the regulations concerning the killing of game and he knows the ways of the game as well. He is always there, too, to back up his client and put in a kill shot if one is needed and his client is incapable of it. The native guide knows the local topography, the whereabouts of animals and even where particular animals are to be found; and you will not be long in Africa before you begin to realize that between the native guide and the animals he hunts, there is a curious kinship—a kinship not of flesh but of the spirit, which was common among all men and animals at one time, I suppose, and has the most curious remnants in both Europe and America.

My car, for instance, is under the protection of the jaguar, that being the mascot with which it is fitted and the name under which it is sold. And my banker, who has all the appearance of an undertaker trying to be jolly, carries a little scrap of rabbit's foot to ward off the evil eye from his piles of gold and stacks of notes receivable. Others, I know, carry the desiccated claw of a grouse on a little chain, and I was amused once, on visiting California, to find the whole state under the protection of a bear called Smokey.

The African kinship is more direct. I do not pretend to be an authority on it, but between man and animal (out in the hunting areas, of course—not in the cities) there is a sense of equality and of mutual respect and even mutual fun that is, I suppose, the product of hundreds of thousands of years of living side by side. Please understand, it is not worship. I don't know anyone in Africa who worships an elephant or a lion or an impala. It is respect—reverence—tolerance. If you will pardon one more digression, it is amusing to reflect that in India and the Near East, the cow, once domesticated, became an object of worship. But in Africa this was never so. The Masai, who domesticated the cow, never worshiped it. Instead they drink its milk and, judiciously bleeding it, also drink its blood. The cow belongs to the Masai, whereas elsewhere the people belong to the cow.

Perhaps the Hindus and Semites were more imaginative. If so, this serves to strengthen a point I want to make. The kind of feeling that existed between César and the game he hunted did not spring from imagination. It sprang from something like knowledge. There were times when I thought César could talk to animals, and not just animals within a few yards of him, but animals miles away. Once, later in the safari, he stopped while filling my canteen from the five-gallon army-type tanks we carried in the jeep and, allowing the water to spill on the ground, said, "An elephant dies." He sounded immensely sad. He looked away into the darkness, for this was the hour before dawn. Then he turned to me reassuringly. "It is not your elephant," he said.

On the night that I had made that huge and unconscious joke about man being master of the creatures of the earth, Thompkins had undertaken to go over the game laws of French Equatorial Africa for me and give me some pointers on hunting elephant.

A brain shot with an elephant, he emphasized, is almost impossible. It is necessary to pierce the heart. The heart is a huge organ, quite as big as a man's head, weighing several pounds and so presenting an excellent target, particularly since it is best to shoot an elephant at close range—a hundred yards is rather far off. You aim two feet behind the shoulder and a little below what you judge to be the center of the joint. If your aim is good, the elephant collapses, tumbling over on his side, and dies almost instantly. Thompkins said that elephants die with their eyes open, unaware of death.

When you have killed your elephant, you have killed the greatest land creature on earth. You have also joined an elite body of big-game hunters, for I do not suppose that there are a thousand men living among all the hundreds of millions on earth who can claim to have killed an elephant. It is a wry thought, and food for the moralists, that more people have killed their fellow creatures than have killed elephants, so you see how rare is the group of elephant hunters. And it is a further wry thought that these hunters must preserve life in order to have life to kill, and so the big-game hunter is of necessity a conservationist and in him are intricately and intimately interwoven those two appalling opposites—life and death.

Looking at Thompkins across the fire that evening, with his big teeth and his long camel face and his bony shoulders, I thought of this and wondered whether he might not be a sort of priest, intimately concerned with a great mystery of which the outward forms—the liturgy and rubrics—lay in the hunting of big game. I am quite sure he was not aware of these thoughts. He went on about the game laws of French Equatorial Africa, and I listened with but half an ear to what he was saying.

"A wounded animal must be killed, irrespective of the convenience of the hunter," he said. "Ammunition is not to be of smaller caliber than .375 (besides being jacketed for the elephant), cows with calves or in calf are not to be shot." And so he went on and on and on. It was irritating, but I bore it with patience, for one of the rules said that the white hunter had to inform his client verbally of all the rules and would be held responsible if this was not done and any rule was broken. It was his livelihood he was protecting as well as the game, so I made grunts of understanding and watched Africa disappear into the dark body of night. After a while there was left only we three floating in the blackness in the circle of light from our fire.

Thompkins finished reciting his creed and César, his acolyte, reported that my sleeping bag was ready. I climbed into it and tried not to think of the real reason that brought me all the way from England to Africa on the pretext of hunting an elephant.

CHAPTER 2

THE GRASS OF Africa sings. There are enough voices in it—chirrups, whistles, croaks, whispers and other sibilants—to provide a respectable wind ensemble. And over it all there is a seething of the wind—a continuing sigh, which dies down a little at night and which knits the whole composition together.

We traveled across the singing grass of Africa eastward from Fort Lamy for a hundred miles or so and then struck south and east on a game trail.

Here on this trail we met the dust of Africa, fine and golden and all-pervading. Looking back along the track of the jeep, I could see the plume of dust behind us, borne off westward by the east wind, which strikes inland even as far as this from the Indian Ocean. The dust got into everything. It had the gift of transmigration in that it could go through what should be impervious barriers. I found this dust, for example, in a can of California peaches immediately the can was opened, and after two days of travel I began to suspect that it had got under my skin and formed a golden coating between skin and muscle. But that feeling may have been the result of the constant jogging in the jeep as we stumbled along the track or took detours over the singing grass to avoid areas where the dust lay too deep.

Such deep places provide the dust baths of the big game. Here all kinds of creatures wallowed with delight—lion and zebra and even the lordly buffalo, who is the true king of the grasslands—mighty, sullen and almost as blind as Samson.

Game was plentiful in this region—wildebeest, buffalo, bushbuck, several kinds of antelope, including the kudu with his wavy, twisted horns, blocky shoulders and surprising white stripes against a coat of buff. Even the antelope wallowed in the dust baths, though they could not roll on their backs as could zebras and other unhorned beasts. The dust bathing is a method of killing ticks—the fine golden dust, bone dry, rubbed thoroughly into pelt and hair, desiccates the parasites and they die off.

We watched, from a distance, a massive eland cow lower her sweaty flanks into the cool dust and ponderously move her great haunches about in slow, deliberate delight. I very much wished, with my shirt sticking to my back like pasted paper, that I could do the same.

The African grasslands are magnificent in their extent and in their abundance of game. They are not like the South American pampas or the Russian steppes—the other two great grass areas remaining in the world—for they are studded with the curious twisted acacias whose leaves grow not in mounds but in stratalike plates, and cast dense shadows upon the ground. Wherever you look, there are the acacias, at times blazing with yellow or pink blossoms and at others, according to the season, drooping their long withered pods, which, becoming twisted and black with the heat, pop their seeds to the dry ground below in the hope of future life.

"Do you suppose," I asked Thompkins as we jogged along through a rather thicker growth of these trees, "that the acacia of Africa is the mandragora—the tree that lies on the eastern approach to Paradise and of which the elephant must eat before it can copulate and produce its young?"

Thompkins, who was driving, had been communicating with his Something for hours when I asked this question, but he dragged himself back into my dimension long enough to say that elephants were not fond of acacia except in the spring, when the shoots were tender. A little later, moving closer to the foothills of the mountains, we came on a small herd of females with three young, feeding happily on acacia. This, contradicting Thompkins, delighted me. Thompkins said that the cows were lactating, and in that condition browsed on the acacia pods, which increased their flow of milk.

"Where did you hear about mandragora?" he asked.

"In a bestiary of the twelfth century," I replied.

"What else did it say?" he asked. I think he was repenting himself for his silence and had decided to make some conversation since it was I, and not his Something, who was paying his fee.

"It said that elephants have no natural desire to copulate, but when as a matter of duty they must produce young, male and female go to the mandragora tree, which, as I said, lies on the eastern road to Paradise, and the female breaks off a portion of the tree and gives some to the male and eats some herself. They are then seduced by the tree and the female conceives. When the calf is to be born, the mother walks into a lake until the water is up to her udders, the male meanwhile standing guard over her, lest a particular serpent, inimical to elephants, should harm her."

"Sounds like Adam and Eve," said Thompkins.

"That is precisely where the story came from," I said. "The mandragora is the tree of knowledge of good and evil, and the elephants are symbols of our biblical ancestors."

Thompkins was interested. "Anything else?" he said.

"You mean about elephants?"

"Yes."

"Some odd bits," I said. "If an elephant falls down, he cannot get up, but he cries out and a large guardian elephant appears and tries to lift him. He fails, however, and so they both cry out and twelve more elephants appear, but they are not able to lift the one who has fallen. Then they all cry out and a very small elephant appears and with his insignificant trunk lifts up the fallen one. The small elephant is the symbol of Christ and the big elephant, I think, is the old Hebrew law. The way to hunt elephants, according to the bestiary, is to saw a tree in half so that it will collapse when an elephant leans against it. Then you can kill the elephant—provided you get there before that little fellow arrives."

Thompkins was very much interested in this. "Whoever wrote that bestiary must have spent some time with elephants," he said. "It is quite true that they will help each other. If one is disabled, the others will try to get him onto his feet. They also try to defend each other. The bulls put themselves between the enemy and the cows. And the cows put their calves under their bellies or close to their flanks. They have a strong sense of concern for their fellows. And they are masters at disappearing. Watch."

We had been traveling along obliquely past the little herd of cows. Thompkins swung the jeep to head directly for them, where they stood browsing and ruminating among the acacias. There were perhaps seven cows and the three calves. For a little while they were unaware of us, for although we made the usual plume of dust, their sight was too poor to pick this up. Then one of the calves gave a little squeak, rather like the squeal of a pig, and trunks began snaking about here and there, groping for a scent of the intruders. One of the cows homed in on us, with her trunk stretched before her like a vast antenna, and then the others zeroed in and knew immediately whence the threat came.

Thompkins stopped the jeep and we were for a moment the focus of half a dozen waving, questing trunks. Then there was the slightest movement among the elephants, and they melted into nothingness. Before me there was only the acacia grove, with the sun striking like splintered glass against the flat strata of boughs and leaves and below these the purple splotches of shadow. Half a dozen elephants and three calves had disappeared as far as I was concerned. God, how I wished that all realities could disappear as well, so that the one reality which for me made a pretense of all the world would vanish, giving me—rebirth?

Thompkins could see the elephants, however. Reality did not disappear for him. It merely changed its shape. He showed me how here and there a dark shadow was invaded by a lighter shade, or the trunk of one of the trees was slightly interrupted before it reached the foliage above, and for a moment I could make out an elephant. And then the eye would lose the evidence and the creature would be lost, though actually standing within a quarter of a mile of me.

"We see always what we expect to see," said Thompkins. "When what we expect to see assumes an unexpected shape, then it disappears. You are looking for the shape of an elephant. But the elephant shape has disappeared into an acacia-elephant shape and that shape is so new to you, you cannot see it."

So it was. Thompkins could see five of the elephants—César confessed he could see only four—but I could only see what I hoped to be part of one. And I was wrong. For when, to satisfy my curiosity, we came up on the grove (from which the elephants had, of course, retreated) what I had thought was the pronounced and distinguishing hump that marks the back of an African elephant proved to be the eroded base of an ancient anthill. I was annoyed to be so deceived; but Thompkins, expanding on the elephant's ability to merge with its background, said it was possible to follow an elephant to within ten feet and still miss seeing him.

"Oh, come on," I said crossly. "A creature ten or twelve feet high and weighing several tons would be hard to miss."

"The size is part of the camouflage," said Thompkins. "You cannot believe that anything that big is alive. You see only what you are expecting to see and, close up, you are not expecting something the size of an elephant."

We were not interested in the little herd among the acacias as game. There were two reasonable tuskers among them, for the female African elephant has tusks quite as splendid as the male, these being used in rooting up food.

But Thompkins, in consultation with César and the small tribe or clan from which César came, had long before my arrival in Africa selected a particular elephant for me to kill—a lone bull of great size and undetermined age. It was known among white hunters as Pétain's elephant, for the reason that it had previously been selected as the elephant to be killed by General Pétain in the days before the tragedy that had overtaken the man who had once been one of France's greatest soldiers.

This business of setting aside, as it were, special elephants for important people to kill is an old tradition in Africa, dating back to

the days of Teddy Roosevelt and perhaps even further. It arose out of the desire that no important person coming to hunt elephant should be unable to find a worthy trophy. Bulls are, of course, the great trophies and they are solitary creatures, only seeking out herds of cows when they are in *masht*—an Indian word, by the way.

Sometimes you will find a great bull and one or two smaller bulls traveling together, but this is reckoned a temporary arrangement. The big bulls, standing perhaps eleven feet high or over, and weighing as much as eight tons and having tusks that are ten feet long, normally travel alone. They are august, noble personages of the African wilds. They are known, individually, to thousands of tribal Africans, who speak of them with respect. Their migrations from place to place are noted, and news of their whereabouts is passed among the people.

At any given time the people of these tribes can tell you where any particular bull elephant is within a radius of twenty miles and often within closer limits. They know these bulls by name and they know their peculiarities, for it is not true that only man is individual and that animals of a species are all of a kind. Some bulls are fastidious and will not drink from a water hole used by buffalo, which are indeed messy creatures. Others slash with their tusks the highest point they can reach on a tree, ripping off bark and wood and branches as if to say, "Behold, I, a great elephant of Africa, passed here!"

Some, passing an anthill in the grasslands—the African elephant is a woodland creature but is not averse to the singing, sunlit grasslands—will sidle around it, distrusting the mechanical and merciless colony inhabiting such a castle of earth. All, then, have their personalities and the greatest, as I say, are picked out as trophies for visiting dignitaries. There is, for instance, a crown prince's elephant roaming Tanganyika to this day. He was selected as the trophy of the crown prince of Germany, who was coming to Africa—to Tanganyika, which was then German territory—in 1913. The crown prince never arrived. The elephant's life was saved by the outbreak of World War I. The crown prince is gone now—indeed I do not know in what circumstances he died. The elephant is still alive and a great lord in Tanganyika. And so it might be with my own elephant.

Pétain's elephant, as I say, had been reserved for me and he was to be found in those wooded highlands that we were now approaching over a plain that in the last day's travel had become inceasingly arid. I do not know why so famous an elephant had been allocated to me. It would be flattering to think that literary fame had brought me as a prize the elephant once reserved for a marshal of France. But I am a realist. I decided that some measure of public relations was involved. Perhaps this was so. But now that I come to reflect on it all much later, I believe there was a connection between the selection of this particular elephant and the Something Thompkins and César were so involved with.

You must remember that both Thompkins and César were hunters, and there is a mystique to hunting that transcends mere killing. Hunters do not merely hunt game but also, I think, the minds and souls of both animals and men, outguessing them, tracking them down, and driving them into predetermined corners.

Furthermore, this hunting mystique is, I believe, as old as man himself. Look at the Cro-Magnon cave drawings of southern France—which are certainly more alive than any art of later times. What is the hunter depicting—the mere spearing and bludgeoning of animals? No. Among all the paintings of buffalo and deer and mastodons spurting blood from their mouths, you will sense something else—the real quarry that the hunter is after.

But at this point in my story, I did not know what that quarry was.

CHAPTER 3

We camped that afternoon in the shade of one of those odd masses of billowing rock that thrust up from the African plains here and there and are lookout points for the traveler. They are very strange, these rock masses, smooth and rounded, one globular rock flowing over the top of another and sometimes the whole edifice standing two hundred feet high. My geology is of the poorest, and I cannot make up my mind whether these rock masses are of volcanic or marine origin. Shrubs often grow on them, their roots striking down through the crevices in search of nourishment, and you must be careful in climbing about them, for there are at times scorpions and centipedes in the cooler and darker parts.

César set up the tent and Thompkins, pointing to a herd of bushbuck, suggested that we kill one for meat. These are smallish antelope, extremely wary, but not great jumpers like springbok and impala. Springbok can clear ten feet in a standing jump with ease and a herd of them jumping is more graceful in its motion than a flock of birds in flight.

The bushbuck were a couple of miles away and between us and the foothills, which were now within easy travel. We would approach them, then, from the dry grass area over which we had been traveling, and we covered three quarters of the distance in the jeep.

African game are not afraid of jeeps and automobiles. They know the game laws, which forbid shooting from a moving vehicle. It is amazing how in a generation or two wild game can learn whether something entirely new in its experience is a danger to its species or not. Thompkins said that when automobiles of various kinds first appeared on the African gamelands, they were often charged by rhino and elephant. Now, the surliest rhino will scarcely do more than sniff the air as a truck or jeep goes by. But let a man get out of the vehicle and the rhino immediately knows the situation has changed and he is in danger.

The bushbuck then took no notice of us when we approached in the jeep and stopped, but when we got out, the herd was immediately tense and uneasy and a beautifully horned male took a number of stiff steps in our direction and stood with his neck extended, his nostrils dilated, sensing the menace of our approach.

The wind, however—it was only the slightest movement of the air—was from the foothills and mountains in the east and flowing toward us, produced by the colder air sliding slowly down from the heights toward the baking plain. This put the bushbuck upwind and after a while he relaxed, as did the herd behind him. The relaxation was not much—just the drooping of an ear and slight lowering of his head. Thompkins moved off to the right and I to the left, or north, at the same time recalling what a Swiss hunter had once told me about stalking game—make everything flow, don't speed up or slow down suddenly.

Actually it is amazing how we are all instinctively hunters. Man has cultivated the soil, I suppose, for five thousand years, but he has been a hunter for two million years, and the genetic memory of the hunt remains strongly with him. You can take the most stricken of city dwellers—one whose landscape has been always steel and concrete and glass—and put him or her in a woodland, intent upon surprising some wild creature, and at once the muscles soften, the tread lightens, the whole figure stoops, the nostrils dilate, and the eyes squint to give sharper focus. The hunter takes over and the urbanite is drowned in the old deep tide of the hunt.

I enjoyed my stalk of the bushbuck. I could almost feel the stiff grass and the warm dust through the soles of my boots as I moved off north and then eastward to both close the distance and get a better angle for my shot. My skin developed a wonderful aliveness as if a million antennae were feeding messages to it—messages about wind and light and shadow and movement. I felt more alive at that moment than I had since childhood, and I actually forgot that sense of burning in the soft part of my palate that time and again in the last few months had set my heart pounding. I seemed now to have not one but several pairs of eyes, for I could watch the bushbuck and the ground before my feet and also Thompkins moving to the south, and even be aware of the general attitude of the herd beyond, feeding, but a trifle disturbed and restless, their unease increased by the absence of the tick birds, which had, for the time being, taken up their station on the ground.

At last I reached a position where I could take my shot. The bushbuck did not offer an ideal target, facing into the sun, which was still so bright that it softened the outline of the animal so that it merged into the surrounding gold and dun of the grasslands. I raised the medium Winchester I was using, making the gun flow upward to my shoulder, and zeroed in on the heart area. The bushbuck sensed the movement, or perhaps Death sent ahead a shadow as a warning of her approach, as was held in the Dark Ages. Whatever the explanation, an ear flicked toward me, the head was raised and the neck extended, and as soon as I took the initial squeeze, the bushbuck stiffened as if to whirl and dart away. But the moment for salvation passed. The head moved slightly and I fired.

The flat dry crack produced panic, I think, throughout the whole of Africa. The bushbuck leaped into the air, fell down, rolled over, got up, ran, and fell again. The herd behind disappeared in an explosion of dust. Indeed there were several dust explosions all over the place as other creatures, unseen in my concentration on the bushbuck, erupted into life and took off in whatever direction panic dictated; some across each other, some into each other, each producing its jet trail of dust and all fleeing, fanwise, away from the killer, which is to say, from me.

I ran immediately to my quarry, but Thompkins was there before me. He took his knife and cut its throat with one swift twist of his arm, but even so the bushbuck, summoning together all its force against the imminence of death, gave its head a tremendous convulsive jerk, which brought one of the horns, with immense impact, against Thompkins' left shoulder. The blow was so shrewd that he cried out. And then the bushbuck was dead, and we examined the carcass for my bullet. My aim had been good in the circumstances, the bullet hitting the right shoulder blade, smashing it, and missing the heart by centimeters. It wasn't a clean shot straight into the heart, but it was a kill shot, and Thompkins congratulated me. He felt relieved, I think, that I was a hunter and not merely a wealthy client with a gun.

He rubbed his shoulder, on which the skin had been heavily grazed through his shirt by the dying convulsion of the bushbuck. It looked swollen and he had difficulty moving the joint, but he said only the muscle was bruised and it would be well in a day or two.

Back at camp, César cut off the best meat from the carcass and, using the jeep, drove off and took the offal a few miles away and dumped it in the open. It soon disappeared under a host of vultures, whose wings glistened like the shells of black beetles as they poured over it.

That evening Thompkins opened up a little more than he had done previously, and instead of lecturing me on the game rules, talked about elephants—individual elephants and in particular Pétain's elephant, which had now been allocated to me.

"Nobody knows how old he is, but a hundred years might be a good guess, which would mean that he was roaming around Africa shortly after the American Civil War. Odd, isn't it? He was probably born before there was an automobile or an airplane and when rimfire cartridges were still common."

"A hundred years?" I said. "I thought elephants had about the same life span as human beings."

"Nobody knows the life span of an elephant," Thompkins said. "The gestation period is uncertain, but it is reckoned to be about eighteen to twenty-two months. The theory is that having twice the gestation period of humans, elephants have also twice the life span. Six score years and twenty or close to a century and a half. If this is so, your elephant is still in his mature years. It makes him very knowing, for he has been hunted a great deal."

"But not by General Pétain," I said.

"No," said Thompkins. He rubbed his shoulder for a moment, for it pained him. "Not by General Pétain. I have hunted him three times and without success. He is not Pétain's elephant and he is not my elephant. He is somebody else's elephant. Maybe yours."

"Anybody with a license can kill him," I said because I wanted to be practical and head off Thompkins from that detached mood of his in which he communicated with his Something. I could feel it coming on. If I hadn't shot the bushbuck, I think he would have relapsed into one of his irritating silences at this point. But I had established a rapport with him now. I had shown that I was worth talking to, so he bared his acorn-shell teeth in a smile and said, "Maybe. But I couldn't, and Pétain—well, the Riff revolt prevented him from trying. That was in 1925. Of course it's reasonable to think of that as a coincidence, but the life of that elephant has been saved by a revolt of the Riffs, a steel strike in the United States, and by the moon."

"I would guess that the steel strike canceled out the plans of a wealthy American hunter," I said. "Tell me about the moon."

"I had been stalking him for two weeks," said Thompkins. "But whenever I came on him something was wrong—a kill shot was impossible, or I wasn't ready. Something. So I laid out a plan—a plan that could not fail to work. I studied his habits and decided my best chance was to get him at nighttime on his way down to the water hole where he drank. This wasn't easy because there was high bush on all sides and this water hole in the middle of it. The bush wasn't dense but it was there, and you have seen what elephants can do in daylight in bush. But there was one spot on the trail that was clear, a place where he had to step into the open to get to the water hole. And it was at that spot that I decided to bag him. I wasn't in a hurry. I just wanted to make sure of him, and I decided it would be better to wait for the full moon so as to have plenty of light.

"As it turned out, that night the full moon was somewhat overcast. There was partial cloud with a diminishing of the amount of light in the clearing, which bothered me. Not that I wouldn't be able to see the elephant. There would be enough light for that. But in the periods of gloom I couldn't see my sights. I made a little reflector out of the tinfoil from a pack of cigarettes and that threw the front sight into a sharper silhouette for me, even in the dark. That done, I waited, confident that every preparation had been made and the elephant was mine." He shifted awkwardly on his stool, the pain of his shoulder making the movement laborious, and continued.

"After a little while," he said, "I could sense the elephant approaching. I am not going to say that I could hear him, for elephants can move through woodland and heavy brush with no more noise than a soap bubble going through the air. But there was an awareness of him coming closer and closer, and though, as I say, I could not hear or see anything, I raised the rifle and aimed it at the precise spot that I had picked as being the place I would kill him.

"He materialized out of the darkness of the woods like a gigantic ghost. He was there for a full second before I realized it. In fact, his presence was revealed not by his several tons of mass but by two very slight signs—a smear of soft light on the tip of one tusk, and the outline of the upper edge of one enormous ear. This materialization of the elephant was something I won't ever forget—this flowing into solidity of his vast mass, coming from nothingness.

"First it was only the gleam of light on his tusk and the top of his ear that I could see, and then more and more of him could be seen—the massive, noble forehead with the two dark indentations over his eyes, the long graceful sweep of his trunk, hanging straight down and softly curled to raise the prehensile tip off the ground, and the magnificent forelegs, strong as Grecian columns. I cannot tell you his height. He seemed as lofty as a mountain, and I think now that it was in the elephant and not in man that evolution reached its peak.

"He moved toward me, unhurried and unafraid, and I got him in my sights. I had only to wait for him to move another foot when the moon saved him. The light had been diminishing all the time and I now found that even with the aid of my tinfoil reflector, I could not see my front sight at all. I thought I would try for a shot anyway, for the range was no more than thirty yards. But just at that moment darkness descended on the whole world—the darkness not of night but of the outer void. I couldn't see the end of my rifle, let alone the sight. The elephant disappeared, as did everything else around. I waited, thinking the cloud over the moon would pass and I would still get my shot. But it was no cloud that had cut off the light. The moon had gone into eclipse, which became total at precisely the moment the elephant stepped into the sights of my gun."

When you hear a story such as that, whatever your reaction, the best thing to do is to say nothing. The modern tendency, of course, would be to scoff at the whole thing, and to ask Thompkins why he hadn't tried for the elephant on the following night, since an eclipse of the moon could hardly be expected to occur twice in succession to save the life of an elephant.

I am afraid that was my view, but I had the tact to say nothing for a while. Then I asked him whether he had not tried for the elephant on another occasion.

"No," he said. "That was enough for me. I realized he was not my elephant."

I said nothing to that piece of mysticism and it was Thompkins' turn to ask a question. He put it kindly. "How long have you got?" he asked.

"Two years—more or less," I said, and the nightmare was back.

CHAPTER 4

IT IS CURIOUS the things one remembers about the dramatic and crushing events of life. When I think back to my brother's death, I think of toasted muffins, well buttered, but with the butter congealing as they grew cold. For that was what we were eating when the telephone rang to tell us he had died, and in the immensity of the shock I could only think of the muffins going cold and wondering whether we ought not to eat them. I did eat one, slowly and solemnly, as a kind of duty, but nobody noticed, or if they did, they did not comment on it.

Thus, when Haller, my doctor, came to call on me years later on that rainy night in London, what I remember most vividly is the raindrops falling off the roof of the porch onto the gravel below. They glittered in the light of the porch like twisted pieces of glass, and they made a *splat* as they fell on the gravel. They had already washed many of the pebbles as white as bones.

Haller pretended that he had dropped by just to say hello, but as soon as I saw him I knew otherwise. Oddly enough, I felt more sorry for him at the moment than I did for myself. He had on a thick dark overcoat and a yellow woolen scarf around his neck—the yellow scarf being the attempt of an English doctor to exorcise some of the stuffiness of his profession. I felt so sorry for him that I asked him in and took his coat and gave him a whiskey and soda by the fire and did everything possible to ease for him the telling of news that must have been a terrible burden to him.

When he eventually got around to it, it was a tremendous relief for me instead of a disastrous blow, so great was my concern for him. Do not for a moment think that I am a kindly man. Not at all. I can be just as miserable and mean to people and as selfish as anybody else in the world, and at times I think I can be rather more so. But I am not a cruel man, and when I see someone suffering, I suffer too, and in a selfish desire to relieve my own suffering, I hasten to relieve theirs. The world is our own selves and we see it and experience it only through ourselves and in no other way. Calmly viewed, there is no such thing as an unselfish action, and I think that the improvement of society will depend upon an increase in our sensitivity or awareness of when our own selfishness will do whatever is needed to improve matters.

The news that Haller brought and finally got out over his whiskey and soda was that for me the world would shortly disappear. I would die. Of course, being a doctor, he couldn't be absolutely sure that I would die, but the prognosis was very poor and the best I could hope for was two years from that date—quickly qualified by the phrase "more or less."

If the malignancy had been situated somewhere else—on my buttocks, for instance, or on the thigh—then it would be of little more concern than a rather large wart that could readily be removed. But being in the palate, close to the brain and to the spinal cord, an operation was out of the question. Treatment with drugs and with radiation could be given to slow the growth and just might possibly arrest it for a while. But the verdict, plainly faced, was death, and the odd thing is that when I faced it squarely, I felt relieved and, in fact, exhilarated.

For one thing, I was halfway through a tedious and troublesome novel, which would not come into being but lingered always in the limbo that surrounds reality. I saw immediately that I did not have to finish the thing—I could put it aside and never look at it again. Indeed, I did not have to write another line for the rest of my days, and that thought was an immense relief—like being released from prison or at least from school with nothing ahead but glorious holidays. At this point, you will perceive that I did not understand myself very well, for the fact of the matter is that in common with many writers, I have to write. There was a condition laid down at my birth to that effect, and it must be fulfilled.

I also felt myself relieved from the cares and burdens of the world. I could look on now, a disinterested observer, slightly amused but in no way concerned. Whether there was a war here or there; whether the tax rate increased or decreased; whether in fact my bills were paid or unpaid did not in the slightest concern me. I was free, and the removal of all these cares filled me with exuberance. I had not been aware of how much they pressed me down until they were removed.

This, of course, was merely the first stage. It lasted for maybe a month or six weeks and it was replaced by another mood—a mood not of detachment and of unconcern, but of isolation—a terrible increasing isolation as if the world could no longer hear me nor I talk to the world. I felt as if I were already being shoveled off the earth's surface, as mere lumber that was encumbering the place and should be got rid of.

Even Haller, kind though tactless Haller, whom I now had to visit twice a week for as much treatment as he could give me, began to adopt, or to seem to adopt, an attitude as if I were dead already. The trouble was that so much of human life depends on the future. We do not live in the present. We do not live in the past. We live in the future. Life is a future thing, always turned expectantly to what is to come. And if you have no future, then you have no life. My future was so short that it might be said not to exist at all. One step beyond that thought would make me dead already. The loneliness of the grave was upon me while I yet walked around.

My exuberance then turned to loneliness and that loneliness—that utter solitude, as it became—was tinged with fear. Lord, how dreadful not to exist—to walk out of this something into nothing; to go to bed one night and never wake again.

If you think I am being morbid, I am not, for as I have said before, I am a practical man and I have no use for exploring the blind alleys of human feeling. I remember once reading a story about a man who through witchcraft had summoned a devil into the world. This was more than he had bargained for; he had merely been amusing himself with black magic and was appalled that it should work. He learned that he could send the devil back to the infernal regions only by drawing a triangle with a circle contained in it. The devil would be compelled to enter this magical design (which I fancy came out of Pythagoras), but if it had not been put in the right place, two devils would immediately emerge. Only if triangle and circle were rightly located could the wretch be sure of getting rid of the evil spirit. He thought about it a great deal and came up with a solution that has perhaps occurred to you already. He caused the devil to lie naked on the floor and then drew the triangle around his navel, which compelled the evil one, with a great shriek, to disappear into himself and so be gone.

I mention this in connection with my attitude toward morbidity and other dead-end feelings. They are examples of disappearing into yourself and, if persisted in, they will destroy you. So it is not morbidity of disposition on my part that inspires me to describe the towering solitude that overtook me, but rather a desire to describe the state of my mind with accuracy.

I sensed a withdrawal of my friends—as if I had leprosy and was being shunned. This was natural enough. Life hates death and the living have an aversion to the dying. And then there was that matter of the future. People who did come to see me—without my wishing it, news of my sentence somehow got around—were very careful not to talk about "plans." Haller himself stopped in midsentence in discussing what his son would do when he left school—he wouldn't leave for three years or so. And Pennystone at the yacht club wouldn't say a word about a big cruising yawl that he was building with the intention of taking his family to the West Indies when he retired—five years hence. This banishing of the future was kindly meant, but it had the effect of cruelty, and many of my friends stopped calling on me because the one question everybody asks of everybody—"How are you feeling?"—was obviously taboo in my case.

So the initial exuberance gave way to loneliness and the loneliness to terror. In the first few weeks or so after Haller had so unwillingly passed sentence, I began to take an interest in cemeteries and funeral parlors, and I once went into a funeral parlor and looked over the coffins, some of which were quite sumptuous. I rather fancied myself in an elegant one of limed elm with some very attractively placed flashes of gold here and there. But that was in the exuberant stage. Later, I hated funeral parlors and cemeteries and began to notice what an enormous number of them there were around and how smug all the healthy people who ran them looked—as if they possessed a secret that would relieve them of any need for purchasing their own wares.

It was this isolation that led to my decision to go to Africa. I could get away from the place of my condemnation, which was London, and I had no faith in Haller's pathetic delaying-tactic treatments anyway. I wanted life—not merely the postponement of death. I could get away from my friends, who now regarded me as good as dead—and there might be a measure of resurrection in that. I could have one last hunt and I could hunt the greatest of the earth's creatures, the elephant.

Even the prospect of getting away from all my mourning friends and from England, which I now associated with doom, cheered me immensely. It was as if I had received a reprieve. My literary earnings were not enough to finance the trip, and though in normal circumstances I could have raised the needed cash by signing contracts for future books, this was out of the question since I lacked a future. But I had a rather ugly cottage in one of the Hertfordshire villages now strangling in vast entrails of highways, and I sold it, and with one or two other sales of securities, life savings and so on, I got together all that was needed.

I thought I had left the whole doom behind for a while, but I hadn't. Thompkins knew about it. It was natural enough that he should. A white hunter, taking an unknown client a very long way from medical help, has a right to know something of his client's physical condition. And blundering Haller, who might have confined his remarks to the condition of my heart and lungs, had mentioned the cancer. So when Thompkins asked me how long I had got I knew that the thing had caught up with me, even in the heart of French Equatorial Africa.

But with Thompkins I had a future. There was my elephant to hunt and there was time in which to do it. Before we turned in for the night, he made one more remark about my ability in stalking, which was complimentary. It made me feel part of the living world, not one of the dying, and that was the happiest thing that had happened to me since I had watched the rain dripping off the porch roof in England and whitening the pebbles while Haller fumbled with his yellow scarf and said he had just dropped by for a moment.

CHAPTER 5

WE LEFT THE singing, shining grasslands the next day, climbing up into foothills cut through the valley. In ten miles of travel we were a good two thousand feet above the level of the plain, which was itself, by the way, a thousand feet above sea level. Now there was a very dense undergrowth around, and, dramatically there before us, was the line of the forest—a green wall, garlanded with liana vines, festooned with flowers of the convolvulus and cutting off the true mountains beyond from our view.

César became excited as we approached the forest, for it was there, in that strip of cool, lofty wood, that the lone bull elephant that was once Pétain's and had become mine was to be found. His face shone with expectancy and his eyes sparkled. Out on the grasslands he had seemed to me silent and ruminative (though you will remember how much we had laughed over that unknowing joke of mine). Now he was happy and expectant.

"Soon we will find the elephant," he said. "It's been a long time since I saw him. Four years." He made a little clucking sound with his tongue to indicate that that was far too long a period, and then in sheer exuberance he patted the top of his head several times with the palm of his hand.

"*Aie—aie—aie*," he said. "Maybe even today."

Thompkins' shoulder was much worse. His arm was badly swollen at the shoulder joint and, curiously, also at the wrist. He kept insisting that it was nothing but a sprain that would yield to massage and time, but meanwhile he did not have the use of his left arm. I helped César set up our camp that day and unload from the jeep all the stores we would need, for this would be a stop of several days.

We had plenty of canned foods and several pounds of the meat from the bushbuck. César produced a round iron pot—a miniature of the ones cartoonists use to cook missionaries in—and into it he put the meat and a couple of fresh bones and made a vast stew with which to vary the canned diet we now faced. We couldn't hunt more game now, for the firing would frighten off my elephant.

"How do you know he is around?" I asked.

"Boss," said César, "I just know."

I thought we might go out and look for the elephant immediately, but Thompkins was a methodical hunter of the kind that lays down a plan for a campaign before launching it. So we spent the whole of that first day, once the camp was established, surveying the area in order to fix its topography in our minds.

The forest, which started a quarter of a mile from our camp, extended eastward into a kind of bay formed by massive cliffs. If you think of the forest as a thick green sea, of a depth of perhaps two hundred feet, washing into that bay, you have a good picture of it. It was eight miles in extent from one horn of the bay to the other, and at the ends the forest petered out into scrubland, for here the igneous rocks that formed the cliffs lay split and tumbled about in a great cataract of black and grayish boulders. Lizards skittered about in this place and were hunted by kites, several of which soared far, far up in the sky—tattered little scraps of menace watching the earth.

Skirting the forest and lying between it and the great dry grassland over which we had crossed from Fort Lamy was a greasy river, which looked as though it contained dirty kerosene rather than water. The river came out of the mountains to the east, but at this point, having reached fairly level ground, it was broad, serpentine and swift.

In my childhood I was given a vastly erroneous picture of the nature of rivers and I have never been able to correct it. This picture was based on the principle that if a river is straight in its course, then it flows swiftly. But if it meanders, then it has but a sluggish flow. This particular river meandered very considerably and had a current sufficient to produce streaks of greasy foam and sinister dark welts on the downstream sides of rocks and tree stumps.

We camped on the grassland side of it for the very good reason that, on the other side, the mosquitoes and sand flies, breeding in every stagnant pool of the forest, would be beyond bearing. That meant that to get to the forest, in its great embrasure of rock, we had each day to cross the river. At the only place where the current was weak enough to make the river crossable, the riverbed was enlarged to the size of a small lake. There was actually a little island in the middle of it, supporting a clump of *cypre*, which is a species of mahogany, I think, and this island appeared to be the undisputed

domain of two white herons that spent the greater part of their time admiring their reflections in the opaque waters of a tiny bay.

A short way upstream of this island was a long mudbank—an island-to-be—and this was the territory of an enormous crocodile; a reptilian horror, contemplating murder. I didn't see the crocodile right away. Thompkins had to point him out to me, letting me sight along his gun barrel. These things are concealed even in the open, so good is their camouflage. The horny plates of his vast back looked like the dried ripples of the mudbank, and his blunt head part of a fallen tree or of a rock protruding from the mud. Nobody knows how many lives a year are taken by crocodiles in Africa. There is not a river or a lake that is not teeming with them. They are commonly acknowledged the greatest killers: the killers of more people—mostly women washing clothing in the rivers—than lions, snakes, leopards or any other wild creatures. "Not thousands but scores of thousands," Thompkins said, and I believed him.

Crossing the river—I will call it the lake from here on because it was at the lake area that we always crossed—was no problem, for there was not one but three dugouts on our side. This is not unusual in Africa, where boats are communal property. Two of the dugouts were small but one was bigger and better made, and its outrigger had been but recently relashed to its poles with those special knots that have a propitiatory significance and are akin, I am told, to knots used for the same purpose in the Fiji Islands.

We crossed in this large dugout, César at the bow and I at the stern, while Thompkins sat in the middle, unable to paddle because of his arm. As we passed the mudbank, toward which the current carried us, the vast crocodile heaved himself up on his stubby claws and waddled a few feet toward the water. I reached for my gun, putting the paddle aside, but Thompkins said, "No shooting."

The crocodile didn't enter the water. He was an excellent judge of trajectory and calculated that the canoe would pass the end of the mudbank too far away to be reached in the time available. He would wait until the dugout was swept down on the mudbank or until it overturned or was swamped. We got over safely, then, and hauled the dugout into the soft mud of the bank and set off into the cool, verdant, dark forest where my elephant had taken up residence for the duration of the dry season, which was now starting.

He had picked his retreat well. He had about fifteen square miles of lush forest available to him. He had a nice, quiet bay by the lake's edge of water, one end of it being a quagmire in which he could wallow with delight, caking himself with mud that would then be scraped off against the sides of trees. He also had an escape route, for there was at the south side of the forest a vast slope leading up those formidable cliffs to the highlands beyond.

We did not see him on that first day. But we found his sign. We found trees, a foot in diameter, pushed carelessly down like stalks of straw, and great gouges in the soft ground where he had rooted for wild yam and cassava. There was one big mahogany so terribly ripped and scarred around its trunk that I thought it had been struck by lightning. The bark and wood fiber hung from it in tatters.

"Your elephant," said Thompkins.

Some of the scars made by his tusks were fourteen feet above the ground.

CHAPTER 6

THOMPKINS HAD TO leave us the next day. His arm was quite useless, the swollen shoulder covered by a drum-tight skin, mildly purple. The wrist was also swollen so that it appeared that he had possibly suffered a fracture in the shoulder and a heavy sprain in the wrist. The shoulder would have to be X-rayed and this meant going back to Fort Lamy. I offered to drive him, but he insisted on going alone, his duty to his client, which was that I should get my elephant, coming ahead of his own hurts. It is the code, perhaps, of the white hunter. The client comes first, as the ship comes first with the captain, and I suppose he would have lost face with other white hunters if a safari had had to be canceled or interrupted because of an injury to himself. He would not hear of my returning with him.

"The elephant is right here," he said on parting. "You really don't need me now, though I would very much like to be with you. Still, he's your elephant and my being absent will make him all the more yours." Having said this, he couldn't resist giving me some perfectly obvious instructions on hunting the elephant. "Study his habits," he said. "He will have a definite pattern of living—certain places he goes to at certain times. You know that yourself, for you have hunted big game before." This was a bit of a concession on Thompkins' part, taking me out of the neophyte class. It was not tact. He was incapable of tact. But it was part of the change in his attitude that had come about since I had brought down the bushbuck.

"The thing to do is to know the elephant before you kill him," he went on. "That's important. Otherwise it isn't hunting—it's just luck." That last went home with me, for I had thought of luck being a very important element of hunting, but for Thompkins the part luck played was unworthy and should be rejected. One had to rely entirely on understanding the nature, the habits and the mind of the prey. This mental conquest of the hunted before his actual killing plainly meant a great deal to Thompkins and to César too, though, to be frank, it had never occurred to me before. Oh, I admit I had spent ten days bagging a particular bear once, and in that time had come to know a great deal about him. But if he had presented himself as a clear target on the first day of the hunt, I would have killed him then and there. This, from Thompkins' point of view, would have been only slaughter.

Thompkins seemed to approach the killing of an elephant as a matador is said to approach the killing of a bull. He hunted not merely the physical life of the animal but its mind and its soul as well. It made of hunting a mystery close to religion. I wondered, as he cautioned me further against hastiness, whether Thompkins might not also be a hunter of men; whether he had not, for instance, been hunting me with the object of bringing me to bay, not at the end of a rifle, but with that question, "How long have you got?" which he had put to me over the fire and which had struck me with all the impact of a bullet.

The human mind is capable of the wildest fancies, or at least mine is, and as he collected his long figure into the driver's seat of the jeep and bent down to say a last word, thrusting that camel face forward with its huge teeth, I thought of him for a moment as a witch doctor—a shaman of hunters. Perhaps one of those who had done the lovely paintings of bison on the Cro-Magnon caves. He was gone then with a wave of his hand, and the trail of dust that he made hung lonely and diminishing over the vast grassland.

The dust stayed a long time hanging in the air, indicating that the wind had dropped. Having seen Thompkins off, we went to the lake and climbed into the dugout and crossed over to the elephant's territory, for I wanted to take advantage of the still air, which would make tracking him easier.

The crocodile was still there on the mudbank, waiting for us. He made the same three or four staggering paces toward us as the outrigger approached the end of his island and then settled down again, deciding that this was not the time. He was, of course, studying me as I was to study the elephant. If and when he ate me, I would not, I reflected, be just a chunk of raw meat that had come his way. I would be a person of whom he had some knowledge. He would have made a mental conquest of me and thus have devoured something more than food. I suppose that that might make his meal more enjoyable. When the crocodile had settled down he opened his jagged mouth and little white and gray birds started cleaning his teeth. I flicked some water in his direction with my paddle and he snapped his jaws together with a report like two boards being banged one against the other. Then he reopened them and the birds fell once more to their work. César said nothing but I sensed he thought my gesture foolish.

The elephant had, during the night, visited the area where we had beached the dugout on the previous day. He had walked all about that area, his huge footprints overlapping each other and obliterating all the evidence of our landing. He had flattened out a great deal of the tall grass nearby, questing about with his trunk, looking for us. He had been quite methodical in his search, covering the whole of the area before deciding that whoever had invaded his territory was no longer there. His spoor led eventually away from the beach into the forest. He had been in no hurry to regain the woods, but had meandered around here and there, stopping every now and then to scent the air.

The elephant knew of us then. He was extraordinarily suspicious and would be on his guard against us and watching for us. This was not entirely a comfortable thought, for lone bulls have a reputation for charging and there was plenty of cover for him.

We went on following his trail into the forest, very much on the alert, and for upwards of a mile the elephant was at no pains at all to conceal his path. Indeed, I got the impression that he was deliberately leading us on, to some place of his own choosing. Three times he stopped to scrape mud off his hide against trees, the smear of mud being plastered against the crushed vines on the bark eight feet off the ground. I am not quite six feet tall so these plasterings of mud were two feet over my head and I could just touch them by stretching up with my hand. My previous concept of elephants, obtained from pictures and zoos, was obviously quite wrong.

The elephants I had seen in zoos would be midgets compared with this fellow. He would stand, I estimated, about eleven feet at the shoulder, which was not quite twice my height. There were places where, fifteen feet from the ground—say, nine feet over my head—he had wrenched away the branch of a tree for a snack. When I saw from these signs how immense this bull was—Pétain's elephant, which was now mine unless I failed to get him, when he would become someone else's—I felt that I had stepped out of reality and was hunting some creature on another planet, for surely nothing as huge as he walked the face of earth.

He was not all dignity, however, but seemed to have a sense of fun. There was a place on a steep slope of great length that was covered with forest mold, where he had apparently sat down on his huge behind and slid to the bottom as I had done many a time myself as a boy on a muddy hill in England. Even the gods, I thought, play games, and there occurred to me a line from Shakespeare's *Troilus and Cressida*—"The elephant hath joints, but none fo. courtesy." Some for fun, however.

At the bottom of this slope was a ravine with a small river in it, and here the elephant had first of all gone upstream and then at a very obvious place, before a thicket of cassava, had changed his mind and gone down again. This was remarkable. In sliding down the hill on his behind he had been at no pains to conceal his trail. Nor indeed had he done so before. Why then, should he now become cautious—why now begin to try to shake off whoever might be following him?

You see immediately that at this point I was beginning to try to encompass and capture the mind of the elephant, as Thompkins had cautioned me to do. Thompkins the Shaman—the priest of elephant hunting. The answer that satisfied me was that the elephant had decided to test our skill as trackers. He had led us deep into his kingdom to see what kind of creatures we were, what was our physical endurance, what were our mental abilities, what was our experience, what was the extent of our determination. The contest between us was now under way, and I rejoiced and wished him well, and knew even then that if I killed him, I would mourn him as I hoped he would mourn me if he killed me—and with a mourning deeper than the mere regret of those embarrassed friends in London.

Cassava, in case you are not familiar with it, grows in thickets of tall canes—perhaps eight feet in height. From the canes grow not branches, but leaves of a medium size and with red veins, which look as if, cut, they would ooze blood. The root only is eaten and then it has to be cooked, for raw it is poisonous. Such a thicket was thrown across the river, which was very shallow at this point—and the elephant had not passed through it or even investigated it. He had plainly turned around and gone downstream, suddenly cautious, for in his previous mood he could have gone straight through the cassava, oblivious to the trail he left.

Seeing the cassava undisturbed, we turned and went back downstream, past the place where he had had his slide, and found his tracks on the other side of the river. Here he had apparently reentered the riverbed. I thought he had continued on downstream, pointing out that the cassava patch upstream, which reached across the riverbed and extended on both sides, had not been disturbed. But César gestured to a slab of white rock, quite flat and thrusting an inch or so above the surface of the water. It was dry.

"If he went downstream, he would have put his foot on that rock, and he didn't," said César.

"The footprint would have dried by now," I countered.

"There would be dead ants," said César. I examined the rock. Sure enough, there were tiny ants scurrying here and there on it (there are ants on everything in Africa), but none dead. Among the traces of the elephant are dead ants and uprooted trees, I thought. It seemed to me something that should be added to that twelfth-century bestiary with its lore about the mandragora tree and the guardian elephant that comes to the aid of those that are stricken.

We went back then to the cassava growth and found what we should have found on our previous visit. The elephant had stepped delicately through a tangle of bayonet grass, traveling along the margin between the grass and cassava in such a way that the leaves, swinging back, helped to hide the bruised grass. It was a beautiful piece of concealment and from this place the trail became more and more difficult to follow. There was no more slashing of trees or ripping off branches or plunging through thickets, but an extremely careful progression with many checks and a great deal of touring about by the elephant, so that we followed him in circles, as foolish as mice in a maze.

I had thought it would be quite easy to follow the trail of an elephant. After all, a creature that weighs several tons can scarcely tread lightly and is bound to leave a hefty impression on soft earth. So he did, leaving massive prints here and there with disdain, and then leading us into some gloomy copse where we would spend our time poking around in the mold for his prints, uncertain, when we did find them, in which direction they led. Nor was the ground about all soft and covered with the droppings of the forest. There were ridges of rock and small streams also, and he delighted in traveling these, leaving scarcely any sign at all.

By noon he had tired me out and we stopped to eat. I was hot, sticky and desperately thirsty, and Haller's London treatment seemed to have weakened me—or perhaps it was the enemy within, expanding to sap my vigor. The sweat was pouring off me, but in the moist air of the forest it would not evaporate. I had to wipe myself dry with a towel that César carried in his knapsack. I was winded and my limbs ached and I would have been quite content to call it a day at this point and go back to camp. In fact, such a languor overcame me after lunch that I had difficulty keeping my eyes open, and César said that I should rest and he would reconnoiter and come back to me after a while.

Off he went, and I, making a little couch for myself in the grass, fell asleep. I don't think I slept long, perhaps not more than fifteen minutes, and I woke from no cause other than the sense of being alone. It took a little while to recall where I was, and since César did not return, I decided to explore a little in the tangle of shrubs and trees, grasses and vines with which I was surrounded.

Somewhere I had read that tropical forests are cool and dark, like the interior of a cathedral, the tall, vine-clad trunks of the trees taking the place of stone columns and the mold of the floor representing a heavy carpeting.

This wasn't at all like that. The trees were for one thing not all of the same species. Some had spreading branches and small leaves while others had scarcely a branch on them until they had reared themselves upward for a hundred feet. The leaves of these might have been big, but at that distance they would scarcely be distinguished, and they formed billows of green blazing almost gold where the sun struck them squarely. The forest actually grew in three levels. There was the underbrush of thick grasses and big-leaved plants and some bushes, hopelessly entangled with vines. There were the higher trees with wide-spreading branches forming a second tier. And then, in clumps here and there, were the huge tall trees from whose distant tops a trapeze of liana vines sloped to the ground or to other trees lower and some distance off.

On the far side from where I had been sleeping there was a big growth of wild yam, the massive, spear-shaped leaves reaching over my head. A game path led around this and I followed it and came on the other side to a clump of bamboo, the green stems so thick that they made a living palisade through which nothing much larger than a rabbit could pass. It was quite impossible for me to go through the bamboo, and I stepped into that vast growth of wild yams with their enormous emerald leaves and their cool stalks as thick as a man's arm. The change was delightful. I was now in a green world, with a green sky above me and green air about me. It was rather like diving into a sea of light emerald and seeing all about the lovely underwater shapes, themselves green. The stalks of the yams were as smooth and translucent as jade. They had serenity and grace and I delighted in them and thought, in my entrancing green world, that Paradise itself could not equal this.

The ground of Paradise, alas, was muddy, for yams love a quagmire, and I soon found my boots had sunk well over the soles in a thick black goo. It took considerable effort to move them, and I made a great deal of noise doing so. And then when I had finally floundered, though still among the yams, to firmer ground, I heard another noise. It was no more than a rustling, a moving of those giant leaves. For a moment I thought it might be the wind until I recalled that there was no wind. Some creature was moving about among the yams, but I did not think of the elephant until I saw him. He moved aside the greater part of the leaves and stalks that lay between us and there he was, looming over me like a building. His head was noble and lofty, and the sweep of the one massive tusk I could see was a thing of tremendous power.

He stood head on to me, looking at me, and after a patient inquiry, as it were, he extended his huge trunk in my direction. It moved around, snaking in the air, and then he held it straight out toward me. I could see the black hole of his nostril, and I almost heard the sound he made as he sucked in the air and tasted it to see if it was really I that stood before him among the stems of the giant yams. I was horrified at the seeking out of me by this huge organ. He homed in on me, the end of his trunk quivering at my scent.

Then he withdrew the trunk and turned slowly away. As he did so I saw the appalling thing that had happened to him. His left eye was gone. Where it had once been there was a black, gaping horror, crawling with flies.

CHAPTER 7

I SHOULD HAVE shot and killed the elephant then, but I didn't. Thompkins probably would have done so, but I was overwhelmed by his sudden appearance, by his immense size (far greater than I had even imagined), by his terrible seeking out of me with his trunk, and by the appalling leprous horror of his blinded eye.

He turned from me, his huge ears, as big as doors, moving rather clumsily, and then the moment for killing him had gone. His back was toward me, his mountain of a back with its almost comical tail dangling down, and he moved off quickly, and I was left alone among the trampled stalks and leaves of the yams. I didn't even think of following him. I stayed there, staring, and then César found me and I explained to him all that had happened.

When I described the horror of the elephant's eye, César said immediately, "Ivory poachers," and added, shaking his head, "Bad men." The way in which he pronounced these two utterly banal words, which as I write them sound like something out of a very old Tarzan movie, gave a quality to the badness of the men that had something almost superevil about it, as if these were men who were contrary to all the nature of the world.

We set out after the elephant then, but time was against us. We followed his trail for an hour, but he was moving fast, and as the light began to fade, prudence suggested that we return to our camp and follow him on the next day. Certainly it is a foolhardy thing to hunt a wounded elephant in a forest after sunset.

On our way back across the lake the crocodile was still there, watching for us, studying the distance at which the outrigger would pass the end of the mudbank. For a moment he seemed hopeful, for he took two of his staggering steps toward us, but his heart was not really in it. He did not raise his great belly off the ground as these creatures do when they charge, but was content to slither along. Then he came again to rest and indulged his thoughts of murder as we paddled past.

We had dinner of some of the bushbuck and a can of plums from Petaluma, California, wherever that may be, and during the preparation and eating of dinner César kept clucking his tongue and shaking his head in his disgust and anger over the ivory poachers.

We of the Western world think of ivory largely in terms of billiard balls and have a comfortable feeling that most billiard balls are made of the new plastics, and so elephants are not killed to give us our pleasure. But this is only partly true. The very best billiard balls are still made of elephant ivory and from small tusks weighing perhaps seven pounds. These tusks command the highest prices and out of each of them no more than eight billiard balls can be produced. A young elephant then will provide sixteen billiard balls, of which six are of the finest quality and the others not so good, and the fondness for billiards, plus the invention of the piano, has been, to a very great degree, responsible for the thinning of the elephant herds and their confinement now to the central portions of Africa, though a century ago they roamed the whole continent from the Cape to the fringes of the northern deserts.

Ivory, however, is also the marble of the Orient. It is the delight of the artists and artisans of China and of Japan and of Malaysia and indeed of the whole East. It is readily carved, it has a slight elasticity, it will not split or chip under the carver's tools (though dramatic changes of temperature will cause it to split), and it will hold its carved shape without the slightest distortion. Thus vast tonnages of ivory find their way to the oriental markets and there is no wastage at all, for even the shavings are used in polishing, and the minute particles amounting to dust are used in the manufacture of India ink. Christian saints and Chinese dragons, cigarette holders and knife handles, ladies' bracelets, serviette rings and opium pipes—all are made of ivory, and the price is so high that the temptation to poachers is very great—and increases as elephants become harder to find.

Poachers, César insisted, had been after Pétain's elephant, which was now mine. And poachers, of course, are not bound by the game laws of French Equatorial Africa. If they wound an animal, they will kill him only if this is possible without danger to themselves. In this case César speculated that the poachers, having wounded the elephant with a round that had taken out his eye, had been discovered. They would not have admitted to wounding the elephant, which had fled, for that would be first-class evidence against them. They had paid their fine or served their sentences, leaving the elephant to stagger about blinded in the forest, awaiting death.

Clearly the elephant was doomed. It was no longer a case of my hunting and killing an elephant for pleasure or, to be more accurate, to get away from that doom that had been pronounced on me in England and which I felt still awaited me there. Now I had to kill the elephant because that was the law. He must not be allowed to escape. I was to be the sure and certain instrument of his death as that lump in the soft part of my palate was to be the sure and certain instrument of mine. It did not occur to me at this time that that lump might be obeying a law too, that it might stand in the same relationship to me as I did to the elephant. Had such a thought occurred to me, I would have rejected it as puerile. But what did occur to me was that we were both doomed, that we were both halfway out of the world, creatures with only a limited supply of tomorrows. And that thought brought with it an affection, an involvement with the elephant deeper than I have felt for any other creature on earth. There is nothing in all literature to capture the closeness I now felt for that great beast, staggering like blinded Samson about the forest, for whom all the lovely world was soon to disappear into blackness, as it would for me.

There is a comradeship of the condemned of which those uncondemned know nothing. Think for a moment of the biblical lepers and indeed of lepers until the end of the Dark Ages. They were, as soon as their infection was certified, pronounced dead.

They attended one last Requiem Mass of the Church. They heard the Offices for the Dead recited over them, they were given all the blessings and forgiveness extended to the dead, and then they were banished and forbidden the company of the living forever. They were not really dead, but they were doomed. And in the period between their ecclesiastical death and their medical death, they had only each other for company; whatever the hates and the strifes among them, they were all linked by that chain that is stronger even than life—death. So I felt toward the elephant, and though I accepted the law that said I must shoot him, I would much rather have stayed with him in the forest, following him about, a companion of his, until one or the other of us died to leave his fellow mourning.

I said nothing of this to César, who himself recognized the deep change that had now taken place in our safari. When it was just a hunting safari, I had proposed using .375 ammunition, which was adequate but not brutal. César now suggested that I put aside the lighter gun and instead take the heavier Winchester I had, which used .45-90. I will not bother you with a technical discussion of the difference between these two rifles, for you will appreciate that the heavier bullet had more penetrating power and with it I might be able to succeed with a brain shot through the massive skull of that enormous creature. Purists may insist that the .375 would have been sufficient, but decision in these cases lies in the hands of the hunter. Since I was now an executioner, I chose the heavier gun.

We sat for a long time over the fire that night talking about the elephant. César's disgust at the ivory poachers was mixed with a curious practicality that suggested to me that in certain areas he was quite insensitive. He said, for instance, that since the elephant picked for me had been wounded, I could demand another one in full health. There was indeed another bull that spent the early part of the dry season in the southern part of the highlands about two days from where we were.

He was not as big as my elephant, for he was not as old. But César knew where he was and I had a right to him if I wished to exercise it. I said that I didn't, and I think César was quite surprised, for he knew that the fees for this safari had cost me a lot of money. Nor did he particularly honor me for my refusal. I gathered that he, in my place, would have undertaken first to execute the blinded elephant and then go off and hunt another and healthy animal. But then, César was far more easy in the world than I. What code he had was not as elaborate as mine. His was the hunter's code, which insisted that the hunter had a right to hunt and that hunting was a fine occupation for men and for animals and brought the two close together in a proper relationship.

Having ascertained that I did not wish to go after another elephant, César then said, with considerable tact, that I did not have to kill the blinded elephant. If the job was anybody's, it was either Thompkins', since he was licensed as a professional white hunter, or it was a game warden's job. A wounded elephant, César emphasized, was dangerous, and as I had not inflicted the wound, I did not have to accept this additional measure of danger in killing him.

I told César that I would kill the elephant myself and that I would do this as soon as possible and not wait for Thompkins to get back from Fort Lamy. He would be a week at least and I could not abide the thought of the elephant with that terrible eye living through seven additional days of agony in the forest until Thompkins arrived. This, of course, was at variance with my desire to go to the forest unarmed and live out my days with the elephant and he with me. But recall I was talking to César and so giving him the answer that he expected from a man in my position. If we do not give these answers, as you are aware yourself, we are taken to be eccentric and perhaps unbalanced. I knew indeed that the elephant must be suffering terribly. And I knew also that alone in that forest, in his condition, it would be better if he were killed. But I felt that if I, who was also doomed, joined him, there would be a companionship that would reduce his agony. I understood only too well that it is the aloneness that makes death so terrible. If death could be shared and the aloneness thus banished, it would lose a great deal of its horror.

César considered my attitude, staring with brooding eyes and a quite comically wrinkled forehead (for he rarely worried about anything) for a short while, and then he understood. If I killed the elephant, not only would I be entitled to the ivory but I would also be entitled to a very considerable bonus offered by the French authorities for killing a wounded animal at large in the bush. He smiled without guile as he mentioned this explanation. And then he laughed in exactly the same frank and honest manner with which he had greeted my unknowing and stupendous joke about man being the master of the earth, during our first acquaintance.

I can give you only this explanation of his conclusions and his laughter. César was more "natural" than I. The world had fewer mysteries for him. Men like me (white men who arranged expensive safaris) were by their natures avaricious for trophies and for money, so it was natural that I should elect to kill the elephant and collect the bounty. This was nothing for which I was to be blamed—there was no moral value attached to the nature of man in César's view. That I should feel any compassion for the elephant never entered his head. When I had deduced this I was puzzled at his indignation over the ivory hunters, for I had thought that that indignation had been aroused over the suffering of the elephant.

This, it turned out, was not the case at all. César's indignation was aroused because these poachers were not really hunters. They were just killers. As killers only, they offended nature. They were "bad men."

That night, as I lay in my sleeping bag, I found it intriguing to ponder this definition of "bad men." Was there really, I wondered, a universal law for all creatures on earth that animals were obliged to follow (having no powers of reason or of will), but men were not? Was this universal law a law of nature, to use a term that defies definition but still conveys some sense to all but the splitters of hairs? Did nature lay down rules for the conduct of all things on earth, their birth, their growth and their dying? Did "goodness" for men consist of first establishing these rules and then obeying them scrupulously? And did "badness" consist of interfering with these rules or setting them at nothing?

Not very deep thinking, as you see, but I plunged on. Supposing that this was the case, and the "goodness" of a tree, for instance, consisted of its putting out its leaves at the appointed time and bearing fruit in the right season (I suddenly remembered the fig tree that had not, and that had been cursed and caused to die in what had seemed to me a fit of pure spite) . . . if this was the case, what now was the position of man, who is given or has developed both reason and free will?

Well, he had the choice between "goodness" and "badness." But hadn't he also more than that? With all that science had placed at his disposal, hadn't he reached the point where he could decide for himself what was "goodness" and what was "badness"? With his multiplication of all kinds of fruit flies and of plants he was approaching mastery of evolution in other species and even mastery of evolution in his own. Would not "goodness" then be what man decided was good, in his own human wisdom? Or was there still that other law— César's and Thompkins' Something, maybe—with which man's definition of good must accord, or man would be placed in terrible peril?

I would have gone on from there, but I didn't. I fell asleep, my last efforts at ethical reflection being a fleeting recollection of Thompkins with his long camel face expounding on the game laws of French Equatorial Africa.

CHAPTER 8

THE NEXT DAY the wind came up and came up hard. It began to rise during the night, so that the walls of the tent flapped like a flag and I had to stumble out into the darkness with César and tighten the guy lines. The wind had turned around completely. Previously it had blown from the highlands and the forest out over the grasslands. Now it blew from the grasslands toward the highlands. It rose fretfully at first, as if it had sent ahead outriders to report on the territory. There would be a sudden gust under which the tent would strain like a sail, and then calm and then another gust from a slightly different direction. But by dawn the wind was with us steadily, strong and increasing in strength, and César said it would blow for four days or maybe five. It was a wind peculiar to the dry season and until it died down there was nothing we could do but remain in camp. To go after the elephant was impossible. We could not cross the lake in the dugout, which would be swamped, and if we weren't drowned, the crocodile would get us.

I did not altogether believe this, for the English (and Americans as well, I suppose) are brought up to doubt the word, the judgment and the experience of people who are foreign to themselves. Although I respected César, I had the feeling that he and his people lacked real daring. So after breakfast I went down to look at the lake, lashed by that thundering wind and choking with dust. It was an utterly foolish thing to do, but I did it, and I found that, as César had said, the lake was impassable. The waves on it were remarkable. They rose out of that kerosene-colored water three or four feet high, and crested as they went, a pattern of lacy spume flying over them such as one sees in the Channel in a rising gale.

The wind gave to the water an appearance of hardness as if it were covered with a casing of metal. It had a wicked look, and beyond the borders of the lake the forest writhed and lashed here and there, trees swaying and bending and rearing back from the gale, and the ends of vines whipping about in the air like dark threads.

I could hear branches being torn off with the splintering sound that accompanies the crushing of matchboxes. The furious motion of the forest, normally a silent and stationary presence, was frightening. I felt as if some powerful malevolence were abroad in the world and that the world might not survive this fury but gradually be stripped of all its living envelope and reduced to wind-blasted rocks and streaming piles of sand.

Such a wind as this I had experienced only once before—in the spring on the west coast of Ireland. Then it was a westerly wind, straight off the Atlantic, and it blew with glitter and steadiness for a solid week. I say "glitter" because all the time the wind blew, the sun was out, and stone walls and the upper sides of the stricken grass and the waving frantic branches of the trees all glittered in the sunlight, which nonetheless was quite without warmth. At the end of the week, the windward side of all the trees was brown, as in deep autumn, for the wind had dried out all the moisture in the leaves.

This African wind brought with it dust. It turned the whole surface of the earth into a streaming, writhing fabric, and the dust rose to a great height so that the sun lost its edge. It was only the ghost of the sun, brightening and diminishing in the dust clouds.

I had had the wind at my back in going down to the lake, which was but a quarter of a mile away. But returning, I faced it and had to put my hand over my mouth to stop my throat and lungs from filling with the fine golden powder. This wind, César said, was a great killer of game. The animals quickly became exhausted in it and some of them took leave of their senses, dashed panic-stricken downwind, hoping to run away from it, and so died. I think they died of something more than physical discomfort. I think they died of anxiety, for all the secure, normal sights and sounds of the world had been swept away by the wind and everything was strange and threatening. In my own little walk back from the lake I felt, caught in that motion of air and of earth, that I would sink into the ground, and was dizzy and disoriented. When I reached it I sat in the lee of the tent for some time before I could gain control of my senses and of my brain and think with any degree of calm. The wind seemed to blow away my reason.

There was nothing to do in this gale, it seemed, but wait for it to end. I could not even occupy myself with dismantling and cleaning my rifles—not that they needed this. The dust would have got into the mechanism and ruined them. I lay on my camp cot and at times talked to César and at times read from the two books I had brought with me. But every now and then in the midst of a conversation with César or of a passage in one of my books, the elephant, with his leprous eye, would intrude, reaching his long probing trunk toward me. He was my comrade in doom and I knew he needed me. Time and again I went over that encounter I had had with him among the yams. I recalled how he had come so close that I could see the black hole of his nostril in the end of his trunk. Surely he had known that I was there. It was impossible that he should not have picked up my scent. But instead of seizing me and dashing me to the ground or tossing me into the air, he had merely turned and gone away. Why?

César was of the opinion that the elephant had not surely scented me, but had suspected that there was some creature before him and, recalling the poachers and the terrible extinguishing of his eye when they fired, had taken fright in his uncertainty and run off. He pointed out that in the yam patch not only was there no movement of the air to carry my scent strongly to him, but also the strong, sappy smell of the crushed stalks and leaves of the yams would have overlain my own scent. Furthermore, the elephant was in pain and his senses disoriented.

That was all very sensible, and for two days I tried to be satisfied with César's view. But as that gale continued to blow and the elephant appeared more and more to me, I grew increasingly disturbed. I kept thinking of him out there in that gale-lashed forest, in a world that had gone insane, with his eye crawling with flies. It seemed more and more that he wanted me to help him; and that if I did not help him, then I would fail in a very important trust. Not only would I have failed him but I would also have failed all creation; I would have severed an essential link uniting all living creatures, and the betrayal entailed in this would spell the doom of all.

It is curious how the mind works. Reason leads us plodding and hopefully in what seems the right direction and then bogs down or takes a different road, and then some kind of voice tells us that reason is wrong. For a moment we get a glimpse of a vaster and deeper picture than ever reason could produce; a picture that embraces all things in proper proportion. It is gone in a moment, of course, and reason starts to efface even its memory. But for the moment we glimpse that picture, we know it to be true beyond all truth; to be the very source and font of truth. It is, to use another simile, like a tiny light flashed in the great heavy darkness of the sea and seen for but a moment, announcing another dimension. And then it is gone and reason tells us that it was not there and that we saw it only because we hoped to see it and it was all an illusion.

So it was with the elephant. Reason told me that in the condition of the wind and the lake and the tossing of the forest, I could not do what I was required to do, which was to shoot him. But the elephant kept haunting me with his outstretched trunk, ignoring wind and waves and breaking branches; pleading for me to come. For one moment I felt that here was a plea that I could not ignore.

On the third day of the wind, when it had not lessened in the slightest, I told César that I was going to cross the lake to find the elephant. I told him this right after breakfast, and I did not wait for him to reply but took up that heavy Winchester, which was

already loaded with the .45-90 ammunition, and set out. I didn't really expect César to come with me, but he did. Maybe he sensed also that there are some cries that cannot be disregarded, to which the response may not be delayed for mere reason. He stopped long enough only to bring a saucepan with him, which I thought ridiculous until he started using it to bail out the dugout.

César set me in the back of the dugout with my rifle slung high on my back by the strap and told me to steer. He bailed, and no paddling was needed. César bailed with an endurance and a tenacity of which only human beings are capable. Animals would give up in half the time. I saw nothing of him all the way across the lake but his bulging bush shirt, ballooned up by the wind, rising and falling as he raised and lowered his torso, and the bright flash of water that burst time and again from his hand as he flung the contents of the saucepan over the side, where they were immediately turned to spray. He bailed without ceasing, without taking a breath, without stopping to look to the right or the left or even in front of him. He put more energy into that bailing than I put into my physical living in a month, and even so we were three times swamped as, with a roar like a load of gravel being dumped from a truck, a wave rose behind us, crested and swept the dugout from end to end.

In all this fury of air and water I almost forgot about the crocodile. I remembered him when through the scud I saw that low mudbank of his, of which only the very surface was above the waves, the rest being awash with foam. I thought he must certainly have gone to some terrible mudhole of his on the lake bottom. But no. There he was, lying in what little lee there was to his island, watching us. But he took no step toward us as we shot by, jouncing through the waves

and driven before the wind. A third of the way across the lake I discovered something interesting about the dugout. If by paddling I could get it going a little faster and if by good luck I happened to have the right angle, it would catch on the back of a wave and lance forward at remarkable speed until finally the wave passed beneath it. But I did not always catch the wave right and, as I have said, we were three times swamped before we got to the other side.

The tall reeds and grasses that lined the lake's edge were flattened to matting, and we drove down on the land so hard that I was tumbled from my seat in the dugout and thrown on top of César, who himself had not moved fast enough to get out. Indeed the dugout drove right up on the shore and broke one of the outriggers. We paid no attention to that but struggled over the flattened matting of reeds to the writhing wall of the forest, with its tossing, tortured boughs and flailing vines, and thrust inside it. We had gone a third of a mile before the wind diminished.

Even so, though on the forest floor there now blew nothing but an erratic breeze, the sensation was like being inside some kind of tent or envelope that a great beast was trying to break into. Overhead the tops of the trees swayed and twisted and there was a continuing patter of twigs and leaves and pieces of vine falling from above to the floor below. The stout trunks of the mahogany trees reeled back and forth as if the trees had gone mad and wanted to pull themselves out of the ground and run in a herd across the earth. Great vine-clad trunks, four feet and more in thickness, reeled about like saplings and there was a tremendous clashing of branches overhead. Every now and then there was a vast tearing sound as some branch was twisted free of its trunk and fell to the ground.

In this raging world we set out to find the elephant, itself more stricken than the forest around us.

CHAPTER 9

CÉSAR, THOMPKINS had told me, was the best tracker in that part of French Equatorial Africa, but in the present shambles and confusion of that forest his skill was of little use. You will understand, of course, that the whole art of tracking rests on the premise that things should be undisturbed or disturbed in a predictable manner after the prey has passed by.

There was nothing in that whole forest that was not being violently and unpredictably disturbed every moment by the gale that seethed and roared over our heads. César did his best and he did find a place where the elephant had passed through a devastated copse of tree ferns and some bamboo. But I soon began to realize that if we found the elephant at all, it would be largely a matter of happenstance. We would just stumble upon him, as he himself stumbled about in that stricken forest.

It is a long time since I read *Paradise Lost*, but I seem to recall somewhere in it a description of hell that is given in terms of noise—noise everywhere; noises above, below and on all sides; noise from which there is no rest or even a moment's surcease.

This was the condition inside the forest.

The noise of the wind, because of the resistance of the trees and the tremendous crashing together of their branches overhead, was far greater in the interior of the forest than outside on the grasslands. I cannot describe to you the fury of those branches clashing together, at times with a sound like huge castanets, and at others with a deep groan breaking through the hiss and boom and whistle of the wind. When we came to a more open place it was to walk into a leaf storm—a pelting of leaves from the treetops to the ground or, more properly, across the clearing almost parallel with the ground, to crash into the stricken, swaying trees on the other side. And in the forest groves there was the furious sound, above and about, which made conversation a matter of shouting or of gesticulation.

The floor of the forest was by no means even. It consisted of a series of ridges, which were perhaps the exposed roots of the great highlands lying beyond the cliffs. When we were in the valleys between these ridges we were in an island of comparative calm, for even the trees thrusting up from these valleys were deprived of fifteen or twenty feet of growth and so did not meet the full fury of the wind overhead.

It needed no great hunting instinct to decide that the elephant would likely be found in one of these quieter valleys and that our best chance of finding him would be to search them one by one for signs of his passing. It is curious that while I had thought of the elephant

as waiting for me and begging me to come to him with his outstretched trunk, it did not occur to me that he might also be looking
for me—that just as I was staggering about seeking him, so also he
might be staggering about seeking me.

I sought for him in the yam patch, and up the river valley where
we had first encountered him, and deep in the forest and up several
valleys where there was comparative calm; and it was midafternoon
before it occurred to me that if he were really waiting for me to come,
he might be near the area where we had landed our dugout.

So we struck out toward that area, and while still within the forest
we came upon him. I was climbing up a ridge separating one of those
valleys from the other when I saw him. In fact, he came to meet me,
for he was climbing up the other side and he halted on the top of the
ridge facing me. He stood there—enormous in the raging forest—
and we two who were doomed faced each other in the great gladiato-
rial ring of the world.

He took a step forward and reached out his trunk toward me with
that questing motion that was a salute, a recognition, and almost a
gesture of friendship. He was so big that he seemed to diminish the
trees. All my mind had room for was this creature of power and
dignity and grace. I could not see the ruined eye, for he was head on
to me, his trunk reaching out. He advanced another step, his huge
ears moving forward, his trunk still extended so that there was no
question that he knew I was there. Then he stopped. He lowered his
trunk and stood quite still. There was only the slightest movement of
those huge ears as I took the safety catch off the big Winchester. I
brought the gun up to my shoulder slowly and fired. He went down
in a moment, jerking a little from me and tumbling over in a tremendous heap on his side. He was dead instantly, snatched out of the
world between one second and the next.

I cannot describe the terrible sense of loss I felt when he was gone.
I went to him and when I reached him the tears burst from me as
from a child.

ALL THIS HAPPENED six months or so ago. I have written the whole
account while in the hospital back in London, undergoing the
various tests essential to an operation that Haller says has a fifty-
fifty chance of success. You are surprised? Well, so was I. Haller

called on me as soon as I got back from Africa, on a dismal March day, wearing that same yellow scarf that has become almost a badge of his. He was excited and doing his very best to appear calm. He said I looked fit and didn't listen to a thing I told him about Africa in his anxiety to tell me his news. But he did wait until I had given him a cup of tea, and then he announced that a technique had been developed in America with which to operate on my condition. He said it had an excellent chance for success, but when I pressed him for a mathematical definition of "excellent," he said, "Fifty-fifty," which of course isn't excellent at all. But from his point of view it was, because it meant that out of one hundred people doomed to die of the condition from which I suffered, fifty could be saved.

It is strange, but I received this news of a reprieve almost with distaste. No, I hadn't become accustomed to being condemned to death, but I had, to a degree, adjusted my spiritual muscles, or whatever it is that makes a man different from an animal, to carrying the load. They groaned under it. They broke down under it. But somehow they carried it. The breakdowns, however, were unpredictable. Would you believe, for instance, that on the plane back from Africa, thinking of Thompkins, the shaman of elephant hunters, bidding me good-bye at the airport, I broke into tears at the stark realization that I would never see that camel face of his again? A hunt is like a life. It doesn't last very long—neither does life itself. But it has the depth of a lifetime, and we had hunted together, Thompkins and I. (It is only in putting that down now that I have realized that the reverse is true, and life itself is a hunt. But what is the quarry?)

Haller, over his cup of tea, gave me the details of this technique and the news that there was one doctor at St. Bartholomew's who was trained in it. He would operate. I had only to agree. And for a while I resented this prospect of reprieve—it wasn't reprieve itself—this removal of certainty, to have put in its place, uncertainty. It was actually in my mind to refuse the operation. But there was Haller, his pudding-white face, which I noticed for the first time had the lines of middle age, shining with hope like a boy's. He was so happy that I had to make a joke to restore his equilibrium. I told him that I would undergo the operation on one condition, which was that if it proved successful, he would undertake to finish that wretched novel of mine that after twenty chapters contained not one singing word.

And so, I have been lying in this hospital, undergoing these tests and doing a lot of thinking. Take that remark of Thompkins to the effect that we see only what we expect to see. He made it, you will remember, in connection with the little herd of elephants that had been able to disappear in the grove of acacia. I thought it a remarkable finding of his at the time, proved by the fact that I had been looking for an elephant shape and so could not see, plainly before me, an acacia-elephant shape. And then, lying here in the hospital, I suddenly realized how old was that saying of Thompkins. It was first given to us, in different words, two thousand years ago—"All is in the eye of the beholder."

My eye, for some time, had been self-centered and I could see no shape that was not in the shape of myself and my own death. All things turned into that shape: all my friends, the whole of London and in fact the whole of England. But after Thompkins' remark and my African experience, I began to see other shapes—the shape of Haller's kindness and concern, and the kindness of my friends who were not really hustling me off the earth, but wishing very much that I could stay here and share it with them. It is not too much to say, I think, that I recognized for the first time the shape of love. And it was only then that I realized how very cold I had been and for how very long. I thought of other things, too, out of which, after a while, some meaning began to seep like sap out of the cut bark of a tree.

Take the bestiary, for instance, and the description given in it of the elephant. In the case of that great elephant that was Pétain's and then mine, was I not in truth the smaller elephant that came to the aid of the big one when he cried out for help? And did I not lift him up out of his misery? I fancy this is so. In fact, I cannot see it any other way. At first, I admit, thinking back on that elephant and how a rising of the Riff and then an American steel strike and then an eclipse of the moon had each saved him, that I was horrified that all this should have taken place only for him to be mutilated by ivory poachers. But then I remembered the bestiary and how the elephant had cried out to me in that terrible wind and how I had gone to him and helped him. And now how about me? Do I not cry out? And will not someone come and lift me up in my great need?

Then there is Thompkins and his devotion to the game laws of

French Equatorial Africa, designed, he maintained, for the improvement of man. So they are, of course, teaching man compassion—even in killing; teaching him that when he has hurt another creature he must forfeit his own life rather than let that creature live in agony. That much is rather obvious, though it is amusing and enlightening to reflect that the game laws of French Equatorial Africa find their source in the Christian Testament, and so may be thought of as an extension of the Bible.

Thompkins' mystique of hunting puzzled me for a long time until I realized what he was hunting, which was not deer and lions and elephants at all. And then it was all quite clear to me, and I began to understand that Something with which he and César communicated, to my intense annoyance in the early days of our acquaintance.

To conclude the physical account of my story, I didn't kill the crocodile, though I had intended to. We were compelled by the wind to remain on the forest side of the lake for two days. Then, when we returned, I thought about the crocodile and was ready for him. I actually had him in the sights of the Winchester when I changed my mind. To be sure, there was nothing in the bestiary concerning the killing of crocodiles, but I remembered Thompkins' words about the game laws being designed for the improvement of man. I couldn't see that man would be improved by the crocodile's death, and so I left him. Hunting must never be murder—murder defiles man. Was it not the first of our crimes—Cain's murder of Abel?

And about death itself. Is death, then, a hunter too—not merely a killer, a murderer? Does death study the nature of the prey, tracking him down, watching his habits of body and of mind and of spirit, until he is thoroughly understood and absorbed, and does death, only then, take aim? Is death Thompkins' Something—a purpose, and not an end? Had I been looking at death wrongly and mistaking the shape of it, not seeing that it might be a beginning and not a conclusion?

I am to stop now. They are gathering around the bed to take me to the operating theater. I am afraid, and like the stricken elephant I cry out, hoping as I approach that dark door through which I must go alone that there will be another there on the other side to lift me up in my great need.

I . . .

CHAPTER 10

THE WRITER of the foregoing account fell into a coma during the operation, from which he did not recover, and died four hours later. He left some remarkable directions in his will, which were carried out faithfully by his friends.

At his request his body was shipped to Africa and buried in the grasslands close to the forest in which he had killed the elephant. The tusks of the elephant were laid on each side of him, and the body was powdered with red ocher. He said that this was the custom among Cro-Magnon men and that it was an expression of faith on their part—the red coloring symbolizing their belief in the continuance of life. He said they were great artists and hunters. As artists they knew the truth, and as hunters they understood the mystery of hunting, which is a search not for death but for life.

His friends find the world diminished now that he is gone.

PHILLIP HALLER, M.D.

THE SAINTMAKER'S
CHRISTMAS EVE

The Saintmaker's
Christmas Eve

by Paul Horgan
ILLUSTRATED BY ROBERT QUACKENBUSH

Despite the hardships life had thrust
upon him, Roberto Castillo was sustained by two things.
One was his abiding faith and trust in God.
The other was his skill at crafting wood and
plaster saints to adorn the Spanish missions in what
later became the New Mexico Territory of
the American Southwest.

Thus, on Christmas Eve in the year 1809,
Roberto set out on his burro to deliver a statue of
Saint Christopher holding the Christ Child to
the tiny mountain village of San Cristóbal. But as
sunset approached the snow began to fall and,
lost and freezing, Roberto realized that
only a miracle could save him. . . .

"Beautifully told in strong, simple prose that
has a desert clarity about it."

The New York Times

CHAPTER 1

To a northern village of the Rio Grande in the royal Spanish kingdom of New Mexico, Roberto Castillo came home on December 30, 1809, bringing his invoice, and accompanied by Governor, his burro, whose pack was empty.

Awaiting him in the swept yard of their small earthen house was his younger brother, Carlos Castillo, who, though his eagerness to hear all the news was so great that it made his bones dance within him, now lounged against the faded blue wooden door case to give a picture of indifference. Roberto saw him from a distance but for his part made no sign. The brothers lived in an intimacy so habitual and so intuitive that only by preserving a certain formality, even an outer coldness, could they work together at their trade in harmony.

Ever since their boyhood in this same village, whose little houses like boxes of earth clung in squares to the ditch sides that ran from the river, the brothers had made their living as saintmakers.

They learned their craft from a strange Franciscan missionary who appeared one day riding a horse and announcing that he would stay a fortnight to fulfill the spiritual needs of the villagers. He was an irritable man. Everyone feared him, not knowing that what irritated him most of all was his own weakness when there was so much to be done with so few resources in the beautiful and impoverished valley of the Rio Grande. He was at his best with children and old people, for in the one he saw beginnings, and in the other, endings, both of which were closer to God, the source and the goal, and less trying than middles, when people thought they knew what they wanted. He stormed at the congregation in their crumbling chapel for not having kept up the church, in which there was not a single statue or holy object. What were they thinking of? Did they need nothing in their lives to venerate, so that their attention might be translated to the saints and the powers that could help?

The villagers wondered if he knew that over a hundred years ago all sacred figures were violated and burned when the Pueblo Indians arose in revolt; since then no saints had come from Spain, or even from Mexico, to this little northern town. They could hardly answer the missioner in church, but they said in their thoughts, Where would we get any statues? We have no money to buy them—we have never had any money, or anything else except what we grow and fashion for ourselves.

The preacher saw some such miserable facts in their faces and said in his grating voice, "Very well, suppose you have no money to buy statues, or even to give to me for my poor families among the Indians. What is wrong with taking off your shirts and going to work and making some statues yourselves?"

From his cadaverous height he glared at them with the red eyes of a hawk. They humbled themselves for their lack of talent and ambition. If they loved Saint Francis enough (he was their village patron), they felt that long ago they would have hacked out his image, however crudely, to do him honor. Seeing them crestfallen before him, the Franciscan had a pang, which he concealed.

How can I, he asked himself, with my shortcomings, sneer at theirs? Therefore he said aloud, yet somehow in spite of himself making it sound like an insult, "Very well, I will remain here a few extra days, which I will spend in making a statue to stand in this church."

He finished by asking for volunteers to help him; and later was almost struck with joy to see the adolescent Castillo brothers, who were clever with their hands, come around after Mass and report to him.

"*Chamacos,*" he remarked sandily, "brats," but he knew that here lay hope, as in all the young; and shutting his mouth to conceal his gratification, he set to work with the brothers.

CHAPTER 2

HE SHOWED THEM all the steps of making a saint, many of which were humble. From the cottonwood grove they took up dried limbs that had fallen from age. The missioner turned the branches critically this way and that, harshly asking questions the while.

"What does this look like?"

"An arm."

"And this?"

Silence.

"What donkeys! Don't you see Raphael the Archangel and his fish here in this bent twig?"

"Oh, yes—now."

"Learn to see what is already there before you cut up a lot of fine wood and waste it. Is this piece good enough to use?"

"Don't know, Father."

"Don't know! Did you feel it? Is it dry?"

"No. It's not dry."

"Then you don't dare to use it. Come on."

He led them back to their house, where they stripped bark off their chosen logs and dried them further by the fire overnight. In the morning, he had the boys carry the wood out in back of the house under the shade of a tree, where there would be no one about to bother them; and with an excitement that they felt, he selected a cottonwood log, turned it before him several times and said, "I must find the best for the front."

As he turned it again, Roberto put out his hand, pointed and said, "There, Father. That is the front."

"Oh, you think so, do you?" said the visitor, but with inner delight, for the boy was correct. "Very well, it will be your fault if this turns out to look more like a back."

He took up a little iron saw and cut into the log a collar that would be taken away to suggest where the neck supported the head and widened to the shoulders. He stripped down the back of the log to thin it to the flatness of a body. The log was only as wide as the shoulders.

"Don't ask where the arms are," said the sculptor. "You will see."

When the time came he carved separate arms and held them up to their sockets. The blind and hacked figure assumed a gesture. Life was being made here. Entranced, the boys stared at the missioner as if he had magic. With a grudging laugh he laid down the arms and went on to carve something else.

"This is to be Saint Francis of Assisi, of course," he said, "who is my dear father. We shall show him holding a cross in one hand, a skull in the other." He scrabbled about among small bits of cottonwood fallen to the ground from the work of carving and found a piece that suited his purpose. He worked on it for a while, and then held up a tiny skull. "How do you like this?" he asked. The answers of the brothers suggested the differences in their characters.

"It is wonderful, the way it looks when you hold it to make the eyes so dark, just like a real one," said Roberto, longing to touch the skull but hardly daring to. The Franciscan looked at him and saw an imagination.

"*Bu-hu-hu,*" shivered Carlos comically, "a skull, it turns me cold," betraying to the Franciscan an innocent view of the world that looked back to what people had always said, and made no discoveries for itself.

This contrast in the makeup of the brothers was further illustrated for their instructor. He saw that each took interest in different details of the work they watched. Roberto could not conceal his excitement at the process of selection, design, the carving and enlivening of the wood; while Carlos barely paid attention, but jiggled his mind and his muscles in abstraction.

But when it came time to study the tasks of measuring, mixing, stewing and transforming raw materials into usable substances, Carlos grew hot-cheeked and absorbed, watching, while Roberto had to work to pay attention.

Their instructor took them up the valley to a gypsum ledge overhanging the river and made them cut out a sackful of whiting, which they brought home and stewed up in a pot till they had cream. Carlos stirred the brew, hoping Roberto would not ask to do it. In the corral the missioner poked about till he found remnants of hide and old horn and hoof. These he cooked out-of-doors, where their stench could go free, and showed the boys how to make glue, and then how to mix it with the rich white of the gypsum wash.

"Why?" he asked. Why did they go to all this trouble, with careful measuring and fearful stinks?

"To make it all finer," said Roberto.

"To make the plaster stick on," said Carlos.

"Both!" he snapped. And then showed them how to make a brush with yucca fibers bound tightly to a stick, and set it to soak till it was as pliant as a beaver tail. With this brush he then took up the gypsum soup and approached the statue, whose parts were now assembled. When the white creamy flow went over the wood, there was a sudden transformation from something raw to something refined. In the attention of the brothers, the missioner felt again their qualities that completed one another, and he had to hold his breath lest he believe what he knew: the brothers were fashioned by God to constitute, between them, that which it took to make a work of faith, which was the same thing as saying a work of art. Roberto had the eye, the swift and careful hand, to see what lay hidden in a stick of wood and to carve it free; while Carlos had the patient and musing joy to work by measure, like an apothecary, and never by the flash of certainty that comes from nowhere.

The reverend missioner in all his life had lost himself absolutely in prayer only a very few times. He had begged for the grace of it constantly, but without reward. Yet if only once in his life, and that briefly, he had felt complete identity with God, that would have been enough to confirm his calling and justify whatever humility he could practice.

Now in teaching the Castillo brothers he had a glimpse of the same kind of pure affirmation that dwelt beyond his powers to sustain; and in the perfect meeting in this river village of the need, the workers, the talents and the materials, he saw completed by the passing on of his own knowledge a design whose meaning brought him delight.

He scowled at the boys, in their thick caps of glossy black hair, and read the awed admiration in their shining black eyes, and saw their hot mouths open with hunger for more learning. They were two years apart in age. A few years from now they would be men. Already they had silky shadows of mustaches on their upper lips, and knew how to farm, hunt and travel.

What would be their future? The missioner knew what he wished for, but he must dismiss it abruptly, to save himself disappointment if after all the brothers fell back among their own people, content never to do more than query the weather, scratch the soil, fight off Apaches, mock the government at Santa Fe even while paying it reverence, and grow heavy in the soul.

"Look at that!" said the brothers, peering closely at the now completely whitened statue.

"We're not done, by a long shot," said their teacher. "If you think *that* looks right as it is, you don't know very much. What's it need?"

"Color," said Roberto.

"Color, color, who has any color," rasped the missioner, turning to Carlos. "Do you know how to make color?"

"No, Father."

"Well, the Indians know how. Are they that much better than you? Come on."

He took them to the farmyard and the riverside and even the foothills that lay back and above the river, and found what would yield color. He got his black out of charcoal. From different bands of clay exposed in an arroyo below the foothills, he took red, yellow and orange. Out of blue beans, cooked and pressed, he took a pale grayish blue. If there was time for a journey, he said, they could go to the mines far to the southwest and bring back copper ore, from which a brilliant green-blue could be had. Meanwhile, they would do with what was here, and obtain through mixing what they had not found in nature.

Between smooth stones the colors were ground, until there were handsome little piles of each to be put into little Indian dishes. The Franciscan was not above a taste for small dramas, based mostly upon surprise.

"You keep domestic fowl, of course?" he asked.

"Yes, Father."

"They shall now do their part in our work."

Chickens? How ridiculous, thought the brothers, and the missioner observed their incredulity, which was just what he hoped for, and said with a flare of his red-rimmed eyes, "Go bring me a handful of nice clean chicken feathers and an egg."

Wondering, they did as he ordered. He dipped the feathers in water till they were soft, and showed how here he had fine brushes to draw with.

"And the egg?" they asked.

"An egg is a mysterious affair," he replied.

He threw back his voluminous and ragged sleeves and took up the egg. He delicately broke it and separated the yolk from the white into two shallow clay vessels. Then on a clean stone palette he mixed his powdered color with the egg yolk, and had his paint. The first thing he mixed was a rich brown, out of charcoal, red clay, blue bean and a touch of yellow. His hand shook a little as he approached the pure gypsum surface with his heavied little chicken feather. The brothers observed this.

He must be getting old, thought Carlos.

He loves to do this, thought Roberto warmly.

The brown paint flowed on beautifully, making the Franciscan robe on the statue. After its first trembling, the painter's touch was sure. He took care of the edges first, leaving much creamy white to be covered.

Suddenly on an intuition, he handed the feather, newly loaded, to Roberto.

The boy took it, and with something choking him, he made his first touch upon a work of art, and though it took only a second to happen, a new boy, a new man, was created in him. Watching him, the missioner knew what he had wrought and gave thanks.

Saint Francis was represented in his robe, which was easier to make than legs, as the sculptor pointed out. The robe was now covered in brown. The head was still all white, also the hands, one of which held the skull, the other a cross. He was about a foot high, and already stood on a squared block of wood. In his face his nose protruded like a fish's fin, and his jaw was long and sharp—too long, Roberto believed. Nobody had a chin as long as that. A face should look like somebody, he felt. This one never would.

THE SAINTMAKER'S CHRISTMAS EVE

But he was wrong. The missioner rinsed and licked his feather till he had a fine point, and then he took up pure black and painted the saint's tonsure on the smooth white dome. Squinting as if to project upon the blind plaster face the memory of features he had known somewhere, he then carefully drew two heavy arched eyebrows that seemed both to frown in pain and rise in doubt. He then drew upper and lower eyelids, just the line of the lashes, and then scrubbed into the centers of the whites two large, intense pupils that stared more or less at the skull in the left hand.

"Mary most holy!" exclaimed Roberto softly. The saint was already human—and that was the whole purpose of the venture. His nose was now a nose.

"Yes, yes, don't say anything yet; we are not done," said the missioner, and took up more black, with which he painted the line of Saint Francis' beard down the long jaw, taking in what Roberto in his impatience and ignorance had thought was to be all chin.

"You see?" asked the teacher. "If you mean to paint a beard, you must have some place to *put* the paint. So I carved it. You must always plan *two* steps ahead, at least."

Roberto was glad he had not spoken out about the overlong chin, which was now a glossy beard. In another moment, there was a black mustache curving across the lip and meeting the beard just under the wooden cheekbones.

"Now," sighed the painter, rinsing and taking up red on his brush, "the really deciding expression," and leaned forward to paint the mouth. He pursed his own, and what he painted was thus also somewhat pursed. There was now a complete character arrested in the carved, plastered and painted wood. The brothers sat back on their heels and gave every effect of applauding without actually doing so. The figure was the more amazing because it looked like someone they knew or had seen. Who was it?

Soon the last details were colored—a little blur of red on the cheeks, which made a hectic glow come into the expression; an ivory cast over the skull held by the saint; a pale earth color on the hands that knew work; more shining black for the cross; and around the waist of the brown robe, the coarse white rope cincture of the Brothers of Saint Francis.

Now, for the first time, the people of the village were permitted to see the figure. It was carried in solemn procession to the church, and there installed as the tutelary saint of the little settlement. Everyone was grateful. All venerated the statue. Standing beside it, the missioner preached his farewell sermon, full of worthy admonitions, which he delivered gracelessly.

Hardly listening, but gazing at him with half-closed eyes and his head on one side, Roberto suddenly saw that in all its stiffness, its glaring eyes, its cheeks, its gaunt beard, its long robe, the statue, though not intended to be, was a self-portrait. Nobody else saw the likeness. In the eyes of everyone else there stood in the little clay chapel of Saint Francis only a painted figure wearing a look of surprise and misery, such as you might see on any farmer in any dry year. Roberto was moved by his discovery. His heart came into his mouth to think that here was how you fashioned something to look like someone real. His head turned a little dizzy for a moment when he considered that now all the saints—for him, at any rate—were as near and as real as people who walked all about him in daily life.

Completing his sermon, the missioner gave his blessing with a sprawling gesture that hardly made a cross in the air, and left the church. Leaving it, and its people, he was engulfed by a sense of loss. If his home was on high, he yet felt the pull of his fellow beings, and when his work was done he always left them with a sense of desolation. He bit till his jaws were lumpy, mounted his horse and rode away toward Santa Fe. Nobody knew his name, but he left behind him his own likeness—sharp-featured, fever-eyed, fixed in meditation upon man's dead skull.

He left also enough of his craft to serve the Castillo brothers all their lives. These two gifts together were important to Roberto especially. For years he would go back to the chapel to recover in the presence of the image all the first excitement, the power of vocation, that he had felt under the eye of the traveling Franciscan, his teacher.

CHAPTER 3

FOR THE CASTILLOS went on making saints.

The products of the first few years were similar to drawings by children—solemnly out of proportion, hilarious in their abandon, and close to some secret of art that would be lost with maturity. But the more they made, the better the brothers refined their images, and the more confident became the carving of wood, the plastering of surfaces and the painting of features and attributes. A new statue would be added now and then to Saint Francis in the church. From time to time neighbors would come and speak of a decision arrived at through long hours of thought, which was to have a saint of their own to keep in the house. Would the brothers make it for them? Presently someone said the boys should sell their works, only the pity of it was, nobody had any money to pay for them, around here at any rate. Perhaps in Santa Fe, the capital, or in river cities like Bernalillo, Albuquerque, Tomé, Socorro? True, those were far away, and travel was dangerous without an escort of soldiers from the Flying Company of the Santa Fe garrison to repel the Apache if they should strike. As the saying went, only a Franciscan or a fool took to the roads alone.

But the brothers were young and venturesome. They went out one spring to try their luck with a pack of six saints. They were gone for many weeks, but when they came back, their goods were all sold, and they were bringing an unbelievable surprise for their father and mother. This was a little soft buckskin bag heavy with coins—real money, silver royals, such as passed only in the most important commerce in the great cities of Albuquerque, El Paso and Chihuahua.

They felt like men.

They came home to hard news that made them men when they heard it.

In their absence, the Apache of the Mescalero tribe had come, slender and clever like foxes, along the far side of the mountains, and passing through canyons at night, had struck the village early one morning. They were after food and clothing, which they took,

along with many lives. The Castillo
parents were among those killed and
dragged away behind horses by the
Indians until lost and left.

A committee of village men went to
Santa Fe to mourn bitterly before the
governor that such a worthy settlement, living at peace, raising children
and adoring God, could receive no
protection against the terrible enemy
who was such a wild beast with such
crafty human ways.

The governor was unable to promise any help, but mentioned the distance between the Rio Grande and the

King of Spain, and the fact that the governor's salary was itself
months in arrears. The committee first felt that they and their fellow
townsmen were condemned to death by such indifference, and they
went home raging; and then they realized that in effect they were
condemned to life, and in their natural pride, the terms of this fate
were hard to endure. In that village "governor" became a scornful
epithet.

The brothers remained in their family house. Their surviving
neighbors took pity on them and traded meager supplies of food
and clothing for the statues they continued to create. Presently the
Castillo brothers were somebody at home, and even in the nearby
river settlements.

For fifteen years they made up a fresh stock every year, and
Roberto took it upon himself to go out to sell and see the world,
while Carlos waited at home to help defend the village if need be
and to anticipate the profits from the year's sale. The prices varied,
for much depended on good crops and the variable social conven-
tions of haggling. Carlos had persuaded his brother never to accept
anything in trade, never to barter, but to turn all he took with him
into cash before coming home. There was something about those soft
little buckskin purses, heavy with what was inside them. There was
no doubt about it, as the years passed, Carlos Castillo came to
love money.

CHAPTER 4

HE COULD HARDLY wait to see the invoice now as Roberto came into the yard and tied Governor to a post. He noted that Roberto was limping, and he wondered. But he was unable to ask about it. If there was anything to tell, Roberto would tell it in his own time. For various small reasons Carlos was never quite able to forget that he was the younger brother, though only by two years. He was exasperated by this, and the respect he should properly have shown to Roberto came out more times than not as a show of bad temper. Roberto, though older, was smaller than Carlos, and this too went oddly with the fact that Roberto never seemed to need physical power to make his point. There was a sparkling energy deep down in Roberto. It shone in his black, deeply shadowed eyes. He moved with small gestures scaled to his compact little body. He gazed up into the face of the world with great confidence. When he smiled his whole face broke with joy. It was curious, but as he grew older his features took on something of an animal charm, almost a monkey's plain, clever countenance, yet at the same time without losing the look of a handsome little man. His skin was a dry earth brown. He wore a short leather jacket with silver buttons, a white woolen shirt, a high leather belt studded with beaten coins, tight trousers with silver buttons from thigh to foot, and much-scarred boots. Over his shoulder was draped his serape, or blanket-shaped cloak. His hat was an old-fashioned Spanish tricorne edged with frayed ostrich feathers.

Carlos, much taller and bigger in every physical way, was dressed similarly, though more richly. He was considered the handsomer of the two, with his tall brow, his straight nose and his close-trimmed beard. There was less general love and good humor in his face, but to make up for this there was a reassuring seriousness that burned steady in his gaze like the flame of a candle in a perfectly still room. The brothers were the most successful men of the village.

"Well," said Carlos, opening the door so that they could pass through to the low, dark, immaculate interior of the house, where a fire hissed and cracked in the earthen fireplace, "I see your pack is empty."

"As a snakeskin," declared Roberto. "Here's the list."

Carlos took it and read it with care. The brothers knew just enough of reading, writing and ciphering to keep their uncomplicated accounts. Two thirds of the way down the page of soft Mexican paper that was like cloth in the fingers, Carlos frowned and asked, "What's this?"

Roberto leaned to read what was at the end of his brother's finger. On his pleased little face with its open nostrils he put an expression of surprise that was not convincing.

"Where?" he asked with false alertness.

"Right here, the Christopher," said Carlos sharply, offended by his brother's playacting. "Can't you read? It says, just as I wrote it in the first place, 'Item, one Saint Christopher with Holy Child, arm extended, large, twelve royals.' "

"That's right," said Roberto warmly.

"But then it has a line drawn through it, and in the column it is not marked paid, though everything else is. Why isn't it?"

They were sitting at a heavy table that stood before the fireplace. Roberto leaned far out on the table toward his brother, and with an air of coming to the inevitable, he blinked both his eyes to invoke good feeling and said, "I gave it to them."

Carlos sat back. His jaw dropped and his cheeks were sucked in. His look of marble health deserted him.

"You mean you did not collect the price? Is that what you mean?"

"I do."

"But the price was agreed upon in advance! Twelve royals. The church of San Cristóbal ordered it a year ago. We worked on it like dogs. We are not in this for our health!"

Roberto smiled. Some sort of wise sweetness came over his face and infuriated Carlos, making him aware of his juniority.

"I used to think just as you do," said Roberto, "but now I am not so sure."

"Just what do you mean by that?"

"Wait till I tell you."

"Wait till you give me the money you collected for the other things," said Carlos bitterly.

Roberto opened his jacket and his shirt and took from next to his warm belly three soft little bags that he threw on the table, where they made a muffled chime. Carlos immediately opened them, stacked the silver royals, and saw that aside from missing the price of the Christopher, the accounts were correct. He cupped his fingers tenderly over the little stacks of money as though in his touch he would feel consolation for what was missing. His eyes smoldered as he looked at Roberto.

"In all our years of working together," he said, "nothing like this has ever happened. And you don't seem to care at all."

"Only listen—"

"I am not sure I want to hear." A sense of injury that was almost dear came over Carlos. "I haul wood. I chop it up. I dry it. I strip off the bark, and I set the lumber where you can work on it with the tools that I keep shining and sharp for you. I scrape whiting out of the river walls and I heat it, and I boil that stinking glue out of horns and hooves, just to get things to the point where you can sit down and hack out a figure and slop it over with paint."

"*Hola*, little brother," said Roberto gently. He was shocked at the sudden pouring out of long-buried resentments that he had never suspected. His sympathy was infuriating to Carlos, who needed no reminder that he was the "little brother," though he stood a foot taller.

Carlos went on, "I can do all that and not mind. You get all the credit. You are the famous artist. I didn't care, so long as the money came in and our savings grew and there was no question about any of it. But now it turns out *this* way. To throw away the most beautiful saint, the largest, and the first Christopher we ever made. And the Infant Jesus on his shoulder—holding His little hand out in a blessing—you just gave that away? Have you forgotten how hard it was to carve that hand, with two fingers up and the others under the thumb? We never did that before, either. Very few statues have that feature. I thought we would really start something with that. And now—I never expected my brother to cheat me."

It was difficult for Roberto to be patient, even though he knew his brother's temper was quick. He was pricked by resentment that Carlos should say "we" when it came to carving. Then he despised himself for his ungenerous thought. He held his breath until his heartbeat slowed down, and then he said, "All I ask is for you to be quiet and let me tell you. Then you can decide if I did wrong."

"And if I decide that you did wrong?"

"Then we shall see."

Roberto smiled, and his family feeling reached Carlos, who was further irritated by it. But some authority told from the older to the younger man, and after a pause during which Carlos searched aside with his eyes for further excuses to wrangle, he said thinly, "Very well. But I warn you—"

"Yes. I know, I know. All right. Now, this is what happened."

CHAPTER 5

ON THE DAY before Christmas Roberto was going up the Rio Grande valley north of Santa Fe, driving Governor with a willow switch and congratulating himself that only one saint remained in the worn wooden packsaddle on the burro's spine. It was the large Saint Christopher, two and a half feet high. The figure presented a packing problem, for the Infant's left arm was extended as if to indicate a direction and make a blessing, while the right arm was hooked about the neck of the stalwart saint on whose shoulder He rode. The statue was wrapped in an old green cloth that was part of a discarded Spanish uniform. It was destined for the church of the village of San Cristóbal, which sat huddled in mountain country several miles east of the river. Roberto had promised on his previous journey that he would complete and deliver the work to his patrons in time for Christmas this year. As he estimated, he now had just enough time to reach San Cristóbal before true darkness fell.

The afternoon was cold but brilliant under a sky white with thin cloud. At about half past four Roberto followed the river upstream between rising hills that were like arms folded but not quite touching. Between the arms he was in general shadow. The river way turned again, and now canyon walls rose above him on both sides. It was suddenly warmer. The dry, bare willows stood like pale scratches against the slate-blue air, and the valley cottonwoods, holding their leaves of beaten thin bronze, were perfectly still. There was a flavor in the air that made Roberto think of spring—some moist goodness that seemed to lift up the scents of the land. He was happy.

He should have known better, but even when Governor suddenly

stopped his little trotting steps and shook himself and then emitted a
gut-emptying bray, Roberto thought of nothing more significant
than how idiotic a burro could be, and he whipped the little beast and
told him to stop shaking if he didn't want to shake Saint Christopher
entirely apart. Governor made another noise that actually resembled
a sigh, lowered his white eyelashes half across his large brown eyes,
and took up his rapid walk again.

"That is better," remarked Roberto. "You should be ashamed,
after all the years you—" but he felt something on his lips that
stopped his talk. His lips were stung by a sensation that was faint but
certain. He looked upward along the dark canyon walls. It was
beginning to snow. That was what Governor was talking about.

It was, as always, amazing how quickly the storm came to full
power. Roberto fixed his landmark ahead: a huge, ancient cottonwood on a little stony beach opposite which the side road turned off
to San Cristóbal. Before his eyes the tree turned into a spirit, fading
and fading, until it must vanish entirely behind the falling snow.
Daylight was dying two hours ahead of its proper time. When he
closed his eyes to blink the furry flakes off his lashes, he saw in his
own darkness a crimson image of the falling sky. When he opened
his eyes again, he saw how much blacker the world was; and he began
to feel how much colder. He watched Governor, who walked along
priggishly with his ears divided—one forward into the increasing
storm, one backward toward his master. Roberto could not help
smiling uneasily at the notion that each traveler thought the other in

charge. It was a way to confess that a man, an animal, alone in a December snow at nightfall in the northern river mountains, could find himself in extreme, perhaps mortal, danger before he was done.

Would it do any good to hurry? He whipped Governor and both trotted for a little way; but there was small value in giving in to a moment of concern. If they had to travel far into the night, it would be much wiser to conserve their strength. On the other hand, it was regrettable, and it was true, that the later the hour, the colder they would be. It was hard to decide what choice to make, or even, indeed, whether any alternative was to be had.

It was not surprising that Roberto should have his own scrape foremost in his mind. But this storm would work trouble for others too, and he recalled how the people of San Cristóbal were expecting him to arrive with their new saint; how there was to be a great feast, with bonfires, a procession and midnight Mass, for which the father resident from Santa Cruz was to come. Roberto hoped the priest was already there. It would be enough of a wonder if he and Governor and Christopher and little Jesus got through the blizzard.

Snow was driving now so thick and fast that he feared that he might go right past his big cottonwood, and so miss the turn to the right that he must make in order to follow a troughlike canyon full of odd, rocky falls and age-old rubble in its white, sandy bed. This would lead him to the mesa where the town of San Cristóbal sat below mountains. He moved to his left, closer to the river, and plodded ahead, straining his eyes to see the tree. He would have missed it, except for Governor, whose instinct for repose and shelter was highly developed. Before they knew it, Governor was standing in the lee of the thick trunk like someone who has come home and means to stay.

Roberto shivered. He knew the way to San Cristóbal, but it was odd how the storm that wiped out vision seemed almost to wipe out memory as well. It was surely the effect of the sudden cold. He decided to make a little fire out of deadwood scraps under the big tree and warm his hands for a moment. Then he could push ahead on his journey with renewed spirit. He pulled a few dried branches together and with his tinderbox lighted the smallest. A little flame came with a burst into the air. Governor, who had seen many camp-fires, chose this one to be startled by. He lunged against Roberto, knocking him over, and then stepped delicately back to his tree.

"You—" and Roberto cursed him. "You have knocked my tinder-box out of my hand into the snow. I should starve you until you find it for me."

He crawled on his hands and knees, feeling under the thickening snow that made all things—rock, hummock, twig—into the same soft shapes.

"This is absurd," he said. "It could have flown off only in this direction. It must be there." But he could not find it. He threw the snow aside. It would be awkward, perhaps serious, to be out in a mountain snowstorm without the means of making fire. The wind came pressing harder, and the snow fell thicker. Perhaps time was more precious to him than fire, he thought. Before the storm grew any worse, he had better be on his way. After one more thrust into the snow for his tinderbox, he gave up his search and turned angrily to Governor.

They said a burro's memory was in his feet. Good. Let us remember, my friend—and he grimly took Governor by the hackamore and turned him away from the tree and led him across the riverside trail. There should be a V-shaped opening in the canyon that they must enter. Carefully they made their way in the swirling air; and then Roberto felt a little lift of resolution in Governor and gave him his head. The burro led the way to the side canyon, and they entered at about the time when total darkness closed over the river and all its hidden veins.

It was natural to hope that on leaving the big river canyon and entering this narrower way a traveler might feel that he was more at home; that little familiar places would appear one by one; and that shelter from the falling sky would be provided by a reduction in scale, so to speak, of the forms of earth through which he traveled.

But Roberto was unable to discover any change in his surroundings or any lessening of his trouble. Leaning forward against the wind, he tried to get a sense of how the land rose steadily away from the river. He revived pictures in his mind of what the San Cristóbal Arroyo looked like—the sharply cut banks of earth, tufted with dark olive-green juniper bushes and heavy-limbed piñon trees; the occasional ledges of rock that obtruded from the walls and even crossed the waterless bed of the draw here and there; the waste of deadwood, left by lightning strikes, or washed out of the ground, roots and all, by violent flood, or dropped by the axes of wood gatherers or of soldiers and hunters out for mountain game. It was fearsome to feel lost in surroundings wholly familiar.

A rift in the spiraling snow showed him that nightfall was not yet total above the clouds. Suddenly the storm was divided overhead, a silver flight of thin cloud and fretted daylight showed, and then with raging manes the snow clouds came together like a herd of wild horses. All sense of movement, and hope, in the sky was lost, and the snow fell like darkness and the darkness itself was the snow.

He braced himself a little angrily.

"Not at all," he said aloud, for to be alone in such wilderness was to be at large with your thoughts in the utmost privacy. There was no one to overhear what a man said to himself. "Nothing can happen. The storm and the mountains can't hurt me."

He recalled with a hard smile what he had once told Carlos—their name, Castillo, meant castle, or fortress. A great fortress did not fall at the first attack, from whatever source. He never thought of himself as a small man, and was always amazed when, standing beside a big man, or seeing his own shadow on a wall where he lounged to watch the setting sun, he was reminded again of how short he was and slight of build. He did not feel small now in the storm. To express his contempt for the danger that gathered about him, he spat into the wild air. His spittle was blown against his cheek. In disgust he wiped it away.

CHAPTER 6

"Stop it! Stop, I tell you!" he shouted later.

He spoke to the snow that would not let him alone. It came and came and touched him and stayed on him, and pressed into his eyes, his nose; it clung to his boots, and tried with every power to hold him back and take him to the ground and cover him. He was playing blindman's buff, only he was not a child who called aloud in glee to fix under his reach those who would elude him in a playtime instant of the childhood village of long ago. What a joke it used to be to get turned around and not know which way you were shuffling, so that often when reaching for a certain tree trunk you ended up holding a corral post far opposite to it. Roberto now felt the spiraling snow so much in his mind that he was suddenly convinced that he had reversed his steps and was walking in arrested desperation back toward the Rio Grande. Violently he shook his head against the idea.

"Look here," he said, leaning down to Governor's ear, "you keep going perfectly straight, do you understand? I'll hold on to you for a while, and then I will take the lead and you can follow me. How far do you suppose we have come from the river?"

He grasped his beard and broke the ice that felt like someone else's fingers pulling at his face.

"Now what time do you suppose it is?" he asked.

His head was pierced by pains that traveled inward from his freezing ears. The pains drove all power of steady thought out of his mind. He could only keep moving, asking of his hope that he was going in the right direction, and that it was yet early, and that perhaps as they missed him, the people of San Cristóbal might send out a search party with lanterns and a jug full of the whiskey of Taos or the brandy of El Paso. At the thought of how it would be to swallow a mouthful of that fire, his bones clattered with the cold.

Suddenly his left arm was wrenched and his grasp on Governor's hackamore was violently broken free. Governor was gone just as if the trail had vanished from under him. That was just the case. In another instant Roberto fell forward across the lip of a ledge that came out from the arroyo wall. He crashed to the rubble ground, bearing his weight on his right knee when he struck. Dead limbs lay there, and fallen stones. He lay facedown. The snow fell on him and the wind took it around him, describing the fine sweep with which it piled snow in a crescent like the shape of an enfolding, a loving, arm.

He lay mindless with surprise and pain.

What brought him back was a nudge from Governor, who stood over him unharmed and composed. Roberto tried to rise up, but he was twisted again to the ground by a shock of pain in his knee.

"So," he said, with his eyes shut against the snowfall that he could not see in any case, but only feel as it touched and touched him— every touch so tender and simple, yet together so overpowering and heavy with a wooing appeal to lie still and rest. "So it is like this, then. Ah-ha."

He remembered where this place must be. In open weather, the rock ledge over which he had fallen could be seen and avoided by a trail that skirted it against the opposite wall of the draw. By a freak of the wind, snow was now piled in an eddy out from the cliff, so that much of its shoulder was dry. He drowsily imagined how intelligent he was about the whole situation. He was lying still for a moment to conserve his strength. He was thinking things over cleverly, and when he had made up his mind what to do, he would rise and do it.

Meanwhile, how good it was not to move, if moving rammed the breath out of him with pain. He carefully inched his hand down toward his hurt knee to feel what he could feel. It encountered some little rocks lying free and various pieces of fallen wood, weathered and brittle. He sighed for his tinderbox. How good a fire would feel now, though he felt more tired than cold. He closed his mind in the ease of a sleeper. What was the strange desire—he had heard of it—the desire that came to creatures lost in snowstorms to bank the fires of living in their minds and lie down and go to sleep forever?

He heard something. He raised his head. Who was singing there, beyond the wind, a multitude of voices rising and falling? How beautiful the sound. He smiled and lifted his face to the moving air. What were they singing, in long lines like the winds that spent their power against the lower slopes after tearing down past the black mountaintops so far away and high? They sang his name, "Roberto Castillo, Roberto Castillo," calling for him.

The imagined music was enough to tell him who he was. Should Roberto Castillo press his face down upon the freezing rocks, hugging his arms and legs together, and wait there for whatever might come, until, occupying as little space as possible in the world that enfolded him, he was frozen to death in the attitude of an unborn child?

"No!" he cried.

Raising himself against his pain so that his hands were free, he made the sign of the cross out of habit, and out of habit an answer cleared in his mind.

"Governor!" he called.

The burro moved closer to him. The animal was velveted with snow. Roberto clung to him and, hauling on the belly strap of the saddle, lifted himself against the shocks in his knee until he could handle the ties by which the pack was fastened. In the darkness he had to work entirely by touch. The cords were frozen. Nevertheless, he wrenched at them until they slid free. Sweating, he took the old military tunic with its contents to the ground. He opened the bundle and freed the statue and set it upright at a little distance. He put his hands together in veneration before Saint Christopher, who gave his protection to all who traveled.

A lovely warmth began to spread through Roberto. He closed his eyes, and even before he began to pray for help from Saint Christopher, he knew that not mountains with their inhuman peaks where storms came from, nor wind with its piercing words, nor the darling seductive snow, nor pain and break in his own body could prevail against him now. In the snowy darkness he humbled himself before the image that he could not even see and called upon his own likeness of the saint who more than any other must in this circumstance hear his cry. He did not know how long it was before he raised his head and opened his eyes against the endless brushing of the snow.

What he then saw was something that amazed him, and yet did not amaze him. In a queer way he expected it. But of course when he saw it, it made his heart turn over and his breath hold up just the same. It was very much like having a thought in your mind so strongly that suddenly it left you and dwelled outside—there, where you could actually see it, and perhaps others could too. In any case, what he saw far off in the snow-blackness was a silvery light, moving toward him, strong and clear.

He bowed his head in thanks. This must be light from a lantern carried by friends from San Cristóbal.

He looked up again. This was no lantern. The light was tall. He could not say how far away it was, but he knew now what it looked like. It was light shaped like a man clothed in a long robe, bearing a staff. Held against the left shoulder of the figure was a child lost in radiance who put forth its left hand with the first two fingers extended, the others folded under the thumb, in the sign of blessing.

There in the arroyo stood the real Saint Christopher with the Divine Child.

Roberto knew it was the real one because it was all—except for the light and the great size of the figures— just the same as his own image of the saint. The clothes were alike, the gestures, the bold, piercing eyes. Roberto was amazed to realize how well he must have known how Saint Christopher really looked to have made a carving of him that was so close to the truth.

"Yes, Roberto Castillo?" was what the vision asked in ways beyond words or voice.

Roberto sprang to his feet like anything but a man with a ruined knee. He was stupefied not with awe or fear but with splendor. The vision was so radiant that it threw daggers of light in a great circle about itself and cast a moving ray of shadow from each snowflake that fell around it. It was so beautiful beyond the imagination that Roberto could only feed upon it in the staring hunger of his eyes.

"Well, there, Roberto," he understood it to convey to him, "you called upon me. What do you want?"

Roberto came to himself with a shake. If he had been briefly lost in wonder, he now felt like himself to an extraordinary degree, so to speak, and he answered with a strange ease, "Yes. Thank you. I am lost and hurt. I am cold. I must go to San Cristóbal."

"Well, then, come"—and the great shining saint turned away and began to lead him through the bitter darkness. Roberto found that he could proceed readily. He had only to think of the idea of passing through and over the snow to do so.

They went a little distance before Roberto stopped and clapped his hands in remorse. He had started to walk off from his carved statue and from Governor, who was standing back there in the snow.

"You, there, Saint Christopher," he called, like one practical man to another. "Please wait a minute. Just a little minute. I have forgotten something. I'll be right back."

He watched to see—yes, the figure of light paused and turned, regarding him, and then it indicated that of course he must go and gather whatever he had left behind; let him attend to his business; it would wait for him. The saint stood waiting, a self-contained element of white fire that shed none of its light on the surroundings.

Roberto scraped his way back through the snow, holding his hands before him to feel for Governor. He found him. The burro perversely backed about a little, scattering the deadwood on the ground.

"Be quiet! Stand! Governor! We are going to march immediately, as soon as I load my pack again."

The burro then waited quietly while Roberto went to the ground, feeling for his statue. It had fallen down during Governor's small commotion. Roberto touched and touched until he felt an extended wooden arm, and the little gnarled presence of the Infant Jesus on the left shoulder, and the thick trunk of the body (for Saint Christopher was a big man).

"Thank God I found it," said Roberto, wrapping it carefully in the ragged green coat. "What luck. Though no thanks to you," he added to Governor. "Now." He put the pack on the saddle, and taking Governor by the harness, he turned again to the light that waited for him and that resumed its way as soon as he was ready.

He had no idea how long it took, for the rest of the journey passed in what seemed disembodied glory. No man ever traveled with such ease. No animal was ever so docile and nimble as Governor. The drifts of snow were there, all the time, and the snowy wind, the driving cold. The ground was hard, uneven and slippery. The night was pitch-black. And yet every step was a joy. The radiant man and Child who led the way toiled like any mortals against a storm, and the storm abated none of its violence, but those who led and those who followed seemed really to be not of the experience, though they were in it. But suddenly—it must have been after ten o'clock—the glorious light vanished in a gesture of farewell, and Roberto in his return of blindness after such brilliance was at first unable to see anything. The pain in his knee returned and he nearly collapsed, saving himself only by hanging over Governor's shoulder. All the radiant powers of his journey up the arroyo were gone. He was abandoned.

"Saint Christopher!" he called like a lost child.

He was immediately ashamed of himself. Now used to the darkness again, he saw that he had no further need of his dazzling friend and that his journey was over, for there ahead of him was the first lanternlike window of the village of San Cristóbal. Gasping and stumbling, Roberto came to safety among friends at that house.

They were amazed at how he had come through the storm. They had given up all hope. How on earth had he managed?

While the women of the house laid him down and exposed his knee and treated it, the men, after turning Governor into a corral, brought in his packsaddle. Roberto told them what had come to him after his fall and had remained with him until right here, at the edge of the village, it had vanished, leaving him safely among all to whom he spoke.

CHAPTER 7

THEY FOUND IT hard to believe him. The saints did not often come to poor people lost in storm-closed mountains. He was out of his head from exhaustion.

Roberto was offended.

"Explain, then, if you can," he said, "how I managed to walk miles on a broken knee?"

"It is not broken," said the mother of the house kindly, "just a deep cut."

He leaned to see. There across his knee and down inside his calf was a long blue wound shaped like a knife blade. In the warm air, and addressed with kindness, it was hurting in a new way. He swallowed at the pain.

"Still," said someone, "it is unbelievable that he got here at all, and yet there he is."

There was general agreement as to this, and for some minutes the storm was described and compared to previous ones. Terrible memories of those who had died in the mountain ways during nights like this came back and were spoken of in Roberto's honor. He had endured much for them, just to bring them what he had promised.

"You have the statue?"

"Yes. In my pack. Bring it near my bed, and I will open it."

The pack was carried to him, and at the same time the people spoke miserably of their misfortune on this Christmas Eve. The fires were laid all along the way to the church. The church was decorated with fresh pine boughs. New candles were waiting in profusion to be lighted. The saint's niche in the altar was outlined with bright paper flowers, and more paper flowers were arranged in bouquets. Did he know where the paper came from to make them? At Taos, during the fair last October, crockery from China, brought across the Pacific Ocean to Mexico and shipped north in the yearly wagon train, had been unpacked from straw hampers. Every dish and cup was wrapped in Chinese paper—yellow, blue, pink or green—and when an article was displayed, the paper was thrown on the ground. People of this town had earnestly gathered the rumpled little sheets and had brought them home to fashion for tonight. The whole town—men, women, boys and girls—had put their hearts and their arms into making ready for this feast day. And now what was the use? There could be no midnight Mass, no procession amid fire and song.

"Why not?" asked Roberto. "I have come with your saint as I promised to do."

Yes. They thanked him. He had been faithful. But he might have spared himself all the hardships he had endured to come among them all tonight, for it was only an hour before midnight and the priest from Santa Cruz was nowhere to be seen.

"Ah," said Roberto, understanding very well that all depended upon the arrival of the resident father from Santa Cruz, and knowing better than any that if he was abroad in the storm, he would never arrive.

"Let us hope, then," he said, completing his thought aloud, "let us hope that the father never started out at all. We could not expect in one night two miracles."

At the word, his friends in silence consulted one another again. Their doubt and pity almost made a rustle in the room. Roberto stared at them sickly. He liked people. He spent his life creating for them out of common materials those objects of veneration that could fill their eyes with beauty and lift their hearts to heaven. Sometimes he had been made to feel that he was not quite of their world; and the feeling troubled him. But at such times, looking about him, he would see that all the creatures of God had their appointed forms and ways of life, differing one from another and yet living on the same earth; and he would conclude that if his fellows, or indeed he himself, hardly understood his nature and his duty, he  could but obey creation as it was shown in him and bring it forth upon the world in his carvings. Now amid their doubts he took refuge once again in his work and pulled at the pack that lay on the floor beside his low bed.

"Yes, at least let us see our new statue," they said in their various ways, crowding close.

"It is the finest I have yet made," replied Roberto, budging his knotted thongs with difficulty. "The largest, with the most colors and, I believe, the most real faces I have ever succeeded in making in all my fifteen years of work."

"Hurry up, then," they urged, leaning over the pack.

He finally got it open.

"Bring the lamp," he said with a touch of acerbity, to let them know that it meant something to him, if not to them, under just what conditions a new work of the imagination was revealed for the first time. Until the lamp was brought and at his direction held high and to one side so that fine shadows would result on the figure, he reserved his revelation. But satisfied at last, he flung back the heavy green cloth of the old Spanish coat and lifted up the contents.

As he did so he knew a shock. He quickly glimpsed the faces about him to see if there was any possibility that they had not yet seen what he had seen. But they had seen. They were openmouthed in perplexity, which in another instant gave way to anger. They pointed to what he held. It was a meaningless piece of dead cottonwood, weathered, gray and light with decay.

Like an arm extended as if pointing a way, a branch extended from the main trunk. A gnarled knot at the top of the trunk protruded like a secondary growth. The whole thing was about two and a half feet long. In the dark, under the hastening snow, with only touch to go by, it very well could have been taken for the carved statue of Saint Christopher and the Infant.

"Another miracle, so," said someone with shocking ill will.

" 'Bring the lamp,' " mocked someone else.

"A most dreadful mistake," gasped Roberto softly.

A woman or two began to weep at this last of a series of disappointments. An old man said, with heavy gentleness that saddened Roberto more than insults, "We made our bargain in good faith. This is not a very faithful way to keep it on your part—though it may be an excellent joke."

At cost of much pain Roberto tried to stand to speak to them, but he could not. He lay back and groaned, "I know exactly where the real statue is. I prayed to it in the dark, and in the dark I had to feel for it when it was time to walk again. I took this branch by mistake, feeling for the arm, the head. Tomorrow, even if I have to drag myself over the ground by my hands and elbows, I will go back and find the piece I made for you and bring it to you. Until then I do not ask you to believe me."

"Thank you," remarked a sour voice from a hidden face.

Roberto put his hands over his eyes. Once, years ago, he had watched for hours a monkey that had traveled to Santa Fe with a troupe of tattered acrobats. The little creature wore a look of incessant concern, and now and then as though the burdens of life overcame it, it would sit down and cover its face with a shudder, in a burlesque of a troubled man. This picture came back to him now. It was what he must look like, as his animal nature tried to conceal his spiritual suffering. The little crowd in the room continued to murmur, but he fled them in his mind. He thought that otherwise he would go crazy.

The women changed the bacon-fat poultice on his knee, where pain sliced against the bone every time his blood beat. The wind pulled and questioned vastly about the village of San Cristóbal.

Roberto Castillo kept asking himself his own question, which was, Why had he been saved by divine intervention only to make a fool of himself? The fury and anguish of his thought lost him his mind for a little while. He drifted into unconsciousness and slept.

CHAPTER 8

HE WAS AWAKENED by a commotion at the door.

Half awake and witless with pain, he thought that the people of the town were coming for him to do him justice and harm, and he pulled himself toward the wall by his cot and stared as everyone turned together to see the door open violently before the loud, shuddering wind.

There stood a tall figure muffled to the eyes and shaking with cold. It was a man, blind for a second in the lamplight of the little earthen room. His dark serape made him loom out of the shadows like an apparition. In a voice that a few of his hearers knew, he said impatiently, "Will someone please take this before my arms drop off?"

"Father!" they cried, falling to their knees. It was the priest from Santa Cruz, and he was carrying the statue of Saint Christopher and the Child. The statue was a pillar of ice, robed in snow like a king's mantle. Two women, by their sex custodians of sacred objects, hurried forward and took the figure to the fire to thaw.

"And will someone please see to my poor horse?" declared the visitor in tones of reproof. A man near the door at once went out to this duty.

His arms now free, the newcomer whirled his blanket cloak about him like a dark cloud until, rising, it left his shoulders and sailed to the floor like some ominous bird with spread wings. This action filled everyone with awe, and they crowded back to let him pass as he strode toward the fire, extending his blue hands to warm them over the statue that stood on the hearth.

"There, look, all of you," called Roberto, "there is my Christopher, just as I told you!"

The priest turned with a fiery glare to see who spoke. There followed an immediate recognition.

"Do I know you?" he asked in a grating voice.

"Yes, Father. I am Roberto Castillo, the saintmaker."

"Yes," declared the priest with a shake of his bones as he began to feel the fire behind him, "my brat of fifteen years ago. Well, do you habitually scatter your fabrications around on mountainsides?"

"No, Father," replied Roberto, feeling strangely tongue-tied and restored to the relationship between master and boy.

There was some exchange of established understanding between the two of them that made the other people draw into themselves with respect, though they continued to peer and listen curiously. The priest, with his familiar wryness of speech that was powerless to conceal an inner excitement now, spoke to them all. "First I have a few curious facts for you. After that, I may have one or two comments."

He swept their faces and had the effect of extinguishing the respectful joy that his arrival had put there. He groaned silently at what he always did to people out of the best of motives; then, in a manner of speech that sounded like a Spanish novel of romance to some of his more educated listeners, he continued.

"Having promised that I would be here to sing midnight Mass, I set out, with my poor wretch of a horse, even when the weather turned bad. If it was dreadful as I came down the river, it was as nothing compared to what I encountered after dark when I turned into the arroyo. How I found my turnoff it will never be given to me to know. My horse knew better than I did. We came, slipping and scraping, up to the draw until I had to get down and lead my animal, who had reached the point of coming to a standstill too often. I was a greater fool, and preferred to keep on walking.

"But an hour ago I reached the end. I could neither see nor feel nor even hear my way forward. The snow was laid across the draw like mountain ranges and valleys to challenge any palmer in his voyage. I consulted my conscience. Had I done all I could to get here and keep my promise? It seemed to me so. Should I not choose to live for another day to do broader duties for many more people than a handful of probably indifferent families in San Cristóbal? I thought so. Reflecting upon my condition, I concluded that as a man of goodness, I must preserve myself that my goodness could serve the world on the morrow, and when I came to a shelter by a little cliff where providentially scattered was a lot of dried wood, I got down, huddled out of the wind and resolved to take refuge for the night."

He paused and grappled for their secret minds with a glance like a fishhook. He suddenly changed his storytelling character, whose every word Roberto lodged in memory, and in a flare of scorn for the human talent for self-deception, he rasped out at the little gathering,

"Look out if you ever make up your minds that you are people of goodness, look out! That is the beginning of damnation, as it nearly was for me tonight." He lifted and let fall his long arms in a buzzard's settling gesture and resumed his narrative manner. "To continue: I had my tinder, and I scraped up a fire and lit it. What do you think was the first thing I saw?"

Silent and moonfaced, they hung on his words.

"I'll tell you," he proceeded, with a distortion of his thin, bearded face. "I saw that statue of Saint Christopher and the Infant lying on the snow. And what was Jesus doing? He was pointing up the arroyo. And what did He mean by that? He meant, 'Get up, you faithless wretch, you self-indulgent, self-important cheat, and walk your feet raw if you have to, but keep faith!' "

He permitted a brief silence that was like a whipping, and then continued. "As you may or may not know, I am not familiar with your country hereabouts. Years ago I made one trip up the river, and after that I was sent to Spain, to my old college, where I taught students for the priesthood what miseries awaited them when in their turn they should come here as missioners. And then I was sent to Peru, and then to Mexico again. When I was assigned to Santa Cruz this winter I was informed that your town would be one of my mission towns, and I knew that sooner or later I should be obliged to learn the way. I learned it tonight, in darkness and wind and ice. I picked up the saint and, leading my horse, started to walk again.

"We felt our way up out of the arroyo, and then on the open mesa I was without the smallest idea of where to turn. Do you know what told me? The Christopher. In my frozen arm he turned, and the arm of the Christ Child pointed where I must go. Out of some faint glimmer of science in my frosted brain I speculated as to whether I could prevent the movement within my grasp, and I would hold the statue tight to my ribs and turn aside from my course. I was powerless. Against my strength, the figure would turn until the arm was pointing the way. I could not but follow it. They say there are men who can find water by holding a forked willow that they are powerless to turn from its attraction toward a buried spring. I came to a greater fountain tonight by grace of a higher power. When I could not see a step ahead of me, I came across the mesa until I finally saw the light of this window."

He sought in their faces the skepticism of the world and asked quietly, "Are you among those who must explain everything? Then let us ask Master Castillo how it happened that Saint Christopher was waiting to make a man of me in that mountain ditch?"

Roberto leaned up on his bed. "I can tell you, Father!" he cried in excitement, and the missioner turned upon him his lidless bird's eye.

"Yes, you could always tell me. Well, go ahead."

"It is one of my statues. I was on my way to deliver it here," and Roberto told all his wonders again. The missioner listened, with his hand in his beard, his thin scarlet mouth pursed in a familiar expression, his eyes fixed on Roberto in points of light. The people watched him to see what he thought, but he was as expressionless as a judge. When Roberto finished and fell silent, the missioner extended an arm toward him like a weapon and asked sharply, "This story of yours, do you believe it?"

Roberto stared at him in dismay.

"It is not a story," he said indignantly.

"This report, then. You were exhausted?"

"Of course I was exhausted."

"Possibly frightened out of your wits?"

"Possibly frightened, yes. Men have been frozen to death in a matter of a few hours in these mountains."

"Spare us your dramatics, if you please. Yes. Exhausted. Frightened. Could you not have imagined the whole thing? Perhaps you did not know what you were doing. Possibly you got up and walked just because one last shred of sense told you you had to do so."

Roberto was perfectly aware of whither the missioner was trying to take him. He was proud and calm. He knew what had befallen him. He was not prepared to repudiate it for anyone. He looked around the room. The faces of his friends were bland with the easy virtue of agreeing with authority. They seemed to assure the priest that they too had listened and refused to believe what Roberto Castillo was saying. They breathed comfortably their luxurious fellowship with the great man who saved or damned according to laws they thought he made up all by himself half the time. They now felt, but not as much as Roberto, what a terrible thing it was when a pupil rose up against his teacher. With sweat standing out upon his brow, he said, "Father, it is true that I got up and walked because it was all I could do. What made me do it was not fear or exhaustion, but the command of our Holy Child and his friend Saint Christopher, who carried Him there in the snow, as I saw, and as I tell."

There were a few muffled snickers in the room, inviting the glance of confederacy from the missioner. He turned upon those of easy opinion and lashed them with his most icy tongue. "Ears and hear not!" he all but whistled through his beard. "I stand like the devil's advocate and tempt this poor man to cease being an honest fool, and he breaks out in a cold sweat of fear and denies me that he may keep his God! And you huddle together to mock because you think I mock! If you disbelieve him, what do you make of my own story tonight? Do you think I lied?" They hung their heads. "Do you? Did Master Castillo come here by accident? Did I? He says he picked up a piece of deadwood by accident, and left Saint Christopher behind by mistake. Is that true? He is a humble man and does not claim more than he can possibly know. Not I, though. On my Lord's business, I am not so humble. Let me tell you that under divine Providence there are no accidents. Not if you truly believe that if we choose it, Paradise awaits at the end of this life, and that what we can feel in our flesh and what we can foresee in our minds must join together in the great design of Almighty God!"

He was shaken and dried by his own heat. He made himself be calm, clamping jaws in his habitual effort to control the bitterness that too often otherwise rushed to his mouth and poured out not God's love but man's anger.

Roberto lay down again on his bed. He was at peace, for he was believed.

At the fireplace a woman was preparing a pot of hot chocolate. Leaning down, she gave a little cry of pity and regret.

"No, this is a shame," she said, lifting the statue from which all ice and snow had now melted away and pointing to its wooden skirt at the right knee. "It is damaged!"

"Damaged?" called Roberto. "Let me see."

She handed it to the missioner, who took it to Roberto. Examining it, Roberto crossed himself and peered up at the burning eyes of his old teacher.

"Look, Father," he said in a dry croak, "it is my wound, exactly as it happened to me."

Crossing the right knee of the statue in its wooden gown and cutting downward over the calf was a gash in the shape of a knife blade.

Whatever its cause, the effect of the wound was to spread throughout the crowded little house visible confirmation of the happenings of that night. The people fell to their knees and began to pray. The missioner did not lead them. He listened. As the power of one was joined to that of another, and of all together, he seemed to rise in his heart and he prayed with them. When the prayer ended, his voice lingered, and they all heard him say what was to them an odd thing. He held his hands together and open like the pages of a book, and he bent his head like a reader, but his eyes were shut, and they saw that

he was speaking something memorized from a book he knew well. "Suffer thy exile in patience, and thy dryness of soul, until again I shall come to thee and make thee free of all anxiety."

Roberto watched him shake his head as if to ask, How long must I wait? and he saw at last that his old friend was really two men—the one outside and the one within. It was a striking discovery, but he could never speak of it generally, for with it came a wave of feeling that would assuredly be considered irreverent directed by a humble man toward so great a figure. What Roberto felt for him now was pity. He prayed that whatever it might be that the missioner must await in patience, it might come to him on this night of wonders.

CHAPTER 9

AND IT DID seem that the portents and mercies of that Christmas Eve knew no end, for when people came out of the little house where the refugees had found safety from the blizzard, all saw that the storm was over. The snow had stopped suddenly, as it could in mountains, where the storm was low on the earth because the earth was so high. Now the sky was calm and clear. The stars seemed immense where they intimately sparkled with light like fire at the heart of ice. In the starlight all the earth was deeply robed in royal snow. Word went like sparks through the village that nothing had been done in vain—the visiting missioner was here, the patronal statue had arrived, the fires would be lighted and the feast would take place after all.

In a few moments boys ran down the village street, setting alight the fires that had been laid since midafternoon—little towers of kindling laid in hollow squares. The snow had drifted about them but had not soaked into the wood, and a handful of dry straw was enough to set each beacon going. For beacons they were, marking the path of the procession, and signaling through the high mountain darkness so that the Christ Child would know where this village was, and accordingly could visit it tonight. Against the smooth, spiraling banks of snow leaped the young firelight, melting away great caldrons of shadow in the surrounding drifts. When all the fires were blazing in their long lane, there came a brazen tongue of sound from the tower of San Cristóbal, where the bell of 1707 rang out to assemble everyone for the procession.

Roberto, with each arm around the neck of a friend, was helped to a position of honor near the church where he could see everything without having to move. He was in that state of double awareness that sometimes came to him at his work. He saw everything as though from afar, and yet he felt everything sharply, as at the center of all experience. Now he saw the high mesa world defined by the black walls of the enclosing mountains. The mesa top lay flat with snow under the starlight. Seen from so far as Roberto's godlike view, the village at first looked like a single bonfire. But the earthen cubes of the houses threw long shadows over the snow, and between the shadows lay wavering blades of warm light. In the dark sides of houses shone windows like embers. Dividing the houses and the darkness was the lane of beacon fires that ran all the way to the church door. In the lane slowly moved the entranced people of the town of San Cristóbal, bathed in firelight and crowned by stars after the storm. They sang together as they walked. Their ancient bell called them closer and closer to itself. Boys ran and jumped over the little fire towers and were chased away by the grotesque figure of a village elder who, masked and false-voiced, acted once a year on Christmas Eve as the bogeyman who must terrify, challenge and delight children.

In the procession young unmarried men came first, followed by unmarried girls. After them walked hand in hand the younger fathers and mothers of the town. Their parents followed them, and then the most elderly of all. Now came four strong youths for whom Roberto watched most keenly, as they bore on their shoulders a platform on which stood his patronal statue of Saint Christopher and the Child. The firelight rippled over the figure, and as Roberto squinted at it, considering it critically as its creator, he received a cold rebuff in his mind. The statue was no longer his. It already had a history. He seemed called upon to venerate it humbly and to forget its simple origin in his own callused fingers. He bent his head. When he looked up again, he saw the missioner at the end of the procession, vested in his shabby cope of white brocade and gold lace, which in spite of its hard experience of much travel in saddlebags, now roiled and sparkled in the windy firelight.

The missioner's face was startling. Roberto looked again. He could not be sure of what he saw. Was that long, ashen face breaking with every instant into different expressions of suffering, so that it looked almost like a succession of masks passed swiftly over a man's soul? Or did the flicker of the fires cause that effect of shattered change to pass and pass on the bones and hollows of a face fixed in some racking plea? He could not say.

The face of the church was plastered with earth and painted a pale yellow that came, as Roberto knew, from the walls of the arroyo. It was waved over with hot light from the nearest fires. The procession entered the portal, whose old wooden doors, carved with the crown of Castile and the keys of Saint Peter, were thrown back. Roberto had always admired them. Passing through the doors, each person was for an instant exposed to the strike of the bronze, brass and silver bell in the tower just overhead. The bell was kept rolling by the sexton, and its halting clangor released downward into the captive air of the church a hard shudder of energy that deafened and shook everyone who entered beneath it. It was a disagreeable sensation, but one so powerful that it came like a privileged ordeal, as though the heavens were opening in judgment. Once past it, the marchers were in the long, plain, boxlike interior of their earthen church, which narrowed at its far end and always reminded Roberto of the head of a coffin. It was a box of earth in which the villagers solemnly met all the stages of human life.

Roberto was helped to a position in the rear of the church where he could lean against the wall. He saw over the heads of the congregation of San Cristóbal the towering glory of their altar, with its galaxy of homemade candles; its banks, garlands and sprays of paper blossoms; and its frontal cloth for ceremonial occasions, which had been made by women who embroidered it with a design of large flowers and leaves in coarse yarns dyed in the pale colors of grasses and plants that grew on the mesa in spring.

CHAPTER 10

INTO THE NICHE framed with paper flowers the statue was lifted. As it faced out over the crowd with the extended arm and hand of its Child, a sigh of consummation arose from everyone spontaneously. It made Roberto shiver that any work of his should have such meaning for so many people.

He watched the missioner fling holy water upward at the statue and heard him speak a blessing. He spoke in an odd voice, wild and distant, almost the wail of an old man, or even more strangely, of a forlorn child. Coming down to the foot of the altar to begin the midnight Mass, he was stooped as if under a heavy burden. His eyes were half shut and his hands were folded against his lips. He seemed hardly to be present as he moved at the Mass in uncertain steps and turns. Once or twice he raised his head and gazed about and upward, perhaps trying to realize where he was. It was plain to Roberto that the missioner was enduring some inner tempest. Sometimes strange notions occurred to Roberto. He often noticed that he understood one thing in terms of something else. So now, watching the missioner, he recalled how in the Rio Grande uplands where he lived it was sometimes possible to know, long before the skies changed, that a break in the weather was coming just by watching the behavior of creatures. For no apparent reason old sheep would toss themselves about like lambkins, and cows would make longing cries like the sound of breath blown through a scraped gourd. Hours would pass, and then faithfully the weather would change, coming with wind, dust and finally rain, and bringing ease to all.

So it was now in the close-aired church. He remembered the missioner praying aloud in the bedroom a while ago. He had prayed for patience in his exile and for his "dryness of soul," desiring what he desired with such passion that he did not seem to care if all heard his cry. What do you suppose it was? Roberto turned it all over in his mind. Who was going to answer the prayer? Who else but the divine Lord? The missioner was longing with all his thorny heart to be one with God. It sobered Roberto to see in the missioner what a shaking experience it must be to carry such a desire.

At the altar the missal was carried from one side to the other, and the missioner, leaning on the table for support, went to meet the book. He read in silence and then faced the people so that they should stand. Their eyes were drawn to his by the dying fire of the glare under his deep, bony brows. He began to read in a worn whisper. It was the Gospel for midnight Mass. They strained to hear him, wondering if he must stop before he was done. Everyone had the half-framed thought that here was someone who had come to the end of something, who must either end with it or start all over again.

They did not have long to wait to see which would happen. In his exhausted rasp he read of the birth of Christ in the stable and of the shepherds in the fields, and then he read:

> "And, lo, the angel of the Lord came upon them, and the glory of the Lord shone round about them; and they were sore afraid.
>
> And the angel said unto them, Fear not: for, behold, I bring you good tidings of great joy, which shall be to all people.
>
> For unto you is born this day in the city of David a Saviour, which is Christ the Lord."

And at this, they saw tears start down his haggard cheeks, and saw him come to stand erect, and heard his voice take power and ring out over them. Finishing the Gospel from memory, he opened his arms to embrace all. His dryness of soul was done with, for the moment, anyway. He wept for joy. His tears eked their way like the break of mountain springs into dry runnels that had waited forever for such assuagement. All who saw could not but weep with him. His love was free. They all knew his old, hard, bitter, earthbound shell. Now from it bloomed his love, like the lily of the yucca bursting its dry gold pod after winter. Roberto thumbed away the sting from his own eyes. He knew how the missioner felt. It was something like what happened to him when a design for a carving was right the first time, except that this tonight was the greater glory, for having been carried so heavily for so long in mankind. He looked about him in the firelit church of San Cristóbal, and was among those who, hearing the missioner, heard the love of God, which they would never, despite the failures and distractions of daily life, entirely forget.

There was no sermon, nor any need of one.

The missioner resumed the Mass, and over one face after another came expressions of joy that now had new fullness. At the elevation of the Blessed Sacrament the little altar bell rang out, and then immediately came the voice of the tower bell of 1707 in its widening circles of jubilation. But even that was not all, for eight young men waited outside the doors for the signal, and when it came, they lifted eight muskets with double charges in them and fired such a blast of devotion that Roberto thought it must be heard up and down the river, where others might remark enviously, "There is San Cristóbal again."

As the echo of the fusillade died away in the church, praise arose from the animal creation. Out in their corral at the edge of town, the missioner's horse heaved a strangled cry, and Governor, the burro, brayed. Roberto heard them and was glad that if they had forgotten when to pay their reverence, the musket blasts had reminded them.

And now within the church another hymn arose. It came from the sagging choir loft above the great doors. Out over the worshipers flew the caroling of many little birds, which pierced their hearts. This jubilant birdsong came from two dozen little boys of the village who had practiced for weeks to make their great effect at the most joyful moment of Christmas Eve. On the floor of the loft were six earthen bowls holding water. Four boys crouched down to each. Into the water they dipped dried reeds that were perforated like flutes. Fingering the stops, the children blew into their reeds, and the bright notes chirping seemed to tell how in the dead of a winter night even the wild birds of the air must lift their songs in praise.

Roberto was sorry that Carlos was not there to witness the events of the night, and in its arch of light to see their handiwork standing like a visible promise above the people of San Cristóbal. Even from his place in the rear of the church he could see the raw wound in the wooden knee, and he felt his own sore leg in awesome kinship. He could hardly wait to be home again to tell Carlos of all this.

CHAPTER 11

THERE WASN'T much more to tell.

The next day Roberto's knee was so stiff that he could not move it. He lay in bed in the house of his friends at the edge of town. Early in the morning he had a visitor. It was the missioner, who was on his way back to Santa Cruz, where he must arrive before noon in order to hold services for his own people. The day was clear and the sun shone again from the snow that lay everywhere.

"Well. I am glad to have seen you again after all these years," said the Franciscan. "I am glad that when I gave you lessons in carving I did not after all waste your time."

"Or yours," replied Roberto, completing the thought that lay behind the older man's sardonic manner. After the exaltations of the night the missioner was himself again. But now when he spoke in his usual finicking style that recalled his Spanish university training, Roberto knew, because he had seen it last night, the depths of devotion to his fellowmen that the missioner ordinarily buried under exasperation with himself. They were no longer master and pupil. They were partners in a powerful experience whose beginnings they had created together a long time ago.

"Take care of that leg," said the missioner. "Come to see me if you are ever in my valley."

"Yes, Father. And let us see you down our way."

"Oh, if I should ever have the time," said the missioner with a rude shrug. "By the way, what can you do about the scar?"

"Mine, you mean?" Roberto touched his leg gingerly. "Or on the statue?"

"It is perfectly clear that you will be walking again in a few days. I can hardly waste any sympathy on you."

"Then you mean the statue. Well, I can fill the gash with plaster and touch it up. I've been thinking about it."

"Yes, I daresay. All right, remember, then," said the missioner, "remember that for patching, you must use more glue in proportion to plaster, to make it hold."

Roberto knew this, but he bowed and said, "Yes, Father."

The missioner glanced impatiently out-of-doors. He must be off, but he could not yet go. He was always pulled by opposites.

"Well," he asked with his lip lifted, "*are* you going to patch it?"

Roberto was not clear about why this was asked. He simply gazed at the missioner, who added, in the manner of the teacher of a backward child, "Let me put it another way. What will people say when they see the scar?"

"Oh, they will ask how it got there."

"Of course they will. And so long as they ask, so long will the story be told. And if they listen, they might learn something. I leave it with you. Here is a blessing." He made his loose, irregular sign in the air, to which Roberto inclined his head. "Good-bye."

"Good-bye, Father."

The missioner went out of the house, tested the straps of his saddlebags, mounted his horse and, holding elbows to his sides, his body somewhat twisted and his head stiffly raised so that his beard stood out sharply before him, rode away.

After a few days Roberto was able to walk, though with a painful limp. He announced that he must soon be leaving for his home downriver. Before he could leave, a committee of elders came to see him. There were a few polite preliminaries, and then the chairman said, "In the matter of the statue, there has been some question as to its damaged condition. The committee wishes to ask whether it can be repaired properly."

Roberto smiled. "It would be very simple to repair it so that nobody would ever know the difference. But are you sure you want it done?"

The chairman, an old man with doleful eyes, looked at him in bewilderment.

"Let me put it another way," said Roberto. "What will people say when they see the scar?"

"Oh," said the chairman, glad to understand, "they will ask how it got there."

"Exactly," said Roberto. "And so long as they ask, so long will the story be told. This town will be famous. And if people listen, they might learn something. I leave it with you."

The chairman turned to his colleagues and withdrew with them out of earshot. After a discussion of about half an hour's duration, they returned, and the chairman declared, "We have considered that the wound to our saint came about by means that should not be questioned, and we therefore consider the wound to be sacred, as part of the statue. Our arrangements are therefore completed with you, except for payment." He produced a small money bag. "Here are the twelve royals we owe you for the statue. It is all in silver. We have kept it for the purpose ever since the Taos Fair last October."

"THAT WAS WHEN I REFUSED," said Roberto to Carlos over their own table at home, "to take their money. I leave it to anyone to say that I didn't do the right thing, after all that took place on Christmas Eve, and all on account of our statue."

Carlos was still under the spell of what he had listened to. His eyes were lost in mystery. He absently murmured a pious ejaculation. Then bringing himself back to common affairs by clinging to a small detail of the whole adventure, he said reflectively, "So that was why you limped."

"Of course. Well? What do you say?"

Carlos took a deep breath and slowly nodded his head in grudging approval of how his brother had disposed of the piece of work that was crossed out on the invoice before him on the table.

Roberto laughed and jumped to his feet. He leaned over and clapped Carlos on the shoulder. He knew his man. He knew how to bring Carlos back to good humor and fill his head with hot thoughts of a future crammed with satisfactions.

"Good!" he exclaimed. "Now that we are agreed, look at this."

He pulled out of his inner pocket another piece of paper, which he put down on the table before Carlos. It was a list of orders for six new Christophers, " 'all two and a half feet tall, the Holy Child on the left shoulder with arm extended, and on the right knee, a deep wound, all to be identical with the statue in the church at San Cristóbal.' "

"What's this?" asked Carlos.

"Just what it says, and each at twelve royals apiece. When I wouldn't take money for the other one, they went off again and talked for a while, and came back with these orders. They all want one in their own houses."

Carlos stared at him and exclaimed, "But that's more money than we've made in five years!"

"You are right. Well?"

Carlos smiled like a boy. He went to a chest that stood on the floor near the fireplace and brought out of it a flask of homemade ink and a sharpened turkey quill. He returned to the table and sat down to cipher on the margin of the new order list.

Roberto watched him and sighed in his mind. People were what they were. He was glad harmony was restored, even if it came out of a combination of piety and covetousness. For himself there were satisfactions—matters of bringing reminders of life into a painted wooden face, a wooden body—that, if they were hard to define, were yet real. He heard Carlos and his quill pen scratching away with loving care, and then heard him say, "Seventy-two royals in all!"

"Seventy-two."

It was plain that Carlos was over his bad temper. The brothers looked at one another. Each was thankful, though in different ways, that Providence still chose to grant him what he so loved: work and the need of his fellowmen of that which he could make for them.

CHAPTER 12

THE CASTILLO brothers made their saints for many more years. A century after their lifetime their works attracted the desire of collectors, until it became almost impossible to find one. Even from the altar of San Cristóbal in the mountains above the Rio Grande in the ancient kingdom of New Mexico vanished, hurt knee and all, the Saint Christopher of 1809. But in any case its work long since had been done.

THE ROYAL GAME

THE
ROYAL
GAME

by Stefan Zweig

ILLUSTRATED BY ERHARD GOTTLICHER

To his fellow passengers aboard the ocean
liner, Mirko Czentovic was a fellow of the most
boorish sort—vain, rude, uncommunicative,
lacking in the most fundamental social graces. In fact,
Czentovic had only one exceptional quality.
And exceptional it was. He was chess champion of the
world; the most brilliant master of the game.

   It is all the more astounding, therefore,
when he is challenged by Dr. B., a Viennese lawyer
who has never played a game of chess
before, except in his own imagination. With
mounting drama and suspense, Stefan Zweig brings
the two men face-to-face across a chessboard
and leads them inexorably toward
their final confrontation.

THE USUAL ELEVENTH-HOUR bustle and commotion reigned on the big liner that was due to sail from New York to Buenos Aires at midnight. Visitors who were not sailing forced their way through the crowds to see their friends off; telegraph boys with caps worn at an angle called out names as they darted through the public saloons; cabin trunks and flowers were being delivered; children ran, full of curiosity, up and down the companionways while the orchestra played imperturbably on deck. I was standing somewhat apart from this turmoil, talking to a friend on the promenade deck, when two or three flashbulbs went off nearby. Apparently some important person was being quickly interviewed and photographed by the press just before we sailed.

My friend looked over and laughed. "There's a rare bird you have on board. That's Czentovic." And as I reacted to this information with a rather obviously blank expression, he went on to explain: "Mirko Czentovic, the world chess champion. He has traipsed around the whole of America from the east coast to the west, playing tournaments, and now he's off to Argentina for fresh triumphs."

In fact I did now recall this young world champion and even a few details connected with his meteoric career. My friend, a more observant reader of the newspapers than I, was able to supplement these with a whole string of anecdotes. At a stroke Czentovic had established himself about a year earlier alongside such reputable past masters of the chess world as Alekhine, Capablanca, Tartakower, Lasker and Bogolyubov. Not since the appearance of the ten-year-old prodigy Reshevsky at the New York chess tournament in 1922 had the breakthrough of a completely unknown person into the magic circle caused quite such a sensation. For Czentovic's intellectual attributes didn't appear in any way to predict at the outset that he would have such a dazzling career. The secret soon leaked out that this champion was, in his private life, incapable of writing any sentence in any language without making spelling mistakes and, as one of his exasperated colleagues angrily jeered, "his lack of education is almost universal in all departments." He was the son of a poverty-stricken southern Yugoslav who worked as a boatman on the Danube, and whose small craft was run down one night by a barge carrying grain. After his father's death the twelve-year-old boy was taken in out of pity by the priest of his remote village. The good man strove honestly, by coaching him at home, to make up for what the taciturn, unresponsive boy with the broad forehead seemed unable to learn at the village school.

But his efforts continued to be fruitless. Mirko went on staring at the letters, which had been explained to him a hundred times, as though he had never seen them before. His slow-functioning brain also lacked any retentive capacity for the simplest lessons in any subject. He had to use his fingers for counting even at the age of fourteen; and to read a book or newspaper required even more effort for this lad already halfway to adulthood. No one, however, could call Mirko unwilling or difficult. Obediently he did as he was told—fetched water, chopped wood, worked in the field, cleaned the kitchen, and always punctiliously completed every task he was given, even if he did it with infuriating slowness. But what upset the good priest most about the strange boy was his total apathy. He did nothing unless someone particularly asked him to; he never asked a question, didn't play with other lads, and never looked for any occupation beyond what had been specifically organized by someone else. As soon as Mirko had finished doing his household chores, he would sit dourly looking around the room, with the empty expression of the sheep in the meadow, utterly ignoring any activity going on around him. In the evenings, when the priest smoked his long, countryman's pipe and played his usual three games of chess with the village police sergeant, the fair-haired lad squatted dumbly beside them and stared from under his heavy lids, apparently half-asleep and with indifference, at the board with the black and white squares. One winter evening, while the two men were deep in their daily game, they heard out on the village street the bells of a fast-approaching sleigh. A farmer, his cap covered with snow, stepped quickly into the house. His old mother lay dying, and he wanted the priest to hurry to be in time to give her Extreme Unction. The priest went with him immediately. The policeman, who hadn't finished his beer, lit up his pipe again. When he was just putting on his heavy knee boots to get ready to leave, he noticed how Mirko's gaze was fixed unwaveringly on the chessboard with the unfinished game.

"Well now, would you like to finish the game?" he said jokingly, convinced that the sleepy youngster had no idea how to move a single piece on the board. The boy looked up shyly, then nodded and sat in the priest's chair. After fourteen moves the police sergeant was beaten and had to admit his defeat was not the result of a careless move on his part. The second game produced the same result.

"Balaam's ass!" the priest exclaimed in astonishment when he returned, explaining to the policeman—who was not so well versed in the Bible—that more than two thousand years ago a similar phenomenon had occurred, when someone who was dumb had suddenly discovered the gift of wise speech. Despite the late hour the priest couldn't resist challenging his semiliterate stand-in to a match. Mirko beat him easily, too. He played toughly, slowly, imperturbably, without once lifting his broad forehead from the board. But he played with undeniable certainty. Neither the policeman nor the priest was able to win one game against him over the next few days. The priest, who was better equipped than almost anyone else to assess the otherwise total backwardness of his protégé, was now eagerly curious to know how far this single, special gift would stand up to a more serious examination. After he had taken Mirko to the village barber to have his unkempt straw-colored hair cut to make him more or less presentable, he took him in his sleigh to the small town nearby. He knew some really keen chess players gathered in a corner of the café in the main square, and that they were more experienced players than himself. There was no small stir among them when the priest pushed the fair-haired, red-cheeked lad of fourteen, with his inside-out sheepskin and heavy knee boots, forward into the café. The youngster stood apart, shyly, in a corner, his eyes cast down, until he was summoned to one of the chess tables. Mirko was beaten in the first game because he had not seen the so-called Sicilian opening played at the good priest's table. In the second game he drew with the best player there. From the third and fourth games on, he beat all his opponents without exception.

Now, exciting things rarely happen in a small provincial town in southern Yugoslavia; so for the assembled worthies the debut of the peasant champion was an instant sensation. It was agreed unanimously that, whatever happened, the boy wonder must stay in the town until the next day, so that the other members of the chess club could be called together; and above all, so that a message could be sent to the castle to tell the elderly Count Simczic, who was a chess fanatic. The priest, who looked on his ward with quite new pride, but who did not wish to neglect his duties at the Sunday service merely on account of the pleasure of his discovery, agreed to leave Mirko behind for a further test. The chess group paid for young Czentovic to be put up at a hotel, and that evening he saw a lavatory for the first time. The chess room was full to capacity the following Sunday afternoon. Mirko sat for four hours at the chessboard and, without saying a word or even looking up, defeated one player after another. Finally a simultaneous game was suggested. It took some time for the uninstructed boy to grasp that in a simultaneous game he had to play alone against a number of the other players at the same time. But once Mirko had grasped this procedure, he quickly got the hang of it, and walked in his heavy, creaking boots slowly from table to table. In the end he won seven of the eight games.

Great consultations now began. Although strictly speaking, this new champion didn't belong to the town, native pride was keenly aroused. Hardly anyone had so far noticed the existence of this little town on the map, but perhaps now, for the first time, it would gain the honor of sending a man destined for fame out into the world. An agent named Koller, who until now had dealt only in singers for the cabaret, declared himself willing, if someone would guarantee his expenses for a year, to have the youngster taught all about chess professionally in Vienna, by an excellent local champion he knew. Count Simczic, who had not met such a notable opponent in sixty years of playing chess daily, guaranteed the sum immediately. That Sunday the astonishing career of the boatman's son began.

After six months Mirko had completely mastered the secrets of chess technique, but with one strange limitation, which was to be much noticed and made fun of later in chess circles. He never managed, even for one single game, to play from memory—or as the experts say, to play blindfold. He completely lacked the ability to visualize the board in the unrestricted space of the imagination. He always had to have the black-and-white board with the sixty-four squares and the thirty-two pieces physically in front of him. Even when he was world famous he carried a folding pocket chess set with him, so that if he wanted to reconstruct a championship game or solve a problem, he could have the positions displayed visually. This defect, trivial in itself, betrayed a flaw in his imaginative power, and it was often discussed within the small world of chess in the same way that musicians talk about an outstanding virtuoso or conductor who proves unable to play or conduct without a written score.

But this odd peculiarity in no way slowed down Mirko's stupendous progress. By the time he was seventeen he had already won a dozen chess prizes. At eighteen he had won the Hungarian championship, and at twenty the world championship. The most audacious champions, each one vastly superior to him in intellectual ability, imagination and daring, were nevertheless beaten by his tough, cold logic, as Napoleon was by the ponderous Kutuzov, or Hannibal by Fabius Cunctator. The latter, according to Livy, had similarly shown in childhood conspicuous signs of impassivity and stupidity. So it came about that a complete outsider, a ponderous, taciturn country lad, from whom even the most cunning reporters were unable to extract one usefully pub-

lishable word, fought his way into the illustrious gallery of chess champions, in whose ranks were assembled men of the most varied types of intellectual superiority—philosophers, mathematicians, calculating, imaginative and often creative temperaments. To be sure, what Czentovic denied the papers in the way of polished speech he soon more than adequately made up for in anecdotes about himself. Inescapably, the moment he left the chessboard, where he was undisputed master, Czentovic became an almost comic figure; despite his formal black suit, his splendid cravat with the somewhat ostentatious pearl tiepin, and his painstakingly manicured nails, he remained in behavior and manners the same limited country bumpkin who had cleaned out the priest's quarters in the village. In a blatantly crude and clumsy way he set about extracting from his gift and his fame whatever money there was to be had. He did this, to the amusement and vexation of his professional colleagues, in a petty way, often showing what amounted to sheer vulgar greed. He traveled from town to town, always staying in the cheapest hotels. He played in the most awful clubs, provided they paid his fee. He allowed himself to appear on advertisements for soap, and even lent his name— ignoring the jokes of his rivals, who knew well that he couldn't put three sentences together correctly—to a *Philosophy of Chess*, which was really written for its commercially aware publisher by an insignificant student from Galicia. As with every truly stubborn person, he lacked a sense of the ridiculous. From the moment he won the world championship he thought he was the most important man in the world; and the knowledge that he had beaten all those clever, intellectual, brilliant speakers and writers in their own field, and above all, the plain fact that he had earned more than they had, turned his initial insecurity into a cold and tactless display of pride.

"But how could such an early rise to fame fail to turn such an empty head?" my friend concluded, having just given me a classic demonstration of Czentovic's childish propensities. "How could a twenty-one-year-old peasant from the Banat fail to succumb to an attack of vanity if, suddenly, by moving a few pieces around on a wooden board, he could earn more in a week than his entire village back home in a whole year of woodcutting and bitter hard work? Besides, isn't it confoundedly easy to think you're a great man if you aren't burdened with the slightest idea that Rembrandt, Beethoven, Dante or Napoleon ever even lived? This lad knows only one thing in that walled-in brain of his: that for months now he hasn't lost a game of chess. And as he really has no idea that anything else in the world apart from chess and money has any value, he has every reason to be pleased with himself."

The information given me by my friend couldn't fail to arouse my particular curiosity. All my life I have been attracted by every kind of monomania, by people obsessed with one single idea. For the more a man limits himself, the nearer he is on the other hand to what is limitless; it is precisely those who are apparently aloof from the world who build for themselves a remarkable and thoroughly individual world in miniature, using their own special equipment, termitelike. So I made no secret of my intention of examining this particular specimen of intellectual one-track-mindedness under the microscope during the twelve-day journey to Rio.

"You won't have much luck there," my friend warned me. "As far as I know, no one's been able to extract the slightest bit of psychological material from Czentovic. Behind his abysmal stupidity the wily peasant conceals the ultimate in cleverness. He leaves no chinks in his armor, thanks to a simple technique. He talks only to fellow Yugoslavs from his own background. He looks for them in small bars. If he gets a whiff of education in a man, he retreats into his shell. Then no one can boast of having heard him say anything stupid."

My friend was right, in fact. During the first day of the voyage it proved absolutely impossible to approach Czentovic without being boorishly importunate, which definitely isn't my way. Sometimes, to be sure, he would walk on the promenade deck, but always with his hands clasped behind his back and with a proud self-absorbed bearing, as in those well-known pictures of Napoleon. Besides, he took his walk around the deck with such speed and thrustfulness that you would have had to follow him at a trot to be able to speak to him. Again, he never appeared in the public rooms, in the bar, in the smoking room. As I was told by the steward of whom I inquired discreetly, he spent most of the day in his cabin practicing or going over games of chess on a large board.

After three days it began really to annoy me that his skillful defense technique was stronger than my determination to approach him. I had never yet in my life had the opportunity of actually meeting a chess champion, and the more concerned I became about fitting a label to this specific type of man, so the thought processes involved seemed to me the more incredible—that a man could spend his whole life revolving exclusively around a space consisting of sixty-four black and white squares. I knew well enough from my own experience the mysterious attraction of "the royal game," that game among games devised by man, which rises majestically above every tyranny of chance, which grants its victor's laurels only to a great intellect, or rather, to a particular form of mental ability.

But are we not already guilty of an insulting limitation in calling chess a game? Isn't it also a science, an art? Isn't it a unique bond between every pair of opponents, ancient and yet eternally new; mechanical in its framework and yet only functioning through use of the imagination; confined in geometrically fixed space and at the same time released from confinement by its permutations; continuously evolving yet sterile; thought that leads nowhere, mathematics that add up to nothing, art without an end product, architecture without substance, and nevertheless demonstrably more durable in its true nature and existence than any books or creative works? Isn't it the only game that belongs to all peoples and all times? And who knows whether God put it on earth to kill boredom, to sharpen the wits or to lift the spirits? Where is its beginning and where its end?

Every child can learn its basic rules, every bungler can try it; and yet it requires, within those unchanging small squares, the production of a special species of master, not comparable to any other kind, men who have a singular gift for chess, geniuses of a particular kind, in whom vision, patience and technique function in just as precise divisions as they do in mathematicians, poets and musicians, only on different levels and in different conjunctions.

At an earlier stage of the great interest in research into physiognomy, someone like Gall would have dissected the brains of chess champions to establish if such geniuses had a unique coil in their gray matter, a kind of chess bump that was more pronounced there than in other skulls. And how a case like Czentovic's would have excited such a physiognomist, where this precise type of genius appears to be deposited in intellectually totally inert matter, like a single vein of gold in a hundredweight of dead rock!

In principle I understood the time-honored fact that such a unique, such an ingenious, game must produce its own special matadors. But how difficult it is, how impossible even, to visualize the life of an alert, intelligent man who reduces the world to the narrow linear traffic between black and white, who looks for his life's apogee in the mere to-ing and fro-ing, back and forth, of thirty-two pieces. How hard it is to understand a man who, through using a new opening, moving the Knight instead of the pawn, achieves a feat, and his tiny little scrap of immortality is tucked away in a chess book reference—a man, an intelligent man, who, without losing his reason, for ten, twenty, thirty, forty years concentrates all his mental energy over and over again on the ludicrous exercise of maneuvering into a corner a wooden king on a wooden board!

And now one such phenomenon, one such genius or incomprehensible fool, was physically near me for the first time, six cabins away on the same ship. And there was I, feeling wretched because my curiosity about how the mind works has always been a kind of passion and I was not in a position to approach him. I began to think up the most absurd stratagems: perhaps to flatter his vanity by pretending to interview him for an important paper, or to arouse his greed by offering him a lucrative tournament in Scotland. But eventually I remembered that the hunter's most successful technique for enticing the black grouse is to imitate its mating call: What could really be more effective in attracting the attention of a chess champion than to play chess oneself?

Now I have never in my life been a serious exponent of the art of chess, the reason being simply that I have always entered into a game lightheartedly and entirely for pleasure. If I sit down at a chessboard for an hour, I am not going to exert myself in any way. Quite the opposite: I shall be seeking relaxation from intellectual tension. I "play" chess in the truest sense of the word while others, the real chess players, work at it. For chess, then, as for love, a partner is essential, and at that time I didn't know if there were any other chess enthusiasts on board. To lure them out of their hiding places I set up a rudimentary trap in the smoking room. Although my wife is an even weaker player than I, she and I sat there at a chessboard like birdcatchers. We hadn't completed six moves before someone passing by stopped, and a second asked permission to watch us. Eventually the partner I was hoping for arrived to challenge me to a game.

His name was McConnor and he was a Scots mining engineer. As I heard it, he had made a large fortune out of oil wells in California. He was stocky in appearance, with a strong, firm, almost square jaw, strong teeth, and a rich ruddy complexion for which, it would appear, a copious intake of whisky was at least in part responsible. His shoulders were strikingly broad and almost athletically mobile. Unfortunately and characteristically they drew one's attention as he played, for this Mr. McConnor was one of that breed of successful self-made men for whom a defeat, even in the most unimportant game, diminishes their self-esteem. Accustomed in life to getting his own way ruthlessly and spoiled by material success, this massive self-made man was so unshakably convinced of his own superiority that any opposition provoked him as being unwarrantable, almost an affront. When he lost the first game he became bad tempered and began to explain dictatorially and at length that it could only have been because his attention must have wandered for a moment. In the third game he blamed the noise in the next room for his failure. He was never prepared to lose without at once seeking a return game. At first this driving determination amused me. In the end I accepted it only as an unavoidable accompaniment to the achievement of my own objective: to lure the world champion to our table.

On the third day it worked, but only by half. It could have been that Czentovic noticed us at our chessboard through the window from the promenade deck, or it could have been by chance that he honored the smoking room with his presence. Anyway, as soon as he saw us amateurs practicing his art, he instinctively took a step over in our direction and from a measured distance cast a searching glance at our board. It was McConnor's move. And this one move was quite sufficient to tell Czentovic how little worthy of his expert interest a closer study of our unskilled efforts would be. With the same obvious gesture that one uses to put down a bad detective novel one has been offered in a bookshop, without even leafing through it, he walked away from our table and left the smoking room. Weighed in the balance and found wanting, I thought to myself, slightly put out by that cool, contemptuous look. To relieve my feelings a little, I said to McConnor, "The champion didn't seem to be very enthusiastic about your move."

"Which champion?"

I explained that the person who had just walked past and given our game a disapproving glance was Czentovic, the chess champion. However, I continued, the two of us would survive and come to terms without his illustrious contempt breaking our hearts; beggars can't be choosers. But to my surprise my offhand remark had quite an unexpected effect on McConnor. He immediately became so excited he forgot our game, and you could almost hear his ambition building up steam. He had no idea Czentovic was on board. Czentovic simply must play him. He had only once in his life played against a world champion, and that was in a simultaneous match with forty others; even that had been frightfully exciting, and he had very nearly won. Did I know the champion personally? I said I didn't. Would I speak to him and ask him over? I declined, on the grounds that I knew Czentovic was not very responsive to new acquaintances. Besides, what sort of attraction would there be for a world champion in playing with third-rate players like us?

Well, I ought not to have spoken of third-rate players to a man of McConnor's overweening nature. He leaned back angrily and declared bluntly that, for his part, he couldn't believe Czentovic would decline the polite challenge of a gentleman; and he would soon see about that. At his request I gave him a brief description of the world champion. With uncontrolled impatience he soon rushed off after Czentovic on the promenade deck, unconcernedly leaving our game abandoned. Again, I felt the owner of the broad shoulders was not to be restrained once he was determined to have something.

I waited quite anxiously. After ten minutes McConnor returned, not looking very pleased, it seemed to me.

"Well?" I asked him.

"You were right," he replied, somewhat annoyed. "He's not a very pleasant gentleman. I introduced myself, told him who I am. He didn't shake hands. I tried to explain how proud and honored we would all be on board if he would play a simultaneous match against us. But he was damnably stiff-necked about it. Said he was sorry, but he had contractual obligations to his agent that expressly forbade him to play on the whole trip without payment of a fee. His minimum is two hundred and fifty dollars a match."

I laughed. "It would never have occurred to me that pushing

pieces about from black to white could be such a profitable business. Well, I hope you said good-by just as politely."

But McConnor remained utterly serious. "The match has been arranged for tomorrow afternoon at three o'clock. Here in the smoking room. I hope we won't let him make mincemeat of us too easily."

"What? You've agreed to pay him two hundred and fifty dollars?" I exclaimed in astonishment.

"Why not? It's his trade. If I had a toothache and there happened to be a dentist on board, I wouldn't ask him to extract the tooth for nothing. The man's right to ask a fat price. In every field the real experts are also the best businessmen. And as far as I'm concerned, the more straightforward the deal, the better. I'd rather pay cash than have to be obliged to our Mr. Czentovic and thank him afterwards. Besides, I've often lost more than two hundred and fifty dollars in an evening at our club and still not played with a world champion. It's no disgrace for a 'third-rate' player like me to be beaten by a Czentovic."

I was amazed to note how deeply I had dented McConnor's self-esteem with that unforgivable phrase "third-rate player." But as he was disposed to pay for this expensive amusement, I had no objection against his misplaced vanity, which was after all to be the means of my meeting the object of my curiosity. Quickly the four or five gentlemen who had already declared themselves chess players were told of the impending event. So that we wouldn't be disturbed too much by passengers walking by, we reserved in advance of the match not only our own table but also the neighboring ones.

The next day our little group mustered in full strength at the appointed hour. The center seat opposite the champion was naturally allotted to McConnor, who relieved his nerves by lighting up one strong cigar after another and frequently looking anxiously at his watch. But—as I suspected he would, after what my friend had told me—the champion kept us waiting a good ten minutes, so that the effect of his coolly superior entry was heightened. He walked quietly and calmly over to the table. Without introducing himself—"You know who I am, and I am not interested in knowing who you are" seemed to be the inference to draw from this rudeness—he began to give the necessary instructions in a dry, professional manner. As it was impossible to play a proper simultaneous match here on the ship owing to a lack of chessboards, he proposed that we should all combine together to play him. So as not to disturb our deliberations, after each move he would go to another table at the far end of the room. As soon as we had made our next move, we should tap on a glass with a spoon, as there was unfortunately no small table bell handy. He suggested ten minutes should be the maximum time for each move, unless we wanted some other arrangement. Of course we accepted every suggestion, like timid schoolchildren. The draw gave Czentovic Black. Without sitting down, he made his first move in reply to ours and went immediately to his appointed table, where he sat back idly and leafed through an illustrated magazine.

There is little point in going into the details of the game. It ended, as of course it had to, with our total defeat, and after only twenty-four moves at that. Well, it wasn't surprising that a world champion had defeated half a dozen average or below-average players, using his left hand. What really did leave a bad impression on us all was the arrogant, unpleasant way Czentovic made us feel very clearly that he was indeed beating us with his left hand. Each time, he appeared to give the board the most casual glance, and looked right through us as though we were wooden chessmen ourselves. This rudeness unconsciously reminded me of how one throws a morsel to a mangy dog without looking at him. In my opinion he might have had the tact to point out our mistakes or to encourage us with a friendly word. But even after the match was over, this inhuman chess automaton never uttered a syllable once he had said "Mate," but waited stolidly at the table to see if we wanted a second game. Being helpless, as one always is in the face of thick-skinned, boorish behavior, I had already decided to indicate by a gesture that now that this dollar transaction had been completed, the pleasure of our acquaintance was at an end, at least as far as I was concerned. To my annoyance McConnor, sitting next to me, said huskily, "Return game!"

I was taken aback by his challenging tone; in fact, at that moment McConnor gave more the impression of being a boxer about to cut loose than a well-mannered gentleman. Was it Czentovic's unpleasant behavior toward us, or just his own pathologically sensitive ego? Whichever it was, McConnor's personality had completely changed. His face flushed right up into the roots of his hair, his nostrils flared stiffly with inner tension; he was visibly perspiring, and there was a

sharp crease between his tight-set lips and his belligerently thrust-out chin. Uneasily I recognized in his eyes that flickering of uncontrolled passion that you sometimes see gripping people at the roulette table when, after they have doubled their stakes six or seven times, the right color doesn't come up. I knew then that this was driving ambition, and if it were to cost him his entire fortune, McConnor would go on playing Czentovic over and over again, for single stakes or double, until he had won at least one game. If Czentovic kept at it, he would find a gold mine in McConnor. He should be able to extract several thousand dollars from him before we reached Buenos Aires.

Czentovic remained impassive. "As you wish," he answered politely. "You gentlemen will take Black this time."

The second game went the same way, the only difference being that our circle was not only enlarged by interested bystanders but through them it became more lively. McConnor stared fixedly at the board as though he wanted to mesmerize the pieces and will them to win. I sensed he would gladly have sacrificed a thousand dollars for the satisfaction of shouting "Mate" at our cold, insensitive opponent. Strange to say, some of the determination in his excitement seemed to rub off unwittingly onto us. Every single move was discussed with considerably more heat than hitherto; repeatedly we would hold one another back until the last moment, before giving Czentovic the signal to return to the table. Eventually we came to the seventeenth move. To our own astonishment a position on the board had been reached that appeared amazingly advantageous to us because it was possible to move one of our pawns from the third file (QB6) to the last square but one, at QB7. We had only to push it forward to QB8 to change it into a second Queen. We weren't, of course, altogether comfortable about this all too obvious chance. To a man, we suspected that Czentovic, who had assessed the situation over a much wider range of moves than we had, must have deliberately put this apparent advantage in our way as a bait. But despite the closest study and discussion we couldn't among us discover the hidden trick. Nearing the agreed time limit, we decided to chance the move. McConnor already had his hand on the pawn to move it to the last square when he felt someone grab his arm. In an urgent undertone a voice whispered, "For God's sake! Don't!"

Involuntarily we all turned around. In the last few minutes a man about forty-five, whose thin, sharp features I recognized—for I had noticed him on the promenade deck on account of his pale, almost chalky complexion—must have come over to us while we were concentrating on our problem. Aware that we were looking at him, he went on rapidly.

"If you make a Queen now, he will take her immediately by moving his Bishop to QB8. You will take that with your Knight. But meanwhile he will move his pawn to Q7, threatening your Rook. And even if you check the King with your Knight, you will lose in nine or ten moves. It is almost the same combination Alekhine used against Bogolyubov at the tournament at Piešťany in 1922."

Astonished, McConnor took his hand off the pawn and stared in no less wonderment than the rest of us at this man, whom we took to be an unexpected guardian angel from heaven. Anyone who could see checkmate nine moves ahead must be a first-class player, possibly in the running for the championship, traveling to the same tournament as Czentovic. His sudden arrival and intervention at precisely such a critical moment had something of the supernatural about it. McConnor was the first to react.

"What would you advise?" he whispered excitedly.

"Don't advance straightaway. For the moment act defensively! First withdraw your King out of the line of fire from KKt1 to KR2. He'll probably then move his line of attack over to the other flank. But you parry that with Rook QB1–QB5; that will cost him two moves, a pawn, and consequently his advantage. Then it will be pawn against pawn, and if your defense is sound, you'll make a draw for it. That's the best you can hope for."

Once more we were astonished. The precision, no less than the speed, of his calculation was quite bewildering. It was as though he had been reading the moves from a book. Anyway, the unexpected chance for us to force a draw in a game with a world champion, thanks to this man's intervention, worked wonders. By common consent we stood back to give him a clearer view of the board.

McConnor asked again, "So it's King from KKt1 to KR2?"

"That's right. Play safe!"

McConnor obeyed, and we tapped on the glass. Czentovic came over to our table at his customary even pace and at a glance assessed the countermove. Then he moved his pawn on the King's side, KR2–KR4, exactly as our unknown helper had forecast.

And immediately our man whispered excitedly, "Advance your Rook, the Rook QB8 to QB4. Then he'll have to cover his pawn. Attack with your Knight QB6–Q4, and you'll be back on even terms again. Press the attack instead of defending!"

We didn't understand what he meant. But once under his spell, McConnor did as he was told, without stopping to think about it. We tapped on the glass again to recall Czentovic. For the first time he didn't decide on his move quickly but looked intently at the board. Then he made his move exactly as the stranger had told us he would, and turned to go. Before he went, though, Czentovic raised his eyes and looked at us all. Clearly he wanted to find out who was offering him such energetic opposition for once.

From this instant our excitement grew immeasurably. We had been playing without any real hope, but now the thought that we might break Czentovic's cold pride made our pulses race. Our new friend soon directed our next move, and we called Czentovic over— my fingers were trembling as I tapped the glass with the spoon. And now we had our triumph. Until this moment Czentovic had played standing up, but now he hesitated, went on hesitating, and finally sat down. He sat down slowly and heavily, but this action was enough to neutralize—purely physically—the "high and mighty" distance between us. We had forced him, at least spatially, to put himself on the same level as ourselves. He reflected for a long time, his eyes fixed on the board, so that you could scarcely see the pupils under the heavy lids. The effort of concentration gradually made his mouth fall open, which gave his round face a slightly silly expression. Czentovic considered for a few minutes, then he made his move and stood up.

Soon our friend was whispering, "A delaying tactic! Good thinking! But don't go along with it! Force an exchange, make him exchange. Then we'll have a draw, and even the gods can't help him."

McConnor did as he was told. In the next few moves between the two—the rest of us had long since been reduced to inactive extras—there began what was to us meaningless interplay. About seven moves later Czentovic, after a long pause for thought, looked up and said, "Draw."

For a moment everything was very still. You could suddenly hear the sound of the waves, and the jazz on the radio in the saloon, you were aware of people walking on the promenade deck and of the light, gentle sighing of the wind as it came in through the open windows. No one breathed: it had happened too suddenly and we were all frankly startled by the improbability of what had occurred—that this unknown man should have imposed his will on the world champion in a game that was already half lost. McConnor leaned back all at once, releasing his pent-up breath from his lips in an audible, happy "Ah!" I looked again at Czentovic. I had already thought he seemed to grow paler while the final moves were being made. But he knew how to conduct himself. He maintained his apparently imperturbable equanimity and merely inquired in an offhand way, while he removed the pieces from the board, "Do you gentlemen want a third game?"

He asked the question in a purely matter-of-fact way, purely businesslike. But what was noteworthy was that he didn't look at McConnor as he spoke, but directed his eyes searchingly and straight at our rescuer. As a horse recognizes a new and better rider from the firmness of his seat, Czentovic must have recognized from the last few moves who his real—his only—opponent was. Instinctively we followed his gaze and looked anxiously at the stranger.

Before he could think about it, however, or have a chance to answer, McConnor, in his boundless excitement had already called out to him triumphantly, "Of course! But now you must play him on your own! Just you against Czentovic!"

Now, however, something unforeseen happened. The stranger, who oddly enough was still staring intently at the now empty chessboard, took fright when he saw everyone was looking at him and how enthusiastically he was being appealed to. He seemed embarrassed.

"Oh, no, gentlemen," he stumbled, visibly disconcerted. "That's quite out of the question . . . count me out . . . it's twenty years, no, twenty-five, since I sat down at a chessboard . . . and I have just realized how rude it was of me to meddle in your game without being asked. Please excuse me for being so presumptuous. I really won't disturb you further." And before we could recover from our surprise he had withdrawn from the group and left the room.

"But that's really quite impossible!" McConnor boomed out boisterously, gesticulating with his fist. "It's not credible that that man hasn't played chess for twenty-five years! He calculated every move, every countermove, five or six moves ahead. No one can do that right off the cuff. It's totally impossible—isn't it?" McConnor had without thinking turned to Czentovic with his last question. But the world champion remained completely impassive.

"It isn't for me to give an opinion on that. However, the gentleman did play a quite surprising and interesting game; that's why I deliberately left him a chance." As he spoke, he stood up languidly and continued in his matter-of-fact way. "If he, or you, should wish to play another game tomorrow, I shall be at your disposal from three o'clock."

We couldn't suppress a mild chuckle. We all knew Czentovic hadn't left our unknown helper a chance out of generosity at all, and that his remark was nothing but a naive excuse to cover up his own failure. It only intensified our desire to see such an unshakably arrogant man humiliated. All at once a wild, overpowering wish to do battle came over us peaceful, relaxed sea voyagers; for we were fascinated in a challenging way by the thought that right here on our ship, in the middle of the ocean, the victory wreath could be taken from the champion—a triumph that would then be flashed around the whole world by the telegraph offices. Moreover, there was the fascination of the mystery of the unexpected intervention of our rescuer at precisely the critical moment, and the contrast of his almost timid diffidence and the unshakable self-confidence of the professional. Who was this unknown man? Had a hitherto undiscovered chess genius been brought to light here by chance? Or was a famous champion keeping his name from us for reasons of his own? We debated all these possibilities in a state of great excitement. Even the most farfetched hypotheses were not outrageous enough for us to reconcile the stranger's puzzling shyness and astonishing avowal with his undeniable ability at the game. In one respect, however, we remained united: whatever happened, we were not going to turn down the spectacle of another contest. We resolved to try every way of inducing our helper to play Czentovic the next day. McConnor undertook to put up the stake. As, meanwhile, inquiries of the steward had established that our man was an Austrian, it fell to me, as his compatriot, to put our request to him.

It didn't take me long to find our swiftly disappearing fugitive on the promenade deck. He was sitting in a deck chair, reading. Before I went up to him I took the opportunity to have a good look at him. His sharply chiseled head was resting on the cushion as though he were a little tired. Once again I was struck by the noticeable pallor of his relatively young face, and by how the hair framing his temples was absolutely white. I had a feeling, I don't know why, that this man must have aged suddenly. I had scarcely approached him before he stood up politely and introduced himself. I recognized the name immediately as belonging to an old and well-respected Austrian family. I recalled that a bearer of that name had been one of Schubert's closest friends, and that one of the physicians of the old emperor came from the same family. When I put our request to Dr. B., that he should take up Czentovic's challenge, he was visibly taken aback. It turned out he had no idea that in that game of ours he had stood up magnificently to a world champion—indeed, the most successful player of the day. For some reason this information seemed to make an impression on him, because he kept on asking me if I was sure his opponent was really an acknowledged grand master. I soon realized this made my task easier, but I thought it advisable nonetheless, in order to spare his sensibilities, not to tell him that McConnor would be taking the financial risk if he were defeated. After hesitating a long time Dr. B. eventually declared he was prepared to play, but not without expressly asking me to warn the others not to set too much store by his ability.

"Because," he went on with a pensive laugh, "I honestly don't know if I'm capable of playing a match according to all the rules. Please believe me, it wasn't false modesty when I said I haven't touched a chess piece since my school days—more than twenty years ago. And even then I wasn't considered a player of any special merit."

He said this so naturally that I couldn't entertain the slightest doubt about his sincerity. Yet I couldn't refrain from expressing my surprise that he had been able to remember every detail of combinations by a variety of champions. At least he must have made a serious study of chess theory?

Dr. B. laughed again in his curiously dreamy way. "A serious study! God knows, that's true. I have studied chess a great deal. But that happened in quite special circumstances; indeed, they were absolutely unique. It's quite a complicated story and one that could be taken, possibly, as a little contribution to the delightful, splendid times we live in. If you have the patience to listen for half an hour . . . ?"

He motioned me toward the deck chair next to his. I accepted his invitation gladly. We had no neighbors. Dr. B. took off his reading glasses, put them away and began.

"You were good enough to say you remembered my family name, being Viennese yourself. But I don't suppose you will have heard of the firm of solicitors I ran with my father, and later alone, because we didn't take any cases that would get into the papers and we avoided new clients on principle. Strictly speaking, we didn't actually have what you could call a proper legal practice. Instead we restricted ourselves exclusively to advising the great monasteries, and above all to administering their estates. My father had connections with them, having been earlier a member of Parliament representing the Catholic party. In addition—now that the empire is part of history, one can talk about these things—we were entrusted with the management of the finances of several members of the imperial family. Our connection with court and Church went back two generations—my uncle was physician to the emperor, another was an abbot in Seitenstellen. We had only to supervise their investments, and it was an unobtrusive, I might say silent, function that was allotted to us through this inherited trust. It called for no more than the utmost discretion and trustworthiness, two qualities my late father possessed in the highest degree. He managed, in fact, substantially to maintain the value of his clients' fortunes through the years of inflation and at the time of the fall of the empire. Then when Hitler took the helm in Germany and began his raids on the property of the Church and the monasteries, negotiations and transactions to save at least the movable assets from confiscation passed through our hands from across the frontier. The two of us knew more about certain secret political matters concerning the Curia and the imperial family than the general public would ever imagine. But it was precisely the inconspicuousness of our office—we didn't even have a nameplate on the door—as well as the precaution we both took of pointedly avoiding all monarchist circles, that gave us the surest protection from overzealous investigation. It was a fact that in all those years no official in Austria ever suspected that the secret couriers of the imperial household collected or delivered their most important mail in our insignificant fourth-floor office.

"But the Nazis had begun, long before they rearmed their military forces against the world, to organize another army—just as dangerous and well trained—in all neighboring countries: the legion of the underprivileged, the downtrodden, the maladjusted. In every office, in every business, they established their so-called cells; in every government department, right up to the private offices of Dollfuss and Schuschnigg themselves, they had their eavesdroppers and spies. They even had their man in our insignificant office, as unfortunately I only found out too late. It's true he was only a wretched, run-of-the-mill clerk, whom I had taken on at the recommendation of a priest, just to give our office the outward appearance of a bona fide business. All we used him for really was running innocent errands, answering the telephone and filing papers—unimportant and harmless papers, that is. He wasn't allowed to open the mail. I typed all the important letters myself, without making copies for the files. I took every important document home with me, and confidential conversations were held exclusively in the priory house of the monastery or in my uncle's consulting room. Thanks to these precautions our eavesdropper obtained no information about what was really going on. But by some unlucky accident this self-seeking and self-important young man must have become aware that he wasn't being trusted and that whatever was of interest was happening behind his back. Perhaps in my absence one of the couriers had carelessly spoken of "His Majesty" instead of the agreed "Baron Bern," or, disobeying instructions, the scoundrel opened letters. Anyway, before it occurred to me to suspect him, he had instructions from Munich or Berlin to watch us. It wasn't until much later, long after my arrest, that I remembered how his initial idleness at work had suddenly changed over the previous few months into enthusiasm, and how more than once he had practically insisted I let him post my letters. I am not free from blame myself, therefore, for a certain amount of negligence; but weren't the most important diplomats and generals craftily outmaneuvered in the end by Hitler?

"How closely and with what loving care the Gestapo had been keeping me under surveillance for so long became tangibly evident from the fact that I was arrested by the SS on the very evening that Schuschnigg announced his resignation, and one day before Hitler took possession of Vienna. Luckily I was able to burn the most important documents the moment I heard Schuschnigg's resignation speech. The rest of the papers, along with the essential certificates for the securities held abroad on behalf of the monasteries and two archdukes, I sent—literally at the last minute, just before those fellows smashed my door in—to my uncle, hiding them in a laundry basket carried by my elderly and reliable housekeeper."

Dr. B. broke off to light a cigar. I saw in the flickering light a nervous tic at the right-hand corner of his mouth. I had noticed it before, and observed that it happened every minute or two. It was only a slight movement, not much stronger than a breath, but it made his whole face look remarkably restless.

"I expect you are thinking I'm going to tell you now about the concentration camp where everyone who was loyal to our old Austria was sent, and about the degradations, suffering and torture I endured there. But nothing of the kind happened. I was in a different category. I wasn't one of those unfortunates on whom they vented their long-accumulated resentment by inflicting physical and spiritual degradation. I belonged to that other quite small group from whom the Nazis hoped to extract money or important information. In my own right I was, of course, too insignificant to be of interest to the Gestapo. They must have discovered, though, that we were the front men, the administrators and confidants of their bitterest opponents. What they hoped to extract from me was incriminating evidence against the monasteries to prove financial malpractice, evidence against the royal family and everyone who devotedly supported the monarchy. They suspected—and, in fact, rightly so—that of the money which had passed through our hands substantial amounts were still hidden and out of reach of their rapacious designs. That's why they sent for me on the first day, to force those secrets out of me by their tried and tested methods. People like me, from whom important information or money might be extracted were, therefore, not bundled into concentration camps, but were reserved for special treatment. You may perhaps recall that Chancellor Schuschnigg, and also Baron Rothschild, from whose relatives they hoped to extort millions, weren't put behind barbed wire in a prison camp at all, but were taken, apparently as a favor, to a hotel, the Hotel Metropole—which was at the same time Gestapo headquarters—where each had his own room. This consideration was also extended to my unimportant person.

"A single room in a hotel—that sounds extremely liberal, doesn't it? But believe me, what they had in mind for us wasn't at all liberal. It was merely using a refined method when they didn't cram us 'bigwigs' twenty to a freezing army barracks, but lodged us in tolerably warm, separate hotel rooms. The pressure they were going to put on us to obtain the required information was to be more subtle than crude beating or physical torture. It was to be through the most complete isolation you could conceive. They did nothing to us—they just placed us in a complete vacuum, for as everyone knows, nothing on earth puts more pressure on the human spirit than a vacuum. Locking each of us up alone in a complete void, in a room hermetically sealed from the outside world, was to produce the pressure from within ourselves that would finally make us speak, without resort to beatings and freezing conditions.

"At first sight the room I was allotted didn't seem at all unpleasant. It had a door, a bed, a chair, a washbasin, a barred window. But the door stayed shut day and night. There was no book, newspaper, sheet of paper or pencil on the table. The window looked out onto a blank wall. A total void surrounded me physically and spiritually. They had taken away every possession: my watch, so I couldn't tell the time; my pencil, so I couldn't write anything; my pocket knife, so I couldn't slash my wrists; even the smallest narcotic, like a cigarette, was denied me. I saw no human face except for the warder, who wasn't allowed to speak or answer any questions. I heard no human voice. Eyes, ears, none of my senses received the slightest stimulus from morning to night, from night to morning. I was alone with myself and the four or five silent objects—table, bed, window, washbasin—inescapably alone. I lived like a diver in his bell in the black ocean of that silence; and, at that, a diver who suspects his cable to the outside world has snapped and he will never be hauled back out of the soundless deep. There was nothing to do, nothing to hear, nothing to see. All around, and unbroken, was a void, a complete vacuum in time and space. I walked up and down, up and down, endlessly. But even thoughts, however trivial, need an anchorage, otherwise they begin to spin and chase themselves in mad circles. And they can't bear a vacuum either. You waited for something to happen, from morning to night, but nothing did. You were waiting, waiting, waiting and thinking, thinking, thinking until your head ached. Nothing happened. You were alone. Alone. Alone.

"I lived out of time and out of the world for a whole fortnight. Had war broken out, I wouldn't have known. My world consisted only of table, door, bed, washbasin, chair, window and wall, and I stared continuously at the same wall.

Then at last the interrogation began. They summoned you suddenly, without your really knowing if it was day or night. They sent for you and you were taken along a corridor or two. You didn't know where you were going. You waited somewhere, and you didn't know where you were.

Then abruptly you were standing in front of a table with a few people in uniform sitting at it. On the table was a pile of documents whose contents you knew nothing about. Then the questions started, genuine and fake, straightforward and crafty, superficial questions and catch questions. And while you answered, the hands of strangers with evil intent leafed through the papers whose contents you didn't know, malicious hands wrote things in a record of the proceedings and you didn't know what they were writing.

But what I found most frightening about this interrogation was that I couldn't guess what the Gestapo already knew about the workings of my office, and what they wanted to get out of me. As I've told you already, at the last moment I had sent my housekeeper to my uncle with the really incriminating documents. But had he received them? And how much had that clerk betrayed? How many letters had they intercepted? How much had they meanwhile wormed out of some naive cleric in one of the German monasteries with which we dealt? And they went on with question after question.

What securities had I bought for this monastery, what banks did I deal with, did I know Mr. So-and-so, did I receive letters from Switzerland or Timbuktu? And as I couldn't tell how much they knew already, every answer was a terrible responsibility. If I gave something away that they didn't know, I might perhaps be needlessly sending someone to his execution. If I told too many lies, I might be putting myself at risk.

"But the interrogation was not the worst part. The worst was being returned afterwards to my vacuum, to the same room with the same table, the same bed, the same washbasin, the same wall. Scarcely was I alone again than I tried to recapitulate, to think what I ought to have said if I had been clever, and what I must say next time to divert any suspicion that a careless remark of mine might perhaps have aroused. I reflected on, pondered over, examined and checked every word of my own testimony, everything I had told the chief interrogator. I repeated every question they had asked me, every answer I had given. I tried to assess what they had been able to put in their report, and yet I knew I couldn't ever possibly do that. But these thoughts, once conjured up in the empty room, wouldn't stop going round in my head, always in new or different combinations, and they seeped into my sleep. After every interrogation by the Gestapo my own thoughts took over, just as relentlessly, the torment of questioning and searching and harassment.

Perhaps it was even more horrible in that every interrogation did end after an hour but this recapitulation never ended, thanks to the insidious torture of my isolation. And still I had only the table, the washbasin, the bed, the wall, the window. No diversion—no book, no newspaper, no other face, no pencil to write with, no matchstick to play with, nothing, nothing, nothing.

"It was then that I first became aware of how devilishly clever, how psychologically murderous the concept of this system of using hotel rooms was. In a concentration camp you might have had to cart stones, perhaps, until your hands bled and your feet froze in your shoes. You might have been crammed together with two dozen others, stinking and shivering. But you would have seen faces, had a field, a square, a tree, a star, something, anything, to look at; instead of here, where everything was never changing, always the same, always unbearably the same. There was nothing here that could release me from my thoughts, from my obsession with them, from my pathological reiteration of them. And that was exactly what they intended. I was to choke on my thoughts until they asphyxiated me, and until I couldn't do anything else but spit them out, in the end to confess, to tell all, everything they wanted, to hand over, finally, information and men.

"Gradually I could feel how my nerves were beginning to break under the terrible pressure of the vacuum; and recognizing the danger, I braced myself to my nerve ends to try to find or invent some kind of diversion. To occupy myself I tried to recite and reconstruct everything I had ever learned by heart: the national anthem, nursery rhymes, schoolboy jokes, clauses of the Code of Civil Law. Then I tried arithmetic, adding and dividing random figures, but I had no power of concentration in that void. The same thought kept flickering in and out of my mind: What do they know? What did I say yesterday? What must I say next time?

"This really indescribable state of affairs lasted four months. Well—four months, that's easy to write: just one figure, one word! Easy to say, too: four months—two syllables. The lips can articulate a sound like that in no time at all: four months! But no one can describe, can measure, can visualize for someone else, for himself even, how long such a time seems within an infinity of time and space. You can't explain to anyone how this vacuum, this void, this nothingness around you corrodes and destroys; how you go mad having nothing but table, and bed, and washbasin and wall, and always the silence, always the same warder pushing the food into the room without looking at you, always the same thoughts going round in circles in the void. I became uneasily aware from small signs that my mind was falling into disarray. At first I had been quite clear in my own mind at the interrogations. I had answered calmly and with deliberation; the process of thinking of both sides—what I should say and what I should not—still functioned.

Now I could only haltingly articulate the simplest sentences, for while I answered, I would be staring hypnotically at the recording pen as it ran across the paper, as though I wanted my own words to run after it. I sensed that my strength was failing. I sensed the moment was drawing ever nearer when, to save myself, I would tell them everything I knew; when, to escape the asphyxiation of this vacuum, I would betray twelve men and their secrets without gaining anything for myself beyond a breathing space. One evening it had really gone that far. When the warder by chance brought me food at that moment of asphyxiation, I suddenly screamed after him, 'Take me for questioning! I'll tell them everything! I'll confess it all! I'll tell them where the papers are, where the money is! I'll tell them everything, everything!' Luckily he was too far away to hear me. Perhaps he didn't want to hear me.

"In my extreme moment of need, however, something unexpected happened. It held out salvation, at least salvation for a certain time. It was the end of July, a dark, gloomy, rainy day. I remember those details quite clearly because the rain was beating on the windows in the corridor along which I was taken for interrogation. I had to wait in the anteroom belonging to the chief interrogator. You always had to wait before every session. Making you wait was also part of the technique. First your nerves would be ripped apart by the summons, by suddenly being fetched from your cell in the middle of the night. Then when you'd adjusted to the idea of being questioned, had tensed your mind and will to resist, they made you wait, pointlessly, one hour, two hours, three, before the interrogation, to exhaust your body and break down your spirit. And they made me wait particularly long that Thursday, the twenty-seventh of July, in this anteroom, where I had never been before. Two solid hours I stood waiting. I remember the exact date because in that anteroom, where—of course I wasn't allowed to sit down—for two hours my legs had to hold my body up, there was a calendar. I don't have to tell you how I stared at those figures, that word on the wall, 'July 27,' in my hunger for the printed or written word. My brain devoured them. And then I went on waiting and waiting and staring at the door to see when it would eventually be opened. I pondered, too, over what my interrogators would ask me this time. I knew even then that they would ask me something quite different from what I expected.

"But despite everything the ordeal of waiting and standing was nevertheless a blessing, a pleasure, because this room was after all different from my own. It was slightly bigger, had two windows instead of one, and had no bed or washbasin, and didn't have the same crack in the windowsill that I had looked at a million times. The door was painted a different color, there was a different chair against the wall, and on the left a filing cabinet with documents, as well as a coatrack with hangers, on which hung three or four wet uniform overcoats, my torturers' coats. So I had something new, something different to look at, at last something else for my staring eyes, and they pounced eagerly on every detail. I noticed every fold of those coats. I noticed, for example, a raindrop hanging on the wet collar of one of them, and however ridiculous it may sound to you, I waited with absurd excitement to see if that droplet would eventually run down the collar or would defy gravity and just stay there. Yes, I stared at that droplet and went on staring for several minutes, with bated breath, as though my life depended on it. Then, when it had rolled down, I counted the buttons on the coats: eight on the first one, eight on the second, ten on the third. Then I compared the insignia of rank. My hungry eyes took in, played with and seized on all those silly, unimportant details with an avidity I can't describe.

"Suddenly my gaze fixed on something. I had discovered that the side pocket of one of the coats was bulging slightly. I stepped nearer and believed I recognized the rectangular shape of the protrusion: what was in the swollen pocket—a book! My knees began to tremble: a BOOK! For four months I hadn't held a book in my hand, and already the mere idea of a book, in which you could see words following one another, lines, pages, a book in which you could read different, new, strange, entertaining thoughts, absorb them into your brain, was both intoxicating and stupefying at the same time. My eyes were hypnotized by that little bump in the pocket made by the book. They bored into that insignificant spot as if they wanted to burn a hole in the coat. In the end I couldn't control my greed; instinctively I drew nearer. Already the thought of at least feeling a book through the material made my fingers tingle. Almost without realizing it, I was going closer and closer. Luckily the warder ignored my odd behavior. Perhaps it seemed natural to him that after two hours of standing a man wanted to lean on the wall. At last I was standing right up against the coat and I deliberately put my hands behind my back so that I could touch the coat unobtrusively. I fingered the material and through it, right enough, I could feel something rectangular, something flexible, that rustled slightly—a book! A thought struck me like a shot: Steal the book! Perhaps you can do it, and you can hide it in your cell and then read and read and read!

"Scarcely had the thought entered my head than it began to work like a strong poison; all at once there was a singing in my ears and my heart began to pound, my hands were ice-cold and unresponsive. But after the first moment of paralysis I moved my hands slowly and slyly into the pocket of the coat. All the time keeping an eye on the warder, and with my hands working behind my back, I lifted the book from the bottom of the pocket higher and higher. And then, gripping it, I gave a slight and cautious tug and suddenly I had the small, slender volume in my hand. Now for the first time I was frightened by what I had done. But there was no going back. Still, where could I put it? Behind my back I pushed the volume inside my trousers, where the belt would hold it, and then gradually moved it round to my hip so that when I walked I could hold it there by keeping my hand pressed, military fashion, against the seam of my trouser leg. Now came the first test. I moved away from the coatrack, one step, two steps, three. It worked. It was possible to keep the book in position while I walked if I pressed my arm against my belt.

"Then came the interrogation. It required more attention from me than ever, for while I was answering, I was concentrating all my effort, not on what I was saying, but above all on holding on to the book without arousing suspicion. Luckily the session was a short one, and I carried the book safely to my room. I won't waste your time with all the details, but once the book slid dangerously down my trouser leg in the middle of a corridor, and I had to pretend to have a bad bout of coughing to be able to bend down and push it safely back up under my belt. But what a moment that was when I went back into my hellhole, alone at last, yet not alone anymore!

"I expect you think I seized upon the book, examined it and read it! Oh, no! First I wanted to enjoy to the full the pleasure of anticipation, of having a book. I wanted the artificially protracted pleasure—which stimulated my senses wonderfully—of daydreaming about what kind of book I most hoped this stolen one would be. Very closely printed, above all, containing many, many letters, many, many thin pages, so that there would be more in it to read. And then I wanted it to be a work that stretched me intellectually, not shallow, light reading; something I could learn, memorize, poetry, and best of all—what a bold dream—Goethe or Homer. But at last I couldn't contain my eagerness and curiosity any longer. Stretched out on the bed so that the warder couldn't catch me by surprise if he opened the door, I pulled the book out from under my belt, trembling.

"The first glance brought disappointment and indeed a kind of bitter anger. This book, captured at such awful risk, anticipated with such glowing expectation, was nothing more than a chess handbook, a collection of a hundred and fifty championship games. If I hadn't been barred and bolted into the room, I would have hurled the book through an open window in my initial rage. For what should I do, what could I begin to do, with this nonsense? As a schoolboy I had tried playing chess from time to time, like most other boys, out of boredom. But what was I to make of this theoretical stuff? You can't very well play chess without an opponent, and certainly not without chessmen and a board. I thumbed through the pages sullenly, hoping even now to find something readable, an introduction, some instructions; but I found nothing except the bare squared-off diagrams of the individual championship games, and beneath them what were to me the almost unintelligible symbols QR2–QR3, KKt1–KB3 and so on. It all seemed a kind of algebra to me, to which I could find no key. Only gradually did I puzzle out that the numbers stood for the ranks and the letters for the files, so that you could establish the position of each piece. That way the purely graphic diagram had a language of its own.

"I wondered if perhaps I could make some sort of chessboard in my cell and then try to play these games through. It seemed like a sign from heaven that my bedspread happened to have a coarse check weave. If I folded it correctly, I could make sixty-four squares out of it. Next I tore the page showing the first game out of the book and put the book under the mattress. I saved some of my bread and began to model little chessmen, King, Queen, and so on, out of it—of course they were comically inadequate. After endless attempts I was finally able to reconstruct the positions shown in the book on the checkered bedspread. But when I tried to play the whole game through, my comical bread men, half of whom I had differentiated by darkening them with dust, failed completely. I repeatedly got into a muddle for the first few days. I had to begin this one game from the beginning five, ten, twenty times. But who on earth had so much spare and useless time as I, the slave of the void? Who could command as much boundless eagerness and patience? After six days I could play this game right through without a mistake. A week later and I didn't even need the bread men on the bedspread to be able to visualize the positions in the book. And another week after that the bedspread was unnecessary. The signs, which had at first been mere abstractions in the book—QR1, QR2, QB7, QB8—were transformed automatically in my head into real objects, actual positions. The transition was indefatigably achieved: I had projected the chessboard and its pieces into my mind and, thanks to the basic rules, could survey the current position in the same way that a musician can hear all the instruments and their harmony just by looking at the full score. In another fortnight I could play every game in the book from memory without effort, or as the terminology has it, blindfold.

"I began for the first time to understand the immense benefit of my daring theft. For I had all at once an occupation—pointless, if you like, but nevertheless an occupation, which negated the vacuum around me. With these hundred and fifty tournament games I possessed a wonderful weapon against the crushing monotony of space and time. To preserve the attractiveness of this new occupation, I divided my day exactly from now on: two games in the morning, two in the afternoon, and a quick recapitulation in the evening. In that way my day, hitherto as formless as unset jelly, took shape. I was occupied without exhausting myself because chess possesses a wonderful quality: it concentrates one's mental energy on one narrow area so that the brain isn't worn out by the most strenuous effort of thought. Its agility and vigor are actually improved.

"I played these championship games quite mechanically at first, but gradually they awoke in me artistic and pleasurable understanding. I learned to appreciate the finer points, the tricks and stratagems in attack and defense. I grasped the technique of thinking ahead, of combinations and counterattacks, and soon came to recognize the personal mark of each chess champion in his individual play as unerringly as one recognizes a poet from just a few of his lines. What began merely as a way of filling in time became a pleasure, and the great chess strategists such as Alekhine, Lasker, Bogolyubov and Tartakower joined me in my isolation like valued friends.

"My silent cell was blessed every day with continuous variety; and, indeed, the regularity of the exercises restored the soundness of my thought processes, which had been disturbed earlier. I was aware that my brain felt refreshed and even newly sharpened by the regular discipline of thinking. It was noticeable at the interrogations that I was thinking more clearly and to the point. Without my realizing it, the chessboard had improved my mental defenses against false threats and concealed tricks. From that time on, I gave them no openings through contradictory statements and even fancied that the Gestapo was beginning to view me with a certain respect. Perhaps when they saw everyone else breaking down, they asked themselves privately what the secret source of strength was that enabled me alone to put up such unshakable resistance.

"This happy time during which I played the hundred and fifty games in that book systematically, day by day, lasted about two and a half to three months. Then unexpectedly I came to a standstill. Suddenly the void opened up again in front of me, because once I had played every single game twenty or thirty times, the pleasure of novelty and surprise was lost, and the power of the games, which had been so exciting and so stimulating until then, was spent. What point was there in playing games over and over again when I long since knew every move by heart? No sooner had I made the opening move than the completion of the game sewed itself up quite automatically in my head. There was no longer any surprise, any tension, any problem. I needed a different book with different games in it to occupy me and elicit the essential exertion and diversion. As this was completely impossible, there was only one way out of this peculiar maze: instead of the old games, I had to invent new ones. I had to try to partner myself, or rather, to play against myself.

"Now, I don't know how much thought you have given to the intellectual character of this royal game. But even the most superficial reflection should be enough to make it clear that, chess being a game of purely mental processes with no element of chance, it is absurd, logically speaking, to want to play against yourself. The attraction of chess lies, therefore, only in the fact that its strategy evolves in two different brains, that in this battle of the mind Black doesn't know what White's next move will be, and he is constantly trying to guess and to thwart it. While for his part, White, countering him, strives to outdo Black and oppose his concealed intentions. Imagine Black and White being one and the same person, then, and you have the contradiction that the same brain knows something, and yet isn't supposed to know it, simultaneously; that when it is functioning as White's partner, it can completely forget on command what a minute earlier it wanted to do and what it intended when it was Black's partner. Such two-way thinking really presupposes a complete split in one's consciousness, an arbitrary ability of the mind to switch on and off as though it were a mechanical machine. Wanting to play chess against oneself involves a real paradox, like jumping over one's own shadow.

"Well, to be brief, I was so desperate that I explored this absurd impossibility for months. But I had no choice apart from this nonsense, if I wasn't to go quite mad or lapse into a total mental decline. The frightful situation I was in forced me at least to try to split myself into this White ego and Black ego, if I was not to be overwhelmed by that awful void."

Dr. B. leaned back in his deck chair and closed his eyes for a minute. It was as though he were trying forcibly to suppress a disturbing recollection. Once again I noticed the nervous tic that he couldn't control at the corner of his mouth. Then he pulled himself up a little in his chair.

"I hope up to now I have explained everything to you reasonably clearly. But I don't know, unfortunately, if I can be as clear about what happened next, because this new occupation required such absolute harnessing of the brain that it made it impossible to exercise self-control at the same time. I have already told you that I think it is absurd to want to play chess against yourself; but even this absurdity might have a minimal chance if you have a real chessboard in front of you. For the board, being real, allows after all a certain distance, a physical separation of territory. Faced with a real board and real pieces, you can introduce pauses for reflection, you can actually stand first at one side of the table and then at the other and see the position from Black's viewpoint and from White's. But to conduct this battle, as I had to, against myself or, if you prefer, with myself, projecting it in space in my imagination, I had to hold firmly in my mind's eye the current positions on the sixty-four squares. And not just the existing configuration. I also had to calculate the possible further moves of both players, and that meant—I know how absurd it all sounds—imagining double or treble, no, six-, eight-, twelve-fold, for both my selves, for Black and White, always four or five moves ahead.

"I apologize for expecting you to follow this madness. In this game in the abstract space of fantasy I had to calculate four or five moves ahead for White and the same for Black. So I had to work out with two brains—a White and a Black—all the combinations for deploying the pieces in given situations. But even this division of myself was not the most dangerous element of my abstruse experiment. Instead, through having to invent my own independent games, there was the risk that I would no longer be standing on firm ground, but would fall into an abyss. Playing through championship games mechanically, as I had done in the earlier weeks, was after all nothing but an achievement of recall, a pure recapitulation of given material, and as such no more demanding than when I had learned poetry by heart or had memorized sections of the Civil Code. It was a limited, disciplined activity and therefore an excellent mental exercise. The two games I played in the morning and the two in the afternoon represented a definite task I could complete without getting worked up about it. They took the place of normal employment, and furthermore, I had the book to fall back on if I went wrong in a game or forgot the next move. This task was healing and calming for my shattered nerves because I could be objective in replaying someone else's game. It didn't matter to me who won, Black or White. It was either Alekhine or Bogolyubov fighting for the champion's laurels, and I personally—my mind, my heart—was involved only as an onlooker, as a connoisseur of the crises and highlights of each game. However, from the moment I began to play against myself I began involuntarily to compete. Each of my egos, my Black self and my White, had to vie with the other and strive ambitiously and impatiently to gain the upper hand and win. After every move as Black I was in a fever to know what my White ego would do. One side of me triumphed as the other made a mistake; and each was equally downcast over its own incompetence.

"All that sounds senseless; and indeed it was a form of artificial schizophrenia, of split personality in fact, which contributed to a dangerous state of inner turmoil inconceivable in a normal person in normal circumstances. But don't forget that I'd been dragged violently away from all normality. I was a prisoner, locked up although I was innocent, and for months suffering intense loneliness. I was a human being who wanted to vent my accumulated rage on something. And as I had nothing but this senseless game against myself, this is what my rage, my lust for revenge, focused on singlemindedly. Something within me wanted to win, but I had only this other ego to fight, so an almost manic state of agitation grew in me while I played.

"At first my thoughts had been calm and deliberate. There had been a pause between one game and the next, so I could recover from the effort involved. But gradually my overwrought nerves wouldn't allow me to wait. My White ego had scarcely made a move before my Black ego feverishly pushed itself forward. Scarcely was one game finished before I was challenging myself to the next, because, of course, every time one of my chess egos was beaten by the other, it wanted a return game. I couldn't ever tell you, even approximately, how many games I played against myself in my room as a result of this insatiable madness—a thousand, perhaps, possibly more. It was an obsession I couldn't resist. From morning to night I thought of nothing else except Bishops and pawns, Rooks and Kings, ranks and files, and castling and mate. My entire being and senses were concentrated on the checkered board. Playing for fun turned into enthusiasm, which became a compulsion, a mania, a frenetic madness that gradually invaded not only my waking hours but my sleep, too. I could think only in terms of chess, chess moves, chess problems. Sometimes I woke with sweat on my forehead and realized I must have been playing a game of chess in my sleep without knowing it. If I dreamed of people, they immediately seemed to move like a Bishop, or a Rook, or jump back or forward like a Knight. Even when I was called for interrogation I couldn't concentrate on my responsibility anymore. I had the feeling I must have expressed myself in a rather confused way at the last few hearings because my questioners sometimes looked at each other in surprise. But while they were asking questions and deliberating, I was really waiting, just wretchedly eager to be returned to my room so I could go on with my game, my mad game: a new one, and then another and another.

"Every interruption disturbed me, even the quarter of an hour when the warder cleaned the room; and the two minutes it took him to bring my food tortured my burning impatience. Sometimes the bowl with my supper in it was left untouched: I had forgotten to eat because I was playing a game. The only physical thing I noticed was a frightful thirst. It must have been the fever of this continuous mental effort and playing. I drank the water jug dry in two gulps and pestered the warder for more; and yet my tongue still felt dry in my mouth a moment later. Eventually my frenzy mounted during the game itself—and I did nothing else from morning to night—to such a pitch that I couldn't sit still anymore. I walked up and down ceaselessly while I thought out the moves, going faster and faster, up and down, up and down; and the nearer I came to the winning move, the more rapidly I walked. The driving desire to win, to dominate, to defeat myself, gradually became a kind of madness.

"I trembled with impatience because the one chess ego in me was always too slow for the other. The one urged the other on. It will seem laughable to you, I'm sure, but I began to berate myself. "Faster, faster," I would shout, or "Move! Do get on with it!" if one of my egos didn't respond quickly enough to the other. I understand perfectly today, of course, that my behavior was nothing less than a thoroughly pathological form of mental overstrain. The only name I can find for it isn't in the medical textbooks: chess poisoning. In the end this monomaniac obsession began to attack my body as well as my mind. I lost weight, my sleep was disturbed and restless. When I woke up, I had to make a special effort every time to force my leaden eyelids open. Sometimes I felt so weak and my hands were shaking so much that I had difficulty in raising a glass to my lips. But as soon as I had begun a game, I was in the grip of an overwhelming force. I rushed up and down with clenched fists, and sometimes I heard my own voice shouting hoarsely and angrily at myself through a red fog, or so it seemed, "Check!" or "Mate!"

"How this horrible, unspeakable situation came to a head I can't tell you myself. All I know about it is that I woke up one morning and the process was different from usual. It was as though I were outside my body. I was lying there comfortably relaxed. A warm, pleasant drowsiness of a kind I hadn't experienced for months caressed my eyelids, so warm and comforting that I couldn't bring myself, at first, to open my eyes. I lay awake for several minutes and savored this languid torpor, just lying there with my senses agreeably numbed. Then I thought I heard voices behind me, living, human voices, using words—and you can't imagine my delight, for it was months, almost a year, since I had heard any speech except the hard, sharp and evil questions of the panel of interrogators. You're dreaming, I told myself. You're dreaming! Whatever you do, don't open your eyes! Let it go on, this dream. Otherwise you'll see that accursed room again, the chair and the washbasin and the wall. You're dreaming—go on dreaming!

"But curiosity got the upper hand. I opened my eyes slowly and cautiously. It was a miracle! I was in a different room, wider, more spacious than my hotel room. An unbarred window let light in freely and gave a view of trees, green trees stirring in the wind, instead of my blank wall. The walls of the room shone white and smooth, the ceiling was white and high above me—surely I was lying in a new, different bed, and indeed, it wasn't a dream, there really were soft human voices whispering behind me. Without realizing it, I must have moved noticeably, I was so surprised, for at once I heard an approaching step behind me. A woman came over—a woman with a white cap on her head, a nurse, a nun. I felt a thrill of delight: I hadn't seen a woman for a year. I stared at this charming apparition, and it must have been a wild, ecstatic look, because she said soothingly but firmly, 'Quiet! Keep still!' But I hung only on her voice—was this really a human being who spoke to me? Was there really still someone on earth who didn't question and torment me? And wasn't it—inconceivable miracle—the gentle, warm, almost tender voice of a woman? Greedily I stared at her mouth, for this year of hell had made it seem unlikely that one person could speak to another in a kindly way. She was smiling at me—yes, smiling. There were still people who could smile sympathetically. Then she put her finger to her lips as a warning, and went gently away. But I couldn't obey her order. I hadn't seen enough yet of this miracle. I struggled to sit up in bed to gaze after this apparition of a human being who was kind. But as I went to support myself on the edge of the bed, I couldn't do it. Where my right hand had formerly been, with fingers and wrist, I discovered something strange: a thick, large, white lump, apparently an all-embracing bandage. I stared at this white, thick, strange object at first without understanding it. Then slowly it began to dawn on me where I was, and I started to consider what could have happened to me. They must have injured me, or I must have damaged my hand myself. I was in a hospital.

"The doctor, a friendly, elderly man, came at midday. He knew my family and made such a deferential reference to my uncle, the physician to the imperial household, that I felt at once he was on my side. In the course of conversation he asked me all sorts of questions, but there was one which particularly astonished me: Was I a mathematician or a chemist? I said no, I wasn't. 'Odd,' he murmured. 'In your fever you kept crying out such strange formulas—QB3, QB4. We didn't know what to make of it.' I asked him what had happened to me. He smiled wryly. 'Nothing serious. An acute nervous upset.'

"After he had looked round cautiously, he went on in a low voice, 'Quite understandable, too. It started on March thirteenth, didn't it?'

"I nodded.

" 'It's no wonder with their way of doing things,' he murmured. 'You aren't the first. But don't worry.'

"I knew from the soothing way he whispered this to me and from his reassuring expression that I was safe with him.

"Two days later the kindly doctor explained to me quite frankly what had happened. The warder had heard me shouting out in my cell and thought at first someone was in there with me and I was fighting him. He had scarcely appeared at the door when I had set upon him and screamed wildly at him, such things as, 'Will you ever move then, you scoundrel, you coward!' I had tried to grab him by the throat and had attacked him so furiously that he had to call for help. As they were dragging me out to be medically examined, I had suddenly broken loose in my mad frenzy, thrown myself at the corridor window, broken the glass and cut my hand. You can still see the deep scar here. The first night in the hospital I had had a kind of brain fever, but now the doctor found my mental faculties quite healthy. 'Of course,' he said in an undertone, 'I had better not report that to the authorities, otherwise they'll take you back there in the end. Leave it to me. I'll do my best.'

"I don't know what that helpful doctor told my torturers about me. At any rate, he achieved his aim: my release. It's possible he declared me insane; or perhaps in the interval I had ceased to be important to the Gestapo, for Hitler had by then occupied Czechoslovakia and that settled the outcome in Austria as far as he was concerned. So I had only to sign an undertaking to leave our homeland within a fortnight; and those two weeks were taken up to such an extent with all the hundred and one formalities the would-be citizen of the world needs today for a journey abroad—military papers, police permit, tax returns, passport, visa, health certificate—that I had no time to dwell on the past. Apparently there is some mysterious regulating capacity in the brain that automatically cuts out anything that can be disturbing or dangerous to the mind. Whenever I wanted to think back about my imprisonment, it was as though a light switched off in my brain. Only now, here on this ship weeks later, have I found the courage to reflect on what happened to me.

"So now you will understand my impertinent and apparently puzzling behavior with your friends. It was quite by chance that I was strolling through the smoking room and saw your friends at the chessboard. Instinctively my feet felt rooted to the spot, I was so surprised and frightened. I had completely forgotten that you can play chess with a real board and real chessmen; that for this game two quite different men sit physically opposite each other. It took me a couple of minutes to remember that what those players were doing was basically the same as I had tried to do, playing against myself while I was helpless all those months. The code I had used in my ferocious exercises had been nothing more than a substitute and a symbol for these solid figures. I was astonished that the movement of figures on the board was the same as the imaginary moves I had made in my head. It must be similar to how an astronomer feels when he has used some complicated method to calculate on paper the position of a new planet and then really sees it in the sky as a white, distinct, substantial object. I stared at the board as though held there by a magnet. I saw my symbols there—Knight, Rook, King, Queen and pawns—as tangible figures carved out of wood. To grasp the state of play, I had first instinctively to change my abstract world of symbols into the moving pieces. Gradually I was overcome with curiosity to watch a real game like this one between two opponents. It was then that I so embarrassingly forgot all good manners and interfered in your game. But that bad move your friend was going to make cut me to the quick. It was pure instinct, an impulsive movement that made me hold him back, as you grab a child who is leaning over a parapet. It was only later that I realized just how rude my impetuous intervention had been."

I hastened to assure Dr. B. how very pleased we all were to have made his acquaintance through this occurrence and that I would be doubly interested, after everything he had told me, in seeing him at our improvised tournament the next day.

Dr. B. shifted uneasily. "No, really, don't expect too much. It will just be a test for me . . . a test to see if . . . if I can really play an ordinary game of chess, on a real board with actual chessmen and a live opponent . . . for I'm now more doubtful than ever whether those hundreds or possibly thousands of games I played were in fact played by the rules and weren't just a form of dream chess, fever chess . . . a hallucinatory game in which, as always in dreams, intermediate steps were left out. I hope you don't seriously expect me to presume I can stand up to a grand master, and the best in the world at that. What interests me is purely retrospective curiosity, to establish whether it was really chess I played in my cell or if it was madness—if I was right on the brink of the slippery slope or had already gone down it. That's all, there's no other reason."

At that moment the gong sounded, calling us to dinner. We must have been talking for two hours or so, for Dr. B. had told me everything in much greater detail than I have put down here. I thanked him warmly and said good-by.

I hadn't gone the length of the deck before he came after me and said nervously and somewhat haltingly, "One more thing. Would you please tell your friends in advance, so that I don't appear to be uncivil later on, that I'll play one game only? . . . It has to be the closing line beneath an old account—a final settlement, not a new beginning. I mustn't fall into that passionate obsession with the game a second time. It fills me with horror to recall it. And besides—besides, the doctor warned me, expressly: the victim of any mania is always in danger. With chess poisoning—even if you are cured—it's better not to go near a chessboard. So, you understand—just this one trial game for my own sake—and no more."

The next day we gathered in the smoking room punctually at the agreed time of three o'clock. Our circle had increased by two more lovers of the royal game, ship's officers who had sought leave from their duties to watch the match. Even Czentovic didn't keep us waiting as he had the day before. After the necessary choice of colors the memorable game between this *homo obscurissimus* and the famous world champion began. I regret it was played before such thoroughly incompetent spectators as we were, and that its course is as lost to the annals of chess as Beethoven's piano impromptus are to music. True, we tried the next afternoon to reconstruct the game among us from memory, but without success. Quite possibly we had all concentrated too much on the two players during the game instead of taking note of its progress. For in the course of the game the intellectual contrast between the two opponents became more and more physically apparent in their manner. Czentovic, the man of routine, remained as immovably solid as a rock the whole time, his eyes fixed unwaveringly on the board. Thinking seemed almost to cause him actual physical effort, as though he had to engage all his senses with the utmost concentration. Dr. B., on the other hand, was completely relaxed and unconstrained. Like the true dilettante in the best sense of the word, who plays for the pure joy—the *diletto*—of playing, he was physically relaxed and chatted to us during the early pauses, explaining the moves. He lit a cigarette with a steady hand and, when it was his move, looked at the board only for a minute. Each time it seemed as though he had expected the move his opponent made.

The routine opening moves were made quite quickly. It was only at about the seventh or eighth move that a definite plan seemed to emerge. Czentovic was taking longer over his pauses for thought; from that we sensed the real battle for domination had begun. But to tell you the truth, the gradual unfolding of the positional play was something of a disappointment for us nonspecialists—as in every true tournament game. For the more the pieces wove in and out in a strange design, the more impenetrable the actual position seemed to us. We couldn't perceive what either opponent had in mind or which of the two really had the upper hand. We noticed only that individual pieces were being moved like levers to breach the enemy front, but we were unable to grasp the strategic objective behind these maneuvers. For with these two experienced players every move was combined in advance with other projected moves.

We were gradually overtaken by mild fatigue, principally because of Czentovic's interminable pauses for reflection. These began to annoy our friend as well. I noticed uneasily how the longer the game went on, the more he began to fidget. Soon he was so tense he began to light one cigarette after another. Then he grabbed a pencil to make a note of something. Then he ordered mineral water, which he gulped down, one glass after another. It was obvious that he could plan his moves a hundred times faster than Czentovic. Every time the latter, after endless reflection, decided to move a piece forward with his heavy hand, our friend smiled like someone who had seen something he had long expected, and made his countermove immediately. With his agile mind he must have worked out in advance all the possibilities open to his opponent. The longer Czentovic delayed his decision, the more Dr. B.'s impatience grew, and as he waited, his lips were pressed together in an angry line. But Czentovic didn't allow himself to be hurried. He studied the board stubbornly and silently and his pauses became longer the more the field was emptied of chessmen. By the forty-second move, after two and three-quarter hours had gone by, we were all sitting wearily around the tournament table, almost indifferent to it. One of the ship's officers had already gone, the other had taken out a book to read and looked up for a moment only when a move was made. But then, suddenly, the unexpected happened, following a move by Czentovic. As soon as Dr. B. saw Czentovic touch his Knight to move it forward, he gathered himself together like a cat about to pounce. His whole body began to tremble, and scarcely had Czentovic moved his Knight than Dr. B. pushed his Queen forward with a flourish, and said loudly and triumphantly, "There! That settles it!" He leaned back, folded his arms on his chest and looked challengingly at Czentovic. His eyes were suddenly aglow with a burning light.

We bent over the board to try to understand this move that had been proclaimed so triumphantly. At first sight no direct threat was visible. Our friend's exclamation must therefore have referred to a development we, as amateurs who couldn't think far ahead, were unable to calculate as yet. Czentovic was the only one among us who hadn't stirred when the challenging statement was made. He sat quite unmoved, as though he had completely missed the insulting "That settles it!" Nothing happened. You could hear us all involuntarily draw in our breath and also the ticking of the clock that had been placed on the table to measure the time for each move. Three minutes, seven, eight passed—Czentovic didn't stir, but it seemed to me that his wide nostrils were flaring as a result of inner tension.

Our friend found this silent waiting just as unbearable as we did. He stood up suddenly in one movement, and began to pace up and down the smoking room. At first he walked slowly, but then faster and faster. Everyone looked at him in surprise, but none as uneasily as I. For it struck me that in spite of the vigor of the way he paced up and down, his steps covered only a precisely measured area: it was as though in the middle of this spacious room he ran up against an invisible cupboard that forced him to turn back every time. And I recognized with a shudder that without his being aware of it, this reproduced the limits of the area of his former room. He must have paced rapidly up and down like a caged animal in exactly this way during the months of his incarceration, with his hands clenched and his shoulders hunched. He must have rushed up and down exactly like this a thousand times, with the glowing light of madness in his staring expression.

His thought processes seemed completely unimpaired, however, for occasionally he would turn to the table impatiently to see if Czentovic had made a decision yet. But nine minutes, ten minutes went by. Then what no one had expected finally happened. Czentovic slowly lifted his heavy hand, which until then had rested motionless on the table. Intently we all hung on his decision. But Czentovic didn't move a piece; with a sweep of his hand he pushed all the pieces off the board. It took us a moment to grasp the situation: Czentovic had conceded the match. He had given in to avoid being checkmated. The improbable had happened. The world champion, winner of countless tournaments, had struck his colors in the face of an unknown player—and one who hadn't touched a chessboard for twenty or twenty-five years. Our friend—anonymous, unknown—had beaten the strongest chess player on earth in open battle!

Without thinking, we all jumped up, we were so excited. We felt we had to say or do something to release our pent-up joy. The only one who remained calmly unmoved was Czentovic. After a measured interval he raised his head and looked stonily at our friend.

"Another game?" he asked.

"Of course," Dr. B. answered with an eagerness that made me apprehensive. He sat down again before I could remind him of his intention of being satisfied with one game only, and began to set up the pieces with desperate haste. He assembled them with such passionate intensity that twice a pawn slipped to the floor through his shaking fingers. My earlier embarrassed unease in the face of his abnormal agitation grew to alarm. This hitherto calm, quiet man was now visibly overexcited. The nervous tic at the corner of his mouth was more frequent, and his body was quivering.

"No!" I whispered to him softly. "Not now! That's enough for one day! It's too much of a strain for you."

"Strain! Ha!" He laughed loudly and with contempt. "I could have played seventeen games in the time instead of dawdling like that. The only strain I have, playing at that speed, is to stop myself from falling asleep! Well! Go on, begin!"

He addressed these last remarks to Czentovic in a vehement, almost churlish, tone. Czentovic looked at him calmly and evenly but his stony expression had something of the clenched fist in it. All at once a new element had sprung up between the two players: a dangerous tension, a violent hatred. They were no longer two opponents wanting to test each other's playing skill, but two enemies who had sworn to annihilate each other. Czentovic hesitated a long time before he made the first move, and I had a definite feeling his delay was deliberate. Clearly this trained tactician had already noted that he wearied and annoyed his opponent by playing slowly. So he sat for at least four minutes before he made the most normal and simplest of all openings, pushing the King's pawn the customary two squares forward. Our friend immediately followed by advancing his own King's pawn, but again Czentovic created an almost unbearably long pause. It was like seeing a fierce flash of lightning and waiting with bated breath for the thunder—and then the thunder not happening. Czentovic didn't move. He thought silently and slowly, and I was increasingly certain his slowness was malicious. However, he gave me ample time to observe Dr. B., who had just gulped down a third glass of water. I recalled how he had told me about the feverish thirst he had had in his cell. He was showing clearly all the symptoms of abnormal excitement. I saw the perspiration on his forehead, and the scar on his hand growing redder and standing out more distinctly than it had before. But he was still self-controlled. It was not until the fourth move, when Czentovic again went on thinking interminably, that he could no longer restrain himself.

"For heaven's sake, make a move, will you!"

Czentovic looked up coldly. "As I recall, we agreed on ten minutes per move. I don't play to a shorter limit on principle."

Dr. B. bit his lip. I noticed how he was moving his foot up and down under the table more and more restlessly and I became uncontrollably more nervous myself. I had an awful premonition that some kind of madness was working itself up inside him. In fact, there was a further incident at the eighth move. Dr. B. had been growing increasingly impatient while he waited and couldn't contain his tension any longer. He shifted about on his chair and started involuntarily to drum on the table with his fingers. Once again Czentovic lifted his heavy peasant's head.

"Would you mind not drumming, please? It disturbs me. I can't play if you do that."

"Ha!" Dr. B. gave a curt laugh. "That's obvious."

Czentovic went red in the face. "What do you mean by that?" His question was sharp and angry.

Dr. B. gave another tight and malicious laugh. "Nothing. Only that you are obviously feeling the strain."

Czentovic was silent and lowered his head again.

It was seven minutes before he made his next move, and the game dragged on at this funereal pace. Czentovic became more like a block of stone than ever, in the end always taking the maximum of agreed time for thought before deciding on a move. And from one interval to the next our friend's behavior grew stranger. It seemed as though he was no longer interested in the game but was occupied with something quite different. He stopped walking up and down and remained motionless on his chair. He had a fixed and almost crazed expression as he stared into space, ceaselessly muttering unintelligible words to himself. Either he was lost in endless combinations or—as I suspected deep down—he was working through completely

different games. For whenever Czentovic eventually moved, Dr. B. had to be brought back from his private reverie. Then he always needed a whole minute to find out exactly how the game stood. The suspicion was borne in on me more and more that he had long since quite forgotten Czentovic and the rest of us in this chilling form of madness, which could suddenly explode in violence of some kind. And indeed the crisis came at the nineteenth move. Czentovic had scarcely made his move when Dr. B. suddenly, without looking at the board properly, pushed his Bishop forward three squares and shouted out so loudly that we all jumped, "Check! The King's in check!"

We looked at the board at once in expectation of a particularly significant move. But after a minute what happened was not what any of us had anticipated. Czentovic raised his head very, very slowly toward our circle—something he hadn't done before—and looked from one man to the next. He seemed to be relishing something immensely, because slowly a satisfied and clearly sarcastic smile began to play about his lips. Only after he had savored to the full the triumph that we still didn't understand did he turn with pretended courtesy to our group.

"I'm sorry—but I see no check. Do any of you gentlemen see a check against my King, by any chance?"

We looked at the board and then uneasily at Dr. B. The square Czentovic's King occupied was in fact fully protected from the Bishop by a pawn, so the King couldn't possibly be in check. We were uneasy. Had our friend in his excitement mistakenly pushed a piece one square too far or too short? Roused by our silence, Dr. B. now gazed at the board and began to stammer and protest.

"But the King should be on KB7 . . . its position is wrong, quite wrong. You've moved incorrectly! Everything is quite wrong on this board . . . the pawn should be on KKt5, not on KKt4. That is a completely different game. . . . That's . . . "

He stopped abruptly. I had gripped his arm so tightly that even in his fevered and confused state he must have felt my hold on him. He turned round and stared at me like a sleepwalker.

"What do you want?"

All I said was "Remember!" and lightly drew my finger at the same time over the scar on his hand. Involuntarily he followed my movement, his eyes staring glassily at the inflamed line. Then he began to shiver suddenly and his whole body shook.

"For God's sake," he whispered, his lips pale. "Have I said or done anything untoward? Has it really happened again?"

"No," I whispered gently. "But you must stop playing at once. It's high time you did. Remember what the doctor told you!"

Dr. B. stood up quickly. "Please excuse me for my stupid mistake," he said in his earlier polite voice. He bowed to Czentovic. "What I said was complete nonsense. Clearly, it's your game." Then he turned to us. "I must also ask you to forgive me. But I did warn you not to expect too much. Excuse me for making a fool of myself— that's the last time I shall try my hand at chess." He bowed and left us, in the same modest and mysterious way as he had first appeared. I alone knew why this man would never again touch a chessboard. The others remained slightly bewildered. They had a vague feeling they had only just escaped something unpleasant and dangerous. "Damned fool!" McConnor growled with disappointment. The last person to stand up was Czentovic. He glanced at the half-finished game.

"Pity," he said generously. "The attack was quite well conceived. That gentleman is really exceptionally able. For an amateur."

THE GRASS HARP

THE GRASS HARP

by Truman Capote

ILLUSTRATED BY BERNIE FUCHS

To others there was nothing at all special
about the China tree. It had a makeshift tree-house,
around which the branches hung down and
moved softly, sighing in the wind. But
to young Collin Fenwick, his maiden-lady cousin,
Miss Dolly, and Dolly's friend, Catherine, it
became a home, a haven and a sanctuary against
a world that neither understood them
nor wanted to.

With a sensitivity and style uniquely his
own, Truman Capote has created as mixed
and memorable a group of characters as any
to be found in modern fiction.

Said the New York *Herald Tribune* when
the book was originally published, "A charming
human warmth pervades these pages, a
feeling for the positive quality of life, despite life's
abiding sadness."

CHAPTER 1

WHEN WAS IT that first I heard of the grass harp? Long before the autumn we lived in the China tree; an earlier autumn, then; and of course it was Dolly who told me, no one else would have known to call it that, a grass harp.

If on leaving town you take the church road you soon will pass a glaring hill of bonewhite slabs and brown burnt flowers: this is the Baptist cemetery. Our people, Talbos, Fenwicks, are buried there; my mother lies next to my father, and the graves of kinfolk, twenty or more, are around them like the prone roots of a stony tree. Below the hill grows a field of high Indian grass that changes color with the seasons: go to see it in the fall, late September, when it has gone red as sunset, when scarlet shadows like firelight breeze over it and the autumn winds strum on its dry leaves sighing human music, a harp of voices.

Beyond the field begins the darkness of River Woods. It must have been on one of those September days when we were there in the woods gathering roots that Dolly said: Do you hear? that is the grass harp, always telling a story—it knows the stories of all the people on the hill, of all the people who ever lived, and when we are dead it will tell ours, too.

AFTER MY MOTHER died, my father, a traveling man, sent me to live with his cousins, Verena and Dolly Talbo, two unmarried ladies who were sisters. Before that, I'd not ever been allowed into their house.

For reasons no one ever got quite clear, Verena and my father did not speak. Probably Papa asked Verena to lend him some money, and she refused; or perhaps she did make the loan, and he never returned it. You can be sure that the trouble was over money, because nothing else would have mattered to them so much, especially Verena, who was the richest person in town. The drugstore, the drygoods store, a filling station, a grocery, an office building, all this was hers, and the earning of it had not made her an easy woman.

Anyway, Papa said he would never set foot inside her house. He told such terrible things about the Talbo ladies. One of the stories he spread, that Verena was a morphodyte, has never stopped going around, and the ridicule he heaped on Miss Dolly Talbo was too much even for my mother: she told him he ought to be ashamed, mocking anyone so gentle and harmless.

I think they were very much in love, my mother and father. She used to cry every time he went away to sell his frigidaires. He married her when she was sixteen; she did not live to be thirty. The afternoon she died Papa, calling her name, tore off all his clothes and ran out naked into the yard.

It was the day after the funeral that Verena came to the house. I remember the terror of watching her move up the walk, a whip-thin, handsome woman with shingled peppersalt hair, black, rather virile eyebrows and a dainty cheekmole. She opened the front door and walked right into the house. Since the funeral, Papa had been breaking things, not with fury, but quietly, thoroughly: he would amble into the parlor, pick up a china figure, muse over it a moment, then throw it against the wall. The floor and stairs were littered with cracked glass, scattered silverware; a ripped nightgown, one of my mother's, hung over the banister.

Verena's eyes flicked over the debris. "Eugene, I want a word with you," she said in that hearty, coldly exalted voice, and Papa answered: "Yes, sit down, Verena. I thought you would come."

That afternoon Dolly's friend Catherine Creek came over and packed my clothes, and Papa drove me to the impressive, shadowy house on Talbo Lane. As I was getting out of the car he tried to hug me, but I was scared of him and wriggled out of his arms. I'm sorry now that we did not hug each other. Because a few days later, on his way up to Mobile, his car skidded and fell fifty feet into the Gulf.

When I saw him again there were silver dollars weighting down his eyes.

Except to remark that I was small for my age, a runt, no one had ever paid any attention to me; but now people pointed me out, and said wasn't it sad? that poor little Collin Fenwick! I tried to look pitiful because I knew it pleased people: every man in town must have treated me to a Dixie Cup or a box of Crackerjack, and at school I got good grades for the first time. So it was a long while before I calmed down enough to notice Dolly Talbo.

And when I did I fell in love.

Imagine what it must have been for her when first I came to the house, a loud and prying boy of eleven. She skittered at the sound of my footsteps or, if there was no avoiding me, folded like the petals of shy-lady fern. She was one of those people who can disguise themselves as an object in the room, a shadow in the corner, whose presence is a delicate happening. She wore the quietest shoes, plain virginal dresses with hems that touched her ankles. Though older than her sister, she seemed someone who, like myself, Verena had adopted. Pulled and guided by the gravity of Verena's planet, we rotated separately in the outer spaces of the house.

In the attic, a slipshod museum spookily peopled with old display dummies from Verena's drygoods store, there were many loose boards, and by inching these I could look down into almost any room. Dolly's room, unlike the rest of the house, which bulged with fat dour furniture, contained only a bed, a bureau, a chair: a nun might have lived there, except for one fact: the walls, everything was painted an outlandish pink, even the floor was this color. Whenever I spied on Dolly, she usually was to be seen doing one of two things: she was standing in front of a mirror snipping with a pair of garden shears her yellow and white, already brief hair; either that, or she was writing in pencil on a pad of coarse Kress paper. She kept wetting the pencil on the tip of her tongue, and sometimes she spoke aloud a sentence as she put it down: *Do not touch sweet foods like candy and salt will kill you for certain.* Now I'll tell you, she was writing letters. But at first this correspondence was a puzzle to me. After all, her only friend was Catherine Creek, she saw no one else and she never left the house, except once a week when she and Catherine went to River Woods where they gathered the ingredients of a dropsy remedy

Dolly brewed and bottled. Later I discovered she had customers for this medicine throughout the state, and it was to them that her many letters were addressed.

Verena's room, connecting with Dolly's by a passage, was rigged up like an office. There was a rolltop desk, a library of ledgers, filing cabinets. After supper, wearing a green eyeshade, she would sit at her desk totaling figures and turning the pages of her ledgers until even the streetlamps had gone out. Though on diplomatic, political terms with many people, Verena had no close friends at all. Men were afraid of her, and she herself seemed to be afraid of women. Some years before she had been greatly attached to a blonde jolly girl called Maudie Laura Murphy, who worked for a bit in the post office here and who finally married a liquor salesman from St. Louis. Verena had been very bitter over this and said publicly that the man was no account. It was therefore a surprise when, as a wedding present, she gave the couple a honeymoon trip to the Grand Canyon. Maudie and her husband never came back; they opened a filling station nearby Grand Canyon, and from time to time sent Verena Kodak snapshots of themselves. These pictures were a pleasure and a grief. There were nights when she never opened her ledgers, but sat with her forehead leaning in her hands, and the pictures spread on the desk. After she had put them away, she would pace around the room with the lights turned off, and presently there would come a hurt rusty crying sound as though she'd tripped and fallen in the dark.

That part of the attic from which I could have looked down into the kitchen was fortified against me, for it was stacked with trunks like bales of cotton. At that time it was the kitchen I most wanted to spy upon; this was the real living room of the house, and Dolly spent most of the day there chatting with her friend Catherine Creek. As a child, an orphan, Catherine Creek had been hired out to Mr. Uriah Talbo, and they had all grown up together, she and the Talbo sisters, there on the old farm that has since become a railroad depot. Dolly she called Dollyheart, but Verena she called That One. She lived in the back yard in a tin-roofed silvery little house set among sunflowers and trellises of butterbean vine. She claimed to be an Indian, which made most people wink, for she was dark as the angels of Africa. But for all I know it may have been true: certainly she dressed like an Indian. That is, she had a string of turquoise beads, and wore enough rouge to put out your eyes; it shone on her cheeks like votive taillights. Most of her teeth were gone; she kept her jaws jacked up with cotton wadding, and Verena would say Dammit Catherine, since you can't make a sensible sound why in creation won't you go down to Doc Crocker and let him put some teeth in your head? It was true that she was hard to understand: Dolly was the only one who could fluently translate her friend's muffled, mumbling noises. It was enough for Catherine that Dolly understood her: they were always together and everything they had to say they said to each other: bending my ear to an attic beam I could hear the tantalizing tremor of their voices flowing like sapsyrup through the old wood.

To reach the attic, you climbed a ladder in the linen closet, the ceiling of which was a trapdoor. One day, as I started up, I saw that the trapdoor was swung open and, listening, heard above me an idle sweet humming, like the pretty sounds small girls make when they are playing alone. I would have turned back, but the humming stopped, and a voice said: "Catherine?"

"Collin," I answered, showing myself.

The snowflake of Dolly's face held its shape; for once she did not dissolve. "This is where you come—we wondered," she said, her voice frail and crinkling as tissue paper. She had the eyes of a gifted person, kindled, transparent eyes, luminously green as mint jelly: gazing at me through the attic twilight they admitted, timidly, that I meant her no harm. "You play games up here—in the attic? I told Verena you would be lonesome." Stooping, she rooted around in the depths of a barrel. "Here now," she said, "you can help me by looking in that other barrel. I'm hunting for a coral castle; and a sack of pearl pebbles, all colors. I think Catherine will like that, a bowl of goldfish, don't you? For her birthday. We used to have a bowl of tropical fish—devils, they were: ate each other up. But I remember when we bought them; we went all the way to Brewton, sixty miles. I never went sixty miles before, and I don't know that I ever will again. Ah see, here it is, the castle." Soon afterwards I found the pebbles; they were like kernels of corn or candy, and: "Have a piece of candy," I said, offering the sack. "Oh thank you," she said, "I love a piece of candy, even when it tastes like a pebble."

We were friends, Dolly and Catherine and me. I was eleven, then I was sixteen. Though no honors came my way, those were the lovely years.

I never brought anyone home with me, and I never wanted to. Once I took a girl to the picture-show, and on the way home she asked couldn't she come in for a drink of water. If I'd thought she was really thirsty I would've said all right; but I knew she was faking just so she could see inside the house the way people were always wanting to, and so I told her she better wait until she got home. She said: "All the world knows Dolly Talbo's gone, and you're gone too." I liked that girl well enough, but I gave her a shove anyway, and she said her brother would fix my wagon, which he did: right here at the corner of my mouth I've still got a scar where he hit me with a Coca-Cola bottle.

I know: Dolly, they said, was Verena's cross, and said, too, that more went on in the house on Talbo Lane than a body dared to think about. Maybe so. But those were the lovely years.

On winter afternoons, as soon as I came in from school, Catherine hustled open a jar of preserves, while Dolly put a foot-high pot of coffee on the stove and pushed a pan of biscuits into the oven; and the oven, opening, would let out a hot vanilla fragrance, for Dolly, who lived off sweet foods, was always baking a pound cake, raisin bread, some kind of cookie or fudge: never would touch a vegetable, and the only meat she liked was the chicken brain, a pea-sized thing gone before you've tasted it. What with a woodstove and an open fireplace, the kitchen was warm as a cow's tongue. The nearest winter came was to frost the windows with its zero blue breath. If some wizard would like to make me a present, let him give me a bottle filled with the voices of that kitchen, the ha ha ha and fire whispering, a bottle brimming with its buttery sugary bakery smells—though Catherine smelled like a sow in the spring. It looked more like a cozy parlor than a kitchen; there was a hook rug on the floor, rocking chairs; ranged along the walls were pictures of kittens, an enthusiasm of Dolly's; there was a geranium plant that bloomed, then bloomed again all year round, and Catherine's goldfish, in a bowl on the oilcloth-covered table, fanned their tails through the portals of the coral castle. Sometimes we worked jigsaw puzzles, dividing the pieces among us, and Catherine would hide pieces if she thought you were going to finish your part of the puzzle before she finished hers. Or they would help with my homework; that was a mess. About all natural things Dolly was sophisticated; she had the subterranean intelligence of a bee that knows where to find the sweetest flower: she could tell you of a storm a day in advance, predict the fruit of the fig tree, lead you to mushrooms and wild honey, a hidden nest of guinea hen eggs. She looked around her, and felt what she saw. But about homework Dolly was as ignorant as Catherine. "America must have been called America before Columbus came. It stands to reason. Otherwise, how would he have known it was America?" And Catherine said: "That's correct. America is an old Indian word." Of the two, Catherine was the worst: she insisted on her infallibility, and if you did not write down exactly what she said, she got jumpy and spilled the coffee or something. But I never listened to her again after what she said about Lincoln: that he was part Negro and part Indian and only a speck white. Even I knew this was not true. But I am under special obligation to Catherine; if it had not been for her who knows whether I would have grown to ordinary human size? At fourteen I was not much bigger than Biddy Skinner, and people told how he'd had offers from a circus. Catherine said don't worry yourself honey, all you need is a little stretching. She pulled at my arms, legs, tugged at my head as though it were an apple latched to an unyielding bough. But it's the truth that within two years she'd stretched me from four feet nine to five feet seven, and I can prove it by the breadknife knotches on the pantry door, for even now when so much has gone, when there is only wind in the stove and winter in the kitchen, those growing-up scars are still there, a testimony.

Despite the generally beneficial effect Dolly's medicine appeared to have on those who sent for it, letters once in a while came saying Dear Miss Talbo we won't be needing any more dropsy cure on account of poor Cousin Belle (or whoever) passed away last week bless her soul. Then the kitchen was a mournful place; with folded hands and nodding heads, my two friends bleakly recalled the circumstances of the case, and Well, Catherine would say, we did the best we could Dollyheart, but the good Lord had other notions. Verena, too, could make the kitchen sad, as she was always introducing a new rule or enforcing an old one: do, don't, stop, start: it was as though we were clocks she kept an eye on to see that our time jibed with her own, and woe if we were ten minutes fast, an hour slow: Verena went off like a cuckoo. That One! said Catherine, and Dolly would go hush now! hush now! as though to quiet not Catherine but a mutinous inner whispering. Verena in her heart wanted, I think, to come into the kitchen and be a part of it; but she was too like a lone man in a house full of women and children, and the only way she could make contact with us was through assertive outbursts: Dolly, get rid of that kitten, you want to aggravate my asthma? who left the water running in the bathroom? which one of you broke my umbrella? Her ugly moods sifted through the house like a sour yellow mist. That One. Hush now, hush.

Once a week, Saturdays mostly, we went to River Woods. For these trips, which lasted the whole day, Catherine fried a chicken and deviled a dozen eggs, and Dolly took along a chocolate layer cake and a supply of divinity fudge. Thus armed, and carrying three empty grain sacks, we walked out the church road past the cemetery and through the field of Indian grass. Just entering the woods there was a double-trunked China tree, really two trees, but their branches were so embraced that you could step from one into the other; in fact, they were bridged by a tree-house: spacious, sturdy, a model of a tree-house, it was like a raft floating in the sea of leaves. The boys who built it, provided they are still alive, must by now be very old men; certainly the tree-house was fifteen or twenty years old when Dolly first found it and that was a quarter of a century before she showed it to me. To reach it was easy as climbing stairs; there were footholds of gnarled bark and tough vines to grip; even Catherine, who was heavy around the hips and complained of rheumatism, had no trouble. But Catherine felt no love for the tree-house; she did not know, as Dolly knew and made me know, that it was a ship, that to sit up there was to sail along the cloudy coastline of every dream. Mark my word, said Catherine, them boards are too old, them nails are slippery as worms, gonna crack in two, gonna fall and bust our heads don't I know it.

Storing our provisions in the tree-house, we separated into the woods, each carrying a grain sack to be filled with herbs, leaves, strange roots. No one, not even Catherine, knew altogether what went into the medicine, for it was a secret Dolly kept to herself, and we were never allowed to look at the gatherings in her own sack: she held tight to it, as though inside she had captive a blue-haired child, a bewitched prince. This was her story: "Once, back yonder when we were children (Verena still with her babyteeth and Catherine no higher than a fence post) there were gipsies thick as birds in a blackberry patch—not like now, when maybe you see a few straggling through each year. They came with spring: sudden, like the dogwood pink, there they were—up and down the road and in the woods around. But our men hated the sight of them, and daddy, that was your great-uncle Uriah, said he would shoot any he caught on our place. And so I never told when I saw the gipsies taking water from the creek or stealing old winter pecans off the ground. Then one evening, it was April and falling rain, I went out to the cowshed where Fairybell had a new little calf; and there in the cowshed were three gipsy women, two of them old and one of them young, and the young one was lying naked and twisting on the cornshucks. When they saw that I was not afraid, that I was not going to run and tell, one of the old women asked would I bring a light. So I went to the house for a candle, and when I came back the woman who had sent me was holding a red hollering baby upside down by its feet, and the other woman was milking Fairybell. I helped them wash the baby in the warm milk and wrap it in a scarf. Then one of the old women took my hand and said: Now I am going to give you a gift by teaching you a rhyme. It was a rhyme about evergreen bark, dragonfly fern— and all the other things we come here in the woods to find: *Boil till dark and pure if you want a dropsy cure*. In the morning they were gone; I looked for them in the fields and on the road; there was nothing left of them but the rhyme in my head."

Calling to each other, hooting like owls loose in the daytime, we worked all morning in opposite parts of the woods. Towards afternoon, our sacks fat with skinned bark, tender, torn roots, we climbed back into the green web of the China tree and spread the food. There was good creek water in a mason jar, or if the weather was cold a thermos of hot coffee, and we wadded leaves to wipe our chicken-stained, fudge-sticky fingers. Afterwards, telling fortunes with flowers, speaking of sleepy things, it was as though we floated through the afternoon on the raft in the tree; we belonged there, as the sun-silvered leaves belonged, the dwelling whippoorwills.

ABOUT ONCE A YEAR I GO OVER to the house on Talbo Lane, and walk around in the yard. I was there the other day, and came across an old iron tub lying overturned in the weeds like a black fallen meteor: Dolly—Dolly, hovering over the tub dropping our grain-sack gatherings into boiling water and stirring, stirring with a sawed-off broomstick the brown as tobacco spit brew. She did the mixing of the medicine alone while Catherine and I stood watching like apprentices to a witch. We all helped later with the bottling of it, and because it produced a fume that exploded ordinary corks, my particular job was to roll stoppers of toilet paper. Sales averaged around six bottles a week, at two dollars a bottle. The money, Dolly said, belonged to the three of us, and we spent it fast as it came in. We were always sending away for stuff advertised in magazines: Take Up Woodcarving, Parcheesi: the game for young and old, Anyone Can Play A Bazooka. Once we sent away for a book of French lessons: it was my idea that if we got to talk French we would have a secret language that Verena or nobody would understand. Dolly was willing to try, but "Passez-moi a spoon" was the best she ever did, and after learning "Je suis fatigué," Catherine never opened the book again: she said that was all she needed to know.

Verena often remarked that there would be trouble if anyone ever got poisoned, but otherwise she did not show much interest in the dropsy cure. Then one year we totaled up and found we'd earned enough to have to pay an income tax. Whereupon Verena began asking questions: money was like a wildcat whose trail she stalked with a trained hunter's muffled step and an eye for every broken twig. What, she wanted to know, went into the medicine? and Dolly, flattered, almost giggling, nonetheless waved her hands and said Well this and that, nothing special.

Verena seemed to let the matter die; yet very often, sitting at the supper table, her eyes paused ponderingly on Dolly, and once, when we were gathered in the yard around the boiling tub, I looked up and saw Verena in a window watching us with uninterrupted fixity: by then, I suppose, her plan had taken shape, but she did not make her first move until summer.

Twice a year, in January and again in August, Verena went on buying trips to St. Louis or Chicago. That summer, the summer I reached sixteen, she went to Chicago and after two weeks returned accompanied by a man called Dr. Morris Ritz. Naturally everyone wondered who was Dr. Morris Ritz? He wore bow ties and sharp jazzy suits; his lips were blue and he had gaudy small swerving eyes; altogether, he looked like a mean mouse. We heard that he lived in the best room at the Lola Hotel and ate steak dinners at Phil's Café. On the streets he strutted along bobbing his shiny head at every passerby; he made no friends, however, and was not seen in the company of anyone except Verena, who never brought him to the house and never mentioned his name until one day Catherine had the gall to say, "Miss Verena, just who is this funny looking little Dr. Morris Ritz?" and Verena, getting white around the mouth, replied: "Well now, he's not half so funny looking as some I could name."

Scandalous, people said, the way Verena was carrying on with that little Jew from Chicago: and him twenty years younger. The story that got around was that they were up to something out in the old canning factory the other side of town. As it developed, they were; but not what the gang at the pool-hall thought. Most any afternoon you could see Verena and Dr. Morris Ritz walking out toward the canning factory, an abandoned blasted brick ruin with jagged windows and sagging doors. For a generation no one had been near it except schoolkids who went there to smoke cigarettes and get naked together. Then early in September, by way of a notice in the *Courier*, we learned for the first time that Verena had bought the old canning factory; but there was no mention as to what use she was planning to make of it. Shortly after this, Verena told Catherine to kill two chickens as Dr. Morris Ritz was coming to Sunday dinner.

During the years that I lived there, Dr. Morris Ritz was the only person ever invited to dine at the house on Talbo Lane. So for many reasons it was an occasion. Catherine and Dolly did a spring cleaning: they beat rugs, brought china from the attic, had every room smelling of floorwax and lemon polish. There was to be fried chicken and ham, English peas, sweet potatoes, rolls, banana pudding, two kinds of cake and tutti-frutti ice cream from the drugstore. Sunday noon Verena came in to look at the table: with its sprawling centerpiece of peach-colored roses and dense fancy stretches of silverware, it seemed set for a party of twenty; actually, there were only two places. Verena went ahead and set two more, and Dolly, seeing this, said weakly Well, it was all right if Collin wanted to eat at the table, but that she was going to stay in the kitchen with Catherine. Verena put her foot down: "Don't fool with me, Dolly. This is important. Morris is coming here expressly to meet you. And what is more, I'd appreciate it if you'd hold up your head: it makes me dizzy, hanging like that."

Dolly was scared to death: she hid in her room, and long after our guest had arrived I had to be sent to fetch her. She was lying in the pink bed with a wet washrag on her forehead, and Catherine was sitting beside her. Catherine was all sleeked up, rouge on her cheeks like lollipops and her jaws jammed with more cotton than ever; she said, "Honey, you ought to get up from there—you're going to ruin that pretty dress." It was a calico dress Verena had brought from Chicago; Dolly sat up and smoothed it, then immediately lay down again: "If Verena knew how sorry I am," she said helplessly, and so I went and told Verena that Dolly was sick. Verena said she'd see about that, and marched off leaving me alone in the hall with Dr. Morris Ritz.

Oh he was a hateful thing. "So you're sixteen," he said, winking first one, then the other of his sassy eyes. "And throwing it around, huh? Make the old lady take you next time she goes to Chicago. Plenty of good stuff there to throw it at." He snapped his fingers and jiggled his razzle-dazzle, dagger-sharp shoes as though keeping time to some vaudeville tune: he might have been a tapdancer or a soda-jerk, except that he was carrying a brief case, which suggested a more serious occupation. I wondered what kind of doctor he was supposed to be; indeed, was on the point of asking when Verena returned steering Dolly by the elbow.

The shadows of the hall, the tapestried furniture failed to absorb her; without raising her eyes she lifted her hand, and Dr. Ritz gripped it so ruggedly, pumped it so hard she went nearly off balance. "Gee, Miss Talbo; am I honored to meet you!" he said, and cranked his bow tie.

We sat down to dinner, and Catherine came around with the chicken. She served Verena, then Dolly, and when the doctor's turn came he said, "Tell you the truth, the only piece of chicken I care about is the brain: don't suppose you'd have that back in the kitchen, mammy?"

Catherine looked so far down her nose she got almost cross-eyed;

and with her tongue all mixed up in the cotton wadding she told him that, "Dolly's took those brains on her plate."

"These southern accents, Jesus," he said, genuinely dismayed.

"She says I have the brains on my plate," said Dolly, her cheeks red as Catherine's rouge. "But please let me pass them to you."

"If you're sure you don't mind . . ."

"She doesn't mind a bit," said Verena. "She only eats sweet things anyway. Here, Dolly: have some banana pudding."

Presently Dr. Ritz commenced a fit of sneezing. "The flowers, those roses, old allergy . . ."

"Oh dear," said Dolly who, seeing an opportunity to escape into the kitchen, seized the bowl of roses: it slipped, crystal crashed, roses landed in gravy and gravy landed on us all. "You see," she said, speaking to herself and with tears teetering in her eyes, "you see, it's hopeless."

"Nothing is hopeless, Dolly; sit down and finish your pudding," Verena advised in a substantial, chin-up voice. "Besides, we have a nice little surprise for you. Morris, show Dolly those lovely labels."

Murmuring "No harm done," Dr. Ritz stopped rubbing gravy splotches off his sleeve, and went into the hall, returning with his brief case. His fingers buzzed through a sheaf of papers, then lighted on a large envelope which he passed down to Dolly.

There were gum-stickers in the envelope, triangular labels with orange lettering: Gipsy Queen Dropsy Cure: and a fuzzy picture of a woman wearing a bandana and gold earloops. "First class, huh?" said Dr. Ritz. "Made in Chicago. A friend of mine drew the picture: real artist, that guy." Dolly shuffled the labels with a puzzled, apprehensive expression until Verena asked: "Aren't you pleased?"

The labels twitched in Dolly's hands. "I'm not sure I understand."

"Of course you do," said Verena, smiling thinly. "It's obvious enough. I told Morris that old story of yours and he thought of this wonderful name."

"Gispy Queen Dropsy Cure: very catchy, that," said the doctor. "Look great in ads."

"*My* medicine?" said Dolly, her eyes still lowered. "But I don't need any labels, Verena. I write my own."

Dr. Ritz snapped his fingers. "Say, that's good! We can have labels printed like her own handwriting: personal, see?"

"We've spent enough money already," Verena told him briskly; and, turning to Dolly, said: "Morris and I are going up to Washington this week to get a copyright on these labels and register a patent for the medicine—naming you as the inventor, naturally. Now the point is, Dolly, you must sit down and write out a complete formula for us."

Dolly's face loosened; and the labels scattered on the floor, skimmed. Leaning her hands on the table she pushed herself upward; slowly her features came together again, she lifted her head and looked blinkingly at Dr. Ritz, at Verena. "It won't do," she said quietly. She moved to the door, put a hand on its handle. "It won't do: because you haven't any right, Verena. Nor you, sir."

I HELPED Catherine clear the table: the ruined roses, the uncut cakes, the vegetables no one had touched. Verena and her guest had left the house together; from the kitchen window we watched them as they went toward town nodding and shaking their heads. Then we sliced the devil's-food cake and took it into Dolly's room.

Hush now! hush now! she said when Catherine began lighting into That One. But it was as though the rebellious inner whispering had become a raucous voice, an opponent she must outshout: Hush now! hush now! until Catherine had to put her arms around Dolly and say hush, too.

We got out a deck of Rook cards and spread them on the bed. Naturally Catherine had to go and remember it was Sunday; she said maybe we could risk another black mark in the Judgment Book, but there were too many beside her name already. After thinking it over, we told fortunes instead. Sometime around dusk Verena came home. We heard her footsteps in the hall; she opened the door without knocking, and Dolly, who was in the middle of my fortune, tightened her hold on my hand. Verena said: "Collin, Catherine, we will excuse you."

Catherine wanted to follow me up the ladder into the attic, except she had on her fine clothes. So I went alone. There was a good knothole that looked straight down into the pink room; but Verena was standing directly under it, and all I could see was her hat, for she was still wearing the hat she'd put on when she left the house. It was a straw skimmer decorated with a cluster of celluloid fruit. "Those are facts," she was saying, and the fruit shivered, shimmered in the blue dimness. "Two thousand for the old factory, Bill Tatum and four carpenters working out there at eighty cents an hour, seven thousand dollars' worth of machinery already ordered, not to mention what a specialist like Morris Ritz is costing. And why? All for you!"

"All for me?" and Dolly sounded sad and failing as the dusk. I saw her shadow as she moved from one part of the room to another. "You are my own flesh, and I love you tenderly; in my heart I love you. I could prove it now by giving you the only thing that has ever been mine: then you would have it all. Please, Verena," she said, faltering, "let this one thing belong to me."

Verena switched on a light. "You speak of giving," and her voice was hard as the sudden bitter glare. "All these years that I've worked like a fieldhand: what haven't I given you? This house, that . . ."

"You've given everything to me," Dolly interrupted softly. "And to Catherine and to Collin. Except, we've earned our way a bit: we've kept a nice home for you, haven't we?"

"Oh a fine home," said Verena, whipping off her hat. Her face was full of blood. "You and that gurgling fool. Has it not struck you that I never ask anyone into this house? And for a very simple reason: I'm ashamed to. Look what happened today."

I could hear the breath go out of Dolly. "I'm sorry," she said faintly. "I am truly. I'd always thought there was a place for us here, that you needed us somehow. But it's going to be all right now, Verena. We'll go away."

Verena sighed. "Poor Dolly. Poor poor thing. Wherever would you go?"

The answer, a little while in coming, was fragile as the flight of a moth: "I know a place."

LATER, I WAITED in bed for Dolly to come and kiss me goodnight. My room, beyond the parlor in a faraway corner of the house, was the room where their father, Mr. Uriah Talbo, had lived. In his mad old age, Verena had brought him here from the farm, and here he'd died, not knowing where he was. Though dead ten, fifteen years, the pee and tobacco old-man smell of him still saturated the mattress, the closet, and on a shelf in the closet was the one possession he'd carried away with him from the farm, a small yellow drum: as a lad my own age he'd marched in a Dixie regiment rattling this little yellow drum, and singing. Dolly said that when she was a girl she'd liked to wake up winter mornings and hear her father singing as he went about the house building fires; after he was old, after he'd died, she sometimes heard his songs in the field of Indian grass. Wind, Catherine said; and Dolly told her: But the wind is us—it gathers and remembers all our voices, then sends them talking and telling through the leaves and the fields—I've heard Papa clear as day.

On such a night, now that it was September, the autumn winds would be curving through the taut red grass, releasing all the gone voices, and I wondered if he was singing among them, the old man in whose bed I lay falling asleep.

Then I thought Dolly at last had come to kiss me goodnight, for I woke up sensing her near me in the room; but it was almost morning, beginning light was like a flowering foliage at the windows, and roosters ranted in distant yards. "Shhh, Collin," Dolly whispered, bending over me. She was wearing a woolen winter suit and a hat with a traveling veil that misted her face. "I only wanted you to know where we are going."

"To the tree-house?" I said, and thought I was talking in my sleep.

Dolly nodded. "Just for now. Until we know better what our plans will be." She could see that I was frightened, and put her hand on my forehead.

"You and Catherine: but not me?" and I was jerking with a chill. "You can't leave without me."

The town clock was tolling; she seemed to be waiting for it to finish before making up her mind. It struck five, and by the time the note had died away I had climbed out of bed and rushed into my clothes. There was nothing for Dolly to say except: "Don't forget your comb."

Catherine met us in the yard; she was crooked over with the weight of a brimming oilcloth satchel; her eyes were swollen, she had been crying, and Dolly, oddly calm and certain of what she was doing, said it doesn't matter, Catherine—we can send for your goldfish once we find a place. Verena's closed quiet windows loomed above us; we moved cautiously past them and silently out the gate. A fox terrier barked at us; but there was no one on the street, and no one saw us pass through the town except a sleepless prisoner gazing from the jail. We reached the field of Indian grass at the same moment as the sun. Dolly's veil flared in the morning breeze, and a pair of pheasants, nesting in our path, swept before us, their metal wings swiping the cockscomb-scarlet grass. The China tree was a September bowl of green and greenish gold: Gonna fall, gonna bust our heads, Catherine said, as all around us the leaves shook down their dew.

CHAPTER 2

IF IT HADN'T BEEN for Riley Henderson, I doubt anyone would have known, or at least known so soon, that we were in the tree.

Catherine had loaded her oilcloth satchel with the leftovers from Sunday dinner, and we were enjoying a breakfast of cake and chicken when gunfire slapped through the woods. We sat there with cake going dry in our mouths. Below, a sleek bird dog cantered into view, followed by Riley Henderson; he was shouldering a shotgun and around his neck there hung a garland of bleeding squirrels whose tails were tied together. Dolly lowered her veil, as though to camouflage herself among the leaves.

He paused not far away, and his wary, tanned young face tightened; propping his gun into position he took a roaming aim, as if waiting for a target to present itself. The suspense was too much for Catherine, who shouted: "Riley Henderson, don't you dare shoot us!"

His gun wavered, and he spun around, the squirrels swinging like a loose necklace. Then he saw us in the tree, and after a moment said, "Hello there, Catherine Creek; hello, Miss Talbo. What are you folks doing up there? Wildcat chase you?"

"Just sitting," said Dolly promptly, as though she were afraid for either Catherine or I to answer. "That's a fine mess of squirrels you've got."

"Take a couple," he said, detaching two. "We had some for supper last night and they were real tender. Wait a minute, I'll bring them up to you."

"You don't have to do that; just leave them on the ground." But he said ants would get at them, and hauled himself into the tree. His blue shirt was spotted with squirrel blood, and flecks of blood glittered in his rough leather-colored hair; he smelled of gunpowder, and his homely well-made face was brown as cinnamon. "I'll be damned, it's a tree-house," he said, pounding his foot as though to test the strength of the boards. Catherine warned him that maybe it was a tree-house now, but it wouldn't be for long if he didn't stop that stamping. He said, "You build it, Collin?" and it was with a happy shock that I realized he'd called my name: I hadn't thought Riley Henderson knew me from dust. But I knew him, all right.

No one in our town ever had themselves so much talked about as Riley Henderson. Older people spoke of him with sighing voices, and those nearer his own age, like myself, were glad to call him mean and hard: that was because he would only let us envy him, would not let us love him, be his friend.

Anyone could have told you the facts.

He was born in China, where his father, a missionary, had been killed in an uprising. His mother was from this town, and her name was Rose; though I never saw her myself, people say she was a beautiful woman until she started wearing glasses; she was rich too, having received a large inheritance from her grandfather. When she came back from China she brought Riley, then five, and two younger children, both girls; they lived with her unmarried brother, Justice of the Peace Horace Holton, a meaty spinsterish man with skin yellow as quince. In the following years Rose Henderson grew strange in her ways: she threatened to sue Verena for selling her a dress that shrank in the wash; to punish Riley, she made him hop on one leg around the yard reciting the multiplication table; otherwise, she let him run wild, and when the Presbyterian minister spoke to her about it she told him she hated her children and wished they were dead. And she must have meant it, for one Christmas morning she locked the bathroom door and tried to drown her two little girls in the tub: it was said that Riley broke the door down with a hatchet, which seems a tall order for a boy of nine or ten, whatever he was. Afterwards, Rose was sent off to a place on the Gulf Coast, an institution, and she may still be living there, at least I've never heard that she died. Now Riley and his uncle Horace Holton couldn't get on. One night he stole Horace's Oldsmobile and drove out to the Dance-N-Dine with Mamie Curtiss: she was fast as lightning, and maybe five years older than Riley, who was not more than fifteen at the time. Well, Horace heard they were at the Dance-N-Dine and got the Sheriff to drive him out there: he said he was going to teach Riley a lesson and have him arrested. But Riley said Sheriff, you're after the wrong party. Right there in front of a crowd he accused his uncle of stealing money that belonged to Rose and that was meant for him and his sisters. He offered to fight it out on the spot; and when Horace held back, he just walked over and socked him in the eye. The Sheriff put Riley in jail. But Judge Cool, an old friend of Rose's, began to investigate, and sure enough it turned out Horace had been draining Rose's money into his own account. So Horace simply packed his things and took the train to New Orleans where, a few months later, we heard that, billed as the Minister of Romance, he had a job marrying couples on an excursion steamer that made moonlight cruises up the Mississippi. From then on, Riley was his own boss. With money borrowed against the inheritance he was coming into, he bought a red racy car and went skidding round the countryside with every floozy in town; the only nice girls you ever saw in that car were his sisters—he took them for a drive Sunday afternoons, a slow respectable circling of the square. They were pretty girls, his sisters, but they didn't have much fun, for he kept a strict watch, and boys were afraid to come near them. A reliable colored woman did their housework, otherwise they lived alone. One of his sisters, Elizabeth, was in my class at school, and she got the best grades, straight A's. Riley himself had quit school; but he was not one of the pool-hall loafs, nor did he mix with them; he fished in the daytime, or went hunting; around the old Holton house he made many improvements, as he was a good carpenter; and a good mechanic, too: for instance, he built a special car horn, it wailed like a train-whistle, and in the evening you could hear it howling as he roared down the road on his way to a dance in another town. How I longed for him to be my friend! and it seemed possible, he was just two years older. But I could remember the only time he ever spoke to me. Spruce in a pair of white flannels, he was off to a dance at the clubhouse, and he came into Verena's drugstore, where I sometimes helped out on Saturday nights. What he wanted was a package of Shadows, but I wasn't sure what Shadows were, so he had to come behind the counter and get them out of the drawer himself; and he laughed, not unkindly, though it was worse than if it had been: now he knew I was a fool, we would never be friends.

Dolly said, "Have a piece of cake, Riley," and he asked did we always have picnics this early in the day? then went on to say he considered it a fine idea: "Like swimming at night," he said. "I come down here while it's still dark, and go swimming in the river. Next time you have a picnic, call out so I'll know you're here."

"You are welcome any morning," said Dolly, raising her veil. "I daresay we will be here for some while."

Riley must have thought it a curious invitation, but he did not say so. He produced a package of cigarettes and passed it around; when Catherine took one, Dolly said: "Catherine Creek, you've never touched tobacco in your life." Catherine allowed as to how she may have been missing something: "It must be a comfort, so many folks speak in its favor; and Dollyheart, when you get to be our age you've got to look for comforts." Dolly bit her lip; "Well, I don't suppose there's any harm," she said, and accepted a cigarette herself.

There are two things that will drive a boy crazy (according to Mr. Hand, who caught me smoking in the lavatory at school) and I'd given up one of them, cigarettes, two years before: not because I thought it would make me crazy, but because I thought it was imperiling my growth. Actually, now that I was a normal size, Riley was no taller than me, though he seemed to be, for he moved with the drawn-out cowboy awkwardness of a lanky man. So I took a cigarette, and Dolly, gushing uninhaled smoke, said she thought we might as well all be sick together; but no one was sick, and Catherine said next time she would like to try a pipe, as they smelled so good. Whereupon Dolly volunteered the surprising fact that Verena smoked a pipe, something I'd never known: "I don't know whether she does any more, but she used to have a pipe and a can of Prince Albert with half an apple cut up in it. But you mustn't tell that," she added, suddenly aware of Riley, who laughed aloud.

Usually, glimpsed on the street or seen passing in his car, Riley wore a tense, trigger-tempered expression; but there in the China tree he seemed relaxed: frequent smiles enriched his whole face, as though he wanted at last to be friendly, if not friends. Dolly, for her part, appeared to be at ease and enjoying his company. Certainly she was not afraid of him: perhaps it was because we were in the tree-house, and the tree-house was her own.

"Thank you for the squirrels, sir," she said, as he prepared to leave. "And don't forget to come again."

He swung himself to the ground. "Want a ride? My car's up by the cemetery."

Dolly told him: "That's kind of you; but really we haven't any place to go."

Grinning, he lifted his gun and aimed it at us; and Catherine yelled You ought to be whipped, boy: but he laughed and waved and ran, his bird dog barking, booming ahead. Dolly said gaily, "Let's have a cigarette," for the package had been left behind.

BY THE TIME Riley reached town the news was roaring in the air like a flight of bees: how we'd run off in the middle of the night. Though neither Catherine nor I knew it, Dolly had left a note, which Verena found when she went for her morning coffee. As I understand it, this note simply said that we were going away and that Verena would not be bothered by us any more. She at once rang up her friend Morris Ritz at the Lola Hotel, and together they traipsed off to rouse the Sheriff. It was Verena's backing that had put the Sheriff into office; he was a fast-stepping, brassy young fellow with a brutal jaw and the bashful eyes of a cardsharp; his name was Junius Candle (can you believe it? the same Junius Candle who is a Senator today!). A searching party of deputies was gathered; telegrams were hurried off to sheriffs in other towns. Many years later, when the Talbo estate was being settled, I came across the handwritten original of this telegram—composed, I believe, by Dr. Ritz. *Be on lookout for following persons traveling together. Dolly Augusta Talbo, white, aged 60, yellow grayish hair, thin, height 5 feet 3, green eyes, probably insane but not likely to be dangerous, post description bakeries as she is cake eater. Catherine Creek, Negro, pretends to be Indian, age about 60, toothless, confused speech, short and heavy, strong, likely to be dangerous. Collin Talbo Fenwick, white, age 16, looks younger, height 5 feet 7, blond, gray eyes, thin, bad posture, scar at corner of mouth, surly natured. All three wanted as runaways.* They sure haven't run far, Riley said in the post office; and postmistress Mrs. Peters rushed to the telephone to say Riley Henderson had seen us in the woods below the cemetery.

While this was happening we were peaceably setting about to make the tree-house cozy. From Catherine's satchel we took a rose and gold scrapquilt, and there was a deck of Rook cards, soap, rolls of toilet paper, oranges and lemons, candles, a frying pan, a bottle of blackberry wine, and two shoeboxes filled with food: Catherine bragged that she'd robbed the pantry of everything, leaving not even a biscuit for That One's breakfast.

Later, we all went to the creek and bathed our feet and faces in the cold water. There are as many creeks in River Woods as there are veins in a leaf: clear, crackling, they crook their way down into the little river that crawls through the woods like a green alligator. Dolly looked a sight, standing in the water with her winter suit-skirt hiked up and her veil pestering her like a cloud of gnats. I asked her, Dolly, why are you wearing that veil? and she said, "But isn't it proper for ladies to wear veils when they go traveling?"

Returning to the tree, we made a delicious jar of orangeade and talked of the future. Our assets were: forty-seven dollars in cash, and several pieces of jewelry, notably a gold fraternity ring Catherine had found in the intestines of a hog while stuffing sausages. According to Catherine, forty-seven dollars would buy us bus tickets anywhere: she knew somebody who had gone all the way to Mexico for fifteen dollars. Both Dolly and I were opposed to Mexico: for one thing, we didn't know the language. Besides, Dolly said, we shouldn't venture outside the state, and wherever we went it ought to be near a forest, otherwise how would we be able to make the dropsy cure? "To tell you the truth, I think we should set up right here in River Woods," she said, gazing about speculatively.

"In this old tree?" said Catherine. "Just put that notion out of your head, Dollyheart." And then: "You recall how we saw in the paper where a man bought a castle across the ocean and brought it every bit home with him? You recall that? Well, we maybe could put my little house on a wagon and haul it down here." But, as Dolly pointed out, the house belonged to Verena, and was therefore not ours to haul away. Catherine answered: "You wrong, sugar. If you feed a man, and wash his clothes, and born his children, you and that man are married, that man is yours. If you sweep a house, and tend its fires and fill its stove, and there is love in you all the years you are doing this, then you and that house are married, that house is yours. The way I see it, both those houses up there belong to us; in the eyes of God, we could put That One right out."

I had an idea: down on the river below us there was a forsaken houseboat, green with the rust of water, half-sunk; it had been the property of an old man who made his living catching catfish, and who had been run out of town after applying for a certificate to marry a fifteen-year-old colored girl. My idea was, why shouldn't we fix up the old houseboat and live there?

Catherine said that if possible she hoped to spend the rest of her life on land: "Where the Lord intended us," and she listed more of His intentions, one of these being that trees were meant for monkeys and birds. Presently she went silent and, nudging us, pointed in amazement down to where the woods opened upon the field of grass.

There, stalking toward us, solemnly, stiffly, came a distinguished party: Judge Cool, the Reverend and Mrs. Buster, Mrs. Macy Wheeler; and leading them, Sheriff Junius Candle, who wore high-laced boots and had a pistol flapping on his hip. Sunmotes lilted around them like yellow butterflies, brambles brushed their starched town clothes, and Mrs. Macy Wheeler, frightened by a vine that switched against her leg, jumped back, screeching: I laughed.

And, hearing me, they looked up at us, an expression of perplexed horror collecting on some of their faces—it was as though they were visitors at a zoo who had wandered accidentally into one of the cages. Sheriff Candle slouched forward, his hand cocked on his pistol. He stared at us with puckered eyes, as if he were gazing straight into the sun. "Now look here . . ." he began, and was cut short by Mrs. Buster, who said: "Sheriff, we agreed to leave this to the Reverend." It was a rule of hers that her husband, as God's representative, should have first say in everything. The Reverend Buster cleared his throat, and his hands, as he rubbed them together, were like the dry scraping feelers of an insect. "Dolly Talbo," he said, his voice very fine-sounding for so stringy, stunted a man, "I speak to you on behalf of your sister, that good gracious woman . . ."

"That she is," sang his wife, and Mrs. Macy Wheeler parroted her.

". . . who has this day received a grievous shock."

"That she has," echoed the ladies in their choir-trained voices.

Dolly looked at Catherine, touched my hand, as though asking us to explain what was meant by the group glowering below like dogs gathered around a tree of trapped possums. Inadvertently, and just, I think, to have something in her hands, she picked up one of the cigarettes Riley had left.

"Shame on you," squalled Mrs. Buster, tossing her tiny baldish

head: those who called her an old buzzard, and there were several, were not speaking of her character alone: in addition to a small vicious head, she had high hunched shoulders and a vast body. "I say shame on you. How can you have come so far from God as to sit up in a tree like a drunken Indian—sucking cigarettes like a common . . ."

"Floozy," supplied Mrs. Macy Wheeler.

". . . floozy, while your sister lies in misery flat on her back."

Maybe they were right in describing Catherine as dangerous, for she reared up and said: "Preacher lady, don't you go calling Dolly and us floozies; I'll come down there and slap you bowlegged." Fortunately, none of them could understand her; if they had, the Sheriff might have shot her through the head: no exaggeration; and many of the white people in town would have said he did right.

Dolly seemed stunned, at the same time self-possessed. You see, she simply dusted her skirt and said: "Consider a moment, Mrs. Buster, and you will realize that we are nearer God than you—by several yards."

"Good for you, Miss Dolly. I call that a good answer." The man who had spoken was Judge Cool; he clapped his hands together and chuckled appreciatively. "Of course they are nearer God," he said, unfazed by the disapproving, sober faces around him. "They're in a tree, and we're on the ground."

Mrs. Buster whirled on him. "I'd thought you were a Christian, Charlie Cool. My ideas of a Christian do not include laughing at and encouraging a poor mad woman."

"Mind who you name as mad, Thelma," said the Judge. "That isn't especially Christian either."

The Reverend Buster opened fire. "Answer me this, Judge. Why did you come with us if it wasn't to do the Lord's will in a spirit of mercy?"

"The Lord's will?" said the Judge incredulously. "You don't know what that is any more than I do. Perhaps the Lord told these people to go live in a tree; you'll admit, at least, that He never told you to drag them out—unless, of course, Verena Talbo is the Lord, a theory several of you give credence to, eh Sheriff? No, sir, I did not come along to do anyone's will but my own: which merely means that I felt like taking a walk—the woods are very handsome at this time of year." He picked some brown violets and put them in his buttonhole.

"To hell with all that," began the Sheriff, and was again interrupted by Mrs. Buster, who said that under no circumstances would she tolerate swearing: Will we, Reverend? and the Reverend, backing her up, said he'd be damned if they would. "I'm in charge here," the Sheriff informed them, thrusting his bully-boy jaw. "This is a matter for the law."

"Whose law, Junius?" inquired Judge Cool quietly. "Remember that I sat in the courthouse twenty-seven years, rather a longer time than you've lived. Take care. We have no legal right whatever to interfere with Miss Dolly."

Undaunted, the Sheriff hoisted himself a little into the tree. "Let's don't have any more trouble," he said coaxingly, and we could see his curved dog-teeth. "Come on down from there, the pack of you." As we continued to sit like three nesting birds he showed more of his teeth and, as though he were trying to shake us out, angrily swayed a branch.

"Miss Dolly, you've always been a peaceful person," said Mrs. Macy Wheeler. "Please come on home with us; you don't want to miss your dinner." Dolly replied matter-of-factly that we were not hungry: were they? "There's a drumstick for anybody that would like it."

Sheriff Candle said, "You make it hard on me, ma'am," and pulled himself nearer. A branch, cracking under his weight, sent through the tree a sad cruel thunder.

"If he lays a hand on any one of you, kick him in the head," advised Judge Cool. "Or I will," he said with sudden gallant pugnacity: like an inspired frog he hopped and caught hold to one of the Sheriff's dangling boots. The Sheriff, in turn, grabbed my ankles, and Catherine had to hold me around the middle. We were sliding, that we should all fall seemed inevitable, the strain was immense. Meanwhile, Dolly started pouring what was left of our orangeade down the Sheriff's neck, and abruptly, shouting an obscenity, he let go of me. They crashed to the ground, the Sheriff on top of the Judge and the Reverend Buster crushed beneath them both. Mrs. Macy Wheeler and Mrs. Buster, augmenting the disaster, fell upon them with crow-like cries of distress.

Appalled by what had happened, and the part she herself had played, Dolly became so confused that she dropped the empty orangeade jar: it hit Mrs. Buster on the head with a ripe thud. "Beg pardon," she apologized, though in the furor no one heard her.

When the tangle below unraveled, those concerned stood apart from each other embarrassedly, gingerly feeling of themselves. The Reverend looked rather flattened out, but no broken bones were discovered, and only Mrs. Buster, on whose skimpy-haired head a bump was pyramiding, could have justly complained of injury. She did so forthrightly. "You attacked me, Dolly Talbo, don't deny it, everyone here is a witness, everyone saw you aim that mason jar at my head. Junius, arrest her!"

The Sheriff, however, was involved in settling differences of his own. Hands on hips, swaggering, he bore down on the Judge, who was in the process of replacing the violets in his buttonhole. "If you weren't so old, I'd damn well knock you down."

"I'm not so old, Junius: just old enough to think men ought not to fight in front of ladies," said the Judge. He was a fair-sized man with strong shoulders and a straight body: though not far from seventy, he looked to be in his fifties. He clenched his fists and they were hard and hairy as coconuts. "On the other hand," he said grimly, "I'm ready if you are."

At the moment it looked like a fair enough match. Even the Sheriff seemed not so sure of himself; with diminishing bravado, he spit between his fingers, and said Well, nobody was going to accuse him of hitting an old man. "Or standing up to one," Judge Cool retorted. "Go on, Junius, tuck your shirt in your pants and trot along home."

The Sheriff appealed to us in the tree. "Save yourselves a lot of trouble: get out of there and come along with me now." We did not stir, except that Dolly dropped her veil, as though lowering a curtain on the subject once for all. Mrs. Buster, the lump on her head like a horn, said portentously, "Never mind, Sheriff. They've had their chance," and, eyeing Dolly, then the Judge, added: "You may imagine you are getting away with something. But let me tell you there will be a retribution—not in heaven, right here on earth."

"Right here on earth," harmonized Mrs. Macy Wheeler.

They left along the path, erect, haughty as a wedding procession, and passed into the sunlight where the red rolling grass swept up, swallowed them. Lingering under the tree, the Judge smiled at us and, with a small courteous bow, said: "Do I remember you offering a drumstick to anybody that would like it?"

HE MIGHT HAVE BEEN PUT TOGETHER from parts of the tree, for his nose was like a wooden peg, his legs were strong as old roots, and his eyebrows were thick, tough as strips of bark. Among the topmost branches were beards of silvery moss the color of his center-parted hair, and the cowhide sycamore leaves, sifting down from a neighboring taller tree, were the color of his cheeks. Despite his canny, tomcat eyes, the general impression his face made was that of someone shy and countrified. Ordinarily he was not the one to make a show of himself, Judge Charlie Cool; there were many who had taken advantage of his modesty to set themselves above him. Yet none of them could have claimed, as he could, to be a graduate of Harvard University or to have twice traveled in Europe. Still, there were those who were resentful and felt that he put on airs: wasn't he supposed to read a page of Greek every morning before breakfast? and what kind of a man was it that would always have flowers in his buttonhole? If he wasn't stuck up, why, some people asked, had he gone all the way to Kentucky to find a wife instead of marrying one of our own women? I do not remember the Judge's wife; she died before I was old enough to be aware of her, therefore all that I repeat comes second-hand. So: the town never warmed up to Irene Cool, and apparently it was her own fault. Kentucky women are difficult to begin with, keyed-up, hellion-hearted, and Irene Cool, who was born a Todd in Bowling Green (Mary Todd, a second cousin once removed, had married Abraham Lincoln), let everyone around here know she thought them a backward, vulgar lot: she received none of the ladies of the town, but Miss Palmer, who did sewing for her, spread news of how she'd transformed the Judge's house into a place of taste and style with Oriental rugs and antique furnishings. She drove to and from church in a Pierce-Arrow with all the windows rolled up, and in church itself she sat with a cologned handkerchief against her nose: *the smell of God ain't good enough for Irene Cool.* Moreover, she would not permit either of the local doctors to attend her family, this though she herself was a semi-invalid: a small backbone dislocation necessitated her sleeping on a bed of boards. There were crude jokes about the Judge getting full of splinters. Nevertheless, he fathered two sons, Todd and Charles Jr., both born in Kentucky where their mother had gone in order that they could claim to be natives of the bluegrass state. But those who tried to make out the Judge got the brunt of his wife's irritableness, that he was a miserable man, never had much of a case, and after she died even the hardest of their critics had to admit old Charlie must surely have loved his Irene. For during the last two years of her life, when she was very ill and fretful, he retired as circuit judge, then took her abroad to the places they had been on their honeymoon. She never came back; she is buried in Switzerland. Not so long ago Carrie Wells, a schoolteacher here in town, went on a group tour to Europe; the only thing connecting our town with that continent are graves, the graves of soldier boys and Irene Cool; and Carrie, armed with a camera for snapshots, set out to visit them all: though she stumbled about in a cloud-high cemetery one whole afternoon, she could not find the Judge's wife, and it is funny to think of Irene Cool, serenely there on a mountain-side still unwilling to receive. There was not much left for the Judge when he came back; politicians like Meiself Tallsap and his gang had come into power: those boys couldn't afford to have Charlie Cool sitting in the courthouse. It was sad to see the Judge, a fine-looking man dressed in narrow-cut suits with a black silk band sewn around his sleeve and a Cherokee rose in his buttonhole, sad to see him with nothing to do except go to the post office or stop in at the bank. His sons worked in the bank, prissy-mouthed, prudent men who might have been twins, for they both were marshmallow-white, slump-shouldered, watery-eyed. Charles Jr., he was the one who had lost his hair while still in college, was vice-president of the bank, and Todd, the younger son, was chief cashier. In no way did they resemble their father, except that they had married Kentucky women. These daughters-in-law had taken over the Judge's house and divided it into two apartments with separate entrances; there was an arrangement whereby the old man lived with first one son's family, then the other. No wonder he'd felt like taking a walk to the woods.

"Thank you, Miss Dolly," he said, wiping his mouth with the back of his hand. "That's the best drumstick I've had since I was a boy."

"It's the least we can do, a drumstick; you were very brave." There was in Dolly's voice an emotional, feminine tremor that struck me as unsuitable, not dignified; so, too, it must have seemed to Catherine: she gave Dolly a reprimanding glance. "Won't you have something more, a piece of cake?"

"No ma'am, thank you, I've had a sufficiency." He unloosened from his vest a gold watch and chain, then lassoed the chain to a strong twig above his head; it hung like a Christmas ornament, and its feathery faded ticking might have been the heartbeat of a delicate thing, a firefly, a frog. "If you can hear time passing it makes the day last longer. I've come to appreciate a long day." He brushed back the fur of the squirrels, which lay curled in a corner as though they were only asleep. "Right through the head: good shooting, son."

Of course I gave the credit to the proper party. "Riley Henderson, was it?" said the Judge, and went on to say it was Riley who had let our whereabouts be known. "Before that, they must have sent off a hundred dollars' worth of telegrams," he told us, tickled at the thought. "I guess it was the idea of all that money that made Verena take to her bed."

Scowling, Dolly said, "It doesn't make a particle of sense, all of them behaving ugly that way. They seemed mad enough to kill us, though I can't see why, or what it has to do with Verena: she knew we were going away to leave her in peace, I told her, I even left a note. But if she's sick—is she, Judge? I've never known her to be."

"Never a day," said Catherine.

"Oh, she's upset all right," the Judge said with a certain contentment. "But Verena's not the woman to come down with anything an aspirin couldn't fix. I remember when she wanted to rearrange the cemetery, put up some kind of mausoleum to house herself and all you Talbos. One of the ladies around here came to me and said Judge, don't you think Verena Talbo is the most morbid person in town, contemplating such a big tomb for herself? and I said No, the only thing morbid was that she was willing to spend the money when not for an instant did she believe she was ever going to die."

"I don't like to hear talk against my sister," said Dolly curtly. "She's worked hard, she deserves to have things as she wants them. It's our fault, someway we failed her, there was no place for us in her house."

Catherine's cotton-wadding squirmed in her jaw like chewing tobacco. "Are you my Dollyheart? or some hypocrite? He's a friend, you ought to tell him the truth, how That One and the little Jew was stealing our medicine. . . ."

The Judge applied for a translation, but Dolly said it was simply nonsense, nothing worth repeating and, diverting him, asked if he knew how to skin a squirrel. Nodding dreamily, he gazed away from us, above us, his acornlike eyes scanning the sky-fringed, breeze-fooled leaves. "It may be that there is no place for any of us. Except we know there is, somewhere; and if we found it, but lived there only a moment, we could count ourselves blessed. This could be your place," he said, shivering as though in the sky spreading wings had cast a cold shade. "And mine."

Subtly as the gold watch spun its sound of time, the afternoon curved toward twilight. Mist from the river, autumn haze, trailed moon-colors among the bronze, the blue trees, and a halo, an image of winter, ringed the paling sun. Still the Judge did not leave us: "Two women and a boy? at the mercy of night? and Junius Candle, those fools up to God knows what? I'm sticking with you." Surely, of the four of us, it was the Judge who had most found his place in the tree. It was a pleasure to watch him, all twinkly as a hare's nose, and feeling himself a man again, more than that, a protector. He skinned the squirrels with a jackknife, while in the dusk I gathered sticks and built under the tree a fire for the frying pan. Dolly opened the bottle of blackberry wine; she justified this by referring to a chill in the air. The squirrels turned out quite well, very tender, and the Judge said proudly that we should taste his fried catfish sometime. We sipped the wine in silence; a smell of leaves and smoke carrying from the cooling fire called up thoughts of other autumns, and we sighed, heard, like sea-roar, singings in the field of grass. A candle flickered in a mason jar, and gipsy moths, balanced, blowing about the flame, seemed to pilot its scarf of yellow among the black branches.

There was, just then, not a footfall, but a nebulous sense of intrusion: it might have been nothing more than the moon coming out. Except there was no moon; nor stars. It was dark as the blackberry wine. "I think there is someone—something down there," said Dolly, expressing what we all felt.

The Judge lifted the candle. Night-crawlers slithered away from its lurching light, a snowy owl flew between the trees. "Who goes there?" he challenged with the conviction of a soldier. "Answer up, who goes there?"

"Me, Riley Henderson." It was indeed. He separated from the shadows, and his upraised, grinning face looked warped, wicked in the candlelight. "Just thought I'd see how you were getting on. Hope you're not sore at me: I wouldn't have told where you were, not if I'd known what it was all about."

"Nobody blames you, son," said the Judge, and I remembered it was he who had championed Riley's cause against his uncle Horace Holton: there was an understanding between them. "We're enjoying a small taste of wine. I'm sure Miss Dolly would be pleased to have you join us."

Catherine complained there was no room; another ounce, and those old boards would give way. Still, we scrunched together to make a place for Riley, who had no sooner squeezed into it than Catherine grabbed a fistful of his hair. "That's for today with you pointing your gun at us like I told you not to; and this," she said, yanking again and speaking distinctively enough to be understood, "pays you back for setting the Sheriff on us."

It seemed to me that Catherine was impertinent, but Riley grunted good-naturedly, and said she might have better cause to be pulling somebody's hair before the night was over. For there was, he told us, excited feelings in the town, crowds like Saturday night; the Reverend and Mrs. Buster especially were brewing trouble: Mrs. Buster was sitting on her front porch showing callers the bump on her head. Sheriff Candle, he said, had persuaded Verena to authorize a warrant for our arrest on the grounds that we had stolen property belonging to her.

"And Judge," said Riley, his manner grave, perplexed, "they've even got the idea they're going to arrest you. Disturbing the peace and obstructing justice, that's what I heard. Maybe I shouldn't tell you this—but outside the bank I ran into one of your boys, Todd. I asked him what he was going to do about it, about them arresting you, I mean; and he said Nothing, said they'd been expecting something of the kind, that you'd brought it on yourself."

Leaning, the Judge snuffed out the candle; it was as though an expression was occurring in his face which he did not want us to see. In the dark one of us was crying, after a moment we knew that it was Dolly, and the sound of her tears set off silent explosions of love that, running the full circle round, bound us each to the other. Softly, the Judge said: "When they come we must be ready for them. Now, everybody listen to me. . . ."

CHAPTER 3

"We must know our position to defend it; that is a primary rule. Therefore: what has brought us together? Trouble. Miss Dolly and her friends, they are in trouble. You, Riley: we both are in trouble. We belong in this tree or we wouldn't be here." Dolly grew silent under the confident sound of the Judge's voice; he said: "Today, when I started out with the Sheriff's party, I was a man convinced that his life will have passed uncommunicated and without trace. I think now that I will not have been so unfortunate. Miss Dolly, how long? fifty, sixty years it was that far ago that I remember you, a stiff and blushing child riding to town in your father's wagon—never getting down from the wagon because you didn't want us town-children to see you had no shoes."

"They had shoes, Dolly and That One," Catherine muttered. "It was me that didn't have no shoes."

"All the years that I've seen you, never known you, not ever recognized, as I did today, what you are: a spirit, a pagan . . ."

"A pagan?" said Dolly, alarmed but interested.

"At least, then, a spirit, someone not to be calculated by the eye alone. Spirits are accepters of life, they grant its differences—and consequently are always in trouble. Myself, I should never have been a Judge; as such, I was too often on the wrong side: the law doesn't admit differences. Do you remember old Carper, the fisherman who had a houseboat on the river? He was chased out of town—wanted to marry that pretty little colored girl, I think she works for Mrs. Postum now; and you know she loved him, I used to see them when I went fishing, they were very happy together; she was to him what no one has been to me, the one person in the world—from whom nothing is held back. Still, if he had succeeded in marrying her, it would have been the Sheriff's duty to arrest and my duty to sentence him. I sometimes imagine all those whom I've called guilty have passed the real guilt on to me: it's partly that that makes me want once before I die to be on the right side."

"You on the right side now. That One and the Jew . . ."

"Hush," said Dolly.

"The one person in the world." It was Riley repeating the Judge's phrase; his voice lingered inquiringly.

"I mean," the Judge explained, "a person to whom everything can be said. Am I an idiot to want such a thing? But ah, the energy we spend hiding from one another, afraid as we are of being identified. But here we are, identified: five fools in a tree. A great piece of luck provided we know how to use it: no longer any need to worry about the picture we present—free to find out who we truly are. If we know that no one can dislodge us; it's the uncertainty concerning themselves that makes our friends conspire to deny the differences. By scraps and bits I've in the past surrendered myself to strangers—men who disappeared down the gangplank, got off at the next station: put together, maybe they would've made the one person in the world— but there he is with a dozen different faces moving down a hundred separate streets. This is my chance to find that man—you are him, Miss Dolly, Riley, all of you."

Catherine said, "I'm no man with any dozen faces: the notion," which irritated Dolly, who told her if she couldn't speak respectably why not just go to sleep. "But Judge," said Dolly, "I'm not sure I know what it is you have in mind we should tell each other. Secrets?" she finished lamely.

"Secrets, no, no." The Judge scratched a match and relighted the candle; his face sprang upon us with an expression unexpectedly pathetic: we must help him, he was pleading. "Speak of the night, the fact there is no moon. What one says hardly matters, only the trust with which it is said, the sympathy with which it is received. Irene, my wife, a remarkable woman, we might have shared anything, and yet, yet nothing in us combined, we could not touch. She died in my arms, and at the last I said, Are you happy, Irene? have I made you happy? Happy happy happy, those were her last words: equivocal. I have never understood whether she was saying yes, or merely answering with an echo: I should know if I'd ever known her. My sons. I do not enjoy their esteem: I've wanted it, more as a man than as a father. Unfortunately, they feel they know something shameful about me. I'll tell you what it is." His virile eyes, faceted with candle-glow, examined us one by one, as though testing our attention, trust. "Five years ago, nearer six, I sat down in a train-seat where some child had left a child's magazine. I picked it up and was looking through it when I saw on the back cover addresses of children who wanted to correspond with other children. There was a little girl in

Alaska, her name appealed to me, Heather Falls. I sent her a picture postcard; Lord, it seemed a harmless and pleasant thing to do. She answered at once, and the letter quite astonished me; it was a very intelligent account of life in Alaska—charming descriptions of her father's sheep ranch, of northern lights. She was thirteen and enclosed a photograph of herself—not pretty, but a wise and kind looking child. I hunted through some old albums and found a Kodak made on a fishing trip when I was fifteen—out in the sun and with a trout in my hand: it looked new enough. I wrote her as though I were still that boy, told her of the gun I'd got for Christmas, how the dog had had pups and what we'd named them, described a tent-show that had come to town. To be growing up again and have a sweetheart in Alaska—well, it was fun for an old man sitting alone listening to the noise of a clock. Later on she wrote she'd fallen in love with a fellow she knew, and I felt a real pang of jealousy, the way a youngster would; but we have remained friends: two years ago, when I told her I was getting ready for law school, she sent me a gold nugget—it would bring me luck, she said." He took it from his pocket and held it out for us to see: it made her come so close, Heather Falls, as though the gently bright gift balanced in his palm was part of her heart.

"And that's what they think is shameful?" said Dolly, more piqued than indignant. "Because you've helped keep company a lonely little child in Alaska? It snows there so much."

Judge Cool closed his hand over the nugget. "Not that they've mentioned it to me. But I've heard them talking at night, my sons and their wives: wanting to know what to do about me. Of course they'd spied out the letters. I don't believe in locking drawers—seems strange a man can't live without keys in what was at least once his own house. They think it all a sign of . . ." He tapped his head.

"I had a letter once. Collin, sugar, pour me a taste," said Catherine, indicating the wine. "Sure enough, I had a letter once, still got it somewhere, kept it twenty years wondering who was wrote it. Said Hello Catherine, come on to Miami and marry with me, love Bill."

"Catherine. A man asked you to marry him—and you never told one word of it to me?"

Catherine lifted a shoulder. "Well, Dollyheart, what was the Judge saying? You don't tell anybody everything. Besides, I've known a peck of Bills—wouldn't study marrying any of them. What worries my mind is, which one of the Bills was it wrote that letter? I'd like to know, seeing as it's the only letter I ever got. It could be the Bill that put the roof on my house; course, by the time the roof was up—my goodness, I have got old, been a long day since I've given it two thoughts. There was Bill that came to plow the garden, spring of 1913 it was; that man sure could plow a straight row. And Bill that built the chicken-coop: went away on a Pullman job; might have been him wrote me that letter. Or Bill—uh uh, his name was Fred—Collin, sugar, this wine is mighty good."

"I may have a drop more myself," said Dolly. "I mean, Catherine has given me such a . . ."

"Hmn," said Catherine.

"If you spoke more slowly, or chewed less . . ." The Judge thought Catherine's cotton was tobacco.

Riley had withdrawn a little from us; slumped over, he stared stilly into the inhabited dark: I, I, I, a bird cried, "I—you're wrong, Judge," he said.

"How so, son?"

The caught-up uneasiness that I associated with Riley swamped his face. "I'm not in trouble: I'm nothing—or would you call that my trouble? I lie awake thinking what do I know how to do? hunt, drive a car, fool around; and I get scared when I think maybe that's all it will ever come to. Another thing, I've got no feelings—except for my sisters, which is different. Take for instance, I've been going with this girl from Rock City nearly a year, the longest time I've stayed with one girl. I guess it was a week ago she flared up and said where's your heart? said if I didn't love her she'd as soon die. So I stopped the car on the railroad track; well, I said, let's just sit here, the Crescent's due in about twenty minutes. We didn't take our eyes off each other, and I thought isn't it mean that I'm looking at you and I don't feel anything except . . ."

"Except vanity?" said the Judge.

Riley did not deny it. "And if my sisters were old enough to take care of themselves, I'd have been willing to wait for the Crescent to come down on us."

It made my stomach hurt to hear him talk like that; I longed to tell him he was all I wanted to be.

"You said before about the one person in the world. Why couldn't

I think of her like that? It's what I want, I'm no good by myself. Maybe, if I could care for somebody that way, I'd make plans and carry them out: buy that stretch of land past Parson's Place and build houses on it—I could do it if I got quiet."

Wind surprised, pealed the leaves, parted night clouds; showers of starlight were let loose: our candle, as though intimidated by the incandescence of the opening, star-stabbed sky, toppled, and we could see, unwrapped above us, a late wayaway wintery moon: it was like a slice of snow, near and far creatures called to it, hunched moon-eyed frogs, a claw-voiced wildcat. Catherine hauled out the rose scrapquilt, insisting Dolly wrap it around herself; then she tucked her arms around me and scratched my head until I let it relax on her bosom—You cold? she said, and I wiggled closer: she was good and warm as the old kitchen.

"Son, I'd say you were going at it the wrong end first," said the Judge, turning up his coat-collar. "How could you care about one girl? Have you ever cared about one leaf?"

Riley, listening to the wildcat with an itchy hunter's look, snatched at the leaves blowing about us like midnight butterflies; alive, fluttering as though to escape and fly, one stayed trapped between his fingers. The Judge, too: he caught a leaf; and it was worth more in his hand than in Riley's. Pressing it mildly against his cheek, he distantly said, "We are speaking of love. A leaf, a handful of seed— begin with these, learn a little what it is to love. First, a leaf, a fall of rain, then someone to receive what a leaf has taught you, what a fall of rain has ripened. No easy process, understand; it could take a lifetime, it has mine, and still I've never mastered it—I only know how true it is: that love is a chain of love, as nature is a chain of life."

"Then," said Dolly with an intake of breath, "I've been in love all my life." She sank down into the quilt. "Well, no," and her voice fell off, "I guess not. I've never loved a," while she searched for the word wind frolicked her veil, "gentleman. You might say that I've never had the opportunity. Except Papa," she paused, as though she'd said too much. A gauze of starlight wrapped her closely as the quilt; something, the reciting frogs, the string of voices stretching from the field of grass, lured, impelled her: "But I have loved everything else. Like the color pink; when I was a child I had one colored crayon, and it was pink; I drew pink cats, pink trees—for thirty-four years I lived in a pink room. And the box I kept, it's somewhere in the attic now, I must ask Verena please to give it to me, it would be nice to see my first loves again: what is there? a dried honeycomb, an empty hornet's nest, other things, oh an orange stuck with cloves and a jaybird's egg—when I loved those love collected inside me so that it went flying about like a bird in a sunflower field. But it's best not to show such things, it burdens people and makes them, I don't know why, unhappy. Verena scolds at me for what she calls hiding in corners, but I'm afraid of scaring people if I show that I care for them. Like Paul Jimson's wife; after he got sick and couldn't deliver the papers any more, remember she took over his route? poor thin little thing just dragging herself with that sack of papers. It was one cold afternoon, she came up on the porch her nose running and tears of cold hanging in her eyes—she put down the paper, and I said wait, hold on, and took my handkerchief to wipe her eyes: I wanted to say, if I could, that I was sorry and that I loved her—my hand grazed her face, she turned with the smallest shout and ran down the steps. Then on, she always tossed the papers from the street, and whenever I heard them hit the porch it sounded in my bones."

"Paul Jimson's wife: worrying yourself over trash like that!" said Catherine, rinsing her mouth with the last of the wine. "I've got a bowl of goldfish, just 'cause I like them don't make me love the world. Love a lot of mess, my foot. You can talk what you want, not going to do anything but harm, bringing up what's best forgot. People ought to keep more things to themselves. The deepdown ownself part of you, that's the good part: what's left of a human being that goes around speaking his privates? The Judge, he say we all up here 'cause of trouble some kind. Shoot! We here for very plain reasons. One is, this our tree-house, and two, That One and the Jew's trying to steal what belongs to us. Three: you here, every one of you, 'cause you want to be: the deepdown part of you tells you so. This last don't apply to me. I like a roof over my own head. Dolly-heart, give the Judge a portion of that quilt: man's shivering like was Halloween."

Shyly Dolly lifted a wing of the quilt and nodded to him; the Judge, not at all shy, slipped under it. The branches of the China tree swayed like immense oars dipping into a sea rolling and chilled by the far far stars. Left alone, Riley sat hunched up in himself like a pitiful orphan. "Snuggle up, hard head: you cold like anybody else," said Catherine, offering him the position on her right that I occupied on her left. He didn't seem to want to; maybe he noticed that she smelled like bitterweed, or maybe he thought it was sissy; but I said come on, Riley, Catherine's good and warm, better than a quilt. After a while Riley moved over to us. It was quiet for so long I thought everyone had gone to sleep. Then I felt Catherine stiffen. "It's just come to me who it was sent my letter: Bill Nobody. That One, that's who. Sure as my name's Catherine Creek she got some nigger in Miami to mail me a letter, thinking I'd scoot off there never to be heard from again." Dolly sleepily said hush now hush, shut your eyes: "Nothing to be afraid of; we've men here to watch out for us." A branch swung back, moonlight ignited the tree: I saw the Judge take Dolly's hand. It was the last thing I saw.

CHAPTER 4

RILEY WAS THE FIRST to wake, and he wakened me. On the skyline three morning stars swooned in the flush of an arriving sun; dew tinseled the leaves, a jet chain of blackbirds swung out to meet the mounting light. Riley beckoned for me to come with him; we slid silently down through the tree. Catherine, snoring with abandon, did not hear us go; nor did Dolly and the Judge who, like two children lost in a witch-ruled forest, were asleep with their cheeks together.

We headed toward the river, Riley leading the way. The legs of his canvas trousers whispered against each other. Every little bit he stopped and stretched himself, as though he'd been riding on a train. Somewhere we came to a hill of already about and busy red ants. Riley unbuttoned his fly and began to flood them; I don't know that it was funny, but I laughed to keep him company. Naturally I was insulted when he switched around and peed on my shoe. I thought it meant he had no respect for me. I said to him why would he want to do a thing like that? Don't you know a joke? he said, and threw a hugging arm around my shoulder.

If such events can be dated, this I would say was the moment Riley Henderson and I became friends, the moment, at least, when there began in him an affectionate feeling for me that supported my own for him. Through brown briars under brown trees we walked deep in the woods down to the river.

Leaves like scarlet hands floated on the green slow water. A poking end of a drowned log seemed the peering head of some river-beast. We moved on to the old houseboat, where the water was clearer. The houseboat was slightly tipped over; drifts of waterbay sheddings were like a rich rust on its roof and declining deck. The inside cabin had a mystifying tended-to look. Scattered around were issues of an adventure magazine, there was a kerosene lamp and a line of beer empties ranged on a table; the bunk sported a blanket, a pillow, and the pillow was colored with pink markings of lipstick. In a rush I realized the houseboat was someone's hide-out; then, from the grin taking over Riley's homely face, I knew whose it was. "What's more," he said, "you can get in a little fishing on the side. Don't you tell anybody." I crossed an admiring heart.

While we were undressing I had a kind of dream. I dreamed the houseboat had been launched on the river with the five of us aboard: our laundry flapped like sails, in the pantry a coconut cake was cooking, a geranium bloomed on the windowsill—together we floated over changing rivers past varying views.

The last of summer warmed the climbing sun, but the water, at first plunge, sent me chattering and chicken-skinned back to the deck where I stood watching Riley unconcernedly propel himself to and fro between the banks. An island of bamboo reeds, standing like the legs of cranes, shivered in a shallow patch, and Riley waded out among them with lowered, hunting eyes. He signaled to me. Though it hurt, I eased down into the cold river and swam to join him. The water bending the bamboo was clear and divided into knee-deep basins—Riley hovered above one: in the thin pool a coal-black catfish lay dozingly trapped. We closed in upon it with fingers tense as fork-prongs: thrashing backwards, it flung itself straight into my hands. The flailing razory whiskers made a gash across my palm, still I had the sense to hold on—thank goodness, for it's the only fish I ever caught. Most people don't believe it when I tell about catching a catfish barehanded; I say well ask Riley Henderson. We drove a spike of bamboo through its gills and swam back to the houseboat holding it aloft. Riley said it was one of the fattest catfish he'd ever seen: we would take it back to the tree and, since he'd bragged what a great hand he was at frying a catfish, let the Judge fix it for breakfast. As it turned out, that fish never got eaten.

All this time at the tree-house there was a terrible situation. During our absence Sheriff Candle had returned backed by deputies and a warrant of arrest. Meanwhile, unaware of what was in store, Riley and I lazed along kicking over toadstools, sometimes stopping to skip rocks on the water.

We still were some distance away when rioting voices reached us; they rang in the trees like axe-blows. I heard Catherine scream: roar, rather. It made such soup of my legs I couldn't keep up with Riley, who grabbed a stick and began to run. I zigged one way, zagged another, then, having made a wrong turn, came out on the grass-field's rim. And there was Catherine.

Her dress was ripped down the front: she was good as naked. Ray Oliver, Jack Mill, and Big Eddie Stover, three grown men, cronies of the Sheriff, were dragging and slapping her through the grass. I wanted to kill them; and Catherine was trying to: but she didn't stand a chance—though she butted them with her head, bounced them with her elbows. Big Eddie Stover was legally born a bastard; the other two made the grade on their own. It was Big Eddie that went for me, and I slammed my catfish flat in his face. Catherine said, "You leave my baby be, he's an orphan"; and, when she saw that he had me around the waist: "In the booboos, Collin, kick his old booboos." So I did. Big Eddie's face curdled like clabber. Jack Mill (he's the one who a year later got locked in the ice-plant and froze to death: served him right) snatched at me, but I bolted across the field and crouched down in the tallest grass. I don't think they bothered to look for me, they had their hands so full with Catherine; she fought them the whole way, and I watched her, sick with knowing there was no help to give, until they passed out of sight over the ridge into the cemetery.

Overhead two squawking crows crossed, recrossed, as though making an evil sign. I crept toward the woods—near me, then, I heard boots cutting through the grass. It was the Sheriff; with him was a man called Will Harris. Tall as a door, buffalo-shouldered, Will Harris had once had his throat eaten out by a mad dog; the scars were bad enough, but his damaged voice was worse: it sounded giddy and babyfied, like a midget's. They passed so close I could have untied Will's shoes. His tiny voice, shrilling at the Sheriff, jumped with Morris Ritz's name and Verena's: I couldn't make out exactly, except something had happened about Morris Ritz and Verena had sent Will to bring back the Sheriff. The Sheriff said: "What in hell does the woman want, an army?" When they were gone I sprang up and ran into the woods.

In sight of the China tree I hid behind a fan of fern: I thought one of the Sheriff's men might still be hanging around. But there was nothing, simply a lonely singing bird. And no one in the tree-house: smoky as ghosts, streamers of sunlight illuminated its emptiness. Numbly I moved into view and leaned my head against the tree's trunk; at this, the vision of the houseboat returned: our laundry flapped, the geranium bloomed, the carrying river carried us out to sea into the world.

"Collin." My name fell out of the sky. "Is that you I hear? are you crying?"

It was Dolly, calling from somewhere I could not see—until, climbing to the tree's heart, I saw in the above distance Dolly's dangling childish shoe. "Careful, boy," said the Judge, who was beside her, "you'll shake us out of here." Indeed, like gulls resting on a ship's mast, they were sitting in the absolute tower of the tree; afterwards, Dolly was to remark that the view afforded was so enthralling she regretted not having visited there before. The Judge, it developed, had seen the approach of the Sheriff and his men in time for them to take refuge in those heights. "Wait, we're coming," she said; and, with one arm steadied by the Judge, she descended like a fine lady sweeping down a flight of stairs.

We kissed each other; she continued to hold me. "She went to look for you—Catherine; we didn't know where you were, and I was so afraid, I . . ." Her fear tingled my hands: she felt like a shaking small animal, a rabbit just taken from the trap. The Judge looked on with humbled eyes, fumbling hands; he seemed to feel in the way, perhaps because he thought he'd failed us in not preventing what had happened to Catherine. But then, what could he have done? Had he gone to her aid he would only have got himself caught: they weren't fooling, the Sheriff, Big Eddie Stover and the others. I was the one to feel guilty. If Catherine hadn't gone to look for me they probably never would have caught her. I told of what had taken place in the field of grass.

But Dolly really wanted not to hear. As though scattering a dream she brushed back her veil. "I want to believe Catherine is gone: and I can't. If I could I would run to find her. I want to believe Verena has done this: and I can't. Collin, what do you think: is it that after all the world is a bad place? Last night I saw it so differently."

The Judge focused his eyes on mine: he was trying, I think, to tell me how to answer. But I knew myself. No matter what passions compose them, all private worlds are good, they are never vulgar places: Dolly had been made too civilized by her own, the one she shared with Catherine and me, to feel the winds of wickedness that circulate elsewhere: No, Dolly, the world is not a bad place. She passed a hand across her forehead: "If you are right, then in a moment Catherine will be walking under the tree—she won't have found you or Riley, but she will have come back."

"By the way," said the Judge, "where *is* Riley?"

He'd run ahead of me, that was the last I'd seen of him; with an anxiety that struck us simultaneously, the Judge and I stood up and started yelling his name. Our voices, curving slowly around the woods, again, again swung back on silence. I knew what had happened: he'd fallen into an old Indian well—many's the case I could tell you of. I was about to suggest this when abruptly the Judge put a finger to his lips. The man must have had ears like a dog: I couldn't hear a sound. But he was right, there was someone on the path. It turned out to be Maude Riordan and Riley's older sister, the smart one, Elizabeth. They were very dear friends and wore white matching sweaters. Elizabeth was carrying a violin case.

"Look here, Elizabeth," said the Judge, startling the girls, for as yet they had not discovered us. "Look here, child, have you seen your brother?"

Maude recovered first, and it was she who answered. "We sure have," she said emphatically. "I was walking Elizabeth home from her lesson when Riley came along doing ninety miles an hour; nearly ran us over. You should speak to him, Elizabeth. Anyway, he asked us to come down here and tell you not to worry, said he'd explain everything later. Whatever that means."

Both Maude and Elizabeth had been in my class at school; they'd

jumped a grade and graduated the previous June. I knew Maude
especially well because for a summer I'd taken piano lessons from
her mother; her father taught violin, and Elizabeth Henderson was
one of his pupils. Maude herself played the violin beautifully; just a
week before I'd read in the town paper where she'd been invited to
play on a radio program in Birmingham: I was glad to hear it. The
Riordans were nice people, considerate and cheerful. It was not
because I wanted to learn piano that I took lessons with Mrs. Riordan—rather, I liked her blond largeness, the sympathetic, educated
talk that went on while we sat before the splendid upright that
smelled of polish and attention; and what I particularly liked was
afterwards, when Maude would ask me to have a lemonade on the
cool back porch. She was snub-nosed and elfin-eared, a skinny excit-
able girl who from her father had inherited Irish black eyes and from
her mother platinum hair pale as morning—not the least like her
best friend, the soulful and shadowy Elizabeth. I don't know what
those two talked about, books and music maybe. But with me
Maude's subjects were boys, dates, drugstore slander: didn't I think it
was terrible, the awful girls Riley Henderson chased around with?
she felt so sorry for Elizabeth, and thought it wonderful how, despite
all, Elizabeth held up her head. It didn't take a genius to see that
Maude was heartset on Riley; nevertheless, I imagined for a while
that I was in love with her. At home I kept mentioning her until
finally Catherine said Oh Maude Riordan, she's too scrawny—nothing on her to pinch, a man's crazy to give her the time of day. Once I
showed Maude a big evening, made for her with my own hands a
sweet-pea corsage, then took her to Phil's Café where we had Kansas
City steaks; afterwards, there was a dance at the Lola Hotel. Still she
behaved as though she hadn't expected to be kissed goodnight. "I
don't think that's necessary, Collin—though it was cute of you to take
me out." I was let down, you can see why; but as I didn't allow myself
to brood over it our friendship went on little changed. One day, at
the end of a lesson, Mrs. Riordan omitted the usual new piece for
home practice; instead, she kindly informed me that she preferred
not to continue with my lessons: "We're very fond of you, Collin, I
don't have to say that you're welcome in this house at any time. But
dear, the truth is you have no ability for music; it happens that way
occasionally, and I don't think it's fair on either of us to pretend

otherwise." She was right, all the same my pride was hurt, I couldn't help feeling pushed-out, it made me miserable to think of the Riordans, and gradually, in about the time it took to forget my few hard-learned tunes, I drew a curtain on them. At first Maude used to stop me after school and ask me over to her house; one way or another I always got out of it; furthermore, it was winter then and I liked to stay in the kitchen with Dolly and Catherine. Catherine wanted to know: How come you don't talk any more about Maude Riordan? I said because I don't, that's all. But while I didn't talk, I must have been thinking; at least, seeing her there under the tree, old feelings squeezed my chest. For the first time I considered the circumstances self-consciously: did we, Dolly, the Judge and I, strike Maude and Elizabeth as a ludicrous sight? I could be judged by them, they were my own age. But from their manner we might just have met on the street or at the drugstore.

The Judge said, "Maude, how's your daddy? Heard he hasn't been feeling too good."

"He can't complain. You know how men are, always looking for an ailment. And yourself, sir?"

"That's a pity," said the Judge, his mind wandering. "You give your daddy my regards, and tell him I hope he feels better."

Maude submitted agreeably: "I will, sir, thank you. I know he'll appreciate your concern." Draping her skirt, she dropped on the moss and settled beside her an unwilling Elizabeth. For Elizabeth no one used a nickname; you might begin by calling her Betty, but in a week it would be Elizabeth again: that was her effect. Languid, banana-boned, she had dour black hair and an apathetic, at moments saintly face—in an enamel locket worn around her lily-stalk neck she preserved a miniature of her missionary father. "Look, Elizabeth, isn't that a becoming hat Miss Dolly has on? Velvet, with a veil."

Dolly roused herself; she patted her head. "I don't generally wear hats—we intended to travel."

"We heard you'd left home," said Maude; and, proceeding more frankly: "In fact that's all anyone talks about, isn't it, Elizabeth?" Elizabeth nodded without enthusiasm. "Gracious, there are some pecular stories going around. I mean, on the way here we met Gus Ham and he said that colored woman Catherine Crook (is that her name?) had been arrested for hitting Mrs. Buster with a mason jar."

In sloping tones, Dolly said, "Catherine—had nothing to do with it."

"I guess someone did," said Maude. "We saw Mrs. Buster in the post office this morning; she was showing everybody a bump on her head, quite large. It looked genuine to us, didn't it Elizabeth?" Elizabeth yawned. "To be sure, I don't care who hit her, I think they ought to get a medal."

"No," sighed Dolly, "it isn't proper, it shouldn't have happened. We all will have a lot to be sorry for."

At last Maude took account of me. "I've been wanting to see you, Collin," she said hurrying as though to hide an embarrassment: mine, not hers. "Elizabeth and I are planning a Halloween party, a real scary one, and we thought it would be grand to dress you in a skeleton suit and sit you in a dark room to tell people's fortunes: because you're so good at . . ."

"Fibbing," said Elizabeth disinterestedly.

"Which is what fortune-telling is," Maude elaborated.

I don't know what gave them the idea I was such a story-teller, unless it was at school I'd shown a superior talent for alibis. I said it sounded fine, the party. "But you better not count on me. We might be in jail by then."

"Oh well, in that case," said Maude, as if accepting one of my old and usual excuses for not coming to her house.

"Say, Maude," said the Judge, helping us out of the silence that had fallen, "you're getting to be a celebrity: I saw in the paper where you're going to play on the radio."

As though dreaming aloud, she explained the broadcast was the finals of a state competition; if she won, the prize was a musical scholarship at the University: even second prize meant a half-scholarship. "I'm going to play a piece of daddy's, a serenade: he wrote it for me the day I was born. But it's a surprise, I don't want him to know."

"Make her play it for you," said Elizabeth, unclasping her violin case.

Maude was generous, she did not have to be begged. The wine-colored violin, coddled under her chin, trilled as she tuned it; a brazen butterfly, lighting on the bow, was spiraled away as the bow swept across the strings singing a music that seemed a blizzard of butterflies flying, a sky-rocket of spring sweet to hear in the gnarled fall woods. It slowed, saddened, her silver hair drooped across the violin. We applauded; after we'd stopped there went on sounding a mysterious extra pair of hands. Riley stepped from behind a bank of fern, and when she saw him Maude's cheeks pinked. I don't think she would have played so well if she'd known he was listening.

Riley sent the girls home; they seemed reluctant to go, but Elizabeth was not used to disobeying her brother. "Lock the doors," he told her, "and Maude, I'd appreciate it if you'd spend the night at our place: anybody comes by asking for me, say you don't know where I am."

I had to help him into the tree, for he'd brought back his gun and a knapsack heavy with provisions—a bottle of rose and raisin wine, oranges, sardines, wieners, rolls from the Katydid Bakery, a jumbo box of animal crackers: each item appearing stepped up our spirits, and Dolly, overcome by the animal crackers, said Riley ought to have a kiss.

But it was with grave faces that we listened to his report.

When we'd separated in the woods it was toward the sound of Catherine that he'd run. This had brought him to the grass: he'd been watching when I had my encounter with Big Eddie Stover. I said well why didn't you help me? "You were doing all right: I don't figure Big Eddie's liable to forget you too soon: poor fellow limped along doubled over." Besides, it occurred to him that no one knew he was one of us, that he'd joined us in the tree: he was right to have stayed hidden, it made it possible for him to follow Catherine and the deputies into town. They'd stuffed her into the rumble-seat of Big Eddie's old coupé and driven straight to the jail; Riley trailed them in his car. "By the time we reached the jail she seemed to have got quieted down; there was a little crowd hanging around, kids, some old farmers—you would have been proud of Catherine, she walked through them holding her dress together and her head like this." He tilted his head at a royal angle. How often I'd seen Catherine do that, especially when anyone criticized her (for hiding puzzle pieces, spreading misinformation, not having her teeth fixed); and Dolly, recognizing it too, had to blow her nose. "But," said Riley, "as soon as she was inside the jail she kicked up another fuss." In the jail there are only four cells, two for colored and two for white. Catherine had objected to being put in a colored people's cell.

The Judge stroked his chin, waved his head. "You didn't get a chance to speak to her? She ought to have had the comfort of knowing one of us was there."

"I stood around hoping she'd come to the window. But then I heard the other news."

Thinking back, I don't see how Riley could have waited so long to tell us. Because, my God: our friend from Chicago, that hateful Dr. Morris Ritz, had skipped town after rifling Verena's safe of twelve thousand dollars in negotiable bonds and more than seven hundred dollars in cash: that, as we later learned, was not half his loot. But wouldn't you know? I realized this was what baby-voiced Will Harris had been recounting to the Sheriff: no wonder Verena had sent a hurry call: her troubles with us must have become quite a side issue. Riley had a few details: he knew that Verena, upon discovering the safe door swung open (this happened in the office she kept above her drygoods store) had whirled around the corner to the Lola Hotel, there to find that Morris Ritz had checked out the previous evening: she fainted: when they revived her she fainted all over again.

Dolly's soft face hollowed; an urge to go to Verena was rising, at the same moment some sense of self, a deeper will, held her. Regretfully she gazed at me. "It's better you know it now, Collin; you shouldn't have to wait until you're as old as I am: the world is a bad place."

A change, like a shift of wind, overcame the Judge: he looked at once his age, autumnal, bare, as though he believed that Dolly, by accepting wickedness, had forsaken him. But I knew she had not: he'd called her a spirit, she was really a woman. Uncorking the rose and raisin wine, Riley spilled its topaz color into four glasses; after a moment he filled a fifth, Catherine's. The Judge, raising the wine to his lips, proposed a toast: "To Catherine, give her trust." We lifted our glasses, and "Oh Collin," said Dolly, a sudden stark thought widening her eyes, "you and I, we're the only ones that can understand a word she says!"

CHAPTER 5

THE FOLLOWING DAY, which was the first of October, a Wednesday, is one day I won't forget.

First off, Riley woke me by stepping on my fingers. Dolly, already awake, insisted I apologize for cursing him. Courtesy, she said, is more important in the morning than at any other time: particularly when one is living in such close quarters. The Judge's watch, still bending the twig like a heavy gold apple, gave the time as six after six. I don't know whose idea it was, but we breakfasted on oranges and animal crackers and cold hotdogs. The Judge grouched that a body didn't feel human till he'd had a pot of hot coffee. We agreed that coffee was what we all most missed. Riley volunteered to drive into town and get some; also, he would have a chance to scout around, find out what was going on. He suggested I come with him: "Nobody's going to see him, not if he stays down in the seat." Although the Judge objected, saying he thought it foolhardy, Dolly could tell I wanted to go: I'd yearned so much for a ride in Riley's car that now the opportunity presented itself nothing, even the prospect that no one might see me, could have thinned my excitement. Dolly said, "I can't see there's any harm. But you ought to have a clean shirt: I could plant turnips in the collar of that one."

The field of grass was without voice, no pheasant rustle, furtive flurry; the pointed leaves were sharp and blood-red as the aftermath arrows of a massacre; their brittleness broke beneath our feet as we waded up the hill into the cemetery. The view from there is very fine: the limitless trembling surface of River Woods, fifty unfolding miles of ploughed, windmilled farmland, far-off the spired courthouse tower, smoking chimneys of town. I stopped by the graves of my mother and father. I had not often visited them, it depressed me, the tomb-cold stone—so unlike what I remembered of them, their aliveness, how she'd cried when he went away to sell his frigidaires, how he'd run naked into the street. I wanted flowers for the terracotta jars sitting empty on the streaked and muddied marble. Riley helped me; he tore beginning buds off a japonica tree, and watching me arrange them, said: "I'm glad your ma was nice. Bitches, by and large." I wondered if he meant his own mother, poor Rose Hender-

son, who used to make him hop around the yard reciting the multiplication table. It did seem to me, though, that he'd made up for those hard days. After all, he had a car that was supposed to have cost three thousand dollars. Second-hand, mind you. It was a foreign car, an Alfa-Romeo roadster (Romeo's Alfa, the joke was) he'd bought in New Orleans from a politician bound for the penitentiary.

As we purred along the unpaved road toward town I kept hoping for a witness: there were certain persons it would have done my heart good to have seen me sailing by in Riley Henderson's car. But it was too early for anyone much to be about; breakfast was still on the stove, and smoke soared out the chimneys of passing houses. We turned the corner by the church, drove around the square and parked in the dirt lane that runs between Cooper's Livery and the Katydid Bakery. There Riley left me with orders to stay put: he wouldn't be more than an hour. So, stretching out on the seat, I listened to the chicanery of thieving sparrows in the livery stable's haystacks, breathed the fresh bread, tart as currant odors escaping from the bakery. The couple who owned this bakery, County was their name, Mr. and Mrs. C. C. County, had to begin their day at three in the morning to be ready by opening time, eight o'clock. It was a clean prosperous place. Mrs. County could afford the most expensive clothes at Verena's drygoods store. While I lay there smelling the good things, the back door of the bakery opened and Mr. County, broom in hand, swept flour dust into the lane. I guess he was surprised to see Riley's car, and surprised to find me in it.

"What you up to, Collin?"

"Up to nothing, Mr. County," I said, and asked myself if he knew about our trouble.

"Sure am happy October's here," he said, rubbing the air with his fingers as though the chill woven into it was a material he could feel. "We have a terrible time in the summer: ovens and all make it too hot to live. See here, son, there's a gingerbread man waiting for you—come on in and run him down."

Now he was not the kind of man to get me in there and then call the Sheriff.

His wife welcomed me into the spiced heat of the oven room as though she could think of nothing pleasanter than my being there. Most anyone would have liked Mrs. County. A chunky woman with no fuss about her, she had elephant ankles, developed arms, a muscular face permanently fire-flushed; her eyes were like blue cake-icing, her hair looked as if she'd mopped it around in a flour barrel, and she wore an apron that trailed to the tips of her toes. Her husband also wore one; sometimes, with the fulsome apron still tied around him, I'd seen him crossing the street to have a time-off beer with the men that lean around the counter at Phil's Café: he seemed a painted clown, flopping, powdered, elegantly angular.

Clearing a place on her work table, Mrs. County set me down to a cup of coffee and a warm tray of cinnamon rolls, the kind Dolly relished. Mr. County suggested I might prefer something else: "I promised him, what did I promise? a gingerbread man." His wife socked a lump of dough: "Those are for kids. He's a grown man; or nearly. Collin, just how old are you?"

"Sixteen."

"Same as Samuel," she said, meaning her son, whom we all called Mule: inasmuch as he was not much brighter than one. I asked what was their news of him? because the previous autumn, after having been left back in the eighth grade three years running, Mule had gone to Pensacola and joined the Navy. "He's in Panama, last we heard," she said, flattening the dough into a piecrust. "We don't hear often. I wrote him once, I said Samuel you do better about writing home or I'm going to write the President exactly how old you are. Because you know he joined up under false pretenses. I was darned mad at the time—blamed Mr. Hand up at the schoolhouse: that's why Samuel did it, he just couldn't tolerate always being left behind in the eighth grade, him getting so tall and the other children so little. But now I can see Mr. Hand was right: it wouldn't be fair to the rest of you boys if they promoted Samuel when he didn't do his work proper. So maybe it turned out for the best. C. C., show Collin the picture."

Photographed against a background of palms and real sea, four smirking sailors stood with their arms linked together; underneath was written, God Bless Mom and Pop, Samuel. It rankled me. Mule, off seeing the world, while I, well, maybe I deserved a gingerbread man. As I returned the picture, Mr. County said: "I'm all for a boy serving his country. But the bad part of it is, Samuel was just getting where he could give us a hand around here. I sure hate to depend on nigger help. Lying and stealing, never know where you are."

"It beats me why C. C. carries on like that," said his wife, knotting her lips. "He knows it irks me. Colored people are no worse than white people: in some cases, better. I've had occasion to say so to other people in this town. Like this business about old Catherine Creek. Makes me sick. Cranky she may be, and peculiar, but there's as good a woman as you'll find. Which reminds me, I mean to send her a dinner-tray up to the jail, for I'll wager the Sheriff doesn't set much of a table."

So little, once it has changed, changes back: the world knew us: we would never be warm again: I let go, saw winter coming toward a cold tree, cried, cried, came apart like a rain-rotted rag. I'd wanted to since we left the house. Mrs. County begged pardon if she'd said anything to upset me; with her kitchen-slopped apron she wiped my face, and we laughed, had to, at the mess it made, the paste of flour and tears, and I felt, as they say, a lot better, kind of lighthearted. For manly reasons I understood, but which made me feel no shame, Mr. County had been mortified by the outburst: he retired to the front of the shop.

Mrs. County poured coffee for herself and sat down. "I don't pretend to follow what's going on," she said. "The way I hear it, Miss Dolly broke up housekeeping because of some disagreement with Verena?" I wanted to say the situation was more complicated than that, but wondered, as I tried to array events, if really it was. "Now," she continued thoughtfully, "it may sound as though I'm talking against Dolly: I'm not. But this is what I feel—you people should go home, Dolly ought to make her peace with Verena: that's what she's always done, and you can't turn around at her time of life. Also, it sets a poor example for the town, two sisters quarreling, one of them sitting in a tree; and Judge Charlie Cool, for the first time in my life I feel sorry for those sons of his. Leading citizens have to behave themselves; otherwise the entire place goes to pieces. For instance, have you seen that wagon in the square? Well then, you better go have a look. Family of cowboys, they are. Evangelists, C.C. says—all I know is there's been a great racket over them and something to do with Dolly." Angrily she puffed up a paper sack. "I want you to tell her what I said: go home. And here, Collin, take along some cinnamon rolls. I know how Dolly dotes on them."

As I left the bakery the bells of the courthouse clock were ringing eight, which meant that it was seven-thirty. This clock has always run a half-hour fast. Once an expert was imported to repair it; at the end of almost a week's tinkering he recommended, as the only remedy, a stick of dynamite; the town council voted he be paid in full, for there was a general feeling of pride that the clock had proved so incorrigible. Around the square a few storekeepers were preparing to open; broom-sweepings fogged doorways, rolled trashbarrels berated the cool cat-quiet streets. At the Early Bird, a better grocery store than Verena's Jitney Jungle, two colored boys were fancying the window with cans of Hawaiian pineapple. On the south side of the square, beyond the cane benches where in all seasons sit the peaceful, perishing old men, I saw the wagon Mrs. County had spoken of—in reality an old truck contrived with tarpaulin covering to resemble the western wagons of history. It looked forlorn and foolish standing alone in the empty square. A homemade sign, perhaps four feet high, crested the cab like a shark's fin. Let Little Homer Honey Lasso Your Soul For The Lord. Painted on the other side there was a blistered greenish grinning head topped by a ten-gallon hat. I would not have thought it a portrait of anything human, but, according to a notice, this was: Child Wonder Little Homer Honey. With nothing more to see, for there was no one around the truck, I took myself toward the jail, which is a box-shaped brick building next door to the Ford Motor Company. I'd been inside it once. Big Eddie Stover had taken me there, along with a dozen other boys and men; he'd walked into the drugstore and said come over to the jail if you want to see something. The attraction was a thin handsome gipsy boy they'd taken off a freight train; Big Eddie gave him a quarter and told him to let down his pants: nobody could believe the size of it, and one of the men said, "Boy, how come they keep you locked up when you got a crowbar like that?" For weeks you could tell girls who had heard that joke: they giggled every time they passed the jail.

There is an unusual emblem decorating a side wall of the jail. I asked Dolly, and she said that in her youth she remembers it as a candy advertisement. If so, the lettering has vanished; what remains is a chalky tapestry: two flamingo-pink trumpeting angels swinging, swooping above a huge horn filled with fruit like a Christmas stocking; embroidered on the brick, it seems a faded mural, a faint tattoo, and sunshine flutters the imprisoned angels as though they were the spirits of thieves. I knew the risk I was taking, parading around in plain sight; but I walked past the jail, then back, and whistled, later whispered Catherine, Catherine, hoping this would bring her to the window. I realized which was her window: on the sill, reflecting beyond the bars, I saw a bowl of goldfish, the one thing, as subsequently we learned, she'd asked to have brought her. Orange flickerings of the fish fanned around the coral castle, and I thought of the morning I'd helped Dolly find it, the castle, the pearl pebbles. It had been the beginning and, chilled suddenly by a thought of what the end could be, Catherine coldly shadowed and peering downward, I prayed she would not come to the window: she would have seen no one, for I turned and ran.

Riley kept me waiting in the car more than two hours. By the time he showed up he was himself in such a temper I didn't dare show any of my own. It seems he'd gone home and found his sisters, Anne and Elizabeth, and Maude Riordan, who had spent the night, still lolling abed: not just that, but Coca-Coca bottles and cigarette butts all over the parlor. Maude took the blame: she confessed to having invited some boys over to listen to the radio and dance; but it was the sisters who got punished. He'd dragged them out of bed and whipped them. I asked what did he mean, whipped them? Turned them over my knee, he said, and whipped them with a tennis shoe. I couldn't picture this; it conflicted with my sense of Elizabeth's dignity. You're too hard on those girls, I said, adding vindictively: Maude, now there's the bad one. He took me seriously, said yes he'd intended to whip her if only because she'd called him the kind of names he wouldn't take off anybody; but before he could catch her she'd bolted out the back door. I thought to myself maybe at last Maude's had her bait of you.

Riley's ragged hair was glued down with brilliantine; he smelled of lilac water and talcum. He didn't have to tell me he'd been to the barber's; or why.

Though he has since retired, there was in those days an exceptional fellow running the barbershop. Amos Legrand. Men like the Sheriff, for that matter Riley Henderson, oh everybody come to think of it, said: that old sis. But they didn't mean any harm; most people enjoyed Amos and really wished him well. A little monkeyman who had to stand on a box to cut your hair, he was agitated and chattery as a pair of castanets. All his steady customers he called honey, men and women alike, it made no difference to him. "Honey," he'd say, "it's about time you got this hair cut: was about to buy you a package of bobbypins." Amos had one tremendous gift: he could tattle along on matters of true interest to businessmen and girls of ten—everything from what price Ben Jones got for his peanut crop to who would be invited to Mary Simpson's birthday party.

It was natural that Riley should have gone to him to get the news. Of course he repeated it straightforwardly; but I could imagine Amos, hear his hummingbird whirr: "There you are, honey, that's how it turns out when you leave money lying around. And of all people, Verena Talbo: here we thought she trotted to the bank with every dime came her way. Twelve thousand seven hundred dollars. But don't think it stops there. Seems Verena and this Dr. Ritz were going into business together, that's why she bought the old canning factory. Well get this: she gave Ritz over ten thousand to buy machinery, mercy knows what, and now it turns out he never bought one blessed penny's worth. Pocketed the whole thing. As for him, they've located not hide nor hair; South America, that's where they'll find him when and if. I never was somebody to insinuate any monkeyshines went on between him and her; I said Verena Talbo's too particular: honey, that Jew had the worst case of dandruff I've ever seen on a human head. But a smart woman like her, maybe she *was* stuck on him. Then all this to-do with her sister, the uproar over that. I don't wonder Doc Carter's giving her shots. But Charlie Cool's the one kills me: what do you make of him out there catching his death?"

We cleared town on two wheels; pop, pulp, insects spit against the windshield. The dry starched blue day whistled round us, there was not a cloud. And yet I swear storms foretell themselves in my bones. This is a nuisance common to old people, but fairly rare with anyone young. It's as though a damp rumble of thunder had sounded in your joints. The way I hurt, I felt nothing less than a hurricane could be headed our way, and said so to Riley, who said go on, you're crazy, look at the sky. We were making a bet about it when, rounding that bad curve so convenient to the cemetery, Riley winced and froze his brakes: we skidded long enough for a detailed review of our lives.

It was not Riley's fault: square in the road and struggling along like a lame cow was the Little Homer Honey wagon. With a clatter of collapsing machinery it came to a dead halt. In a moment the driver climbed out, a woman.

She was not young, but there was a merriness in the seesaw of her hips, and her breasts rubbed and nudged against her peach-colored blouse in such a coaxing way. She wore a fringed chamois skirt and knee-high cowboy boots, which was a mistake, for you felt that her legs, if fully exposed, would have been the best part. She leaned on the car door. Her eyelids drooped as though the lashes weighed intolerably; with the tip of her tongue she wettened her very red lips. "Good morning, fellows," she said, and it was a dragging slow-fuse voice. "I'd appreciate a few directions."

"What the hell's wrong with you?" said Riley, asserting himself. "You nearly made us turn over."

"I'm surprised you mention it," said the woman, amiably tossing her large head; her hair, an invented apricot color, was meticulously curled, and the curls, shaken out, were like bells with no music in them. "You were speeding, dear," she reproved him complacently. "I imagine there's a law against it; there are laws against everything, especially here."

Riley said, "There should be a law against that truck. A broken-down pile like that, it oughtn't to be allowed."

"I know, dear," the woman laughed. "Trade with you. Though I'm afraid we couldn't all fit into this car; we're even a bit squeezed in the wagon. Could you help me with a cigarette? That's a doll, thanks." As she lighted the cigarette I noticed how gaunt her hands were, rough; the nails were unpainted and one of them was black as though she'd crushed it in a door. "I was told that out this way we'd find a Miss Talbo. Dolly Talbo. She seems to be living in a tree. I wish you'd kindly show us where . . ."

Back of her there appeared to be an entire orphanage emptying out of the truck. Babies barely able to toddle on their rickety bowlegs, towheads dribbling ropes of snot, girls old enough to wear brassieres, and a ladder of boys, man-sized some of them. I counted up to ten, this including a set of crosseyed twins and a diapered baby being lugged by a child not more than five. Still, like a magician's rabbits, they kept coming, multiplied until the road was thickly populated.

"These all yours?" I said, really anxious; in another count I'd made a total of fifteen. One boy, he was about twelve and had tiny steel-rimmed glasses, flopped around in a ten-gallon hat like a walking mushroom. Most of them wore a few cowboy items, boots, at least a rodeo scarf. But they were a discouraged-looking lot, and sickly too, as though they'd lived years off boiled potatoes and onions. They pressed around the car, ghostly quiet except for the youngest who thumped the headlights and bounced on the fenders.

"Sure enough, dear: all mine," she answered, swatting at a mite of a girl playing maypole on her leg. "Sometimes I figure we've picked up one or two that don't belong," she added with a shrug, and several of the children smiled. They seemed to adore her. "Some of their daddies are dead; I guess the rest are living—one way and another: either case it's no concern of ours. I take it you weren't at our meeting last night. I'm Sister Ida, Little Homer Honey's mother." I wanted to know which one was Little Homer. She blinked around and singled out the spectacled boy who, wobbling up under his hat, saluted us: "Praise Jesus. Want a whistle?" and, swelling his cheeks, blasted a tin whistle.

"With one of those," explained his mother, tucking up her back hairs, "you can give the devil a scare. They have a number of practical uses as well."

"Two bits," the child bargained. He had a worried little face white as cold cream. The hat came down to his eyebrows.

I would have bought one if I'd had the money. You could see they were hungry. Riley felt the same, at any rate he produced fifty cents and took two of the whistles. "Bless you," said Little Homer, slipping the coin between his teeth and biting hard. "There's so much counterfeit going around these days," his mother confided apologetically. "In our branch of endeavor you wouldn't expect that kind of trouble," she said, sighing. "But if you kindly would show us—we can't go on much more, just haven't got the gas."

Riley told her she was wasting her time. "Nobody there any more," he said, racing the motor. Another driver, blockaded behind us, was honking his horn.

"Not in the tree?" Her voice was plaintive above the motor's impatient roar. "But where will we find her then?" Her hands were trying to hold back the car. "We've important business, we . . ."

Riley jumped the car forward. Looking back, I saw them watching after us in the raised and drifting road dust. I said to Riley, and was sullen about it, that we ought to have found out what they wanted. And he said: "Maybe I know."

HE DID KNOW a great deal, Amos Legrand having informed him thoroughly on the subject of Sister Ida. Although she'd not previously been to our town, Amos, who does a little traveling now and then, claimed to have seen her once at a fair in Bottle, which is a county town not far from here. Nor, apparently, was she a stranger to the Reverend Buster who, the instant she arrived, had hunted out the Sheriff and demanded an injunction to prevent the Little Homer Honey troupe from holding any meetings. Racketeers, he called them; and argued that the so-called Sister Ida was known throughout six states as an infamous trollop: think of it, fifteen children and no sign of a husband! Amos, too, was pretty sure she'd never been married; but in his opinion a woman so industrious was entitled to respect. The Sheriff said didn't he have enough problems? and said: Maybe those fools have the right idea, sit in a tree and mind your own business—for five cents he'd go out there and join them. Old Buster told him in that case he wasn't fit to be Sheriff and ought to hand in his badge. Meanwhile, Sister Ida had, without legal interference, called an evening of prayers and shenanigans under the oak trees in the square. Revivalists are popular in this town; it's the music, the chance to sing and congregate in the open air. Sister Ida and her family made a particular hit; even Amos, usually so critical, told Riley he'd missed something: those kids really could shout, and that Little Homer Honey, he was cute as a button dancing and twirling a rope. Everybody had a grand time except the Reverend and Mrs. Buster, who had come to start a fuss. What got their goat was when the children started hauling in God's Washline, a rope with clothespins to which you could attach a contribution. People who never dropped a dime in Buster's collection plate were hanging up dollar bills. It was more than he could stand. So he'd skipped off to the house on Talbo Lane and had a small shrewd talk with Verena, whose support, he realized, was necessary if he were going to get action. According to

Amos, he'd incited Verena by telling her some hussy of a revivalist was describing Dolly as an infidel, an enemy of Jesus, and that Verena owed it to the Talbo name to see that this woman was run out of town. It was unlikely that at the time Sister Ida had ever heard the name Talbo. But sick as she was, Verena went right to work; she rang up the Sheriff and said now look here Junius, I want these tramps run clear across the county line. Those were orders; and old Buster made it his duty to see they were carried out. He accompanied the Sheriff to the square where Sister Ida and her brood were cleaning up after the meeting. It had ended in a real scuffle, mainly because Buster, charging illegal gain, had insisted on confiscating the money gathered off God's Washline. He got it, too—along with a few scratches. It made no difference that many bystanders had taken Sister Ida's side: the Sheriff told them they'd better be out of town by noon the next day. Now after I'd heard all this I said to Riley why, when these people had been wrongly treated, hadn't he wanted to be more helpful? You'd never guess the answer he gave me. In dead earnest he said a loose woman like that was no one to associate with Dolly.

A TWIG FIRE fizzed under the tree; Riley collected leaves for it, while the Judge, his eyes smarting with smoke, set about the business of our midday meal. We were the indolent ones, Dolly and I. "I'm afraid," she said, dealing a game of Rook, "really afraid Verena's seen the last of that money. And you know, Collin, I doubt if it's losing the money that hurts her most. For whatever reason, she trusted him: Dr. Ritz, I mean. I keep remembering Maudie Laura Murphy. The girl who worked in the post office. She and Verena were very close. Lord, it was a great blow when Maudie Laura took up with that whiskey salesman, married him. I couldn't criticize her; 'twas only fitting if she loved the man. Just the same, Maudie Laura and Dr. Ritz, maybe those are the only two Verena ever trusted, and both of them—well, it could take the heart out of anyone." She thumbed the Rook cards with wandering attention. "You said something before—about Catherine."

"About her goldfish. I saw them in the window."

"But not Catherine?"

"No, the goldfish, that's all. Mrs. County was awfully nice: she said she was going to send some dinner around to the jail."

She broke one of Mrs. County's cinnamon rolls and picked out the raisins. "Collin, suppose we let them have their way, gave up, that is: they'd have to let Catherine go, wouldn't they?" Her eyes tilted toward the heights of the tree, searching, it seemed, a passage through the braided leaves. "Should I—let myself lose?"

"Mrs. County thinks so: that we should go home."

"Did she say why?"

"Because—she did run on. Because you always have. Always made your peace, she said."

Dolly smiled, smoothed her long skirt; sifting rays placed rings of sun upon her fingers. "Was there ever a choice? It's what I want, a choice. To know I could've had another life, all made of my own decisions. That would be making my peace, and truly." She rested her eyes on the scene below, Riley cracking twigs, the Judge hunched over a steaming pot. "And the Judge, Charlie, if we gave up it would let him down so badly. Yes," she tangled her fingers with mine, "he is very dear to me," and an immeasurable pause lengthened the moment, my heart reeled, the tree closed inward like a folding umbrella.

"This morning, while you were away, he asked me to marry him."

As if he'd heard her, the Judge straightened up, a schoolboy grin reviving the youthfulness of his countrified face. He waved; and it was difficult to disregard the charm of Dolly's expression as she waved back. It was as though a familiar portrait had been cleaned and, turning to it, one discovered a fleshly luster, clearer, till then unknown colors: whatever else, she could never again be a shadow in the corner.

"And now—don't be unhappy, Collin," she said, scolding me, I thought, for what she must have recognized as my resentment.

"But are you . . . ?"

"I've never earned the privilege of making up my own mind; when I do, God willing, I'll know what is right. Who else," she said, putting me off further, "did you see in town?"

I would have invented someone, a story to retrieve her, for she seemed to be moving forward into the future, while I, unable to follow, was left with my sameness. But as I described Sister Ida, the wagon, the children, told the wherefores of their run-in with the Sheriff and how we'd met them on the road inquiring after the lady in the tree, we flowed together again like a stream that for an instant an island had separated. Though it would have been too bad if Riley had heard me betraying him, I went so far as to repeat what he'd said about a woman of Sister Ida's sort not being fit company for Dolly. She had a proper laugh over this; then, with sudden soberness: "But it's wicked— taking the bread out of children's mouths and using my name to do it. Shame on them!" She straightened her hat determinedly. "Collin, lift yourself; you and I are going for a little walk. I'll bet those people are right where you left them. Leastways, we'll see."

The Judge tried to prevent us, or at any rate maintained that if Dolly wanted a stroll he would have to accompany us. It went a long way toward mollifying my jealous rancor when Dolly told him he'd best tend to his chores: with Collin along she'd be safe enough—it was just to stretch our legs a bit.

As usual, Dolly could not be hurried. It was her habit, even when it rained, to loiter along an ordinary path as though she were dallying in a garden, her eyes primed for the sight of precious medicine flavorings, a sprig of penny-royal, sweetmary and mint, useful herbs whose odor scented her clothes. She saw everything first, and it was her one real vanity to prefer that she, rather than you, point out certain discoveries: a birdtrack bracelet, an eave of icicles—she was always calling come see the cat-shaped cloud, the ship in the stars, the face of frost. In this slow manner we crossed the grass, Dolly amass- ing a pocketful of withered dandelions, a pheasant's quill: I thought it would be sundown before we reached the road.

Fortunately we had not that far to go: entering the cemetery, we found Sister Ida and all her family encamped among the graves. It was like a lugubrious playground. The crosseyed twins were having their hair cut by older sisters, and Little Homer was shining his boots with spit and leaves; a nearly grown boy, sprawled with his back against a tombstone, picked melancholy notes on a guitar. Sister Ida was suckling the baby; it lay curled against her breasts like a pink ear. She did not rise when she realized our presence, and Dolly said, "I do believe you're sitting on my father."

For a fact it was Mr. Talbo's grave, and Sister Ida, addressing the headstone (Uriah Fenwick Talbo, 1844–1922, Good Soldier, Dear Husband, Loving Father) said, "Sorry, soldier." Buttoning her blouse, which made the baby wail, she started to her feet.

"Please don't; I only meant—to introduce myself."

Sister Ida shrugged, "He was beginning to hurt me anyway," and rubbed herself appropriately. "You again," she said, eyeing me with amusement. "Where's your friend?"

"I understand . . ." Dolly stopped, disconcerted by the maze of children drawing in around her; "Did you," she went on, attempting to ignore a boy no bigger than a jackrabbit who, having raised her skirt, was sternly examining her shanks, "wish to see me? I'm Dolly Talbo."

Shifting the baby, Sister Ida threw an arm around Dolly's waist, embraced her, actually, and said, as though they were the oldest friends, "I knew I could count on you, Dolly. Kids," she lifted the baby like a baton, "tell Dolly we never said a word against her!"

The children shook their heads, mumbled, and Dolly seemed touched. "We can't leave town, I kept telling them," said Sister Ida, and launched into the tale of her predicament. I wished that I could have a picture of them together, Dolly, formal, as out of fashion as her old face-veil, and Sister Ida with her fruity lips, fun-loving figure. "It's a matter of cash; they took it all. I ought to have them arrested, that puke-faced Buster and what's-his-name, the Sheriff: thinks he's King Kong." She caught her breath; her cheeks were like a raspberry patch. "The plain truth is, we're stranded. Even if we'd ever heard of you, it's not our policy to speak ill of anyone. Oh I know that was just the excuse; but I figured you could straighten it out and . . ."

"I'm hardly the person—dear me," said Dolly.

"But what would you do? with a half gallon of gas, maybe not that, fifteen mouths and a dollar ten? We'd be better off in jail."

Then, "I have a friend," Dolly announced proudly, "a brilliant man, he'll know an answer," and I could tell by the pleased conviction of her voice that she believed this one hundred per cent. "Collin, you scoot ahead and let the Judge know to expect company for dinner."

Licketysplit across the field with the grass whipping my legs: couldn't wait to see the Judge's face. It was not a disappointment. "Lordylaw!" he said, raring back, rocking forward; "Sixteen people," and, observing the meager stew simmering on the fire, struck his head. For Riley's benefit I tried to make out it was none of my doing, Dolly's meeting Sister Ida; but he just stood there skinning me with his eyes: it could have led to bitter words if the Judge hadn't sent us scurrying. He fanned up his fire, Riley fetched more water, and into the stew we tossed sardines, hotdogs, green bay-leaves, in fact whatever lay at hand, including an entire box of Saltines which the judge claimed would help thicken it: a few stuffs got mixed in by mistake—coffee grounds, for instance. Having reached that overwrought hilarious state achieved by cooks at family reunions, we had the gall to stand back and congratulate ourselves: Riley gave me a forgiving, comradely punch, and as the first of the children appeared the Judge scared them with the vigor of his welcome.

None of them would advance until the whole herd had assembled. Whereupon Dolly, apprehensive as a woman exhibiting the results of an afternoon at an auction, brought them forward to be introduced. The children made a rollcall of their names: Beth, Laurel, Sam, Lillie Ida, Cleo, Kate, Homer, Harry—here the melody broke because one small girl refused to give her name. She said it was a secret. Sister Ida agreed that if she thought it a secret, then so it should remain.

"They're all so fretful," she said, favorably affecting the Judge with her smoky voice and grasslike eyelashes. He prolonged their handshake and overdid his smile, which struck me as peculiar conduct in a man who, not three hours before, had asked a woman to marry him, and I hoped that if Dolly noticed it would give her pause. But she was saying, "Why certain they're fretful: hungry as they can be," and the Judge, with a hearty clap and a boastful nod towards the stew, promised he'd fix that soon enough. In the meantime he thought it would be a good idea if the children went to the creek and washed their hands. Sister Ida vowed they'd wash more than that. They needed to, I'll tell you.

There was trouble with the little girl who wanted her name a secret; she wouldn't go, not unless her papa rode her piggyback. "You are too my papa," she told Riley, who did not contradict her. He lifted her onto his shoulders, and she was tickled to death. All the way to the creek she acted the cut-up, and when, with her hands thrust over his eyes, Riley stumbled blindly into a bullis vine, she ripped the air with in-heaven shrieks. He said he'd had enough of that and down you go. "Please: I'll whisper you my name." Later on I remembered to ask him what the name had been. It was Texaco Gasoline; because those were such pretty words.

The creek is nowhere more than knee-deep; glossy beds of moss green the banks, and in the spring snowy dewdrops and dwarf violets flourish there like floral crumbs for the new bees whose hives hang in the waterbays. Sister Ida chose a place on the bank from which she could supervise the bathing. "No cheating now—I want to see a lot of commotion." We did. Suddenly girls old enough to be married were trotting around and not a stitch on; boys, too, big and little all in there together naked as jaybirds. It was as well that Dolly had stayed behind with the Judge; and I wished Riley had not come either, for he was embarrassing in his embarrassment. Seriously, though, it's only now, seeing the kind of man he turned out to be, that I understand the paradox of his primness: he wanted so to be respectable that the defections of others somehow seemed to him backsliding on his own part.

Those famous landscapes of youth and woodland water—in after years how often, trailing through the cold rooms of museums, I stopped before such a picture, stood long haunted moments having it recall that gone scene, not as it was, a band of goose-fleshed children dabbling in an autumn creek, but as the painting presented it, husky youths and wading water-diamonded girls; and I've wondered then, wonder now, how they fared, where they went in this world, that extraordinary family.

"Beth, give your hair a douse. Stop splashing Laurel, I mean you Buck, you quit that. All you kids get behind your ears, mercy knows when you'll have the chance again." But presently Sister Ida relaxed and left the children at liberty. "On such a day as this . . ." she sank against the moss; with the full light of her eyes she looked at Riley, "There is something: the mouth, the same jug ears—cigarette, dear?" she said, impervious to his distaste for her. A smoothing expression suggested for a moment the girl she had been. "On such a day as this . . .

". . . but in a sorrier place, no trees to speak of, a house in a wheatfield and all alone like a scarecrow. I'm not complaining: there was mama and papa and my sister Geraldine, and we were sufficient, had plenty of pets and a piano and good voices every one of us. Not that it was easy, what with all the heavy work and only the one man to do it. Papa was a sickly man besides. Hired hands were hard to come by, nobody liked it way out there for long: one old fellow we thought a heap of, but then he got drunk and tried to burn down the house. Geraldine was going on sixteen, a year older than me, and nice to look at, both of us were that, when she got it into her head to marry a man who'd run the place with papa. But where we were there wasn't much to choose from. Mama gave us our schooling, what of it we had, and the closest town was ten miles. That was the town of Youfry, called after a family; the slogan was You Won't Fry In Youfry: because it was up a mountain and well-to-do people went there in the summer. So the summer I'm thinking of Geraldine got waitress work at the Lookout Hotel in Youfry. I used to hitch a ride in on Saturdays and stay the night with her. This was the first either of us had ever been away from home. Geraldine didn't care about it particular, town life, but as for me I looked toward those Saturdays like each of them was Christmas and my birthday rolled into one. There was a dancing pavilion, it didn't cost a cent, the music was free and the colored lights. I'd help Geraldine with her work so we could go there all the sooner; we'd run hand in hand down the street, and I used to start dancing before I got my breath—never had to wait for a partner, there were five boys to every girl, and we were the prettiest girls anyway. I wasn't boy-crazy especially, it was the dancing—sometimes everyone would stand still to watch me waltz, and I never got more than a glimpse of my partners, they changed so fast. Boys would follow us to the hotel, then call under our window Come out! Come out! and sing, so silly they were—Geraldine almost lost her job. Well we'd lie awake considering the night in a practical way. She was not romantic, my sister; what concerned her was which of our beaux was surest to make things easier out home. It was Dan Rainey she decided on. He was older than the others, twenty-five, a man, not handsome in the face, he had jug ears and freckles and not much chin, but Dan Rainey, oh he was smart in his own steady way and strong enough to lift a keg of nails. End of summer he came out home and helped bring in the wheat. Papa liked him from the first, and though mama said Geraldine was too young, she didn't make any ruckus about it. I cried at the wedding, and thought it was because the nights at the dancing pavilion were over, and because Geraldine and I would never lie cozy in the same bed again. But as soon as Dan Rainey took over everything seemed to go right; he brought out the best in the land and maybe the best in us. Except when winter came on, and we'd be sitting round the fire, sometimes the heat, something made me feel just faint. I'd go stand in the yard with only my dress on, it was like I couldn't feel the cold because I'd become a piece of it, and I'd close my eyes, waltz round and round, and one night, I didn't hear him sneaking up, Dan Rainey caught me in his arms and danced me for a joke. Only it wasn't such a joke. He had feelings for me; way back in my head I'd known it from the start. But he didn't say it, and I never asked him to; and it wouldn't have come to anything provided Geraldine hadn't lost her baby. That was in the spring. She was mortally afraid of snakes, Geraldine, and it was seeing one that did it; she was collecting eggs, it was only a chicken snake, but it scared her so bad she dropped her baby four months too soon. I don't know what happened to her—got cross and mean, got where she'd fly out about anything. Dan Rainey took the worst of it; he kept out of her way as much as he could: used to roll himself in a blanket and sleep down in the wheatfield. I knew if I stayed there—so I went to Youfry and got Geraldine's old job at the hotel. The dancing pavilion, it was the same as the summer before, and I was even prettier: one boy nearly killed another over who was going to buy me an orangeade. I can't say I didn't enjoy myself, but my mind wasn't on it; at the hotel they asked where was my mind—always filling the sugar bowl with salt, giving people spoons to cut their meat. I never went home the whole summer. When the time came—it was such a day as this, a fall day blue as eternity—I didn't let them know I was coming, just got out of the coach and walked three miles through the wheat stacks till I found Dan Rainey. He didn't speak a word, only plopped down and cried like a baby. I was that sorry for him, and loved him more than tongue can tell."

Her cigarette had gone out. She seemed to have lost track of the story; or worse, thought better of finishing it. I wanted to stamp and whistle, the way rowdies do at the picture-show when the screen goes unexpectedly blank; and Riley, though less bald about it, was impatient too. He struck a match for her cigarette: starting at the sound, she remembered her voice again, but it was as if, in the interval, she'd traveled far ahead.

"So papa swore he'd shoot him. A hundred times Geraldine said tell us who it was and Dan here'll take a gun after him. I laughed till I cried; sometimes the other way round. I said well I had no idea;

there were five or six boys in Youfry could be the one, and how was I
to know? Mama slapped my face when I said that. But they believed
it; even after a while I think Dan Rainey believed it—wanted to
anyway, poor unhappy fellow. All those months not stirring out of
the house; and in the middle of it papa died. They wouldn't let me go
to the funeral, they were so ashamed for anyone to see. It happened
this day, with them off at the burial and me alone in the house and a
sandy wind blowing rough as an elephant, that I got in touch with
God. I didn't by any means deserve to be Chosen: up till then,
mama'd had to coax me to learn my Bible verses; afterwards, I
memorized over a thousand in less than three months. Well I was
practicing a tune on the piano, and suddenly a window broke, the
whole room turned topsy-turvy, then fell together again, and someone was with me, papa's spirit I thought; but the wind died down
peaceful as spring—He was there, and standing as He made me,
straight, I opened my arms to welcome Him. That was twenty-six
years ago last February the third; I was sixteen, I'm forty-two now,
and I've never wavered. When I had my baby I didn't call Geraldine
or Dan Rainey or anybody, only lay there whispering my verses one
after the other and not a soul knew Danny was born till they heard
him holler. It was Geraldine named him that. He was hers, everyone
thought so, and people round the countryside rode over to see her
new baby, brought presents, some of them, and the men hit Dan
Rainey on the back and told him what a fine son he had. Soon as I
was able I moved thirty miles away to Stoneville, that's a town double
the size of Youfry and where they have a big mining camp. Another
girl and I, we started a laundry, and did a good business on account
of in a mining town there's mostly bachelors. About twice a month I
went home to see Danny; I was seven years going back and forth; it
was the only pleasure I had, and a strange one, considering how
it tore me up every time: such a beautiful boy, there's no describing.
But Geraldine died for me to touch him: if I kissed him she'd come
near to jumping out of her skin; Dan Rainey wasn't much different,
he was so scared I wouldn't leave well enough alone. The last time I
ever was home I asked him would he meet me in Youfry. Because for
a crazy long while I'd had an idea, which was: if I could live it again, if
I could bear a child that would be a twin to Danny. But I was wrong
to think it could have the same father. It would've been a dead child,

born dead: I looked at Dan Rainey (it was the coldest day, we sat by the empty dancing pavilion, I remember he never took his hands out of his pockets) and sent him away without saying why it was I'd asked him to come. Then years spent hunting the likeness of him. One of the miners in Stoneville, he had the same freckles, yellow eyes; a goodhearted boy, he obliged me with Sam, my oldest. As best I recall, Beth's father was a dead ringer for Dan Rainey; but being a girl, Beth didn't favor Danny. I forgot to tell you that I'd sold my share of the laundry and gone to Texas—had restaurant work in Amarillo and Dallas. But it wasn't until I met Mr. Honey that I saw why the Lord had chosen me and what my task was to be. Mr. Honey possessed the True Word; after I heard him preach that first time I went round to see him: we hadn't talked twenty minutes than he said I'm going to marry you provided you're not married a'ready. I said no I'm not married, but I've got some family; fact is, there was five by then. Didn't faze him a bit. We got married a week later on Valentine's Day. He wasn't a young man, and he didn't look a particle like Dan Raney; stripped of his boots he couldn't make it to my shoulder; but when the Lord brought us together He knew certain what He was doing: we had Roy, then Pearl and Kate and Cleo and Little Homer—most of them born in that wagon you saw up there. We traveled all over the country carrying His Word to folks who'd never heard it before, not the way my man could tell it. Now I must mention a sad circumstance, which is: I lost Mr. Honey. One morning, this was in a queer part of Louisiana, Cajun parts, he walked off down the road to buy some groceries: you know we never saw him again. He disappeared right into thin air. I don't give a hoot what the police say; he wasn't the kind to run out on his family; no sir it was foul play."

"Or amnesia," I said. "You forget everything, even your own name."

"A man with the whole Bible on the tip of his tongue—would you say he was liable to forget something like his name? One of them Cajuns murdered him for his amethyst ring. Naturally I've known men since then; but not love. Lillie Ida, Laurel, the other kids, they happened like. Seems somehow I can't get on without another life kicking under my heart: feel so sluggish otherwise."

When the children were dressed, some with their clothes inside out, we returned to the tree where the older girls, bending over the fire, dried and combed their hair. In our absence Dolly had cared for the baby; she seemed now not to want to give it back: "I wish one of us had had a baby, my sister or Catherine," and Sister Ida said yes, it was entertaining and a satisfaction too. We sat finally in a circle around the fire. The stew was too hot to taste, which perhaps accounted for its thorough success, and the Judge, who had to serve it in rotation, for there were only three cups, was full of gay stunts and nonsense that exhilarated the children: Texaco Gasoline decided she'd made a mistake—the Judge, not Riley, was her papa, and the Judge rewarded her with a trip to the moon, swung her, that is, high over his head: *Some flocked south, Some flocked west, You go flying after the rest, Away! Awhee!* Sister Ida said say you're pretty strong. Of course he lapped it up, all but asked her to feel his muscles. Every quarter-minute he peeked to see if Dolly were admiring him. She was.

The croonings of a ringdove wavered among the long last lances of sunlight. Chill green, blues filtered through the air as though a rainbow had dissolved around us. Dolly shivered: "There's a storm nearby. I've had the notion all day." I looked at Riley triumphantly: hadn't I told him?

"And it's getting late," said Sister Ida. "Buck, Homer—you boys chase up to the wagon. Gracious knows who's come along and helped themselves. Not," she added, watching her sons vanish on the darkening path, "that there's a whole lot to take, nothing much except my sewing machine. So, Dolly? Have you . . ."

"We've discussed it," said Dolly turning to the Judge for confirmation.

"You'd win your case in court, no question of it," he said, very professional. "For once the law would be on the right side. As matters stand, however . . ."

Dolly said, "As matters stand," and pressed into Sister Ida's hand the forty-seven dollars which constituted our cash asset; in addition, she gave her the Judge's big gold watch. Contemplating these gifts, Sister Ida shook her head as though she should refuse them. "It's wrong. But I thank you."

A light thunder rolled through the woods, and in the perilous quiet of its wake Buck and Little Homer burst upon the path like charging cavalry. "They're coming! They're coming!" both got out at once, and Little Homer, pushing back his hat, gasped: "We ran all the way."

"Make sense, boy: who?"

Little Homer swallowed. "Those fellows. The Sheriff one, and I don't know how many more. Coming down through the grass. With guns, too."

Thunder rumbled again; tricks of wind rustled our fire.

"All right now," said the Judge, assuming command. "Everybody keep their heads." It was as though he'd planned for this moment, and he rose to it, I do concede, gloriously. "The women, you little kids, get up in the tree-house. Riley, see that the rest of you scatter out, shinny up those other trees and take a load of rocks." When we'd followed these directions, he alone remained on the ground; firm-jawed, he stayed there guarding the tense twilighted silence like a captain who will not abandon his drowning ship.

CHAPTER 6

FIVE OF US roosted in the sycamore tree that overhung the path. Little Homer was there, and his brother Buck, a scowling boy with rocks in either hand. Across the way, straddling the limbs of a second syca-more, we could see Riley surrounded by the older girls: in the deepening burnished light their white faces glimmered like candle-lanterns. I thought I felt a raindrop: it was a bead of sweat slipping along my cheek; still, and though the thunder lulled, a smell of rain intensified the odor of leaves and woodsmoke. The overloaded tree-house gave an evil creak; from my vantage point, its tenants seemed a single creature, a many-legged, many-eyed spider upon whose head Dolly's hat sat perched like a velvet crown.

In our tree everybody pulled out the kind of tin whistles Riley had bought from Little Homer: good to give the devil a scare, Sister Ida had said. Then Little Homer took off his huge hat and, removing from its vast interior what was perhaps God's Washline, a thick long rope, at any rate, proceeded to make a sliding noose. As he tested its efficiency, stretched and tightened the knot, his steely miniature spectacles cast such a menacing sparkle that, edging away, I put the distance of another branch between us. The Judge, patrolling below, hissed to stop moving around up there; it was his last order before the invasion began.

The invaders themselves made no pretense at stealth. Swinging their rifles against the undergrowth like canecutters, they swaggered up the path, nine, twelve, twenty strong. First, Junius Candle, his Sheriff's star winking in the dusk; and after him, Big Eddie Stover, whose squint-eyed search of our hiding places reminded me of those newspaper picture puzzles: find five boys and an owl in this drawing of a tree. It requires someone cleverer than Big Eddie Stover. He looked straight at me, and through me. Not many of that gang would have troubled you with their braininess: good for nothing but a lick of salt and swallow of beer most of them. Except I recognized Mr. Hand, the principal at school, a decent enough fellow taken all around, no one, you would have thought, to involve himself in such shabby company on so shameful an errand. Curiosity explained the attendance of Amos Legrand; he was there, and silent for once: no wonder: as though he were a walking-stick, Verena was leaning a hand on his head, which came not quite to her hip. A grim Reverend Buster ceremoniously supported her other arm. When I saw Verena I felt a numbed reliving of the terror I'd known when, after my mother's death, she'd come to our house to claim me. Despite what seemed a lameness, she moved with her customary tall authority and, accompanied by her escorts, stopped under our sycamore.

The Judge didn't give an inch; toe to toe with the Sheriff, he stood his ground as if there were a drawn line he dared the other to cross.

It was at this crucial moment that I noticed Little Homer. He gradually was lowering his lasso. It crawled, dangled like a snake, the wide noose open as a pair of jaws, then fell, with an expert snap, around the neck of the Reverend Buster, whose strangling outcry Little Homer stifled by giving the rope a mighty tug.

His friends hadn't long to consider old Buster's predicament, his blood-gorged face and flailing arms; for Little Homer's success inspired an all-out attack: rocks flew, whistles shrilled like the shriekings of savage birds, and the men, pummeling each other in the general rout, took refuge where they could, principally under the bodies of comrades already fallen. Verena had to box Amos

Legrand's ears: he tried to sneak up under her skirt. She alone, you might say, behaved like a real man: shook her fists at the trees and cursed us blue.

At the height of the din, a shot slammed like an iron door. It quelled us all, the serious endless echo of it; but in the hush that followed we heard a weight come crashing through the opposite sycamore.

It was Riley, falling; and falling: slowly, relaxed as a killed cat. Covering their eyes, the girls screamed as he struck a branch and splintered it, hovered, like the torn leaves, then in a bleeding heap hit the ground. No one moved toward him.

Until at last the Judge said, "Boy, my boy," and in a trance sank to his knees; he caressed Riley's limp hands. "Have mercy. Have mercy, son: answer." Other men, sheepish and frightened, closed round; some offered advice which the Judge seemed unable to comprehend. One by one we dropped down from the trees, and the children's gathering whisper is he dead? is he dead? was like the moan, the delicate roar of a sea-trumpet. Doffing their hats respectfully, the men made an aisle for Dolly; she was too stunned to take account of them, or of Verena, whom she passed without seeing.

"I want to know," said Verena, in tones that summoned attention, ". . . which of you fools fired that gun?"

The men guardedly looked each other over: too many of them fixed on Big Eddie Stover. His jowls trembled, he licked his lips: "Hell, I never meant to shoot nobody; was doing my duty, that's all."

"Not all," Verena severely replied. "I hold you responsible, Mr. Stover."

At this Dolly turned round; her eyes, vague beyond the veiling, seemed to frame Verena in a gaze that excluded everyone else. "Responsible? No one is that; except ourselves."

Sister Ida had replaced the Judge at Riley's side; she completely stripped off his shirt. "Thank your stars, it's his shoulder," she said, and the relieved sighs, Big Eddie's alone, would have floated a kite. "He's fairly knocked out, though. Some of you fellows better get him to a doctor." She stopped Riley's bleeding with a bandage torn off his shirt. The Sheriff and three of his men locked arms, making a litter on which to carry him. He was not the only one who had to be carried; the Reverend Buster had also come to considerable grief:

loose-limbed as a puppet, and too weak to know the noose still hung around his neck, he needed several assistants to get up the path. Little Homer chased after him: "Hey, hand me back my rope!"

Amos Legrand waited to accompany Verena; she told him to go without her as she had no intention of leaving unless Dolly—hesitating, she looked at the rest of us, Sister Ida in particular: "I would like to speak with my sister alone."

With a wave of her hand that quite dismissed Verena, Sister Ida said, "Never mind, lady. We're on our way." She hugged Dolly. "Bless us, we love you. Don't we, kids?" Little Homer said, "Come with us, Dolly. We'll have such good times. I'll give you my sparkle belt." And Texaco Gasoline threw herself upon the Judge, pleading for him to go with them, too. Nobody seemed to want me.

"I'll always remember that you asked me," said Dolly, her eyes hurrying as though to memorize the children's faces. "Good luck. Good-bye. Run now," she raised her voice above new and nearer thunder, "run, it's raining."

It was a tickling feathery rain fine as a gauze curtain, and as they faded into the folds of it, Sister Ida and her family, Verena said: "Do I understand you've been conniving with that—woman? After she made a mockery of our name?"

"I don't think you can accuse me of conniving with anyone," Dolly answered serenely. "Especially not with bullies who," she a little lost control, "steal from children and drag old women into jail. I can't set much store by a name that endorses such methods. It ought to be a mockery."

Verena received this without flinching. "You're not yourself," she said, as if it were a clinical opinion.

"You'd best look again: I am myself." Dolly seemed to pose for inspection. She was as tall as Verena, as assured; nothing about her was incomplete or blurred. "I've taken your advice: stopped hanging my head, I mean. You told me it made you dizzy. And not many days ago," she continued, "you told me that you were ashamed of me. Of Catherine. So much of our lives had been lived for you; it was painful to realize the waste that had been. Can you know what it is, such a feeling of waste?"

Scarcely audible, Verena said, "I do know," and it was as if her eyes crossed, peered inward upon a stony vista. It was the expression I'd seen when, spying from the attic, I'd watched her late at night brooding over the Kodak pictures of Maudie Laura Murphy, Maudie Laura's husband and children. She swayed, she put a hand on my shoulder; except for that, I think she might have fallen.

"I imagined I would go to my dying day with the hurt of it. I won't. But it's no satisfaction, Verena, to say that I'm ashamed of you, too."

It was night now; frogs, sawing insects celebrated the slow-falling rain. We dimmed as though the wetness had snuffed the light of our faces. Verena sagged against me. "I'm not well," she said in a skeleton voice. "I'm a sick woman, I am, Dolly."

Somewhat unconvinced, Dolly approached Verena, presently touched her, as though her fingers could sense the truth. "Collin," she said, "Judge, please help me with her into the tree." Verena protested that she couldn't go climbing trees; but once she got used to the idea she went up easily enough. The raftlike tree-house seemed to be floating over shrouded vaporish waters; it was dry there, however, for the mild rain had not penetrated the parasol of leaves. We drifted in a current of silence until Verena said, "I have something to say, Dolly. I could say it more easily if we were alone."

The Judge crossed his arms. "I'm afraid you'll have to put up with me, Miss Verena." He was emphatic, though not belligerent. "I have an interest in the outcome of what you might have to say."

"I doubt that: how so?" she said, recovering to a degree her exalted manner.

He lighted a stub of candle, and our sudden shadows stooped over us like four eavesdroppers. "I don't like talking in the dark," he said. There was a purpose in the proud erectness of his posture: it was, I thought, to let Verena know she was dealing with a man, a fact too few men in her experience had enough believed to assert. She found it unforgivable. "You don't remember, do you, Charlie Cool? Fifty years ago, more maybe. Some of you boys came blackberry stealing out at our place. My father caught your cousin Seth, and I caught you. It was quite a licking you got that day."

The Judge did remember; he blushed, smiled, said: "You didn't fight fair, Verena."

"I fought fair," she told him drily. "But you're right—since neither of us like it, let's not talk in the dark. Frankly, Charlie, you're not a welcome sight to me. My sister couldn't have gone through with such tommyrot if you hadn't been goading her on. So I'll thank you to leave us; it can be no further affair of yours."

"But it is," said Dolly. "Because Judge Cool, Charlie . . ." she dwindled, appeared for the first time to question her boldness.

"Dolly means that I have asked her to marry me."

"That," Verena managed after some suspenseful seconds, "is," she said, regarding her gloved hands, "remarkable. Very. I wouldn't have credited either of you with so much imagination. Or is it that I am imagining? Quite likely I'm dreaming of myself in a wet tree on a thundery night. Except I never have dreams, or perhaps I only forget them. This one I suggest we all forget."

"I'll own up: I think it is a dream, Miss Verena. But a man who doesn't dream is like a man who doesn't sweat: he stores up a lot of poison."

She ignored him; her attention was with Dolly, Dolly's with her: they might have been alone together, two persons at far ends of a bleak room, mutes communicating in an eccentric sign-language, subtle shiftings of the eye; and it was as though, then, Dolly gave an answer, one that sapped all color from Verena's face. "I see. You've accepted him, have you?"

The rain had thickened, fish could have swum through the air; like a deepening scale of piano notes, it struck its blackest chord, and drummed into a downpour that, though it threatened, did not at once reach us: drippings leaked through the leaves, but the tree-house stayed a dry seed in a soaking plant. The Judge put a protective hand over the candle; he waited as anxiously as Verena for Dolly's reply. My impatience equaled theirs, yet I felt exiled from the scene, again a spy peering from the attic, and my sympathies, curiously, were nowhere; or rather, everywhere: a tenderness for all three ran together like raindrops, I could not separate them, they expanded into a human oneness.

Dolly, too. She could not separate the Judge from Verena. At last, excruciatingly, "I can't," she cried, implying failures beyond calculation. "I said I would know what was right. But it hasn't happened; I don't know: do other people? A choice, I thought: to have had a life made of my own decisions . . ."

"But we have had our lives," said Verena. "Yours has been nothing to despise, I don't think you've required more than you've had; I've envied you always. Come home, Dolly. Leave decisions to me: that, you see, has been my life."

"Is it true, Charlie?" Dolly asked, as a child might ask where do falling stars fall? and: "Have we had our lives?"

"We're not dead," he told her; but it was as if, to the questioning child, he'd said stars fall into space: an irrefutable, still unsatisfactory answer. Dolly could not accept it: "You don't have to be dead. At home, in the kitchen, there is a geranium that blooms over and over. Some plants, though, they bloom just the once, if at all, and nothing more happens to them. They live, but they've had their life."

"Not you," he said, and brought his face nearer hers, as though he meant their lips to touch, yet wavered, not daring it. Rain had tunneled through the branches, it fell full weight; rivulets of it streamed off Dolly's hat, the veiling clung to her cheeks; with a flutter the candle failed. "Not me."

Successive strokes of lightning throbbed like veins of fire, and Verena, illuminated in that sustained glare, was not anyone I knew; but some woman woebegone, wasted—with eyes once more drawn toward each other, their stare settled on an inner territory, a withered country; as the lightning lessened, as the hum of rain sealed us in its multiple sounds, she spoke, and her voice came so weakly from so very far, not expecting, it seemed, to be heard at all. "Envied you, Dolly. Your pink room. I've only knocked at the doors of such rooms, not often—enough to know that now there is no one but you to let me in. Because little Morris, little Morris—help me, I loved him, I did. Not in a womanly way; it was, oh I admit it, that we were kindred spirits. We looked each other in the eye, we saw the same devil, we weren't afraid; it was—merry. But he outsmarted me; I'd known he could, and hoped he wouldn't, and he did, and now: it's too long to be alone, a lifetime. I walk through the house, nothing is mine: your pink room, your kitchen, the house is yours, and Catherine's too, I think. Only don't leave me, let me live with you. I'm feeling old, I want my sister."

The rain, adding its voice to Verena's, was between them, Dolly and the Judge, a transparent wall through which he could watch her losing substance, recede before him as earlier she had seemed to recede before me. More than that, it was as if the tree-house were dissolving. Lunging wind cast overboard the soggy wreckage of our Rook cards, our wrapping papers; animal crackers crumbled, the rain-filled mason jars spilled over like fountains; and Catherine's beautiful scrapquilt was ruined, a puddle. It was going: like the doomed houses rivers in flood float away; and it was as though the Judge were trapped there—waving to us as we, the survivors, stood ashore. For Dolly had said, "Forgive me; I want my sister, too," and the Judge could not reach her, not with his arms, not with his heart: Verena's claim was too final.

Somewhere near midnight the rain slackened, halted; wind barreled about wringing out the trees. Singly, like delayed guests arriving at a dance, appearing stars pierced the sky. It was time to leave. We took nothing with us: left the quilt to rot, spoons to rust; and the tree-house, the woods we left to winter.

CHAPTER 7

FOR QUITE A WHILE it was Catherine's custom to date events as having occurred before or after her incarceration. "Prior," she would begin, "to the time That One made a jailbird of me." As for the rest of us, we could have divided history along similar lines; that is, in terms of before and after the tree-house. Those few autumn days were a monument and a signpost.

Except to collect his belongings, the Judge never again entered the house he'd shared with his sons and their wives, a circumstance that must have suited them, at least they made no protest when he took a room at Miss Bell's boarding house. This was a brown solemn establishment which lately has been turned into a funeral home by an undertaker who saw that to effect the correct atmosphere a minimum of renovation would be necessary. I disliked going past it, for Miss Bell's guests, ladies thorny as the blighted rosebushes littering the yard, occupied the porch in a dawn-to-dark marathon of vigilance. One of them, the twice-widowed Mamie Canfield, specialized in spotting pregnancies (some legendary fellow is supposed to have told his wife Why waste money on a doctor? just trot yourself past Miss Bell's: Mamie Canfield, she'll let the world know soon enough whether you is or ain't). Until the Judge moved there, Amos Legrand was the only man in residence at Miss Bell's. He was a godsend to the other tenants: the moments most sacred to them were when, after supper, Amos swung in the seat-swing with his little legs not touching the floor and his tongue trilling like an alarm-clock. They vied with each other in knitting him socks and sweaters, tending to his diet: at table all the best things were saved for his plate—Miss Bell had trouble keeping a cook because the ladies were forever poking around in the kitchen wanting to make a delicacy that would tempt their pet. Probably they would have done the same for the Judge, but he had no use for them, never, so they complained, stopped to pass the time of day.

The last drenching night in the tree-house had left me with a bad cold, Verena with a worse one; and we had a sneezing nurse, Dolly. Catherine wouldn't help: "Dollyheart, you can do like you please—tote That One's slopjar till you drop in your tracks. Only don't count on me to lift a finger. I've put down the load."

Rising at all hours of the night, Dolly brought the syrups that eased our throats, stoked the fires that kept us warm. Verena did not, as in other days, accept such attention simply as her due. "In the spring," she promised Dolly, "we'll make a trip together. We might go to the Grand Canyon and call on Maudie Laura. Or Florida: you've never seen the ocean." But Dolly was where she wanted to be, she had no wish to travel: "I wouldn't enjoy it, seeing the things I've known shamed by nobler sights."

Doctor Carter called regularly to see us, and one morning Dolly asked would he mind taking her temperature; she felt so flushed and weak in the legs. He put her straight to bed, and she thought it was very humorous when he told her she had walking pneumonia. "Walking pneumonia," she said to the Judge, who had come to visit her, "it must be something new, I've never heard of it. But I do feel as though I were skylarking along on a pair of stilts. Lovely," she said and fell asleep.

For three, nearly four days she never really woke up. Catherine stayed with her, dozing upright in a wicker chair and growling low whenever Verena or I tiptoed into the room. She persisted in fanning Dolly with a picture of Jesus, as though it were summertime; and it was a disgrace how she ignored Doctor Carter's instructions: "I wouldn't feed that to a hog," she'd declare, pointing to some medicine he'd sent around. Finally Doctor Carter said he wouldn't be responsible unless the patient were removed to a hospital. The nearest hospital was in Brewton, sixty miles away. Verena sent over there for an ambulance. She could have saved herself the expense, because Catherine locked Dolly's door from the inside and said the first one to rattle the knob would need an ambulance themselves. Dolly did not know where they wanted to take her; wherever it was, she begged not to go: "Don't wake me," she said, "I don't want to see the ocean."

Toward the end of the week she could sit up in bed; a few days later she was strong enough to resume correspondence with her dropsy-cure customers. She was worried by the unfilled orders that had piled up; but Catherine, who took the credit for Dolly's improvement, said, "Shoot, it's no time we'll be out there boiling a brew."

Every afternoon, promptly at four, the Judge presented himself at the garden gate and whistled for me to let him in; by using the garden gate, rather than the front door, he lessened the chance of encountering Verena—not that she objected to his coming: indeed, she wisely supplied for his visits a bottle of sherry and a box of cigars. Usually he brought Dolly a gift, cakes from the Katydid Bakery or flowers, bronze balloonlike chrysanthemums which Catherine swiftly confiscated on the theory that they ate up all the nourishment in the air. Catherine never learned he had proposed to Dolly; still, intuiting a situation not quite to her liking, she sharply chaperoned the Judge's visits and, while swigging at the sherry that had been put out for him, did most of the talking as well. But I suspect that neither he nor Dolly had much to say of a private nature; they accepted each other without excitement, as people do who are settled in their affections. If in other ways he was a disappointed man, it was not because of Dolly, for I believe she became what he'd wanted, the one person in the world—to whom, as he'd described it, everything can be said. But when everything can be said perhaps there is nothing more to say. He sat beside her bed, content to be there and not expecting to be entertained. Often, drowsy with fever, she went to sleep, and if, while she slept, she whimpered or frowned, he wakened her, welcoming her back with a daylight smile.

In the past Verena had not allowed us to have a radio; cheap melodies, she contended, disordered the mind; moreover, there was the expense to consider. It was Doctor Carter who persuaded her that Dolly should have a radio; he thought it would help reconcile her to what he foresaw as a long convalescence. Verena bought one, and paid a good price, I don't doubt; but it was an ugly hood-shaped box crudely varnished. I took it out in the yard and painted it pink. Even so Dolly wasn't certain she wanted it in her room; later on, you couldn't have pried it away from her. That radio was always hot enough to hatch a chicken, she and Catherine played it so much. They favored broadcasts of football games. "Please don't," Dolly admonished the Judge when he attempted to explain the rules of this game. "I like a mystery. Everybody shouting, having such a fine time: it might not sound so large and happy if I knew why." Primarily the Judge was peeved because he couldn't get Dolly to root for any one team. She thought both sides should win: "They're all nice boys, I'm sure."

Because of the radio Catherine and I had words one afternoon. It was the afternoon Maude Riordan was playing in a broadcast of the state musical competition. Naturally I wanted to hear her, Catherine knew that, but she was tuned in on a Tulane–Georgia Tech game and wouldn't let me near the radio. I said, "What's come over you, Catherine? Selfish, dissatisfied, always got to have your own way, why you're worse than Verena ever was." It was as though, in lieu of prestige lost through her encounter with the law, she'd had to double her power in the Talbo house: we at least would have to respect her Indian blood, accept her tyranny. Dolly was willing; in the matter of Maude Riordan, however, she sided with me: "Let Collin find his station. It wouldn't be Christian not to listen to Maude. She's a friend of ours."

Everyone who heard Maude agreed that she should've won first prize. She placed second, which pleased her family, for it meant a half-scholarship in music at the University. Still it wasn't fair, because she performed beautifully, much better than the boy who won the larger prize. She played her father's serenade, and it seemed to me as pretty as it had that day in the woods. Since that day I'd wasted hours scribbling her name, describing in my head her charms, her hair the color of vanilla ice cream. The Judge arrived in time to hear the broadcast, and I know Dolly was glad because it was as if we were reunited again in the leaves with music like butterflies flying.

Some days afterwards I met Elizabeth Henderson on the street. She'd been at the beauty parlor, for her hair was finger-waved, her nails tinted, she did look grown-up and I complimented her. "It's for the party. I hope your costume is ready." Then I remembered: the Halloween party to which she and Maude had asked me to contribute my services as a fortuneteller. "You can't have forgotten? Oh, Collin," she said, "we've worked like dogs! Mrs. Riordan is making a *wine* punch. I shouldn't be surprised if there's drunkenness and everything. And after all it's a celebration for Maude, because she won the prize, and because," Elizabeth glanced along the street, a glum perspective of silent houses and telephone poles, "she'll be going away—to the University, you know." A loneliness fell around us, we did not want to go our separate ways: I offered to walk her home.

On our way we stopped by the Katydid where Elizabeth placed an order for a Halloween cake, and Mrs. C. C. County, her apron glittering with sugar crystals, appeared from the oven room to inquire after Dolly's condition. "Doing well as can be expected I suppose," she lamented. "Imagine it, walking pneumonia. My sister, now she had the ordinary lying-down kind. Well, we can be thankful Dolly's in her own bed; it eases my mind to know you people are home again. Ha ha, guess we can laugh about all that foolishness now. Look here, I've just pulled out a pan of doughnuts; you take them to Dolly with my blessings." Elizabeth and I ate most of those doughnuts before we reached her house. She invited me in to have a glass of milk and finish them off.

Today there is a filling station where the Henderson house used to be. It was some fifteen draughty rooms casually nailed together, a place stray animals would have claimed if Riley had not been a gifted carpenter. He had an outdoor shed, a combination of workshop and sanctuary, where he spent his mornings sawing lumber, shaving shingles. Its wall-shelves sagged with the relics of outgrown hobbies: snakes, bees, spiders preserved in alcohol, a bat decaying in a bottle; ship models. A boyhood enthusiasm for taxidermy had resulted in a pitiful zoo of nasty-odored beasts: an eyeless rabbit with maggot-green fur and ears that drooped like a bloodhound's—objects better off buried. I'd been lately to see Riley several times; Big Eddie Stover's bullet had shattered his shoulder, and the curse of it was he had to wear an itching plaster cast which weighed, he said, a hundred pounds. Since he couldn't drive his car, or hammer a proper nail, there wasn't much for him to do except loaf around and brood.

"If you want to see Riley," said Elizabeth, "you'll find him out in the shed. I expect Maude's with him."

"Maude Riordan?" I had reason to be surprised, because on the occasions I'd visited Riley he'd made a point of our sitting in the shed; the girls wouldn't bother us there, for it was, he'd boasted, one threshold no female was permitted to cross.

"Reading to him. Poetry, plays. Maude's been absolutely adorable. And it's not as though my brother had ever treated her with common human decency. But she's let bygones be bygones. I guess coming so near to being killed the way he was, I guess that would change a person—make them more receptive to the finer things. He lets her read to him by the hour."

The shed, shaded by fig trees, was in the back yard. Matronly Plymouth hens waddled about its doorstep picking at the seeds of last summer's fallen sunflowers. On the door a childhood word in faded whitewash feebly warned Beware! It aroused a shyness in me. Beyond the door I could hear Maude's voice—her poetry voice, a swooning chant certain louts in school had dearly loved to mimic. Anyone who'd been told Riley Henderson had come to this, they'd have said that fall from the sycamore had affected his head. Stealing over to the shed's window, I got a look at him: he was absorbed in sorting the insides of a clock and, to judge from his face, might have been listening to nothing more uplifting than the hum of a fly; he jiggled a finger in his ear, as though to relieve an irritation. Then, at the moment I'd decided to startle them by rapping on the window, he put aside his clockworks and, coming round behind Maude, reached down and shut the book from which she was reading. With a grin he gathered in his hand twists of her hair—she rose like a kitten lifted by the nape of its neck. It was as though they were edged with light, some brilliance that smarted my eyes. You could see it wasn't the first time they'd kissed.

Not one week before, because of his experience in such matters, I'd taken Riley into my confidence, confessed to him my feelings for Maude: please look. I wished I were a giant so that I could grab hold of that shed and shake it to a splinter; knock down the door and denounce them both. Yet—of what could I accuse Maude? Regardless of how bad she'd talked about him I'd always known she was heartset on Riley. It wasn't as if there had ever been an understanding between the two of us; at the most we'd been good friends: for the last few years, not even that. As I walked back through the yard the pompous Plymouth hens cackled after me tauntingly.

Elizabeth said, "You didn't stay long. Or weren't they there?"

I told her it hadn't seemed right to interrupt. "They were getting on so well with the finer things."

But sarcasm never touched Elizabeth: she was, despite the subtleties her soulful appearance promised, too literal a person. "Wonderful, isn't it?"

"Wonderful."

"Collin—for heaven's sake: what are you sniveling about?"

"Nothing. I mean, I've got a cold."

"Well I hope it doesn't keep you away from the party. Only you must have a costume. Riley's coming as the devil."

"That's appropriate."

"Of course we want you in a skeleton suit. I know there's only a day left. . . ."

I had no intention of going to the party. As soon as I got home I sat down to write Riley a letter. Dear Riley . . . Dear Henderson. I crossed out the dear; plain Henderson would do. Henderson, your treachery has not gone unobserved. Pages were filled recording the origins of our friendship, its honorable history; and gradually a feeling grew that there must be a mistake: such a splendid friend would not have wronged me. Until, toward the end, I found myself deliriously telling him he was my best friend, my brother. So I threw these ravings in a fireplace and five minutes later was in Dolly's room asking what were the chances of my having a skeleton suit made by the following night.

Dolly was not much of a seamstress, she had her difficulties lifting a hemline. This was also true of Catherine; it was in Catherine's makeup, however, to pretend professional status in all fields, particularly those in which she was least competent. She sent me to Verena's drygoods store for seven yards of their choicest black satin. "With seven yards there ought to be some bits left over: me and Dolly can trim our petticoats." Then she made a show of tape-measuring my lengths and widths, which was sound procedure except that she had no idea of how to apply such information to scissors and cloth. "This little piece," she said, hacking off a yard, "it'd make somebody lovely bloomers. And this here," snip, snip, ". . . a black satin collar would dress up my old print considerable." You couldn't have covered a midget's shame with the amount of material allotted to me.

"Catherine, now dear, we mustn't think of our own needs," Dolly warned her.

They worked without recess through the afternoon. The Judge, during his usual visit, was forced to thread needles, a job Catherine despised: "Makes my flesh crawl, like stuffing worms on a fishhook." At suppertime she called quits and went home to her house among the butterbean stalks.

But a desire to finish had seized Dolly; and a talkative exhilaration. Her needle soared in and out of the satin; like the seams it made, her sentences linked in a wiggling line. "Do you think," she said, "that Verena would let me give a party? Now that I have so many friends? There's Riley, there's Charlie, couldn't we ask Mrs. County, Maude and Elizabeth? In the spring; a garden party—with a few fireworks. My father was a great hand for sewing. A pity I didn't inherit it from him. So many men sewed in the old days; there was one friend of Papa's that won I don't know how many prizes for his scrapquilts. Papa said it relaxed him after the heavy rough work around a farm. Collin. Will you promise me something? I was against your coming here, I've never believed it was right, raising a boy in a houseful of women. Old women and their prejudices. But it was done; and somehow I'm not worried about it now: you'll make your mark, you'll get on. It's this that I want you to promise me: don't be unkind to Catherine, try not to grow too far away from her. Some nights it keeps me wide awake to think of her forsaken. There," she held up my suit, "let's see if it fits."

It pinched in the crotch and in the rear drooped like an old man's B.V.D.'s; the legs were wide as sailor pants, one sleeve stopped above my wrist, the other shot past my fingertips. It wasn't, as Dolly admitted, very stylish. "But when we've painted on the bones . . ." she said. "Silver paint. Verena bought some once to dress up a flagpole—

before she took against the government. It should be somewhere in the attic, that little can. Look under the bed and see if you can locate my slippers."

She was forbidden to get up, not even Catherine would permit that. "It won't be any fun if you scold," she said and found the slippers herself. The courthouse clock had chimed eleven, which meant it was ten-thirty. A dark hour in a town where respectable doors are locked at nine; it seemed later still because in the next room Verena had closed her ledgers and gone to bed. We took an oil lamp from the linen closet and by its tottering light tiptoed up the ladder into the attic. It was cold up there; we set the lamp on a barrel and lingered near it as though it were a hearth. Sawdust heads that once had helped sell St. Louis hats watched while we searched; wherever we put our hands it caused a huffy scuttling of fragile feet. Overturned, a carton of mothballs clattered on the floor. "Oh dear, oh dear," cried Dolly, giggling, "if Verena hears that she'll call the Sheriff."

We unearthed numberless brushes; the paint, discovered beneath a welter of dried holiday wreaths, proved not to be silver but gold. "Of course that's better, isn't it? Gold, like a king's ransom. Only do see what else I've found." It was a shoebox secured with twine. "My valuables," she said, opening it under the lamp. A hollowed honeycomb was demonstrated against the light, a hornet's nest and clove-stuck orange that age had robbed of its aroma. She showed me a blue perfect jaybird's egg cradled in cotton.

"I was too principled. So Catherine stole the egg for me, it was her Christmas present." She smiled; to me her face seemed a moth suspended beside the lamp's chimney, as daring, as destructible. "Charlie said that love is a chain of love. I hope you listened and understood him. Because when you can love one thing," she held the blue egg as preciously as the Judge had held a leaf, "you can love another, and that is owning, that is something to live with. You can forgive everything. Well," she sighed, "we're not getting you painted. I want to amaze Catherine; we'll tell her that while we slept the little people finished your suit. She'll have a fit."

Again the courthouse clock was floating its message, each note like a banner stirring above the chilled and sleeping town. "I know it tickles," she said, drawing a branch of ribs across my chest, "but I'll make a mess if you don't hold still." She dipped the brush and skated it along the sleeves, the trousers, designing golden bones for my arms and legs. "You must remember all the compliments: there should be many," she said as she immodestly observed her work. "Oh dear, oh dear . . ." She hugged herself, her laughter rollicked in the rafters. "Don't you see . . ."

For I was not unlike the man who painted himself into a corner. Freshly gilded front and back, I was trapped inside the suit: a fine fix for which I blamed her with a pointing finger.

"You have to whirl," she teased. "Whirling will dry you." She blissfully extended her arms and turned in slow ungainly circles across the shadows of the attic floor, her plain kimono billowing and her thin feet wobbling in their slippers. It was as though she had collided with another dancer: she stumbled, a hand on her forehead, a hand on her heart.

Far on the horizon of sound a train whistle howled, and it wakened me to the bewilderment puckering her eyes, the contractions shaking her face. With my arms around her, and the paint bleeding its pattern against her, I called Verena; somebody help me!

Dolly whispered, "Hush now, hush."

Houses at night announce catastrophe by their sudden pitiable radiance. Catherine dragged from room to room switching on lights unused for years. Shivering inside my wrecked costume I sat in the glare of the entrance hall sharing a bench with the Judge. He had come at once, wearing only a raincoat slung over a flannel nightshirt. Whenever Verena approached he brought his naked legs together primly, like a young girl. Neighbors, summoned by our bright windows, came softly inquiring. Verena spoke to them on the porch: her sister, Miss Dolly, she'd suffered a stroke. Doctor Carter would allow none of us in her room, and we accepted this, even Catherine who, when she'd set ablaze the last light, stood leaning her head against Dolly's door.

There was in the hall a hat-tree with many antlers and a mirror. Dolly's velvet hat hung there, and at sunrise, as breezes trickled through the house, the mirror reflected its quivering veil.

Then I knew as good as anything that Dolly had left us. Some moments past she'd gone by unseen; and in my imagination I followed her. She had crossed the square, had come to the church, now she'd reached the hill. The Indian grass gleamed below her, she had that far to go.

IT WAS A JOURNEY I made with Judge Cool the next September. During the intervening months we had not often encountered each other—once we met on the square and he said to come see him any time I felt like it. I meant to, yet whenever I passed Miss Bell's boarding house I looked the other way.

I've read that past and future are a spiral, one coil containing the next and predicting its theme. Perhaps this is so; but my own life has seemed to me more a series of closed circles, rings that do not evolve with the freedom of a spiral: for me to get from one to the other has meant a leap, not a glide. What weakens me is the lull between, the wait before I know where to jump. After Dolly died I was a long while dangling.

My one idea was to have a good time.

I hung around Phil's Café winning free beers on the pinball machine; it was illegal to serve me beer, but Phil had it on his mind that someday I would inherit Verena's money and maybe set him up in the hotel business. I slicked my hair with brilliantine and chased off to dances in other towns, shined flashlights and threw pebbles at girls' windows late at night. I knew a Negro in the country who sold a brand of gin called Yellow Devil. I courted anyone who owned a car.

Because I didn't want to spend a waking moment in the Talbo house. It was too thick with air that didn't move. Some stranger occupied the kitchen, a pigeon-toed colored girl who sang all day, the wavering singing of a child bolstering its spirit in an ominous place. She was a sorry cook. She let the kitchen's geranium plant perish. I had approved of Verena hiring her. I thought it would bring Catherine back to work.

On the contrary, Catherine showed no interest in routing the new girl. For she'd retired to her house in the vegetable garden. She had taken the radio with her and was very comfortable. "I've put down the load, and it's down to stay. I'm after my leisure," she said. Leisure fattened her, her feet swelled, she had to cut slits in her shoes. She developed exaggerated versions of Dolly's habits, such as a craving for sweet foods; she had her suppers delivered from the drugstore, two quarts of ice cream. Candy wrappers rustled in her lap. Until she became too gross, she contrived to squeeze herself into clothes that had belonged to Dolly; it was as though, in this way, she kept her friend with her.

Our visits together were an ordeal, and I made them grudgingly, resenting it that she depended on me for company. I let a day slip by without seeing her, then three, a whole week once. When I returned after an absence I imagined the silences in which we sat, her offhand manner, were meant reproachfully; I was too conscience-ridden to realize the truth, which was that she didn't care whether or not I came. One afternoon she proved it. Simply, she removed the cotton wads that jacked up her jaws. Without the cotton her speech was as unintelligible to me as it ordinarily was to others. It happened while I was making an excuse to shorten my call. She lifted the lid of a potbellied stove and spit the cotton into the fire; and her cheeks caved in, she looked starved. I think now this was not a vengeful gesture: it was intended to let me know that I was under no obligation: the future was something she preferred not to share.

Occasionally Riley rode me around—but I couldn't count on him or his car; neither were much available since he'd become a man of affairs. He had a team of tractors clearing ninety acres of land he'd bought on the outskirts of town; he planned to build houses there. Several locally important persons were impressed by another scheme of his: he thought the town should put up a silkmill in which every citizen would be a stockholder; aside from the possible profits, having an industry would increase our population. There was an enthusiastic editorial in the paper about this proposal; it went on to say that the town should be proud of having produced a man of young Henderson's enterprise. He grew a mustache; he rented an office and his sister Elizabeth worked as his secretary. Maude Riordan was installed at the State University, and almost every week-end he drove his sisters over there; it was supposed to be because the girls were so lonesome for Maude. The engagement of Miss Maude Riordan to Mr. Riley Henderson was announced in the *Courier* on April Fool's Day.

They were married the middle of June in a double-ring ceremony. I acted as an usher, and the Judge was Riley's best man. Except for the Henderson sisters, all the bridesmaids were society girls Maude had known at the University; the *Courier* called them beautiful debutantes, a chivalrous description. The bride carried a bouquet of jasmine and lilac; the groom wore spats and stroked his mustache. They received a sumptuous table-load of gifts. I gave them six cakes of scented soap and an ashtray.

After the wedding I walked home with Verena under the shade of her black umbrella. It was a blistering day, heatwaves jiggled like a sound-graph of the celebrating Baptist bells, and the rest of summer, a vista rigid as the noon street, lengthened before me. Summer, another autumn, winter again: not a spiral, but a circle confined as the umbrella's shadow. If I ever were to make the leap—with a heartskip, I made it. "Verena, I want to go away."

We were at the garden gate; "I know. I do myself," she said, closing her umbrella. "I'd hoped to make a trip with Dolly. I wanted to show her the ocean." Verena had seemed a tall woman because of her authoritative carriage; now she stooped slightly, her head nodded. I wondered that I ever could have been so afraid of her, for she'd grown feminine, fearful, she spoke of prowlers, she burdened the doors with bolts and spiked the roof with lightning rods. It had been her custom the first of every month to stalk around collecting in person the various rents owed her; when she stopped doing this it caused an uneasiness in the town, people felt wrong without their rainy day. The women said she's got no family, she's lost without her sister; their husbands blamed Dr. Morris Ritz: he knocked the gumption out of her, they said; and, much as they had quarreled with Verena, held it against him. Three years ago, when I returned to this town, my first task was to sort the papers of the Talbo estate, and among Verena's private possessions, her keys, her pictures of Maudie Laura Murphy, I found a postcard. It was dated two months after Dolly died, at Christmas, and it was from Paraguay: *As we say down here, Feliz Navidad. Do you miss me? Morris.* And I thought, reading it, of how her eyes had come permanently to have an uneven cast, an inward and agonized gaze, and I remembered how her eyes, watering in the brassy sunshine of Riley's wedding day, had straightened with momentary hope: "It could be a long trip. I've considered selling a few—a few properties. We might take a boat; you've never seen the ocean." I picked a sprig of honeysuckle from the vine flowering on the garden fence, and she watched me shred it as if I were pulling apart her vision, the voyage she saw for us. "Oh," she

brushed at the mole that spotted her cheek like a tear, "well," she said in a practical voice, "what are your ambitions?"

So it was not until September that I called upon the Judge, and then it was to tell him good-bye. The suitcases were packed, Amos Legrand had cut my hair ("Honey, don't you come back here bald-headed. What I mean is, they'll try to scalp you up there, cheat you every way they can."); I had a new suit and new shoes, a gray fedora ("Aren't you the cat's pajamas, Mr. Collin Fenwick?" Mrs. County exclaimed. "A lawyer you're going to be? And already dressed like one. No, child, I won't kiss you. I'd be mortified to dirty your finery with my bakery mess. You write us, hear?"): that very evening a train would rock me northward, parade me through the land to a city where in my honor pennants flurried.

At Miss Bell's they told me the Judge had gone out. I found him on the square, and it gave me a twinge to see him, a spruce sturdy figure with a Cherokee rose sprouting in his buttonhole, encamped among the old men who talk and spit and wait. He took my arm and led me away from them; and while he amiably advised me of his own days as a law student, we strolled past the church and out along the River Woods road. This road or this tree: I closed my eyes to fix their image, for I did not believe I would return, did not foresee that I would travel the road and dream the tree until they had drawn me back.

It was as though neither of us had known where we were headed. Quietly astonished, we surveyed the view from the cemetery hill, and arm in arm descended to the summer-burned, September-burnished field. A waterfall of color flowed across the dry and strumming leaves; and I wanted then for the Judge to hear what Dolly had told me: that it was a grass harp, gathering, telling, a harp of voices remembering a story. We listened.

THE APPLE TREE

THE
APPLE
TREE

John Galsworthy

ILLUSTRATED BY FRANK MORRIS AND BEN WOHLBERG

They came from different worlds and they
met by chance—Megan, the young and lovely farm
girl, as pure and fresh as the English countryside
that was her home; and Frank Ashurst, well-
born, idealistic and afire with romantic
and poetic sentiments. Yet beneath a flowering apple
tree on the farm where Megan lived,
the two of them confessed their love and pledged a
life together.

Years later, Frank Ashurst stumbles
on the memory of those long-forgotten
vows—and discovers just how time and
circumstances have dishonored them.

"The Apple-tree, the singing, and the gold."
    —from Gilbert Murray's translation of
    THE HIPPOLYTUS OF EURIPIDES

O<small>N THEIR</small> silver-wedding day Ashurst and his wife were motoring along the outskirts of the moor, intending to crown the festival by stopping the night at Torquay, where they had first met. This was the idea of Stella Ashurst, whose character contained a streak of sentiment. If she had long lost the blue-eyed, flowerlike charm, the cool, slim purity of face and form, the apple-blossom coloring, which had so swiftly and so oddly affected Ashurst twenty-six years ago, she was still at forty-three a comely and faithful companion, whose cheeks were faintly mottled and whose gray-blue eyes had acquired a certain fullness.

It was she who had stopped the car where the common rose steeply to the left, and a narrow strip of larch and beech, with here and there a pine, stretched out toward the valley between the road and the first long high hill of the full moor. She was looking for a place where they might picnic, for Ashurst never looked for anything; and this, between the golden furze and the feathery green larches smelling of lemons in the last sun of April—this, with a view into the deep valley and up to the long moor heights, seemed fitting to the decisive nature of one who sketched in watercolors and loved romantic spots. Grasping her paint box, she got out.

"Won't this do, Frank?"

Ashurst, bearded, gray at the sides, tall and long-legged, with large remote gray eyes that sometimes filled with meaning and became almost beautiful, with a nose a little to one side and bearded lips just open—Ashurst, forty-eight and silent, grasped the picnic basket and got out too.

"Oh! Look, Frank! A grave!"

By the side of the road, where the track from the top of the common crossed it at right angles and ran through a gate past the narrow wood, was a thin mound of turf, six feet by one, with a moorstone to the west, and on it someone had thrown a blackthorn spray and a handful of bluebells. Ashurst looked, and the poet in him moved.

At crossroads—a suicide's grave! Poor mortals with their superstitions! Whoever lay there, though, had the best of it, no clammy sepulcher among other hideous graves carved with futilities—just a rough stone, the wide sky and wayside blessings!

Without comment he strode away up onto the common, dropped the picnic basket under a wall, spread a blanket for his wife to sit on—she would turn up from her sketching when she was hungry—and took from his pocket Murray's translation of the *Hippolytus*. He had soon finished reading of the Cyprian, the goddess of love, and her revenge, and looked at the sky instead.

Watching the white clouds so bright against the intense blue, Ashurst, on his silver-wedding day, longed for—he knew not what. Maladjusted to life—civilized man! One's mode of life might be high and scrupulous, but there was always an undercurrent of greediness, a hankering and a sense of waste. Did women have it too? Who could tell?

And yet, men who gave vent to their appetites for novelty, their riotous longings for new adventures, new risks, new pleasures, these suffered, no doubt, from the reverse side of starvation, from surfeit. No getting out of it—a maladjusted animal, civilized man! There could be no garden of his choosing, of "the Apple-tree, the singing, and the gold," in the words of that lovely Greek chorus, no achievable Elysium in life, or lasting haven of happiness for any man with a sense of beauty—nothing that could compare with the captured loveliness in a work of art, set down forever, so that to look on it or to read it was always to have the same precious sense of exaltation and intoxication.

Life had moments with that quality of beauty, of unbidden flying rapture, but the trouble was that they lasted no longer than the span of a cloud's flight over the sun; impossible to keep them with you, as art caught beauty and held it fast. They were as fleeting as one of the glimmering or golden visions one had of the soul in nature, glimpses of its remote and brooding spirit. Here, with the sun hot on his face, a cuckoo calling from a thorn tree, and in the air the honey savor of gorse—here among the little fronds of the young fern, the starry blackthorn, while the bright clouds drifted by high above the hills and dreamy valleys—here and now was such a glimpse.

And suddenly he sat up. Surely there was something familiar about this view, this bit of common, that ribbon of road, the old wall behind him. While they were driving he had not been taking notice— he never did; thinking of faraway things or of nothing—but now he saw!

Twenty-six years ago, just at this time of year, from a farmhouse within half a mile of this very spot, he had started for Torquay whence it might be said he had never returned. And a sudden ache beset his heart; he had stumbled on just one of those past moments in his life whose beauty and rapture he had failed to arrest, whose wings had fluttered away into the unknown; he had stumbled on a buried memory, a wild sweet time, swiftly choked and ended. And, turning on his face, he rested his chin on his hands and stared at the short grass where the little blue milkwort was growing. . . .

And this is what he remembered.

CHAPTER 1

ON THE FIRST OF May, after their last year together at college, Frank Ashurst and his friend Robert Garton were on a hike. They had walked that day from Brent, intending to make Chagford, but Ashurst's football knee had given out, and according to their map they had still some seven miles to go. They were sitting on a bank beside the road, where a track crossed alongside a wood, resting the knee and talking of the universe, as young men will. Both were over six feet and thin as rails; Ashurst pale, idealistic, full of absence; Garton eccentric, knotted, curly, like some primeval beast. Both had a literary bent; neither wore a hat. Ashurst's hair was smooth, pale, wavy, and had a way of rising on either side of his brow, as if always being flung back; Garton's was a kind of dark unfathomed mop. They had not met a soul for miles.

"My dear fellow," Garton was saying, "pity's only an effect of self-consciousness; it's a disease of the last five thousand years. The world was happier without it."

Ashurst, following the clouds with his eyes, answered, "It's the pearl in the oyster, anyway."

"My dear chap, all our modern unhappiness comes from our pity. Look at animals—limited to feeling their own occasional misfortunes; then look at ourselves—never free from feeling the toothaches of others. Let's get back to feeling for nobody, and we'll have a better time."

"You'll never practice that."

Garton pensively stirred the hotchpotch of his hair. "To attain full growth, one mustn't be squeamish. To starve oneself emotionally's a mistake. All emotion is to the good. It enriches life."

"Yes, and when it runs up against chivalry?"

"Ah! That's so English! If you speak of emotion, the English always think you want something physical and are shocked. They're afraid of passion but not lust—oh, no!—as long as they can keep it secret."

Ashurst did not answer at once; he had plucked a blue floweret and was twiddling it against the sky. A cuckoo began calling from a thorn tree. The sky, the flowers, the songs of birds! Robert was talking through his hat! Finally, he said, "Well, let's go on, and find some farm where we can put up."

In uttering those words, he was conscious of a girl coming down from the common just above them. She was outlined against the sky, carrying a basket, and you could see the sky through the crook of her arm. And Ashurst, who saw beauty without wondering how it could be of advantage to him, thought, How pretty! The wind, blowing her rough tweed skirt against her legs, lifted her battered peacock tam-o'-shanter; her grayish blouse was worn and old, her shoes were split, her little hands rough and red, her neck browned. Her dark hair waved untidily across her broad forehead, her face was short, her upper lip short, showing a glint of teeth. Her brows were straight and dark, her lashes long and dark, her nose straight; but her gray eyes were the wonder—dewy, as if opened for the first time that day. She looked at Ashurst—perhaps he struck her as strange, limping along without a hat, with his large eyes on her and his hair flung back.

He could not take off what was not on his head, but he put up his hand in a salute and said, "Can you tell us if there's a farm near here where we could stay the night? I've gone lame."

"There's only our farm near, sir." She spoke without shyness, in a pretty, soft, crisp voice.

"And where is that?"

"Down here, sir."

"Would you put us up?"

"Oh! I think we would."

"Will you show us the way?"

"Yes, sir."

He limped on, silent, and Garton took up the inquiry. "Are you a Devonshire girl?"

"No, sir."

"What then?"

"From Wales."

"Ah! I *thought* you were a Celt; so it's not your farm?"

"My aunt's, sir."

"And your uncle's?"

"He is dead."

"Who farms it, then?"

"My aunt and my three cousins."

"But your uncle was a Devonshire man?"

"Yes, sir."

"Have you lived here long?"

"Seven years."

"And how d'you like it after Wales?"

"I don't know, sir."

"I suppose you don't remember?"

"Oh, yes! But it is different."

"I believe you!"

Ashurst broke in suddenly: "How old are you?"

"Seventeen, sir."

"And what's your name?"

"Megan David."

"This is Robert Garton, and I am Frank Ashurst. We wanted to get on to Chagford."

"It is a pity your leg is hurting you."

Ashurst smiled, and when he smiled his face was rather beautiful.

Descending past the narrow wood, they came on it suddenly—a long, low, stone-built dwelling with casement windows, in a farmyard where pigs and fowl and an old mare were straying. A short steep grass hill behind was crowned with a few Scotch firs, and in front, an old orchard of apple trees, just breaking into flower, stretched down to a stream and a long wild meadow. A little boy with dark almond-shaped eyes was shepherding a pig, and by the house door stood a woman, who came toward them.

The girl said, "It is Mrs. Narracombe, my aunt."

Mrs. Narracombe had quick dark eyes, like a mother wild duck's, and something of the same snaky turn about her neck.

"We met your niece on the road," said Ashurst. "She thought you might perhaps put us up for the night."

Mrs. Narracombe, taking them in from head to heel, answered, "Well, I can, if you don't mind one room. Megan, get the spare room ready, and a bowl of cream. You'll be wanting tea, I suppose."

Passing through a sort of porch made by two yew trees and some flowering currant bushes, the girl disappeared into the house, her peacock tam-o'-shanter momentarily bright against that rosy pink and dark green of the yews.

"Will you come into the parlor and rest your leg? You'll be from college, perhaps?"

"We were, but we've graduated now."

Mrs. Narracombe nodded sagely.

The parlor, brick-floored, with a bare table and shiny chairs and a sofa stuffed with horsehair, seemed never to have been used, it was so terribly clean. Ashurst sat down at once on the sofa, holding his lame knee between his hands, and Mrs. Narracombe gazed at him. He was the only son of a late professor of chemistry, but people found a certain lordliness in one who was often so sublimely unconscious of them.

"Is there a stream where we could bathe?"

"There's the stream at the bottom of the orchard, but sittin' down you'll not be covered!"

"How deep?"

"Well, 'tis about a foot and a half, maybe."

"Oh! That'll do fine. Which way?"

"Down the lane, through the second gate on the right, an' the pool's by the big apple tree that stands by itself. There's trout there, if you can tickle them."

"They're more likely to tickle us!"

Mrs. Narracombe smiled. "There'll be the tea ready when you come back."

The pool, formed by the damming of a rock, had a sandy bottom; and the big apple tree, lowest in the orchard, grew so close that its boughs almost overhung the water; it was in leaf, and all but in flower—its crimson buds just bursting. There was not room for more than one at a time in that narrow bath, and Ashurst waited his turn, rubbing his knee and gazing at the wild meadow, all rocks and thorn trees and field flowers, with a grove of beeches beyond, raised up on a mound. Every bough was swinging in the wind, every spring bird calling, and a slanting sunlight dappled the grass. He thought of the moon, and the maiden with the dewy eyes; of so many things that he seemed to think of nothing; and he felt absurdly happy.

CHAPTER 2

DURING A LATE and sumptuous tea with eggs to it, cream and jam, and thin, fresh cakes touched with saffron, Garton improvised on the history of the Celts. It was during the period of the Celtic awakening, and the discovery that there was Celtic blood in this family had excited one who believed that he was a Celt himself. Sprawling on a horsehair chair, with a handmade cigarette dribbling from the corner of his curly lips, he had been plunging his cold pinpoints of eyes into Ashurst's and praising the refinement of the Welsh. To come out of Wales into England was like the change from china to earthenware! Frank, as an Englishman, had not of course perceived the exquisite refinement and emotional capacity of that Welsh girl! And, delicately stirring the dark mat of his still wet hair, he explained how exactly she illustrated the writings of the Welsh bard Morgan-ap-Something in the twelfth century.

Ashurst, full length on the horsehair sofa, and jutting far beyond its end, smoked a pipe and did not listen, thinking of the girl's face when she brought in a relay of cakes. It had been exactly like looking at a flower, or some other pretty sight in nature—till, with a funny little shiver, she had lowered her glance and gone out, quiet as a mouse.

"Let's go to the kitchen," said Garton, "and see some more of her."

The kitchen was a whitewashed room with rafters, to which were attached smoked hams; there were flowerpots on the windowsill and guns hanging on nails, queer mugs, china and pewter, and portraits of Queen Victoria. A long, narrow table of plain wood was set with bowls and spoons, under a string of high-hung onions; two sheepdogs and three cats lay here and there. On one side of the recessed fireplace sat two small boys, idle and good as gold; on the other side sat a stout, light-eyed, red-faced youth with hair and lashes the color of the flaxen yarn he was running through the barrel of a gun; between them Mrs. Narracombe dreamily stirred some savory-scented stew in a large pot.

Two other youths, almond-eyed, dark-haired, rather sly-faced, like the two little boys, were talking together and lolling against the wall; and a short, elderly, clean-shaven man in corduroys, seated in the window, was perusing a battered journal. The girl Megan seemed the only active creature—drawing cider and passing with the jugs from cask to table. Seeing them about to eat, Garton said, "Ah! If you'll let us, we'll come back when supper's over," and without waiting for an answer they withdrew again to the parlor. But the color in the kitchen, the warmth, the scents and all those faces heightened the bleakness of their shiny room, and they resumed their seats moodily.

"Regular gipsy type, those boys. There was only one Saxon—the fellow cleaning the gun. That girl is a very subtle study psychologically," Garton said.

Ashurst's lips twitched. Garton seemed to him an ass just then. Subtle study! She was a wildflower. A creature it did you good to look at. Study!

Garton went on. "Emotionally she would be wonderful. She wants awakening."

"Are you going to awaken her?"

Garton looked at him and smiled. "How coarse and English you are!" that curly smile seemed to be saying.

And Ashurst puffed his pipe. Awaken her! This fool had the best opinion of himself! He threw up the window and leaned out. Dusk had gathered thick. The farm buildings were all dim and bluish, the apple trees but a blurred wilderness; the air smelled of woodsmoke from the kitchen fire. From the stable came the snuffle and stamp of a feeding horse. And away over there was the loom of the moor, and away and away the shy stars that had not as yet full light, pricking white through the deep blue heavens. A quavering owl hooted.

Ashurst drew a deep breath. What a night to wander out in! A padding of unshod hooves came up the lane, and three dim, dark shapes passed—ponies on an evening march. Their heads, black and fuzzy, showed above the gate. At the tap of his pipe and a shower of little sparks, they shied round and scampered away. A bat went fluttering past, uttering its almost inaudible *chip, chip*. Suddenly from overhead he heard little burring boys' voices, little thumps of boots thrown down, and another voice, crisp and soft—the girl putting them to bed, no doubt—and nine clear words: "No, Rick, you can't have the cat in bed"; then came a skirmish of giggles and gurgles, a soft slap, a laugh so low and pretty that it made him shiver a little. Silence reigned. Ashurst withdrew into the room and sat down; his knee was hurting him, and his soul felt gloomy.

"You go to the kitchen," he said. "I'm going to bed."

CHAPTER 3

FOR ASHURST the wheel of slumber was wont to turn noiseless and slick and swift, but though he seemed sunk in sleep when his companion came up, he was really wide awake; and long after Garton, smothered in the other bed of that low-roofed room, was sound asleep, he heard the owls. Barring the discomfort of his knee, it was not unpleasant—the cares of life did not loom large in night watches for Frank Ashurst. In fact he had none; just enrolled as a barrister, with literary aspirations, the world before him, no father or mother, and four hundred a year of his own. Did it matter where he went, what he did or when he did it? He lay, sniffing the scent of the night that drifted into the low room through the open casement close to his head. Ashurst's memories and visions that sleepless night were kindly and wistful and exciting. One vision, specially clear and unreasonable, for he had not even been conscious of noting it, was the face of the youth cleaning the gun—intent, stolid, yet startled as he looked up at the kitchen doorway, quickly shifting to the girl carrying the cider jug. This red, blue-eyed, light-lashed, tow-haired face stuck as firmly in his memory as the girl's own face, so dewy and simple. But at last, in the square of darkness through the uncurtained casement, he saw day coming and heard one hoarse and sleepy caw. Then followed silence, dead as ever, till the song of a blackbird, not properly awake, adventured into the hush. And, from staring at the framed brightening light, Ashurst fell asleep.

The next day his knee was badly swollen; for him the walking tour was obviously over. Garton, due back in London on the morrow, departed at noon with an ironical smile that left behind a scar of irritation—healed the moment his loping figure vanished round the corner of the steep lane. All day Ashurst rested his knee, in a green-painted wooden chair on the patch of grass by the yew-tree porch, where the sunlight distilled the scent of stocks and carnations. Beatifically he smoked, dreamed, watched.

A farm in spring is all birth—young things coming out of bud and shell, and human beings watching over the process with faint excitement, feeding and tending what has been born. So still the young man sat that a mother goose with a stately cross-footed waddle brought her six yellow-necked gray-backed goslings to strop their little beaks against the blades of grass at his feet. Now and again Mrs. Narracombe or Megan would come and ask if he wanted anything, and he would smile and say, "Nothing, thanks. It's splendid here." Toward teatime they came out together, bearing a poultice of some dark stuff in a bowl, and, after a long and solemn scrutiny of his swollen knee, bound it on. When they were gone, he thought of the girl's soft "Oh!"—of her pitying eyes and the little wrinkle in her brow. And again he felt that unreasoning irritation against his departed friend, who had talked such rot about her. When she brought his tea, he said, "How did you like my friend, Megan?"

She forced down her upper lip, as if afraid that to smile was not polite. "He was a funny gentleman; he made us laugh. I think he is very clever."

"What did he say to make you laugh?"

"He said I was a daughter of the bards. What are they?"

"Welsh poets who lived hundreds of years ago."

"And why am I their daughter?"

"He meant that you were the sort of girl they sang about."

She wrinkled her brow. "I think he likes to joke. Am I?"

"Would you believe me, if I told you?"

"Oh, yes."

"Well, I think he was right."

She smiled.

And Ashurst thought, You *are* a pretty thing!

"He said, too, that Joe was a Saxon type. What would that be?"

"Which is Joe? With the blue eyes and red face?"

"Yes. My uncle's nephew."

"Not your cousin, then?"

"No."

"Well, he meant that Joe was like the men who came over to England about fourteen hundred years ago and conquered it."

"Oh! I know about them; but is he?"

"Garton's crazy about that sort of thing; but I must say Joe does look a bit Early Saxon."

"Yes."

That "yes" tickled Ashurst. It was so crisp and graceful, so conclusive and politely acquiescent in what was evidently Greek to her.

"He said that all the other boys were regular gipsies. He should not have said that. My aunt laughed, but she didn't like it, of course, and my cousins were angry. Uncle was a farmer—farmers are not gipsies. It is wrong to hurt people."

Ashurst wanted to take her hand and give it a squeeze, but he only answered, "Quite right, Megan. By the way, I heard you putting the little ones to bed last night."

She flushed a little. "Please to drink your tea—it is getting cold. Shall I get you some fresh?"

"Do you ever have time to do anything for yourself?"

"Oh, yes."

"I've been watching, but I haven't seen it yet."

Megan wrinkled her brow in a puzzled frown, and her color deepened.

When she was gone, Ashurst thought, Did she think I was making fun of her? I wouldn't for the world! Never very conscious of his surroundings, it was some time before he was aware that the youth whom Garton had called a Saxon type was standing outside the stable door; and a fine bit of color he made in his soiled brown corduroys, muddy gaiters and blue shirt; red-armed, red-faced, the sun turning his hair to flax; immovably stolid, persistent, unsmiling he stood. Then, seeing Ashurst looking at him, he crossed the yard at that gait of the young countryman always ashamed not to be slow and heavy-dwelling on each leg, and disappeared round the end of the house toward the kitchen entrance. A chill came over Ashurst's mood. Clods! With all the goodwill in the world, how impossible to get on terms with them! And yet—see that girl! Her shoes were split, her hands rough; but—what was it? Was it really her Celtic blood, as Garton had said? She was a lady born, a jewel, though probably she could do no more than barely read and write!

The elderly, clean-shaven man he had seen last night in the kitchen had come into the yard with a dog, driving the cows to their milking. Ashurst saw that he was lame. "You've got some good ones there!"

The lame man's face brightened. He had the upward look in his eyes that prolonged suffering often brings.

"Yes; they'm proper beauties; good milkers too."

"I bet they are."

" 'Ope as your leg's better, surr."

"Thank you, it's getting on."

The lame man touched his own. "I know what 'tis, meself; 'tis a main worritin' thing, the knee. I've a 'ad mine bad this ten year."

Ashurst made the sound of sympathy that comes so readily from those who have an independent income, and the lame man smiled again.

"Mustn't complain, though—they mighty near 'ad it off."

"Ho!"

"Yes; an' compared with what 'twas, 'tis almost so good as new."

"They've put a poultice of splendid stuff on mine."

"The maid, she picks et. She'm a good maid wi' the flowers. There's folks zeem to know the healin' in things. My mother was a rare one for that. 'Ope as you'll sune be better, surr. Goo ahn, there!"

Ashurst smiled. "Wi' the flowers!" A flower herself.

That evening, after his supper of cold duck, junket and cider, the girl came in.

"Please, auntie says—will you try a piece of our Mayday cake?"

"If I may come to the kitchen for it."

"Oh, yes! You'll be missing your friend."

"Not I. But are you sure no one minds?"

"Who would mind? We shall be very pleased."

Ashurst rose too suddenly for his stiff knee, staggered and sank down. The girl gave a little gasp and held out her hands. Ashurst took them, small, rough, brown; checked his impulse to put them to his lips and let her pull him up. She came close beside him, offering her shoulder. And, leaning on her, he walked across the room. Her shoulder seemed quite the pleasantest thing he had ever touched.

That night he slept like a top and woke with his knee almost normal size. He again spent the morning in his chair on the grass patch, scribbling down verses; but in the afternoon he wandered about with the two little boys, Nick and Rick. It was Saturday, so they were home from school; quick, shy, dark little rascals of seven and six, soon talkative, for Ashurst had a way with children. By four o'clock they had shown him all their methods of destroying life, except the tickling of trout; and with breeches tucked up, they lay on their stomachs beside the trout stream, pretending they had this accomplishment also. They tickled nothing, of course, for their giggling and shouting scared every spotted thing away. Ashurst, on a rock at the edge of the beech clump, watched them till Nick, the elder and less persevering, came up and stood beside him.

"The gipsy bogle sets on that stone," he said.

"What gipsy bogle?"

"Dunno; never seen 'e. Megan says 'e sets there; an' old Jim seed 'e once. 'E was settin' there night afore our pony kicked in father's 'ead. 'E plays the viddle."

"What tune does he play?"

"Dunno."

"What's he like?"

" 'E's black. Old Jim says 'e's all over 'air. 'E's a proper bogle. 'E don' come only at night." The little boy's dark eyes slid round. "D'you think 'e might want to take me away? Megan's feared of 'e."

"Has she seen him?"

"No. She's not afeared o' you."

"I should think not. Why should she be?"

"She says a prayer for you."

"How do you know that, you little rascal?"

"When I was asleep, she said, 'God bless us all, an' Mr. Ashes.' I yeard 'er whisperin'."

"You're a little ruffian to tell what you hear when you're not meant to hear it!"

The little boy was silent. Then he said aggressively, "I can skin rabbits. Megan, she can't bear skinnin' 'em. I like blood."

"Oh, you do! You little monster!"

"What's that?"

"A creature that likes hurting others."

The little boy scowled. "They'm only dead rabbits, what us eats."

"Quite right, Nick. I beg your pardon."

"I can skin frogs, too."

But Ashurst had become absent. "God bless us all, an' Mr. Ashes!" And puzzled by his sudden inaccessibility, Nick ran back to the stream, where the giggling and shouting began again at once.

When Megan brought his tea, he said, "What's the gipsy bogle, Megan?"

She looked up, startled. "He brings bad things."

"Surely you don't believe in ghosts?"

"I hope I will never see him."

"Of course you won't. There aren't such things. What old Jim saw was probably a pony."

"No! There are bogles in the rocks—men who lived long ago."

"They aren't gipsies, anyway; those old men were dead long before gipsies came."

She said simply, "They are all bad."

"Why? If there are any, they're only wild things, like the rabbits. The flowers aren't bad for being wild; the thorn trees were never planted—and you don't mind them. I shall go down at night and look for your bogle, and have a talk with him."

"Oh, no! Oh, no!"

"Oh, yes! I shall go and sit on his rock."

She clasped her hands together. "Oh, please!"

"Why! What does it matter if anything happens to me?"

She did not answer; and peevishly he added, "Well, I daresay I shan't see him, because I suppose I must be off soon."

"Soon?"

"Your aunt won't want to keep me here."

"Oh, yes! We always let lodgings in summer."

Fixing his eyes on her face, he asked, "Would you like me to stay?"

"Yes."

"I'm going to say a prayer for *you* tonight!"

She flushed crimson, frowned and went out of the room. He sat cursing himself, till his tea was stewed. It was as if he had hacked with his thick boots at a clump of bluebells. Why had he said such a silly thing? Was he just a townie college ass like Robert Garton, and as far from understanding this girl?

CHAPTER 4

ASHURST SPENT the next week confirming the restoration of his leg by exploration of the country within easy reach. Spring was a revelation to him this year. In a kind of intoxication he would watch the pink-white buds of some beech tree sprayed up in the sunlight against the deep blue sky, or the trunks and limbs of the few Scotch firs, tawny in violent light, or again on the moor, the gale-bent larches that had such a look of life when the wind streamed in their young green above the rusty black underboughs.

It was certainly different from any spring he had ever known, for spring was within him as well as without. In the daytime he hardly saw the family; and when Megan brought in his meals she always seemed too busy in the house or among the young things in the yard to stay talking long. But in the evenings he installed himself in the window seat in the kitchen, smoking and chatting with the lame man, Jim, or Mrs. Narracombe while the girl sewed, or moved about, clearing the supper things away. And sometimes with the sensation a cat must feel when it purrs, he would become conscious that Megan's

eyes—those dew-gray eyes—were fixed on him with a sort of lingering soft look that was strangely flattering.

On a Sunday in the evening, when he was lying in the orchard and
composing a love poem, he heard the gate swing to and saw the girl
come running among the trees, with the red-cheeked, stolid Joe in
pursuit. About twenty yards away the chase ended, and the two stood
confronting each other, not noticing the stranger in the grass—the
boy pressing on, the girl fending him off. Ashurst could see her face,
angry, disturbed; and the youth's—who would have thought that
yokel could look so distraught! And painfully affected by that sight,
he jumped up. They saw him then. Megan dropped her hands and
shrank behind a tree trunk; the boy gave an angry grunt, rushed at
the bank, scrambled over and vanished. Ashurst went slowly up to
her. She was standing quite still, biting her lip—very pretty with her
hair blown loose about her face and her eyes cast down.

"I beg your pardon," he said.

She gave him one upward look, from eyes much dilated; then,
catching her breath, turned away. Ashurst followed. "Megan!"

But she went on; and taking hold of her arm, he turned her gently
round to him. "Stop and speak to me."

"Why do you beg my pardon? It is not to me you should do that."

"Well, then, to Joe."

"How dare he come after me?"

"In love with you, I suppose."

She stamped her foot.

Ashurst uttered a short laugh. "Would you like me to punch his
head?"

She cried out with passion, "You laugh at me—you laugh at us!"

He caught hold of her hands, but she shrank back, till her passionate little face and loose dark hair were caught among the pink
clusters of the apple blossoms. Ashurst raised one of her imprisoned
hands and put his lips to it. He felt how chivalrous he was, and
superior to that clod Joe—just brushing that small, rough hand with
his mouth! Her shrinking ceased suddenly; she seemed to tremble
toward him. A sweet warmth overtook Ashurst from top to toe. This
slim maiden, so simple and fine and pretty, was pleased, then, at the
touch of his lips! And, yielding to a swift impulse, he put his arms
round her, pressed her to him and kissed her forehead. Then he was

frightened—she went so pale, closing her eyes so that the long, dark lashes lay on her pale cheeks; her hands, too, lay inert at her sides. The touch of her breast sent a shiver through him. "Megan!" he sighed out. She knelt beside the tree, he over her.

In the utter silence a blackbird shouted. Then the girl seized his hand, put it to her cheek, her heart, her lips, kissed it passionately, rose and fled away among the mossy trunks of the apple trees, till they hid her from him.

Ashurst sat down on a twisted old tree growing almost along the ground and, throbbing and bewildered, gazed vacantly at the blossoms that had crowned her hair—those pink buds with one white open apple star. What had he done? How had he let himself be thus stampeded by beauty—pity—or—just the spring! He felt curiously happy, all the same; happy and triumphant, with shivers running through his limbs, and a vague alarm. This was the beginning of—what? The midges bit him, the dancing gnats tried to fly into his mouth, and all the spring around him seemed to grow more lovely and alive; the songs of the cuckoos and the blackbirds, the level-slanting sunlight, the apple blossoms that had crowned her head—! He got up from the old trunk and strode out of the orchard, wanting space, an open sky, to get on terms with these new sensations. He made for the moor, and from an ash tree in the hedge a magpie flew out to herald him.

Of man—at any age from five years on—who can say he has never been in love? Ashurst had loved his partners at his dancing class; loved his nursery governess; girls on school holidays; perhaps never been quite out of love, cherishing always some more or less remote admiration. But this was different, not remote at all. Quite a new sensation; terribly delightful, bringing a sense of completed manhood. To be holding in his fingers such a wildflower, to be able to put it to his lips and feel it tremble with delight against them! What intoxication, and—embarrassment! What to do with it—how meet her next time? His first caress had been cool, pitiful; but the next could not be, now that, by her burning little kiss on his hand, by her pressure of it to her heart, he knew that she loved him. Some natures are coarsened by love bestowed on them; others, like Ashurst's, are swayed and drawn, warmed and softened, almost exalted, by what they feel to be a sort of miracle.

And up there among the tors he was racked between the passionate desire to revel in this new sensation of spring fulfilled within him and a vague but very real uneasiness. At one moment he gave himself up completely to his pride at having captured this pretty, trustful, dewy-eyed thing! At the next he thought with factitious solemnity, Yes, my boy! But look out what you're doing! You know what comes of it!

Dusk dropped down without his noticing—dusk on the carved masses of the rocks. And the voice of nature said, "This is a new world for you!" As when a man gets up at four o'clock and goes out into a summer morning, and beasts, birds, trees stare at him and he feels as if all had been made new.

He stayed up there for hours, till it grew cold, then groped his way down the stones and heather roots to the road, back into the lane, and came again past the wild meadow to the orchard. There he struck a match and looked at his watch. Nearly twelve! It was black and unstirring in there now, very different from the lingering, bird-befriended brightness of six hours ago! And suddenly he saw this idyll of his with the eyes of the outer world—had a mental vision of Mrs. Narracombe's snakelike neck turned, her quick dark glance taking it all in, her shrewd face hardening; saw the gipsylike cousins coarsely mocking and distrustful; Joe stolid and furious; only the lame man, Jim, with the suffering eyes, seemed tolerable to his mind. And the village pub!—the gossiping matrons he passed on his walks; and then—his own friends—Robert Garton's smile when he went off that morning ten days ago; so ironical and knowing! Disgusting! For a minute he literally hated this earthly, cynical world to which one belonged, willy-nilly.

The gate where he was leaning grew gray, a sort of shimmer passed before him and spread into the bluish darkness. The moon! He could just see it over the bank behind; red, nearly round—a strange moon! And turning away, he went up the lane, which smelled of the night and cow dung and young leaves.

In the straw yard he could see the dark shapes of cattle, broken by the pale sickles of their horns, like so many thin moons fallen ends up. He unlatched the farm gate stealthily. All was dark in the house. Muffling his footsteps, he gained the porch and, blotted against one of the yew trees, looked up at Megan's window. It was open. Was she sleeping, or lying awake perhaps, disturbed—unhappy at his absence? An owl hooted while he stood there peering up, and the sound seemed to fill the whole night, so quiet was all else, save for the never-ending murmur of the stream running below the orchard. The cuckoos by day, and now the owls—how wonderfully they voiced this troubled ecstasy within him! And suddenly he saw her at her window, looking out. He moved a little from the yew tree and whispered, "Megan!" She drew back, vanished, reappeared, leaning far down. He stole forward on the grass patch, hit his shin against the green-painted chair and held his breath at the sound. The pale blur of her stretched-down arm and face did not stir; he moved the chair and noiselessly mounted it. By stretching up his arm he could just reach. Her hand held the huge key of the front door, and he clasped that burning hand with the cold key in it. He could just see her face, the glint of teeth between her lips, her tumbled hair. She was still dressed—poor child, sitting up for him, no doubt! "Pretty Megan!" Her hot, roughened fingers clung to his; her face had a strange, lost look. To have been able to reach it—even with his hand! The owl hooted, a scent of sweetbriar crept into his nostrils. Then one of the farm dogs barked; her grasp relaxed, she shrank back.

"Good night, Megan!"

"Good night, sir!" She was gone! With a sigh he dropped back to earth and, sitting on that chair, took off his boots. Nothing for it but to creep in and go to bed; yet for a long while he sat unmoving, his feet chilly in the dew, drunk on the memory of her lost, half-smiling face and the clinging grip of her burning fingers pressing the cold key into his hand.

CHAPTER 5

HE AWOKE feeling as if he had eaten heavily overnight, instead of having eaten nothing. And far off, unreal, seemed yesterday's romance! Yet it was a golden morning. Full spring had burst at last—in one night the "goldie-cups," as the little boys called them, seemed to have made the field their own, and from his window he could see apple blossoms covering the orchard as with a rose-and-white quilt. He went down almost dreading to see Megan; and yet, when not she but Mrs. Narracombe brought in his breakfast, he felt vexed and disappointed. The woman's quick eye and snaky neck seemed to have a new alacrity this morning. Had she noticed?

"So you an' the moon went walkin' last night, Mr. Ashurst! Did you have your supper anywheres?"

Ashurst shook his head.

"We kept it for you, but I suppose you was too busy in your brain to think o' such a thing as that?"

Was she mocking him in that voice of hers, which still kept some Welsh crispness against the invading burr of the West Country? If she knew! And at that moment he thought, No, no; I'll clear out. I won't put myself in such a beastly false position.

But after breakfast the longing to see Megan began and increased with every minute, together with fear lest something might have been said to her that had spoiled everything. Sinister that she had not appeared, not given him even a glimpse of her! And the love poem, whose manufacture had been so important and absorbing yesterday afternoon under the apple trees, now seemed so paltry that he tore it up and rolled it into pipe cleaners. What had he known of love till she seized his hand and kissed it! And now—what did he not know?

But to write of it seemed mere insipidity! He went up to his bedroom to get a book, and his heart began to beat violently, for she was in there making the bed. He stood in the doorway watching; and suddenly, with turbulent joy, he saw her stoop and kiss his pillow, just at the hollow made by his head last night. How let her know he had seen that pretty act of devotion? And yet if she heard him stealing away, it would be even worse. She took the pillow up, holding it as if reluctant to shake out the impress of his cheek, dropped it and turned round.

"Megan!"

She put her hands up to her cheeks, but her eyes seemed to look right into him. He had never before realized the depth and purity and touching faithfulness in those dew-bright eyes, and he stammered, "It was sweet of you to wait up for me last night."

She still said nothing, and he stammered on, "I was wandering about on the moor; it was such a jolly night. I—I've just come up for a book."

Then, the kiss he had seen her give the pillow afflicted him with sudden headiness, and he went up to her. Touching her eyes with his lips, he thought with queer excitement, I've done it! Yesterday all was sudden—anyhow; but now—I've done it! The girl let her forehead rest against his lips, which moved downward till they reached hers. That first real lovers' kiss—strange, wonderful, still almost innocent—in which heart did it make the most disturbance?

"Come to the big apple tree tonight after they've gone to bed. Megan—promise!"

She whispered back, "I promise!"

Then, scared of her white face, scared of everything, he let her go and went downstairs again. Yes! He had done it now! Accepted her love, declared his own! He went out to the green chair as devoid of a book as ever; and there he sat staring vacantly before him, triumphant and remorseful, while under his nose and behind his back the work of the farm went on. How long he had been sitting in that curious state of vacancy he had no notion when he saw Joe standing a little behind him to the right. The youth had evidently come from hard work in the fields, and stood shifting his feet, breathing loudly, his face colored like a setting sun, and his arms, below the rolled-up sleeves of his blue shirt, showing the hue and furry sheen of ripe peaches. His red lips were open, his blue eyes with their flaxen lashes stared fixedly at Ashurst, who said ironically, "Well, Joe, anything I can do for you?"

"Yes."

"What, then?"

"You can goo away from yere. Us don' want you."

Ashurst's face, never too humble, assumed its most lordly look. "Very good of you, but, do you know, I prefer the others should speak for themselves."

The youth moved a pace or two nearer, and the scent of his honest heat afflicted Ashurst's nostrils.

"What d'you stay yere for?"

"Because it pleases me."

" 'Twon't please you when I've bashed your head in!"

"Indeed! When would you like to begin that?"

Joe answered only with the loudness of his breathing, but his eyes looked like those of a young and angry bull. Then a sort of spasm seemed to convulse his face. "Megan don' want you."

A rush of jealousy, of contempt and anger with this thick, loud-breathing rustic got the better of Ashurst's self-possession; he jumped up and pushed back his chair. "You can go to the devil!"

And as he said those simple words, he saw Megan in the doorway with a tiny brown spaniel puppy in her arms. She came up to him quickly.

"Its eyes are blue!" she said.

Joe turned away; the back of his neck was literally crimson.

Ashurst put his finger to the mouth of the little brown bullfrog of a creature in her arms. How cosy it looked against her!

"It's fond of you already. Ah! Megan, everything is fond of *you*."

"What was Joe saying to you?"

"Telling me to go away because you didn't want me here."

She stamped her foot; then looked up at Ashurst. At that adoring look he felt his nerves quiver, just as if he had seen a moth scorching its wings.

"Tonight!" he said. "Don't forget!"

"No." And smothering her face against the puppy's little fat, brown body, she slipped back into the house.

Ashurst wandered down the lane. At the gate of the wild meadow he came on the lame man and his cows.

"Beautiful day, Jim!"

"Ah! 'Tis brave weather for the grass. The ashes be later than th' oaks this year."

Ashurst said idly, "Where were you standing when you saw the gipsy bogle, Jim?"

"It might be under that big apple tree, as you might say."

"And you really do think it was there?"

The lame man answered cautiously, "I shouldn't like to say rightly that '*twas* there. 'Twas in my mind as 'twas there."

"What do you make of it?"

The lame man lowered his voice. "They do say old master, Mist' Narracombe, come o' gipsy stock. But that's tellin'. They'm a wonderful people, you know, for claimin' their own. Maybe they knew 'e was goin', and sent this feller along for company. That's what I've a-thought about it."

"What was he like?"

" 'E 'ad 'air all over 'is face, an' goin' like this, he was, same as if 'e 'ad a viddle. They say there's no such thing as bogles, but I've a-seen the 'air on this dog standin' up of a dark night, when I couldn' see nothin' meself."

"Was there a moon?"

"Yes, very near full, but 'twas on'y just risen, goldlike be'ind them trees."

"And you think a ghost means trouble, do you?"

The lame man pushed his hat up; his ascending eyes looked at Ashurst more earnestly than ever.

" 'Tis not for me to say that—but 'tis they bein' so unrestin'-like. There's things us don' understand, that's for sure. There's people that see things, too, an' others that don't never see nothin'. Now, our Joe—you might put anything under 'is eyes an' 'e'd never see it; and them other boys, too, they'm good fellers. But you take an' put our Megan where there's suthin', she'll see it, an' more too, or I'm mistaken."

"She's sensitive, that's why."

"What's that?"

"I mean, she feels everything."

"Ah! She'm very lovin'-'earted."

Ashurst, who felt color coming into his cheeks, held out his tobacco pouch. "Have a fill, Jim?"

"Thank 'ee, sir. She'm one in an 'underd, I think."

"I expect so," said Ashurst shortly and, folding up his pouch, walked on.

"Lovin'-'earted!" Yes! And what was he doing? What were his intentions—as they say—toward this loving-hearted girl? The thought dogged him, wandering through fields bright with buttercups, where the red calves were feeding and the swallows flying high.

Yes, the oaks were before the ashes, brown-gold already; every tree in different stage and hue. The cuckoos and a thousand birds were singing; the little streams were very bright. The ancients believed in a golden age, in the garden of the Hesperides! . . . A queen wasp settled on his sleeve. Each queen wasp killed meant two thousand fewer wasps to thieve the apples that would grow from those blossoms in the orchard; but who, with love in his heart, could kill anything on a day like this? He entered a field where a young red bull was feeding. It seemed to Ashurst that he looked like Joe. But the young bull took no notice of this visitor, a little drunk himself, perhaps, on the singing and the glamour of the golden pasture under his short legs.

Ashurst crossed unchallenged to the hillside above the stream. From that slope a tor mounted to its crown of rocks. The ground there was covered with a mist of bluebells, and nearly a score of crab-apple trees were in full bloom. He threw himself down on the grass. The change from the buttercup glory and oak-goldened glamour of the fields to this ethereal beauty under the gray tor filled him with a sort of wonder; nothing the same, save the sound of running water and the songs of the cuckoos. He lay there a long time, watching the sunlight wheel till the crab-apple trees threw shadows over the bluebells, his only companions a few wild bees. He was not quite sane, thinking of that morning's kiss, and of tonight under the apple tree. In such a spot as this, surely fauns and dryads lived; nymphs, white as the crab-apple blossom, retired within those trees; fauns, brown as the dead bracken, with pointed ears, lay in wait for them.

The cuckoos were still calling when he woke, there was the sound of running water; but the sun had couched behind the tor, the hillside was cool and some rabbits had come out. Tonight! he thought. Just as from the earth everything was pushing up, unfolding under the soft insistent fingers of an unseen hand, so were his heart and senses being pushed, unfolded. He got up and broke off a spray from a crab-apple tree. The buds were like Megan—shell-like, rose-pink, wild and fresh; and so, too, the opening flowers, white and wild and touching. He put the spray into his coat. And all the rush of the spring within him escaped in a triumphant sigh. But the rabbits scurried away.

CHAPTER 6

IT WAS NEARLY eleven that night when Ashurst put down the pocket *Odyssey*, which for half an hour he had held in his hands without reading, and slipped through the yard down to the orchard. The moon had just risen, very golden, over the hill, and like a bright, powerful, watching spirit peered through the bars of an ash tree's half-naked boughs.

In among the apple trees it was still dark, and he stood making sure of his direction, feeling the rough grass with his feet. A black mass close behind him stirred with a heavy grunting sound, and three large pigs settled down again close to each other, under the wall. He listened. There was no wind, but the stream's burbling, whispering chuckle had gained twice its daytime strength. One bird, he could not tell what, cried "Pip—pip. Pip—pip," with perfect monotony; he could hear a nightjar spinning very far off; an owl hooting. Ashurst moved a step or two, and again halted, aware of a dim living whiteness all round his head.

On the dark unstirring trees innumerable flowers and buds all soft and blurred were being bewitched to life by the creeping moonlight. He had the oddest feeling of actual companionship, as if a million white moths or spirits had floated in and settled between dark sky and darker ground, and were opening and shutting their wings on a level with his eyes. In the bewildering, still, scentless beauty of that moment he almost forgot why he had come to the orchard. The glamour that had clothed the earth all day had not gone now that night had fallen, but only changed into this new form. He moved on through the thicket of stems and boughs covered with that live powdery whiteness till he reached the big apple tree. No mistaking that tree, even in the dark, nearly twice the height and size of any other, and leaning out toward the open meadows and the stream. Under the thick branches he stood still again, to listen. The same sounds exactly, and a faint grunting from the sleepy pigs. He put his hands on the dry, almost warm tree trunk, whose rough mossy surface gave forth a peaty scent at his touch. Would she come— would she? And among these quivering, haunted, moon-witched trees he was seized with doubts of everything! All was unearthly here, fit for no earthly lovers; fit only for god and goddess, faun and nymph—not for him and this little country girl. Would it not be almost a relief if she did not come? But all the time he was listening. And still that unknown bird went "Pip—pip. Pip—pip," and there rose the busy chatter of the little trout stream, whereon the moon was flinging glances through the bars of her tree-prison. The blossoms on a level with his eyes seemed to grow more living every moment, seemed with their mysterious white beauty more and more a part of his suspense. He plucked a fragment and held it close—three blossoms. Sacrilege to pluck fruit-tree blossoms—soft, sacred, young blossoms—and throw them away! Then suddenly he heard the gate close, the pigs stirring again and grunting; and leaning against the trunk, he pressed his hands to its mossy sides behind him and held his breath.

She might have been a spirit threading between the trees, for all the noise she made! Then he saw her quite close—her dark form part of a little tree, her white face part of its blossom; so still, and peering toward him. He whispered, "Megan!" and held out his hands. She ran forward, straight to his breast. When he felt her heart beating against him, Ashurst knew to the full the sensations of chivalry and passion. Because she was not of his world, because she was so simple and young and adoring and defenseless, how could he be other than her protector, in the dark! Because she was all simple nature and beauty, as much a part of this spring night as were the living blossoms, how should he not take all that she would give him—how not fulfill the spring in her heart and his! And torn between·these two emotions, he clasped her close and kissed her hair.

How long they stood there without speaking he knew not. The stream went on chattering, the owls hooting, the moon kept stealing up and growing whiter; the blossoms all round them and above brightened in suspense of living beauty. Their lips had sought each other's, and they did not speak. The moment speech began, all would be unreal! Spring has no speech, nothing but rustling and whispering. Spring has so much more than speech in its unfolding flowers and leaves, and in the coursing of its streams, and in its sweet restless seeking! And sometimes spring will come alive, and, like a mysterious presence, stand, encircling lovers with its arms, laying on them the fingers of enchantment, so that, standing lips to lips, they forget everything but just a kiss. While her heart beat against him and her lips quivered on his, Ashurst felt nothing but simple rapture—destiny meant her for his arms, love could not be flouted! But when their lips parted for breath, division began again at once. Only, passion now was so much the stronger, and he sighed, "Oh! Megan! Why did you come?"

She looked up, hurt, amazed. "Sir, you asked me to."

"Don't call me 'sir,' my pretty sweet."

"What should I be callin' you?"

"Frank."

"I could not. Oh, no!"

"But you love me—don't you?"

"I could not help lovin' you. I want to be with you—that's all."

"All!"

So faint that he hardly heard, she whispered, "I shall die if I can't be with you."

Ashurst took a mighty breath. "Come and be with me, then!"

"Oh!"

Intoxicated by the awe and rapture in that "oh!" he went on, whispering, "We'll go to London. I'll show you the world. And I *will* take care of you, I promise, Megan. I'll never be a brute to you!"

"If I can be with you—that is all."

He stroked her hair and whispered on. "Tomorrow I'll go to Torquay and get some money, and get you some clothes that won't be noticed, and then we'll steal away. And when we get to London, soon perhaps, if you love me well enough, we'll be married."

He could feel her hair quiver with the shake of her head.

"Oh, no! I could not. I only want to be with you!"

Drunk on his own chivalry, Ashurst went on murmuring. "It's I who am not good enough for you. Oh! Megan, when did you begin to love me?"

"When I saw you in the road, and you looked at me. The first night I loved you; but I never thought you would want me."

She slipped down suddenly to her knees, trying to kiss his feet.

A shiver of horror went through Ashurst; he lifted her up bodily and held her fast—too upset to speak.

She whispered, "Why won't you let me?"

"It's I who will kiss your feet!"

Her smile brought tears into his eyes. The whiteness of her moonlit face so close to his, the faint pink of her opened lips, had the living unearthly beauty of the apple blossoms.

And then, suddenly, her eyes widened and stared past him painfully; she writhed out of his arms and whispered, "Look!"

Ashurst saw nothing but the brightened stream, the furze faintly gilded, the beech trees glistening, and behind them all the wide loom of the moonlit hill. Behind him came her frozen whisper: "The gipsy bogle!"

"Where?"

"There—by the stone—under the trees!"

Exasperated, he leapt the stream and strode toward the beech clump. Prank of the moonlight! Nothing! In and out of the boulders and thorn trees, muttering and cursing, yet with a kind of terror, he rushed and stumbled. Absurd! Silly! Then he went back to the apple tree. But she was gone; he could hear a rustle, the sound of a gate closing. Instead of her, only this old apple tree! He flung his arms round the trunk. What a substitute for her soft body; the rough moss against his face—what a substitute for her soft cheek; only the scent, as of the woods, a little the same! And above him, and around, the blossoms, more living, more moonlit than ever, seemed to glow and breathe.

CHAPTER 7

DESCENDING FROM the train at Torquay station, Ashurst wandered uncertainly along the seafront, for he did not know this particular queen of English seaside resorts. Having little sense of what he had on, he was quite unconscious of being remarkable among its inhabitants, and strode along in his rough Norfolk jacket, dusty boots and battered hat without observing that people gazed at him rather blankly. He was seeking a branch of his London bank, and having found one, found also the first obstacle to his mood. Did he know anyone in Torquay? No. In that case, if he would wire to his bank in London, they would be happy to oblige him on receipt of the reply. That suspicious breath from the matter-of-fact world somewhat tarnished the brightness of his visions. But he sent the telegram.

Nearly opposite to the post office he saw a shop full of ladies' garments, and he examined the window with strange sensations. To have to undertake the clothing of his rustic love was more than a little disturbing. He went in. A young woman came forward; she had blue eyes and a faintly puzzled forehead. Ashurst stared at her in silence.

"Yes, sir?"

"I want a dress for a young lady."

The young woman smiled. Ashurst frowned—the peculiarity of his request struck him with sudden force.

The young woman added hastily, "What style would you like—something modish?"

"No. Simple."

"What figure would the young lady be?"

"I don't know; about two inches shorter than you, I should say."

"Could you give me her waist measurement?"

Megan's waist!

"Oh! Anything usual!"

"Quite!"

While she was gone he stood disconsolately eyeing the models in the window, and suddenly it seemed to him incredible that Megan—his Megan—could ever be dressed save in the rough tweed skirt, coarse blouse and tam-o'-shanter cap he was wont to see her in. The young woman had come back with several dresses in her arms, and Ashurst eyed her holding them against her own modish figure. There was one whose color he liked, a dove gray, but to imagine Megan clothed in it was beyond him. The young woman went away and brought some more. But on Ashurst there had now come a feeling of paralysis. How could he choose? She would want a hat too, and shoes and gloves; and suppose when he had got them all, they commonized her, as Sunday clothes always commonized village folk! Why should she not travel as she was? Ah? But conspicuousness would matter; this was a serious elopement. And, staring at the young woman, he thought, I wonder if she guesses and thinks me a blackguard?

"Do you mind putting aside that gray one for me?" he said desperately at last. "I can't decide now; I'll come in again this afternoon."

The young woman sighed. "Oh! Certainly. It's a very tasteful costume. I don't think you'll get anything that will suit your purpose better."

"I expect not," Ashurst murmured and went out.

Freed again from the suspicious matter-of-factness of the world, he took a long deep breath and went back to visions. In fancy he saw the trustful, pretty creature who was going to join her life to his; saw himself and her stealing forth at night, walking over the moor under the moon, he with his arm round her and carrying her new garments, till, in some far-off wood, when dawn was coming, she would slip off her old things and put on these, and an early train at a distant station would bear them away on their honeymoon journey, till London swallowed them up and the dreams of love came true.

"Frank Ashurst! Haven't seen you since Rugby, old chap!"

Ashurst's frown dissolved; the face, close to his own, was blue-eyed, suffused with sun—one of those faces where sun from within and without join in a sort of luster. And he answered, "Phil Halliday, by Jove!"

"What are you doing here?"

"Oh, nothing. Just looking round, and getting some money. I'm staying on the moor."

"Are you lunching anywhere? Come and lunch with us; I'm here with my young sisters. They've had measles."

Hooked in by that friendly arm, Ashurst went along, up a hill, down a hill, away out of the town, while the voice of Halliday, redolent of optimism as his face was of sun, explained how "in this moldy place the only decent things are the swimming and boating," and so on, till presently they came to a crescent of houses a little above and back from the sea, and into the center one—a hotel—made their way.

"Come up to my room and have a wash. Lunch'll be ready in a jiffy."

Ashurst contemplated his visage in a looking glass. After his farmhouse bedroom, the comb and one spare shirt regime of the last fortnight, this room littered with clothes and brushes seemed incredibly luxurious; and he thought, Queer—one doesn't realize— But what—he did not quite know.

When he followed Halliday into the sitting room for lunch, three faces, very fair and blue-eyed, were turned suddenly at the words: "This is Frank Ashurst—my young sisters."

Two were indeed young, about eleven and ten. The third was perhaps seventeen, tall and fair-haired too, with pink-and-white cheeks just touched by the sun, and eyebrows, rather darker than the hair, running a little upward from her nose to their outer points. The voices of all three were like Halliday's, high and cheerful; they stood up straight, shook hands with a quick movement, looked at Ashurst critically, away again at once, and began to talk of what they were going to do in the afternoon. A regular Diana and attendant nymphs! After the farm this crisp, slangy, eager talk, this cool, clean, offhand refinement, was queer at first, and then so natural that what he had come from became suddenly remote. The names of the two little ones seemed to be Sabina and Freda; of the eldest, Stella.

Presently the one called Sabina turned to him and said, "I say, will you come shrimping with us? It's awful fun!"

Surprised by this unexpected friendliness, Ashurst murmured, "I'm afraid I've got to get back this afternoon."

"Oh!"

"Can't you put it off?"

Ashurst turned to the new speaker, Stella, shook his head and smiled. She was very pretty!

Sabina said regretfully, "You might!" Then the talk switched off to caves and swimming.

"Can you swim far?"

"About two miles."

"Oh!"

"I say!"

"How jolly!"

The three pairs of blue eyes, fixed on him, made him conscious of his new importance. The sensation was agreeable. Halliday said, "I say, you simply must stop and have a swim. You'd better stay the night."

"Yes, do!"

But again Ashurst smiled and shook his head. Then suddenly he found himself being quizzed about his physical achievements. He had rowed—it seemed—with his college crew, played on his college football team, won his college mile; and he rose from table a sort of hero. The two little girls insisted that he must see "their" cave, and they set forth chattering like magpies, Ashurst between them, Stella and her brother a little behind. In the cave, damp and darkish like any other cave, the great feature was a pool with the possibility of creatures that might be caught and put into bottles. Sabina and Freda, who wore no stockings on their shapely brown legs, exhorted Ashurst to join them in the middle of it and help sieve the water. He too was soon bootless and sockless. Time goes fast for one who has a sense of beauty when there are pretty children in a pool and a young Diana on the edge to receive with wonder anything you can catch! Ashurst never had much sense of time. It was a shock when, pulling out his watch, he saw it was well past three. No cashing his check

today—the bank would be closed before he could get there. Watch
ing his expression, the little girls cried out at once, "Hurrah! Now
you'll have to stay!"

Ashurst did not answer. He was seeing again Megan's face when at
breakfast he had whispered, "I'm going to Torquay, darling, to get
everything; I shall be back this evening. If it's fine, we can go tonight.
Be ready." He was seeing again how she quivered and hung on his
words. What would she think? Then he pulled himself together,
conscious suddenly of the calm scrutiny of this other young girl, so
tall and fair and Diana-like, at the edge of the pool, of her wondering
blue eyes under those brows that slanted up a little. If they knew
what was in his mind—if they knew that this very night he had
meant—! Well, there would be sounds of politely concealed shock,
and he would be alone in the cave. And with a curious mixture of
anger, chagrin and shame, he put his watch back into his pocket and
said abruptly, "Yes; I'm dished for today."

"Hurrah! Now you can swim with us."

It was impossible not to succumb a little to the contentment of
these pretty children, to the smile on Stella's lips, to Halliday's "Ripping, old chap! I can lend you things for the night!" But again a
spasm of longing and remorse throbbed through Ashurst, and he
said moodily, "I must send a wire!"

The attractions of the pool palling, they went back to the hotel.
Ashurst sent his wire, addressing it to Mrs. Narracombe: "Sorry, de-
tained for the night, back tomorrow." Surely Megan would understand
that he had too much to do; and his heart grew lighter. It was a lovely
afternoon, warm, the sea calm and blue, and swimming his great
passion; the favor of these pretty children flattered him, the pleasure
of looking at them, at Stella, at Halliday's sunny face; the slight
unreality, yet extreme naturalness of it all—as of a last peep at
normality before he took this plunge with Megan! He got his borrowed bathing suit, and they all set forth. Halliday and he undressed
behind one rock, the three girls behind another. He was first into the
sea, and at once swam out with the bravado of justifying his self-given
reputation. When he turned he could see Halliday swimming along the
shore, and the girls flopping and dipping and riding the little waves in
the way he was accustomed to despise but now thought pretty and
sensible, since it gave him the distinction of being the only deep-

water fish. But drawing near, he wondered if they would like him, a stranger, to come into their splashing group; he felt shy, approaching that slim nymph. Then Sabina summoned him to teach her to float, and between them the little girls kept him so busy that he had no time even to notice whether Stella was accustomed to his presence, till suddenly he heard a startled sound from her. She was standing submerged to the waist, leaning a little forward, her slim white arms stretched out and pointing, her wet face puckered by the sun and an expression of fear.

"Look at Phil! Is he all right? Oh, look!"

Ashurst saw at once that Phil was not all right. He was splashing and struggling out of his depth, perhaps a hundred yards away; suddenly he gave a cry, threw up his arms and went down. Ashurst saw the girl launch herself toward him, and crying out, "Go back, Stella! Go back!" he dashed out. He had never swum so fast, and reached Halliday just as he was coming up a second time. It was a case of cramp, but to get him in was not difficult, for he did not struggle. The girl, who had stopped where Ashurst told her to, helped as soon as he was in her depth, and once on the beach they sat down one on each side of him to rub his limbs while the little ones stood by with scared faces. Halliday was soon smiling. It was—he said—rotten of him, absolutely rotten! If Frank would give him an arm, he could get to his clothes all right. Ashurst gave him the arm, and as he did so caught sight of Stella's face, wet and flushed and tearful, all broken up out of its calm; and he thought, I called her Stella! Wonder if she minded?

While they were dressing, Halliday said quietly, "You saved my life, old chap!"

"Rot!"

Clothed, but not quite in their right minds, they went up all together to the hotel and sat down to tea, except Halliday, who was lying down in his room. After some slices of bread and jam, Sabina said, "I say, you know, you *are* a brick!"

And Freda chimed in, "Rather!"

Ashurst saw Stella looking down; he got up in confusion and went to the window. From there he heard Sabina mutter, "I say, let's swear blood bond. Where's your knife, Freda?" and out of the corner of his eye he could see each of them solemnly prick herself, squeeze out a drop of blood and dabble a bit on paper. He turned and made for the door.

"Don't be a weasel! Come back!" His arms were seized; imprisoned between the little girls he was brought back to the table. On it lay a piece of paper with an effigy drawn in blood, and the three names Stella Halliday, Sabina Halliday, Freda Halliday—also in blood, running toward it like the rays of a star. Sabina said, "That's you. We shall have to kiss you, you know."

And Freda echoed, "Oh! Yes!"

Before Ashurst could escape, some wettish hair dangled against his face, something like a bite descended on his nose, he felt his left arm pinched and other teeth softly searching his cheek. Then he was released, and Freda said, "Now, Stella."

Ashurst, red and rigid, looked across the table at a red and rigid Stella. Sabina giggled; Freda cried, "Buck up—it spoils everything!"

A queer, ashamed eagerness shot through Ashurst. Then he said quietly, "Shut up, you little demons!"

Again Sabina giggled. "Well, then, she can kiss her hand, and you can put it against your nose. It *is* to one side!"

To his amazement the girl did kiss her hand and stretch it out. Solemnly he took that cool, slim hand and laid it to his cheek. The two little girls broke into clapping, and Freda said, "Now, we shall have to save your life at any time; that's settled. Can I have another cup, Stella, not so beastly weak?"

Tea was resumed, and Ashurst, folding up the paper, put it in his pocket. The talk turned on the advantages of measles—tangerines, honey on a spoon, no lessons and so forth. Ashurst listened, silent, exchanging friendly looks with Stella, whose face was again of its normal sun-touched pink and white. It was soothing to be so taken to the heart of this jolly family, fascinating to watch their faces. And after tea, while the two little girls pressed seaweed, he talked to Stella on the window seat and looked at her watercolor sketches. The whole thing was like a pleasurable dream; time hung up, importance and reality suspended. Tomorrow he would go back to Megan, with nothing of all this left save the paper with the blood of these children in his pocket. Children! Stella was not quite that—as old as Megan! Her talk—quick, rather hard and shy, yet friendly—seemed to flourish on his silences, and about her there was something cool and virginal—a maiden in a bower. At dinner, to which Halliday, who had swallowed too much seawater, did not come, Sabina said, "I'm going to call you Frank."

Freda echoed, "Frank, Frank, Franky."

Ashurst grinned and bowed.

"Every time Stella calls you Mr. Ashurst, she's got to pay a forfeit. It's ridiculous."

Ashurst looked at Stella, who grew slowly red. Sabina giggled; Freda cried, "Yah!"

Ashurst reached out to right and left and grasped some fair hair in each hand. "Look here," he said, "you two! Leave Stella alone, or I'll tie you together!"

Freda gurgled, "Ouch! You *are* a beast!"

Sabina murmured cautiously, *"You* call *her* Stella, you see!"

"Why shouldn't I? It's a jolly name!"

"All right; we give you leave to!"

Ashurst released the hair. Stella! What would she call him—after this? But she called him nothing, till at bedtime he said deliberately, "Good night, Stella!"

"Good night, Mr.— Good night, Frank! It *was* jolly of you, you know!"

"Oh—that! Bosh!"

Her quick, straight handshake tightened suddenly, and as suddenly became slack.

Ashurst stood motionless in the empty sitting room. Only last night, under the apple tree and the living blossoms, he had held Megan to him, kissing her eyes and lips. And he gasped, swept by that rush of remembrance. Tonight it should have begun—his life with Megan, who only wanted to be with him! And now, twenty-four hours and more must pass, because—of not looking at his watch! Why had he made friends with this family of innocents just when he was saying good-bye to innocence and all the rest of it? But I mean to marry her, he thought; I told her so!

He took a candle, lighted it and went to his bedroom, which was next to Halliday's. His friend's voice called as he was passing, "Is that you, old chap? I say, come in."

He was sitting up in bed, smoking a pipe and reading.

"Sit down a bit."

Ashurst sat down by the open window.

"I've been thinking about this afternoon, you know," said Halliday rather suddenly. "They say you go through all your past. I didn't. I suppose I wasn't far enough gone."

"What did you think of?"

Halliday was silent for a little, then said quietly, "Well, I did think of one thing—rather odd—of a girl at Cambridge that I might have—you know; I was glad I hadn't got her on my mind. Anyhow, old chap, I owe it to you that I'm here; I should have been in the big dark by now. No more bed, no more anything. I say, what d'you suppose happens to us?"

Ashurst murmured, "Go out like flames, I expect."

"Phew!"

"We may flicker and cling about a bit, perhaps."

"H'm! I think that's rather gloomy. I say, I hope my young sisters have been decent to you?"

"Awfully decent."

Halliday put his pipe down, crossed his hands behind his neck and turned his face toward the window. "They're not bad kids!" he said.

Watching his friend lying there with that smile and the candlelight on his face, Ashurst shuddered. Quite true! He might have been lying there with no smile, with all that sunny look gone out forever! He might not have been lying there at all but at the bottom of the sea, waiting for resurrection on the—ninth day, was it? And that smile of Halliday's seemed to him suddenly something wonderful, as if in it were all the difference between life and death—the little flame—the all! He got up and said softly, "Well, you ought to sleep, I expect. Shall I blow out?"

Halliday caught his hand. "I can't say it, you know; but it must be rotten to be dead. Good night, old boy!"

Stirred and moved, Ashurst squeezed his hand and went downstairs. The hall door was still open, and he passed out onto the lawn. The stars were bright, and by their light the lilacs had that mysterious color of flowers by night. Ashurst pressed his face against a spray; and before his closed eyes Megan started up, with the tiny spaniel pup against her breast. "I thought of a girl that I might have—you know; I was glad I hadn't got her on my mind!" He jerked his head away from the lilacs and began pacing up and down over the grass.

He was with her again under the living, breathing whiteness of the blossoms, the stream chattering by, the moon glinting steel-blue on the swimming pool; back in the rapture of his kisses on her upturned face of innocence and humble passion, back in the suspense and beauty of that pagan night.

He stood still once more in the shadow of the lilacs. A window of the hotel, high up, was lighted; he saw a shadow move across the blind. And the most queer sensations stirred within him, a sort of churning and twining and turning of a single emotion on itself, as though spring and love, bewildered and confused, seeking the way, were baffled. This girl, who had called him Frank, whose hand had given his that sudden little clutch, this girl so cool and pure—what would *she* think of such wild, unlawful loving? He sank down on the grass, sat there cross-legged with his back to the house, motionless. Was he really going to break through innocence and steal? Sniff the scent out of a wildflower and—perhaps—throw it away? "Of a girl at Cambridge that I might have—you know!" What am I going to do? he thought. Perhaps Megan was at her window, looking out at the blossoms, thinking of him! Poor little Megan! Why not? he thought. I love her! But do I—really love her? Or do I only want her because she is so pretty, and loves me? What am I going to do?

The stars winked; and Ashurst gazed out before him at the dark sea, as if spellbound. He got up at last, cramped and rather chilly. There was no longer light in any window. And he went in to bed.

CHAPTER 8

OUT OF a deep and dreamless sleep he was awakened by the sound of thumping on the door. A shrill voice called, "Hi! Breakfast's ready."

He jumped up. Where was he—? Ah!

He found them already eating marmalade, and sat down in the empty place between Stella and Sabina, who, after watching him a little, said, "I say, do buck up; we're going to start at half-past nine."

"We're going to Berry Head, old chap; you *must* come!"

Ashurst thought, Come! Impossible. I shall be getting things and going back. He looked at Stella. She said quickly, "Do come!"

Sabina chimed in, "It'll be no fun without you."

Freda got up and stood behind his chair. "You've got to come, or else I'll pull your hair!"

Ashurst thought, Well—one day more—to think it over! One day more! And he said, "All right! You needn't tweak my mane!"

"Hurrah!"

At the station he wrote a second telegram to the farm, and then—tore it up; he could not have explained why. From Brixham they drove in a very little wagonette. There, squeezed between Sabina and Freda, with his knees touching Stella's, the gloom he was feeling gave way to frolic. In this one day more to think it over, he did not want to think! They ran races, wrestled, paddled—for today nobody wanted to swim—they sang rounds, played games and ate all they had brought. The little girls fell asleep against him on the way back, and his knees still touched Stella's in the narrow wagonette. It seemed incredible that thirty hours ago he had never set eyes on any of those three flaxen heads. In the train he talked to Stella of poetry, discovering her favorites, and telling her his own with a pleasing sense of superiority; till suddenly she said, rather low, "Phil says you don't believe in a future life, Frank. I think that's dreadful."

Disconcerted, Ashurst muttered, "I don't either believe or not believe—I simply don't know."

She said quickly, "I couldn't bear that. What would be the use of living?"

Watching the frown of those pretty oblique brows, Ashurst answered, "I don't believe in believing things because one wants to."

"But why should one *wish* to live again, if one isn't going to?"

And she looked full at him.

He did not want to hurt her, but an itch to dominate pushed him on to say, "While one's alive, one naturally wants to go on living forever; that's part of being alive. But it probably isn't anything more."

"Don't you believe in the Bible at all, then?"

Ashurst thought, Now I shall really hurt her! "I believe in the Sermon on the Mount, because it's beautiful and good for all time."

"But don't you believe Christ was divine?"

He shook his head.

She turned her face quickly to the window, and there sprang into his mind Megan's prayer, repeated by little Nick: "God bless us all, an' Mr. Ashes!" Who else would ever say a prayer for him except Megan, who at this moment must be waiting—waiting to see him come down the lane? And he thought suddenly, What a scoundrel I am!

All that evening this thought kept coming back; but, as is not unusual, each time with less poignancy, till it seemed almost a matter of course to be a scoundrel. And—strange!—he did not know whether he was a scoundrel if he meant to go back to Megan, or if he did not mean to go back to her.

They played cards till the children were sent off to bed; then Stella went to the piano. From over on the window seat, where it was nearly dark, Ashurst watched her fair head on the long white neck bending to the movement of her hands. She played fluently, without much expression; but what a picture she made—the faint golden radiance, a sort of angelic atmosphere hovering about her! Who could have passionate thoughts or wild desires in the presence of that swaying white-clothed girl with the seraphic head? She played a thing of Schumann's called "Warum?" Then Halliday brought out a flute, and the spell was broken. After this they made Ashurst sing, Stella playing him accompaniments from a book of Schumann songs, till two small figures clad in blue dressing gowns crept in and tried to conceal themselves beneath the piano. The evening broke up in confusion and what Sabina called "a splendid rag."

That night Ashurst hardly slept at all. He was thinking, tossing and turning. The intense domestic intimacy of these last two days, the strength of this Halliday atmosphere, seemed to make the farm and Megan—even Megan—seem unreal. Had he really promised to take her away to live with him? He must have been bewitched by the spring, the night, the apple blossoms! The notion that he was going to make her his mistress—that simple child not yet eighteen—now filled him with a sort of horror. He muttered to himself, "It's awful what I've done—awful!" And the sound of Schumann's music throbbed and mingled with his fevered thoughts, and he saw again Stella's cool, white, fair-haired figure, the angelic radiance about her. I must have been—I must be—mad! he thought. What came over me? Poor little Megan! "God bless us all, an' Mr. Ashes!" "I want to be with you—only to be with you!" And burying his face in his pillow, he smothered down a fit of sobbing. Not to go back was awful! To go back—more awful still!

Emotion, when you are young and give real vent to it, loses its power of torture. And he fell asleep, thinking, What was it—a few kisses—all forgotten in a month!

Next morning he got his check cashed, but avoided the shop of the dove-gray dress like the plague; and, instead, bought himself some necessaries. He spent the whole day in a queer mood, cherishing a kind of sullenness against himself. Instead of the hankering of the last two days, he felt nothing but a blank—all passionate longing gone, as if quenched in that outburst of tears. After tea Stella put a book down beside him and said shyly, "Have you read that, Frank?"

It was Farrar's *Life of Christ*. Ashurst smiled. Her anxiety about his beliefs seemed to him comic but touching. Infectious, too, perhaps, for he began to have an itch to justify himself, if not to convert her. And in the evening, when the children and Halliday were mending their shrimping nets, he said, "At the back of orthodox religion, there's always the idea of reward—what you can get for being good; a kind of begging for favors. I think it all starts in fear."

She was sitting on the sofa making reef knots with a bit of string. She looked up quickly. "I think it's much deeper than that."

Ashurst felt again that wish to dominate.

"You think so," he said; "but wanting the quid pro quo is about the deepest thing in all of us! It's jolly hard to get to the bottom of it!"

She wrinkled her brows in a puzzled frown. "I don't think I understand."

He went on obstinately. "Well, think, and see if the most religious people aren't those who feel that this life doesn't give them all they want. I believe in being good because to be good is good in itself."

"Then you do believe in being good?"

How pretty she looked now—it was easy to be good with her! And he nodded and said, "I say, show me how to make that knot!"

With her fingers touching his in maneuvering the bit of string, he felt soothed and happy. And when he went to bed he willfully kept his thoughts on her, wrapping himself in her fair, cool, sisterly radiance.

Next day he found they had arranged to go by train to Totnes and picnic at Berry Pomeroy Castle. He took his place in the landau beside Halliday, back to the horses. And then, along the seafront, nearly at the turning to the railway station, his heart almost leaped into his mouth. Megan—Megan herself!—was walking on the far pathway, in her old skirt and jacket and tam-o'-shanter, looking up into the faces of the passersby. Instinctively he threw his hand up for cover, then made a feint of clearing dust out of his eyes; but between his fingers he could see her still, moving, not with her free country step, but wavering, lost-looking, pitiful—like some little dog that has lost its master and does not know whether to run on, to run back— where to run. How had she come here? What excuse had she found to get away? But with every turn of the wheels bearing him away from her, his heart revolted and cried to him to stop them, to get out and go to her! When the landau turned the corner to the station he could stand it no more and, opening the carriage door, muttered, "I've forgotten something! Go on—don't wait for me! I'll join you at the castle by the next train!" He jumped, stumbled, spun round, recovered his balance and walked forward while the carriage with the astonished Hallidays rolled on.

From the corner he could only just see Megan, a long way ahead now. He ran a few steps, checked himself and dropped into a walk. With each step nearer to her, farther from the Hallidays, he walked more and more slowly. How did it alter anything—this sight of her? How make the going to her, and that which must come of it, less ugly? For there was no hiding it—since he had met the Hallidays he had become gradually sure that he would not marry Megan. It would only be a wild love-time, a troubled, remorseful, difficult time—and then—well, then he would get tired, just because she gave him everything, was so simple and so trustful, so dewy. And dew—wears off! The little spot of faded color, her tam-o'-shanter, wavered on far in front of him; she was looking up into every face, and at the house windows. Had any man ever such a cruel moment to go through? Whatever he did, he felt he would be a beast. And he uttered a groan that made a nursemaid turn and stare. He saw Megan stop and lean against the seawall, looking at the sea; and he too stopped. Quite likely she had never seen the sea before, and even in her distress could not resist that sight. Yes—she's seen nothing, he thought; every- thing's before her. And just for a few weeks' passion, I shall be cutting her life to ribbons. I'd better go and hang myself rather than do it! And suddenly he seemed to see Stella's calm eyes looking into his, the wave of fluffy hair on her forehead stirred by the wind. Ah! It would be

madness, would mean giving up all that he respected, and his own self-respect. He turned and walked quickly back toward the station.

But the memory of that poor, bewildered little figure, those anxious eyes searching the passersby, smote him too hard again, and once more he turned toward the sea. The cap was no longer visible; that little spot of color had vanished in the stream of noon promenaders. And impelled by the passion of longing, the dearth that comes on one when life seems to be whirling something out of reach, he hurried forward.

She was nowhere to be seen; for half an hour he looked for her; then on the beach flung himself face downward in the sand. To find her again he knew he had only to go to the station and wait till she returned from her fruitless quest to take her train home; or to take the train himself and go back to the farm, so that she found him there when she returned. But he lay inert in the sand, among the indifferent groups of children with their spades and buckets. Pity at her little figure wandering, seeking, was well-nigh merged in the spring-running of his blood; for it was all wild feeling now—the chivalrous part, what there had been of it, was gone. He wanted her again, wanted her kisses, her soft body, her abandonment, all her quick, warm, pagan emotion; wanted the wonderful feeling of that night under the moonlit apple boughs; wanted it all with a horrible intensity, as the faun wants the nymph. The quick chatter of the little bright trout stream, the dazzle of the buttercups, the rocks of the old "wild men"; the calling of the cuckoos, the hooting of the owls; and the red moon peeping out of the velvet dark at the living whiteness of the blossoms; and her face just out of reach at the window, lost in its love-look; and her heart against his, her lips answering his, under the apple tree—all this besieged him. Yet he lay inert. What was it that struggled against pity and this feverish longing, and kept him there paralyzed in the warm sand? Three flaxen heads—a fair face with friendly blue-gray eyes, a slim hand pressing his, a quick voice speaking his name—"So you do believe in being good?" Yes, and a sort of atmosphere as of some old walled-in English garden, with pinks, and cornflowers, and roses, and scents of lavender and lilac—cool and fair, untouched, almost holy—all that he had been brought up to feel was clean and good.

And suddenly he thought, She might come along the seafront

again and see me! And he got up and made his way to the rock at the far end of the beach. There, with the spray biting into his face, he could think more coolly.

To go back to the farm and love Megan out in the woods, among the rocks, with everything around wild and fitting—that, he knew, was impossible, utterly. To transplant her to a great town, to keep, in some little flat or rooms, one who belonged so wholly to nature—the poet in him shrank from it. His passion would be a mere sensuous revel, soon gone; in London, her very simplicity, her lack of all intellectual quality, would make her his secret plaything—nothing else. The longer he sat on the rock, with his feet dangling over a greenish pool from which the sea was ebbing, the more clearly he saw this; but it was as if her arms and all of her were slipping slowly, slowly down from him, into the pool, to be carried out to sea; and her face looking up, her lost face with beseeching eyes and dark, wet hair, possessed, haunted, tortured him! He got up at last, scaled the low rock cliff and made his way down into a sheltered cove. Perhaps in the sea he could get back his control—lose this fever! And stripping off his clothes, he swam out. He wanted to tire himself so that nothing mattered, and swam recklessly, fast and far; then suddenly, for no reason, felt afraid. Suppose he could not reach shore again—suppose the current sent him out—or he got a cramp, like Halliday! He turned to swim in.

The red cliffs looked a long way off. If he drowned, they would find his clothes. The Hallidays would know; but Megan perhaps never—they took no newspaper at the farm. And Phil Halliday's words came back to him again: "—a girl at Cambridge I might have—glad I haven't got her on my mind!" And in that moment of unreasoning fear he vowed he would not have her on his mind. Then his fear left him; he swam in easily enough, dried himself in the sun and put on his clothes. His heart felt sore, but no longer ached; his body was cool and refreshed.

When one is as young as Ashurst, pity is not a violent emotion. And, back in the Hallidays' sitting room, eating a ravenous tea, he felt much like a man recovered from a fever. Everything seemed new and clear; the tea, the buttered toast and jam tasted absurdly good; tobacco had never smelled so nice. And walking up and down the empty room, he stopped here and there to touch or look. He took up

Stella's workbasket, fingered the cotton reels and a gaily colored plait of sewing silks, sniffed at the little bag filled with woodruff she kept among them. He sat down at the piano, playing tunes with one finger, thinking, Tonight she'll play; I shall watch her while she's playing; it does me good to watch her. He took up the book, which still lay where she had placed it beside him, and tried to read. But Megan's little sad figure began to come back at once, and he got up and leaned out the window, listening to the thrushes in the hotel gardens, gazing at the sea, dreamy and blue below the trees. A waiter came in and cleared the tea away, and he still stood, inhaling the evening air, trying not to think. Then he saw the Hallidays coming through the gate of the hotel, Stella in front of Phil and the children with their baskets, and instinctively he drew back. His heart, too sore and discomfited, shrank from this encounter, yet wanted its friendly solace—bore a grudge against this influence, yet craved its cool innocence, and the pleasure of watching Stella's face. From against the wall behind the piano he saw her come in and stand looking a little blank as though disappointed; then she saw him and smiled, a swift, brilliant smile that warmed yet irritated Ashurst.

"You never came after us, Frank."

"No; I found I couldn't."

"Look! We picked such lovely late violets!" She held out a bunch. Ashurst put his nose to them, and there stirred within him vague longings, chilled instantly by a vision of Megan's anxious face lifted to the faces of the passersby.

He said shortly, "How jolly!" and turned away. He went up to his room and, avoiding the children, who were coming up the stairs, threw himself on his bed and lay there with his arms crossed over his face. Now that he felt the die really cast and Megan given up, he hated himself, and almost hated the Hallidays and their atmosphere of healthy, happy English homes. Why should they have chanced here, to drive away first love—to show him that he was going to be no better than a common seducer? What right had Stella, with her fair, shy beauty, to make him know for certain that he would never marry Megan; and, tarnishing it all, bring him such bitterness of regretful longing and pity? Megan would be back by now, worn out by her miserable seeking—poor little thing!—expecting, perhaps, to find him there when she reached home. Ashurst bit at his sleeve to stifle a groan of remorseful longing. He went to dinner glum and silent, and his mood threw a dinge over even the children. It was a melancholy, rather ill-tempered evening, for they were all tired; several times he caught Stella looking at him with a hurt, puzzled expression, and this pleased his evil mood. He slept miserably; got up quite early and wandered out. He went down to the beach. Alone there with the serene, the blue, the sunlit sea, his heart relaxed a little. Conceited fool—to think that Megan would take it so hard! In a week or two she would almost have forgotten! And he—well, he would have the reward of virtue! A good young man! If Stella knew, she would give him her blessing for resisting that devil she believed in; and he uttered a hard laugh. But slowly the peace and beauty of sea and sky, the flight of the lonely seagulls, made him feel ashamed. He turned homeward.

In the hotel gardens Stella herself was sitting on a camp stool, sketching. He stole up close behind. How fair and pretty she was, bent diligently, holding up her brush, measuring, wrinkling her brow.

He said gently, "Sorry I was such a beast last night, Stella."

She turned around, startled, flushed very pink and said in her quick way, "It's all right. I knew there was something. Between friends it doesn't matter, does it?"

Ashurst answered, "Between friends—and we are, aren't we?"

She looked up at him, nodded vehemently, and her upper teeth gleamed again in that swift, brilliant smile.

Three days later Ashurst went back to London, traveling with the Hallidays. He had not written to the farm. What was there he could say?

On the last day of April in the following year he and Stella were married. . . .

SUCH WERE Ashurst's memories, sitting against the wall among the gorse, on his silver-wedding day. At this very spot, where he had laid out the lunch, Megan must have stood outlined against the sky when he had first caught sight of her. Of all the queer coincidences! And there moved in him a longing to go down and see again the farm and the orchard, and the meadow of the gipsy bogle. It would not take long; Stella would be an hour yet, perhaps.

How well he remembered it all—the little crowning group of pine trees, the steep grass hill behind! He paused at the farm gate. The low stone house, the yew-tree porch, the flowering currants—not changed a bit; even the old green chair was out there on the grass under the window, where he had reached up to her that night to take the key. Then he turned down the lane, and stood leaning on the orchard gate—a gray skeleton of a gate, as then. A black pig even was wandering in there among the trees. Was it true that twenty-six years had passed, or had he dreamed and awakened to find Megan waiting for him by the big apple tree? Unconsciously he put up his hand to his beard and brought himself back to reality. Opening the gate, he made his way down through the weeds and nettles till he came to the edge and the old apple tree itself. Unchanged! A little more of the gray-green lichen, a dead branch or two, and for the rest it might have been only last night that he had embraced that mossy trunk after Megan's flight and inhaled its woody savor, while above his head the moonlit blossoms had seemed to breathe and live. In that early spring a few buds were showing already; the blackbirds shouting their songs, a cuckoo calling, the sunlight bright and warm. Incredibly the same—the chattering trout stream, the narrow pool he had lain in every morning, splashing the water over his flanks and chest; and out there in the wild meadow the beech clump and the stone where the gipsy bogle was supposed to sit. And an ache for lost youth, a hankering, a sense of wasted love and sweetness, gripped Ashurst by the throat. Surely, on this earth of such wild beauty, one was meant to hold rapture to one's heart, as this earth and sky held it! And yet, one could not!

He went to the edge of the stream and, looking down at the little pool, thought: Youth and spring! What has become of them all, I wonder? And then, in sudden fear of having this memory jarred by human encounter, he went back to the lane and pensively retraced his steps to the crossroads.

Beside their car an old, gray-bearded laborer was leaning on a stick, talking to the chauffeur. He broke off at once, as though guilty of disrespect, and, touching his hat, prepared to limp on down the lane.

Ashurst pointed to the narrow green mound. "Can you tell me what this is?"

The old fellow stopped; on his face had come a look as though he were thinking, You've come to the right shop, mister!

" 'Tis a grave," he said.

"But why out here?"

The old man smiled. "That's a tale, as you may say. An' not the first time as I've a-told et—there's plenty folks asks 'bout that bit o' turf. 'Maid's Grave' us calls et, 'ereabouts."

Ashurst held out his tobacco pouch. "Have a fill?"

The old man touched his hat again, and slowly filled an old clay pipe. His eyes, looking upward out of a mass of wrinkles and hair, were still quite bright.

"If you don' mind, surr, I'll set down—my legs 'urtin' a bit today." And he sat down on the mound of turf.

"There's always a flower on this grave. An' 'tain't so very lonesome, neither; brave lot o' folks goes by now, in they new motorcars an' things—not as 'twas in th' old days. She've a-got company up 'ere. 'Twas a poor soul killed 'erself."

"I see!" said Ashurst. "Crossroads burial. I didn't know that custom was kept up."

"Ah, but 'twas a long time ago. Us 'ad a parson as was very God-fearin' then. Let me see, I've 'ad my pension six year come Michaelmas, an' I were just on fifty when t'appened. There's none livin' knows more about et than what I do. She belonged close 'ere; same farm as where I used to work along for Mrs. Narracombe—'tis Nick Narracombe's now; I does a bit for 'im still, odd times."

Ashurst, who was leaning against the gate, lighting his pipe, left his curved hands before his face for long after the flame of the match had gone out.

"Yes?" he said, and to himself his voice sounded hoarse and queer.

"She was one in an 'underd, poor maid! I puts a flower 'ere every time I passes. Pretty maid an' good maid she was, though they wouldn't bury 'er up to th' church, nor where she wanted to be buried neither." The old laborer paused and put his hairy, twisted hand flat down on the turf beside the bluebells.

"Yes?" said Ashurst.

"In a manner of speakin'," the old man went on, "I think as 'twas a love story—though there's no one never knew for sure. You can't tell what's in a maid's 'ead—but that's what I think about it." He drew his hand along the turf. "I was fond o' that maid—don' know as there was anyone as wasn' fond of 'er. But she was too lovin'-'earted—that's what 'twas, I think." He looked up.

Ashurst, whose lips were trembling in the cover of his beard, murmured again, "Yes?"

" 'Twas in the spring, 'bout now as 't might be, or a little later—blossom time—an' we 'ad one o' they young college gentlemen stayin' at the farm—nice feller too, with 'is 'ead in the air. I liked 'e very well, an' I never see nothin' between 'em, but to my thinkin' 'e turned the maid's fancy."

The old man took the pipe out of his mouth, spat and went on. "You see, 'e went away sudden one day, an' never come back. They got 'is knapsack and bits o' things down there still. That's what stuck in my mind—'is never sendin' for 'em. 'Is name was Ashes, or somethin' like that."

"Yes?" said Ashurst once more.

The old man licked his lips. " 'Er never said nothin', but from that day 'er went kind of dazed lookin'; didn' seem rightly there at all. I never knew a 'uman creature so changed in me life—never. There was another young feller at the farm—Joe Biddaford 'is name were, that was properly sweet on 'er, too; I guess 'e used to plague 'er wi' 'is attentions. She got to look quite wild. I'd see her sometimes of an evenin' when I was bringin' up the calves; there she'd stand in th' orchard, under the big apple tree, lookin' straight before 'er. 'Well,' I used t'think, 'I dunno what 'tis that's the matter wi' you, but you'm lookin' pitiful, that you be!' "

The old man relit his pipe and sucked at it reflectively.

"Yes?" said Ashurst.

"I remembers one day I said to 'er, 'What's the matter, Megan?'—'er name was Megan David, she come from Wales same as 'er aunt, ol' Mrs. Narracombe. 'You'm frettin' about somethin',' I says. 'No, Jim,' she says, 'I'm not frettin'.' 'Yes, you be! ' I says. 'No,' she says, and two tears came rollin' out. 'You'm cryin'—what's that, then?' I says. She puts 'er 'and over 'er 'eart: 'It 'urts me,' she says; 'but 'twill soon be better,' she says. 'But if anything should 'appen to me, Jim, I wants to be buried under this apple tree.' I laughed. 'What's goin' to 'appen to you?' I says, 'Don't be foolish.' 'No,' she says, 'I won't be foolish.' Well, I know what maids are, an' I never thought no more about et, till two days arter that, 'bout six in the evenin' I was comin' up wi' the calves, when I see somethin' dark lyin' in the stream, close to that big apple tree. I says to meself, 'Is that a pig—funny place for a pig to get to!' an' I goes up to et, an' I see what 'twas."

The old man stopped: his eyes, turned upward, had a bright, suffering look.

" 'Twas the maid, in a little pool there that's made by the stoppin' of a rock—where I see the young gentleman bathin' once or twice. 'Er was lyin' on 'er face in the water. There was a plant o' goldie-cups growin' out o' the stone just above 'er 'ead. An' when I come to look at 'er face, 'twas lovely, beautiful, so calm's a baby's—wonderful beautiful et was. When the doctor saw 'er, 'e said, ' 'Er couldn' never a-done it in that little bit o' water ef 'er 'adn't a-been in an extarsy.' Ah! an' judgin' from 'er face, that was just 'ow she was. Et made me cry proper—beautiful et was! 'Twas June then, but she'd a-found a little bit of apple blossom left over somewheres, and stuck et in 'er 'air. That's why I thinks 'er must a-been in an extarsy, to go to et gay, like that. Why! There wasn't more than a foot and 'arf o' water. But I tell 'ee one thing—that place, et's 'aunted. I knew et, an' she knew et; an' no one'll persuade me as 'tisn't. I told 'em what she said to me 'bout bein' buried under th' apple tree. But I think that turned 'em—made et look too much 's ef she'd 'ad it in 'er mind deliberate; an' so they buried 'er up 'ere. Parson we 'ad then was very particular, 'e was."

Again the old man drew his hand over the turf.

" 'Tis wonderful, et seems," he added slowly, "what maids 'll do for love. She 'ad a lovin' 'eart; I guess 'twas broken. But us never *knew* nothin'!"

He looked up as if for approval of his story, but Ashurst had walked past him as if he were not there.

Up on the top of the hill, beyond where he had spread the lunch, over, out of sight, he lay down on his face. So had his virtue been rewarded, and the Cyprian, goddess of love, taken her revenge! And before his eyes, dim with tears, came Megan's face with the sprig of apple blossoms in her dark, wet hair. What did I do that was wrong? he thought. What did I do?

But he could not answer. Spring, with its rush of passion, its flowers and song—the spring in his heart and Megan's! Was it just

Love seeking a victim! Euripides was right, then—the words of his *Hippolytus* as true today!

> "For mad is the heart of Love,
> And gold the gleam of his wing;
> And all to the spell thereof
> Bend when he makes his spring.
> All life that is wild and young
> In mountain and wave and stream,
> All that of earth is sprung,
> Or breathes in the red sunbeam;
> Yea, and Mankind. O'er all a royal throne,
> Cyprian, Cyprian, is thine alone!"

Megan! Poor little Megan—coming over the hill! Megan under the old apple tree waiting and looking! Megan dead, with beauty printed on her! . . .

A voice said, "Oh, there you are! Look."

Ashurst rose, took his wife's sketch and stared at it in silence.

"Is the foreground right, Frank?"

"Yes."

"But there's something wanting, isn't there?"

Ashurst nodded. Wanting? The Apple-tree, the singing, and the gold!

WINTER THUNDER

WINTER THUNDER

by Mari Sandoz

ILLUSTRATED BY MITCHELL HOOKS

The morning gave no hint of the ferocity
with which the day would end. Then suddenly the
blizzard was upon them, deepening with every
passing minute and threatening to engulf the school
bus. For Lecia Terry, the young schoolteacher,
who had grown up on the
Nebraska prairie, sudden winter storms were not
a new experience. But she also knew how
deadly some of them could be.

Still, as the windblown snow swirled into
drifts and the progress of the bus became more
difficult, Lecia had no way of knowing what fate
awaited her or the young children in her care. Nor
could she guess just how much strength, stamina and
courage the ensuing days and nights
would ask of all of them.

THE SNOW BEGAN quietly this time, like an afterthought to the gray Sunday night. The moon almost broke through once, but toward daylight a little wind came up and started white curls, thin and lonesome, running over the old drifts left from the New Year storm. Gradually the snow thickened, until around eight thirty the two ruts of the winding trails were covered and undisturbed except down in the Lone Tree district, where an old yellow bus crawled heavily along, feeling out the ruts between the choppy sand hills.

As the wind rose, the snow whipped against the posts of a ranch fence across the trail and caked against the bus windows, obscuring the young faces pressed to the glass. The storm increased until all the air was a powdery white and every hill, every trace of road, was obliterated.

The bus wavered and swayed in its direction, the tracks filling in close upon the wheels as they sought out the trail lost somewhere far back, and then finally grasped at any footing, until it looked like some great snowy, bewildered bug seen momentarily through the shifting wind. But it kept moving, hesitating here, stalling there in the deepening drifts, bucking heavily into them, drawing back to try once more while the chains spun out white fans that were lost in the driving snow that seemed almost as thick, as dense.

Once the bus had to back down from a steep little patch that might have led into a storm-lost valley with a ranch house and warmth and shelter. It started doggedly around, slower now, but decisive, feeling cautiously for traction on the drifted hill side. Then the wheels began to slip, catch, and then slip again, the bus tipping precariously in the push of the wind, a cry inside lost under the rising noise of the storm.

For a long time it seemed that the creeping bus could not be stopped. Even when all discernible direction or purpose was finally gone, it still moved, backing, starting again, this way and that, plowing the deepened slope, swaying, leaning until it seemed momentarily very tall and held from toppling only by the thickness of the flying snow.

Once more a wheel caught and held under the red-hot smoking exhaust. It slipped and held again, but now the force of the wind was too great. For a moment the tilting bus seemed to lift. Then it pivoted into a slow skid and turned half around, broadside. Slowly it went over on its side, almost as though without weight at all, settling lightly against a drift, to become a part of it at that thickening place where the white storm turned into snowbanks, lost except that there were frightened cries from inside and a hiss of steam and smoke from the hot engine against the snow.

In a moment the door was forced outward, the wind catching a puff of smoke as dark, muffled heads pushed up and were white in an instant. They were children, most of them in snowsuits and in sheepskin coats, being thrust down over the side of the bus, coughing and gasping as the force of the blizzard struck them, the older ones hunching their shoulders to shield themselves and some of the rest.

Again, the engine roared and the upper back wheel spun on its side, free and foolish in the awkward caking of snow. Then the young woman who had handed the children down followed them, her sheepskin collar turned up about her head, her arms full of blankets and lunch boxes.

"You'll have to give it up, Chuck," she called back into the smoky interior. "Quick! Bring the rest of the lunches—"

With Chuck, sixteen and almost as tall as a man, beside her, Lecia Terry pushed the frightened huddle of children together and hurried them away downwind into the wall of storm. Once she tried to look back through the smother of snow, wishing that they might have taken the rope and shovel from the toolbox. But there was no time to dig and search for them on the underside of the bus now.

Back at the bus thick smoke was sliding out the door into the snow that swept along the side. Flames began to lick up under the leaning windows, the caking of ice suddenly running from them. The glass held one moment and burst, and the flames whipped out, torn away by the storm as the whole bus was suddenly a wet, shining yellow that blistered and browned with the heat. Then there was a dull explosion above the roar of the wind, and down the slope the fleeing little group heard it and thought they saw a dark fragment fly past overhead.

"I guess that was the gas tank going," Chuck shouted as he tried to peer back under his shielding cap. But there was only the blizzard closed in around them, and the instinctive fear that these swift storms brought to all living creatures, particularly the young.

There was sobbing among the children now, a small one crying out, "Teacher! Teacher!" inside the thick scarf about her face, clutching for Lecia in her sudden panic.

"Sh-h, Joanie. I'm right here," the young woman soothed, drawing the six-year-old to her, looking around for the others, already so white that she could scarcely see them in the storm.

"Bill, will you help Chuck pack all the lunches in two, three boxes, tight, so nothing gets lost? Maggie's big syrup bucket'll hold a lot. Throw all the empties away. We'll have to travel light—" she said, trying to make it sound like a little joke.

"My father will be coming for me soon—" the eight-year-old Olive said primly. "So you need not touch my lunch."

"Nobody can find us here," Chuck said shortly, and the girl did not reply, too polite to argue. But now one of the small boys began to cry. "I want my own lunch box, too, Teacher," he protested, breathless from the wind. "I—I want to go home!"

His older brother slapped him across the ear muffs with a mittened hand. "Shut up, Fritz," he commanded. "You can't go home. The bus is—" Then he stopped, looking toward the teacher, almost lost only an arm's length away, and the full realization of their plight struck him. "We can't go home," he said, so quietly that he could scarcely be heard in the wind. "The bus is burned and Chuck and Miss Lecia don't know where we are—"

"Sure we know!" Chuck shouted against him without looking up from the lunch packing, his long back stooped protectively over his task. "Don't we know, Lecia? Anyway, it won't last. Radio this morning said just light snow flurries, or Dad wouldn't have let me take the bus out 'stead of him, even sick as he was." The tall boy straightened up, the lunch boxes strung to the belt of his sheepskin to bang together in the wind until they were crusted with snow. "Baldy Stever'll be out with his plane with skis on it looking for his girl-friend soon's it clears a little, won't he, Lecia?" he said. "Like he came New Year's."

But the bold talk did not quiet the sobbing, and the teacher's nod was lost in the storm as she tied scarves and mufflers across the faces of the younger children, leaving only little slits for the eyes, with the brows and lashes by now already furred with snow. When that was done she lined up the seven, mixing the ages from six-year-old Joanie to twelve-year-old Bill, who limped heavily as he moved in the deepening snow. One of the blankets she pinned around the thinly dressed Maggie, who had only a short outgrown coat, cotton stockings and torn overshoes against the January storm. The other blanket she tied around herself, ready to carry Joanie on her back, Indian fashion, when the short little legs were worn out.

Awkwardly, one after another, Lecia pulled the left arm of each child from its sleeve, buttoned it inside the coat and then tied the empty sleeve to the right arm of the one ahead. She took the lead, with little Joanie tied to her belt, where she could be helped. Chuck was at the tail end of the clumsy little queue, just behind Bill with the steel-braced ankle.

"Never risk getting separated," Lecia remembered hearing her pioneer grandfather say when he told of burying the dead from the January blizzard of 1888, the one still called the schoolchildren's storm. "Never get separated and never stop moving until you find shelter—"

The teacher squinted back along the line, moving like some long snow-covered, winter-logged animal, the segmented back bowed before the sharpening blizzard wind. Just the momentary turn into the storm took her breath and frightened her for these children hunched into themselves, half of them crying softly, hopelessly, as though already lost. They must hurry. With not a rock anywhere and not a tree within miles to show the directions, they had to seek out the landmark of the ranch country—the wire fence. So the girl started downwind again, breaking the new drifts as she searched for valley ground where fences were most likely, barbed-wire fences that might lead to a ranch, or nowhere except around some hay meadow. But it was their only chance, the girl from the sand hills knew. Stumbling, floundering through the snow, she kept the string moving, the eyes of the older ones straining through frozen lashes for even the top of one fence post, those of the small ones turned in upon their fear as the snow caked on the mufflers over their faces and they stumbled blindly to the pull from ahead.

Once there was a bolt of lightning, milky white in the blizzard, and a shaking of thunder, ominous winter thunder that stopped the moving feet. Almost at once the wind grew sharper, penetrating even Chuck's heavy sheepskin coat, numbing the ears and feet as panting, sobbing, the children plowed on again. The new drifts were soon far above Lecia's boots, and with no visibility, there was no way to avoid them.

With their hands so useless, someone stumbled every few steps, but the first to fall was the crippled Bill. The others, the crying ones too, stood silent in the storm, not even able to slap one frozen hand against another while the boy was helped up. After that others went down, and soon it was all that the teacher and the boy Chuck could do to keep the children moving as they pushed through the chop hills and found themselves going up what seemed a long windswept, frozen slope. Lecia was carrying Joanie on her back most of the time now. But they kept moving somehow, barely noticing even the jack-rabbit that burst out among their feet and was gone into the storm. Otherwise there was nothing.

After a long, long time they reached what seemed a high ridge of hills standing across the full blast of the north wind that bent them low and blinded them. Suddenly Chuck's feet slid off sideways into a hole, a deep-cupped blowout hidden by the storm. Before he could stop, he had drawn the rest tumbling in after him, with an avalanche of snow. Crying, frightened, the smaller ones were set on their feet and brushed off a little. Then they all crouched together under the bank to catch their breath out of the wind, shivering, wet from the snow that had fallen inside their clothes, which were already freezing hard as boards.

"The blowouts are always from the northwest to the southeast,"

Chuck shouted into the teacher's covered ear: "The wind's plainly from the north, so we're being pushed about due south. That direction there can't be a house for five, six miles, even if we could find it—unless we got clear out of our home country—"

The girl shivered, empty with fear. "So that's why we haven't found a fence," she said slowly. "We're probably in the old Bar M summer range, miles and miles across. But we can't go any other direction—"

"I could alone; I could make it out alone!" Chuck shouted suddenly, angrily.

For a moment the teacher was silent, waiting, but when he added nothing more, she said, "You can't leave these little ones now, Chuck. Even if you were sure you could find a ranch—"

There was no reply, except that Bill, the crippled boy, began to cry; a reddening from his ankle was coming up through the snow that was packed into his overshoes around the brace. Others were sobbing too, and shaking with cold, but the younger ones were very quiet now, already drowsing, and so the young teacher had to get to her feet and help lift the children out of the blowout. Slapping at the muffler-covered cheeks, shaking the smaller ones so hard that the caked snow fell from them, she got the line moving again, but very slowly. She was worn out too, and with Joanie in her arms to warm the child, keep her from the sleep of freezing that came upon her on Lecia's back, with only the thin blanket against the ice of the wind.

They seemed to be going down now, through a long deep-drifted slope, plowing into buried yucca clumps, the sharp spears penetrating the snowsuits, even the boot tops. Here a few head of cattle passed them, less than three feet away and barely to be seen. They were running, snow-caked, blinded, bawling, and Lecia squinted anxiously back into the storm for others, for a herd that might be upon them, trample them as surely as stampeding buffalo. But there were no more now, and she could see that Chuck was shouting, "Little chance of its clearing up soon, with that snow thunder and those cattle already drifting so fast—all the way from the winter range!"

Yes, drifting fast with the force and terror of the storm, even hardy, thick-haired range cattle running!

Then suddenly one of the younger boys cried out something. "Teacher," he repeated, "I saw a post!"

But it must have been a trick of the wind, for there was only the driving snow, except that the sharp-eyed Maggie saw one too, ahead and to the right—a snowy post with only the upper foot or so out of the drifts, holding up a strand of gray wire taut and humming in the cold.

For a moment Lecia could not see through the blurring of her eyes. At least this was something to follow, but where? To her signal Chuck lifted his arm and dropped it. He didn't recognize the fence either, and so the teacher took the easier direction, leftward, only side-face to the wind, although it might lead to the hills, to some final drift where the fleeing cattle would end.

Moving slowly along the fence, Lecia knew that it could not be much farther anyway. Her arms were wooden with cold and the weight of the child, her legs so weary in the deepening drifts that with each step it seemed that she could never lift a snow-caked boot again.

Then suddenly Chuck was hurrying up the line. "I think I know where we are! That old split post just back there's where we made a takedown running coyotes with Dad's hounds this fall. If I'm right, this is Miller's north meadow, and there's a strip of willows down ahead there, off to the right—"

For a moment the girl set Joanie into the deep snow, panting, and even when she caught her breath, she was afraid to speak.

"How far to a house?" she finally asked, her lips frozen.

"There's no house along this fence if it's Miller's," Chuck had to admit. "It just goes around the meadow, three, four miles long."

"You're sure—" the teacher asked slowly, "—sure there's no cross fence to the ranch? You might get through, find help in time—"

The boy could only shake his head and then, thinking that the storm hid this, he shouted the words on the wind. No, no cross fence, and the ranch was five miles south. Not even a haystack left in the valley here. Miller had had his hay balers in this fall, hauled it all out for his fancy Angus herd.

Then they must take a chance on the willows, with Bill hardly able to limp along, Joanie too heavy to carry, and several others worn out. So they wallowed through the drifted fence and tried to keep parallel

to its direction, but far enough in the meadow to see any willows. There must be willows now.

Suddenly Lecia went down in what must have been a deep gully, the ground gone, the girl sinking into soft powdery snow to her shoulder. Panting, choking, she managed to get Joanie and the rest back out and the frightened ones quieted a little. Then she swung off along the barer edge of the gully, seeking a place to cross. The wind was blowing in powerful gusts now, so that she could scarcely stand up. Bent low, she dragged at the line behind her, most of the children crawling in the trench she plowed for them. There was no crying now—only the slow, slow moving. Perhaps they should dig into the snow here below the gully bank. Indians and trappers had done that and survived. But they had thick-furred buffalo robes to shut out the cold and snow, and they were grown men, tough, strong—not helpless, worn-out children, their frozen feet heavy as stone, with only an overgrown boy and a twenty-three-year-old girl to lead them, keep them alive.

More and more often Lecia had to stop, her head down, her arms dropping the weight of the little girl. But there seemed to be a shallowing in the gully now. So it was time to try to break a path through it and turn back toward the fence if they were not to wander lost as so many did that other time, long ago, when a teacher and her nine pupils were lost, finally falling to die on the prairie. They must cling to the fence here, if it went no farther than around the meadow. At least it was proof that something existed on the earth except the thick, stinging blizzard, with a white, freezing, plodding little queue caught in the heart of it, surrounded.

Once when the girl looked up through the blowing snow it seemed there was something darkish off to the right, little farther than arm's reach away. She saw it again, something rounded, perhaps a willow clump, low, snow filled, and possibly with more nearby. Signaling to Chuck, Lecia turned down to it—a willow covered as in sleep, but with at least two more bushes just beyond, larger, darker, and standing closer together, their longer upper branches snow-weighted, entwined over the drifts. There, between the clumps, out of the worst of the storm, she left the children squatting close, the blankets over them. With the belts of her coat and Chuck's, they tied the longer brushy tops of the two clumps together as solidly as they could. Then, fighting the grasping wind, they managed to fasten the blankets across the gap between the willows, to hold awhile. Behind this protection Lecia dug through the snow to the frozen ground while Chuck gathered deadwood from the trees. Inside a close little kneeling circle of children they built a fire pile with some dry inner bark and a piece of sandwich wrapping paper for the lighting. Awkwardly, with freezing hands the teacher and Chuck hurried, neither daring to think about dry matches in any pocket.

The two smaller children were dropping into the heavy sleep of exhaustion and cold and had to be held in their places by the older ones while Chuck dug swiftly through his pockets for matches, deeper, then frantically, the circle of peering eyes like those of fearful young animals, cornered, storm-trapped.

Down to his shirt, Chuck found some in his pocket, six in a holder made of two rifle cartridges slipped together. Hurrying clumsily he struck one of the matches. It sputtered and went out, the flames sucked away. They had to try again, making a closer circle. This time the match caught on the waxed paper and the willow began to snap and sizzle in the snow, throwing a dancing light up to the circle of crouching children.

But it seemed even colder now that they had stopped walking. Lecia thought of the night ahead, with the temperature surely down to twenty-five or thirty below zero. Beyond that she would not look now; but to get through this night they must have a great pile of wood, and they must have shelter even to hold the fire.

"We can't both go out at one time," the teacher told Chuck as they made plans. "It's too risky for the children. We might not get back."

The boy looked around from the fire he was nursing, and upward, but there was still no thinning of the storm. The area of snowy visibility was almost as small as the confines of their new meat-freeze room at the ranch. Even so, he gave the girl no sign of agreement.

Lecia set willow poles into the snowbanks as she went to look for wood, placing them no farther apart than the outstretched reach of her arms. She found more willows, so cold now that the green wood snapped off like glass. Each time it was only by the row of sticks in the drifts that she managed to stagger, blinded and panting, back against the wind with her load of wood.

The brushier portions she piled behind the blankets of the shelter to catch the snow and shut out the wind. Some, long as fish poles, she pushed through the willow clumps and across the opening between, in a sort of lattice inside the billowing blankets that Eddie and Calla tried to hold in place. They were the first of the children to separate themselves from the snowy composite, the enforced coordinate that had been the queue driven by the storm, the circle that shielded the sprouting fire. Now they were once more individuals who could move alone, hold the blankets from blowing inward, pile the dry powdery snow from the ground against and between the sticks, trying to work it like plaster, building a wall between the clumps of willows. Even Bill helped a little, as far as he could reach without moving his bad ankle.

By one o'clock the north wind was cut off so that the fire fattened and burned higher, softening the ice caked to their clothing until it could be knocked off, and softening the face of the drift that was struck by the windblown heat. The children packed this against the north wall too, and into the willow clumps both ways, drawing the rounded wall inward toward the top along the bend of the willows, making what looked like half of an Indian snow shelter, or the wickiup Calla had seen at the county fair, just high enough at the center for a seven-year-old to stand up.

"That's a good job!" Chuck shouted over the roar of the storm as he tried to rub circulation into Joanie's waxen feet. The small girl was beginning to cry out of her sleep with the first pain; others began too, their ears and hands swollen and purpling, their toes painful as their boots thawed. But it seemed that the feet of nine-year-old Maggie must be lost, the ragged old overshoes and cotton stockings so frozen that she had to cut them away with Eddie's knife. Under them her feet were like stone, dead white stone, although the girl was working hard to rub life into them. She worked silently and alone, as had become natural for her long ago, her thin face pinched and anxious with the pain and the alarm.

Of them all only Olive seemed untouched. She was dry in her heavy waterproofed snowsuit with attached rubber feet inside her snow boots. And she was still certain that her father would come soon.

"He would not care to leave me in such an unpleasant place—"

When they had the semicircular wall of their shelter drawn in as far as the snow would hold, Lecia decided to pull the blankets away from the outside and use one over the top, with the belt-tied willows sticking through a smoke hole cut in the center. But as the blankets came down, part of the loose snow wall was blown in by the force of the blizzard, the huddle of children suddenly became white again and the fire was almost smothered. So the wall had to be rebuilt in discouragement, but with care, using more brush and sticks, more fire-softened snow to freeze in place as soon as it was struck by the storm. Lecia had to stop several times for her hands too, pounding them hard, holding them over the fire, her diamond sparkling. She tried to turn the ring off before the swelling became too great and then gave it up. The wall must be finished, and when it was solid, Calla came to whisper under the roar of the wind. "Bill's eating the lunch," she said.

"Oh, Bill! That's not fair to the others, to your own little sister Joanie!" Lecia cried. Suddenly not the good teacher, she grabbed up the containers and hung them on high branches out in plain sight for watching, for reminders and derision from the other children. "Why, it may be days before we are found!" she scolded, in her exasperation saying what should have been kept hidden in silence.

Before the boy could defend himself with a plea of hunger or his usual complaint about his crippled foot, some realization of their plight had struck the others. Even little Fritz, with the security of his older sister and brother Calla and Eddie along, began to sob. Only the round-cheeked Olive was calm. The others, angered to see it, wanted to shout against her outsider's assurance, to tell her she was too stupid and green to know that her father could not come for her in such a blizzard, that he would never find her if he could get through. But they were silent under the teacher's admonitory eye. And, as in the schoolhouse and on the playground, Bill had withdrawn, except that now it could not be more than a foot or two.

As the frozen earth between the willow humps became soggy, Calla and Eddie helped move the others around so that there was room to draw the fire first one way and then another, to dry and warm the ground. Lecia watched to see that they set no one afire and then bowed her head out into the storm again. Chuck was dragging in willows for the night. They drove sticks into the hardening drifts around the front of the shelter and piled brush against them to catch the snow. It filled in as fast as they worked until there was no more than a little crawling hole left. Then Chuck laid a mat of brushy sticks on the ground and packed soft snow into them to freeze, making a slab with a handle big enough to close the low doorway. Now, so long as the blanket with the smoke hole stayed tied over the top they could be as warm as they wished in the little shelter that was scarcely longer than a tall man—a close cramping for the teacher, Chuck, and the seven pupils, but easily warmed with a few pieces of wood, an Indian fire. They were safe and warm so long as the shelter stood against the rising ferocity of the blizzard and the willows lasted.

By now the cold stung the nose and burned the lungs; the snow turned to sharp crystals that drew blood from the bare skin. It drove the teacher and Chuck to the fire, shaking, unable, it seemed, ever to be warmed through again. Lecia opened her sheepskin coat, hung up her frozen scarf and cap and shook out her thick brown hair that gleamed in the firelight. Even with her tawny skin red and swollen, her gold-flecked hazel eyes bloodshot, she was still a pretty girl, and the diamond on her hand flashed as she hunted for her stick of white salve to pass around for the raw, bleeding lips. It was all she could do.

Now they tried to plan for what was to come, but here they were as blind as in the flight through the storm. There would be sickness, with the noses already running, Joanie coughing deep from°her chest, and, worst of all, Maggie's feet that seemed to be dying. Besides, the fire must be kept going and the food spread over three, perhaps four, days.

Here Bill raised his complaining voice. "You ain't our boss outside of school! We'll do what we want to. There ain't enough to eat for everybody."

"You mean *isn't*, not *ain't*," the teacher corrected firmly. "And talking like that—when you've barely missed one lunchtime!"

"You ain't never my boss," Chuck said casually, "—only about the kids while in the bus, like you do with my dad when he's driving. I sure can do what I want to here, and I'll do it."

Slowly the girl looked around the ring of drowsy, firelit eyes upon her, some uneasy at this bold talk to their teacher, but some smaller ones aping the defiance of the big boys. Chuck, who sat almost a head taller than Lecia, grinned down at the pretty young teacher with an arrogance that was intended to remind her he saw nothing here as his responsibility, nothing except saving himself.

Unable to reply in words that would not frighten the children more, the teacher looked past the fire into the boy's broad, defiant face, into his unblinking, storm-reddened eyes, until it seemed she dared not turn her gaze away or at that instant the sixteen-year-old boy would assert his victory by plunging out into the storm.

Before this silent, incomprehensible struggle the children were uneasy and afraid; even the coughing stilled, so that the storm seemed very loud outside the smoke hole. But little Fritz was too young to be held so for long. "I'm hungry!" he shouted against the restraining hand of his sister. "I want my lunch!"

As though freed, released, Chuck sat back and grinned a little at the small boy. Matter-of-factly the teacher washed her raw hands with snow and held them over the fire. Then she spread her napkin on her lap and set out all there was in the eight lunches now: fourteen sandwiches, most of them large, six pieces of Sunday cake, a handful of cookies, a few pieces of candy, and six apples and two oranges, frozen hard. There were two thermos bottles of milk, and these Lecia pushed away into the snow wall.

"If somebody gets sick and can't eat solid food," she said to the owners, their eyes following her hands in consternation. Even with the best management, there would be no food of any kind in a few days, but this the small children could not yet understand.

The frozen fruit she handed to Chuck and, without meeting the girl's eyes, he set it around the coals for toasting, to be eaten now because it would not keep well, and might sicken leaner stomachs. In the meantime Lecia set one lunch box filled with snow near the fire and packed away all except four of the big sandwiches into the others, the eyes of the children following her hands here too, even as she hung the containers back above her head. Then she divided the four sandwiches into halves and passed them around.

"Eat very slowly," she cautioned. "Blizzards usually last three days, so we must make what we have here last too, probably clear to Thursday, or longer."

But Bill seemed not to be listening. "Chuck's eating!" he suddenly protested. "He ain't—*isn't*—in on the lunches."

For a moment the teacher looked sternly at the boy. "After Chuck carried you all from the bus, helped get you through the bad places and helped to make the shelter and the fire!" the girl said in astonishment. "Now we'll have no more of this bickering and complaint. Here we are equal partners, and not one of us will get out of this alive unless we keep working together. Even your comic books should have taught you that much! And don't think this is play. You remember what the storm of 1888 was called in your history book—because so many schoolchildren died in it. Most of the children in 1888 died because somebody got panicky, didn't think, or they didn't stick together—"

There was silence all around the fire now. The storm seemed to rise; the children edged closer to each other, glancing fearfully over their shoulders as though there were terrible things stalking outside.

"Oh, we're okay," Chuck said optimistically. "We can last three days easy here—" The rebellion was gone from him, or hidden for the moment.

But Olive, the newcomer, was unconcerned. "I should like another sandwich, Miss Terry. From my own lunch, please," she said, with the formality of an old-fashioned boarding school. "I won't need the remainder. My father will come for me when it is time."

"He won't find you—" Maggie said as she rubbed at her feet. Color was seeping into them now, an angry gray-splotched purple, with pain that twisted her thin face.

"My father will come," Olive repeated, plainly meaning that he was not like the fathers of the others here, particularly Maggie's, who had done nothing since the war except make South Pacific bug juice, as he called it, for himself from chokecherries, wild grapes, or raisins in the way they did in the war. He couldn't make more than enough for himself, yet he managed to get into jail just the same, for crashing his old truck through the window of the county assistance office. But things had not been good before that. Often this fall Maggie was at school when the bus arrived, not waiting at the stop near their crumbling old sod shack but walking the three miles. Sometimes her face was bruised, but she was silent to any questioning. If Maggie lost her feet now, it was because she had no warm snowsuit and high boots like the others, only the short old coat above her skinny knees, the torn overshoes with the soles flopping.

But there was still a cheerful face at the fire. Although Fritz's frosted ears stood away under the flaps of his cap, he could still show his gap-toothed grin in mischief. "If we don't get home till Thursday, Teacher, Baldy'll be mad at you when he comes flying out Wednesday—"

The rest laughed a little, drowsily. "Maybe Baldy won't be flying around that soon," Eddie said, and then he was corrected by Calla's sisterly concern. "Don't say *Baldy*. Say *Mr. Stever*."

But the teacher busied herself hanging up everything loose. Then with Chuck's knife she slit the remaining blanket down the middle and fastened half around each side against the snow wall, like a tepee lining. By the time the white blizzard darkness came, the smaller children had all been taken outside for the last time and lay in fretful, uneasy sleep. Olive had been the last, waiting stubbornly for her father until she toppled forward. Calla caught her and made room for the girl still murmuring, "Papa—"

Finally the last sob was stilled. Even Joanie was asleep, her feverish head in the teacher's lap, her throat raw and swelling, with nothing except hot snow water to ease the hollow cough.

The children were packed around the fire like little puppies on a very cold night. Chuck was at the opposite side from Lecia, the boys on his side, the girls on hers, with Calla and her brothers around the back. The older ones lay nearer the wall, their arms over the younger to hold their restlessness from the fire.

But Bill was still up, drawn back under the willows, his head pulled into his sheepskin collar, his ankle bent to him. He watched the teacher doze in fatigue, met her guilty waking gaze sullenly. But finally he reached down into his pocket and drew out something wrapped in waxed paper. "I didn't eat the piece you gave me—" he said, holding out his half of the sandwich.

"Bill! That was fine of you," the girl said, too worn out to say more as she reached up to put it away.

"No—no, you eat it. I guess you didn't take any."

For a moment Lecia looked at the boy, but he avoided her as he edged himself around Chuck closer to the fire, turning his chilled back to the coals, and so she ate the buttered bread with the thick slice of strengthening cold beef, while more snow was driven in through the smoke hole and settled in sparkling dust around the little fire. There were white flashes too, and the far rumble of winter thunder.

"Is—is there lots of willows left?" the crippled boy asked.

The teacher knew what he meant—how many clumps, and would they be so far out that someone might get lost.

"I think there are quite a few," she replied, needing to reassure the boy but unable to make it a flat lie.

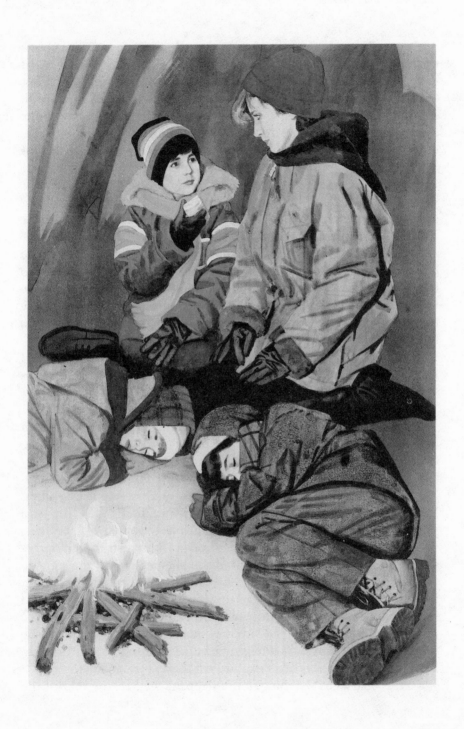

He sat silent a long time. Finally he pulled his cap off and shook the long yellowish hair back from his petulant face. "I wonder what Mother's doing—" he said slowly, looking away, his hand seeking out the tortured ankle. Lecia motioned him to hold it out to her and so she did not need to reply, to ask what all the mothers of these children must be doing, with the telephone lines still down from the other storm and surely nobody foolish enough to try bucking this one, unless it might be Olive's father, the new rancher from the East.

With snow water heated in the lunch tin, Lecia washed the poor stick that was the boy's ankle, gently sponging the bone laid almost bare where the frozen snow and the iron brace wore through the scarred and unhealthy skin.

"It looks pretty bad, Bill, but you probably won't have to put the brace back on for days—" Lecia started to comfort him, but it was too late, and she had to see fear and anger and self-pity darken his face in the firelight. Because nothing could be unsaid, the girl silently bandaged the ankle with half of the boy's handkerchief. "Now get a little sleep if you can," she said gently.

The boy crawled in next to Eddie as though Ed were the older, and for a long time the teacher felt his dark eyes staring at her out of his shadowy coat collar.

SEVERAL TIMES before midnight the girl started to doze but jerked herself awake at the frozen creak of the willow shelter, to push the children's out-tossed arms back and to replenish the fire.

Eddie coughed and moaned, digging at his chest, Calla was helpless beside him, her sleep-weighted eyes anxious on the teacher. Maggie too was finally crying now. Her feet had puffed up and purpled, with graying spots that would surely slough off, perhaps spread in gangrene. Yet all Lecia could do was turn the girl's feet from the fire and push them behind the blanket against the snow to relieve the pain and itching a little. Perhaps only freeze them more. Lecia touched the girl's forehead to calm her but felt her stiffen and start to pull away from this unaccustomed kindly touch. Then Maggie relaxed a little, and as the teacher stroked the hot temples, she wondered how many days it might be before help could get through. Finally Maggie slept, worn out, but still tearing at her feet.

To the weary girl watching, half asleep, at the fire, the roar of the storm rose and fell like the panting of a great live thing, sometimes a little like many great planes warming up together. If only she had married Dale Stever, they would be in the Caribbean now; these children all would be safe at home, with probably no other teacher available so soon. Once Lecia turned her swollen hand to the fire, watching the ring catch and break the light into life, and tried to recall the fine plans Dale had made for them. He wasn't a rancher's son like those who usually took her to parties and dances. Dale had come from outside last summer and bought the sale pavilion in town. Since then he flew all around the surrounding ranch country in a plane the color of a wild canary. Fairtime he took Lecia and her friend Sallie down to the state fair, and several times since on long trips, to Omaha to the ballet and to Denver. To their fathers he called himself the Dutch uncle of the two girls, but gradually he concentrated on Lecia, and at Christmas there was the big diamond and the plane ready to fly south. He even took her to the school board to ask for a release from her contract, but somehow Lecia couldn't break her contract. They must wait until school was out. Dale had been angry. "This is no life for a girl as pretty as you," he said. Truly he was right. Today it was no life for any girl.

Soon after midnight Lecia was startled out of a doze by the sound of cattle bawling somewhere in the roar of the storm, like the herds that passed her home on the night of the May blizzard three years ago, when so many died in the drifts and lakes that the whole region was a stench far into the summer. Then suddenly the girl realized where she was, and hurried bareheaded out into the storm. The bawling was very close; any moment hundreds of storm-blinded cattle might be running over the little willows, over their own two clumps.

Lecia dragged burning sticks from the fire, but in an instant the storm had sucked their flame away. So, with her arms up to shield her eyes from the snow that was sharp as steel dust, she stood behind the shelter shouting the "Hi-ah! Hi-ah!" she had learned when she helped the cowboys push cattle to market. It was a futile, lost little sound against cattle compelled to run by instinct, compelled to flee for survival before the descent of the arctic storm, never stopping until trapped in some drift, or overtaken in some open fence corner to freeze on their feet, as Lecia had seen them standing.

Realizing her danger as a warmth crept over her, the girl tumbled back into the shelter and crouched at the fire. She barely noticed the sting of returning blood in her ears and face while she listened until the drifting herd was surely past, made more afraid by the knowledge of this thing that drove cattle galloping through the night, the power of it and how easily it could overcome the little circle of children here if it were not for the handful of fire, for the walls of the storm's own snow.

Toward morning the weary girl knew that she could not keep awake. She had stirred Chuck to sit up awhile, but he was unable to shake off the weight of sleep, so heavy on an overgrown boy. Trying to remember how the Indians carried their fire—something about moss and damp, rotted wood—Lecia pulled old dead roots from the willow butts and laid them into the coals with the ends sticking far out. Even with waxed paper handy it would be a desperate chance. Willows burned fast as kindlings and there were only five matches, including the one from Eddie's pocket, and no telling how many of them were spoiled by dampness.

Even so it was sweet to let herself sink into darkness, but it seemed that she awoke at once, stiff and cold from the nightmare that reached into the waking black, even the ashes of the fire spot cold. With the waxed paper held ready, the girl blew on the ends of the unburnt roots her hands found, carefully, fearfully. At last a red spark glowed deep in one, and when the fire was going again, she slipped outside for calm in the cold that was like thin, sharp glass fragments in the nose.

There was still no earth and no sky, only the white storm of late dawn blowing hard. But the wood had lasted and now Lecia put on a few extra sticks and heated water to wash the inflamed eyes of the children. She started a rousing song: "Get up! Get up, you sleepy-head!" but even before it was done, Joanie began to whimper, "I'm hungry—"

So the teacher laid out four sandwiches on sticks over the coals and then added another half for herself when she saw Bill watching. "There won't be anything more today except a pinch of cake unless the sun breaks through."

"If it does, we can stomp out a message on the snow," Calla said cheerfully.

"Yes, even if people can't travel for a whole week, Baldy'll come flying over to see about his girlfriend," Bill said boldly.

The younger boys laughed a little, but Chuck was more serious. "If the sky lightens at all and there's no blowing, I'll do the stomping before I leave."

"You'd run away now?" the teacher asked softly as she combed at Joanie's fine brown hair.

"Somebody's got to get help." He defended himself in loud words.

The children around the fire were suddenly quiet, turning their eyes to follow the tall boy as he pulled up his sheepskin collar and crawled out into the storm. And they were silent a long time afterward—all except Joanie, who sobbed softly, without understanding. Even Olive looked up once, but Maggie grated her feet hard along the snow wall and tore at their congestion as though she heard nothing.

Then suddenly there was stomping outside and Chuck came back in, covered with snow, thick frost all over his collar and cap, his brows and lashes icy. The children pushed over toward him, as to one gone, lost. He had brought more wood, and the teacher seemed to have forgotten that he had said anything about leaving. But the children watched him now, even when they pretended they didn't, and watched Lecia too, for suspicion had come in.

The teacher started as for a school day, except that the arithmetic was rote learning of addition and multiplication tables and a quick run through some trick problems: "If I had a fox, a goose, and some corn to get across a river in a boat—" And then, "If I had a dollar to buy a hundred eggs—no, I should take something that won't make us hungry."

"Like a hundred pencils?"

"Well, yes, let's take pencils. I want to buy a hundred for a dollar. Some are five cents each; poor ones, two and a half cents; and broken ones, half a cent. How many of each kind must I buy?"

In history and nature study they talked about the Indians that still roamed the sand hills when Lecia's grandfather came into the country. The Indians lived the winter long in hide tepees something like the shelter here, and almost as crowded, but with piles of thick-furred buffalo robes for the ground and the beds. The girls sat on one side, the boys on the other.

"Like we are here—" Fritz said, his eyes shining in the discovery.

"We're Indians. Whoo-oo-oo!" he cried, slapping his mouth with his palm.

They talked about the food too, the piles of dried and pounded meat, the winter hunts, how the village and lodges were governed, and what the children did, their winter games, one almost like "button, button." The boys learned from the men such things as arrow-making, and later bullet-making, hunting, fighting; and particularly the virtues of resourcefulness, courage, fortitude, and responsibility for all the people. The girls learned from the women beading, tanning hides, and all the other skills needed to live well with modesty, steadfastness and generosity, and with courage and fortitude and responsibility too, for it was thought that the future of the people lay in the palms of the women, to be cherished or thrown away.

"What does that mean, Teacher?" Fritz asked, hitting out in mischief at his brother Eddie despite the fact that Calla and the teacher were both watching, then shouting he was hungry again.

The rest tried to laugh a little as Calla whispered to her small brother, trying to make herself heard against the storm, while Lecia taught them a poem about Indians.

Even Joanie repeated a few lines for her, although the child leaned, weak and feverish, against Calla while Bill comforted his bound ankle and Maggie tried hard to pull herself out of the curious drowsiness that had the teacher frightened.

After a while the children played "button, button," and tried to tell each other poems. When Eddie got stuck on "Snowbound," Bill nudged Fritz and they laughed as easily at his discomfiture here as at school, perhaps because Chuck was back and this was the second day of the storm, with tomorrow the third. Then it would clear up and somebody with a scoop shovel would get his horse along the barer ridges to a telephone.

"Maybe somebody'll just come running over the hills to find us," Eddie teased, looking at Olive, turning his face from the teacher.

Well, even if nobody came for them and Baldy couldn't find a place to land with skis on his plane, he would have sacks of food and blankets and stuff dropped like in the movies and the newspapers.

"I saw it in a movie once, I did," Joanie cried.

So they talked, pretending no one was looking up at the hanging lunch buckets, or sick and afraid. But Lecia did not hear them.

"Oh-oo, Teacher's sleeping—just sitting there!" Eddie exclaimed.

"Sh-h," Calla said in her way. "Let her stretch out here," and with a polite smile Olive moved aside.

THAT NIGHT Joanie was delirious, and once Maggie slipped past the teacher out into the storm to relieve the fire of her feet. By midnight she couldn't stand on them, and the grayish spots were yellow under the thick skin of a barefoot summer, the swelling creeping above the girl's thin ankles, with red streaks reaching almost to the knees. Her eyes glistened, her cheeks were burning, and she talked of wild and dreadful things.

Lecia tried to remember all that she had read of frostbite, all that her grandfather had told her, but she knew that the inflammation spreading past the frozen area was like the cold overtaking the fleeing cattle, and she had to make a desperate decision. She dug two holes deep into the snow wall and laid Maggie with her feet in them almost to her knees, wishing they had something waterproof for covering. The cold would probably freeze the girl more, but it would numb the nerves and perhaps slow the congestion and tissue starvation.

Later, when the girl was restless again and crying, Lecia found the yellow spots spreading, painful and hard as boils. She burned the end of a safety pin, and while Maggie's frightened eyes became caverns in her thin face, Lecia opened one of the spots. Bloody pus burst down over her hand. Turning aside, she wiped it away on the snow, from her ring too, and then slipped the ring from her shrunken finger and hung it on a twig overhead, where it swayed a little, like a morning dewdrop, while she opened the rest of the festering patches.

When the girl's feet were bathed and bound in the sleeves torn from Lecia's white shirt, she thrust them back into the snow. Then she gave Maggie half a cup of the milk, very quietly, hoping no one would awaken and see, although none of them needed it more. Almost at once the girl was asleep, to rest until the pus gathered again. But the first time Lecia returned with firewood she saw the thermos bottle half out. She jerked it from the hole. The milk was all gone, and across the little fire Olive stared at her teacher.

"It was mine," the girl said flatly.

So the time had come when the little food left must be hidden.

Now, with all but Olive sleeping, was the time. When Lecia came back in, the girl held out something—the ring that had been left hanging on the twig and forgotten.

THE NEXT DAY and the next were the same, only colder, the drifts deeper along the willows, the wind so sharp that it froze the eyeballs. Lecia and Chuck covered their faces as they fought their way back against it, dragging the wood tied by a strap of cloth cut off around the bottom of Lecia's coat. One at a time they went out and came back, a hand stretched ahead feeling for the next guide pole before the other let go of the last, the face turned from the storm to save the breath from being torn away by the wind.

All the third day they watched out of the smoke hole for the sky that never appeared. When night finally came without a star or stillness, even Lecia, who had tried to prepare herself for this eventuality, felt that she could not face another day of the blizzard. Maggie no longer sat up, and both Joanie and Eddie were so sick—their fevers high, their chests filling—that the teacher had to try something. She seemed to remember that the early settlers used willow bark to break a fever, so she steeped a handful in Maggie's tin cup until the liquid was strong and dark. She made the children drink it, first experimentally, then more, and after a while they began to sweat. When they awoke they were wet, their hair clinging to their vulnerable young foreheads, but they seemed better all the next day, except weak.

The fourth day was like the rest, colder, with the same white storm outside, the children hunching silent upon themselves inside. Sometimes a small one sobbed a little in sickness and hunger, but it was no more than a soft moaning now, even when Lecia divided most of the little food that was left. The children, even Chuck, took it like animals, and then sat silent again, the deep-socketed eyes watching, some slyly gnawing at willow sticks and roots hidden in the palm.

Everybody around the fire was coughing and fevered now, it seemed to Lecia, the bickering going beyond childish things to quarrels about real or fancied animosities between their families. Once even Calla spoke angrily to Bill, defending her brothers.

"At last they aren't mama babies like you!"

"Mama babies! I wouldn't talk if everybody knew that my family got a start in cattle by stealing calves—"

"You can't say such things!" Calla cried, up and reaching for Bill, caught without his brace and unable to flee into the storm. Joanie cried, "Don't! Don't hit my brother!"

When Lecia returned, Chuck was holding the two apart, shaking them both.

Lecia spoke out in anger and impatience, and Bill's face flushed with embarrassment and shame at her words, the sudden red like fever in his hunger-grayed cheeks.

Only Maggie with her poor feet was quiet, and Olive, sitting as though stunned or somewhere far away. The teacher knew that she should do something for this girl, only eight yet apparently so self-contained. Olive never spoke of her father now, just as none of the boys teased Lecia about Baldy anymore. Olive was as remote about him as everything else since the night she drank the milk and found the ring on a twig.

Too weary to think about it, and knowing she must keep awake in the night, Lecia stretched out for a nap. When she awoke, Olive was sitting exactly the same, but the places of Chuck and Eddie were empty—Eddie was out in the blizzard after his night of sweating. The boys returned with wood, weak, dragging, almost frozen, and with something that Lecia had to be told outside. There seemed only one willow clump left.

One clump? Then they must start digging at the frozen butts, or even pull down their shelter to keep the fire alive, for now the boys too were believing that the storm would blow forever. Yet toward evening there was a thinning above the smoke hole. The sun was suddenly there like a thin disk of milky ice seen from the bottom of a cup. It was almost a promise, even though the storm swept the sun away in a few minutes and the wind shifted around to the south, whipping in past the block the boys had in the hole of their shelter. The children shivered, restless. Once Eddie rose from his sleep and fought to get out, go home. When he finally awakened, he lay down in a chill, very close to the fire, and would not move until a stench of burning cloth helped rouse him. Then he drank the bitter willow bark tea too, and finally he slept.

Friday morning the sun came out again toward ten o'clock, the same cold, pale disk, with the snow still running along the earth, running higher than the shelter or Chuck, shutting out everything except the veiled sun. The boy came in, looked around the starved, listless circle at the fire, at the teacher too, with her face that had been so pretty Monday morning gaunt and sooty now.

He laid two red-tipped matches, half of all he had, in the girl's lap. "I'm getting out," he said, and without a protest from anyone crawled through the hole and was gone.

The children were almost past noticing his desertion now, barely replying when they were spoken to. If the colds got worse or pneumonia struck, it would be over in a few hours. Maggie hadn't sat up since yesterday, lying flat, staring at the white storm blowing thin above the smoke hole. If any of them wondered how Lecia could keep the fire going alone, with nothing much except the willow butts left, no one spoke of it. The teacher sat with her arms hanging between her knees, hopeless.

She finally stirred and put the matches away in waxed paper in her shirt pocket where her ring lay, buttoning the flap down carefully now. Joanie started to cough again, choking, turned red and then very white under the grime and grayness of her face, lying very still. Now Bill made the first gesture toward his small sister.

"Come here, Doll," he said, gently drawing her awkwardly from Lecia's lap, the child lifting her head slowly, holding herself away, looking up at him as a baby might at a stranger, to be weighed and considered. Then she snuggled against him and in a moment she was asleep.

AFTER A LONG TIME there seemed a dull sound outside, and then Chuck was suddenly back, crawling in almost as though he had not left, panting in his weakness from the fight against the wind that had turned north again and colder.

"Scared an eagle off a drift out there," he finally managed to say. "And there's a critter stuck in the snow—beyond the far willows. Small spring calf. Froze hard, but it's meat—"

Then the realization that Chuck was back struck the teacher. She was not alone with the children, and he too was safe for now. But there was something more. The boy who had resented them and his involvement in their plight—he had escaped and come back.

"Oh, Chuck!" the girl exclaimed. Then what he said reached her mind. "A calf? Maybe we could build a fire there so we can cut some off, if we can't get it all out." She reached for her boots. "But we'll have to go work at it one at a time—" looking around the firelit faces that were turned toward her as before, but the eyes alert, watching as though a morsel might be dropped, even thrown.

"I'll go with Chuck, Miss Lecia," Bill said softly. "He can show me and I'll show you. Save time hunting—"

The teacher looked at the crippled boy, already setting Joanie gently aside and reaching for his brace. She felt pride in him, and unfortunate doubt.

"He can probably make it," Chuck said, a little condescending. "It's not over an eighth of a mile, and I found more willows farther along the way, the drifts mostly frozen hard too. I blazed the willows beyond our poles—"

"You'll be careful—mark everything," the girl pleaded.

"We've got to. It's snowing again, and the sun's gone."

IT SEEMED HOURS since the boys went out and finally the teacher had to go after them, appalled that the younger ones had to be left alone, yet it must be done. She moved very carefully, feeling her way in the new storm, going sideways to it, from pole to pole. Then she came to a place where the markers were gone, probably blown down and buried by the turning wind. The boys were out there, lost, in at least fifteen, perhaps twenty, below zero. Without sticks to guide her way back, the girl dared go no farther, but she crouched there, bowed before the wind, cupping her mouth with her mittens, shouting her hopeless: "Boys! Chuck! O-hoo!" the wind snatching it away. She kept calling until she was shaking and frozen. But now she had to keep on, for it seemed that she heard a vague, smothered sound, and yet a little like a reply. Tears froze on her face as she called again and again until suddenly the boys were at her feet, there before she could see them, so much like the snow, like white dragging animals— one bowed, half carrying the other. For a few minutes they crouched together in desperate relief, the snow running over them as something immovable, like an old willow butt. Then, together, they pulled themselves up and started back. When they finally reached the shelter, out of breath and frozen, they said nothing of what had happened, nor spoke at all for a while. Yet all of them, even little Joanie, seemed to sense that the boys had almost been lost.

As soon as the teacher was warmed a little, she started out alone, not certain that she could make it against the storm, but knowing that she must try to get meat. She took Chuck's knife, some dry bark, waxed paper, the two matches in her shirt pocket, and a bundle of poles pulled from their shelter. Moving very carefully beyond the gap in the willow markers, she carefully set the new sticks deep. She found the farther willow clumps with Chuck's blazing, and the brush pile the boys had made, and beside it the ice-covered head of the calf still reaching out of the snow. The hole they had dug around the red hindquarters was drifted in loosely but easily dug out. Lecia set a fire pile there and felt for a match with her numb fingers, fishing in the depths of her pocket. Something round was in the way, her ring.

But she got the match and lighted the fire, using her sheepskin coat as a shield. For a long time she crouched protectively over the flame; the wind carried away the stench of the burning calf hair. As the skin thawed she hacked at it the way Indians must have done here a thousand years ago, their stone knives sharper and more expertly handled.

At a sound she looked over her shoulder and saw a coyote not three feet away, gaunt-bellied too, and apparently no more afraid than a hungry dog. But suddenly he caught the human smell, even against the wind, and was gone. He would have made a soft rug at the fire, Lecia thought, and wondered if he might not return to watch just beyond the wall of storm. But she was too busy to look. As the heat penetrated the meat, she cut off one slice after another until she had a little smoky pile, not much for nine people who had lived five days on less than one lunch apiece, but enough to bring tears that were not all from the storm. In this meat, perhaps three pounds, might lie the life of her pupils.

Lecia scattered the fresh ashes over the calf to keep the coyotes away and piled brush into the fire hole. Then she headed sideways into the storm, so violent that it was a good thing she had the strength of a little cautious meat inside her, for it seemed no one could face the wounding snow. Numb and frightened, she managed to hold herself, not get hurried, panicked, never move until the next broken willow, the next marker was located. So she got back, to find Chuck out near the shelter digging wood from the old clumps, watching for her, uneasy.

It was hard for the children to wait while the thinner slices of meat roasted around the sticks. When the smell filled the little shelter, Lecia passed out toasted bits to be chewed very slowly and well. It tasted fine, and no one asked for bread or salt—not even Olive, still silent and alone. She accepted the meat but returned only distant gravity for the teacher's smile.

By now the white blizzard darkness was coming back, but before they slept there was a little piece of boiled veal for each and a little hot broth. It was a more cheerful sleeping time, even a confident one, although in the night they were struck by the diarrhea that Lecia had expected. But that was from the fresh meat and should not last.

By now Lecia could build a coal bed with rotten wood and ashes to hold a fire a long time, even with willows, and so she dressed Maggie's feet—the girl was now light as a sack of bird bones—and prepared the night fire. For a while Chuck and Eddie kept each other awake with stories of coyote hunts and with plans for another morning of storm, the sixth. The two boys met the day with so much confidence that Lecia had to let them go out into the storm. Eddie, only ten, suddenly became a little old man in his seriousness as he explained their plans. They would make a big brush pile so that they could settle out of the wind and work the fire until they got a whole hindquarter of the calf hacked off. So the teacher watched them go out full of hope, the hope of meat, taking one of the half blankets along to drag their prize in over the snow, like great hunters returning.

Bill had looked sadly after the disappearing boot soles, but without complaint. He helped Lecia with the smaller children, washing at the grime of their faces that would never yield except to soap, and took them out into the storm and back while the teacher soaked Maggie's great swollen feet and tried to keep the girl from knowing that the bone ends of her toes could be seen in the suppurating pits of dying flesh. There were holes on the tops of the toes too, along the edges of her feet, and up the heels as high as the ankle. But above the ankles the swelling seemed looser, the red streaks perhaps no farther up the bony legs than the day before. Once Bill looked over the teacher's shoulder and then anxiously into her face. Others had chilblains—his own feet were swollen from yesterday—but not like this.

"Will she lose—" he started to whisper, but he could not put the rest into words, not with a crippled foot himself.

The air was thick and white with new snow whipped by a northwest wind when Lecia went out for a little wood and to watch for the boys. But they were once more within touching distance before she could see them—very cold and backing awkwardly into the storm through the soft, new drifts, but dragging a whole hindquarter of the calf. It was a lot of meat, and surely soon the wind must finally blow itself out, the clouds be drained.

By the time Eddie and Chuck were warm they knew they had eaten too much roasted veal while they worked. Next Olive became sick, and Fritz, their deprived stomachs refusing the sudden meat, accepting only the broth. During the night the nausea struck Lecia too, and left her so weak that she could scarcely lift her head all the next day. That night Chuck lost his voice for a while and Joanie was worse again, her mind full of terrors, the cough so deep, so exhausting that Bill made a little tent over her face with the skirt of his coat to carry steam from a bucket of boiling snow water to her face. Then sometime toward morning the wind turned and cut into the southeast corner of the shelter, crumbling the whole side inward.

The boys crawled out to patch it with brush and snow softened at the fire; Lecia helped dry off the children as much as she could. Then when they were done and she laid her swimming head down, she heard a coyote's thin, high howl and realized that the wind was dying. Through the smoke hole she saw the running snow like pale windrows of cloud against the sky, and between them stars were shining, far pale stars. As one or another awoke, she directed sleepy eyes to look up. Awed, Joanie looked a second time. "You mean they're really stars—?"

"Yes, and maybe there will be sunshine in the morning."

Dawn came early that eighth day, but it seemed that nothing could be left alive in the cold whiteness of the earth that was only frozen scarves of snow flung deep and layered over themselves. The trailing drifts stretched down from the high ridge of hills in the north, so deep that they made a long, sliding slope of it far over the meadow and up the wind-whipped hills beyond, with not a dark spot anywhere to the horizon—not a yucca or fence post above the snow. In the first touch of the sun the frozen snow sparkled in the deep silence following a long, long storm. Then out of the hills a lone grouse came cackling over the empty meadow, gleaming silver underneath as she flew, her voice carrying loud in the cold stillness.

But the meadow was not completely empty, for out of a little white mound of drifted willows a curl of smoke rose and spread thin and blue along the hill. There was another sound too, farther, steadier than the cackle of the grouse, a sound seeming to come from all around and even under the feet.

"A plane!" Chuck shouted hoarsely, bursting out into the blinding sunlight.

Several other dark figures crept out behind him into the frosty air, their breath a cloud about them as they stood looking northward. A big plane broke from the horizon over the hills, seeming high up, and then another, flying lower. Foolishly Chuck and Eddie started to shout. "Help! Hello! Help!" they cried, waving their arms as they ran toward the planes, as though to hasten their sight, their coming.

But almost at once the sky was empty: the planes circled and then were gone. For a long time the boys stared into the broad, cold sky, pale with nothing in it except wind streaks that were stirring along the ground too, setting feather curls of snow to running.

"Quick! Let's make a big smudge!" Lecia called out, her voice loud in the unaccustomed quiet, and fearful. She threw water on the fire inside, driving smoke out of the hole, while the boys set the snowy woodpile to burning.

Before the smoke could climb far, planes were over the north hills again, coming fast. Now even Fritz got out into the stinging cold—everybody except Joanie, held back by Lecia, and Olive, who did not move from her place. Maggie was lifted up by the teacher to watch through the smoke hole as something tumbled from the higher plane, came falling down. Then it opened out like the waxy white bloom of the yucca, and settled toward the snow, with several other smaller chutes, bright as poppies, opening behind.

There was shouting and talk outside the shelter, and while Lecia was hurrying to get the children into their caps and boots, a man came crawling into the shelter with a bag—a doctor. In the light of the fire and a flashlight he looked swiftly at Joanie and then at Olive, considered her unchanging face, lifted the lids of her eyes, smiled and got no response. Then he examined the poor feet of Maggie, the girl like a skin-bound skeleton in this first sharp light, her eyes dark and fearful on the man's face.

The doctor nodded reassuringly to Lecia, and smiled down at Maggie.

"You're a tough little girl!" he said. "Tough as the barbed wire you have out in this country. But you're lucky somebody thought to try snow against the gangrene—" He filled a little syringe and fingered cotton as he looked around to divert the child.

"All nine of you alive, the boys say. Amazing! Somebody got word to a telephone during the night, but we had no hope for any of you. Small children lost eight days without food, with fifty inches of snow at thirty-eight below zero. Probably a hundred people dead through the country. The radio in the plane picked up a report that six were found frozen in a car stalled on the highway—not over five miles from town. I don't see how you managed here."

The doctor rubbed the punctured place in Maggie's arm a little, covered it, smiling into her fearful eyes, as men with a stretcher broke into the front of the shelter.

When they got outside, the air was filled with the roar of engines. Several planes were flying around overhead; two with skis had landed and approached the shelter and a helicopter, hovering like a brownish dragonfly, was settling. Men in uniform were running toward the children, motioning where they should be brought.

They came along the snow trail broken by the stretcher men, but walking through it as they had through the storm. Lecia, suddenly trembling, her feet unsteady on the frozen snow, was still in the lead, the others behind her, and Chuck once more at the end. Bill, limping awkwardly, carried little Joanie, who clung very close to her brother. They were followed by Calla and Eddie, with Fritz between them, and then the stretcher with Maggie. Only Olive of all the children walked alone, just ahead of Chuck, brushing aside all help. There were men running toward the bedraggled, sooty little string now, men with cameras and others, among them some who cried, and who must be acknowledged soon—Olive's father and Dale Stever of the canary yellow plane.

But for now, for this little journey back from the smoke-holed shelter of snow, the awkward queue stayed together.

NOTES ON THE AUTHORS

JOHN STEINBECK
(1902–1968)

Although he traveled widely throughout his lifetime, John Steinbeck's roots remained in the fertile soil of the Salinas Valley of California, where he was born.

Before becoming a novelist and short story writer he worked at a variety of jobs that ranged from fruit picker, housepainter and ranch hand to journalist and war correspondent. His most renowned novels include *Tortilla Flat, Of Mice and Men, The Winter of Our Discontent* and *The Grapes of Wrath*, which won him the Pulitzer Prize in 1940. Among his nonfiction works, he is best remembered for *Travels with Charley in Search of America*. Several of his novels—*Of Mice and Men* and *The Moon Is Down*— he also dramatized for the stage, and he contributed to the screenplay of the film *Viva Zapata*.

In 1962 he was awarded the Nobel Prize for Literature. In his speech accepting the award, Steinbeck said, "The writer is delegated to declare and to celebrate man's proven capacity for greatness of heart and spirit—for gallantry in defeat—for courage, compassion and love."

JAMES HILTON
(1900–1954)

In 1933, as a struggling young writer, James Hilton found himself confronted with a story deadline for the magazine *British Weekly*. Within four days, and initially without a thought as to his subject, he completed *Good-bye, Mr. Chips*. Its appearance in Great Britain gained little notice from the reading public. But the acclaim following its publication in the United States was instantaneous and within a short time the story was an international success.

Although Hilton wrote several other novels, the one for which he is also well remembered is *Lost Horizons,* with its idyllic mythical kingdom of Shangri-la. During the latter part of his career he lived in Southern California, where he continued to write novels and screenplays, such as the 1942 film classic *Mrs. Miniver,* for which he received an Academy Award.

ANTOINE de SAINT-EXUPÉRY
(1900–1944)

Born in Lyon, France, three years before the Wright Brothers' first successful airplane flight, Saint-Exupéry was taken early with the adventure and romance of aviation. During the 1920s he served in the French Army Air Force and following his discharge he found work as an air mail pilot in Africa and South America. His first two novels, *Southern Mail* and *Night Flight,* were closely based on his own personal experiences. In *Wind, Sand and Stars,* published in 1939, he moved from fiction to more meditative autobiographical pieces.

When France fell to the Nazis in 1940, Saint-Exupéry fled to the United States, where he wrote the charming fairy tale *The Little Prince.* Throughout the early years of the war he continued to organize French resistance to the occupation of his homeland and, in 1943, he joined the Free French Air Force in North Africa. A year later, while on a lone reconnaissance flight over the Mediterranean and the south of France, his plane disappeared.

PAUL GALLICO
(1897–1976)

He was a man of protean energy and enthusiasm, who as a young sports reporter once boxed a round with Jack Dempsey to find out "what it's like." (He lasted one minute thirty-seven seconds before being carried from the ring.) But Gallico was also a prolific writer in a variety of forms. After leaving his job as a reporter and newspaper columnist, he went on to write short stories, children's fiction, film and television scripts and more than forty books.

Among his most popular novels are *The Snow Goose, The Poseidon Adventure, The Hand of Mary Constable* and the popular series of books featuring their own irrepressible heroine, Mrs. 'Arris.

The places where he chose to live were equally wide-ranging, from New York and London to Monaco and Liechtenstein.

LEONARD WIBBERLY
(1915–1983)

The author Robert Nathan, wrote of his friend Leonard Wibberly, "He is an Irishman, a great, bearded teller of tales, a sage, a bard, a good man to have at one's back in a fight. Filled with laughter and impatience, love and indignation, he writes as he talks, with the chuckle of wit, the jab of knowledge and the authority of the master."

Born in Dublin, Wibberly was schooled in England and later went into newspaper work in London. The Great Depression of the 1930s brought him to the United States, where he finally found employment—playing a violin for pennies on the streets of New York City.

Ten years later, and after a variety of jobs, he became a newspaper reporter in Los Angeles. It was in 1955 that one of his books, *The Mouse That Roared*, was published, which later became a popular motion picture starring Peter Sellers. It was followed by *The Mouse on the Moon*. His other works, which range from detective stories to tales of history to travel books and children's fiction, include *The Life of Winston Churchill, Toward a Distant Island* and *The Centurion*.

PAUL HORGAN
(1903–   )

The spirit, as well as the unique history, of the American Southwest, is familiar ground to Paul Horgan, as he demonstrates in his short novel *The Saintmaker's Christmas Eve*. But though many of his books and stories are set in that region, he has not limited himself to it in his many years as novelist, playwright, historian, essayist, short story writer and editor.

Born in Buffalo, New York, he had his introduction to the Southwest when he attended school in New Mexico as a young man. Since then he has traveled throughout this country and abroad.

Among his works of fiction are the novels *Whitewater, One Red Rose for Christmas, Things As They Are, The Fault of Angels, Far from Cibola* and *The Common Heart*. His short stories have been collected in several volumes, including *The Peach Stone* and *Return of the Weed*. His historical writings feature profiles of Abraham Lincoln, Igor Stravinsky and the conquistadors of the Southwest. In 1955 he received the Pulitzer Prize for History for his book *Great River: The Rio Grande in North America*.

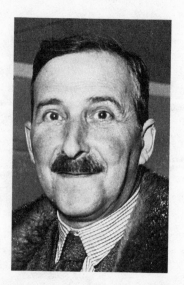

STEFAN ZWEIG
(1881–1942)

Of his own works Stefan Zweig once said that his main interest was in "the psychological representation of personalities and their lives." Indeed, as a study in psychology, Zweig's own life was both fascinating and complex.

Viennese-born, he embarked on a series of journeys as a young man that took him to India and the Far East. He lived much of his adult life in Austria, but in the 1930s became disenchanted with the country and moved to London. In 1940, a continuing wanderlust brought him to the United States, and a year later to Brazil, still seeking, as he admitted, "the land of the future." It was in 1942, near Rio de Janeiro, that he and his young wife died from drinking poison in a double suicide pact.

As well-known for his biographies as for his fiction, Zweig chronicled the lives of such men and women as Balzac, Dickens, Dostoyevsky, Marie Antoinette and Mary, Queen of Scots. He had just completed his autobiography, *The World of Yesterday,* when he died. Among his works of fiction are *Passion and Pain, Conflicts, Amok* and *Letter from an Unknown Woman.*

TRUMAN CAPOTE
(1924–1984)

When Truman Capote won first prize in a short story contest at the age of eight, he knew exactly what his life's work would be. It was not too many years later before readers in the United States and throughout the world knew as well.

Born in New Orleans and orphaned at an early age, he dropped out of school at seventeen and worked at various jobs from being a protégé of a fortune-teller to cataloguing cartoons for *The New Yorker* magazine. When he was twenty-four, his first novel, *Other Voices, Other Rooms,* was published to critical acclaim.

An almost continuous flow of novels and stories were to follow, among them *A Tree of Night and Other Stories, The Grass Harp, Breakfast at Tiffany's, A Christmas Memory* and *The Thanksgiving Visitor,* as well as a musical play, *House of Flowers,* and a collection of travel sketches, *Local Color.* Yet it was what he called his "nonfiction novel," *In Cold Blood,* that brought him his greatest celebrity.

JOHN GALSWORTHY
(1867–1933)

Considered the last great Victorian novelist, John Galsworthy studied law as a young man and was admitted to the bar. Then, on a trip to the Orient he met the novelist Joseph Conrad. It was Conrad's encouragement of Galsworthy's writing that probably deprived the English legal system of an effective advocate.

As both playwright and novelist, Galsworthy had a keen instinct for capturing the spirit of his times while revealing its shortcomings. His first play, *The Silver Box,* produced in 1906, brought a sense of social responsibility to English drama. Later plays such as *Strife* and *Justice* also dealt tellingly with social and ethical issues.

It is his novels, however, that have guaranteed Galsworthy a lasting place in literature, particularly the series of novels collectively entitled *The Forsyte Saga.* Other novels include *Fraternity, Loyalists* and *Caravan.* He was offered a knighthood for his literary achievements and refused it, but accepted the Nobel Prize for Literature in 1932.

MARI SANDOZ
(1901–1966)

From her experience as a country schoolteacher in Nebraska came the ingredients for Mari Sandoz's dramatic and touching novella, *Winter Thunder*.

Raised in the Sand Hills cattle country of the northwest part of the state, she was, in her own words, "the second child of a hot-tempered, violent, gun-toting Swiss immigrant" who considered artists and writers "the maggots of society." As a girl she lost an eye due to snow blindness while battling a winter blizzard.

Her first book, *Old Jules*, which was the story of her father, won the Atlantic Monthly writing award in 1935. Two years later, it was followed by the novel *Slogum House*, and later by such novels as *Miss Morissa*, *The Horsecatcher* and *Christmas of the Phonograph Records*. In addition to *Old Jules*, her biographies include *Crazy Horse* and *Cheyenne Autumn*, plus other nonfiction works, such as *The Cattlemen*, *Love Song of the Plains* and *The Beaver Men*.

As much a woman of her region as any of the fictional characters she depicted, Mari Sandoz listed as her "avocational interests" young writers, justice for the American Indian, and above all, human justice.

The stories in this volume are used by permission of and special arrangement with the publishers and the holders of the respective copyrights.

The Red Pony, copyright 1933, 1937, 1938; renewed © 1961, 1965, 1966 by John Steinbeck, is reprinted by permission of Viking Penguin, Inc., William Heinemann Ltd., and McIntosh & Otis, Inc.

Good-bye, Mr. Chips, copyright 1934 by James Hilton, renewed © 1962 by Alice Hilton, is reprinted by permission of Little, Brown & Co., Inc., and Hodder & Stoughton Ltd.

Night Flight by Antoine de Saint–Exupéry, copyright 1932, 1942 by Reynal & Hitchcock, Inc., copyright 1939 by Antoine de Saint–Exupéry, renewed © 1967 by Lewis Galantiere, is reprinted by permission of Harcourt Brace Jovanovich, Inc., and William Heinemann Ltd.

Love of Seven Dolls, copyright 1954 by Paul Gallico, renewed © 1982 by Virginia Gallico, Robert L. Gallico and William T. Gallico, is reprinted by permission of Harold Ober Associates, Inc., and Hughes Massie Ltd.

Meeting with a Great Beast, copyright © 1971 by Leonard Wibberly, is reprinted by permission of William Morrow & Co., Inc., and McIntosh & Otis, Inc.

The Saintmaker's Christmas Eve, copyright 1955, renewed © 1983 by Paul Horgan, is reprinted by permission of Farrar, Straus & Giroux, Inc.

The Royal Game by Stefan Zweig, copyright © 1943 by Bermann-Fischer AB, Stockholm, English translation by Jill Sutcliffe, copyright © 1981 by Atrium Press Ltd., is reprinted by permission of Crown Publishers, Inc., and Jonathan Cape Ltd.

The Grass Harp, copyright 1952, renewed © 1980 by Truman Capote, is reprinted by permission of Random House, Inc., and Hamish Hamilton Ltd.

The Apple Tree by John Galsworthy, copyright 1918 by Charles Scribner's Sons, renewed © 1946 by Ada Galsworthy, is reprinted by permission of Charles Scribner's Sons.

Winter Thunder by Mari Sandoz, copyright 1951 by The Curtis Publishing Co., copyright 1954 by Mari Sandoz, renewed © 1982 by Caroline Pifer, is reprinted by permission of The Westminster Press, and McIntosh & Otis, Inc.

PHOTO CREDITS:

Pages 599, 604: AP/Wide World Photos. Pages 600 top, 605: The Granger Collection. Pages 600 bottom, 606: Culver Pictures, Inc. Page 601: Keystone Pictures, Inc. Page 603: The Bettmann Archive, Inc. Page 607: Nebraska State Historical Society/Negative #5219-la.